Brilliant Words to Grow By

A Devotional Celebrating the Duality of Life

PAM MALOW-ISHAM

BALBOA.
PRESS

A DIVISION OF HAY HOUSE

Balboa Press books may be ordered through booksellers or by contacting:

Balboa Press
A Division of Hay House
1663 Liberty Drive
Bloomington, IN 47403
www.balboapress.com
1 (877) 407-4847

Because of the dynamic nature of the Internet, any web addresses or links contained in this book may have changed since publication and may no longer be valid. The views expressed in this work are solely those of the author and do not necessarily reflect the views of the publisher, and the publisher hereby disclaims any responsibility for them.

The author of this book does not dispense medical advice or prescribe the use of any technique as a form of treatment for physical, emotional, or medical problems without the advice of a physician, either directly or indirectly. The intent of the author is only to offer information of a general nature to help you in your quest for emotional and spiritual well-being. In the event you use any of the information in this book for yourself, which is your constitutional right, the author and the publisher assume no responsibility for your actions.

Print information available on the last page.

ISBN: 978-1-9822-0006-0 (sc)
ISBN: 978-1-9822-0008-4 (hc)
ISBN: 978-1-9822-0007-7 (e)

Library of Congress Control Number: 2018903518

Balboa Press rev. date: 07/16/2018

Contents

Dedicated to

I would like to dedicate this book to my Pastors, Bruce and Sharon Garner. When I came to them with the idea of starting a "Goal Setting Girlfriend Group" in August of 2010; to meet weekly, set goals, and hold each other accountable, I was given the green light. Each week I would come up with a new word with a handout. We met at the church for over three years. I am still sending out new words every week via email. Thanks so much for believing in me and being the best example of a strong person of character, humility, and humor that I have ever met. This book is the accumulation of those words, and more.

Introduction

The first twenty years of my life were spent trapped in hatred, anger, bitterness, and apathy from all the verbal, physical, and sexual abuse I endured growing up. I wavered between hating God and not believing there was one. I had a foul mouth and used my words to harm people. Now I use my words to lift them up.

I am a searcher of light, truth, and the best way to live. I believe what we focus on expands. When I allowed God to take control of my life, I changed my thinking and speaking, and my life turned around. This book is also the story of my life told from my perspective in small snippets.

As you muse over these words, meditate on these quotes, contemplate the questions, and make the declarations out loud over your life; you will grow in your capacity to love yourself, others, and God, even if you don't believe it now. If you choose to be diligent and do it daily, you will be amazed this time next year how much better, calmer, happier, and more productive your life will be. *I dare you to give it a try*.

1:
Resolution
January 1

Bible Verses

"He will strengthen your resolution to the last, so that no charge will lie against you on the day when our Lord Jesus Christ comes." 1 Corinthians 1:8 (KNOX)

"Each day, while the word today has still a meaning, strengthen your own resolution, to make sure that none of you grows hardened; sin has such power to cheat us." Hebrews 3:13 (KNOX)

Word of the Day

Resolution – The decision to keep your word. A choice to do what you say you are going to do.

Quotes

"Those who gave thee a body furnished it with weakness; but He who gave thee Soul, armed thee with resolution. Employ it, and thou art wise; be wise and thou art happy." Unknown, Elegant Extracts, 1797

"Divide each difficulty into as many parts as is feasible and necessary to resolve it." René Descartes, Discourse on Method

Pam's Perspective

I have broken a lot of New Year's resolutions through the years but, I keep making them, so I have something to look forward to and work toward. I keep on trying. When you have the fortitude to keep your resolutions, nothing can stop you.

Questions

Do I think resolutions are important? What kind of resolutions will I make and keep this year? What steps can I put in place to ensure my success? Why do I find it easy to stick to my resolutions?

Declarations

I do solemnly **resolve** to embrace my wonderful life, and live with a spirit of calm contentment. I have a childlike trust in God to help me keep my **resolutions**. I remember that I am the vessel through which God is revealed. With razor sharp focus, I take affirmative action now to attain my well thought out **resolutions.**

I immerse myself in the possibility of being a **resolution** keeper. I ask for, and get, the help I need to succeed. Divine help is here to inspire me this day on the best course to fulfill my **resolutions**.

I lead with love. I choose to forgive those who have wronged me. I **resolve** to reconcile with those whom I have hurt. My number one **resolution** is to walk in love, grace, and compassion. I **resolve** to be empathetic toward others. I leave the past behind as I pursue love.

I eat fresh fruit and vegetables, say "NO" to sugar, and keep the **resolution** I have made to eat healthily. I **resolve** to exercise and keep fit. I welcome growth. I am vigilant about filling my mind with positive thoughts to grow stronger, happier, wealthy, and wise.

I listen and learn from people who have successfully met their **resolutions**. I educate myself about my financial situation, due diligence, seek wise council about my investments and never spend more than I earn. I honor my **resolutions** to save and invest wisely.

I **resolve** to reorder my life to walk in wisdom and freedom. I put first things first. I **resolve** to move in a progressive pattern. This is the year for breakthroughs! Right now I act on my dreams and see my **resolutions** come to pass. I live in awe at the beauty around me. I choose to keep my word and make this the best year and decade of my life. I have faith in God, and He has **resolved** to have faith in me.

2:
Indecision
January 2

Bible Verse
"Elijah approached all the people and said, 'How long are you going to be paralyzed by indecision? If the Lord is the true God, then follow him, but if Baal is, follow him!' But the people did not say a word." 1 Kings 18:21 (NET)

Word of the Day
Indecision – Not being able to make a choice. Lack of assurance in one's ability to come to a verdict.

Quotes
"There is no more miserable human being than the one in whom nothing is habitual but indecision." William James

"If you acknowledge indecision, face it, and then make a definitive choice, no matter if it is right or wrong, you will not be infected by the cancerous doubts and uncertainty that indecision brings." Pam Malow-Isham

Pam's Perspective
I could not get permission to use Random House's definitions for this book after six months of emailing back and forth. They said they would not permit me unless I knew exactly how many I was going to sell and when the publishing date would be. I could not turn this book into the publisher without the permission, so it was a catch 22. Not being able to know either, I decided I am smart enough to give up the indecision, start over, and make up definitions myself for this book. So that is what I did.

Questions
How have I let indecision affect my life? How fast am I at making decisions? Do I stick with the decisions I make? If not, why not?

Declarations

Facing **indecision** is a part of my life that I continue to deal with responsibly. I can ignore **indecision**, but it is not going away. I can try to fool myself with **indecision**, but in reality, I already chose. Life is a series of decisions that I cannot avoid. Choices are easy to make.

The revelation of God's forgiveness breaks the barriers of **indecision** in my life. **Indecision** has never helped anyone, so I will take a small action step to make a difference in my life. I light the world up with the love of God in my heart. I will not allow **indecision** to keep me from unleashing massive amounts of kindness to all people.

God pardons me from **indecision** and remembers it no more. I am forgiven for all eternity. I have the authority to use boldness in my prayer to loosen bondages, the ties of deception, sin, and **indecision**. At my core belief, I deliver all my **indecision** over to God, listen, and then decide. I redeem every moment and appreciate my life.

I am very thankful that God is not **indecisive** about me. He sees me with all my flaws and loves me anyway. I let go of all **indecision** by trusting in the Presence of the Almighty. God created me and did not make a mistake. He will do awesome things on my behalf.

There will be things that come up that I might tend to be **indecisive** about, as long as I have breath. I can release **indecision** whenever I want. I drop **indecision** and pick the best possible solution for me. I am grateful that I am always divinely guided and protected.

In any situation, I make the grade because my brisk activity liberates my **indecision**. I get the job done. I will ask intelligent questions to motivate people to reject **indecision** and make a choice. No matter what I elect to do, I will be happy, insightful, and content.

3:
Brilliant
January 3

Bible Verses
"God, brilliant Lord, your name echoes around the world." Psalm 8:9 (MSG)

"So where does this leave the philosophers, the scholars, and the world's brilliant debaters? God has made the wisdom of this world look foolish." 1 Corinthians 1:20 (NLT)

Word of the Day
Brilliant – Outstanding skill and wit. Very wise and astute. Magnificent. Incandescent and showy.

Quotes
"Jewels arranged upon a lady's person appear far more brilliant, beautiful, and valuable, than when lying confusedly in the casket." Ebenezer Cobham Brewer

"Beautiful is the star-light of nature to man, clear is the moonlight of reason, and brilliant is the meteor-light of genius; but more beautiful, more clear, more brilliant than all these is the sunlight of Divine Revelation." Edward P. Day

"The more brilliant the lightning, the quicker it disappears." Avicenna

Pam's Perspective
Everyone is brilliant at something. When I started my Goal Setting Girlfriend Group, I was unsure if I was brilliant. But with declaring how brilliant I am with the affirmations in this book while writing it, now I believe it, and like myself too.

Questions
What brilliant thing will I do and say today? Who are some brilliant people I can model after? Why is being brilliant natural for me?

Declarations

I **brilliantly** do **brilliant** things. I am well-mannered and **brilliant**. As I become **brilliant** at the basics, I quickly master the difficult. I surprise and delight my friends with my **brilliant** humor and wit.

God created me to be **brilliant**, so as I study His word, He reveals His **brilliant** wisdom to me. I have mighty, **brilliant** forces working in my favor. I realize God's ways are more **brilliant** than mine. God's **brilliant** grace never gives up on me. I feel secure with Him.

I remember to smile. By elevating the conversations around me, I will be considered **brilliant**. I stand out in the crowd by my **brilliant** insights. I hang around **brilliant** people. We love encouraging each other to do our best. My **brilliant** actions produce miracle results. I am sharp, respectful, self-controlled and confidently **brilliant.**

I see the **brilliance** and gifts in people. I help them realize just how **brilliant** they really are. I focus on **brilliant** solutions and efficiently solve problems. I am inventive. Because I am accountable and persevere despite obstacles, I am thought of as a **brilliant** co-worker.

I can express my **brilliant** contribution to the world by radiating love. I will honor God and myself by my **brilliant** practices. I inspire excellence by following through on my commitments. I identify my target, and go for it! I succeed on purpose. I am aware of the things I lack, so therefore I am **brilliant**. Today I will celebrate my **brilliance**.

I am enthusiastically **brilliant** and believe I can achieve whatever I set my mind to. I will stimulate my mind by auto-suggestion, so I reap the **brilliant** rewards of thinking positive. There are no limits to my **brilliant** mind. I will create my happiness by what I do right now. I accept myself for who I am. I am beautiful and **brilliant!**

4:
Stupid
January 4

Bible Verses

"People who worship idols are stupid and foolish. The things they worship are made of wood!" Jeremiah 10:8 (NLT)

"Have nothing to do with stupid and senseless controversies; you know that they breed quarrels." 2 Timothy 2:23 (NRSV)

Word of the Day

Stupid – Defective in making smart choices. Missing common sense.

Quotes

"People are stupid if they don't investigate what they say they believe. They will be fickle and sensitive, unable to answer rightly." Pam Malow-Isham

"Stupidity, - unconscious ignorance." Henry Wheeler Shaw

"Against stupidity, the very gods fight un-victorious." Friedrich Schiller

"We are all born ignorant, but one must work hard to remain stupid." Benjamin Franklin

Pam's Perspective

Not until I gave myself permission to believe in myself, and share my talents with the world did I release the thought that I was too stupid to write a book.

Questions

Why do I find learning so much fun? Will I forgive people who act stupid and unwittingly hurt me? What's one thing I have learned I now enjoy, that I once thought was stupid? What can I do to increase my knowledge?

Declarations

It is no big deal that I have made some **stupid** mistakes in the past. We all have. I am glad for the understanding I have received thus far in my life. I read a Proverb a day to keep **stupid** away. I forgive myself for the **stupid** things I have done because I have learned valuable lessons from them. It is OK for me to be smart.

Today is a new day to start fresh. Instead of **stupid** choices, I make wise decisions from a new place of divine wisdom where everything is possible. I know I am forever connected to my Creator, always forgiven, eternally loved, divinely guided, and incredibly blessed.

I remember that I'm human, and so is everyone else. When I see someone do something **stupid**, I remind myself; 'but for the Grace of God, there go I. So instead of judging them, I lend a helping hand or send a prayer. I am acquiring more tolerance and goodwill each day.

I get smarter and smarter as I grow closer to God. I respect myself for who I am. I find joy in every little **stupid** thing I do. I love feeling happy and adept. I'm nobody's fool. I am a savvy mentor. I play positive tapes in my head to replace the **stupid** negative ones.

I have become a master at being thankful. Everywhere I look I see the splendor of God's beauty. I connect to my sixth sense and follow the leads. I recognize the voice of Spirit and ignore **stupid** thoughts.

I am a well-read person who finds many things interesting. Even if I am **stupid** in some subjects, I am brilliant in others. Reading is an adventure that takes me to beautiful places. I love to investigate different topics finding hidden nuggets of truth. I never judge a book by its cover, but jump in to see what I can discover. Even books that others think are **stupid** I enjoy because I am a genius.

5:
Impossible
January 5

Bible Verses
"I am the Lord, the God of every person on the earth. Nothing is impossible for me." Jeremiah 32:27 (NCV)

"But Jesus looked at them and said, with men this is impossible, but all things are possible with God." Matthew 19:26 (AMP)

Word of the Day
Impossible – Preposterous; nonsensical; contradictory of things thought possible. Totally ridiculous. Unattainable. Futile to try.

Quotes
"The whole Godhead is at your disposal; there is nothing impossible with Him, and there ought to be nothing impossible with us because there is nothing impossible with Him." Rev. Arthur T. Pierson

"Nothing is impossible to the willing mind." English Proverb

Pam's Perspective
I think the word impossible is used by cowards and people too lazy to try. There have been many times in my life that people I looked up to, told me "that is impossible!" I am glad I did not listen, or this book, among many other accomplishments, would never have been finished. A publisher told me my book was too long and it wouldn't sell. If you have a dream, don't listen to anyone who tells you it is impossible. Just smile as you go about proving them all wrong.

Questions
What is one thing that I thought was impossible for me to do, until I did it? Why do impossible endeavors seem effortless for me to tackle?

Declarations

My **impossible** vision becomes my reality as I work toward my goals with diligence. I act like nothing is **impossible**, so I turn things around for my good. I feel terrific today, so I take on the **impossible**.

What doctors' say is **impossible** to cure is an easy fix for my God who loves keeping His promises to me. Nothing is **impossible** to heal or restore. I run into the loving arms of a mighty God. I feel healthy and bold. I remember I can live my **impossible** dream!

I observe **impossible** situations doing an about-face. I am tenacious. I am devoted to my cause. It is a joy to laugh at the **impossible** knowing full well that I can accomplish anything I set my mind to with God's help. All things are working in my favor today. The absolute unexpected happens to bring me treasures and assistance.

Just because someone tells me it is **impossible** does not make it a fact. I can delight "to choose" to do the **impossible**, smoothly turning it into a job well done. I love adventure, and I dare to attempt the **impossible**. I charge forth in victory as I defeat every doubt that comes my way. I am blessed with **impossible** insights.

I feed my mind good thoughts. I never repeat scandal or calamity. I am careful with the use of my words. My words are power packed with love. I use my words to edify and uplift. I am willing to take on **impossible** tasks finishing them with ease and grace. I see precisely the way to turn **impossibilities** into possibilities effortlessly.

I am patient with myself, giving myself time to work my plan. I encourage myself. Fortunately for me, I know that God is a God of possibilities, not **impossibilities**. I think outside the box. Inspired to do the **impossible**, I win. **Impossibilities** are natural for me to try.

6:
Possible
January 6

Bible Verses

"'What do you mean, 'If I can?' Jesus asked. 'Anything is possible if a person believes.'" Mark 9:23 (NLT)

"If possible, to the best of your ability, live at peace with all people." Romans 12:18 (CEB)

Word of the Day

Possible – Able to take place, materialize or come about. Very likely to be accomplished. Conceivable; doable.

Quotes

"My experience has taught me that the next best thing to being truly great, is to emulate the great, by feeling and action, as nearly as possible." Napoleon Hill

"All men dream, but not equally. Those who dream by night in the dusty recesses of their minds wake in the day to find that it was vanity: but the dreamers of the day are dangerous men, for they may act on their dreams with open eyes, to make it possible. This I did." T. E. Lawrence

"It is essential that the dreamer be stronger than the dream. Otherwise danger. Every dream is a struggle. The possible does not verge upon the real without a certain mysterious anger." Victor Hugo

"It is possible to be happy any moment of any day if you want to be. It is as easy as a decision. So smile and choose to be happy." Pam Malow-Isham

Questions

How many possible opportunities will I see, and act on? Is it possible for me to let go of past hurts? Will I? Why do I believe all things are possible?

Declarations

Yes, all things are **possible**. I believe I am destined for greatness. I possess all the **possible** strength and intelligence I need to get the job done. I dream big. I move every **possible** part of my body and stretch it to keep it limber, healthy and flexible. I like to stay active. I reap fantastic rewards from every **possible** direction.

I see all the **possible** solutions to every situation, and I make the right choice. I start with the **possible,** doing it with ease and then I accomplish the impossible. I am experiencing favor from every **possible** source. I am on fire as I blaze a new trail of **possibilities**.

I release all tension. I am what I think I am. My cheerful attitude and dogged determination help make my dreams **possible**. I breeze through roadblocks. My **possible** aspiration now comes to pass.

I look for every **possible** opening to turn the conversation around to be positive. Just the right connections align at the perfect moment to help me today. Thank you, God, for all the joy and love you send my way from every **possible** direction. It is always **possible** to forgive.

I outperform my competition. I am intrigued by how things work. I am top-notch and **possibly** the best in my field. I think about what's **possible**. I put out great work, and I pay my employees the best **possible** wage. I am worthy of special consideration and network with the elite in my field. I set goals, and I achieve each one. I recognize what I want. I dare to take on challenging tasks.

I appreciate my loved ones and enjoy every **possible** minute I can spend with them. I accept our differences and love completely. I like to experiment on how many **possible** ways there are to be kind. I prosper every **possible** way. I become the best I **possibly** can.

7:
Gratitude
January 7

Bible Verses

"Go through His gates, giving thanks; walk through His courts, giving praise. Offer Him your gratitude and praise His holy name." Psalm 100:4 (VOICE)

"Let the word of Christ dwell in you richly as you teach and admonish one another with all wisdom, and as you sing psalms, hymns, and spiritual songs with gratitude in your hearts to God." Colossians 3:16 (NIV)

Word of the Day

Gratitude – A deep state of appreciation for what you have. Thankful.

Quotes

"Gratitude is the fairest blossom which springs from the soul: and the heart of man knoweth none more fragrant." Hosea Ballou

"The thing that awakens the deepest well of gratitude in a human being is that God has forgiven sin." Oswald Chambers

"Gratitude is the prayer, while Celebration is the song and the dance of praise." Jonathan Lockwood Huie

"Gratitude warms God's heart, and fills ours with delight." Pam Malow-Isham

"Gratitude, warm, sincere, intense, when it takes possession of the bosom, fills the soul to overflowing and scarce leaves room for any other sentiment or thought." John Quincy Adams

Questions

How do I allow gratitude to shape my life? Do I have a gratitude journal? If so, how often do I write in it? What else could I be grateful for today?

Declarations

I am **grateful** that God's Spirit leads me. I trust God to take care of my life and direct me where I am supposed to go that would be for my highest good. I am loved so very much. I am confident God is good. I remember the giver of gifts. I express **gratitude** at all times.

I am **grateful** for the fantastic gifts I have received and for the ones to come. **Gratitude** is how I choose to look at life. I appreciate the lessons I have learned and the ones I will learn. Even the hard ones have taught me something that has helped me along my path to grow stronger. There is something to be **grateful** for, always.

I believe in my dreams and act on them. I practice **gratitude**. With love in my heart, I am a force for good. I am **grateful** that the world around me is a constant source of amusement and fun. I have an attitude of **gratitude,** so I allow myself to feel great joy right now.

I am **grateful** for my eyes to see the beauty all around me. I am **grateful** for a sound mind that I can focus on right things and make wise choices. I am **grateful** for a muscular body that I can serve and be a blessing to those in my community. I am **grateful** for friends.

I live in **gratitude** as I realize the blessings of life. I live in a beautiful world and take steps to have a successful day. I put my attention on the good that has already manifested in my life, so then more can materialize. I am **grateful** for everything with no complaints.

I enjoy following my bliss, whatever that may be today. I find it easy to fill my **gratitude** journal with hundreds of new things each day that I am **grateful** for. I reaffirm my joy by acting upbeat and happy. I am **grateful** for my legs. I dance just for the fun of it. I don't care who is watching. I am **grateful** to be me and express myself freely.

8:
Ingratitude
January 8

Bible Verse

"The people of God are being instructed by Moses, but they are being led by God Himself. They can see the cloud of God before them and hear the blowing of trumpets telling them to move, but at the very front of their column is the chest of the covenant. God's presence and His promises go before them as they wander through this wilderness. One of the great truths of Scripture is that God may send His people out, but they are never alone, and He is ever before them. In the same way the Hebrews have led their sheep rather than driving them, God leads His people rather than forcing them to go first into the unknown or into battle. The people griped about life in the wilderness, how hard they felt things were for them, and these evil complaints came up to the ears of the Eternal One. He was furious about this ingratitude, faithlessness, and lack of vision. His anger was kindled, and His fire raged among them and devoured some of the camp's perimeter." Numbers 11:1 (VOICE)

Word of the Day

Ingratitude – Being blind to all the blessings you have right in front of yourself. Self-absorbed. An ingrate.

Quotes

"There be three usual causes of ingratitude upon a benefit received - envy, pride, and covetousness; envy, looking more at other's benefits than our own; pride, looking more at ourselves than at the benefit; covetousness, looking more at what we would have than at what we have." Joseph Hall

"If there be a crime of deeper dye than all the guilty train of human vices, it is ingratitude." Brooke's Earl of Warwick (Francis Greville)

Questions

Where have I let ingratitude slip into my life? Will I ward off ingratitude?

Declarations

As I start my day off right, it goes really well the rest of the day. I am in control of my behavior, able to trust others and enjoy life. I just show up and have fun. Regardless of the **ingratitude** of the people around me, I can still have a great day because I choose to.

I hang around happy people who are encouraging and optimistic. I stay away from people who are full of **ingratitude**. I arrange to surround myself with positive people. **Ingratitude** is like the plague and infects people who are unaware. I choose my friends wisely.

I respect my life. When I notice **ingratitude** creeping into my mind, I immediately choose to change the way I am thinking and appreciate all the blessings I have. I look inside and ponder contentment. I feel overwhelmed by joy as I count all the things God has done for me.

I focus on the infinite ways my body can heal itself. I do what I need to do and eat healthily. I release all the **ingratitude** in my heart now and give God the green light to heal me. I have God's supernatural power to produce miracles in me. I am infused with vitality.

I am a good steward of everything that God gives to me. I serve the Lord with gladness in my heart. I remember to remain thankful and express my gratitude so I will not be perceived as **ungrateful**. I pray for people who are filled with **ingratitude** because I know they are miserable. I am happy when people succeed, and I tell them.

I release all **ingratitude** now. I keep a smile on my face. **Ingratitude** is never an option because I am thankful for everything I have and for all the blessings I continue to obtain. I know God is not finished with me. God has thousands of ways to provide for me, and I am open to receiving them all. I honor God with my life and work.

9:
Understand
January 9

Bible Verses

"But the seed falling on good soil refers to someone who hears the word and understands it. This is the one who produces a crop, yielding a hundred, sixty or thirty times what was sown." Matthew 13:23 (NIV)

"May you experience the love of Christ, though it is too great to understand fully. Then you will be made complete with all the fullness of life and power that comes from God." Ephesians 3:19 (NLT)

Word of the Day

Understand – To figure out the significance of; be conscious of; recognize what something means. Possess knowledge of, or make sense of.

Quotes

"Life is an unfoldment, and the further we travel the more truth we can comprehend. To understand the things that are at our door is the best preparation for understanding those that lie beyond." Hypatia

"You don't need strength to let go of something. What you really need is understanding." Guy Finley

Pam's Perspective

If you never take the time to get to know someone, you will never understand where they are coming from, what they have been through or who they are. Jesus ate with and hung around the so-called rejects because he could see their heart.

Questions

What is the best way for me to understand the person I am talking to? How can I learn to understand others better? Why do I listen?

Declarations

I seek to **understand** what I don't know. I ask intelligent questions. I love to listen to people tell me about themselves. I find people fascinating. I am empathetic, kind and a loyal friend. I research and look for new ways to **understand** the people around me.

I don't worry about what I can't **understand**, so I turn it over to God who gives me peace and contentment. I learn to love. I **understand** we are all different, so I give people a break. I listen with the intent to **understand** the perspective of the other person. I also love myself.

I recognize where my emotions are in my body to **understand** what is happening to me. I **understand** that God loves me and wants me to prosper in all I do. I am full of pep and zeal. I am thoughtful and worthy of all the great things God continues sending my way. With the faith of a child, I totally **understand** I am loved by God.

I am well connected. I **understand** I can accomplish any goal I set for myself. I am open to change. I focus on my goals. Every day, in every way, I **understand** more and more. I help others **understand** the enormous potential inside of them through my positive words.

I am above playing guessing games. I ask my mate precisely what he or she wants and likes, so I **understand** how to make him or her happy. I look for new ways to enhance our relationship to increase our **understanding** of each other. I **understand** my greatness.

I **understand** that I must read great wisdom to recall it. I memorize encouraging words so I can remember them. I am generously given sufficient **understanding** when I need it. I open the doors of success with my winning personality. Today I **understand** that it is my time to seize the day with a smile on my face and hope in my heart.

10:
Misunderstand
January 10

Bible Verses

"Don't misunderstand why I have come. I did not come to abolish the Law of Moses or the writings of the prophets. No, I came to accomplish their purpose." Matthew 5:17 (NLT)

"Why do you misunderstand what I say? It is because you are unable to hear what I am saying. [You cannot bear to listen to My message; your ears are shut to My teaching.]" John 8:43 (AMP)

Word of the Day

Misunderstand – To be confused, bewildered or perplexed. Not able to judge correctly. To miss the point given.

Quotes

"When we release all assumptions and preconceptions, then listen earnestly, misunderstandings will be a thing of the past." Pam Malow-Isham

"To be great is to be misunderstood." Ralph Waldo Emerson

"A fixed hear is a well of water, a river of life, a stream of joy, and a peace that passes all misunderstanding! Well, glory to our Christ." Bud Robinson

"We're all islands shouting lies to each other across seas of misunderstanding." Rudyard Kipling

Questions

Do I ask people to be clear and decisive so I won't misunderstand them? Do I pause and listen? Why do I find it simple to communicate so people won't misunderstand me? Could there be a misunderstanding between a family member or friend that I have not resolved yet? Why is that?

Declarations

I honor myself by accepting my humanness. There are going to be times when I feel like someone **misunderstands** me and doesn't know what I am going through, so I articulate to the best of my ability my thoughts and feelings. I release all **misunderstandings** and live on a higher moral plane of acceptance and mutual respect. I forgive those who **misunderstand** me and open my heart to love.

I resist the urge to get bitter and play the victim game about how people **misunderstand** me. Instead, I choose to rise above the incident with love. I accept responsibility for not being clear in my communications. I never assume people know what I want, think, need, or expect. I naturally communicate clearly and precisely. I like being polite, kind, understanding, and caring to people around me.

God never **misunderstands** my motives. He sees right through me and knows every aspect of my existence. He is with me in every situation, comforting me with His Divine grace and mercy. I feel an inner peace knowing I am safe, highly thought of and well preserved. I pray for God to show me where I **misunderstand** Him.

I may **misunderstand** people, yet I am persistent enough to keep trying to appreciate them. I explore what it is like to be the other person who is **misunderstood**. I empathize to make sense of what people are saying. I remember to be courteous, kind, and conscious of other people's needs, so I don't **misunderstand** them.

Misunderstanding is natural depending on what perception I am coming from. I come across as being open and approachable. I never guess what someone is thinking so I don't **misunderstand** them. I improve my personality by being charitable. I multiply my happiness by sharing it with others even if they **misunderstand** me.

11:
Absence
January 11

Bible Verse
"Therefore, my beloved, as you have always obeyed, not as in my presence only, but now much more in my absence, work out your own salvation with fear and trembling." Philippians 2:12 (ESV)

Word of the Day
Absence – Condition of being unaware, gone, and distant. Not there. AWOL. Deserted.

Quotes
"Absence extinguishes small passions and increases great ones, as the wind will blow out a candle and blow in a fire." Francois De La Rochefoucauld

"What hurt we have caused in our absence. 'Elvis has left the building.' We have checked out. The fear has shut us down. Years ago we flipped onto cruise control, busying ourselves with every important thing. We all know the script, but what is a script with a closed soul? As my friend Billy Blue says, 'She looks like an angel, but she's a cripple on the inside.' We cannot give what we do not have so we work to look the part and hope no one knows the difference. Hiding behind the script, we rob our husbands and wives and friends of real fellowship and shared life. Do you not see how your absence has left your spouse without a friend?" C. Baxter Kruger

Pam's Perspective
The absence of God was not possible, no matter how far I tried to run from Him.

Questions
Why would I allow another person's absence to affect me? Have there been times when I was physically present but mentally absent?

Declarations

I never miss the **absence** of God for He is at home in me. I give from the depths of my heart. I never cease bearing fruit. I look forward to being engaged with my family. My **absence** from my loved ones makes me appreciate them more when I am with them.

Even if I suffered from the **absence** of a parent growing up, I know God's love never fails and will never leave me. I hang around kind people who have my back. Our **absence** from each other strengthens our friendship. Their love and acceptance gratify me.

There is always an **absence** of strife in my home because we get along splendidly, giving each other room to grow. There is no **absence** of appreciation for all the little things that my family does for me. Nothing gets by me. Trusting my family for support is ok.

I have an **absence** of dirt in my home because I like to keep it clean, well-organized and clutter free. I like to relax at home in the **absence** of people. I recognize what I cannot do, so I get help taking care of any daunting tasks by asking. It is OK to ask for help and advice.

The **absence** around my house of sugary foods prevents me from being tempted to snack. I have very healthy cells living in my body, and I want to keep them that way. I take the initiative to stay active. I am in great shape and looking good. Having fun is my priority.

I give myself permission to like myself. There is no **absence** of confidence in me. I am great, and I know it. I am the source of my own happiness. I have an **absence** of sarcasm in me because it is not beneficial. With an **absence** of fear, I make significant decisions. I have the power within me to make the grade at every turn, boosting things in my favor. I am connected to peace and delight in sharing it.

12:
Presence
January 12

Bible Verse

"[That you may really come] to know [practically, through experience for yourselves] the love of Christ, which far surpasses mere knowledge [without experience]; that you may be filled [through all your being] unto all the fullness of God [may have the richest measure of the divine Presence, and become a body wholly filled and flooded with God Himself]!" Ephesians 3:19 (AMP)

Word of the Day

Presence –Poise. Stance. Essence. Being here in the now. Companionship.

Quotes

"I just make it my business only to persevere in His holy presence, wherein I keep myself by a simple attention, and a general fond regard to God, which I may call an actual presence of God; or, to speak better, a habitual, silent, and secret conversation of the soul with God, which often cause me joys and raptures inwardly, and sometimes also outwardly." Brother Lawrence

"The best effect of the fine persons is felt after we have left their presence." Ralph Waldo Emerson

Pam's Perspective

When I learned my presence could cheer up and motivate someone, or demean them, I made the conscious choice to be a presence for good. Now I make sure that my presence brightens every room I enter. Wherever I go, I carry the presence of peace, happiness, and love with me.

Questions

How do I respond in Love's presence? What does my presence convey? Why is my presence important? Do I recognize the presence of God?

Declarations

My **presence** is welcomed everywhere I go. I am brave. Anything is possible today. I am willing to receive Divine direction. I have a dynamite personality. I dare to believe in my ability to get the job done. I have a maverick **presence** that only concentrates on good.

I have the **presence** of mind to keep quiet when I get upset so I can respond in love. I stop and think before I speak and ask myself, is this going to edify anyone? I release the past and keep an open **presence**. I hold my peace, breathe deeply, and stay centered. I bring my whole **presence** into every conversation. I remember who I am.

I am thankful that God's **presence** is always with me, and will never leave me, whether I feel it or not. I habitually listen to the Holy Spirit. I am kind to myself when I make a habit of dwelling in God's **presence**. God's unstoppable **presence** gives me great peace.

I am looking for excellent companions to be in my **presence**. I attract great role models as friends. I budget my time to spend with people whose **presence** most enhance my life. I make my **presence** readily accessible to my family and friends. I love deeply and freely.

I challenge myself to work with the **presence** of acting like I am valuable for ninety days to see what happens. I persistently demand more from myself. I astound myself at how capable I really am. My **presence** is a force to be reckoned with. I am at the top of my game. I recognize substantial opportunities with my honorable **presence**.

I stand taller as I choose to take on the **presence** of a champion. People love to promote my business. I listen for golden nuggets as I remain teachable and realize I can learn from everyone. I give myself license to rejoice and be happy every day. I am a **presence** for good.

13:
Authentic
January 13

Bible Verses

"For the one whom God sent speaks the authentic words of God—and there can be no measuring of the Spirit given to him!" John 3:34 (PHILLIPS)

"Don't be nitpickers; use your head – and heart! – To discern what is right, to test what is authentically right." John 7:24 (MSG)

Word of the Day

Authentic – The real deal: Being legitimate, not phony: Credible personality, faithful, pure: True blue.

Quotes

"True freedom comes from accepting ourselves unconditionally and being totally authentic about who we are, no matter what." Pam Malow-Isham

"'Tis nature's system of divinity and every student of the night inspires. 'Tis elder scripture, writ by God's own hand: Scripture authentic! Uncorrupt by man." Edward Young's Night Thoughts

"Accepting the reality of our sinfulness means accepting our authentic self. Judas could not face his shadow; Peter could. The latter befriended the impostor within; the former raged against him." Brennan Manning

"The ultimate goal of being ourselves in an authentic way is actually about loving ourselves in a generous way." Mike Robbins

Questions

Why is it natural for me to be authentic in all my relationships? Is there any area of my life where I have not been authentic to myself? If so, why is that? What can I do to rectify any inauthenticity?

Declarations

I live an **authentic** life to the best of my ability. I love being real and showing the world the magnificent person I am. As I am **authentic** with others, it opens the doors for them to be **authentic** with me. Everything works out perfectly as I live **authentically**, on purpose.

I am very good looking. I do not care about the opinions of other people or what they think about me because I am on the **authentic** path. I choose to show up and keep it real. I am what I say I am and I am happy to be me. People appreciate an **authentic** person, so they appreciate me. I live with passion and exuberance when I am faithful to my **authentic** self. My life is liberating and full of joy.

I remember that I am adored. I am only accountable to God who believes I am **authentically** beautiful. I have a loving mindset that is full of tolerance. I know, 'but for the grace of God there go I,' so I let go of judgment which allows me to accept others **authentically**. I have loving thoughts about the people around me. I keep an open mind; **authentically** looking at all sides of the story before I decide.

I am **authentic** to myself realizing my strengths, weakness and taking 100% responsibility for every area of my life. I choose to let my **authentic** self be seen. I desire more **authenticity** and honesty from my friends, so I show them how easy it is to be vulnerable and open. Although scary at times, being **authentic** accelerates intimacy. I am willing to be **authentic** even if I might feel uncomfortable.

People listen to me because I am **authentic**. I radiate contentment and have an overflow of joy. I am stunning today, full of vitality. Living **authentically** for me is a lifelong journey full of lessons to learn. I am grateful for who God **authentically** created me to be. I say yes to **authenticity**. I have a capacity to care, and I show it.

14:
Hypocrite
January 14

Bible Verses

"Hypocrite! First get rid of the log in your own eye; then you will see well enough to deal with the speck in your friend's eye." Matthew 7:5 (NLT)

"Jesus replied, 'You hypocrites! Isaiah was right when he prophesied about you, for he wrote, 'These people honor me with their lips, but their hearts are far from me.'" Mark 7:6 (NLT)

Word of the Day

Hypocrite – An unauthentic person. Someone who says they are honorable while being deceptive, deceitful and fraudulent in their actions.

Quote

"Take care lest you play the hypocrite by spending all your time trying to get others right before you worship God yourself." Oswald Chambers

Pam's Perspective

I remember the first time I quit smoking thinking, praise God, glad I am not like those smokers anymore. I will never do that again. Only to find myself smoking and stopping several times before it finally stuck. Seeing myself like the Pharisee in Luke 18:11 did not feel right. Admitting I was a hypocrite is humbling and freeing at the same time, but the only way to live authentically. Realizing where I needed to change, accepting it, and then evolving was vital to being real. As I progress, I continue to find myself being a hypocrite and I probably always will. But now I can face my hypocrisy without fear and share it with the world.

Questions

Is it possible I have judged people when I have done the same thing? Why do I justify my actions and condemn others?

Declarations

When I realize I am a **hypocrite**, I free myself from egotism. I know my faults. Even though I may have thoughts and deeds of envy, greed, jealousy, pride, lust, sloth, gluttony, wrath, and judgments about others every day, I forgive myself and work on being my best.

God knows that I am a **hypocrite** and that I make mistakes. He does not expect perfection, only willingness. God laughs at my **hypocrisy**. I cheerfully follow His lead as I go from glory to glory, growing ever more in His likeness. I admit when I am a **hypocrite**. I choose to think good thoughts, do excellent work, speak good news, and show kindness to everyone. I am prepared to share smiles and hugs.

When I see someone acting like a **hypocrite**, I say a prayer for him or her. I look at myself to see where I could be a **hypocrite** too. There are ways I could use some improvement, so I take deliberate action. I like being honest with myself, even when it hurts my ego.

I remember to stay real. I absolve myself for being a **hypocrite** and move on. I am liberated from the bondage of perfection and pride as I walk in humility and unconditional love. I am rare, special, and beautiful, and so is every other person on this planet. We all belong.

Being a **hypocrite** does not mean that I am a terrible person. It just means I am human. We are all mortal. I realize just as I can see when someone is a **hypocrite**; they also can see when I am a **hypocrite**. I am thankful for this happy life will all the **hypocrites** in it.

I train my brain to focus on being authentic, so I can face the **hypocrite** in the mirror. I am an open book. I write new adventures in the pages to come that is free from **hypocrisy**. I surrender to a loving God who wants to give me good gifts, despite my **hypocrisy**.

15:
Declare
January 15

Bible Verses
"Declare His glory among the nations, His marvelous works among all the peoples." 1 Chronicles 16:24 (NRSV)

"This is the message we have heard from him and declare to you: God is light; in him there is no darkness at all." 1 John 1:5 (NIV)

Word of the Day
Declare – To affirm out loud and make your intention known. Notify.

Quotes
"Real political issues cannot be manufactured by the leaders of political parties, and real ones cannot be evaded by political parties. The real political issues of the day declare themselves, and come out of the depth of that deep which we call public opinion." James A. Garfield

"Stand upright, speak thy thoughts, declare the truth thou hast, that all may share; be bold, proclaim it everywhere: They only live who dare." L. Morris

"The same words conceal and declare the thoughts of men." Dionysius Cato

Pam's Perspective
The power of declarations has transformed my life. I used to be shy, insecure and depressed. Now I start the day with enthusiasm as I declare I am going to have a great day and end it with a smile. Declarations continually create my existence, good or bad.

Questions
Why is it automatic for me to declare God's promises over my life? Does what I declare coincide with what I want and believe? If not, why not?

Declarations

I **declare** I am blessed with God's supernatural creativity, wisdom, and ability. I appreciate my healthy mind. I **declare** all my plans succeed. I **declare** I always have a great attitude and a progressive outlook on life. I recognize and pay attention to wisdom.

I declare I have the mind of Christ. As I turn all my cares over to Him, I have peace of mind and excellent understanding. I **declare** I can hear God speaking to me, leading me, and I gladly obey. I am always trustworthy. I am a reflection of God's love. I **declare** God's provision meets my needs. I **declare** I still have enough.

I **declare** I am courageous, healthy and rich. I gain respect from my co-workers as I remember to speak up for myself. God promotes me at just the right time. I **declare** my ultimate victory today. I feel great. I prosper in all my endeavors. I **declare** I am a wealthy person.

I **declare** I am covered by a divine security blanket when I travel. I love traveling first class. I **declare** wherever I am; I am safe. I pray over every decision I make and then move in that direction. I listen to my inner voice and receive the perfect answer. I feel powerful.

I **declare** any negative word or curse that has been spoken over me is broken. I **declare** God's fabulous favor shines on me. Those who bless me, God blesses. I forgive myself for any negative words I have spoken to myself or others. I **declare** wholeness and strength are mine. I **declare** all is well despite the negativity in the world.

I **declare** I have the spunk, self-discipline, self-respect, fortitude, and determination to achieve my goals. I **declare** I am blessed with loyal, loving, lifelong allies. I am willing to be on top and stay there. I **declare** I keep getting healthier every single day in every way.

16:
Deny
January 16

Bible Verses
"If we are unfaithful, he remains faithful, for he cannot deny who he is." 2 Timothy 2:13 (NLT)

"I know all the things you do, and I have opened a door for you that no one can close. You have little strength, yet you obeyed my word and did not deny me." Revelation 3:8 (NLT)

Word of the Day
Deny – To recant what was thought to be factual. To withhold something from someone. To place doubt, contradict.

Quotes
"We, ignorant of ourselves, beg often our own harms, which the wise powers deny us for our good; so we find profit, by losing of our prayers." Shakespeare

"Never deny your greatness. You are a child of God." Pam Malow-Isham

"In all intellectual debates, both sides tend to be correct in what they affirm, and wrong in what they deny." John Stuart Mill

Pam's Perspective
Denying my abuse happened intensified the torment for me because I kept silent. I should have screamed and reported it immediately. Now I know better.

Questions
Have I denied myself happiness or love? What else do I deny myself? Is it a hardship for me to deny myself something when it will help me reach my goal? Can I choose to be happy when I deny myself?

Declarations

I can't **deny** the fact that almost everyone likes me and most people love me. I never **deny** a warm embrace or hold back a smile. It feels good to laugh in the face of hardships. I **deny** myself the immediate gratification of purchasing something on credit to feel the overwhelming satisfaction of paying for it with cash.

I work on the areas in my life where I am not performing well and **deny** myself from getting lackadaisical. I learn and grow from my past blunders; I don't **deny** them. I don't **deny** I need help, so I ask for it when I need it. I **deny** myself trivial activities, so I can enjoy the reward of a well done completed job. I love being useful.

By **denying** myself junk food, I enjoy a healthier body. I **deny** the comfort of sitting on the couch and replace it with the exhilarating feeling I get after working out. I like feeling energetic and strong. I **deny** striving for perfection so I can enjoy my reality right now.

I can't **deny** God's love for me or mine for Him. I **deny** holding a grudge, so I can release forgiveness and live in complete freedom. I am attuned to the whispers of the Spirit. I testify of what God has done for me. It is up to me to be someone's miracle today. I can't **deny** the power of God within me. I stay open to love.

I won't **deny** myself the pleasure of cheering up someone, even though I may feel down. I can't **deny** spreading my joy and laughter. I have awesome friends. My joy comes from the Lord who reigns over me. I go within to find peace, satisfaction, and contentment.

At no time will I **deny** my unlimited potential. I am excited to be alive. I **deny** the security of a safe harbor to go out and face the storms to reach my goals. I am daring to live on the edge and thrive.

17:
Tranquil
January 17

Bible Verses

"The Lord lift up His [approving] countenance upon you and give you peace (tranquility of heart and life continually)." Numbers 6:26 (AMP)

"A tranquil heart is life to the body, but jealousy is rottenness to the bones." Proverbs 14:30 (HCSB)

Word of the Day

Tranquil – Calm and undisturbed by the environment; peace-loving, still:

Quotes

"We think a happy life consists in tranquility of mind." Marcus Tullius Cicero

"Teachers of truth and ministers of love; Love for all moral power - all mental grace - Love for the humblest of the human race - Love for the tranquil joy that virtue brings - Love for the Giver of all goodly things." John Critchley Prince

Pam's Perspective

I named my massage business "The Tranquility Center" with a tagline "A Resting Place For Sore And Tired Muscles." I created a tranquil space to work despite living in a chaotic world. I feel very fortunate to have found vocations that I love. People look forward to seeing me and are happy when they leave. Living with tranquil power through mind training was worth the time and investment. Anyone can experience a life full of joy and tranquility if they only choose to.

Questions

Is my mind tranquil? If not, what can I do to make it so? Is my home a place of tranquility? If not, what can I do to make it so? How can I create and maintain a more tranquil life? Why is tranquility so vital to me?

Declarations

I have a calm and **tranquil** mind. I bring **tranquility** with me in all my endeavors. God's **tranquil** presence inside of me is a constant source of strength. I have the **tranquil** assurance of eternal life because I am God's child. We are forever united together.

I live in a way that is **tranquil** and peaceful. I encourage others to be **tranquil** and live in love. By living this **tranquil** way, no matter what is happening around me, I stay grounded in love and blissfully happy. I have positive emotions around my desires. I love myself.

My home is a cozy haven of **tranquility**. I remember to slow down and enjoy life. I am in control. From the time I get out of bed to the time I go to sleep, I am filled with **tranquil** joy. Doing things is easy.

I have **tranquil** power to overcome anything, and I am not moved by what other people think or say. By being **tranquil,** I improve the relationships I have with other people as I manifest patience and tolerance. I have noteworthy intentions. I am calm and **tranquil**.

God's love fills me with dynamic energy and **tranquil** brilliance to achieve my dreams. I realize the blessing I am to others. I am good-natured. Love fuels me, and my **tranquil** presence is very magnetic.

Tranquility is my natural state of mind. I have serene thoughts. I live in faith and grow stronger every day. I am grateful for **tranquil** moments. With **tranquility**, I accomplish my God-given dreams.

Now is my time. I am ready to step into **tranquil** greatness. I am **tranquil** and dynamic. I put on my creative hat and allow the ideas flow. I live in a **tranquil** world of joy, harmony, and inspiration. Things naturally are **tranquil** around me and filled with peace.

18:
Chaos
January 18

Bible Verses

"When the earth and everyone living upon it spin into chaos, I am the One who stabilizes and supports it. [Pause]" Psalm 75:3 (VOICE)

"Any place where you find jealousy and selfish ambition, you will discover chaos and evil thriving under its rule." James 3:16 (VOICE)

Word of the Day

Chaos – The disorder and discord of a confused group of people. Pandemonium. Clutter and mess of surroundings. Turmoil of spirit.

Quotes

"Free will makes us responsible for the chaos we create." Pam Malow-Isham

"Invention, it must be humbly admitted, does not consist in creating out of void, but out of chaos." Mary Shelley

Pam's Perspective

The chaos in my mind and the chaos happening at home reflected in how chaotic my bedroom looked when I was young. I yearned for order and safety. When I left home, I attracted friends who thrived on chaos. Not until I learned how to quiet my mind did the chaos stop. Going within was a scary place for me. Feeling unworthy of peace was part of the problem. Learning to believe in myself and my abilities empowered me to sit in silence and be comfortable amidst any chaos.

Questions

Do I have chaos in my life now? What purpose is it serving? Is there something I can do today to make my life more peaceful? Do I have any clutter that I need to get rid of? Can I be OK without stuff?

Declarations

I make a schedule of my activities to stave off **chaos**. I release blame and take responsibility for the **chaos** I have created. I am fruitful and see myself with fresh eyes. I recognize my feelings and admit the **chaos** when it is happening. I forgive myself for the **chaos** I have generated and take action for putting order back into my life. I conform to God's will. It feels remarkable living **chaos** free.

I choose to grow up and be accountable for all my actions. I am the master of my life and destiny. I minimize the **chaos** and my stress level by asking for help when I need it. I renew my strength by getting enough sleep, eating healthy and working out. I am calm and at peace during **chaos** because the Lord is by my side.

I live a well-organized life. I am satisfied with what I have. I am diligent about keeping the **chaos** at bay in my home by keeping it clean and putting stuff away immediately after I use it. I frequently un-clutter my house by donating things I no longer need to charity.

I feel grounded in peace and love. I am cheery. I distance myself from **chaotic** people. I enjoy having a calm and still demeanor in the midst of **chaos**. I am happy, full of vigor and ready to meet every challenge that comes my way. I improve my mood by cheering someone up who is in a **chaotic** situation. I surround myself with people who know how to give and receive compliments. I feel renewed as I remember to trust my inner guidance while in **chaos**.

I battle the spirit of fear, **chaos**, and negativity by speaking positive declarations. I sooth the **chaos** in my head by visualizing what I want to see. I accept myself unconditionally, just like God does. I ease the **chaos** in my mind by meditating on God's Word. God has made something wonderful out of the **chaos** in my life.

19:
Certain
January 19

Bible Verses
"So let everyone in Israel know for certain that God has made this Jesus, whom you crucified, to be both Lord and Messiah!" Acts 2:36 (NLT)

"Our great desire is that you will keep on loving others as long as life lasts, in order to make certain that what you hope for will come true." Hebrews 6:11 (NLT)

Word of the Day
Certain – Convinced about outcome or authenticity. Assured; Positive; Unconcerned; Self-confident.

Quotes
"Researchers have found under some circumstances that people, when claiming to be 99% certain of something, are wrong 40% of the time." Tim Brownson

"A doubtful friend is worse than a certain enemy. Let a man be one thing or the other, and we then know how to meet him." Aesop

Pam's Perspective
When I was in high school, I was certain all the planets would line up, and the world would come to an end in nineteen eighty-two. I was distraught thinking why go to school if we are just going to be blown up in a few years. When nothing happened, I wished I had paid better attention in school. One thing I know for certain is I do not know much. That keeps me curious and open to learning.

Questions
What am I certain of today? Are there things I was certain of in the past that I now disagree with? If so, what are they? Who am I certain in?

Declarations

God is in a good mood today and wants to give me **certain** valuable gifts. I keep myself open to receive. I have a devotional practice that is right for me. I am **certain** I am loved and adored by God. He is **certain** to show me His mercy daily. I am a reflective genius of the Wisest Spirit. I celebrate how God uses me in **certain** ways.

I am honest about the kind of person I am in **certain** circles. I am hopeful and energetic. I enjoy every step I take toward my goals. I am **certainly** grateful. I release stories I have told myself about how I can't do something. I break free and shatter the invisible field that has held me back from **certain** achievements and move ahead.

I make **certain** to get enough exercise so, I stay strong, healthy and vibrant. I am responsible for everything I eat. I **certainly** do things the right way and in the correct order. I abound with vitality. I **certainly** win at the game of life, and I am happy to be here. I use my mind to make **certain** my body continually performs well.

I take **certain** steps to keep myself positive. Listening to motivational speakers and reading great books **certainly** helps my mood. I choose to be around **certain** people with positive attitudes who lift me up and support my goals. I will do what it takes to achieve the **certain** success I want. I act for **certain** like the guaranteed winner that I am.

Certain synchronistic opportunities and connections are drawn to me as I go about doing great things. I let go of having to know for **certain** how something is going to turn out and leap ahead in faith believing for the best possible outcome. I **certainly** keep going and never give up. God has my back. I stand **certain** on my ability to get a job done. I am happy with my resourcefulness. For **certain** I get what I focus on. So I make **certain** to focus on the good I desire.

20:
Dream
January 20

Bible Verses
"Here comes the dreamer!" they said. Genesis 37:19 (NLT)

"Then, after doing all those things, I will pour out my Spirit upon all people. Your sons and daughters will prophesy. Your old men will dream dreams, and your young men will see visions." Joel 2:28 (NLT)

Word of the Day
Dream – The image of the things you desire. The thoughts you envision that create your future success. A vision or goal.

Quotes
"If one advances confidently in the direction of his dreams, and endeavors to live the life which he has imagined, he will meet with a success unexpected in common hours." Henry David Thoreau

"Dream lofty dreams, and as you dream, so shall you become." James Lane Allen

Pam's Perspective
"Dream on" by Aerosmith was my favorite song growing up. I dreamed of being happy, healthy and wealthy as I traveled around the world encouraging people. I made vision boards of exotic places. My dreams are coming true. So far, I have gone to twenty-five different countries and forty-seven states.

Questions
"Are you building a case for or against your dreams? Do you spend more time thinking of how it can work or more time around why it won't? Are you all in or one foot in and one foot out with your dreams and goals?" Tiffany Peterson

Declarations

I am completely capable of realizing my **dreams**. What is impossible is not a fact and what is impossible with man is possible with God. God would not give me these **dreams** if He did not want me to fulfill them. I am a partner with God, so everything is possible.

My passionate desire to achieve my **dreams** is unmatched. I know I have what it takes. I am essential and very valuable. I have faith in my **dreams**. My impossible **dream** becomes a reality as I move forward. I look for blessings in disguise as I **dream** new **dreams**.

I am a **dreamer**. As I verbalize my **dreams** to experts, they endorse me to their colleagues. I **dream** big audacious **dreams**. I visualize my **dreams** fulfilled as I act on accomplishing them. I am a hard worker who realizes my **dreams**. I study the techniques of champions. I create a neighborhood of unity and teamwork around me.

I am willing to see my **dreams** come true so I take powerful, decisive steps to reach them. Excessive kindness is directed my way, and people are inspired to help me accomplish my **dreams**. My godly thought life precedes my ultimate success. I invite discovery and creativity to come forth as I lie down at night to **dream**.

I permit myself to **dream** big. I remember how to have fun again, **dreaming** of good times. Being curious is amusing and a great way to learn. I am always up for the challenge. I **dream** up new goals. I spend a minute every hour relaxing, focusing on my **dreams**.

God created me for a unique purpose and cares about my **dreams**. No **dream** is too big or small. As my **dreams** come true, I flourish and bring blessings to others. With single-minded focus, I achieve the task at hand to accomplish my fantastic God-inspired **dreams**.

21:
Flow
January 21

Bible Verses

"Then your store-houses will be filled with many good things, and your barrels will flow over with new wine." Proverbs 3:10 (NLV)

"Send your grain across the seas, and in time, profits will flow back to you." Ecclesiastes 11:1 (NLT)

Word of the Day

Flow – To calmly move without hindrance. To conveniently scatter and share the wealth that is part of our lives. Movement.

Quotes

"In a state of grace, the soul is like a well of limpid water, from which flow only streams of clearest crystal. Its works are pleasing both to God and man, rising from the River of Life, beside which it is rooted like a tree." Saint Teresa of Avila

"Praise God, from whom all blessings flow! Praise Him, all creatures here below! Praise Him above, ye heavenly host! Praise Father, Son, and Holy Ghost." Thomas Ken

"All the life of God is a flow of the divine self-giving charity. Charity itself is sacrifice – the self-impartation of the Divine Being." Frederick William Robertson

"A laugh to be joyous must flow from a joyous heart, but without kindness, there can be no true joy." Jean-Baptiste-Louis Gresset

Questions

What is the best way to flow through life with ease and grace? Have I interrupted my flow of abundance by my words? If so, what will I do to reinstall the flow of opulence? Why is my life in the flow of good?

Declarations

Kind words **flow** from my lips. As I step into the **flow** of inspiration from on High, I create the great things I desire. I am enveloped with multiple options. The **flow** of good energy around me is a constant source of happiness. I **flow** up to the head of the line. I **flow** with creativity as I immerse myself with joy in what I am doing.

The **flow** of abundance rushes through my windows as I fling them open, ready to receive all the good God has for me. I feel light and vibrant, as I imagine myself to be in the **flow** of grace. I confidently trust God to **flow** with me. I listen to whispers **flowing** from above.

I believe God is the path to the **flow** of abundance. The **flow** of natural resources is unending for me. Feeling God's love is enough for me. I don't have to do anything to justify myself to God. I am always enough. I **flow** through fear and come out courageous.

Walking in the **flow**, I stream toward success. I easily **flow** through stressful situations with great ease and abundant energy. I enjoy myself as I go with the **flow** and clear away distractions that impede my growth. I do the hard things first. The pleasure of getting into the **flow** allows me to complete my tasks happily and on time.

I allow my love to **flow** to my friends and family. I was created for fellowship. I allow joy to **flow** from my heart to assist the people around me. Smiles naturally **flow** to my face and light up the room.

I allow the Holy Spirit to **flow** through my body healing everything that needs healing. I love my beautiful body that is full of health and vigor. I eat for health and treat my body with respect. I am willing to rest and meditate when I feel like I am getting overwhelmed. After I take a break, I jump back into the **flow** of life and charge ahead.

22:
Overflow
January 22

Bible Verses

"Bring the whole tithe into the storehouse, so that there may be food in My house, and test Me now in this," says the Lord of hosts, "if I will not open for you the windows of heaven and pour out for you a blessing until it overflows." Malachi 3:10 (NASB)

"May the God of hope fill you with all joy and peace as you trust in him, so that you may overflow with hope by the power of the Holy Spirit." Romans 15:13 (NIV)

Word of the Day

Overflow – To flood with a surplus. Having a plethora of excess.

Quote

"There are two ways of loving: from our overflow or from our reserve. Loving from our overflow means that we are taking the time to give love, appreciation, and tenderness to ourselves. Our hearts have learned to take in love, and we have shifted the direction of our loving inward until our "cup runneth over." This is the healthiest way to love others. The love we give from a full cup is clean, pure, and free of expectation, need, or manipulation. The other way to love is from our reserve. This is love that is diluted by need, pain, and co-dependence. Loving from our reserve leaves us feeling empty instead of full. It is transactional because we expect to get something in return for the love we are giving, and we are always disappointed regardless of how much or how little love we actually receive. Can we ever love too much? No, not if we are loving from our overflow; yes, if we are loving from our reserve." Frankie Waldo Perez

Questions

What does living in the overflow of blessings feel like to me? How do I create that overflow? Why is living in the overflow the norm for me?

Declarations

I start fresh today with a positive outlook on life. I take vitamins and supplements daily to enhance my health. I have an **overflow** of options. I give myself permission to be healthy. I have an **overflow** of strong muscles because I work out and take care of myself. I live a delighted fulfilled life and inspire others to let their love **overflow**.

Many cherish me as I let my unique gifts and talents be on display. I frolic in the **overflow** of love. I spread happiness wherever I go. My life is a constant stream of **overflowing** miracles. Abundance flows into my life in surprising and miraculous ways. I say yes to me.

God crushes and breaks down the walls of fear and strife with His **overflowing** love. I walk under the anointing of God, full of power and strength. I serve my community from the **overflow** of peace and goodwill that is in my heart. I bless the good in my world.

I **overflow** with the favor of God because of His great love for me. I like being God's favorite child. I claim my power and show up prepared and ready for the **overflow** headed my way. It is safe for me to grow up and be in charge. I give from my financial **overflow**.

My bank account **overflows** with plenty, so I always have more than enough for my family and to help out with worthy causes. I am comfortable attracting success. I receive unexpected checks in the mail and an **overflow** of thank you cards for my many kind deeds.

I gladly receive the **overflow** of gifts that God has for me. I ask, and I win. I **overflow** with laughter, just because I can. I **overflow** with good vibes as I dance on happy feet. I like being in a positive mood so I can **overflow** with joy. I have a lot of friends. I **overflow** with pride because my children are happy, healthy and full of wisdom.

23:
Worthy
January 23

Bible Verses
"The elders who direct the affairs of the church well are worthy of double honor, especially those whose work is preaching and teaching." 1 Timothy 5:17 (NIV)

"Jesus has been found worthy of greater honor than Moses, just as the builder of a house has greater honor than the house itself." Hebrews 3:3 (NIV)

Word of the Day
Worthy – A person or thing of immense value. Worthwhile; reputable; praiseworthy. A person thought of with great respect and honor.

Quotes
"Where you confer a benefit on those worthy of it, you confer a favour on all." Publilius Syrus

"We all dream of being exactly what we are – powerful, beautiful, and worthy." Vironika Tugaleva

Pam's Perspective
The realization that Christ thought I was worthy enough to come, die for me and rise again because He loves me unconditionally, even if I had been the only person on the planet, opened my eyes to see my worth. Nothing in heaven or on earth can keep His love from me. Now my goal is to help people realize how much God loves them and help them discover how worthy they are.

Questions
What determines my worthiness? Why is that? What or who have I looked to in the past for my sense of worth? Why is that? Why do I feel worthy of love from God and everyone else? How can I show my worth?

Declarations

We are all God's children **worthy** of love. Since God has done for others, He can do the same for me and more! I am deserving and **worthy** of love. I am secure and take back my **worth** and power. As I operate from love, God works everything out for my highest good.

I am free to love others and myself in a healthy and **worthy** way. Being considerate of others shows I care about their **worth**. I have **trustworthy** friends. I know how to give and receive compliments. I am a **worthwhile** friend, confidant, companion, and co-worker.

I get things done, am pleasant to look at and **worthy** of the good life. I am appreciated for my **worthy** efforts and endeavors. I immerse my energy in activities I enjoy. I am flexible and go with the flow.

I am **worthy** of breathing slowly and deeply relaxing into this Divine moment. I am very important. I believe what God has to say about me. I receive my **worth** from within. I open my mind to my own **worth**. I think **worthy** thoughts and my awareness expands exponentially. I decide to treat myself with **worth** and honor.

I am **worthy** of perfect health, so I eat healthy food. I appreciate my beautiful body. I am thankful I don't have to prove my **worth** to God to be loved. I speak positively about my good traits and my ability to do a great job. I open my heart and allow love to come rushing in.

I give myself permission to love and respect myself. Only I can decide my **worthiness**. I give myself praise often. I live present to joy. I love being **worthy**. I am God's beloved. I am **worthy** of luxurious things. I have a lovely home. I am conscious of being awake to this **worthy** life. Simply because I am alive today makes me **worthy** of love. My **worth** is a blessing to the world.

24:
Unworthy
January 24

Bible Verses
"Take care lest there be an unworthy thought in your heart and you say, 'The seventh year, the year of release is near,' and your eye look grudgingly on your poor brother, and you give him nothing, and he cries to the Lord against you, and you be guilty of sin." Deuteronomy 15:9 (ESV)

"And if the household is worthy, let your peace be on it. But if it is unworthy, let your peace return to you." Matthew 10:13 (HCSB)

Word of the Day
Unworthy – Not good enough; disgraceful: Valueless. Without worth.

Quotes
"If rain can fall on the just and the unjust alike, so can success befall the unworthy. Success is the fruit of natural laws, not supernatural interventions." Richard Gaylord Briley

"How manifestly is this the constitution of grace; that, when perfect obedience can claim no recompense, such unworthy defiled work, should be so honored with an infinite, overwhelming acceptance!" Charles Bridges

Pam's Perspective
Being told I was dumb and ugly by my Dad made me feel unworthy of love or anything else. God healed my brokenness and revealed to me my worth. He can heal you too. Feeling loved, worthy and respected is priceless.

Questions
How do I measure my worth or unworthiness? Am I realistic? Is there any area of my life where I feel unworthy? If so, how can I feel worthy again?

Declarations

I am free from the chains of **unworthy** condemnation because I am a child of the most High God. I am fearfully and wonderfully made in the likeness of God. I release all **unworthy** feelings and take on the revelation of being a person of worth. I bring pleasure to God just by being me. I am joyful and cute. God likes being with me.

I am an ambassador of God and bring good news with me wherever I go. I repent of any **unworthy** thoughts I may have of myself in the past and choose to be clothed in the righteousness of Christ with a positive attitude and a healthy mind. Regardless if others may think I am **unworthy** of prosperity, I see myself succeeding on purpose.

I am highly regarded for the contributions I make in the world. I am dependable, and people know they can count on me. No matter how **unworthy** I may feel, I stop and take care of myself during challenging times. I never treat anyone like they are **unworthy**.

I think about what is good, what is going right and give thanks. I remember to appreciate my great worth and not fret over **unworthy** actions of the past. I see myself beyond **unworthy** and where I am going. I hang around people of high quality who are reliable like me.

I repent of any **unworthy** deeds I have done. I am a person of immense value. I act in an honorable way. I choose to do everything with excellence. I abstain from **unworthy** gossip and profanity. I am above that. I speak words of value that enlighten the world.

I am ready to move beyond **unworthiness** and into abundance. I am lovely and have beautiful gifts. I am **unworthy** to fail, and I shun negativity. I clear my mind and let go of every **unworthy** thing. I am a winner and **unworthy** of anything less than dignity and greatness.

25:
Laughter
January 25

Bible Verses
"Then the young women will dance for joy; the young and old men will join in. I will turn their mourning into laughter and their sadness into joy; I will comfort them." Jeremiah 31:13 (CEB)

"You never saw him, yet you love him. You still don't see him, yet you trust him—with laughter and singing." 1 Peter 1:8 (MSG)

Word of the Day
Laughter – To chuckle, giggle or shriek for glee. To rejoice. The ability to exude joy and hilarity vocally. Snicker; Crack-up.

Quotes
"Laughter is the sound of the soul dancing. My soul probably looks like Fred Astaire." Jarod Kintz

"The most wasted of all days is that on which one has not laughed." Nicolas Chamfort

"With mirth and laughter let old wrinkles come." William Shakespeare

Pam's Perspective
I have a very distinctive, infectious, loud laugh. I was ridiculed by my Dad and told I would never get a man laughing like that, but I didn't change. There is not a day that goes by that I am not laughing at something.

Questions
Have I ever held back from laughter because of the fear of looking silly? What did that cost me? Will I benefit from being a laughter facilitator?

Declarations

I start each day with thanksgiving and **laughter**. God is in a superb mood today and is excited to send gifts my way. I let go of my inhibitions and **laughter** comes quickly, freely and often. God rejoices over me with **laughter** and fills my heart with abundant joy.

I bridge the gap between people with my **laughter**. I fill others with joy by releasing my **laughter**. My **laughter** ignites the **laughs** of others. My **laughter** is the link to sharing good feelings. There is always a reason to **laugh** at all the funny things around me.

I **laugh** at myself when I make a mistake. Spontaneous **laughter** bubbles up inside me and overflows to bless those around me. People become involved with my **laughter**. As they hear it in their heart, they release it with their mouth. I gleefully chuckle as I network with people who like to **laugh**. I love being funny.

The Holy Spirit delights in my singing and **laughter**. My spirit explodes with **laughter**. I trust the Source of my supply. I pay attention to where the Universe is guiding me. I give my attention to what brings me joy. I remember to play and **laugh** often.

I instinctively gravitate toward **laughter**. I fasten **laughter** around my heart with cords of joy. I spread the wealth of **laughter's** benefits and promote healthy living. My contagious **laughter** infects everyone around me with great feelings of joy and bliss.

I bring a heaping measure of joy and **laughter** with me where ever I go. I am filled with happy feelings as I remember the **laughter** of the past. I learn three clean jokes so I can hear anyone **laugh**. I yuck it up with my friends. I contribute to my friend's pleasure by sharing my **laughter** with them. **Laughter** is my constant friend and sidekick.

26:
Despair
January 26

Bible Verses

"He lifted me out of the pit of despair, out of the mud and the mire. He set my feet on solid ground and steadied me as I walked along." Psalm 40:2 (NLT)

"We are often troubled, but not crushed; sometimes in doubt, but never in despair." 2 Corinthians 4:8 (GNT)

Word of the Day

Despair – Depression of the soul. Discouragement. Despondent. Gloomy.

Quotes

"He who learns must suffer. And even in our sleep, pain that cannot forget falls drop by drop upon the heart, and in our own despair, against our will, comes wisdom to us by the awful grace of God." Aeschylus

"Every composer knows the anguish and despair occasioned by forgetting ideas which one has not time to write down, and which thus escape." Hector Berlioz

"Despair – the last dignity of the wretched." Henry Giles

Pam's Perspective

I know what it is like to suffer from depression. Having someone say, cheer up does not help. I must deliberately smile and take a walk or another action to get the despair to leave. One way I have found to make myself feel better is to do volunteer work. When I am helping others, I have no time to wallow in despair.

Questions

Why do I despair? What is the fastest way to lift despair when it comes? What can I do to prevent it? How well do I help others in despair?

Declarations

I set appropriate boundaries when dealing with difficult people in **despairing** situations. I commit several acts of goodwill every day to help those who **despair**. I console those who are in **despair** and alleviate their burden if I can while keeping my sense of humor.

It is no big deal if I feel **despair** occasionally because I am human and I know it is part of life. I feel grateful for my friends. I am totally honest about my feelings. I work through any sorrow I may be feeling by sharing my **despairing** thoughts with someone trusted.

When I fall into **despair**, I quickly turn my attention to my good qualities. I am health-conscious and cook the most nutritious meals for my family. I love to be active and fit. I don't **despair** about my weight because I am working on being healthier every day in every way. I use aromatherapy to lift **despair.** I elevate my mood by diffusing and smelling essential oils. I live a peaceful existence.

Even when there is **despair** all around me, I stay calm and centered without letting it affect me, because I am the master of my thoughts. Showing kindness boosts my spirits and reveals God's love to a **despairing** world. God shows me many options to alleviate **despair**, live in harmony, maintain forgiveness, be happy, and stay peaceful.

God's mercy lifts me from the depths of **despair** and places me on high ground. I feel His comfort satisfying my soul as I am renewed with strength. I celebrate every day to keep **despair** from coming my way. I sing joyfully to lift any **despair** because life is good.

I can choose **despair** or happiness at any given moment, so I choose wisely. I teach others how to be cheerful in trying times. I am enthusiastic and enjoy the happiness that most people dream of.

27:
Purpose
January 27

Bible Verses
"We know that all things work together for good for those who love God, to those who are called according to his purpose." Romans 8:28 (WEB)

"Now the purpose of the commandment is love from a pure heart, from a good conscience, and from sincere faith." 1 Timothy 1:5 (NKJV)

Word of the Day
Purpose – The understanding of why something is brought about. To know why and plan for a specific target. Objective; aspiration; mission.

Quotes
"The purpose of life is to expand in the capacity to love." Marci Shimoff

"We ought not look back unless it is to derive useful lessons from past errors, and for the purpose of profiting by dear-bought experience." George Washington

"Worry ducks when purpose flies overhead." Terri Guillemets

"The purpose of trials is to grow in wisdom." Pam Malow-Isham

Pam's Perspective
My purpose has changed over the years and will continue to improve as I grow and evolve into the masterpiece God designed me to be. Living my purpose causes my life to be brilliant, exciting, and a grand adventure.

Questions
Why does finding my purpose in life mean so much to me? Am I on the right path? If not, why not? Do I have long and short-term goals?

Declarations

I was born for a definite **purpose** and live a life of significance. I am successful in fulfilling my **purpose**. I give myself permission to love myself and see myself the way God does. I have diplomacy and skill at making friends. I enjoy serving people and making a difference. People know that I live on **purpose**. They have respect for me and respond with love. I love contributing positively to others.

I remind myself daily that I am God's favorite child. God has given me a unique **purpose**. In His strength, I can accomplish His **purpose** on earth. I am gifted and use my talents wisely to fulfill my **purpose**.

My **purposeful** and accelerated learning catapults me to the head of the line. I create and live the good life. I help others find and live their **purpose**. I am practical but remember I have limitless options available. I live my passion-filled, **purpose**-filled life on **purpose**.

I visualize my **purpose** being realized. I impress my subconscious mind with the things I want to experience. I **purpose** to be happy every day regardless of circumstances. God has worked in unique ways to create in me a whole new **purpose** for His glory.

I have an abundance mentality and share big ideas to arrive at my **purpose**. I was created to solve problems. I have a conscious lifestyle of being grateful on **purpose**. There is no limitation to my **purposeful** manifestation. I **purpose** to be around people who lift me up. Unlimited generosity is directed my way because I believe it.

My primary **purpose** is spreading the love of God. Because I know my **purpose**, I have a great reason to sing as I accomplish my goals. Great favor is bestowed on me as I work toward my **purpose** with ease and grace. I **purpose** to live happy and free. I smile on **purpose**.

28:
Opportunity
January 28

Bible Verses
"Therefore, whenever we have the opportunity, we should do good to everyone - especially to those in the family of faith." Galatians 6:10 (NKJV)

"Make the most of every opportunity in these evil days." Ephesians 5:16 (NLT)

Word of the Day
Opportunity – Good fortune is impending. The probability of a good break coming to pass. A lucky event. The likelihood of victory.

Quotes
"Opportunities are unlimited, but ambition is rare." Pam Malow-Isham

"He did not wait and sigh for a great opportunity, but he set to preparing himself for a great opportunity." Augusta C. Bristol

"A wise man will make more opportunities than he finds." Francis Bacon

Pam's Perspective
As a new gardener, I jumped at the opportunity to become the president of the Open Gate Garden Club with one hundred and fifty members. I figured it would be a great way to learn the names of the other members and make new friends while learning about gardening. I listened to people share their expertise, went on some grand garden tours and had fun. Gardeners are great people to be around.

Questions
Are there opportunities I have missed because of fear? What can I do to be more prepared for future opportunities? Am I taking advantage of all the opportunities available? What opportunities can I create?

Declarations

I look for **opportunities** in front of me, beside me, above me, around me, and behind every door. I am connected to Eternal clarity and inspiration. My eyes stay open for o**pportunities**. No **opportunity** gets by me. I attract the coolest **opportunities** from the nicest people.

I am a winner and eager to do my best. I forgive myself for missed **opportunities** and choose to move forward taking advantage of future ones. I never stay down long. I am excellent at bouncing back and rising to the top. I create **opportunities** from every challenge. I learn the lessons I need to learn. I am resourceful and recognize that problems are **opportunities** to grow, so I work on solving them.

I like saving money. By being financially responsible, I always have a reserve for all the **opportunities** that come my way. I am acquiring high returns on my investments. I am grateful for my good fortune. I act on the **opportunities** that resonate with me. I think of ingenious new ways to support myself and give birth to greater **opportunities**.

I am grateful for every **opportunity**. With effortless magnetism, I attract **opportunities**. I easily communicate financial **opportunities** to dedicated, trustworthy friends. I design **opportunities** that flourish. I share my wealth and **opportunities** with who I want. I am an **opportunity** maker creating a lavish bounty. I am bold enough to ask for every **opportunity** I get. They continue to multiply.

I always have the **opportunity** to say kind things about myself. I am experiencing the joy of being me. I enjoy walking in liberty and optimum health. God opens supernatural doors of **opportunity** for me so I can be a blessing to my family and the world. I seek out **opportunities** to show God's love. I am a conduit for peace. There is always an **opportunity** for me to do the right thing and I do it.

29:
Kindness
January 29

Bible Verses
"The Teachings were given through Moses, but kindness and truth came into existence through Jesus Christ." John 1:17 (GW)

"He poured out his kindness by giving us every kind of wisdom and insight." Ephesians 1:8 (GW)

Word of the Day
Kindness – The act of being courteous. Tolerance of different behavior than what you are used to. Thoughtfulness and good will.

Quotes
"The words of kindness are more healing to a drooping heart than balm or honey." Sarah Fielding

"No act of kindness, however small, is ever wasted." Aesop

"On that best portion of a good man's life, his little, nameless, unremembered acts of kindness and of love." William Wordsworth

Pam's Perspective
Looking back over my life, I remember acts of kindness more than people's gifts. My dear mother would spend so much time trying to work to get us beautiful things, and all we wanted was to spend some quality time with her.

Questions
Who has shown me the greatest kindness? How can I aspire to be more like them? Is showing kindness always my first response? What acts of kindness in words, deeds, and gifts will I show today?

Declarations

I show **kindness** to everyone I meet. I allow God's **kindness** to fill my soul. I set the process in motion to be peaceful and **kind**. The **kinder** I am, the more people are **kind** to me. I am grateful for my ability to choose **kindness** over sarcasm. It feels good to be **kind**. The **kindness** in my heart shines out of my bright eyes. I transform into the person I wish to become and have lots of fun doing it.

I am open to receive all the **kindness** that is directed my way. I show **kindness** to myself by eating healthy food and thinking positive thoughts. I treat my body with **kindness** by embracing daily exercise. Staying active is the way I roll. I display **kindness** to myself by getting regular massages, facials, manicures, and pedicures.

I receive God's **kindness** as I give Him access to my hurts. I am changed from the inside out. He turned disdain into **kindness**. I give thanks for His daily blessings. I am thrilled by the **kindness** of God towards me, so I choose to show **kindness** to mean-spirited people.

My **kind** greeting and cheerful smile show my coworkers that I am a delight to work with. My benevolent **kindness** pays with great rewards in friends and future profitable joint ventures. I become adaptable and **kind** in hard circumstances. I recognize that I am a beautiful, **kind** person who inspires everyone I meet.

I am determined to benefit in my community by exhibiting **kindness** and good works. I perform great actions with **kindness** and grace. I live in harmony with my neighbors and transform my neighborhood with my **kindness**. The demonstration of my **kindness** has a vast ripple effect, far beyond what I will ever know. **Kindness** heals and unites my city. There is an abundance of **kindness** in our town. We look out for each other and know each other by name.

30:
Criticism
January 30

Bible Verses
"If you listen to constructive criticism, you will be at home among the wise."
Proverbs 15:31 (NLT)

"In the end, people appreciate honest criticism far more than flattery."
Proverbs 28:23 (NLT)

Word of the Day
Criticism – An adverse assessment of a thing or person. Negative review.

Quotes
"Animals are such agreeable friends - they ask no questions; they pass not criticism." George Eliot

"To announce that there must be no criticism of the President, or that we are to stand by the President, right or wrong, is not only unpatriotic and servile, but is morally treasonable to the American Public." Theodore Roosevelt

"The man who is anybody and who does anything is surely going to be criticized, vilified and misunderstood. This is a part of the penalty for greatness, and every man understands it; and understands, too, that it is no proof of greatness. The final proof of greatness lies in being able to endure contumely without resentment." Elbert Hubbard

"By inviting criticism, I learn how to grow and improve." Pam Malow-Isham

Questions
Why do I stay away from people who like to criticize? When I find myself given to criticism, what do I do? What is my first response to criticism?

Declarations

I am so thankful that I am successful enough to get **criticism**. When I get **criticism,** I learn from it and grow into a better person. **Criticism** is a part of life that I can easily handle. With constant focus, I reach my dreams. I set my intentions and believe God will carry me where I need to go. I stay flexible along my path when **criticism** comes.

When someone **criticizes** me, instead of getting defensive, I look for the grain of truth that is there so my level of understanding can improve. I give people the benefit of the doubt when they **criticize,** believing they are trying to help. I am grateful for **criticism** as I listen with an open and receptive heart. I am glad I can listen and hear. I am thankful that I am changing according to my goals.

I also have been known to **criticize** others, so I make allowances for people. I ignore **criticism** when it comes from a **critical** person. I see with the eyes of wisdom and seek out wise counsel. When I get feedback, I listen with nothing on my mind, so I do not take it as **criticism** but as an opportunity to grow. I take learning seriously. I like to study. I practice tolerance, long-suffering, and patience.

Just as God is gracious to me with unending love and tenderness, I am considerate and kind to those who **criticize** me. I have grace and peace while being **criticized.** Nothing can affect my state unless I allow it. I live in a settled, peaceful state undeterred by **criticism.**

I am grateful that God is not **critical** of me, but loves me just as I am. I feel accepted, loved, vibrant, and beautiful today. I love my beautiful family, even the **critical** complainers. They give balance to life. I never miss a chance to hug a **critical** one. It gives me great pleasure sharing my joy. I smile at everyone, especially those prone to **criticism.** I am the living expression of divine serenity.

31:
Abundance
January 31

Bible Verses
"For by [His clouds] God executes judgment upon the peoples; He gives food in abundance." Job 36:31 (AMP)

"But the meek shall inherit the earth, and shall delight themselves in the abundance of peace." Psalm 37:11 (KJV)

Word of the Day
Abundance – A plethora of prosperity. A bounty of surplus. Plenty of skill and know-how. A stockpile of resources. Opulence.

Quotes
"This blessed Book (Bible) brings such life and health and peace, and such an abundance that we should never be poor anymore." Smith Wigglesworth

"Not what we have, but what we enjoy, constitutes our abundance." J. Petit-Senn

"Troubles are usually the brooms and shovels that smooth the road to a good man's fortune, and many a man curses the rain that falls upon his head, and knows not that it brings abundance to drive away hunger." St. Basil

"Abundance arrives in the physical world when the inner world is ready to receive it. When we give ourselves permission to experience abundance, it always shows up." Pam Malow-Isham

Questions
Do I take for granted the abundance around me? How can I share abundance? Do I compare what I have with the abundance of others? If so, why is that? Am I grateful for the abundance in my life?

Declarations

Abundance is my birthright as a child of God, and I claim it now. I walk in God's **abundant** approval, wisdom and love. I am at peace with my **abundant** state. I am worthy of **abundance**. I receive the **abundant** good as it comes with open arms. I am benevolent as I share my **abundance**. I believe I can live in an **abundance** of good health, friends, and finances. I have an **abundance** of love.

I release any resistance to **abundance**. It is easy to surrender to God's **abundant** care. I just let go. I am my true self as I share my **abundant** love. Goodness floods over me in a continual stream of happiness and **abundance**. I receive an **abundance** of healing now. Every cell in my body is **abundantly** infused with divine health. I radiate **abundant** beauty. I feel **abundantly** healthy and vibrant.

I like thinking of **abundance** and increasing my earnings so I can contribute to great causes. I delight in my work, and the rewards of my labor are **abundant.** I receive an **abundance** of capital. I am willing to do my part and allow God to do the rest. I give freely from my **abundance**. I have the right to make an **abundant** difference.

God slathers an **abundance** of favor on me. I do not worry about any recessions because God is my source. I have developed **abundant** skills. I have an **abundant** perception for my business ventures. I am well educated, **abundantly** charismatic and zealous to try new things. I live in the **abundance** of God's grace.

I am willing to experience a breakthrough in **abundance** in every area. Today is the day of my **abundant** good fortune. I am energetic with **abundant** enthusiasm. Ever-increasing **abundance** is my way of life. I have an unshakable center because of my **abundant** trust in God. Holy Spirit bliss bubbles out of me in billows of **abundance**.

32:
Lack
February 1

Bible Verses
"The Lord is my shepherd; I lack nothing." Psalm 23:1 (NIV)

"Fear the Lord, you his holy people, for those who fear him lack nothing. The lions may grow weak and hungry, but those who seek the Lord lack no good thing." Psalm 34:9-10 (NIV)

Word of the Day
Lack – Insufficiency of something desired. The meagerness of the quantity of something, or the shortage of goods. Having poverty in your spirit.

Quotes
"A lack of tact is one of the greatest stumbling-blocks in the road to success." Orison Swett Marden

"And one who is just of his own free will shall not lack for happiness, and he will never come to utter ruin." Aeschylus

"Look what I lack, my mind supplies; lo, thus I triumph like a king, my mind's content with anything." William Byrd

Pam's Perspective
Although I lack a lot of formal education, I have a doctorate in hard knocks. I never liked school as a kid. I thought I lacked smarts when in truth, I just lacked confidence. Now I enjoy taking classes and stay open to learning anything.

Questions
Do I lack a purpose or worthy goal? Do I lack or is it my perception? Is there another story I can tell myself? How can lack be a good thing?

Declarations

In God, there is no **lack**. I renounce my **lackadaisical** thinking. I am a King's kid and an heir of the Almighty. I am blessed with the riches of my Father who owns the cattle on a thousand hills. I **lack** concern over my next meal because God always provides.

I **lack** the capacity to stay mad because forgiveness is always my first choice. I am patient, kind and **lack** the ability to hold a grudge. I reap many rewards from past good deeds. I collect cool friends. I **lack** loneliness because I am valued, loved and adored by a few.

I never **lack** for an idea because of Divine inspiration. God knows no **lack**. What I **lack** in know-how, I make up for in enthusiasm. I am endowed with wisdom from on High as I step into my success. I give thanks that all **lack** is wiped out of my mind. I arm myself with the thoughts of Christ. I recognize miracles that others **lack** to see.

I have more than enough today because I trust God. I **lack** the ability to stay down because of my inner strength and unsinkable attitude. My **lack** of fear is replaced with faith. Now is my appointed time. I rise from **lack** with accelerated speed, receiving unexpected glory.

I am whole and complete, **lacking** nothing! My awareness is focused on releasing **lack**. I let go of every expectation of **lack**. I receive an ample supply of whatever I need when I need it. Abundance is my birthright, so I experience no **lack**. No matter what I think I might **lack**, I can choose to be happy regardless of any **lacking** situation.

I live in a friendly world where there is no **lack** of smiles, love or charity. As I sow, so shall I reap. I tell myself to harvest what I **lack**. I love receiving kindness and gathering new friends. I embrace new beginnings. Today is my harvest-time, there is no **lack**.

33:
Freedom
February 2

Bible Verses
"So I will live in freedom, because I do my best to know your instructions." Psalm 119:45 (ERV)

"We have freedom now, because Christ made us free. So stand strong in that freedom. Don't go back into slavery again." Galatians 5:1 (ERV)

Word of the Day
Freedom – The right to be free. The privilege of living without incarceration. The flexibility to do what one wants. Unrestrained.

Quotes
"Love transformed, Spirit formed people bring freedom to the oppressed. Freed people, free people." Jeff Ryal

"The freedom of all is essential to my freedom." Mikhail Bakunin

"Our greatest happiness does not depend on the condition of life in which chance has placed us, but is always the result of a good conscience, good health, occupation, and freedom in all just pursuits." Thomas Jefferson

"Thought takes man out of servitude into freedom." Ralph Waldo Emerson

"Man is free at the instant he wants to be." Voltaire

Questions
Why is freedom vital to me? Do I embrace the freedom I have? What must I do to be free from guilt, shame, and self-condemnation? Will I forgive others and myself so I can walk in freedom? What must I do to be free from unhealthy habits? Will I choose to walk in freedom?

Declarations

I am pleased with the **freedom** I have to do work I love and spend time with the people I love. I am light, **free** and breezy. I practice the ability to surrender to God and the **freedom** of inner peace. I live in a wonderful world of **freedom** and possibility. I serve a happy God.

I exercise **freedom** of choice to eat more vegetables. I am **free** to take great care of myself. I am in top condition, getting stronger every day. I love the **freedom** of movement I experience as I stretch my muscles. I enjoy the **freedom** to choose pleasant thoughts over negative ones. I love feeling confident being **free** to be myself.

I am **free** to love, live and laugh! God has given me the **freedom** to live victorious in every situation. His will is done in my affairs. I am rewarded with blessings for no other reason than I am His child.

I have the **freedom** to be debt **free** with a lot of money in the bank because I am responsible for my finances. I am very delighted. I have excess for unexpected emergencies and fun travel too. I am thankful for the **freedom** to travel around the world and meet new friends. I go where I want when I want. That is the **freedom** I enjoy.

I value the **freedom** I have and gladly vote in all political elections. My vote counts. I am **free** to vote for whomever I choose. I also have the **freedom** to voice my concerns to government officials. I pray for our leaders and ask God to give them wisdom and strength.

I easily forgive childhood hurts and release old memories of pain. I can experience more **freedom** every day. I give up any resentment to enjoy **freedom** and happiness. God has set me **free** from the curse of being judgmental. I enjoy walking in **freedom**. It is easy to walk in **freedom** when I let go and let God be in charge. I like living **free**.

34:
Confinement
February 3

Bible Verses

"So that you can open blind eyes, free the prisoners from confinement, those living in darkness from the dungeon. I am Adonai; that is my name. I yield my glory to no one else, nor my praise to any idol." Isaiah 42:7-8 (CJB)

"Then I, God, will burst all confinements and lead them out into the open. They'll follow their King. I will be out in front leading them." Micah 2:13 (MSG)

Word of the Day

Confinement – To be in custody or jail. Detention. To restrict movement.

Quotes

"The most magnificent palace would appear to him a prison who was confined to it." Turkish Spy (Giovanni Paolo Marana)

"Some minds corrode and grow inactive under the loss of personal liberty; others grow morbid and irritable, but it is the nature of the poet to become tender and imaginative in the loneliness of confinement. He banquets upon the honey of his own thoughts, and, like the captive bird, pours forth his soul in melody." Washington Irving

"You find peace in the confinement of silence." Pam Malow-Isham

"True happiness is to no place confined, but still is found in a contented mind." Horace

Questions

Why can confinement be good? What have I learned from it? Do I need to confine myself more to spend time in reflection? Or do I need to break free from the confinement of solitude and make new friends?

Declarations

Dreams come true, and I am proof of that fact. I get stronger every day by breaking free the chains of **confinement** of bad habits. I build life-giving habits that develop my strengths. I think before I act. I like being healthy; healthy looks good on me. The **confinement** of eating raw fruits and vegetables has productive benefits. I love being physically fit. I eat like a slim person. I think like a lean person.

In solitary **confinement**, I enjoy the special time when I meditate, and commune with God. God is good to me. I feel God's presence telling me I am OK with Him in the **confinement** of our quiet time.

I do not let a busy schedule keep me **confined** or bothered. I am compassionate to myself when I make a mistake. I shout for joy for the freedom I receive from God's mercy. I release the **confinement** of bitterness as I walk in love. Choosing to forgive unfetters the **confinement** of the tormentor and releases grace and peace.

I know how to unplug. I am not **confined** to electronics; email, phone, twitter, and Facebook. I go outside and experience the incredible beauty of nature. I take deep breaths of fresh air, release stress and feel calm. I relax, taking time to enjoy the moment and experience inner peace. I leave my work at the office and enjoy the **confinement** of being present with my family as we play together.

Love shatters the **confinement** of prejudice and accepts with open arms all of God's children to fellowship together in unity. I see the **confinement** of narrow-minded thinkers who are intolerant of the viewpoints of others and pray for their hearts to expand. I remember to think for myself. I choose to be open, understanding and humble. I am soft-hearted and kind to the people around me; so much so, that it melts their **confinement** of anger and hatred. Love wins.

35:
Individual
February 4

Bible Verses

"But when God is silent, who can declare Him guilty? When He hides His face, who can see Him? Yet He watches over both individuals and nations." Job 34:29 (HCSB)

"Let your conversation always be gracious and interesting, so that you will know how to respond to any particular individual." Colossians 4:6 (CJB)

Word of the Day

Individual – One person. Separate. Unique, set apart from the crowd.

Quotes

"Every theory of love, from Plato down, teaches that each individual loves in the other sex what he lacks in himself." G. Stanley Hall

"Individual eccentricity is normal and makes life interesting." Pam Malow-Isham

"That man's best works should be such bungling imitations of nature's perfection, matters not much; but that he should make himself an imitation, this is the fact which nature moans over, and depreciates beseechingly. 'Be spontaneous, be truthful, be free, and thus be individuals!' is the song she sings through warbling birds, and whispering pines, and roaring waves, and screeching winds." Lydia M. Child

"A pure heart does not demean the spirit of an individual, it, instead, compels the individual to examine his spirit." Criss Jami

Questions

How can I be individual and yet stand out and get recognized? What are my individual talents? What can I do to make myself more employable?

Declarations

I stand out in the crowd by my **individual** style, smile, humor, and wit. I do not need to copy someone else because I am the best. My **individual** talents are improving daily. My mind is priceless. I am an **individual** in awe of how I continue to grow and nurture myself in this fun adventure called life. I love being extraordinary.

I have survived **individual** attacks and have become stronger. I am confident that I can handle whatever comes my way. I have intuitive intelligence for effective communication with every **individual**. I know how to how to listen, so people feel heard and understood.

I have a well-defined **individual** purpose. I allow God to take control of the outcome. God has given me an **individual** mission that only I can accomplish, so I accept it with gratitude and joy in my heart. I use my **individual** talents to bring harmony and peace to every situation. I am a unique **individual**, perfectly made.

I associate with other great **individuals** who believe in their dreams. We applaud and energize each other. I radiate good feelings. My group of committed **individuals** works together in unity to make the world beautiful. We make a great team. I freely use my **individual** gifts today so that wealth easily transfers into my hands.

I am welcoming. I recharge my batteries in ways that support my **individual** needs. I take time off and laugh. I am an ordinary **individual** with the extraordinary power to reach my goals.

I extend my mind from **individual** goals to quantum possibilities. I am a smart **individual**. I am sought out for my **individual** strengths and abilities to generate great results. New possibilities are popping up now. My expertise as a wise **individual** is world renowned.

36:
Community
February 5

Bible Verses
"Those who accepted Peter's message were baptized. God brought about three thousand people into the community on that day." Acts 2:41 (CEB)

"Don't let any foul words come out of your mouth. Only say what is helpful when it is needed for building up the community so that it benefits those who hear what you say." Ephesians 4:29 (CEB)

Word of the Day
Community – An association of people who live in the same vicinity or who work together for a common cause or social benefit. A close-knit group of friends you hang with. The neighborhood you live in.

Quotes
"If a talent is anywhere born into the world, the community of nations is enriched; and much more, with a new degree of probity." Ralph Waldo Emerson

"Surplus wealth is a sacred trust which its possessor is bound to administer in his lifetime for the good of the community." Andrew Carnegie

Pam's Perspective
We need to be engaged with our community to thrive. I used to be a loner, and I was lonely. Imagine that! I now help the "Friends of the Burton Library." You meet the nicest people by volunteering, you feel good, and it cures loneliness.

Questions
Do I believe that I live in a loving community? If not, what can I do to foster that feeling? What can I do to create a friendly, supportive community? Why is it easy to impact my community in positive ways?

Declarations

I am an asset to my **community**. I help people wherever I go. I bless the people around me, even when I don't want to, or feel like they deserve it. I unite people together from different backgrounds, races, and cultures. Being patient with other people is the norm for me.

I live in a beautiful **community** that is filled with peace, laughter, and joy. I take responsibility for improving my **community**. I love to show hospitality and live a life of service. It is natural for me to help. I am busy making a difference and volunteering in my **community**.

I practice radical acceptance everywhere I go. I immerse myself in my **community** and encourage people to care for one another. I receive great inspiration from my **community** of faith.

I grow stronger as a person when I do **community** service. I love being appreciated. Volunteering is fun. I reach out and bond with people in my **community** creating lifelong friendships. I live in a harmonious Universe of unconditional love. I am charitable. I have a **community** of friends. I care about my **community**. I like to share. I live in a **community** where teamwork and grace is the norm.

I am my own hero. I expect the healing not only of my mind, body, soul, and finances but also my **community**. There are miraculous ways that good comes to me. I serve a miracle working God. I am proud of my **community**. I am happy because I go the way of peace.

I get a sense of connectedness when I help people in my **community**. We need each other to survive and thrive, so I stay linked to my **community**. Connecting to all human beings is valuable and builds a healthy **community**. I will do good things today. I have a mission from heaven to heal this planet, and it starts with my **community**.

37:
Growth
February 6

Bible Verses
"I planted, Apollos watered, but God was causing the growth." 1 Corinthians 3:6 (NASB)

"So neither he who plants nor he who waters is anything, but only God who gives the growth." 1 Corinthians 3:7 (RSV)

Word of the Day
Growth – The improvement of a person's knowledge, skill, character or inner drive. Maturity. Evolving to become a better person. Increase.

Quotes
"The keener the want, the lustier the growth." Wendell Phillips

"Few things have ever impeded either mental or spiritual growth more than a blind adherence to tradition without inquire and reflection." W. W. Davies

"Success is a fruit of slow growth." Henry Fielding

Pam's Perspective
For thirty years I was a personal growth junkie. I read books, attended seminars and webinars, spending over seventy-five thousand dollars, hoping that would fix me. I was a slow learner. My growth was small and steady until I finally realized I wasn't broken. God loves me just as the way I am, and He created me to enjoy my life. I am grateful for the trials that added to my growth along the way.

Questions
How do I view growth? Do I eagerly embrace growth or do I shrink back? What are the areas of growth that I can make this week, month and year?

Declarations

I am committed to constant learning and **growth**. I have a creative mind. Rapid **growth** is the norm for me. I love feeling confident. I give thanks for the mistakes I have made in my life as they are just tools for **growth**. As I **grow** in awareness, I use information to help me live a better, more productive life. I focus my activity on **growth**.

I appreciate being disciplined. The more I save, the more **growth** occurs in my wealth. The **growth** of my bank account is increasing exponentially. I am pleased with my path of **growth** on my job. The **growth** of my paychecks is visible for my excellent work. The **growth** of my generosity continues as I give from a pure heart.

My professional **growth** improves as I listen to audiobooks on the way to work. My **growth** depends on me, so I take authority over what I put into my mind. I shift my thoughts to foster **growth** and repel stagnation. Benevolence **grows** from how I behave.

Apparent **growth** of my memory happens when I make a habit of reviewing what I have learned on a frequent basis. I **grow** smart by repetition. My outlook is always positive. I **grow** happier every day.

My preferred way of living is to see God in everything and believe in the best in people. I love **growing** in being supportive, courteous and kind. God accelerates the speed of my **growth** as I meditate on His Word. An unlimited supply of ideas is available to me. I live above circumstances, putting my hope in God and **growing** in faith.

My **growth** has been phenomenal, and there is joy in my journey as I vocalize my positive declarations every morning. I value my **growth** time. It is safe for me to **grow** up and become responsible. I like the way I feel being in charge of my life as I continue to **grow**.

38:
Reduction
February 7

Bible Verse
"Go get straw yourselves wherever you can find it, but there will be no reduction at all in your workload." Exodus 5:11 (HCSB)

Word of the Day
Reduction – The shrinkage of something. A lower price for something. The decline of perceived value.

Quotes
"Man was the highest note in the scale of creation, and when he descended, through all nature there followed a corresponding reduction." Richard C. Trench

"People who drink four or more cups of coffee a day – it doesn't matter whether it is caffeinated or decaffeinated – have a reduction in Type 2 diabetes, or a reduced incidence of Type 2 diabetes, of about fifty percent. The same with Parkinson's, although there is more related to the caffeine." Gregory Stock

"It is cheaper to reduce crime than to build jails." James A. Garfield

Pam's Perspective
The reduction of harmful thoughts was not easy for me. I prayed, read positive books, listened to positive audiobooks and said a lot of positive declarations. I also reduced the amount of TV I watched and the amount of time I spent with negative people. It took me quite a while to reduce the negative, but it was well worth it. It can be done. It just takes perseverance and a desire to live a happy, contented life.

Questions
Why have I focused on reduction? What area of my life will I make a reduction in today? How can reduction be a good thing?

Declarations

The **reduction** of unproductive activities has produced a great value in the accomplishment of my goals. I get things done on time. I **reduce** anxiety by staying composed. I remember that I am a genius.

By accelerating the **reduction** of negative thoughts by infusing my mind with positive thoughts, I live a joy-filled life. I appreciate things now that I used to take for granted. With the **reduction** of complaints, I have turned my views around to be grateful for life.

I like being organized. The **reduction** of clutter has been freeing. By being generous, I have donated things I no longer need. The **reduction** of those things allows room for new things to come in.

Being conscious about my **reduction** of sugar and junk food, I have caused my body to regenerate and heal itself. I energize myself as I care for my body by choosing healthy fruits and vegetables.

Choosing the **reduction** of sitting in front of the TV or computer and getting up and exercising has strengthened and toned my body. I am an invigorated machine that takes on any challenge with vim and vigor expecting victory from every direction. I turn on the charm.

I am thankful that I have been successful with the **reduction** of my fears by facing them head on and doing it despite being fearful. I **reduce** my limiting beliefs with each fear I conquer. I am resilient.

By the **reduction** of letting go of my petty complaints and choosing to help a friend or volunteer for a worthy cause, I become joyous. I am full of intelligence and compassion. The **reduction** of fear in my life is evident in my confidence. I honor other people's viewpoints. I help **reduce** evil by propagating love, generosity, and faith.

39:
Meditate
February 8

Bible Verses
"I will meditate on your precepts and consider your ways." Psalm 119:15 (WEB)

"They speak of the glorious splendor of your majesty and I will meditate on your wonderful works." Psalm 145:5 (NIV)

Word of the Day
Meditate – To ruminate over. To speculate. To consider in thought.

Quotes
"There has never been a time when religious meditation was more important than in this strenuous age." W. Gardner Thrall

"When the mild sun his paling lustre shrouds in gorgeous draperies of golden clouds; then wander forth, mid beauty and decay, to meditate alone – alone to watch and pray." Emma C. Embury – Autumn Evening

Pam's Perspective
Growing up, I thought meditation was some esoteric nonsense that weirdos did. In my twenties, I thought meditation was for people on a higher spiritual plane than I. Then I assumed it would be hard and I would have to take classes to learn how. Fortunately, God is not complicated. Giving up the struggle of trying to make something happen was all I needed to do. God is in the simple things, a gentle breeze. Meditation is easy. Working and talking are not involved. Being still is all it takes. Set aside time to be with God and listen. He is always there.

Questions
When I meditate on God and what is right, honorable and lovely, why does my life go so well? Do I meditate on what is going wrong? Why?

Declarations

I often **meditate** on God's infinite love for me as an individual. I align my life with God and walk free. I am awakened to the atmosphere of positivity as I **meditate** on the Almighty. **Meditation** is essential in my life. I am grateful that I am learning the nature of God. That which I do not understand, I ask to be shown.

I **meditate** on the good that is bestowed on my family and me. I feel good. There is not a spot where God is not so I can **meditate** if only for a moment and connect with Spirit. I call forth love to guide and fill my life with the overflowing peace of the One who resides in me.

I listen with my whole being as I sit and **meditate** in God's presence. I enjoy our intimacy. I experience a profound revitalization of my spirit, soul, and body as I **meditate**. I am Spirit-filled. I have a purposeful intent as I continue with my daily **meditation** practice.

God reveals deep insights to me as I **meditate** on His Word. Just when I need it, a memorized scripture comes to mind to help me. Because I have read and **meditated** on what is true, I know the truth. I **meditate** on being divinely guided as I operate in love.

I am secure inside myself. I remember that I am in control of my thoughts, feelings, and actions, so I continue to **meditate** on what is valuable. I am reliable, honest, creative and fun to be around. I allow harmony to fill my day. I know that God is always with me and that makes me smile as I continue in my **meditation** exercises.

I **meditate** on what God has for me and realize how highly valued I am. I have many gifts and talents. **Meditating** that all is working in my favor, I feel great. I visualize magnetizing perfect clients, friends, funds, and opportunities. My life is absolutely amazing!

40:
Dismiss
February 9

Bible Verses

"When he attends to the prayer of the wretched. He won't dismiss their prayer." Psalm 102:17 (MSG)

"Sovereign Lord, as you have promised, you may now dismiss your servant in peace. For my eyes have seen your salvation." Luke 2:29-30 (NIV)

Word of the Day

Dismiss – To release a group. To disperse or let go. To cast out or reject.

Quotes

"My thoughts are my company; I can bring them together, select them, detain them, and dismiss them." Walter Savage Landor

"Will we encourage individuals to dismiss from their minds the feeling of responsibility toward our homeless little ones, whose cries and entreaties are heard in every section of our great land?" R. A. Longman

"Man may dismiss compassion from his heart, but God will never." William Cowper

Pam's Perspective

I have had people dismiss me because I am not in the in-crowd, or do not have a degree. To their loss, they prevent themselves from learning from the simple, but wise.

Questions

What negative habit will I dismiss today? What do I do when I feel like someone has rejected and dismissed me? Do I respond in love? Have I ever done the same to someone else? How is that different?

Declarations

I **dismiss** all negative thoughts that pop into my head and replace them with positive ones. I remember to embrace the goodness inside myself. I have the power to choose to **dismiss** habits that no longer serve me. I **dismiss** destructive patterns and create good ones.

I **dismiss** unproductive tasks that take time away from my goals. Once I have decided to move forward, I take bold action. I **dismiss** and release knowing how my goals will arrive. I believe God will always make it work out for my highest good, and He does.

I never **dismiss** someone for their beliefs or pre-judge them. That is between them and God. I must make my own decisions and come to my own conclusions about what matters to me in my life, and so do everyone else. I remember to let people learn their own lessons. I treat people with dignity and respect without **dismissing** them.

I give myself permission to **dismiss** the old, no longer needed things, and pick up new treasures that enhance my surroundings. I **dismiss** the notion of hanging on to something just in case.

My Father smiles on me and gives me brilliant wisdom for daily living. I never **dismiss** an intuitive lead for I know it is God guiding me in the direction I should go. I **dismiss** the roaring winds and listen to the whispers. I am awakened to life. I **dismiss** hate and let love rule as tenderness and kindness is exemplified in me.

I value myself, telling myself how capable I am, never **dismissing** myself as anything but great. I remember to take responsibility for everything that is going on in my life. I do what matters most. I **dismiss** immaturity and quit playing the blame game, as I trust my power to succeed. I love feeling confident, happy, and free.

41:
Cause
February 10

Bible Verses
"The Eternal is on my side, a champion for my cause; so when I look at those who hate me, victory will be in sight." Psalm 118:7 (VOICE)

"Learn to do right; seek justice. Defend the oppressed. Take up the cause of the fatherless; plead the case of the widow." Isaiah 1:17 (NIV)

Word of the Day
Cause – The origin or purpose of an outcome. The real motivation behind a person's actions. A call to action.

Quotes
"Good culture is born of a good disposition; and since the cause is more to be praised than the effect, I will rather praise a good disposition without culture, than good culture without the disposition." Leonardo da Vinci

"The humblest citizen of all the land, when clad in the armor of a righteous cause, is stronger than all the hosts of error." William Jennings Bryan

"The Lord is not compelled to use theologians. He can take snakes, sticks or anything else, and use them for the advancement of his cause." Billy Sunday

"The cause of freedom is the cause of God." C. Bowles

"If you would win a man to your cause, first convince him that you are his sincere friend." Abraham Lincoln

Questions
What is my favorite cause? Why does my cause pull me to action? Why is being at cause beneficial to my life? How can I cause happiness?

Declarations

I **cause** my happiness because I know it comes from within. I speak with conviction about the **cause** closest to my heart. Love is my **cause**, and God is my source. Love is a **cause** more significant than I am and it compels me to be compassionate and kind to everyone.

I risk standing up for the **causes** I believe in. My confidence in God **causes** me to have gigantic dreams. It is God's pleasure to give me the kingdom and express His fullness through me to fulfill His worthy **cause**. Now is the time for me to demonstrate my spiritual legacy. A double portion of favor is bestowed on me to complete my **cause**. I am at **cause** for good. Love **causes** miracles all around me.

I attract help for my noble **cause**. I am passionate about this **cause** as it touches my heart and moves my soul. Energy is always present for my **cause**. I show up and leave nothing overlooked. I am God's representative and **cause** hope, mercy, and charity to thrive.

I do things that **cause** positive results. I like being mature. I rule over myself. I am the creator of how I want to live my life, and I **cause** it to be fabulous. My exercise routine has **caused** my body to become fit, strong, and healthy. I **cause** outcomes to manifest in my favor.

I work only on the **causes** I believe in and can commit to. I make my own decisions about what **causes** are important to me. I exhibit stamina for my **cause**. I break down any and every obstacle that gets in the way of my **cause**. I like seeing my **cause** completed.

My mind is the **cause** of my pleasure or pain, and what I choose to think about determines my experience. I **cause** people to smile and laugh. I love encouraging people. I **cause** great pleasure to fill my mind because I am always focusing on excellence and beauty.

42:
Effect
February 11

Bible Verses

"If they inherit because of the Law, then faith has no effect and the promise has been canceled." Romans 4:14 (CEB)

"And let endurance have its perfect effect, so that you will be perfect and complete, not deficient in anything." James 1:4 (NET)

Word of the Day

Effect – The reaction of an event, activity or impression of something or someone. The reason something happened.

Quotes

"The best effect of any book is that it excites the reader to self-activity." Thomas Carlyle

"Having a positive effect on the people I encounter is worth more than gold and is so easy to do. I have that power anytime I choose. A simple smile is all it takes." Pam Malow-Isham

"I have no faith in human perfectibility. I think that human exertion will have no appreciable effect upon humanity. Man is now only more active – not more happy – nor more wise, than he was 6000 years ago." Edgar Allan Poe

"Adversity has the effect of eliciting talents, which in prosperous circumstances would have lain dormant." Horace

Questions

What effect is my mood having on my productivity? How do effect change in me? What is the effect of my current habits? Is that serving me well? What effect am I willing to create to have a happy, fulfilling life?

Declarations

I am conscious of the wonderful **effect** I have on the world. I live an inspired life. I determine the **effect** I want to have in every area of my life ahead of time. People feel the **effects** of my laughter and good mood. My joy reminds people that it is OK to play again.

I continually do meaningful work that generates remarkable results and positive **effects**. The **effect** of my increased influence in leadership is because I prepared for it. I respect the people I work for and complete my tasks ahead of schedule. My strong work ethic has had an advantageous **effect** on my promotions in this company. I focus on consistency, and the **effect** is being on the winner's list.

My healthy eating habits have had a rejuvenating **effect** on my body. I enjoy exercise. My well-groomed appearance has a genuine **effect** on how people constructively perceive me. I take good care of my skin. My hygienic skin care regimen has had a youthful **effect** on my face. I am always more than enough. Joy is the **effect** of my love.

God is smiling on me today. I can feel the **effect** of His love. I use the power of prayer to help me **effect** this day. I am a supernatural minded person. Miracles are the norm for me. The **effect** of releasing my worries and cares to God has had a peaceful **effect** on my life.

My wisdom of saving, investing and living beneath my means has had a growing **effect** on my wealth. I make wise choices today. I set a good example for my children. I am funny and resourceful.

The way I listen has the **effect** of being heard and understood by the person who is speaking. Every action I take has an undeniable ripple **effect** influencing countless individuals for good. I like expressing gratitude and seeing the **effect**. I have a positive **effect** on the planet.

43:
Spontaneous
February 12

Bible Verses

"Give freely and spontaneously. Don't have a stingy heart. The way you handle matters like this triggers God, your God's, blessing in everything you do, all your work and ventures." Deuteronomy 15:10 (MSG)

"Please, Lord, accept my spontaneous gifts of praise. Teach me your rules!" Psalm 119:108 (CEB)

Word of the Day

Spontaneous – An unplanned action or event. Unintentional occurrence. Free-spirited. Impromptu.

Quote

"Try everything that can be done. Try it in every possible way. Be deliberate. Be spontaneous. Be thoughtful and painstaking. Be abandoned and impulsive. Learn your own possibilities. Have confidence in your self-reliance!" George Bellows

Pam's Perspective

Being spontaneous makes life entertaining. In the fall of 2007, I went to Orlando with my husband for a business trip. I met a girl the same age as me from Munich Germany, Bettina Heiß who was staying at our hotel. We decided to go to Disney World for two hours before they closed. When we got there at 5:00, we found they were having a Pirate & Princess Party from 7-12:00 AM. So we were able to skip down the main street, ride all the rides without waiting in line and saw the Parade & Fireworks twice. We have stayed friends and visited each other.

Questions

Is it normal for me to be spontaneous? How do I respond when spontaneous opportunities show up? How will I be spontaneous today?

Declarations

I am **spontaneous** with my laughter that bubbles up from the joy in my heart. **Spontaneous** praise flows from my lips as I tell of the miraculous things I have received from a marvelous God. **Spontaneous** cheerfulness and amusement is my way of life.

My **spontaneous** glances at the beauty of nature uplift my soul. I cannot help but say thank you God for all your wonderful works. I show **spontaneous** grace and forgiveness to those who try to hurt me. **Spontaneous** mercy is how I react. I am irresistible with the **spontaneous** joy that I circulate from within. My **spontaneous** smile radiates the happiness within my heart and affects my company.

I am reliable and do the best job possible. I am a generous person. I give **spontaneously** from my vast resources. I **spontaneously** get raises because I dare to ask. I face rejection head on and become heroic. I get things done right away. I take short **spontaneous** breaks during the day to relax and rejuvenate, so I stay productive.

I am daring as I **spontaneously** get up and bust a move on the dance floor. **Spontaneous** boldness shows up for me just when I need it. I am secure in my ability to trust God for all my wants and needs. I courageously pursue my dreams unencumbered by fear. I maintain positive cash flows. **Spontaneous** gifts show up at my door, and unexpected acts of kindness are steadily directed my way.

I can **spontaneously** express what I think, feel and need to my friends. Authenticity is the norm for me. I am true to myself and can cope with whatever comes my way. Great feelings **spontaneously** appear as I appreciate what is right in front of me. I enroll my mind in doing what is right. **Spontaneous** ideas unfold as I step out in faith. Without thought, I **spontaneously** hug the people I love.

Deliberate
February 13

Bible Verses
"This man was handed over to you by God's deliberate plan and foreknowledge; and you, with the help of wicked men, put him to death by nailing him to the cross." Acts 2:23 (NIV)

"Both the apostles and the elders met together to deliberate about this matter." Acts 15:6 (NET)

Word of the Day
Deliberate – Calculated thought. A well-pondered choice. A decision that is weighed purposefully and meticulously acted upon.

Quotes
"Men are impatient and for precipitating things; but the Author of Nature appears deliberate throughout his operations, accomplishing his natural ends by slow successive steps." Bishop Butler

"Faith is deliberate confidence in the character of God whose ways you may not understand at the time." Oswald Chambers

Pam's Perspective
I have found when I deliberate too long over a subject I get restless and indecisive, rather than when I go with my gut instinct and decide quickly. Rarely have my decisions been unsatisfactory. Deliberate choices are how I create a wonderful life.

Questions
Have I been deliberate in showing my loved ones how much I care? Have I been deliberate in growing kinder? Am I deliberate in setting my goals? What deliberate action will I take today?

Declarations

I write out my goals, put them in the most important order, make my plans and then take **deliberate** actions toward them. I go happily through my day and it goes smoothly as I make **deliberate** choices as to what kind of day I am going to have in the morning.

I am **deliberate** about the time I spend with God who inspires me and gives me strength. I am a splendid torch to shine the goodness of God by my **deliberate** acts of kindness and love. I transmit good news **deliberately** to the people I work with and everyone I meet.

I **deliberately** care about who I am talking with. Ultimate influence is mine because I am **deliberate** about listening with my whole being. I ask **deliberate** questions that pertain to our conversation. I provide a space for people to be heard, cherished, and open.

Deliberate good food choices keep me healthy and full of life. I am **deliberate** about being present and enjoying every bite of delicious food I eat. I am conscious of what I put in my mouth. **Deliberate** self-control at turning down sweets has kept me sexy and slim. I **deliberately** keep my body trained, well-prepared and healthy.

I **deliberately** think about what is honorable and worthy of my attention. I **deliberately** receive counsel from my mastermind group regularly. We encourage each other to reach beyond what we before thought was impossible, to now achieving extraordinary tasks.

Deliberately recognizing all the small miracles and little blessings that continue to come my way, makes me appreciate the big ones even more. I **deliberately** express who I really am. I am capable of handling strife and success. I am **deliberate** on modeling how to live a happy, fulfilling life. I am **deliberate** about being grateful.

45:
Love
February 14

Bible Verses

"Love is patient and kind. Love is not jealous or boastful or proud or rude. It does not demand its own way. It is not irritable, and it keeps no record of being wronged. It does not rejoice about injustice but rejoices whenever the truth wins out. Love never gives up, never loses faith, is always hopeful, and endures through every circumstance." 1 Corinthians 13:4-7 (NLT)

Word of the Day

Love – An emotion of caring for someone very deeply. Devotedness and yearning to be with your heart's desire. Strong sentiment or respect for.

Quotes

"It is not that love is blind. It is that love sees with a painter's eye, finding the essence that renders all else background." Robert Brault

"Supreme love to God and equal love to man is our banner of victory and peace." Charles Sumner

Pam's Perspective

On February fourteenth, nineteen eighty-nine, I came home ready to commit suicide. I turned on the TV, and there was an evangelist on it. I listened and said, OK God, if you're real, show me. All of a sudden the weight of the world lifted off my shoulders, and I was filled with a love, and peace I had never experienced before. Then I knew God was real, and I continually feel His love and peace. The more love I give away, the more love I get in return. Bonus!

Questions

Do I love myself? Who do I love? Do I know how to receive love? Do I realize how much God loves me? Why do I see people through eyes of love? How can I show more love to everyone I meet?

Declarations

I am **loving**, **lovable** and **loved**. God's **love** fills my mind, body, and soul. If God being omniscient knows me and **loves** me just the way I am, then I can **love** me too. I am happy that I don't have work for, or prove that I am worthy of **love** to God or anyone else. I **love** God, and God **love's** me. I give my **love** freely and unashamed.

Divine **Love** flows through my mind bringing to light what needs to be forgiven. I **love** everyone, and everyone **loves** me. Because I **love** my enemy, they become my friend. I **love** being taught humility. Continuous growth and service is a part of my daily existence.

My **loving** self-talk is creating my fantastic life. I show myself **loving-kindness** by taking care of my body, mind, soul, and spirit. I **love** myself just the way I am, and I am happy to be alive. The idea of beauty, **love**, and integrity is being expressed through me now.

God continues working wonders and **loving** miracles in my life. I operate from a heart of gratitude and **love**. I live in harmony with Spirit. My **love** is sacred and pure. I **love** myself more by performing **loving** deeds. I have a standard practice of being calm, confident, and full of **loving-kindness**. I am proud of who I am becoming.

I am a child of the Living God, and I am now expressing more and more of God's **love**, harmony, and peace, every moment of every day. There is no ceiling on my **love** for others or God's **love** for me. I matter and make a huge mark in the lives of the people around me.

I **love** my life with all the ups and downs. It is still a beautiful world. **Love** is the most significant healing force in the entire universe, and I am glad it is working through me. I **love** openly and draw people to me because **love** is my first response. **Love** is the solution we seek.

46:
Hate
February 15

Bible Verses

"But to you who are willing to listen, I say, love your enemies! Do good to those who hate you." Luke 6:27 (NLT)

"If anyone claims, "I am living in the light," but hates a Christian brother or sister, that person is still living in darkness." 1 John 2:9 (NLT)

Word of the Day

Hate – To loath someone or something with passion. To have enmity towards someone. To feel scorn and spiteful with no love lost.

Quote

"The man or woman who is filled with Love sees Love on all sides and attracts the Love of others. The man with Hate in his heart gets all the Hate he can stand. The man who thinks Fight generally runs up against all the Fight he wants before he gets through. And so it goes, each gets what he calls for over the wireless telegraphy of the Mind." William Walker Atkinson

Pam's Perspective

Being consumed with hate and bitterness is a terrible existence. I hated more people than I loved. I was hurting and would lash out. I thought if I gave up the hate it would give more predators access to harm me. I was wrong. I had layers of hate like an onion. Once I was willing to let the hate go, I said, God, I give this over to you. I kept releasing more and more until there was only love left.

Questions

Is there any hate in my heart? If so, do I want to keep it there? Do I hate people I don't know or fear? Do I hate people who are a different religion than I? Why do I feel so free and light when I release hate and bitterness?

Declarations

Today is a great day to release **hate** and spread benevolence. Even if I **hate** the actions of someone; I can still be kind to the person. Being mean never changed anyone over to good, so I refrain from **hatred**.

I see the pain in **hateful** people, so I steer my heart to be in a loving place. I am tolerant of people who **hate** and pray God would fill them with His joy, and peace. Sweet words ooze out of my mouth. By being so nice to the **haters** with kind words and deeds, they leave me alone or decide to change. I continue to smile regardless.

If I find out someone **hates** me, I try to figure out why and work on that area of my life that might need improvement. I am always up to develop into a wiser person. I trust myself to do well. I get better every day. I move forward with purpose and leave **hate** behind.

I forgive everyone regardless of if they deserve it or not. I forgive, and I am free from **hate**. I allow people the right to change if they want to or stay the same. I ignore the tendency to get upset or **hate** what is going on in the world. I see it as another challenge to take on and conquer. I give myself permission to thrive and live **hate** free.

I **hate** evil and love God. I am sensitive that some people will **hate** what I stand for. I stand anyway. I put the **haters** to remorse by my kindness. I am willing to let go of **hate** when it tries to creep in my heart. I am a representative of love everywhere I go. I exist and deserve the good things in life regardless if people **hate** me or not.

In social situations, people **hate** to see me leave because I am the life of the party. I choose what I get my brain to think about, and **hate** is not on my radar. I feel positive about myself. I find it easy to release **hatred** and bitterness. I freely express who I truly am.

47:
Focus
February 16

Bible Verses

"Turn your ear and hear the words of the wise; focus your mind on my knowledge." Proverbs 22:17 (AMP)

"Focus on your life and your teaching. Continue to do what I've told you. If you do this, you will save yourself and those who hear you." 1 Timothy 4:16 (GW)

Word of the Day

Focus – To see clearly. To hone in on an object, thought or vision. To aim at a target. To zoom in on a photo or opportunity. To recognize what is important and look at it.

Quotes

"A happy man or woman is a better thing to find than a five-pound note. He or she is a radiating focus of good-will, and their entrance into a room is as though another candle had been lighted… they practically demonstrate the livableness of life." Robert Louis Stevenson

"Focus is the foundation for success." Pam Malow-Isham

Pam's Perspective

When I was young, I focused on everything that was going wrong. When I was seventeen, I read my first positive thinking book. It changed my focus and my life. Since then I realize what I focus on is what I materialize or become.

Questions

Why do I always focus on the best in people? What do I need to focus on more? When I get off center, what is the best way to re-focus and stay on track? Why is it advantageous to focus on the solution?

Declarations

I see clearly the positive changes taking place in my life by **focusing** on what I want. I use every second of my time productively. My **focused** desire is a constant help in manifesting my total success.

I enjoy inspiring others to **focus** on their goals and dreams. By doing so, I attain my own. I **focus** on growing harmonious relationships. I know that what I **focus** on is responsible for creating my life today.

When I **focus** on all the blessings in my life, they expand. I **focus** my thinking on what is right, just, pure, and praiseworthy. I am patient as I **focus** on and learn new things. I have lots to learn. I am self-disciplined and **focused**. When I am calm, I am more creative.

I **focus** on the amazing future I am constructing. I see God's plan for me perfectly. I have a clean slate to **focus** on my goals. I can start over and **focus** on what I want. Anything is possible. My strength is renewed as I **focus** on God. I am more productive than ever before. I **focus** on what is beneficial to me now and then take action.

With a happy heart, I **focus** on completing the task at hand. I care about what I do. What I **focus** on multiplies rapidly for my highest good. My heart is full of love. Peace is the norm in my life.

Because I **focus** on things working out beautifully, they do. I am filled with lots of energy as I **focus** on health. Entering my promised land with ease, I manifest my dreams. I master what I **focus** on.

God **focuses** His attention on me and reveals to me the answer to every problem that comes my way. I am talented very adaptable. I feel safe because God is my provider. I find great joy in **focusing** on the solutions and enjoying this incredible journey called life.

48:
Imagine
February 17

Bible Verses
"And the Lord said, Behold, they are one people and they have all one language; and this is only the beginning of what they will do, and now nothing they have 48imagined they can do will be impossible for them." *Genesis 11:6 (AMP)*

"Glory to God, who is able to do far beyond all that we could ask or imagine by his power at work within us;" *Ephesians 3:20 (CEB)*

Word of the Day
Imagine – To envision things, as you would like them to be. To depict in your mind the outcome you want to see. To fantasize. Dream big.

Quotes
"Whatever you vividly imagine, ardently desire, sincerely believe, and enthusiastically act upon... must inevitably come to pass!" *Paul J. Meyer*

"To know is nothing at all, to imagine is everything." *Anatole France*

"Experience has convinced me that there is a thousand times more goodness, wisdom, and love in the world than men imagine." *Johann Carl Gehler*

"A man, to be greatly good, must imagine intensely and comprehensively; he must put himself in the place of another and of many others; the pains and pleasures of his species must become his own." *Percy Bysshe Shelley*

Questions
What great thing will I imagine today? What can I do to spark my imagination? Is there anything I want to accomplish but don't know how? What if I imagined I could do it, what would that look like?

Declarations

I let my **imagination** run wild with possibilities to enhance my world and benefit the people around me. I enter a new reality where what I **imagine** comes to past. I am an **imaginative** leader who excels. I **imagine** the completion of impossible tasks done easily.

I **imagine** getting along with people. I **imagine** bringing peace to stressful situations and watching things work out perfectly. I **imagine** giving love, happiness, and respect to everyone I meet.

I **imagine** uniting my community to work together, so everyone thrives and lives in harmony. I **imagine** doing great things in a great way. I see the good I **imagine** and bring it about. I celebrate little, and big win's as I **imagine** even greater blessing coming my way.

I am grateful for my creative **imagination**. I **imagine** being a torch to assist people out of their darkness and into God's glorious light. God uses **imaginative** ways to show me how much He cares for me.

I like being healthy. I **imagine** maintaining my perfect weight easily. I **imagine** every cell in my body regenerating and restored to its ideal healthful state. I **imagine** building muscles and getting stronger as I exercise throughout my day. I **imagine** my body craving vegetables over bread and fruit over sugar.

I **imagine** leaving a legacy of inspiration and contribution, so future generations are blessed. I **imagine** being a role model for people on how to live a happy, healthy, fun, productive, and prosperous life.

I **imagine** the delight of making friends everywhere I go. I **imagine** the laughter I facilitate because I dare to act silly. I wink at the reflection in my mirror. I reflect all the good I **imagine** myself to be.

49:
Ability
February 18

Bible Verses
"Then the Lord gave the donkey the ability to speak. "What have I done to you that deserves your beating me three times?" it asked Balaam." Numbers 22:28 (NLT)

"Then the disciples, each according to his ability, determined to send relief to the brethren dwelling in Judea." Acts 11:29 (NKJV)

Word of the Day
Ability – The skill to do what is expected. The strength to perform well. Having the know-how to accomplish something. Competence.

Quotes
"Our love of truth is evinced by our ability to discover and appropriate what is good wherever we come upon it." Johann Wolfgang von Goethe

"Of course you can but will you? It is not your ability but your accountability that ultimately determines your success." Kip Kint

"Ability is a poor man's wealth." Mathew Wren

"Everyone has the ability to choose their mental state. It is up to us to program our minds productively." Pam Malow-Isham

"There is only one proof of ability, - action." Marie Ebner-Eschenbach

Questions
What ability will I enhance today? Have I made a list of all my abilities? How is my ability at getting along with cantankerous people? How is my ability to stay peaceful? Why is my ability to forgive substantial?

Declarations

I am confident and competent with all the **abilities** I have to make my life extraordinary. I have a sharp mind and the **ability** to make wise decisions quickly and with ease. My ability to grow wealth expands. I regularly cultivate new **abilities** that inspire me to try new things. I have many gifts and the **ability** to succeed today.

My **ability** to hear God increases as I draw close to Him. He is eager to boost my **ability** to receive. I tune in to peace. My **ability** to reign grows ever expansive as I shower people with the love of God.

I am kind and have the **ability** to release judgments and forgive freely. By treating everyone as someone significant, I have the **ability** to make friends. I am very approachable and well rounded.

I have the **ability** to be confident, even if I am not the smartest person in the room. I am the author of my life. The pen is in my hand, and the outcome is whatever I choose. My **ability** to see my vision already accomplished and believe that it is so; invigorates me.

I have the **ability** to remember what I read and recall it instantly when I need it. My **ability** to remember people's names is outstanding. My **ability** to attract peak, loving experiences is because of the thoughts I think. I think charitable thoughts.

I have the **ability** to laugh at myself when I make a mistake and see the humor in the littlest things. By looking at both sides of a story, I create the **ability** to be compassionate to everyone around me.

My **abilities** expand each day. I am willing to act with bravery and faith knowing I have the **ability** to make my dreams come true. I have the **ability** to win. I have the **ability** to create a life that works.

50:
Inability
February 19

Bible Verses

"His faith did not weaken when he thought about his own body (which was already as good as dead now that he was about a hundred years old) or about Sarah's inability to have children, nor did he doubt God's promise out of a lack of faith. Instead, his faith became stronger and he gave glory to God." Romans 4:19-20 (ISV)

"Since it was because of the work of Christ that he almost died. He risked his life so that he could make up for your inability to serve me." Philippians 2:30 (NET)

Word of the Day

Inability – A deficiency in talent, competence, and skills. Ineffective.

Quote

"The highest purpose of intellectual cultivation is to give a man a perfect knowledge and mastery of his own inner self; to render our consciousness its own light and its own mirror. Hence there is the less reason to be surprised at our inability to enter fully into the feelings and characters of others. No one who has not a complete knowledge of himself will ever have a true understanding of another." Novalis

Pam's Perspective

I had an inability to stand up for myself, say what was on my mind, or even question someone because of my insecurities. As I built up confidence with action and affirmations, I had more to say. Believing what I say is of value is key.

Questions

Do I ever look at the inabilities of others and judge them? Why or why not? Do I ever tell myself I can't do something because of an inability?

Declarations

My **inability** to accept defeat keeps me going full speed ahead. It is fantastic to share my unique inventiveness with people who have different gifts than me so that we can work together beautifully creating a masterpiece. I have an **inability** to quit. I never give up.

I have an **inability** to think or talk negatively because of the way I have programmed my mind with uplifting words and images. I purpose to be successful. Spontaneous happiness is my way of life.

I have an **inability** to stay stagnant. I move and keep active. My stomach and colon easily assimilate all the nutrients from my food and readily eliminates all toxins. Every cell of my body is working correctly to deliver the maximum health and vitality I deserve.

I realize the **inabilities** that I have in some areas of my life. I then delegate those tasks to people better qualified than me so I can focus my energies on what I do best. I have special capabilities that enable me to be celebrated in specific areas, and I know what they are. My **inability** to get distracted keeps me living on purpose. Miraculous is always my outcome. I continually choose the best path for me.

I have an **inability** to stay angry because I forgive. I focus my attention on people's good qualities. I have an **inability** to hold a grudge because releasing bitterness feels so good. I am a grace magnet. I let go of comparison and embrace diversity. My strength is made perfect in God's power, so I am strong and fearless.

I never let my **inability** to see how something is going to happen, stop me from starting. **Inability** to finance a project cannot stop me because I know God is my source. He has massive resources eagerly waiting to rain down on me. I welcome God's tremendous blessings.

51:
Moment
February 20

Bible Verses
"Lies last only a moment, but the truth lasts forever." Proverbs 12:19 (ERV)

"The woman came behind Jesus and touched the bottom of his coat. At that moment, her bleeding stopped." Luke 8:44 (ERV)

Word of the Day
Moment – The point in time where you are. The present minute. The significance of recognizing right now.

Quotes
"Every hour is more than golden; every moment is a gem, treasure up these hours and moments, there are princely pearls in them." Horatius Bonar

"You must live in the present, launch yourself on every wave, find your eternity in each moment." Henry David Thoreau

"He who neglects the present moment throws away all he has." Friedrich Schiller

"Success is brought by continued labor and continued watchfulness. We must struggle on, not for one moment hesitate, nor take one backward step." William Jennings Bryan

"Each moment is sacred. We are not promised more, so take pleasure in the now, and enjoy each one." Pam Malow-Isham

Questions
How can I stay in the moment? What are the consequences of not staying in the present moment? What have I lost and what has it cost me in pleasure, connection, and success by not being in the moment?

Declarations

I live in the only **moment** that I can control, this **moment** right now. I am intent on embracing each **moment**. I spotlight what is clearly in front of me or around me or on me. I feel the fabric of my clothes and focus on the texture. I am grounded in peace this **moment**.

With childlike awe, I welcome every **moment**. I forget the past and release **moments** of painful memories. I reflect on positive **moments** and leave the rest behind. I only focus on what serves me well this **moment**. I receive every good thing from above every **moment**.

I remember to hydrate myself properly. I take deep breaths and just focus this **moment** on inhaling and exhaling. I feel good, look good and enjoy every **moment**. I connect with my deeper self and become more awake as I center myself in this present **moment**.

As I focus in the **moment** to the conversations I have, things flow naturally. I feel centered and relaxed while working or playing. I am a survivor and relish every **moment** I have with my beautiful family. I take care of my family by being strong mentally and physically.

I can create at will a positive emotional state at any **moment** I choose. I am excited this **moment** to be alive. I train people the **moment** I catch them doing something right with words of praise and encouragement. I like living healthy, being wise, keeping fit, staying active and having fun. I practice abiding in the **moment**.

I take my imaginary limits off God and watch Him work miracles this very **moment**. I believe every **moment** is precious and worth living. I am prevailing over every fear that tries to come at me. I keep my attitude optimistic and cheery. My future is full of possibilities. I love this **moment**. This **moment** is fabulous!

52:
Time
February 21

Bible Verses
"There is a time for everything, and a season for every activity under the heavens: a time to be born and a time to die, a time to plant and a time to uproot, a time to kill and a time to heal, a time to tear down and a time to build, a time to weep and a time to laugh, a time to mourn and a time to dance, a time to scatter stones and a time to gather them, a time to embrace and a time to refrain from embracing, a time to search and a time to give up, a time to keep and a time to throw away, a time to tear and a time to mend, a time to be silent and a time to speak, a time to love and a time to hate, a time for war and a time for peace." Ecclesiastes 3:1-8 (NIV)

Word of the Day
Time – The past, present, and future. The duration that something is measured. To measures minutes with a clock.

Quotes
"The bad news is time flies. The good news is you're the pilot." Michael Althsuler

"Time is a great teacher, but unfortunately it kills all its pupils." Hector Berlioz

"How we spend our time determines our outcomes and what we value in life." Pam Malow-Isham

"Waste no more time arguing what a good man should be. Be one." Marcus Aurelius

Questions
How do I budget my time on any given day, week or month? In what areas do I tend to allow too little or too much time? Do I value my time? Do I get paid a good wage? If not, why not? Do I make good use of my time? Do I spend time appreciating life, God, family, nature and myself?

Declarations

I am the author of my day, so I make sure I use my **time** wisely. I keep a list of all my appointments in detail. I allow enough **time** for each one, in order of importance. I make sure **time** is on my side.

I appreciate the **time** I have here on earth, so I choose to make the most of it. I ordain myself into believing I am confident and brilliant. And so it is. My maverick attitude promotes me ahead of **time** to a place of honor. Since **time** is the most valuable resource I have, I use it wisely. I accomplish in less **time** what others only dream of.

I strive to complete my job in a **timely** manner. My resourcefulness quickly pays off. I am a valuable person. I rapidly return phone calls, emails and correspondence to stay on top of things and show people I value their **time**. I take my **time** seriously and never neglect myself or my family. I like myself so, I am my number one priority.

I arrive at all my appointments on **time** or a few minutes before. I give myself extra **time** when I promise to do something, so I have leeway for unexpected emergencies. I practice patience and efficacy.

With the right amount of **time**, I can learn anything I set my mind to. I have plenty of **time** to do it. My **time** to succeed is now. I leave my competition in the dust. I am getting smarter just in the nick of **time**.

I spend **time** with the people I love. I balance my **time** between work, play and rest. I make the **time** to do the fun things I like to do. God redeems my **time**. I happily set aside **time** for God in my day.

Everywhere I look I see beauty, all the **time.** Lovable holy people surround me. I give myself permission to take the **time** to make my daily declarations on how I am living a happy, productive life.

53:
Complete
February 22

Bible Verses

"And the church is his body; it is made full and complete by Christ, who fills all things everywhere with himself." Ephesians 1:23 (NLT)

"You see, his faith and his actions worked together. His actions made his faith complete." James 2:22 (NLT)

Word of the Day

Complete – Being entirely whole. Faultless. Unreduced, intact.

Quotes

"The thief upon the cross and the beloved John were alike complete in Christ." Anna Shipton

"There is no revenge so complete as forgiveness." Josh Billings

"It is the act of an ill-instructed man to blame others for his own bad condition; it is the act of one who has begun to be instructed, to lay the blame on himself; and of one whose instruction is completed, neither to blame another, nor himself." Epictetus

Pam's Perspective

I am the complete collection of all my thoughts, actions and experiences. Without the tragedies that I have been through, I completely would be someone else with different beliefs. I do not have to wait to feel complete because I already am.

Questions

Do I complete things I start? What will I complete today that I have been putting off? What will be said of me when my life is complete?

Declarations

I easily **complete** what I set out to do. I live in **complete** harmony with people, making allowances for them because I choose to live in love. I am effervescent bubbling over with **complete** gladness and glory. I have **complete** authority to reign as a King's kid with all the privileges that affords. I am **completely** reconciled to God and beautiful in His sight. I am **completely** adorable just the way I am.

I take **complete** control over what I put in my mind, what I read and what I say to myself. I watch what I put in my mouth and what comes out of it. I have **complete** restraint over what I eat and speak. Before I overeat, I push away the remainder of food on my plate.

I confront problems and work on them until there is **complete** satisfaction. I gain **complete** consideration and outright grace in all of my business dealings. I have more than enough talent to do the job. I **complete** what I start. I have **complete** confidence in myself.

I am glad I have friends who challenge me and aren't afraid to tell me when they feel I am steering off course. I can't **complete** this journey of life alone successfully, so it is encouraging to have friends who care enough to stand up to me and say, you need to change.

The Lover of the Universe loves me **completely** despite my faults. I am **completely** liberated and free from bondage because Christ is working through me. I gladly surrender **complete** control over to God. He wants to offer me good gifts, and I choose to receive them.

Every obstacle that comes my way, I **completely** blast with love. I enjoy a good challenge. I am glad for opportunities to learn and grow. I get more assurance and wisdom with every trial I **complete.** I love myself **completely.** I am whole and **complete** in Christ!

54:
Incomplete
February 23

Bible Verse
"Now we see things imperfectly as in a cloudy mirror, but then we will see everything with perfect clarity. All that I know now is partial and incomplete, but then I will know everything completely, just as God now knows me completely." 1 Corinthians 13:12 (NLT)

Word of the Day
Incomplete – Fragmented; insufficient. Not whole. Not perfected or accomplished. Needing something to complete it.

Quote
"We need to see and agree that what we seek already lives within us and we within it. Now we know our one great task: watch for whatever promises us freedom, and then quietly, consciously refuse to see ourselves through the eyes of what we know is incomplete. Then we live wholeness itself, instead of spending our lives looking for it." Guy Finley

Pam's Perspective
I struggled feeling incomplete, looking for an outside source to make me feel complete. I thought I needed a man and he could complete me. Nope. I figured if I got a better job that would complete me. Nope. I thought if I accomplished great goals that would complete me. Nope. It wasn't until I allowed Christ to fill the void in me that I finally felt complete. And I didn't even have to work for it!

Questions
Do I ever feel incomplete? How many things have I left incomplete in the last week, month, and year? Is it normal for me to procrastinate and leave things incomplete? If so, why? Do I have any incomplete relationships that I need to mend (Things that I need to say or offer forgiveness)?

Declarations

When an **incomplete** task frustrates me, I ask the Holy Spirit for help, and I receive what I ask for. What I am unable to accomplish by myself, I am well able with God. Not only is God inside me, but also happy to see every **incomplete** thing restored. I am thoroughly equipped for every **incomplete** job that needs my assistance.

I tackle **incomplete** tasks first and see to it they are completed with excellence. I wrap up **incomplete** jobs easily. I believe I have the power to accomplish great things. I am not waiting for permission from anyone but plunge ahead to get every **incomplete** thing done.

I am grateful for all the help I receive to stay healthy and fit. I eat whole, organic, fresh food. I enjoy quality over quantity. A meal is **incomplete** without vegetables. I love to stay hydrated throughout my day. A day is **incomplete** without eight glasses of pure water. I always carry a container of pure water with me, everywhere I go.

I enjoy maintaining my perfect goal weight. Exercise is **incomplete** without proper nutrition, so I stay away from sugar-laden foods. I upgrade my appetite about what tastes good to me, so I crave healthy choices instead of **incomplete,** highly processed, and deficient food. I set my fork down and chew in-between bites.

I realize when I am **incomplete** in my knowledge of certain things. I am guided in the perfect direction, so I find the right answers. The solution is always just around the corner. I am very fortunate.

I discover new resources within this **incomplete** vessel. I am persistent. I receive guidance for **incomplete** projects through meditation. **Incomplete** is not how God views me. He sees me as happy, hearty, healthy, and perfect. Being alive is a wonderful gift.

55:
Easy
February 24

Bible Verses
"But he who listens to me will live free from danger, and he will rest easy from the fear of what is sinful." Proverbs 1:33 (NLV)

"For my yoke is easy to bear, and the burden I give you is light." Matthew 11:30 (NLT)

Word of the Day
Easy – No problem accomplishing the task. Simple and straightforward. Effortless and accessible.

Quotes
"Have patience. All things are difficult before they become easy." Saadi

"How strangely easy difficult things are!" Charles Buxton

"Anticipate the difficult by managing the easy." Lao Tzu

"Letters should be easy and natural." Philip Stanhope, 4ᵗʰ Earl of Chesterfield

Pam's Perspective
When I stopped dreading and started smiling, everything became easier. I have an easy life now because I choose to think that decisions are easy to make, friendships are easy to form, jobs are easy to find and life is easy to handle.

Questions
When I look at a problem do I immediately say, 'this is going to be hard' or do I say 'this is going to be easy'? What makes the difference? What area of my life is complicated? How can I make it easier to handle?

Declarations

It is **easy** to write down my goals, set a plan and **easily** achieve them. I attain my mission in life with **ease**. I love my **easy** life. It is **easy** for me to make a substantial difference in the world just by loving people. I add to the positive vibrations of the world with my **easygoing** way. I keep grinning bigger as the day goes on.

My pleasant feeling about how **easy** it is to share with others entices me to give more. I **easily** create felicity. God made me as a gift to the world. It is **easy** to accept God's unconditional love for me that is beyond measure. I am keen about grace. I **easily** give mercy and forgiveness everywhere I go. I am extraordinary, and so are others.

I **easily** get the job done. I find it **easy** to do my work because I tackle it with joyful elation, knowing that nothing is hard unless I think it is. I believe life can be **easy**, even if hard circumstances come my way. I stick with my plan and **easily** complete it with grace.

It is **easy** for me to embody great joy because I let go of suffering. I give myself permission to breathe in lots of fresh air, and **easily** breathe out all the toxins, and everything that does not serve me.

People gravitate toward me because I am **easy** to be their friend. I **easily** find things in common that we can talk about. I found it **easy** to accept the people around me because I look at them through God's eyes. I am warmly received as being very neighborly.

I find it **easy** to stay in good condition because I stay active and eat healthily. I glow from within. I **easily** embrace the beautiful body I now have. I like riding my bike and having fun. It is **easy** to manifest bliss-filled experiences as I radiate love to the world. I am **easy** to talk to, relaxed, spontaneous, **easygoing**, and operating in the flow.

56:
Hard
February 25

Bible Verses
"Anything I wanted, I would take. I denied myself no pleasure. I even found great pleasure in hard work, a reward for all my labors." Ecclesiastes 2:10 (NLT)

"We never accepted food from anyone without paying for it. We worked hard day and night so we would not be a burden to any of you." 2 Thessalonians 3:8 (NLT)

Word of the Day
Hard – Concrete, hardened and inflexible. Laborious to move, plan or comprehend. Tough to perform. Challenging.

Quotes
"If you choose to think a task is hard before you begin, it will be as you have chosen." Pam Malow-Isham

"Giving yourself a hard time just trains you to give yourself a hard time." Tim Brownson

"Employ your time in improving yourself by other men's writings, so that you shall come easily what others have labored hard for." Socrates

Pam's Perspective
The hard lessons in my past have increased my wisdom. It is hard to watch family and friends who are hard on themselves but won't change. The hardest thing for me is keeping my mouth shut when I want to help and they don't want my help.

Questions
Do I think anything is too hard for God to handle? Do I think life is hard? If so, do I whine about it or do I create it into something beautiful?

Declarations

I do the **hard** things first. I ask the **hard** questions. I enjoy working **hard** and reaping all the benefits of my labor. I approach every **hard** task with the mentality that it is going to be easy to do. It just takes a little longer, that's all. I can quickly complete **hard** assignments.

People with a **hard** face are softened when they see me smiling at them, and they smile back. I invite kindness and generosity. I am agreeable to **hard** people and shower them with tenderness. It is **hard** to get mad at me because I pass out lots of hugs and smiles.

I stimulate my mind with great books. I accomplish **hard** feats by asking for help and sharing the responsibility and the credit with my peers. I have a willingness to put into words the **hard** things I am going through and share them with my support group of friends.

It is **hard** to hear with a lot of noise around. When I slow down, I can breathe deep and listen to the still small voice within. I receive instruction on how to quickly handle any **hard** task. God is for me, and everything is easy for Him. As I trust God to pull me through **hard** times, He never fails and always surpasses my expectations.

Once I let go of the idea that things were **hard**; Shazam! They became a piece of cake. I am thankful I saw the light on how easy life can be and embraced it. I watch so-called **hard** situations turn into sweet delight. In **hard** times, I use my words to confess that God is my helper. Every **hard** thing is accomplished when I trust God.

Perfect peace is mine as I rest after a **hard** day's work. I drift into sleep in a tranquil state, meditating on what is good and lovely, counting my blessings and giving thanks. I look to God and **hard** days disappear. I live the life of my dreams even on **hard** days.

57:
Content
February 26

Bible Verses
"The righteous eat to their hearts' content, but the stomach of the wicked goes hungry." Proverbs 13:25 (NIV)

"A godly life brings huge profits to people who are content with what they have." 1 Timothy 6:6 (GW)

Word of the Day
Content – Being gratified. Being happy with life and yourself. Cheerful.

Quotes
"Humility is a virtue all preach, none practice, and yet everybody is content to hear. The master thinks it good doctrine for his servant, the laity for the clergy, the clergy for the laity." John Selden

"Who hopes in God's help, his help cannot start: Nothing is impossible to a willing heart, and will may win my heart, herein to consent, to take all things as it comes, and be content." John Heywood

"He that questioneth much, shall learn much, and content much; but especially if he apply his questions to the skill of the persons whom he asketh." Francis Bacon

Pam's Perspective
Being content is a choice. That does not mean I don't work or that I don't want finer things. I can be content while aspiring for more and working on my goals.

Questions
Am I content with my spiritual life? How difficult is it for me to feel content? Why will I choose to be content today no matter what?

Declarations

I consider the possibility of living a **contented** life. I have a mental habit of releasing the negative so I can be **content** with the positive stuff I already have. I am energized with goodness and warmth. I remember what is essential. I show appreciation to my family and friends with a kind word, a smile, or a hug. I am always **content.**

I focus on the pleasing things in my life. I have developed a thankful attitude for all the blessings that God gives me each day. I am **content** with what I have. I whip up laughter and joy to share. I give myself permission to have a carefree, **contented** existence.

Praise is continually on my lips for the serenity and **contentment** I feel. I trust that the promises of God are true. He guards my heart and mind, filling me with **contentment** and peace. I choose to let go all resentments and let Love rule my life. I have a **contented** heart.

I am **content** winning the game of life. Although I always strive to improve the circumstances of my life, I am **content** with what God has already given me. God never gives up on me, His favorite child. Abundance and **contentment** follow me wherever I go.

When I see something I want to buy, I stop and ask myself, is this a want or a need? Can I choose to be happy and **content** without it? I do not need to keep up appearances with anyone. I turn to God for wisdom, so I make wise choices on how I spend my money. I am **content** with my savings and investment programs.

I consciously practice **contentment** because God is my assurance. I am **content** with who I am and who I am becoming. God is **content** with me just as I am. I am loved regardless of what I have or have not done. I am living my life in front of Jesus, **content** to be His.

58:
Discontent
February 27

Bible Verse
"By all means you must give to him, and you must not be discontented at your giving to him, because on account of this very thing, Yahweh your God will bless you in all your work and in all that you undertake." Deuteronomy 15:10 (LEB)

Word of the Day
Discontent – Uneasiness with oneself or what one has. Unhappy or ungratified with the outcome of a situation. Miserable and sad.

Quotes
"Despondency is the most unprofitable feeling a man can have. One good laugh is a bombshell exploding in the right place, while spleen and discontent is a gun that kicks over the man that shoots it off. Listen for sweet notes rather than for discords." Rev. W. J. Palm, Alexis, Illinois

"The splendid discontent of God with chaos made the world… And from the discontent of man the world's best progress springs." Ella Wheeler Wilcox

Pam's Perspective
I used to get discontented with the people around me if they were not acting the way I thought they should be behaving. I was discontented with myself and felt the things I had were not good enough. When I started to become grateful, my discontent melted away. Becoming content with myself and allowing people room to be their selves changed my perspective and improved my relationships.

Questions
Is it possible that the discontent I am feeling towards others has more to do with me than them? What will I put in place to ward off any discontentment? How many ways can I use my discontent to my benefit?

Declarations

Discontent is my friend. It spurs me on to greater and better things. I am **discontented** to settle for anything less than all that God has promised me. God wants me to be everything He created me to be. I declare joy and satisfaction are mine now as I work on my goals. I am grateful for all that is happening now and for what that I have.

Discontent has allowed me to give up unhealthy habits. I have a bright future. The **discontentment** of feeling weak has encouraged me to lift weights to strengthen and tone my muscles. Because I have made physical fitness a priority in my life, I reap the benefits of a healthy and robust body. I am **discontented** to let myself get or stay sick or fat. I keep pushing on to be as healthy as I can be.

I am glad I am **discontent** with what I know because it encourages me to study and learn new things. I have a great memory. A fresh avenue opens up for expanding my consciousness. I have a smart mind that is capable of absorbing anything I choose. I naturally pick up and implement better ways to live my life free from **discontent**.

I am **discontent** when I don't trust God. It is not the disposition of God to be **discontent** with me because I am His cherished heir. I am accepted. I no longer feel **discontent** in my relationship with God because I am free from condemnation. God has made up His mind about loving His prized creation, and He is not **discontent** with me.

My **discontentment** at living with the status quo urges me to rise above mediocrity and work toward transcendence in all that I do. Everything I do is valuable and worthwhile. I am gratefully included in God's family. I am humbled by the grace I continue to receive. I believe there is no darkness in God, just love. There is no **discontent** in my heart because the Holy Spirit lives in me.

59:
Accomplish
February 28

Bible Verses

"I cry out to God Most High, to God who accomplishes my requests for me." Psalm 57:2 (WEB)

"God revealed his hidden design to us, which is according to his goodwill and the plan that he intended to accomplish through his Son." Ephesians 1:9 (CEB)

Word of the Day

Accomplish – To get a specific task done. To realize a dream fulfilled. To produce desired results.

Quotes

"If one only wished to be happy, this could be easily accomplished; but we wish to be happier than the other people, and this is always difficult, for we believe others to be happier than they are." Charles de Montesquieu

"Love accomplished what fear could not." Pam Malow-Isham

"Patience, accomplish thy labour; accomplish thy work of affection. Sorrow and silence are strong, and patient endurance is godlike, therefore accomplish thy labour of love, till the heart is made godlike, purified, strengthened, perfected, and rendered more worthy of heaven!." Henry Wadsworth Longfellow

"Books still accomplish miracles; they persuade men." Thomas Carlyle

"He who thinks too much will accomplish little." Friedrich Schiller

Questions

What do I want to accomplish this week? This month? This year? What has stopped me in the past from accomplishing my goals? Why is that?

Declarations

I **accomplish** what I say I am going to **accomplish**. I am a person who keeps my word and gets the job done well. With my head held high, I am confident, knowing I can handle any setback that comes my way. I am unstoppable and can **accomplish** the impossible.

When threatened, I just laugh and persevere, even more, determined than ever to **accomplish** my goals. I choose to do what is right and live in joy. I am highly **accomplished** in what I do. I enjoy my work.

I am a child of God. I tell of all the **accomplishments** that God has done for me. I listen for myself and hear clearly the fresh word that He is saying to me through His Word. I **accomplish** mighty things today with ease by relying on Divine wisdom, favor, and blessings.

I prime my brain with positivity every morning. Because of my willpower, I **accomplish** staying at my perfect weight. I find it elementary to eat healthily and keep moving. I choose mental habits that benefit me in realizing my **accomplishments**. I help change the world with my happiness by sharing my joy and laughter.

I put my foot on the gas and go. I have the internal clarity to know where I am going easily. I get my work **accomplished** in record time. I live without limits and **accomplish** my dreams. I am known for my small and great **accomplishments.** I keep going and never give up. I enjoy being free to **accomplish** the things I desire.

I know I can **accomplish** whatever task is before me as I outshine the rest. I intend to succeed in all my **accomplishments** today and the future. I put excitement into everything I do by my steady optimism, so I clear the path for even more exceptional **accomplishments**. My **accomplishments** stand out and speak for themselves.

60:
Abandon
February 29

Bible Verses
"Do not be afraid or discouraged, for the Lord will personally go ahead of you. He will be with you; he will neither fail you nor abandon you."
Deuteronomy 31:8 (NLT)

"Even if my father and mother abandon me, the Lord will hold me close."
Psalm 27:10 (NLT)

Word of the Day
Abandon – To reject someone or something. To renounce or leave something. A person given to spontaneity, reckless emotions, or deeds.

Quote
"Do not abandon the substance for the shadow." Proverb

Pam's Perspective
Being abandoned was one of my biggest fears. My parents got divorced when I was six months old. Then they dated for six months on, six months off until I was ten. Then they got remarried. I told my mother not to since they fought all the time. Two years later they had divorced again. I felt abandoned by God and both my parents, but especially my dad. He never called, sent cards, gifts or attended any of my school activities and when he was around, he was abusive. It wasn't until I saw how loving, polite and involved my husband was with his children that I could relate to God as a loving heavenly father who wouldn't abandon me.

Questions
Have I ever felt abandoned? How did that make me feel? Have I put up any walls to prevent people from getting close? How has this served me? Has it also hurt me? What thought pattern or habit will I abandon today?

Declarations

I **abandon** the notion of the perfect life with no struggles. During the difficult times is where I learn the greatest lessons and hone my many abilities. Life is what it is, and I go with the flow, enjoying all the adventures as I **abandon** fear. I stand accepted and righteous.

I feel confident and assured in all I do for I know God is on my side and will never **abandon** me. With reckless **abandon**, I put my faith in a loving God. I take responsibility for my actions and **abandon** blame. No one is responsible for me, but me. I take charge.

It is such a joy since I have **abandoned** complaining as I look for the good in people and situations. I **abandon** the negative chatter in my head and replace it with God's positive, life-enriching thoughts about how He wants to bless me and see me prosper in everything I do. I live in harmony with God, and I am at peace with myself.

I **abandon** habits that no longer serve me. I **abandon** grudges, resentments, bitterness, and strife. I **abandon** and release all childhood hurts and animosity. I give them all to God. I enter difficult situations from a blessed place. I focus on forgiveness.

As I **abandon** my care about other people's opinion of me, I live true to my heart. I transmit happiness to the people I meet. I **abandon** putting up walls; let my armor down, and I allow love to come in. I am a treasure to behold. I am the architect of my future. I am enthusiastic, and engineer plans to make my life the best it can be.

I dream with **abandon**. Everything is feasible. I lead with quantum possibilities where everything can happen for my good. I **abandon** thoughts that make me doubt what I can do. I am mighty, fully capable of achieving my dreams. I have a can-do spirit.

61:
Light
March 1

Bible Verses

"In the same way, let your light shine before others, that they may see your good deeds and glorify your Father in heaven." Matthew 5:16 (NIV)

"For you were once darkness, but now you are light in the Lord. Live as children of light." Ephesians 5:8 (NIV)

Word of the Day

Light – Brightness of clear color. Shining vivid glow. Fair; Cheery; Effervescent. To see unobscured.

Quotes

"Knowledge once gained casts a faint light beyond its own immediate boundaries." Tyndall

"It is a great deal better to live a holy life than to talk it. We are told to let our light shine, and if it does, we won't need to tell anybody it does. The light will be its own witness. Lighthouses don't ring bells and fire cannons to call attention to their shining – they just shine." Unknown

"The Bible is a book in comparison with which all others in my eyes are of minor importance, and which in all my perplexities and distresses has never failed to give me light and strength." Gen. Robert E. Lee

"Every moment we choose to walk in either light or darkness. If we choose light, love eradicates the darkness and illuminates our way." Pam Malow-Isham

Questions

How can I light up my neighborhood? Do I light up a room when I walk in? What lights me up? How will I let my light shine today?

Declarations

I have a clear intention about how much peace, love, happiness, success, and **lightness** I want to experience today. I rise above problems and enjoy the good life. I listen to the **Light** within.

I am open to seeing things in a new **light**. I burn brightly with the **light** of Christ inside of me. I give off the **light** of compassion and joy to disperse darkness. I am on the **light** path where I free myself from heavy burdens and strife, by receiving the freedom of Christ.

I have a laser beam focus on the goals I am creating today. I focus on the **light**. I have a green **light** to success. I do what is best for all concerned. I spark a **light** of passion for fueling magnificent dreams.

I am a beacon of **light** in dark places. I am choosing to be in a state of total appreciation. I accept my success. I am an instrument of love and **light** to my community. A windfall of good fortune is mine.

I have a warm glow of the **light** of heaven inside of me that radiates peace to the people around me. I **light** up like a Christmas tree as I thrive in helping people achieve their dreams. I help **light** the way for others to see the bright side of life. I let my **light** shine wherever I go. I am **lighthearted** and carefree. I choose to be shining **light**.

I seek out mentors of **light**. I like spending time with people who support me and **light** me up. Turning on my **light**, I share my brilliance without restraint. Every day I **light** up my world.

I open myself up to the **Light**. I follow the principles of the Universe that God has put in place to help me. I am powerful in His strength and **light**. I have the perception that God wants me to thrive. I leave footprints of peace and **light** everywhere I go. I walk in the **light**.

62:
Dark
March 2

Bible Verses
"Then Solomon said, 'The Lord has said that he would dwell in a dark cloud;'" 2 Chronicles 6:1 (NIV)

"Even the darkness will not be dark to you; the night will shine like the day, for darkness is as light to you." Psalm 139:12 (NIV)

Word of the Day
Dark – The opposite of light. Black or dull in color. Drab. Sunless. Bad.

Quotes
"As in the rankest soil the most beautiful flowers are grown, so in the dark soil of poverty the choicest flowers of humanity have developed and bloomed." James Allen

"To me, every hour of light and dark is a miracle." Walt Whitman

"We must walk consciously only part way toward our goal, and then leap in the dark to our success." Henry David Thoreau

Pam's Perspective
The dark parts of me are just as valid as the light. I have gone through a couple of dark nights of the soul. I went for a time when I could not seem to hear God. I felt empty. I don't have any answers as to why it occurred, other than being able to help someone else who is there now. I told myself, this too shall pass, and it did.

Questions
Why do I trust God in the dark to bring me out into the light? What have I learned from the darkness? Will I heed the lesson and move on?

Declarations

As I travel down the **dark** path, I cannot outrun God. I live with a grateful heart knowing there is no **dark** place God cannot enter. I had times when I felt like the **dark** cloud of despair would surround me, but I choose to pierce the **darkness** with my praise. There is always a reason to praise God, even in **darkness**. I can trust my God.

Even in the **darkest** night, I do not fear because I know God is near. I endure the **dark** night for I know daylight is coming. God works in my **darkness** to bring healing and growth. I cling to and wait on God to carry me through the **darkest** night and heal my soul.

All powers of **darkness** vanish as Christ lights the way. I look for more opportunities to learn something new every day. I shy away from **dark** movies that scare me or make me feel fearful. I disregard **dark** thoughts and focus on things that make me feel good.

I rely on God who created the **darkness** and the light to teach me how to live. I appreciate the light much more after being in **darkness**. Although there may be times in the **dark** that I don't feel God's presence, I can rest assured that He is always there keeping me safe. God lives in me and is not afraid of any of my **darkness**.

The dawn of refreshment arrives as I release my **darkness**, stress and cares. I change **dark** tendencies into a new positive attitude. I am free to be light-hearted. I shine forth God's love to illuminate the **dark** places and blaze a path for others to see and embrace the light.

I endure difficult **dark** situations knowing I am loved. When I feel **dark** inside, I send love to the very part of me that needs it the most. I celebrate both the **dark** and the light sides of myself for they complete me. I am wonderfully made in the image of God.

63:
Responsibility
March 3

Bible Verses

"If you see your neighbor's ox or sheep or goat wandering away, don't ignore your responsibility. Take it back to its owner." Deuteronomy 22:1 (NLT)

"Arise! For this matter is your responsibility, but we will be with you; be courageous and act." Ezra 10:4 (NASB)

Word of the Day

Responsibility – Being accountable for one's thoughts, words, and deeds.

Quotes

"Power to do good and evil, what is that? It is liberty. And what more is it? It is responsibility. Liberty here, responsibility elsewhere. Splendid discovery! Liberty is the soul! Liberty implies resurrection, for resurrection is responsibility." Victor Hugo

"I am here, and I must do the best I can, and bear the responsibility of taking the course which I feel that I ought to take." Abraham Lincoln

Pam's Perspective

I was raised in a church that believed they were the only ones going to heaven and everyone else in the world is going to hell. I felt so sad since there were so few of us. Now my blinders are off, and I serve a loving God full of grace. Every person has a responsibility to think, seek, study, and come to their own conclusions.

Questions

What am I responsible for? Who am I responsible for? What does my boss say about how responsible I am? Is there an area of my life that I need to be more responsible? What is stopping me? Why am I so responsible?

Declarations

I enjoy taking **responsibility** for my choices and not leaving things up to chance. I like creating my life as I go. God has given me the **responsibility** of having dominion over every area of my life. I honor Him by being **responsible** for all my wonderful choices.

Since I alone am **responsible** for the condition of my physical well-being, I choose to eat healthily, exercise daily, and wisely discern what type of material I want to put in my mind, or before my eyes.

I write things down and look at my calendar so I can be **responsible** for the things that must be done and for being on time. I respond to emails and phone calls right away. I am **responsible** for how I spend my time. I do not waste it on social media or surfing the internet.

I am **responsible** for how I respond to stressful situations, so I choose not to let people push my imaginary buttons. I think before I answer. I am **responsible** for the things I notice and the things I ignore. Because I meditate on God's Word, I convey the wisest response. Being **responsible**, I stay in a state of calm tranquility.

I rise to the challenge. My success is my **responsibility**, and I take charge. I am greatly rewarded for my work. I am consistent with whom I hold myself to be. I am smart and open to advancement.

I live in peace with my neighbors. I like keeping my yard neat and clean since I'm **responsible** for its beauty. I am a **responsible** friend. I am engaged in my community and **responsible** for togetherness.

I love taking charge. I am **responsible**, so I save for the future. I earn my own living and depend on me to support myself. I pay my bills on time. I increase my **responsibility** as I learn, grow, and flourish.

64:
Irresponsible
March 4

Bible Verses

"So live responsible as a citizen. If you're irresponsible to the state, then you're irresponsible with God, and God will hold you responsible." Romans 13:2 (MSG)

"And we exhort you, brothers: warn those who are irresponsible, comfort the discouraged, help the weak, be patient with everyone." 1 Thessalonians 5:14 (HCSB)

Word of the Day

Irresponsible – Being fool hearted and witless. Not taking ownership of one's thoughts, words or actions. Untrustworthy.

Quotes

"God was not irresponsible when He gave us free-will." Pam Malow-Isham

"Oppression is but another name for irresponsible power, if history is to be trusted." William Pinkney

Pam's Perspective

I used to be irresponsible and would give my power away. I did not realize no one could make me angry, disrespect me or hurt my feelings without my permission. I would choose to get upset every time someone said or did something I didn't like. I was living upset and blaming everyone for my unhappiness except myself. It wasn't until I changed my perspective and took back my power that I stayed in control. Now I am unshakeable, and I don't allow outside forces to upset me.

Questions

Is there any area of my life where I have been irresponsible? What steps will I put in place today to make sure I stay responsible? Have I been irresponsible with my thought life? Do I stay alert to what I think?

Declarations

Holding myself to a higher standard, I do more than is expected, so I can never be found **irresponsible** in my dealings with other people. I am considerate. I look to see where I could take more responsibility in some area where I might have been **irresponsible** in the past.

I know I am the one with the power and control over my actions, so I think before I act or speak. My words are powerful and create my exciting, beautiful life. I am never **irresponsible** with my words. I keep my vision in mind about what I want to see, be, have, and do.

I pay for things with cash, so I will not be **irresponsible** with my credit cards. I refuse to play the blame game. I never make excuses or practice **irresponsible** behavior. I have an extensive portfolio of a wide variety of investments. Cash is king, and I have lots of money.

I forgive myself for the things I have been **irresponsible** for in the past and move forward with a clean slate and a humble spirit. I have learned my lessons. God is never **irresponsible** and supplies the right contacts for the perfect opportunities to bless me. I am happy, brave and content. I live where miracles are a daily occurrence.

I live my life in the now, not **irresponsibly** in the future or the past. When I see someone acting **irresponsibly**, I am tactful when I ask him or her to take responsibility for their selves. I realize we all make mistakes, so I am easy going. I broadcast joy and light.

I reexamine my **irresponsible** tendencies, so I don't lie to myself. I let go of thinking it is the other person's job to help me. I do what is needed. I expose myself to truth and believe in my message. I am thankful that I am forgiven. I am always accepted and approved by God even though I can be **irresponsible**. I plunge into joyous living.

65:
Pain
March 5

Bible Verses
"Many are the pains of the wicked, but for the one who trusts Yahweh loyal love surrounds him." Psalm 32:10 (LEB)

"And God will wipe away every tear from their eyes; there shall be no more death, nor sorrow, nor crying. There shall be no more pain, for the former things have passed away." Revelation 21:4 (NKJV)

Word of the Day
Pain – Aches, and discomfort in the body. Sickness or inner turmoil.

Quotes
"We cause ourselves most of the pain we undergo in this life by the way we treat ourselves and the way we perceive our experiences." Pam Malow-Isham

"Learning is not child's play; we cannot learn without pain." Aristotle

Pam's Perspective
I decided to get permanent eyeliner about twenty years ago. Karen spent an hour on my right eye. Then I got up to go to the bathroom and asked the fatal question, 'what are you using because it feels like a feather tickling me?' When she showed me the needle, my brain started screaming inside my head, Oh my God, She is going to poke you in the eye with a needle. I was in so much pain when she did the left eye, and I could hardly stand it. And I did it to myself.

Questions
Is there any pain in my life now? What have I done to cause it and what can I do to prevent it happening again? Do I ever inflict pain on myself?

Declarations

Pain is a part of life and an opportunity to praise God regardless of any circumstance. It is time I packed my belongings and bid farewell to all the **pain** that is no longer needed in my life. I believe God for the unbelievable today. He is healing all my **pain** this very moment.

The **pain** class was tough, but I easily learned my lessons. There is no time for looking back, just forward. I remember to pray and forgive. I permit myself to release any **pain** and anger now. I like living **pain**-free. I relinquish all **pain** now and let it go. I look beyond my **pain** and reach for what the **pain** might be teaching me.

The more I take care of my spiritual life the more at peace I am. Even in **pain**, I am completely protected by God. As **pain** appears in my life, I learn from it how to be more compassionate to others in **pain**. I am exchanging my **pain** for peace of mind and joy in my spirit.

I invest in gold and silver so I can have a prosperous future, so I don't end up with the debtor's **pain**. I say goodbye to my **pain**. I say hello to peace, prosperity and good health. I say hello to love. Love is what is awaiting me. I travel light and stay in a peaceful existence.

By choosing healthy food and staying active, I ward off the **pain** of being sick. I like to laugh because it feels good and it is good medicine. I like the **pain** I feel as I push my muscles to lift more weight each time I work out. I am getting healthier every day.

I recognize that I live in a miraculous world filled with **painful** gifts. Even if I am in **pain,** I don't have to moan or suffer. Someone will always have it worse than I do. No matter what **pain** is happening in my life, I bless it and call it good! I turn every **painful** concern over to the Almighty and observe myself transforming this very instant.

66:
Comfort
March 6

Bible Verses

"You will increase my honor and comfort me once more." Psalm 71:21 (NIV)

"This is my comfort and consolation in my affliction: that Your word has revived me and given me life." Psalm 119:50 (AMP)

Word of the Day

Comfort – The security of being cared for all the time. Knowing the satisfaction of a true friend. Warmth and contentment.

Quotes

"Prosperity is not without many fears and distastes, and adversity is not without comforts and hopes." Francis Bacon

"The unhappy derive comfort from the misfortunes of others." Aesop

"Comfort is a state of mind." Pam Malow-Isham

"If I had to sum up friendship in one word, it would be comfort." Terri Guillemets

"When the superior man eats he does not try to stuff himself; at rest, he does not seek perfect comfort; he is diligent in his work and careful in speech." Confucius

"Cure sometimes, treat often, comfort always." Hippocrates

Questions

What do I take comfort in? Do I accept the comfort of friends when they try to help? Do I stay in my comfort zone or do I venture out and take chances? Have I settled for comfort instead of going for my dreams?

Declarations

I appreciate my beautiful life and all the wonderful **comforts** in it. I am grateful for my **comfortable** home. It is **comforting** to have a safe roof over my head and healthy food to eat. Relaxing in the **comfort** of our home is **comforting** to my children and family.

I believe in my ability to succeed and break out of my **comfort** zone. By staying in a positive space and pursuing my goals, I do not need to binge on fatty **comfort** foods that bring me down. I am proactive about my self-care, so I eat what will nourish my body the most.

I **comfort** others with my kind words and deeds. I feel great being able to help others out. I take concentrated effort to **comfort** those in need. I enjoy the fellowship and **comfort** of my supportive friends.

I have a **comfortable** temperament. I live the life of my dreams because I do not let the fear of stepping out of my **comfort** zone stop me. I soar above the crowd. By not settling for less than I am capable of, I **comfort** myself. I am open to opportunities and joint ventures. I choose to be **comfortable** while reaching my goals.

I change little habits that keep me too **comfortable** and stretch out for new adventures. Every possibility of **comfort** and joy is waiting for me to magnetize with it. I change my perception of what is possible and dream new dreams again. It is safe to build a mental picture of what I want to accomplish. I emit strength and **comfort**.

The **comfort** of my pets brings me great joy. I smile just watching them play. I am ever expanding my happiness. I receive **comfort** in my sleep as I put my trust in God. The **comfort** of being accepting and accepted is a grand thing. The **comfort** of knowing God loves me gives me the strength to face the day with peace in my heart.

67:
Trust
March 7

Bible Verses
"Whoever gives attention to the Lord's word prospers, and blessed is the person who trusts the Lord." Proverbs 16:20 (GW)

"The Lord is good, a refuge in times of trouble. He cares for those who trust in him." Nahum 1:7 (NIV)

Word of the Day
Trust – Having assurance of a belief, someone or something. Faith

Quotes
"All I have seen teaches me to trust the creator for all I have not seen." Ralph Waldo Emerson

"Obedience is a way of being trustful." Bruce Garner

"Trust not to your own strength, but with your hand in the hand of the risen Christ, go forth conquering and to conquer." E. M. C.

"You may be deceived if you trust too much, but you will live in torment if you do not trust enough." Frank Crane

Pam's Perspective
Being nominated and then elected as a trustee for the board of my church is an honor and humbling. I would rather be trusted than praised.

Questions
Why am I counted as a trustworthy person? Do I trust freely or am I cynical? Do I give people the benefit of trust? Could I be too trusting?

Declarations

I **trust** God completely. I **trus**t that I will receive insights from on high at just the right time. I admit I need it. I put my **trust** in God, and I let the love of God fill me to overflowing. I live my life as an example of what God can do. I always **trust** my inner guidance.

I am a partner who is **trusted** to do an outstanding job. I **trust** myself to do the right thing, even if no one is looking. I am true blue. I like being open-minded and **trusting**. I easily live my life **trusting** God.

I am an upfront person who speaks with love. I **trust** myself to make sound judgments. I **trust** people to help me along the way. My friends are steadfast and **trustable**. I am truthful when asked the hard questions. I attract **trustworthy** people to do business with.

I refuse to let dishonest people keep me from **trusting**. I can be **trusted** without being taken advantage of or turning contemptuous. I **trust** myself around mean people to stay positive. I have wisdom.

I **trust** in the healing power of prayer. I rely on the ever-increasing strength of God in me. I don't feel week, or helpless when I am faced with a difficult situation. God illuminates my mind to what I need to do. I **trust** in God's Word to reveal just what I need to know.

I have a high self-image that reflects my **trustworthiness**. I **trust** that if I do stumble, I will get back up. I **trust** that I am forgiven and loved. I **trust** my internal teacher to show me where I need to forgive, take responsibility for my wrongs and show more love.

I **trust** my investments to grow exponentially. I have enough **trust** in whatever may come. I **trust** everything is working in my favor. I **trust** myself to succeed past my wildest dreams. In God I **trust**!

68:
Distrust
March 8

Bible Verses
"Your eyes are windows into your body. If you open your eyes wide in wonder and belief, your body fills up with light. If you live squinty-eyed in greed and distrust, your body is a dank cellar. If you pull the blinds on your windows, what a dark life you will have!" Matthew 6:22-23 (MSG)

"No unbelief or distrust made him waver (doubtingly question) concerning the promise of God, but he grew strong and was empowered by faith as he gave praise and glory to God." Romans 4:20 (AMP)

Word of the Day
Distrust – Skepticism about a person, situation or thing. Disbelief.

Quotes
"What loneliness is more lonely than distrust?" George Eliot

"If we are worrying we are not trusting. If we are trusting, we are not worrying." Kate McVeigh

Pam's Perspective
I distrusted God for allowing the abuse I suffered growing up. I distrusted almost everyone. Fear consumed me. Only the grace of God could break through the walls I had erected. When I surrendered to God, my wounds healed. He filled me with joy and my distrust toward Him melted away. Now I am discerning while trusting because relationships cannot thrive with distrust.

Questions
Where does my distrust come from and how does it affect me? How might I come from a place of trust when I am in doubt? Am I too cautious?

Declarations

Even when times are hard, I trust that everything will work out in my favor. I give people the benefit of the doubt to prove they are a person who keeps their word. I don't have to live in **distrust**.

I know that people with **distrust** issues are hurting and that is their way of showing it. I follow my heart and listen for God's intuitive nudge on every matter. I walk with the light in me. I react from love.

I am open-minded about where people are coming from and look at both sides of every situation. I **distrust** people who say we can't live peaceful, happy lives. I instigate togetherness and community.

I break free from old prejudices and look at people with trusting eyes. I am above **distrusting** my neighbor just because they may be different from me. I believe we are all God's children trying our best to survive. My family is loved and accepted by God, no matter what.

I am keenly aware of the **distrust** I have had at times toward God when my prayers seem unanswered. As I admit to God how I feel and release the **distrust** from my heart, I am filled with serenity. No amount of **distrust** can keep God from hearing me. He is God.

I rectify the **distrust** I have around my self-reliance by being upright and reliable. I say nice things to myself. I can increase and improve my confidence with ease by declaring it so and taking action.

I never let the **distrust** of negative people get me down. I overflow with spontaneous gratitude for all the spectacular blessings I continue to notice. I have a bright future. Thank you is forever on my lips. I listen to what positive people say and **distrust** the nay-sayers who like to live in chaos. I believe in myself and live in peace.

69:
Sunshine
March 9

Bible Verses

"Your life will be brighter than sunshine at noon, and life's darkest hours will shine like the dawn." Job 11:17 (GNT)

"The Lord said to me: I will quietly watch from my own place, like the shimmering heat of sunshine, like a cloud's shade in the harvest heat." Isaiah 18:4 (CEB)

Word of the Day

Sunshine – Illuminated by the sun. Intense glowing light. Daytime.

Quotes

"Climb the mountains and get their good tidings. Nature's peace will flow into you as sunshine flows into trees. The winds will blow their own freshness into you, and the storms their energy, while cares will drop off like autumn leaves." John Muir

"A flower cannot blossom without sunshine, and man cannot live without love." George P. Upton

"But friendship is precious, not only in the shade, but in the sunshine of life, and thanks to a benevolent arrangement the greater part of life is sunshine." Thomas Jefferson

"Those who bring sunshine into the lives of others cannot keep it from themselves." James M. Barrie

Questions

How many ways can I bring more sunshine into my life and the life of others? Is there a lack of sunshine in my heart? If so, why is that?

Declarations

Now is my time to **shine**. I have a **sunny** disposition and radiate love to everyone I meet. I let the essence of God **shine** forth from the core of my being and permeate every scope of my experience. I walk on the **sunshiny** side of the street where things continually go my way. I feel the positive energy of the **sunshine** radiating on me.

I see the bright **sunshine** smiling on me. I am cheerful and attract level-headed people. I am very efficient in my work and well accepted by my peers. Infinite possibilities are always present.

I'm **sunshiny** inside and out. My mind is clear, and my heart is light as I attract more friends with a **sunny** disposition. My strength, energy, stamina, and vitality are multiplied in the **sunshine**.

I let the **Son shine** through me, touching everything and everyone in my world. The **sunshine** of God illuminates my mind with wisdom to meet the day. I shed light on dark places. You can even see a glow around me. I circulate trust, afford openness and broadcast **sunshine** wherever I go. I am always expanding my luminosity.

I love walking in the **sunshine**, taking in all the vitamin D my body needs. I appreciate the beauty of nature and feel a deep connection to Spirit as I see His magnificent work. As I dance in the **sunshine**, work in the garden or just sit still, I am thankful for the warmth of the **sun**. I enjoy the **sunshine** with friends as we laugh together.

I warm people's hearts with my kind words and spark them to do the same. What was once a cold, dark neighborhood turns into a blazing flame of laughter, **sunshine**, and friendship as the spark of one ignites another until our whole community **shines** like the light of heaven. I transmit love, kindness, **sunshine**, and hope.

70:
Obscurity
March 10

Bible Verses

"These words Jehovah spoke to all your congregation on the mountain from the midst of the fire, of the cloud, and of the obscurity, with a great voice, and he added no more; and he wrote them on two tables of stone, and gave them to me." Deuteronomy 5:22 (DARBY)

"And in that day the deaf shall hear the words of the book, and out of darkness and obscurity the eyes of the blind shall see." Isaiah 29:18 (DRA)

Word of the Day

Obscurity – Vagueness. Not seen or known. Ambivalence.

Quotes

"There is no defense against criticism except obscurity." Joseph Addison

"Learn to be pleased with everything; with wealth, so far as it makes us beneficial to others; with poverty, for not having much to care for, and with obscurity, for being unenvied." Plutarch 46-119 AD

"Biography, especially the biography of the great and good, who have risen by their own exertions from poverty and obscurity to eminence and usefulness, is an inspiring and ennobling study. Its direct tendency is to reproduce the excellence it records." Horace Mann

"Serve the Lord in obscurity and be rewarded abundantly." Pam Malow-Isham

Questions

What gift inside me can I resurrect from obscurity? What are the benefits of living in obscurity and what are the cons? Do I prefer to share my life and business with the world or stay in obscurity?

Declarations

I can be **obscure** and do a bang up job without any praise. I am peaceful, pleasant and pleasing to the eye. I don't have to be in the limelight to know that I am valuable. **Obscurity** is fine with me. I am OK just the way I am. I am enthusiastic about my wonderful life.

I guard my mind to keep it as innocent as possible because the allure of what is evil **obscures** all that is good and honorable. Doing my work in front of God, I gain stability in **obscurity**. In **obscurity**, I sit with God and listen for instructions. We have a close relationship.

I love seeking for truth as I study in the quiet **obscurity** of my home. I love the adventure of learning something new daily. I like looking up and reading **obscure** books of great people from the past. I am content no matter if my station in life is fame or **obscurity**.

I am comfortable with the ups and downs of life. I am well balanced. In **obscurity**, I give generously of my time, talent and finances, just for the fun of it. I enjoy being sensible and finish more than is expected of me. I ooze wisdom. I attract the perfect connections to help me fulfill my purpose. I rise from a place of **obscurity** to a place of honor where my peers respect me as an expert in their field.

The **obscurity** of negativity is a relief as I go about my day. I release old **obscure** hurts and resentments. I no longer need to carry such weight around. I lose excess weight with ease. I **obscure** the junk food from my sight, so I will eat lots of vegetables. I grant myself permission to have a productive, happy day in **obscurity**.

I rekindle **obscure** goals from my past. I am ready to thrive. I bounce back with zeal igniting **obscure** dreams. I never let the cares of this life **obscure** all the possibilities waiting for me around the corner.

71:
Healing
March 11

Bible Verses

"But for you who revere my name, the sun of righteousness shall rise, with healing in its wings. You shall go out leaping like calves from the stall." Malachi 4:2 (NRSV)

"God gave Jesus of Nazareth the Holy Spirit and power. He went around doing good and healing all who were troubled by the devil because God was with Him." Acts 10:38 (NLV)

Word of the Day

Healing – Recovery from sickness. Mending something that is broken. Advantageous to one's health. Recovering your strength from sickness.

Quotes

"The practice of forgiveness is our most important contribution to the healing of the world." Marianne Williamson

"Why should you carry troubles and sorrows unhealed? There is no bodily wound for which some herb doth not grow, and heavenly plants are more medical. Bind up your hearts in them, and they shall not only give healing but leave with you the perfume of the blessed gardens where they grew." Henry Ward Beecher

"The miracles of the church seem to me to rest not so much upon faces or voices or healing power coming suddenly near to us from afar off, but upon our perceptions being made finer, so that for a moment our eyes can see, and our ears can hear what is there about us always." Willa Cather

Questions

What do I need healing in today? What is preventing my healing? Have I benefited from being sick? How can I bring healing to the people I meet?

Declarations

I am thankful for my marvelous **healing** taking place now. I know God is mighty to **heal**. I am remarkably made in the image of God. He loves **healing** all his children; even the ones who think they don't deserve it, or that He can't do it. I claim my **healing** now because I know my God is more than able to **heal** anything.

I declare **healing** in my mind. God's love now **heals** and overthrows every wrong condition in my thinking. I give all my wounds to God to **heal**. Divine **health** is the natural state I choose to walk in.

I am reminded of whom I need to forgive so I can **heal**. By choosing the way of love, I accept apologies easily and release all resentments and hurts. I forgive everyone for all past offenses committed towards me. I ask people whom I have offended for forgiveness so we both can **heal**. I am thankful for peace and deliverance.

I miraculously recover as **healing** prayers are sent my way. I never allow appearances or a doctor's prognosis to determine my level of wellness. I have a great physician that has given me jurisdiction over my mind, body, **health**, and affairs. My desire for **health** is perfect.

I have the audacity to believe and act as if my **healing** is now complete. I receive God's **healing** as I trust my amazing **healing** Creator. God's love is all-powerful and renders everything not divine defenseless. Every cell of my body is **healing** now. I love my body, and I speak **healing** to each cell declaring its wholeness.

I claim **healing** in my finances as I experience prosperity. Wealth and riches are mine, as I seek to do good work. I am **healed** from an impoverished mindset. There is no shortage with God. **Healing** is normal for me. God in me is my **healing**, right here and now!

72:
Hurt
March 12

Bible Verses
"Am I the one they are hurting?" asks the Lord. "Most of all, they hurt themselves, to their own shame." Jeremiah 7:19 (NLT)

"Bless those who curse you. Pray for those who hurt you." Luke 6:28 (NLT)

Word of the Day
Hurt – To inflict a wound or cause distress to the body or the mind.

Quotes
"Little minds are too much wounded by little things; great minds see all, and are not even hurt." Sophie von La Roche

"By ruminating over past hurts, I re-inflict myself with undue pain. But now, I can make the pain stop by revising the way I think." Pam Malow-Isham

"Many words hurt more than swords." English Proverb

Pam's Perspective
Being on the ski patrol I have to refresh my CPR and first aid skills every year, so when someone gets hurt on the hill, I am equipped to help them. I also carry in my car or put in my dry sack when I kayak, a first aid kit. I like being prepared for anything. We have a saying on patrol. It is not if you will get hurt, but when, if you have been on the ski patrol long enough, but we don't let that stop us from having fun. We are a different breed. A little crazy and a lot humanitarian.

Questions
Who have I hurt that I need to ask forgiveness? Who has hurt me that I need to forgive? What hurt will I release of today?

Declarations

I never blame people who **hurt** me unconsciously. Some people are just unaware. I tell them how I feel as I sit down with them, and how they are **hurting** me, so we can resolve it calmly and quietly. If I choose to respond with a **hurt** feeling when someone lashes out at me, that is my choice. Getting frustrated with someone and angry will not improve a situation. Or I can choose to let it go and be free.

Making up stories in my head about what has happened to me only **hurts** me. My interpretation of what someone has said or done is just that, and my attachment to that interpretation is what **hurts** me. So I choose to release it now. I diffuse all **hurts** with forgiveness.

I am healthy. I spring into action bringing restoration to broken and **hurting** relationships. I proliferate peace and community. I make a great effort to help everyone I can. I release every bit of bitterness that tried to get a hold of me and walk free. By forgiving myself for the **hurt** I have caused myself, I grow in freedom and self-respect.

I know **hurting** people are the ones who **hurt** people, so I don't take it personally when someone criticizes me. I hold my peace. I see the little child in them crying out for help, wanting to be loved but not knowing how. I pray for God to heal their **hurting** wounds.

I help restore **hurting** people and remind them that I care. I am the overflow of tenderness and generosity as I comfort the **hurting**. I have confidence in God to heal others who are **hurting** and in need.

Every **hurt** that tries to lay claim to my mind is dissolved now, in Jesus name. I rise above all **hurts**. I choose to walk in liberty as I forgive the people who have **hurt** me. I can clear the debts of those who have wronged me for I am stronger than any **hurt** they caused.

73:
Perseverance
March 13

Bible Verses

"Therefore, since we are surrounded by such a great cloud of witnesses, let us throw off everything that hinders and the sin that so easily entangles. And let us run with perseverance the race marked out for us." Hebrews 12:1 (NIV)

"Because you know that the testing of your faith produces perseverance. Let perseverance finish its work so that you may be mature and complete, not lacking anything." James 1:3-4 (NIV)

Word of the Week

Perseverance – Consistent work to complete a task. Endurance no matter what. Zeal or Moxie.

Quotes

"Patience and perseverance have a magical talisman, before which difficulties disappear and obstacles vanish into air." John Quincy Adams

"Perseverance. – The falling drops at last will wear the stone." Lucretius

"With ordinary talent and extraordinary perseverance, all things are attainable." Thomas Buxton, 1ˢᵗ Baronet

"Perseverance creates miracles." Pam Malow-Isham

"The difference between perseverance and obstinacy is that one often comes from a strong will, and the other from a strong won't." Author Unknown

Questions

What does perseverance look like to me? Do I apply perseverance to all my tasks? Why do I make perseverance a part of my daily life?

Declarations

Perseverance is my middle name. People know I follow through and get the job done, no matter how long it takes or how hard it is. I just **persist**. I divide every project into small sections so it is manageable and I can complete it smoothly. I live by the creed of **Perseverance.**

My motto is **perseverance** because I never quit. I prepare for my future by speaking, thinking and acting upon the Word of God. I am counted as trustworthy and relentless at achieving my goals because of my **perseverance**. With the **perseverance** of stating my positive declarations, I psych myself up when I am feeling down.

The practice of self-control and **perseverance** is part of my daily life. With **perseverance,** I stay focused till the task is achieved. I dare to push my limits and climb higher than I thought possible. I give it my all. I **persevere** until I bring to pass what seemed impossible.

Step by step I keep going, building character and **perseverance**. I am a role model for what it takes to succeed. With **perseverance** in keeping my word, I am thought of as one who can be trusted.

I pray for the happiness of my enemies. I rejoice in my suffering for it produces **perseverance**. As trials come, I **persevere** by giving myself compassion during difficult times. I stay the course and keep the faith. I joyfully **persevere** through every hardship that comes my way. My success is sure. I remember to give thanks always.

I **persevere** in giving out compliments to the people around me. I can afford to share nice words. God's **perseverance** at chasing me down with wonderful blessings, kindles deep gratitude in my heart. I deserve to succeed, and I do because I **persevere**. I develop into the kind of person I can be proud of as I practice **perseverance**.

74:
Lazy
March 14

Bible Verses

"If someone is too lazy to work, their house will begin to leak, and the roof will fall in." Ecclesiastes 10:18 (ERV)

"Do not be lazy. Be like those who have faith and have not given up. They will receive what God has promised them." Hebrews 6:12 (NLV)

Word of the Day

Lazy – Someone that is apathetic, indifferent and doesn't like to work. Slothful and lethargic, slow.

Quotes

"Any man who reads too much and uses his own brain too little falls into lazy habits of thinking." Albert Einstein

"Human nature is above all things - lazy." Harriet Beecher Stowe

Pam's Perspective

When I was young, I was lazy because I did not have a goal, purpose worth living for, or a mission. Loving myself, having a dream and a purpose cured my lazy tendencies. I was working five jobs in three cities, volunteering and still hearing my Dad's voice in my head calling me lazy. Until I gave myself permission to be lazy once in a while and take a well-deserved break, whatever I did was never enough. I realize I can be lazy once in a while and still be valuable.

Questions

What does lazy look like to me? Do I condemn myself when I am lazy or am I ok with it? Do I judge others for being lazy? Do I set aside time for myself to be lazy? What industrious thing will I do today?

Declarations

I permit myself to fail, be **lazy** and make mistakes. I know I can't be perfect every second, so I give myself the opportunity to be human. **Laziness** is part of being human. I am enthusiastically **lazy**.

I drown out the negative voice of the past that is telling me I am **lazy** when I know I am doing my best and working as hard as I can. I am amazing. I have staying power to get any and every job done well.

I am careful to catch myself from judging people who I think are **lazy**. I remind myself of the times I have been **lazy**, so I give people a break. God loves me even if I decide to be **lazy**. I accept that we all develop at different paces, and I allow people to progress at their own, **lazy** speed. I remember none of us are perfect, and that's OK.

I commend myself for my diligence and ability to keep going. I take the bull by the horns and throw off **lazy** tendencies to complete every task. I plow through my problems and face them head-on.

I have well-informed mentors who give me great techniques on how to change my **lazy** ways. I like taking action. I persuade myself to change my brain from being **lazy** to unstoppable. I am approachable and willing to learn from people who are very industrious and **lazy**.

Despite being **lazy**, I am a pleasure to be around. I appreciate everything I have learned from my **lazy** ways. I honor my word and do what I say. I am tenacious in going for my dreams. I remind myself of all my accomplishments and my strong work ethic.

I amplify my joy by taking things lightly and laughing at myself. On the days that I set aside to rest and be **lazy**, I enjoy it and do not condemn myself. Being **lazy** is OK. It is good to relax occasionally.

75:
Integrity
March 15

Bible Verses

"There once was a man named Job who lived in the land of Uz. He was blameless—a man of complete integrity. He feared God and stayed away from evil." Job 1:1 (NLT)

"The man of integrity walks securely, but he who takes crooked paths will be found out." Proverbs 10:9 (NIV)

Word of the Day

Integrity – Honest. Keeping your word, no matter the circumstance. Someones incorruptibility when tempted. Completeness.

Quotes

"Integrity without knowledge is weak and useless, and knowledge without integrity is dangerous and dreadful." Samuel Johnson

"No man knows the value of innocence and integrity but he who has lost them." William Godwin

"What comfort does overflow the devout soul from a consciousness of its own innocence and integrity!" John Tillotson

"Nothing demands more caution than the truth: 'tis the lancet of the heart. It requires as much to tell the truth as to conceal it. A single lie destroys a whole reputation for integrity." Baltasar Gracian

Questions

What kind of person am I? Do I value integrity? Am I consistent with keeping my word, no matter what? How am I known by my peers, customers, and friends? Why do I choose to walk in integrity today?

Declarations

I refuse to compromise my honor and **integrity**. I neither understate nor overstate something to gain an advantage or make myself look good. I tell the truth even when it may be a drawback to me getting ahead. Being a person of **integrity** is my most important trait.

I build my **integrity** by first keeping the promises I make to myself, then to others. I value my **integrity** as a hallowed offering I give to God and myself. Then I become a contribution to the world as someone extremely valuable. I am trustworthy and true to myself.

God is my promoter, and He will lift me up as I walk in **integrity**. I respect myself enough to be accountable and responsible for my actions and reactions. I am a keeper of my word and a stand for others to live with **integrity**. I act as a person of **integrity**.

I am washing my brain daily with positive thoughts. All my motives are Godlike and true. I know my most valuable quality is **integrity**, so I protect it by always doing what is right. I am a go-getter. I become a person of **integrity** by acting as a person of **integrity**.

I copy the actions of men and women of **integrity**. I am grateful for autobiographies of people who model **integrity,** who I admire. My role models inspire me to victory. When faced with a dilemma I ask myself if my hero would make the same choice. I know in my heart the right answer. I let love and **integrity** steer me to greatness.

People share with their friends, and the word spreads like wildfire, that I am a person of **integrity** and high value. I am straightforward and allow truth to flow freely. I am expressing God's wisdom, truth and beauty always. I tower above the rest. My foundation is built on honesty, kindness, and **integrity**. I circulate love and live in peace.

76:
Disgrace
March 16

Bible Verses
"No one who trusts in you will ever be disgraced, but disgrace comes to those who try to deceive others." Psalm 25:3 (NLT)

"They will not be disgraced in hard times; even in famine they will have more than enough." Psalm 37:19 (NLT)

Word of the Day
Disgrace – Someone who is a liar and disrespectful to someone or something. Tarnish or discredit.

Quotes
"Whatever disgrace we may have deserved, it is almost always in our power to re-establish our character." Francois De La Rochefoucauld

"No one can disgrace us but ourselves." J. G. Holland

"Labor disgraces no man; unfortunately, you occasionally find men who disgrace labor." Ulysses S. Grant

"If you aspire to the highest place, it is no disgrace to stop at the second or even the third place." Marcus Tullius Cicero

"God's grace is what is needed after disgrace." Pam Malow-Isham

Questions
Have I ever been a disgrace to my family or myself? If so, why was that? How did that make me feel? What steps can I put in place to assure I never disgrace myself? How do I want to be remembered?

Declarations

I have a well-established positive self-image. I stand up to people who try to bully or **disgrace** another human being. I am selective about the people I hang around with and the close friends I choose. I surround myself with people of good character. I investigate the people I do business with to see if they are honest or **disgraceful**.

I have the strength of conviction in doing the right thing, so I am not a **disgrace** to my family. I restrain myself from buying unnecessary items, so I am not **disgraced** with debt that I cannot pay. Being effective with my time and energy, I fulfill my God-given destiny.

I realize being around unsavory, **disgraceful** characters with vile language will only bring me down. It could also implicate **disgrace** upon me because people judge my character by the friends I keep. I am a light to them when they are in my presence, but I don't seek to chum around **disgraceful** individuals. I try to honor God in all I do.

I find value in my life and all the wonderful people and things in it. I pilot my thoughts toward joy, not **disgrace**. I have empathy for the people who feel they have **disgraced** themselves. We all make slip ups now and then. Everyone is redeemable. I easily dispense compassion and grace. I declare I live by truthfulness and love.

I don't **disgrace** my reputation because I think before I speak and act. I am conscious at all times and in all situations. Nothing comes out of my mouth that is **disgraceful** or that I will regret later.

God sees me with my flaws and **disgraceful** ways and still loves me. I am very thankful I do not have to be perfect or 'good enough' to be accepted by God. God believes in me. I live a supercharged life that is getting better every day. I stay on course and get what I want.

77:
Play
March 17

Bible Verses
"And they rose up early on the morrow, and offered burnt offerings, and brought peace offerings, and the people sat down to eat and to drink, and rose up to play." Exodus 32:6 (KJV)

"It is better to be an ordinary person working for a living than to play the part of someone great but go hungry." Proverbs 12:9 (GNT)

Word of the Day
Play – To have a good time. Being entertained by a game.

Quotes
"Dare to err and to dream; a deep meaning often lies in the play of a child."
Friedrich Schiller

"Oh, yes, everything is but child's play to the gentleman." Goethe's Mephisto

Pam's Perspective
I love to play all kinds of card, board, dice, and conversational games. It is a great way to see how competitive someone is and how they respond to winning and losing. In 2001 several family members and I played the game of risk. It came down to three of us, and I thought for sure I was going to lose, but then I drew the exact card I needed and ended up coming back and winning the game. Then the person who lost went to the refrigerator and poured a large glass of orange juice on top of my head at three o'clock in the morning. I never played with him again.

Questions
What do I admire about people who play? Do I enjoy the moments when I do play, or is my mind somewhere else? Why do I schedule playtime?

Declarations

I go out and **play** just for the fun of it. I **play** on purpose. I learn new games and new ways to **play**. I am a lifetime learner. I **play** act; like the way, my hero would be acting, and become that kind of person. I write my own lines and create a wonderful, **playful** life.

I **play** a game to see how many people I can bless, without them knowing whom it came from. By doing random acts of kindness, I increase my level of positive emotions. For fun, I feed a stranger's parking meter or pay for the coffee of the person behind me.

By **playing** full out, I stay healthy, wealthy, and wise. I love to **play** the game of life. I am intentional about my **playtime** and how much fun I am going to have. I love discovering new things. I like being surprised. I seek out pleasure and **play** around with happiness. I am grateful that I always schedule enough **playtime** with my children.

Today I intend to **play** a game seeing how much good I can attract. I gather smiles, hugs, laughter, enjoyment, prosperity, and so much more. I love moving with passion, **playfully** fulfilling my dreams.

I have a **playful** smile. As the sun burst through the clouds of disappointment, I am ready to **play**. God loves to see His children **play** and would like to see more of it. I like **playing** games that stretch me to think and use my imagination. I respect others, their choices and the games they choose to **play**. Variety is fun.

I **play** with my pet and laugh with delight at the love I receive. I am lighthearted, thankful and free, **playing** the gratitude game. I live in the flow of **playful** abundance. I allow **playing** to be a regular part of my day. I love how **playful** I can be for no reason at all. I **play** life from a place that anything is possible. It is safe to **play** now.

78:
Work
March 18

Bible Verses

"But you, be strong and do not lose courage, for there is reward for your work." 2 Chronicles 15:7 (NASB)

"We remember before our God and Father your work produced by faith, your labor prompted by love, and your endurance inspired by hope in our Lord Jesus Christ." 1 Thessalonians 1:3 (NIV)

Word of the Day

Work – The effort put forth to complete a job. Employment. Striving.

Quotes

"Prayer does not fit us for the greater works; prayer is the greater work." Oswald Chambers

"Give us the man who sings at his work! Be his occupation what it may, he will be equal to any of those who follow the same pursuit in silent sullenness. He will do more at the same time; he will do it better; he will persevere longer." Thomas Carlyle

Pam's Perspective

I love exercising my gifts and finding new ones. I am so fortunate to have found professions that excite, fulfill, motivate, and inspire me. I do not consider it work but a method through which I can contribute. My life of service has taken me from poverty to plenty, and I am grateful for all the lessons learned.

Questions

Is my work fulfilling? If not, why not? What kind of work inspires me and sets me on fire? Do I perform my work as unto the Lord?

Declarations

I consistently deliver great **work**. I am highly engaged in everything I do, so for me, it is fun. I never consider **work** hard or drudgery. I whistle while I **work**, enjoying the time it takes to reach my goals.

In all my **work**, no matter how big or small, I do it as unto the Lord. I only care about getting approval from God is always watching and is the one. I **work** on being the best **worker** around. God **works** on the inside of my temple illuminating me with light and wisdom.

I **work** through difficult times with my friends. I belong to a great support group of aware individuals. I am thankful for considerate friends who **work** with my idiosyncrasies and love me nevertheless. I do not have to **work** at creating laughter because it naturally bubbles up and multiplies as we **work** and play together.

I **work** on myself to become the most positive, productive person I know. I alone am responsible for what becomes of my life and how I am remembered. I improve my mind by doing the **work** of reading good books. The **work** of memorization has improved my memory.

I cherish my temple and **work** at keeping it fit and nimble. **Working** out with weights builds my core muscles and increases my strength. I **work** to increase my endurance. I love feeling healthy, so I make my **workouts** fun. I **work** through the pain of sore muscles to take care of myself. Exercise and **work** are a part of my lifestyle.

The **work** I desire comes my way, along with so many opportunities that I don't have time to fit them all in. My **work** is my play, and I play at my **work**. I make my **work** count and do it with pride. I am efficient in all my **work** and do it with ease. God smiles on my **work**. My life **works** synergistically in harmony with what I believe.

79:
Truth
March 19

Bible Verses
"Then you will know the truth, and the truth will set you free." John 8:32 (NIV)

"I have no greater joy than to hear that my children are walking in the truth." 3 John 1:4 (NIV)

Word of the Day
Truth – The legitimacy of a fact. Genuineness. Authenticity. Certainty.

Quotes
"Truth is the truth no matter who the source is." Dottie D. Caldwell, MA, LPC

"Love truth, but pardon error." Voltaire

"Truth may sometimes come out of the devil's mouth." Proverb

"The language of truth is simple." Seneca

"Truth does not become more true by virtue of the fact that the entire world agrees with it, nor less so even if the whole world disagrees with it." Maimonides

Pam's Perspective
There is freedom in telling the truth. When I was a teenager, I would lie about my age. It was exhausting trying to remember who I told what and people always found out the truth. Now I am happy to tell my age no matter how old I get.

Questions
Do I seek truth? Do I ask God to show me the truth? Do I stand up for truth? Do I listen for truth? When I hear the truth, how do I respond?

Declarations

I am a seeker of **truth**. God affirms His **truth** to me from His word. He exhibits **truth** in my friends. I know how to be **truthful**. He uncovers the **truth** to me in the antagonist. He imparts **truth** to me in nature. I walk in **truth** today generating hope, joy, and good-will.

I choose the way of **truth**. I reveal the **truth** of how I feel about myself by how I let others treat me. I am vigilant about the content of my thoughts. I think **true** thoughts. I release thoughts of prejudice and think compassionate thoughts. I think on what is **truthful**.

The **truth** is that I am called to love God and love others. I put my anger in the hands of God and surrender to peace. I let **truth** rule. I transmit **truth** and radiate love. I am gentle with myself as I look for **truth**. I learn a new **truth** each day. I have strong intuition.

Listening to the perspective of others is always interesting. I give myself permission to change my mind when I find a new **truth**. I am continually learning more **truth** because I am open and receptive. I stay in fellowship with **truth** seekers. The **truth** is, I feel powerful.

In **truth**, I become a risk taker. I have a keen sense of business. I have an instinct for attracting **truthful** business partners and trusted advisors. I am **truthful**, trustworthy and a valued co-worker. I make wise choices. I give **truthful**, constructive feedback that enhances every receiver. I get good results and produce good fruit.

I have a great brain that chooses **truth** over lies. Today I am acting from the core of my being and living from the **truth** as I know it. I thrive on the principles of **truth**. There is only one source, and that source is God. I am wholly devoted to a **truthful** God. I grasp **truth** easily and often. I know the **truth**, and the **truth** has set me free!

80:
Falsehood
March 20

Bible Verses
"You shall not take the name of the Lord your God in vain, for the Lord will not hold him guiltless who takes His name in falsehood or without purpose."
Deuteronomy 5:11 (AMP)

"He who will speak truth will reveal righteousness, but the witness of falsehood, deceit." Proverbs 12:17 (LEB)

Word of the Day
Falsehood – The cover-up of the truth. A misstatement. Dishonesty.

Quotes
"Truth indeed rather alleviates than hurts, and will always bear up against falsehood, as oil does above water." Miguel De Cervantes

"Truth is so obscure in these times, and falsehood so established, that, unless we love the truth, we cannot know it." Blaise Pascal

"It is an affront to truth to treat falsehood with complaisance." Thomas Paine

Pam's Perspective
The worst falsehoods I have ever told have been to myself about myself. And the distress I inflicted upon myself by believing them was tragic. I told myself I was ugly, dumb, fat, stupid and a loser. I wouldn't tell my enemy such things, yet I continued to berate myself for years. Praise God; I no longer believe those lies.

Questions
Are there falsehoods in any of my thoughts or beliefs? Have I ever told a falsehood to make myself look good? If I did, how did I feel afterward?

Declarations

People regard me as honorable and someone who can be trusted. I put all **falsehoods** behind me and speak truth to everyone. I stay open to God, so I can be used to help people understand the truth. I do not have to tell a **falsehood** to impress or please anyone. God's truth shines from my face and flows from my lips. I am more than enough just the way I am. I read God's word and apply it in my life.

Falsehood cannot enter my home because the truth is guarding the door. I think about what I am seeing and allowing in my life. I stick up for my friends if someone tries to spread a **falsehood**. I am loyal to God, my friends, and family. I am honest with all my business and personal dealings. I tell the truth even when a **falsehood** would be more advantageous. I trust myself to do good deeds.

I memorize truth. I expose **falsehood** by asking divine questions and thinking for myself. God gave me a smart mind, and I use it for His glory. I am confident that the truth will always come out and conquer any **falsehood** that tries to appear. I like telling the truth.

I am connected to my good and **falsehoods** flee. When people see me coming that spew **falsehood,** they jump up and make a quick getaway. Life happens, and I accept the challenges when someone tells a **falsehood** about me. I forgive, stand my ground and move on. I am a person of dignity. **Falsehood** is not welcome in my presence.

The thoughts of God flood my mind with wisdom. When I think something is a **falsehood**, I look within. I don't tell a **falsehood** to myself. I already know what I need to know to make my life magnificent. The application of that wisdom is the key to success. I become one with God's principles so I cannot be fooled by **falsehoods** when they come. I am smarter than the average kid.

Decide
March 21

Bible Verses
"Whatever you decide on a matter, it will be established for you, and light will shine on your ways." Job 22:28 (NET)

"Be honest in your judgment and do not decide at a glance (superficially and by appearances), but judge fairly and righteously." John 7:24 (AMP)

Word of the Day
Decide – To choose. To agree by a settlement. To make a selection.

Quotes
"Once to every man and nation comes the moment to decide, in strife of Truth with Falsehood, for the good or evil side." James Russell Lowell

"Our everyday practices decide our destiny." Pam Malow-Isham

"Men must be decided on what they will NOT do, and then they are able to act with vigor in what they ought to do." Mencius

Pam's Perspective
When I realize I could decide my fate, life became an adventure instead of a grind. I was no longer a victim of circumstance. Putting off a decision has never made one easier for me. I have found if I decide quickly, after I have the facts, I can live with my choice and I always feel better once I decide, right, wrong or indifferent.

Questions
How quickly will I decide on my next goal? What do I need to decide on today that I have been putting off? Why is that? Do I stick to the decisions I have made? Why or why not? Will I decide to have a great day today?

Declarations

I **decide** to be thankful for everything that comes my way. I **decided** today to focus on doing things right as I work on my goals. I am proactive and **decide** now to make things happen. I **decide** to have a great life full of joy. I quickly and confidently **decide** on what I want.

Indecision comes from fear and doubt, so I release it and make an informed **decision**. I **decide** to go to God first with all my concerns. I **decide** to face challenges head-on, instead of running from them because God directs my steps. I am safe and have no worries. I **decide** to follow God with my whole heart, soul, mind, and body.

I **decide** to return phone calls and emails promptly, so I stay ahead. I **decide** to delegate things that I prefer not to do to someone who can do a great job. I **decide** to free up my time for things that are important to me. I **decide** to leave early, so I arrive on time for all my appointments. I **decide** to make the most of my day.

I increase the probability of having great health because of the way I **decide** to take good care of my body. From this moment on, I **decide** on eating and living healthy. I **decide** to associate with healthy people who encourage me to have fun while working out.

I love feeling carefree. I **decided** to focus on the one great thing that went well today instead of what didn't. I believe in myself to make wise **decisions**. I enjoy being in charge of my life and **deciding** what I want to do. I manifest happiness, prosperity, and great work.

Gladly, all my financial needs are met. I **decide** to be grateful for and enjoy the lessons I am learning. I **decide** to stop playing small and go for it. Yes, my dreams can come true. I **decide** to invest my wealth and be charitable. I always have enough. It is good to **decide**!

82:
Defer
March 22

Bible Verses
"You shall do no injustice in judgment; you shall not be partial to the poor nor defer to the great, but you are to judge your neighbor fairly." Leviticus 19:15 (NASB)

"You shall rise before the aged, and defer to the old; and you shall fear your God: I am the Lord." Leviticus 19:32 (NRSV)

Word of the Day
Defer – To postpone something. Procrastinate. Suspend decision.

Quotes
"I expect to pass through this world but once; any good thing therefore that I can do, or any kindness that I can show to any fellow creature, let me do it now; let me not defer or neglect it, for I shall not pass this way again." Stephan Grellet

"O Time! The beautifier of the dead, adorner of the ruin, comforter and only healer when the heart hath bled time! The corrector where our judgments err, the test of truth, love, sole philosopher, for all besides are sophists, from thy thrift which never loses though it doth defer time, the avenger! Unto thee I lift my hands, and eyes, and heart, and crave of thee a gift." Lord Byron

Pam's Perspective
I used to defer my happiness until I achieved something. The joy I missed out on was great. Now I never defer my joy or take little things for granted.

Questions
Have I deferred success, love or friendships? Have I ever deferred being happy? What can I choose to defer today so I can reach my goals?

Declarations

Deferring a smile is not an option for me because I like to feel great. I **defer** eating every time I feel hungry. I drink lots of pure water. I love water. I **defer** sitting when I would rather be dancing joyfully around. I **defer** taking the elevator when I can easily walk up the stairs. I am a joy magnet. I use my power of choice to stay healthy.

I **defer** procrastination when I can easily accomplish the task right in front of me. I **defer** watching TV when I could be spending time doing something more productive. I love to read and expand my vocabulary. I never **defer** learning and discovering new things. I never **defer** a trip. I notice interesting things wherever I go.

I **defer** getting angry when someone cuts me off in traffic. I **defer** saying a snide remark when someone is rude to me because I always rise above small thinkers. I blast my enemies with love. I **defer** being negative because I am the hands of God extended. I show love to every person and thank God who is the source of everything good.

I **defer** greed and allow abundance. I escalate my wealth by sharing it with who I decide. I **defer** purchasing something on credit until I can pay for it with cash. I like to save money and put things away for a rainy day because they always come, and I always have enough. I **defer** allowing friends or family to borrow money from me, so there is never any crummy feelings between us.

I proliferate a life of great rewards. I never **defer** praising God for the grace and love He freely gives me. I immediately say 'Thank You' for every kind act, word and deed that I receive. I never **defer** giving a compliment when it is so easy to do. I **defer** being lonely because I take the initiative to be friendly. I join like-minded groups. I easily make upbeat, dependable friends in my community.

83:
Future
March 23

Bible Verses
"You will be safe from slander; no need to fear the future." Job 5:21 (TLB)

"Lord You are my portion and my cup of blessing; You hold my future." Psalm 16:5 (HCSB)

Word of the Day
Future – The immensity of time to come. The destiny we reach toward.

Quotes
"Practice whatever you want to be in the future now. If you want to be more patient and less reactionary, then practice patience now. If you want to be a manager of your own personal wealth, start managing your finances now, no matter how much money you earn. If you want to be successful, then practice being successful now. Start small. Engage in things that you're already good at and challenge yourself to be better, even if it's just in small increments." T. Harv Eker

"The decisions that we make in the present must be determined from our future!" Bruce Garner

Pam's Perspective
I spent a majority of my life living in a 'future world' instead of dealing with the present. It was easier to dream of how good it was going to be rather than doing something. I'm glad I didn't stay there. I take action now instead of just daydreaming.

Questions
Have I thought about what I would like to see, be, do or have in my future? Have I written it down an action plan for attaining it?

Declarations

I plan for the **future** I desire. I do not live my **future** rooted in the past. The **future** I am committed to living is one where I am healthy, whole physically, mentally, spiritually and financially. I am enough. I am grateful for **future** friends who are a joy to be around.

I act wisely. I create the **future** I envision where I take charge and have an excuse-free life. I improve my mental game by what I listen to, and the books I read. I win in my mind first, before I win in my everyday life and my **future**. I alone am responsible for my **future**, so I make it a good one. I love feeling brilliant and courageous.

I rise to the challenge of welcoming the unknown and inviting uncertainty, for I trust God who is certain my **future** will be great. I am fortunate my **future** is bright. I stop being a victim and become a victor! I benefit in my **future** by the wise choices I make today.

I take charge of my physical surroundings by making them clean and beautiful. I unclutter my house and unclutter my mind. I bring into existence a beautiful **future** that is constructed from my loveliness. I have joy deep down in my heart. Infinite peace is mine.

My uplifting thoughts create a positive **future**. I slow down to master my craft, so I can be recommended in the **future** as a leader in my profession. I easily expand my business because I have a keen eye for opportunity. I am worthy of compliments now and in the **future**. My **future** world is benefited by my godly work today.

Because I meditate, I have more peace and understanding in the **future**. I spread my wings and fly forward excited about my **future** adventures. I look for opportunities behind every door. I am grateful for everything unfolding perfectly in my brilliant **future**.

84:
Past
March 24

Bible Verses
"None of their past sins will be brought up again, for they have done what is just and right, and they will surely live." Ezekiel 33:16 (NLT)

"Oh, the depth of the riches both of the wisdom and knowledge of God! How unsearchable are His judgments and His ways past finding out!" Romans 11:33 (ESV)

Word of the Day
Past – Something that is over and done. Already completed. History. The time or things that are behind you.

Quotes
"When one is past, another care we have; thus woe succeeds a woe, as wave a wave." Robert Herrick

"Even God cannot change the past." Agathon

"The best prophets of the future is the past." Lord Byron

Pam's Perspective
When I am determining my future with the vision of my past, I get what I do not want. So I forgive, let go, and release my past. Then I can create anything I desire. And with an empty canvas, I can invent a masterpiece for God's glory.

Questions
Are my thoughts centered on the past, future or present? Do I spend too much time dwelling on the past? What have I learned in the past that I can use right now? How can I keep from repeating past errs?

Declarations

I profit from the experiences of my **past** that taught me how to take charge of my life and stand up for myself. I am thankful for the things I learned in my **past**, the good, bad and awful. They have all served me well. I let go of **past** mistakes and cut every useless tie that tries to bind. As I release **past** hurts and wounds, I go free.

The same God, who guided me in the **past**, leads me now. I feel loved, protected and forgiven. I enjoy the happy memories of times **past**. I contemplate **past** advice and use it for my benefit. I have a marvelous life. I let go of **past** grievances so I can thrive.

I know I am responsible for what I eat and how much I exercise. I allow myself the pleasure of being trim. I release **past** habits of eating too much sugar. I decide to think, live and stay healthy. I take charge of my physical body by eating vegetables and working out.

Although I appreciate my **past** successes, I continue to advance and pursue greater achievements in the future. I will explode **past** limitations and create powerful new habits; ideas and ways of being that surpass my dreams. I am poised for prominence and success.

Autobiographies are fun to read and a great way to acquire **past** wisdom. I assimilate the good and disregard the rest. Reading of **past** heroes inspires me today. I extract jewels of wisdom from the bright minds of **past** generations. I improve my **past** knowledge.

I value my **past** while living in the present moment. Nothing in my **past** can stop me from achieving my goals. I am fearless. I will allow prosperity and peace to come forth. I liberate my future by releasing the **past**. I see **past** my failures and believe in myself. I overcome every challenge because I keep the **past** in the **past**.

85:
Refuge
March 25

Bible Verses

"As for God, His way is blameless; the word of the Lord is tested; He is a shield to all who take refuge in Him." 2 Samuel 22:31 (NASB)

"In the fear of the Lord there is strong confidence, and his children will have a place of refuge." Proverbs 14:26 (GW)

Word of the Day

Refuge – A sanctuary where you are safe. A strong tower. A safe hideout away from your enemy. A safe house.

Quotes

"Silence is the universal refuge, the sequel to all dull discourses and all foolish acts, a balm to our every chagrin, as welcome after satiety as after disappointment." Henry David Thoreau

"Being optimistic is a great refuge in this negative world." Pam Malow-Isham

"Simple pleasures are the last refuge of the complex." Oscar Wilde

Pam's Perspective

Music and dancing is the refuge I choose that brightens my day and lifts my spirits. The Bible is my refuge for wisdom. Books are my refuge from the negativity of the world and a great escape when I need a diversion.

Questions

Where do I take refuge? With whom do I take refuge? Is there a place of refuge where I feel safe? Do I have a friend who I can share my ups and downs, be authentic, and always feel accepted? If not, why not?

Declarations

God is my defender and **refuge** in times of trouble and times of joy. He commands His angels to surround and to protect me wherever I go. God's loving embrace is the **refuge** I run to. I trust everything will always work out for my highest good. I continue to spread the good news of grace as I take comfort in His **refuge** of mercy.

I take **refuge** knowing God is always with me and never leaves me. Goodness, grace, and mercy follow me wherever I go. I have confidence in God. He comforts me and gives me peace, day and night. Miracles are my **refuge** and a normal occurrence for me.

I take **refuge** with my friends who cheer me up. I have authentic friends who have my back, and I have theirs. I love sharing my time with happy people who value themselves and help others. I share the **refuge** of kindness with everyone. My friends are precious.

I do an all-encompassing investigation into what I believe and with whom I take **refuge**. I read and search out for myself. I ask questions and get answers. I am as capable as anyone else to hear from God. I release any and all doubts. I have nothing to fear, for God is my **refuge** and an ever-present help in times of trouble.

No matter what storm or trial that comes my way, God is my **refuge** and my strength. I find **refuge,** security, and shelter in His loving embrace. He keeps me safe from all diseases, hidden dangers and people who wish me harm. I am endowed with stability from God.

I feel comfortable trusting God. I take **refuge** in knowing the Lord heals all my conditions, no matter how big or small. God brings the smile back to my eyes. I see my self-worth. I say thank you. I walk in peace, live in love and sing for joy. I blossom wherever I turn.

86:
Risk
March 26

Bible Verses
"I am the Good Shepherd. The Good Shepherd risks and lays down His [own] life for the sheep." John 10:11 (AMP)

"Say hello to Prisca and Aquila, my coworkers in Christ Jesus, who risked their own necks for my life. I'm not the only one who thanks God for them, but all the churches of the Gentiles do the same." Romans 16:3-4 (CEB)

Word of the Day
Risk – Not waiting for certainty. Being uncomfortable but taking action. Opening yourself up to danger, or the possibility of failure.

Quotes
"Love is definitely worth the risk of a broken heart." Pam Malow-Isham

"Most people would rather be certain they're miserable, than risk being happy." Dr. Robert Anthony

"To conquer without risk is to triumph without glory." George de Scudery

Pam's Perspective
The risk of being ridiculed and judged by sharing my life's story in this book was scary and intimidating. I cannot change my past, but hopefully, someone will learn from my mistakes. Authenticity is worth the risk of being laughed at.

Questions
Do I play it safe or am I a risk taker? What risk have I been putting off because of fear? What has that cost me? What will it take for me to risk more? Why will I take more risks today?

Declarations

I am a fearless **risk** taker. I **risk** being vulnerable with my feelings by letting down my walls and opening my heart to love. Love is worth fighting and **risking** everything for. I believe in love, and I show it.

I have the courage to **risk** making a mistake. I can do unbelievable things with God if I am willing to take a **risk**. I take **risks** to help people improve their lives with love. When sharing my faith, I **risk** being ridiculed. I **risk** letting the Holy Spirit to speak through me.

I **risk** asking something of people and being told no or yes. I **risk** making friends with strangers. I dare to **risk** looking like a fool because we all can be a little foolish at times, so what. I **risk** laughing from my gut, unashamed of my joy, and gratified with life.

I grow stronger each day with every new **risk** I take. So what if I fail. At least I did my best, and I am satisfied that I tried. I like stepping up and taking **risks**. **Risking** offers me the opportunity to hone my inner game. My life continues to get better and better the more **risks** I take. Challenging myself with **risks** is a recreation I enjoy.

I love my body and the way I look. I **risk** finding and trying new forms of exercise. I **risk** trying new games. **Risking** is fun. I am filled with immense energy as I keep moving my body. I **risk** trying new foods. I will **risk** taking a bite of something new to challenge myself. I will **risk** again and again and enjoy this great adventure of mine.

I awaken to my unlimited possibilities right now as I **risk** dreaming again. God's faithful promises are true and everlasting for me. I plant my seeds and reap the rewards. I let God surprise me with more than I can even imagine. I am simply delighted as I **risk** taking another chance, opening a new business or making a new friend.

Miserable
March 27

Bible Verses

"When I refused to admit my wrongs, I was miserable, moaning and complaining all day long so that even my bones felt brittle." Psalm 32:3 (VOICE)

"A miserable heart means a miserable life; a cheerful heart fills the day with song." Proverbs 15:15 (MSG)

Word of the Day

Miserable - Having a tormented soul. Brokenhearted and despairing. Unsatisfactory in appearance, pathetic or impoverished.

Quotes

"If you want to spoil all that God gives you, if you want to be miserable yourself, and a maker of misery to others, the way is easy enough. Only be selfish, and it is done at once. Think about yourself, what respect people ought to pay you, what people think of you, and then nothing to you will be pure." Charles Kingsley

"A man who has nothing which he is willing to fight for, nothing which he cares more about than he does his personal safety, is a miserable creature who has no chance of being free unless made and kept so by the exertions of better men than himself." John Stuart Mill

Pam's Perspective

Reliving the abuse, I suffered in my head over and over, made me miserable. The more I dwelt on it, the worse I felt. I had to forgive and release it to heal.

Questions

What can I do to help someone who is miserable? What will I do today to keep a positive attitude when miserable things happen to me?

Declarations

Every moment I get to choose how I want to feel, so I choose to feel great. Instead of feeling **miserable**, I count my blessings. Counting my blessings gives me joy. I love my life even though it can be **miserable** at times. **Miserable** is a lot better than being dead.

Being **miserable** does not help me or anyone around me. I ask myself, 'Do I want myself to appear as a **miserable** example or a happy example of a human being?' I matter and what I do matters. Because I choose to think positively, I attract the joyful life I deserve.

I learn from my mistakes. I never take my **miserable** moods too seriously because I know they can fluctuate depending on if I am sick, had enough sleep or need to eat. So I make sure I get enough rest, eat healthily and get enough exercise so I won't feel **miserable**.

I am willing to let **miserable** thoughts fly by without landing and taking root. I dismiss all **miserable** thoughts now. I allow joy to manifest. I turn from **miserable** thoughts to what is holy, pure, and worthy of my time. I listen to good reports. I am a great thinker.

I choose to put my attention on God. My mind concentrates on what is lovely, not what is **miserable**. I give up being offended, hurt, misunderstood and **miserable**. I turn it all over to God and choose to live in forgiveness, love, peace, harmony, and togetherness.

I possess a loving philosophy, and no **miserable** person can take it from me. I operate in loving ways. I am grateful I do not have to keep **miserable** feelings. Just changing my stance and acting as if I am excited can change a **miserable** perspective. With enthusiasm, I declare I am victorious and a highly favored child of God. I love to feel happy. I decide to put a smile on my face and get moving.

88:
Happy
March 28

Bible Verses
"Happy the people to whom such blessings fall! Happy the people whose God is the Lord!" Psalm 144:15 (RSV)

"If you know these things, you will be happy if you do them." John 13:17 (NLV)

Word of the Day
Happy – Feeling overjoyed and blessed. The feeling of being in a grateful mood. Good spirited and upbeat.

Quotes
"Nothing is miserable but what is thought so, and contrariwise, every estate is happy if he that bears it be content." Anicius Manlius Severinus Boethius

"Very little is needed to make a happy life." Marcus Aurelius

"Happy are they who freely mingle prayer and toil till God responds to the one and rewards the other." Samuel Irenaeus Prime

Pam's Perspective
I work at being happy. I have a large organic garden and grow my own vegetables and fruit. I make a homemade jam called, Happy Pam Jam. I make over a dozen different flavors. It is a labor of love. I spread happiness by giving away jam throughout the year. I look for ways to be a blessing, and in doing so, I become happier. I receive more joy by sharing my jam than eating it all myself.

Questions
What does happy look like to me? How do I make myself happy? How can I make someone else happy? Where do I find my happiness?

Declarations

I start and end every day with a smile. **Happiness** vibrates with every pulse of my heart. I have a lot of creative notions because I practice being **happy**. The **happy** things I offer to the world make a big difference. I allow myself to win. I like people, and it shows.

Happiness is the music of my life. **Happy** feelings manifest because I choose to be **happy** in any circumstance. I am in good spirits all the time. I act **happy**, and therefore I am **happy**. I have a lot of **happy** thoughts inside of me. I attract **happy** people who like to have fun.

Instead of pursuing **happiness**, I create it. I do not have to search for **happiness**; I have it. Now is a great time to laugh and be **happy**. I can be spiritual, **happy**, healthy, likable and rich. Life is good.

I am **happy** as I serve others. It is a joy to help and give what I can. My mind is constantly in touch with the Divine. I **happily** give God room to work in me. I am Spirit-filled with **happiness**. I am bright and cheerful, spreading my **happiness** to everyone around me.

I am **happy** to be alive. I seek God and come out with a vision that is so great that it motivates me to the next level. My heart is full of gratitude for all the **happiness** that continues to inundate my day.

I feel **happiest** when I make time for myself, so I stay **happy**. I am as relevant as everyone else, so I put my **happiness** first, and then the people around me are **happy** too. I do what I love. I open the doors of **happiness** and fame with my winning personality.

I am grateful that I experience inner **happiness** at all times. I believe I create and maintain my own, personal **happiness**, no matter what. I live in a **happy** state by multiplying my infectious, **happy** smile!

89:
Strength
March 29

Bible Verses
"It is God who arms me with strength, and keeps my way secure." Psalm 18:32 (ESV)

"O my Strength, unto Thee I sing praise, for God is my tower, the God of my kindness!" Psalm 59:17 (YLT)

Word of the Day
Strength – Virtuous in character. Having robust health and stamina in the body. Having the intestinal fortitude to stand up for what you believe in.

Quotes
"If you are tired with a long day's work, turn the thought of weariness out of your mind and say to yourself: "My body is made of strength, for my spirit is strong," and you will be filled with strength, and weariness will leave you." Dorothy Grenside

"Love is its own perennial fount of strength. The strength of affection is a proof not of the worthiness of the object, but of the largeness of the soul which loves. Love descends, not ascends." Frederick William Robertson

Pam's Perspective
My strength lies in my positive attitude, my willingness to try new things and the perseverance to keep going until I figure it out.

Questions
Do I acknowledge the strength in others? Do I have a written list of my strengths? Have I asked a close friend to list what they think my strengths are? Why do I accentuate my greatest strengths?

Declarations

I measure up because I get my **strength** and confidence from within. My **strength** originates from the Divine source. I accept only the jobs I have the **strength** to complete. I am honest in all things. I live out a life of virtue, gaining **strength** from every trial and tribulation I face. I am a leader who shares my **strengths** with others in my field.

I develop my existing **strengths** and cultivate new ones. I go from **strength** to **strength** as I walk with the Lord. I am strong and have the **strength** I need to see me through every situation. I choose to learn something new every day to enhance my **strengths**.

People know they can expect impartiality, kindness, and **strength** from me. I do not allow the negative attitudes of others to affect me in any adverse way. I respond with the **strength** of love. I am delicate when talking about sensitive subjects. I am a great friend.

I like building the **strength** of my muscles by lifting weights. I alone can **strengthen** my body or let it waste away. I have a strong memory to recall everything I need at just the right time. I find the inner **strength** I need to pull me through. I am more than capable. I have confidence, poise, and **strength** to follow my passion and win.

All irritation in my life is transformed into insight and new **strength**. I release all negative thoughts and infect myself with an everlasting joy, which gives me stability and lasting **strength**. People gain **strength** from me by seeing that no matter what, I never give up.

I have the **strength** to release the past and move on. Forgiveness is easy for me. I get my **strength** from my bold, trusting heart. I think and act from love. My **strength** is evident in my smile. I am known for my honesty, charitable deeds, encouragement, and **strength**.

Weakness
March 30

Bible Verses

"He said to me, "My grace is enough for you, because power is made perfect in weakness." So I'll gladly spend my time bragging about my weaknesses so that Christ's power can rest on me." 2 Corinthians 12:9 (CEB)

"Our High Priest is not one who cannot feel sympathy for our weaknesses. On the contrary, we have a High Priest who was tempted in every~~ way that~~ we are, but did not sin." Hebrews 4:15 (GNT)

Word of the Day

Weakness – Not being strong. The inclination to give in to one's desires regardless of the consequences. A shortcoming in someone's character.

Quotes

"It is weakness rather than wickedness which renders men unfit to be trusted with unlimited power." John Adams, 2nd US President

"Pride and weakness are Siamese twins." James Russell Lowell

"Pessimism leads to weakness, optimism to power." Ralph Waldo Trine

Pam's Perspective

We all have some form of weakness in our lives, either mental, physical or spiritual. Judging others because of their weakness shows your own weakness of character. Jesus said, he who is without sin, throw the first stone.

Questions

Will I acknowledge my weaknesses without blaming others? Am I honest about what I consider to be a weakness? What weakness can I overcome?

Declarations

God accepts me despite my **weaknesses**. I recognize it is not **weakness** to admit that I am wrong but courageous; so I readily admit every error, so I can continue to grow. With discipline, I turn my areas of **weakness** into strengths. I go for a run and feel good.

I relish my **weakness** of never being able to pass a piece of litter on the ground without being able to pick it up because I leave the world a cleaner place. Even if no one is looking, I always do the right thing. I make my days count even when I don't feel like it.

The **weakness** of my muscles is diminishing as I continue to lift more weight. I love feeling firm. I enjoy my daily workouts and encourage my friends to join me in my healthy lifestyle.

My **weakness** for having compassion for stray animals has helped me rescue precious pets and brought me immeasurable joy. Pets and people are thankful for my contribution to their lives.

In my **weakness** I learn to depend on God, receiving His energy. I pray for the **weaknesses** I see in others without judgment because I know I have **weaknesses** too. I am devoted to showing charity.

My life is absolutely grand, in spite of my **weakness**. I celebrate my strengths and **weaknesses**, respecting all parts of myself. I manifest strength in my **weakness** by persevering against all the odds to attain my goals. I love being hearty, disciplined, and kindhearted.

I laugh when people tell me I can't achieve something because of my **weakness**. I know I will show them with God, all things are possible. Every day I get more in tune with my greatness and ability to press on. I just go for it. I have an endurance kind of personality.

91:
Pride
March 31

Bible Verses

"In his pride, the wicked man does not seek him; in all his thoughts there is no room for God." Psalm 10:4 (NIV)

"Believers in humble circumstances ought to take pride in their high position." James 1:9 (NIV)

Word of the Day

Pride – Taking delight in your accomplishments. Being happy with your actions, self-confident. Self-admiration.

Quotes

"Unfortunately, quite often, we are the cause of our own problems. Pride comes in and blinds us as we claim, "I'm too perfect to have caused this problem." Pride alone can open that door. Always examine yourself for open doors where sickness may have gained entrance." Joan Hunter

"Pride is still aiming at the blest abodes; men would be angels, angels would be gods; aspiring to be gods, if angels fell, aspiring to be angels, men rebel." Pope

Pam's Perspective

I take pride in doing a good job at whatever I am attempting, whether it is sweeping the floor, painting a wall, or cooking. Doing sloppy, half-hearted work does not feel good to me. Doing things with excellence makes me feel excellent.

Questions

Has my pride ever hurt someone I love? If so, what did I do about it? What have I accomplished that has brought me the greatest pride? How can I have pride in my work without being arrogant?

Declarations

I take **pride** in the achievements I have made and continually aim to surpass them. I strive for excellence in all I do. Because I am realistic about what I can and can't do, I am not too **prideful** to ask for help. I know I am neither above anyone nor am I below them. We are all human beings deserving of attention, respect, praise, and **pride**.

I take **pride** in being me. I respect myself for who I am and what I do without the need for outside confirmations. I get my validation from within. I show **pride** in being courteous, kind and useful.

I value myself. I am in tune with the Source of life. I am not **prideful** in believing that I am the source of my existence. I live in a balance between **pride** and modesty. I submit to God knowing He gives me breath and strength to meet the day. God and I make a great team.

With modest **pride**, I tell people how I have overcome challenges and conquered setbacks. I obtain **pride** by earning my own money. I am competent enough to pay my own way and make a good living. I am **proud** of my ability to save a good portion of what I earn.

I can spot a person with inflated **pride**, is self-centered and thinks only of themselves. I pray for such a person and pray for myself that my **pride** will never blindside me. I stay transparent to recognize and admit my own errors and swallow my **pride**. I let go of having to be right. I stay open for corrections, insights, and improvement.

I walk tall with **pride**, with my head held high for whom I am and who I am becoming. I can be strong, confident, and full of **pride**, while also being kind, generous and meek. I graciously accept praise when it is due. I am emotionally balanced, not too **prideful** or docile. I am God's **pride** and joy, and he loves bragging about me.

92:
Humility
April 1

Bible Verses
"The result of humility is fear of the Lord, along with wealth, honor, and life." Proverbs 22:4 (HCSB)

"Let this same attitude and purpose and [humble] mind be in you which was in Christ Jesus: [Let Him be your example in humility:]." Philippians 2:5 (AMP)

Word of the Day
Humility – Having a reluctance to take credit for one's work. Being even-tempered. Unpretentious. Being discreet about one's abilities.

Quote
"At least one-half of what we miscall humility, especially the habit of self-accusation and self-abasement that passes for a deep sense of sin, is the fruit of self-obsession. The chronic depression and despondency that go along with a certain type of religious temperament are simply the outcome of lacerated pride. We are disappointed with ourselves, not because we are humble, but, on the contrary, because we thought too highly of ourselves and are wounded in our pride." Brigid E. Herman

Pam's Perspective
When I started to identify with my humanity, and accept that I had faults like everyone else, then I started to respect people who before I would dislike. Looking at people wondering how I can show the love of Christ to this person is humbling.

Questions
What is my view on humility? What is God's view of humility? Do I see humility as a strength or weakness? How can I make humility work for me? Why do I find it easy to walk in humility?

Declarations

Humility is how I succeed in life. I am unscathed by other people's judgments and opinions of me. I am honest with myself about my qualifications and capabilities. It takes **humility** to admit when I am wrong and say, 'I am sorry.' I surrender my ego to God.

Without **humility**, life gets boring when I stop learning. Nobody likes a "know it all." I recognize my limitations and understand that there is always someone who can do some things better than I.

I seek guidance from above on how I can improve my **humility**. I walk in **humility** realizing we are all God's children. I understand that we all make mistakes. When I catch myself judging someone, I turn it around and judge myself and consider how I might improve.

I ponder and meditate on verses on **humility**. I pick out mentors who personify **humility,** honesty, courage, and perseverance. I stay calm when I recognize my ego going astray. I embody **humility** with my kind heart and loving ways. I remain open to instruction.

I see people as valuable and worthy of respect, no matter who they are. **Humility** helps to heal broken relationships and see both sides of every story. My **humble** demeanor is a building block for growing reliable friends. I am cordial and a joy to be around with my **humble** spirit. I am grateful for what **humility** has taught me.

God demonstrated His **humility** by becoming human and showing us the perfect way to live. During **humbling** moments I pray to a powerful God. I remain at peace, intimately connected to a loving God, no matter what is happening in the world. I live in a genuine flow of lightness, love, and laughter. With **humility** and reverence for God, I succeed in all I do. I remember Jesus is by my side.

93:
Grace
April 2

Bible Verses
"He who loves purity of heart and has grace on his lips, the king will be his friend." Proverbs 22:11 (NKJV)

"For by grace you have been saved through faith; and that not of yourselves, it is the gift of God; not as a result of works, so that no one may boast." Ephesians 2:8 (NASB)

Word of the Day
Grace – Receiving benevolence from God without asking for it. Being forgiven. The generosity of a loving God. To show kindness and love.

Quotes
"May the perfect grace and eternal love of Christ our Lord be our never-failing protection and help." St. Ignatius of Loyola

"If I am not in the state of grace, may God put me there; and if I am, may God so keep me." Joan of Arc

"Simplicity is a captivating grace in woman, as rare as it is attractive." De Finod

Pam's Perspective
Grace chases you down when you are running away. Receiving grace is automatic. As I trust God, His grace is revealed to me even more. It is so simple and easy, just trust. We, silly humans, try to complicate everything.

Questions
Will I allow God's grace to wash over me? What is my perception of grace? Do I think I need it? Do I show grace to those around me?

Declarations

Supernatural favor follows me and covers me with **grace**. God is planning good things for me. I know I can't give what I don't have, so I accept God's love, **grace**, and forgiveness freely. I ask for His direction and **grace** in my life and follow it to the best of my ability.

I forgive myself for the bad choices I have made in the past. I accept my failures, and I look past them with God's **grace**. I go from **grace** to **grace** and glory to glory. I choose to stop being so hard on myself. I say **grace** to all my problems and difficulties. I know God can change every tribulation and turn it into something beautiful.

Grace gives me the power to have a great day. I have hope, courage, strength, and love. I relish the peace in my mind and body. Dynamic health is mine. I genuinely value my mate and offer **grace** when we disagree. I make a point of showing my affection and being **graceful**.

Love spontaneously flows out of me like a bubbling well of **grace**. I have relationships that are interdependent with mutual giving and receiving of God's love and **grace**. Forgiving and forgetting is immediate, spontaneous, and easy for me. I am full of **grace**.

God's love never ends, and there is nothing I can do to earn more **grace**. **Grace** is free for the taking, so praise God, I take it with joy in my heart. **Grace** is a marvelous gift that cannot be bought, acquired, bargained for or sold. God's **grace** is unique and unfathomable.

I cannot outrun God's **grace**, no matter how hard I try, so I proceed with gratitude in my heart. I enjoy all the mercy and **grace** given to me. I live a vibrant life surrounded by beauty, elegance, and **grace**. I cherish my wonderful life. I accept **grace** with my open heart. I appreciate the freedom I have. Abundance is the order of my day.

94:
Judgment
April 3

Bible Verses
"My son, do not let wisdom and understanding out of your sight, preserve sound judgment and discretion." Proverbs 3:21 (NIV)

"You judge by human standards; I pass judgment on no one." John 8:15 (NIV)

Word of the Day
Judgment – The ability to gather information, examine something and come to an informed decision. Having a viewpoint of something.

Quotes
"To begin with myself, then, the utterances of men concerning me will differ widely, since in passing judgment almost everyone is influenced not so much by truth as by preference, and good and evil report alike know no bounds." Petrarch

"Releasing judgment, worry, and cares is as easy as trusting God. Allow God to permeate your spirit with truth, love, and acceptance." Pam Malow-Isham

"An orator without judgment is a horse without a bridle." Theophrastus

Pam's Perspective
I used to see a certain family member as very self-righteous and judgmental. I could only relate to that person in every circumstance as judgmental. Then one day I realized I was judging that person for being judgmental. Ouch!

Questions
Does God love all the people on the earth? Do I pass judgment on Muslims or people who don't agree with me? Why or why not? Do I like it when someone who doesn't know me, passes judgment on me?

Declarations

I am a forgiveness specialist. When I catch myself **judging** someone, I immediately ask God to forgive me and to bless that person. I forgive myself. I release all **judgments** now and follow the way of wisdom. I am a witness of God's power, love, and forgiveness.

It is a pleasure to serve. I feel great joy watching my friends succeed with my help. I show enthusiasm for the little victories of others. I value people's differences without **judging** them. I treat other people as equals and help them because it is the right thing to do.

I let love lead rather than **judgment**. I have the inner fortitude to try one more time despite being **judged**. I am up for the challenge of having enormous responsibilities, regardless of any **judgments**. I keep going no matter what. I balance work and personal projects.

God delights in me and is eager to bless my work. Each moment I let go of the inclination to **judge** others. It is an ongoing process. I train myself to perceive the good in others. I am a forgiver. I am a vessel to do God's work. Happy surprises come to me without **judgment**.

I have a worship mindset that allows God to work through me to minister to all kinds of people. I pay no attention to the **judgments** of negative people. I focus on the positive aspects of my life and how I can be a contribution. I put my hope in God, and I become **judgment** free. God washes my mistakes away, and I am clean.

I am grateful for my adept sight. I have good **judgment** and make wise decisions quickly, easily and often. I am more than capable of handling any situation. I see good things in every circumstance. I am infused with Divine **judgment** and superior understanding. I treat others well and love myself for uniting people to work together.

95:
Excuse
April 4

Bible Verses

"For since the creation of the world God's invisible qualities—his eternal power and divine nature—have been clearly seen, being understood from what has been made, so that people are without excuse." Romans 1:20 (NIV)

"You, therefore, have no excuse, you who pass judgment on someone else, for at whatever point you judge another, you are condemning yourself, because you who pass judgment do the same things." Romans 2:1 (NIV)

Word of the Day

Excuse – To let go of offenses. To trelease something. To try to apologize and rationalize about one's own inadequacies. Cover up.

Quotes

"He that is good for making excuses is seldom good for anything else." Benjamin Franklin

"Excuses only aggravate the person you're telling them to and discredits the person who gives them." Pam Malow-Isham

"I attribute my success to this: - I never gave or took an excuse. Yes, I do see the difference now between me and other men. When a disaster happens, I act, and they make excuses." Florence Nightingale

"I am in earnest – I will not equivocate – I will not excuse – I will not retreat a single inch – and I will be heard!" William Lloyd Garrison

Questions

What excuse have I been holding onto? What will I put in place and whom will I hold myself accountable to, to live excuse free?

Declarations

I kick **excuses** to the curb, as I am fully responsible for all my choices and actions. I never make **excuses** or put the blame on someone else. I keep moving to relieve stress. I choose how I will respond every second of the day. No one can make me say, do, act, feel, eat, or anything else, without my permission. **Excuses** flee in my presence.

By resolving not to make **excuses**, I live with purpose. I am self-aware and receptive to correction. If I see I have done wrong, I do not make **excuses,** but I take responsibility to make better choices.

I exist **excuse** free, one day at a time, and enjoy each new moment. I select joy over despair and rejoice at the opportunity to start anew. I overcome any **excuse** I have about my limitations. I am more than enough right now. I allow success to come my way. My life is good.

There are no **excuses** that I accept for myself when it comes to my health. I have the ability to become physically fit. I get up and move to stay poised and strong. I love myself just as I am. I control what and when I eat. Eating healthy is normal for me. Taking vitamin supplements is a daily routine. I am very intentional about my actions and never make **excuses** for my weight. I look great.

I do ordinary things in an extraordinary way. It is never too late to change **excuses** into action. I face the consequences of the choices I have freely made. I do not have an **excuse** not to love and approve of myself. I am aware of what causes my emotions to feel happy.

I am of greater service to the people around me when I allow God to lead my life. I pray for the healing of myself and for every person on the planet. I believe I am up for any challenge, so I release any and all **excuses**. I choose to live an **excuse**-free life from this day forward.

96:
Diligence
April 5

Bible Verses
"Or he that exhorteth, to his exhorting: he that giveth, let him do it with liberality; he that ruleth, with diligence; he that showeth mercy, with cheerfulness. Let love be without hypocrisy. Abhor that which is evil; cleave to that which is good. In love of the brethren be tenderly affectioned one to another; in honor preferring one another; in diligence not slothful; fervent in spirit; serving the Lord." Romans 12:8-11 (ASV)

Word of the Day
Diligence – The vigilance one uses to get ahead. Being industrious. Not stopping, never giving up. Dogged persistence.

Quotes
"The expectations of life depend upon diligence, and the mechanic that would perfect his work must first sharpen his tools." Confucius

"He who labors diligently need never despair; for all things are accomplished by diligence and labor." Menander of Athens

Pam's Perspective
Diligence paid me great rewards as I saw an overgrown lot filled with trees, brush and weeds turn into a lovely flower garden and a bountiful vegetable garden. I read a lot of gardening books, took classes, became an advanced master gardener and made it happen. I continue to learn throughout my life. Everything I have achieved in life is through diligence. There is no free lunch. What I plant, I reap.

Questions
Why am I diligent with some things and not with others? Am I diligent in reaching my goals? Do I due diligence to acquire the facts before I act?

Declarations

I look out for the best interests of my family and **diligently** work to bring us closer together. I am limitless with my love and **diligently** share it. God is **diligently** chasing after me, showing me His love is unending. Blessings rain down on me as I surrender to His grace.

I infuse my life with charity, action, **diligence**, and ingenuity. When I feel like I can do no more, I add a tiny bit more, and benefits follow. With **diligence**, I work on improving all areas of my life.

I choose whom I want to become. Because of the **diligence** of my study habits, learning comes easily. I improve my brain by the books I read. I show up and make a difference with my **diligence** and creative ideas. People love working with me because I'm special.

Success is my way of life. I keep plugging away with **diligence** and a smile on my face until my work is done. Because of my **diligence**, I reap healthy financial rewards. The exponential growth of riches is common for me. I **diligently** reach the goals I set. I can over-deliver. I am a humanitarian **diligently** giving generously of my finances.

I appreciate the **diligence** of hard-working people and encourage them to keep going. I recognize the rare talents and **diligence** of the people who work for me. Giving praise for good work is an easy thing to do. The kindness I show others makes me feel happy, a win-win for both of us. I associate with people who show **diligence** of keeping their character in check. No one is above the law.

I am street smart and highly productive. With **diligence**, I achieve what I set out to accomplish. Today I choose to live as a grateful, heroic spirit showing **diligence**, knowing that God supports me in every way. Everything is a go; everything says yes to my dreams.

97:
Blessing
April 6

Bible Verses
"And I will make of you a great nation, and I will bless you, and make your name great, so that you will be a blessing." Genesis 12:2 (NLT)

"And I will make them and the places around about my hill a blessing; and I will cause the shower to come down in his season; there shall be showers of blessing." Ezekiel 34:26 (KJV)

Word of the Day
Blessing – A gift from God. Good fortune spoke to someone. Prayer.

Quote
"If one should give me a dish of sand, and tell me there were particles of iron in it, I might look for them with my eyes, and search for them with my clumsy fingers, and be unable to detect them; but let me take a magnet, and sweep through it, and how would it draw to itself the most invisible particles by the mere power of attraction! The unthankful heart, like my finger in the sand, discovers no mercies; but let the thankful heart sweep through the day; and, as the magnet finds the iron, so it will find, in every hour, some heavenly blessings; only the iron in God's sand is gold." Oliver Wendell Holmes

Pam's Perspective
I was listening to a webinar, and this person wanted people to pay him for a blessing. I was surprised people were giving him money to pray. He had no more power than you or I. Everyone is capable of giving and receiving a blessing.

Questions
Do I curse or speak blessings over the people around me? Have I counted my blessings today? Am I a blessing to my neighbors, family, and friends?

Declarations

I allow all of God's **blessings** to flow in my direction. I am endorsed from on high and worthy to sit at the king's table. I am thankful that I am included in the family of God. I am special. God loved and **blessed** me before I did anything good. I didn't even have to ask.

I am overflowing with thanksgiving for all the **blessings** I receive. I sing a love song to God for His beautiful mercy. The people I am with recognize that I hear God's voice. I feel totally supported, and have cheerleaders who encourage me on to even greater **blessings**.

I have a clean conscious. I release generational **blessings** over me, for a healthy body, a long and prosperous life, a wise, discerning mind and an abundance of loving friends. I love helping people. I am a **blessing** to those around me and a **blessing** to myself today.

I cherish myself and actively create my own **blessings** by being nice to myself. I treat myself as a valuable gift to the world. Supernatural **blessings** are the norm for me. I rescript my beliefs and realize that some trials I have been through are actually **blessings** in disguise.

I am a **blessing** to my employer because of my strong work ethic. I am promoted quickly. I am a **blessing** to all who work with me. I am reliable and highly productive. I am developing the skills I need to create and maintain powerful relationships. I have many gifts.

I am feeling great physically, mentally, and emotionally. Taking a few deep breaths, I relax right now. I speak multiple **blessings** to my children and family. I speak **blessings** over my life and see them come to pass. I am attracting really good stuff into my life! I speak **blessings** over the people around me. I am eager to say a **blessing** over my food and friends. I am **blessed**, and I am a **blessing**!

98:
Condemn
April 7

Bible Verses

"Your own mouth condemns you, and not I; your own lips testify against you." Job 15:6 (NRSV)

"Do not judge, and you will not be judged. Do not condemn, and you will not be condemned. Forgive, and you will be forgiven." Luke 6:37 (NRSV)

"Indeed, God did not send the Son into the world to condemn the world, but in order that the world might be saved through him." John 3:17 (NRSV)

Word of the Day

Condemn – To pass sentence. To criticize, reject, and put down.

Quotes

"We do not think much of a man who never contradicts us: that is no sign he loves us, but rather that he loves himself. Do not be deceived by flattery, and thereby have to pay for it: rather condemn it." Baltasar Gracian

"We should speak modestly and circumspectly of such great men, lest we should fall into the faults of many, who condemn what they do not understand." Quintilian

Pam's Perspective

Condemning myself for everything I did wrong never helped me. Being nice to myself and others has created a positive lasting effect that did help me and others.

Questions

Who or what do I condemn? How do I feel when people condemn me? Why do I expect perfection from others when I am not perfect?

Declarations

I believe the people around me are trying to do their best. When I start to **condemn** people I stop and remember, but by the grace of God, there go I. When I start to **condemn** myself, I stop, forgive myself, and affirm to do better next time. I am easy going and fun.

I remind myself that I am living my life in front of Jesus. He does not **condemn** me so why should I **condemn** myself or others. God enjoys being with me, and I enjoy being with Him. I no longer live with **condemnation** or uneasiness. I am a Spirit-empowered partner with God. I share my joy and laughter, easily and often.

I want to be trained by God who does not **condemn** me. I stay open to wisdom and correction. I expose my heart to love. No one learns by being **condemned**. I remember I am highly thought of, and so is others. I am a patient person and attract praiseworthy friends. I love embracing people from every walk of life and every nationality. The internet is a great way to learn about different cultures and customs. I live as an open book, free from **condemnation** and fear.

I release the need to **condemn** the unknown. I manifest tolerance and light. I am a forward thinker who does not **condemn** what I don't understand. The things that I believed and **condemned,** as a child are different than the things I believe today. I wait until I have all the facts in front of me before I make an informed decision. I consider diverse subjects and ponder their meanings. Who am I to **condemn** another's opinion? I am not walking in their shoes.

I never feel justified to **condemn** others for doing some of the very same things that I do. Everyone is beautiful when I take the time to look for the good. I can learn something from every person, or I can choose to **condemn** him or her. So what am I learning?

99:
Need
April 8

Bible Verses
"Both of us need help. I can help make your faith strong, and you can do the same for me. We need each other." Romans 1:12 (NLV)

"And my God will give you everything you need because of His great riches in Christ Jesus." Philippians 4:19 (NLV)

Word of the Day
Need – The belief that what you have is not enough. Not having the something you desire or regard as essential. Being uncomfortable.

Quotes
"Eat few suppers, and you'll need few medicines." Benjamin Franklin

"When you don't get what you want, you know you've just received what you need." Mike Lipkin

"God's love is all we need to feel whole." Pam Malow-Isham

Pam's Perspective
I am grateful I have learned when I give what I need away, it returns to me multiplied. I receive more fulfillment by being of service than getting stuff I want. The older I get, the less stuff I need, and the more I want to help people.

Questions
What do I need? Why do I think I need it? Could there be things in my home that I think I need that are really just wants? Do I need so much stuff? Do I need to work so much or so little? How much time do I need to spend with my family? Work? Friends? Hobbies? What about with God?

Declarations

The Lord is my shepherd. I have everything I **need** and a lot of what I want. As I become more self-reliant and take responsibility for my own **needs**, I become more confident and self-assured. I feel content and powerful because I am providing for my own **needs**.

My **needs** are simple, and I am happy with what I have. When I look back at the things that I thought I desperately **needed**, I can see many were only frivolous wants. God always gives me exactly what I **need** at just the right time. I am vigorous, strong, and beautiful.

I am thankful that my **needs** are met at just the right time. I am well. I am willing to accept all the good that is coming my way by divine order. I am learning what I **need** for today. I am playful, fun and activate my incredible power to be free and release the unnecessary.

I **need** to listen to my intuition. I feel the **need** to simplify. I look around my home at the things I possess and evaluate if I have a use for it any longer. What do I **need** and what can I do without? I release the useless stuff I no longer **need**. I pack and give it away. I can be satisfied with less, and it frees up space to allow newer, better and brighter items to come in that I think I might **need**.

God always surpasses my expectations by meeting my physical, emotional, financial, social and spiritual **needs**. I ask myself before making a purchase, do I **need** this? Then wait for the confirmation. I **need** to hear the voice of God directing my steps, so I listen.

God gives me the work, friends, validation, and inspiration that I **need** for today. I no longer **need** to be a people pleaser. I only **need** approval from God. I choose to feel joy without requiring others to change to suit my desires. My **needs** are fulfilled and satisfied.

100:
Want
April 9

Bible Verses

"O fear the Lord, all you who belong to Him. For those who fear Him never want for anything." Psalm 34:9 (NLV)

"May Your holy nation come. What You want done, may it be done on earth as it is in heaven." Matthew 6:10 (NLV)

Word of the Day

Want – A yearning for something else. To be impoverished. Crave. To be without the something you desire. To be found lacking.

Quotes

"The wise man will want to be ever with him who is better than himself." Plato

"If you desire the benefit of success, you should begin to say what you want and not what you feel." Dr. Clarice Fluitt

"Work, not hope, will get you want you want. Action with determination and a positive attitude will replace wants with accomplishments." Pam Malow-Isham

Pam's Perspective

I have collected quotes since I was in my teens. I love affirmations and great questions. I always wanted an inspirational book with everything that I put in this book. I could never find one, so I created this one. Now I want to encourage as many people as possible to believe in themselves and reach their full potential.

Questions

Do I know what I want? Have I prayed for what I want? What am I willing to do to get what I want? Have I asked for what I want? Why not?

Declarations

I make a list of the things I **want**, and then I release it and turn it over to God. I let go of **wanting**, so I can receive. I am open to receiving more. I can see my goals and dreams completed. I am well able and fully equipped to get what I **want** when I **want.**

I write my own story and live by faith. My **wants** and desires are met. I remember achieving goals in the past, and I know I can create more great experiences to get the new things I **want**. I am worthy of connections, and I attract all the supportive friends I **want**. I value the contribution my friends make in my life. I **want** for nothing.

I attract the perfect clients who **want** what I have to offer. I **want** to be satisfied with my work, so I do a good job. I am service minded. I am willing to work and do what it takes to get what I **want**. I love all the referrals I get from other satisfied customers who got what they **wanted**. I am safe and joyous getting my **wants** and needs met.

My ever-increasing supply gives me the things I **want**. As I give to God, He gives back to me multiplied 100 fold. I testify to the fact that I trust God who is my shepherd and I **want** for nothing. Giving is fun and a practice that has monetary and eternal rewards.

I am grateful for what I already have. I balance my **wants** and needs and live in harmony. I am a disciplined consumer who purchases my **wants** on sale. I have the self-restraint to wait and shop around. I love to get a great deal. I save at least ten percent of my income.

I do what I **want** when I **want**, with whom I **want**. All things are possible, so I act as I believe. I joyfully receive from a generous Father who **wants** to bless me. I feel emotionally safe with God, so no **want** is too great to ask. I think abundance, so I **want** for nothing.

101:
Group
April 10

Bible Verses
"Many more men and women put their trust in Christ and were added to the group." Acts 5:14 (NLV)

"But you are a chosen group of people. You are the King's religious leaders. You are a holy nation. You belong to God. He has done this for you so you can tell others how God has called you out of darkness into His great light." 1 Peter 2:9 (NLV)

Word of the Day
Group – A bunch of things put together. An assortment of things. An organization with more than one person in it. People in society.

Quotes
"An aura brings in others to partake of the love He offers as my group meets. Those who pause to allow the Spirit to fill their lives, rise above the flotsam of confusion." Jan Edward Hulett

"Ants are good citizens; they place group interests first." Clarence Day

Pam's Perspective
The older I get, the more groups I belong too. I love meeting with a diverse group of people and clubs. I learn from them all. I believe we can get stuck in a rut if we never venture out and join different groups. People are eager to be your friend.

Questions
Is there a group that I belong to that I need to drop that is no longer serving me or meeting my needs? How can I be an asset to the groups I am involved with? Do I join groups just for fun?

Declarations

My favorite **group** is the Father, Son, Holy Spirit and I. What a great combo we are. We are fun **groupies**. I love meeting with positive people in small **groups** to share beliefs, challenges, ideas, dreams, and goals. I am vital to every **group** I join. I like doing things with the friends in my **group**. We support each other in a variety of ways.

I always have something I can contribute to my **group**, so I show up to give an encouraging word, a thought-provoking question, a kind deed, a new revelation, a hug, or just a smile. I need to be around **groups** of positive people, so when I see the need, I start a new **group**. My **group** lays the groundwork for other **groups** to start.

I have a diverse **group** of friends. I treasure the wonderful friendship I gain by each of us contributing to each other. The feeling of the instant connection, safety, and awareness of how fortunate we are to be together as a **group** is encouraging. I gain understanding by listening to other people's viewpoints, and it gives me a new way of looking at things. I keep getting smarter every day.

I am careful to surround myself with people and **groups** who are engaging in the behaviors that I would like to see in myself. We are all equals. I profit from the insights I receive from the people in my **group**. I arrive early for my **group** appointments with a smile.

My **group** is buzzing with excitement about all the people who will benefit in the future because of us. We **group** our resources for good and act wisely. We are a **group** of winners and leaders. We fill our consciousness with thoughts of affluence, and the possibilities of what we can accomplish. I engage my **group** to serve our community in multiple ways. We are the movers and shakers who change our world and make it better, one **group** at a time.

102:
Scatter
April 11

Bible Verses
"The Lord will conquer your enemies when they attack you. They will attack you from one direction, but they will scatter from you in seven!" Deuteronomy 28:7 (NLT)

"God rises up and scatters his enemies. Those who hate him run away in defeat." Psalm 68:1 (GNT)

Word of the Day
Scatter – To sprinkle about. To toss in several directions. To split up.

Quotes
"Love of God... descend plentifully into my heart. Enlighten the dark corners of this neglected dwelling, and scatter there thy cheerful beams." Saint Augustine

"Whether I have faith or not, am mindful or oblivious, whether I scatter stones or gather them together, God will be just exactly what God is. Or isn't." Kate Braestrup

"Prosperity gathers smiles, while adversity scatters them." William S. Downey

Pam's Perspective
Before I took gardening classes, I decided to scatter sweet pea and milkweed seeds around in my yard not realizing how invasive they both were, and then they took over everything. They are like gossip when scattered, it is very hard to eradicate.

Questions
What do I scatter? Do I realize the impact of the words that I scatter and how they ricochet back to me for either good or bad? Do I scatter grace?

Declarations

I generously **scatter** thoughtful prayers for the people around me and far away. I have a thankful heart that **scatters** goodwill. The way I **scatter** smiles lights the path for discouraged hearts. I like to **scatter** kindness. I am aware when I serve people; I help myself feel good. I **scatter** refreshments and good deeds to those who need it.

As I put God first in my life, I am **scattered** with His mercy. My life is a reflection of the love of God. I **scatter** contagious joy everywhere I go that I gladly receive from the greatest Source of generosity and love. I rejoice to be alive. God is conspiring to help me **scatter** His grace instead of grief. I **scatter** compassion, peace, and merriment.

Strife **scatters** as I put myself in the other person's shoes. I accept people and **scatter** forgiveness. Because I do not have to work for absolution, I am free to pardon others. I leave my heart open despite the fact that I might get hurt, so what. I voluntarily choose to **scatter** love and aid to people, regardless of the results. I see the rainbows and remember the promises. God smiles on me every day, whether I **scatter** good news or not. Charity is always present around me.

God's magnificent kindness towards me encourages me to **scatter** His abundant benevolence. I see giving as a privilege. I **scatter** financial offerings around my community. My keen imagination finds new opportunities to gain wealth and **scatter** blessings.

I work together well with a variety of people. My superb work **scatters** testimonials about my excellence, and I am overcome with referrals. I have a great work ethic. I am faithful in the little things and the big. My persistence in bringing out the best in people opens doors of conversations for our happiness. I focus on **scattering** integrity, hope, appreciation, peace, kindness, and cheer.

103:
Question
April 12

Bible Verses
"Jesus knew immediately what they were thinking, so he asked them, 'Why do you question this in your hearts?'" Mark 2:8 (NLT)

"Without question, this is the great mystery of our faith: Christ was revealed in a human body and vindicated by the Spirit. He was seen by angels and announced to the nations. He was believed in throughout the world and taken to heaven in glory." 1 Timothy 3:16 (NLT)

Word of the Day
Question – To review. To require more information. To ask for ideas.

Quotes
"Judge a man by his questions rather than by his answers." Voltaire

"Whoever is afraid of submitting any question, civil or religious, to the test of free discussion, is more in love with his own opinion than with truth." Bishop Watson

"To be, or not to be, that is the question." William Shakespeare

Pam's Perspective
When I was younger, I did not realize I could question myself, authority or anyone else. When I started to question my thoughts, actions and beliefs are when I started to grow exponentially. There is power in asking great questions. Without asking questions you never really get to know someone. Questions are fun.

Questions
Do I ask myself questions about the impact of the people I associate with and its effect on me? Do I ask myself questions about who I am becoming?

Declarations

I love asking people **questions** and learning new things. Finding out about people's gifts and talents is very interesting. Asking **questions** is the best way to meet a new friend and get to know them.

I listen to the **questions** people ask, and that lets me know what is in their heart and also what they value. By **questioning** someone, you can find out a lot about him or her. I then **question** if that person would diminish or elevate my life. I choose my friends wisely. I can be courteous to people without inviting them into my inner circle.

When I ask God a **question**, He answers me and is not intimidated by any **question** I have. I am related to God and proud to be His child. It is OK to **question** my Father. There is not a **question** I could ever ask that would stop God from loving me, so I **question** on.

I keep an open door policy. I am available and open to all **questions** that come my way. I lead with **questions** rather than telling people what to do. I inquire and discuss the best way to do things. I never get offended by a simple **question**. I am grateful for curiosity. I think before I speak, so my **questions** get right to the heart of the matter.

I ask **questions** to find out where people are coming from, so I never make assumptions. I ask positive **questions** that produce positive results. I easily bounce back from every adversity with a greater understanding because of the **questions** I choose to ask.

I love being inquisitive. I ask great **questions**. I am the only one who can change my life for the better by the **questions** I ask myself, so I ask myself thought-provoking, intelligent **questions** on a daily basis. I trust that the answer will come and it always does. I welcome **questions** and being **questioned**. I live free with nothing to hide.

104:
Respond
April 13

Bible Verses
"Oh, that we might know the Lord! Let us press on to know him. He will respond to us as surely as the arrival of dawn or the coming of rains in early spring." Hosea 6:3 (NLT)

"When you are arrested, don't worry about how to respond or what to say. God will give you the right words at the right time." Matthew 8:26 (NLT)

Word of the Day
Respond – To acknowledge and talk regarding the question that was just asked. To behave either good or bad because of circumstances.

Quotes
"Mercy softens the hardest of hearts. People notice your competence and care when you respond to an angry individual with kindness." Pam Malow-Isham

"Is childhood dead? Or is there not in the bosom of the wisest and the best some of the child's heart left, to respond to its earliest enchantments?" Charles Lamb

Pam's Perspective
The way I respond to criticism, difficulties and emergencies reveal my true nature and the contents of my heart. Everyone has an off day now and then, but how I respond the majority of the time is who I am. If I do not like what I see, then I need to be proactive and change my perceptions and reactions.

Questions
Do I judge people who are not conscious of how they respond? Will I choose to pause, take a deep breath, and think before I respond? Will I respond with joy, calmness, and wisdom, or anger and frustration?

Declarations

I choose to **respond** with love in every situation. I do not take things personally or read more into a comment or action of another person. What they said or did is just that, nothing more. We all have a bad day now and then, so I **respond** with kind answers and remarks.

I am creative in my problem solving so I wow people with my brilliant **responses.** If someone disagrees with my point of view or I with theirs, I **respond** by accepting them, agreeing to disagree, and remaining friends. I weigh my **responses** carefully and patiently.

God **responded** to my call for help and sent me His peace. I **respond** to God by surrendering my will to His. Love demonstrates its power through me by the way I **respond** to others. I love feeling strong. My playful spirit comes from the Lord. I remain in communication with my friends by **responding** directly and quickly to all inquiries.

Choosing not to **respond** in anger when someone hurts me is a choice. I choose to forgive instead as it is extremely liberating. I downplay what is negative and turn my attention to what is supportive and lifts me up. I am determined to **respond** in love.

I expect a good outcome to every situation and **respond** with hope and hard work. Trusting God is my best **response** to worry, so I choose joy right now. I pay attention to what's helpful to me.

I sometimes know when I am in a low mood I **respond** differently than when I am in a high mood. If I offend anyone, I immediately ask for forgiveness. I establish a climate of calm in my home and work. I **respond** to adversity head-on, knowing I am up for any challenge. If I get myself into trouble, I get myself out of it for I am the only person 100% responsible for my actions and how I **respond**.

105:
Patience
April 14

Bible Verses
"A quick temper causes fights, but patience brings peace and calm." Proverbs 15:18 (ERV)

"By your patience possess your souls." Luke 21:19 (NKJV)

Word of the Day
Patience – Having the poise to be content regardless of the situation. Being even-tempered and serene when trials come.

Quotes
"Patience and diligence, like faith, remove mountains." William Penn

"Have patience with everyone, But especially with yourself." Saint Francis de Sales

"Patience and time do more than strength or passion." Jean de La Fontaine

Pam's Perspective
The best time to practice patience is when people irritate me, or I am in a hurry. Patience is a valuable practice that can be cultivated at all times. I take a deep breath and put myself in their shoes. When relating to people with different viewpoints, I view it as an opportunity for growth. Patience produces miracles.

Questions
How can I embody patience in this hectic world? Do I have patience with the people I love the most? Do I have the patience for people who look different than me? Do I have patience with myself? If not, why not? Why is having an abundant supply of patience important to me?

Declarations

I have **patience**. Maintaining **patience** is natural to me. I let my actions display my intentions. I laugh often and become more **patient** with myself every day. I drink a large glass of water before and after my meals. I find the **patience** I need to wait until dinner to eat. I have **patient** temperance. I am poised, **patient** and placid.

I show kindness and **patience** to my fellow human beings. I choose to be **patient** when others around me are becoming annoyed. I don't let little things get me down. I easily produce **patience** when I need it. I am consistently **patient** with friends. I am very indebted to the people who have the **patience** for my idiosyncrasies and quirks.

Since I am the master of my emotions, I choose **patience** when driving or getting stuck in traffic. It gives me time for reflection. I enjoy my surroundings as I take deep refreshing breaths. I release all anxiety, tension, and stress. **Patience** is the way I operate.

God links me up with the right people at the right time. I am an example of **patience** for people to follow. God's immense **patience** towards me is everlasting. I have perfect **patience** as I wait on God to answer my prayers. I give Jesus all the glory because He has so much **patience** to never give up on me. I am always accepted, loved and adored. My dreams are coming true as I **patiently** wait on God.

No matter how long a job takes, I have the **patience** I need to see it through. I am **patient,** well-organized, and smart. My **patience** has brought me great rewards as I slow down and look at things in a new light. **Patience** is my perspective on how to stay tranquil and powerful. I daily clothe myself with **patience,** grace, and humility. Things are revealed to me as I **patiently** wait and listen. I think with a calm and **patient** mind. People see me as the **patience** guru.

106:
Impatience
April 15

Bible Verses
"Patience leads to abundant understanding, but impatience leads to stupid mistakes." Proverbs 14:29 (CEB)

"We were saved by this hope, but in our moments of impatience let us remember that hope always means waiting for something that we haven't yet got. But if we hope for something we cannot see, then we must settle down to wait for it in patience." Romans 8:24-25 (PHILLIPS)

Word of the Day
Impatience – The shortcoming of not wanting to wait for anything. An insufficiency of peace within. Easily agitated or frustrated.

Quotes
"Impatience is the principal cause of most of our irregularities and extravagances." Laurence Sterne

"No man is poor that does not think himself so: but if, in a full fortune, with impatience he desires more, he proclaims his wants and his beggarly condition." Jeremy Taylor

Pam's Perspective
The times I have been given to impatience is a lot fewer with age. Most all of my regrets are the cause of impatience, so I have learned to slow down and wait.

Questions
What areas of my life do I have impatience? Have I been impatient with myself for not being perfect? Have I been impatient with God for not answering my prayers fast enough? How has impatience served me?

Declarations

I realize I could have some **impatience** in certain areas of my life, so I plan ahead of time on how I will respond when the opportunity arises. That way I will be adorned with restraint. I give myself permission to release **impatience** and walk in love. I turn my **impatience** over to God who can handle all my idiosyncrasies.

I never show **impatience** when someone does not understand my beliefs. I am conscious of the role that my faith plays in my life and its importance to my total wellbeing. When my **impatience** starts to emerge, I slow down and think how God would like me to respond.

I know I have been **impatient** so I pray for God to give me poise when dealing with **impatient** people. I realize they are going through a trial right now and need my prayers more than my condemnation. I smile, pray and send blessings in their direction.

I yield to my **impatience** and embrace all the details of my life. I rise above my **impatient** desires and conquer my flesh. I take charge of my **impatient** mind by staying calm and meditating on God. I delight in silence. I release my **impatient** tendencies now.

I direct my **impatience** to the things that I can change. The things I cannot change, I let be. I use my **impatience** to motivate me to work harder and get more done. I focus on the good I can do with a good attitude and how I can be a blessing to others. I appreciate life.

I choose to redeem my **impatience** by slowing down. I have a quiet restraint with inner fortitude, so **impatience** has no control over me. I live in the now, pleased with every moment of my journey; never deferring my joy, but appreciating all the people, places and experiences right in front of me. I enjoy living the good life.

107:
Attitude
April 16

Bible Verses
"A good attitude will support you when you are sick, but if you give up, nothing can help." Proverbs 18:14 (ERV)

"You must have the same attitude that Christ Jesus had." Philippians 2:5 (NLT)

Word of the Day
Attitude – The practice of responding in a certain fashion. Having an opinion about something, good or bad. A positive or negative disposition.

Quotes
"The best way to overcome the habit of fear is to assume the mental attitude of courage, just as the best way to get rid of darkness is to let in the light." William Walker Atkinson

"Success or failure in business is caused more by the mental attitude even than by mental capacities." Walter Scott

Pam's Perspective
I continually have to work on my attitude. My natural tendency is to be cynical and negative. Throughout my life I noticed when I would stay in the positive zone, life would be great. When I neglected reading, listening to positive things and making positive declarations, my life would turn to crap every single time. For years I went back and forth. Now, for me, I have realized it is no longer an option, but a necessity. I like feeling good more than I like having a bad attitude.

Questions
What type of attitudes do I want to cultivate? Why is choosing the type of attitude I maintain importantly? Will I allow people to affect my attitude?

Declarations

I start my golden era today with my glorious invincible **attitude**. I have faith during rough circumstances because I have a sunny **attitude**. I refuse to live upset with a bad **attitude** just because I cannot get the world to do what I want. I accept that life is not fair and move on. I permit myself to have a happy **attitude**.

I consult with people who have solved the same problems I am going through and came out successful because of their **attitude**. My progressive **attitude** produces positive results. I practice having an uplifting **attitude**, and a bright, warm, and gratifying outlook on life.

I am willing to turn my **attitude** over to God for help. I am not a product of my past, my surroundings or what other people say about me. I am who God created me to be. I am willing to move into the destiny God has prepared for me with a good **attitude.**

I will never quit having a positive **attitude**. It is my birthright to feel great. I am consumed with goodness and grace because God will never give up on me. I decide to have a great **attitude**, no matter what. I keep focused on my vision and my **attitude**, for only I can determine how I feel, or what I get done. Smiling helps my **attitude**. I have a healthy **attitude** about myself, and I am not afraid to show it. I will succeed having the best positive **attitude** in town.

My uplifting **attitude** attracts loyal companions. I direct positive silent prayers at people because they deserve to be blessed, no matter who they are. I say yes to good friends. I activate good vibes by sharing my optimistic **attitude** with others. I encourage people so they realize they can have a triumphant **attitude** too. Because of my positive **attitude**, I have a future that is blessed, fulfilling, surprising and worthwhile. Everything about me is harmonious and happy.

108:
Balance
April 17

Bible Verses
"Honest balances and scales belong to the Lord. He made the entire set of weights." Proverbs 16:11 (GW)

"Let me be weighed in an even balance, that God may know my integrity;" Job 31:6 (ASV)

Word of the Day
Balance – Having symmetry on both sides. The ability to recognize both sides of a story. To have equaled parts. To live in harmony with others.

Quotes
"How seldom we weigh our neighbor in the same balance with ourselves." Thomas Kempis

"There is nothing like fun, is there? I haven't any myself, but I do like it in others. Oh, we need it! We need all the counterweights we can muster to balance the sad relations of life. God has made sunny spots in the heart; why should we exclude the light from them?" Thomas Chandler Haliburton

"A just balance preserves justice." English Proverb

Pam's Perspective
I like balance in all things, so I eat healthily and don't worry if I decide to eat a dessert. As long as I eat a balanced diet and keep moving, I can eat what I want.

Questions
Do I balance my time between work and play, family, educational and my spiritual practice? Do I stay active, so my body stays well balanced?

Declarations

I do what is important first. As I rearrange my priorities, I am on the path of true **balance**. I choose to look at all areas of my life and admit to myself where I need improvement. I make a list of my values and honor them. I make a plan of action and work daily on one area of my life to enhance it so I can maintain a **balanced** life.

When I reach for comfort food, I reach for healthy snacks. I keep a **balance** between fruit and vegetables in my diet. I continue finding better ways to keep fit, active and positive. I am in shape and very good looking. I **balance** my workouts between weight lifting and cardio, walking and running, inside and outside activities.

My actions are those of a healthy, **well-balanced** person. I say no to things that take me away from my goals. I keep a good **balance** of friends from different groups. I **balance** my home and work life. I challenge myself to do more at work and be more present when at home. I live with passion and cultivate my many talents.

I **balance** my debt and spending levels with my income. I save a lot more than I spend. I **balance** my savings and investments, so I do not have all my eggs all in one basket. I have a **balanced** portfolio.

I live a well-defined, **well-balanced** life. I relish every opportunity to live **balanced**. I **balance** my spiritual life and give it equal importance. I trust God to **balance** out everything for my highest good. I like developing my skills to **balance** all the aspects of my life.

I take the time to enjoy the simple pleasures of life. I **balance** the connections of the people I associate with, so I stay around more positive people than negative. I continually express gratitude as I look for more ways to be grateful. I tip my **balance** toward the good.

109:
Celebrate
April 18

Bible Verses
"Praise the Lord, for the Lord is good; celebrate his lovely name with music."
Psalm 135:3 (NLT)

"We had to celebrate this happy day. For your brother was dead and has come back to life! He was lost, but now he is found!" Luke 15:32 (NLT)

Word of the Day
Celebrate – To rejoice over good fortune or hallow a special day. To host a feast and make merry with friends to honor someone or something.

Quotes
"Don't complain about being vulnerable. Celebrate that you still have feelings!" Bettina Heiß

"Celebrate everything, even the failures, for they teach us great lessons if we are willing to learn." Pam Malow-Isham

"Celebrate the little things. In the end, these become our most cherished memories." Kelly Kotarski

Pam's Perspective
For years when I would have a goal I would not celebrate until it was completed and a total success. I missed out on a lot of opportunities to celebrate. Now I celebrate all my little successes along the way, and I accomplish so much more.

Questions
Do I celebrate my little victories or do I wait for the big ones? Am I celebrating enough? Is celebration a part of my daily life?

Declarations

I **celebrate** every moment I am alive because it is a beautiful gift! I embrace change and **celebrate** it. I do something fun every day to **celebrate**. I **celebrate** and savor my life. I live a life worth living, and that deserves **celebration**. I am thankful for everything happening in my life right now. I **celebrate** each day because the day is good.

By **celebrating** my accomplishments, the big and little ones, it makes me feel good. Because I feel good, I have another reason to **celebrate**. I like feeling satisfied with myself, **celebrating** all I have done. I treat myself well, toot my own horn and **celebrate** my journey. I also like to **celebrate** the goodness and light I see in every other person.

I **celebrate** my work, and I am passionate about growth. I look for new ways to **celebrate** my accomplishments. I generate a bunch of new business today. People are attracted to what I have to say and **celebrate** how I say it. I **celebrate** closing the deals and completing the sales. I love helping people and seeing them succeed.

I **celebrate** life with my family and friends over a meal or a friendly conversation. I take time to **celebrate** my time on Earth. I take a walk and enjoy the sunshine, the trees and the smell of flowers. I **celebrate** the beauty around me. I honor myself by eating healthy and staying active. Just watching a sunrise or sunset is reason enough to **celebrate**. I honor myself with unfettered **celebration**.

I laugh as I break the shackles of despair. I release the shame of my past and **celebrate** that I have been forgiven. God uses everything to my advantage. I **celebrate** that I am approved of and adored. As I forgive myself, I choose to **celebrate** my beauty and unique gifts. I am willing to be who God is calling me to be. I am still precious in God's sight. Today is a great day to **celebrate**, have fun and be alive!

110:
Beauty
April 19

Bible Verses
"Charm is deceptive, and beauty does not last; but a woman who fears the Lord will be greatly praised." Proverbs 31:30 (NLT)

"Don't hit back; discover beauty in everyone. If you've got it in you, get along with everybody." Romans 12:17 (MSG)

Word of the Day
Beauty – The adorability of the something or someone. The physical attraction of a person. Awe-inspiring to look at and full of grace.

Quotes
"There is no cosmetic for beauty like happiness." Lady Blessington

"It is not beauty that inspires the deepest passion. Beauty without grace is the hook without the bait. Beauty, without expression, tires." Ralph Waldo Emerson

"Inasmuch as love grows in you, in so much beauty grows; for love is itself is the soul's beauty." Saint Augustine of Hippo

Pam's Perspective
I have never been into hero worship or putting people on a pedestal because of their so-called beauty or talent. We are all the same on the inside, and it is our character, not our outside appearance that reveals our true beauty.

Questions
Do I see myself as beautiful? Why or why not? What is my most beautiful quality? Do I see the beauty in the people around me who are acting ugly? Do I notice and appreciate the beauty of my surroundings?

Declarations

I am responsible for my **beauty**. I like taking care of myself. I am **beautiful** on the inside, and **beautiful** on the outside. I cherish the moment I saw my own **beauty** in the mirror and was able to forgive all the criticism I had said or thought about myself. I let my **beauty** shine through and radiate peace and love to those around me.

I forgive and discover the **beauty** that forgiveness brings to my heart. I claim **beauty** in my family relationships, in each friendship I honor, and in every colleague with whom I interact. When I see people as **beautiful**, they become **beautiful**. Life works like that.

I am filled with the **beauty** of Jesus Christ. I am adored and highly favored. By being conscious of what I eat, and what type of activity I participate in, I take care of my **beautiful** body. Being active feels great, and keeps me fit. I eat nutritious food and drink lots of pure water. I invoke divine health over all my **beautiful** body parts. My smile enhances my **beauty**, and lights every room I enter.

I am a **beautiful** person who loves children and watching them grow. God knows me, loves me, and sees me as **beautiful**. Who am I to question His omniscience? I enjoy the peace I have with God. I show my **beauty** by the thoughts I think, the words I say, and the actions I take. I say yes to me, and yes to life. I bring the greatest good to the world by celebrating everyone's **beauty** and brilliance.

I am very thankful for my **beautiful** home with all the **beautiful** furnishings. I live surrounded by **beauty** on every side. Everywhere I look I see God's **beautiful** creation declaring His glory to me. I see the **beauty** of surrendering my cares to God so I can maintain my joy. I find new strength each day as I lean on God to see me through. I am **beautiful** today, and tomorrow, I will be even more **beautiful**!

111:
Rise
April 20

Bible Verses

"For a righteous man falls seven times and rises again, but the wicked are overthrown by calamity." Proverbs 24:16 (AMP)

"They will flog Him and kill Him; and on the third day He will rise again." Luke 18:33 (AMP)

Word of the Day

Rise – To awake and stand up. To aspire to be more. To climb the ladder of success. To be promoted in rank. To tower above.

Quotes

"There is a certain enthusiasm in liberty that makes human nature rise above itself, in acts of bravery and heroism." Alexander Hamilton

"The ability to rise above adversity starts with a thought, followed by deliberate action." Pam Malow-Isham

"Even as the sun doth not wait for prayers and incantations to rise, but shines forth and is welcomed by all: so thou also wait not for clapping of hands and shouts and praise to do they duty; nay do good of thine own accord, and thou wilt be loved like the sun." Epictetus

"The people should never rise without doing something to be remembered – something notable and striking." John Adams

Questions

Do I rise in a good mood or a bad one? Does it matter? How fast do I rise after a fall? What challenges will I rise to meet today?

Declarations

I **rise** in the morning with a smile on my face and a song in my heart that is full of thanksgiving. I love **rising** early to pray and plan out my day. I am thankful for my radiant health and happiness. With limitless determination, I **rise** to reach my goals. God gives me the solutions I need to **rise** above every difficulty and come out on top.

I **rise** in front of the pack by my excellent work. I promote excellence and **rise** above mediocracy. There is nothing I cannot accomplish. Power **rises** within me to overcome every misfortune. I have great ideas, and the ability to see them materialize. By using my gifts in creative ways, I make a great living. I **rise** to the top of my field.

I am easily satisfied as I **rise** from the table, and push extra food away that I don't need. I **rise** and conquer my propensity to overeat by visualizing myself healthy. When I get knocked down, I **rise** up with fervor, stronger than ever to meet every challenge head-on.

I **rise** to the occasion of being my best. As I allow God's peace to **rise** within me, I stay balanced and poised. I figure things out with God's help. Fire **rises** within my belly to say that nothing is impossible with God. Today is a great day to **rise** up and be counted.

God's ways **rise** above my petty notions. My level of love **rises** by accepting everyone just as they are, without trying to change them into what I think they should be. I am **rising** to new heights of glory. I **rise** above every hardship knowing nothing is too hard for me.

I **rise** to the front of the line as my gifts make room for me. Great favor **rises** around me as people are compelled to be kind to me. I am a promoter of my good works. I have **rising** revenues. I **rise** above the crowd with my brilliant ideas and shine ever so brightly.

112:
Fall
April 21

Bible Verses
"He digs a pit and shovels it out. Then he falls into the hole that he made for others." Psalm 7:15 (NOG)

"He has kept us alive and has not allowed us to fall." Psalm 66:9 (NOG)

Word of the Day
Fall – To lose your footing and go down to the ground fast. To corrupt your integrity and decline your morals for greed or pleasure.

Quotes
"Some rise by sin, and some by virtue fall." William Shakespeare

"Our greatest glory consists, not in never falling, but in rising every time we fall." Oliver Goldsmith

Pam's Perspective
In 2000 I was downhill skiing on snow-blades and had a bad fall. I ended up with a spiral fracture of my tibia, a break in my fibula and a break in my ankle. I was off work for eight months. I could not ski or dance for two years. My shoe size went up a whole size. I went through months of physical therapy. My leg still swells 18 years later. I had to decide, do I want to continue skiing, and if so, I needed to face my fear of falling. Since I am not a quitter, I decided to get back on my skis, and in 2003, I joined the Mt. Holly Ski Patrol. Now I help the fallen.

Questions
Why would I think I was above a fall? What action steps can I take to prevent a fall? What is the first thing I do when I fall? Why? Do I help people who fall short or do I just talk about them? Why is that?

Declarations

I am open to **falling** in love with this crazy adventure called life. I appreciate what God has given me to work with as I look in the mirror. I **fall** in love with myself first before **falling** in love with another person. I practice liking me, so I know how to receive love.

When I **fall**, I jump back up. Nothing keeps me down. I **fall** forward into my success. I initiate good habits so I can better myself. Since I can control the amount of effort I put into winning, I use maximum effort. I make decisions that keep me from **falling** apart. I am resourceful with boundless creativity. I **fall** for fun experiences.

I **fall** into the arms of a loving God as I practice the principle of gentleness. I am at peace knowing there is no depth I could **fall** that God would not be right next to me. I can talk to God about anything without worrying about being condemned or **falling** short of the mark. I **fall** on my knees in prayer and become unstoppable.

I challenge myself to up my game, so I don't get complacent and **fall** back. I realize there is always a chance I could **fall**, so it keeps me humble, and well grounded. Even on hard days when I **fall** in the stinky muck, I come out smelling like a rose for God is on my side.

I become conscious of my inner strengths when I **fall**, so I easily bounce back fast. I release all negative thoughts about past **falls**, and focus on my spectacular future. I attract mentors that **fall** into my orbit along my journey. I **fall** for jokes and make laughter a priority.

I allow my judgmental glasses to **fall** off as I embrace all people. I am inventive at reaching out and making friends who stand by me when I **fall**. I see people as intelligent human beings who are trying to do their best. I am benevolent to lift up people who have **fallen**.

113:
Speak
April 22

Bible Verses

"Do you see someone who speaks in haste? There is more hope for a fool than for them." Proverbs 29:20 (NIV)

"These things speak and exhort and reprove with all authority. Let no one disregard you." Titus 2:15 (NASB)

Word of the Day

Speak – To express what you want to say with words. To tell with a shout or a whisper to get your point across. To talk or declare.

Quotes

"The words I speak create my happy or miserable existence." Pam Malow-Isham

"Speak clearly, if you speak at all; carve every word before you let it fall." Oliver Wendell Holmes, Sr.

"Let us speak what we feel, let us feel what we speak, let our conversation be in accordance with our life." Seneca

"To the valiant actions speak alone." Tobias Smollett

"When angry, count ten, before you speak; if very angry, an hundred." Thomas Jefferson

Questions

How does my ability to speak clearly about what I want, reward me? Do I speak up for myself? Do I speak up for others who are being talked about in my presence? What good will I speak about today?

Declarations

I **speak** only about what I want. I now exercise my fearless faith
in three ways – by thinking, **speaking**, and acting. The things
I **speak** about reveals the essence of my heart. God gives me the
perfect words to **speak** at just the right time. I **speak** of victory and
triumph.

I am living high on the hog as I **speak** life into my old dreams and
see them rise from the dead, to flourish, and thrive again. What I
speak about is sure to manifest. I **speak** to inspire, and to uplift
everyone I meet. I continue to **speak** well of others.

I **speak** of the great exploits God has done for me. I **speak** blessings
over the people around me, including my enemies. I praise God for
all the great things that He has given to me, and my family. I **speak**
of faith as I trust God. I **speak** to God, and God **speaks** to me. We
have an ongoing dialog. I **speak** God's promises over my life.

I **speak** of truth, and wisdom, imparting insights from on High. I
always **speak** by my actions! I finish what I start. I positively **speak**
about my future, creating the life I envision. I **speak** of prosperity,
increase, and abundance. I **speak** very highly of myself.

I **speak** about what is on my mind. What I have to say is important,
and worthy of being heard, so I **speak** up for myself. I smile when
I **speak**. I **speak** of love and forgiveness to all who will listen. I am
believed when I **speak** because truth flows from my lips. I have the
ability to close the sale. I **speak** with reassurance and knowledge.

I **speak** health, vitality, strength, and energy to my body. I think
before I **speak**, knowing I have power in my words, so I use my
words wisely. I motivate myself to be bold by the exhilarating words
I **speak**. I **speak** of opportunity, open doors, and good fortune.

114:
Silence
April 23

Bible Verses

"When Jesus woke up, he rebuked the wind and said to the waves, "Silence! Be still!" Suddenly the wind stopped, and there was a great calm." Mark 4:39 (NLT)

"For it is God's will that by doing good you should silence the ignorant talk of foolish people." 1 Peter 2:15 (NIV)

Word of the Day

Silence – Being without sound or aggravation of distractions. Not having to talk or respond. Being quiet.

Quotes

"Let thy speech be better than silence, or be silent." Dionysius of Halicarnassus

"That you may impose silence upon another, first be silent yourself." Proverb

"The most formidable enemy of the spiritual life is self-deception, and if there is a better cure for self-deception than silence, it has yet to be discovered." Bridgid E. Herman

Pam's Perspective

I used to have a radio continually on, because I could not stand the silence. When I learned how to quiet my mind, silence became my friend. It is as easy as taking deep breaths and then saying to yourself I turn all this anxiety over to God, I release it, and let God have it. Then I was open to hearing His still small voice.

Questions

Am I comfortable or afraid of silence? Why is that? Do I enjoy the silence? How much time will I set aside to be in silence today?

Declarations

I enjoy the **silence** when I awake, and all is calm and peaceful. **Silence** is my friend. Thanking God for another day of life before I get out of bed is the first thing I do. In the **silence**, I stretch, smile, and spring out of bed ready to take advantage of every opportunity.

I love taking good care of myself by eating right, exercise, and getting plenty of sleep. I have a healthy metabolism. Even in the **silence,** my self-talk is positive and caring. I am happy to take my best friend with me everywhere I go. God is conspiring to help me today. I relish our **silent** time together. I love meditating in **silence**.

I hold fast to the peace of God. I walk in the **silence** of nature and enjoy all the beauty that surrounds me. I set apart time in my schedule to have a time of **silence** where I just listen and receive creative ideas from the Ultimate Source. I lean on God for my help.

I turn off all the electronics and meditate in **silence** so I can hear God's voice clearly. I bask in our intimacy, and time together where He tells me, He loves me and shares His truths with me. Through the **silence** of my prayers, I bless people when I am around them.

New understandings come to me as I sit in **silence**. I surrender to the calm **silence** in my room. I give myself permission to listen fully. I break the **silence** by allowing myself to get excited for no reason other than I am happy. I rest free, forgiven, fascinated, and flexible.

In the **silence** of the evening, I write in my gratitude journal. When I lay down in **silence** to sleep, I recount all the blessings of my day. **Silence** gives me strength and renewed energy to make it through the day. With gratitude in my heart, I say thank you God one more time. I rest comfortably in **silence** as I stretch out, and fall asleep.

115:
Train
April 24

Bible Verses

"Train up a child in the way he should go, and when he is old, he will not depart from it." Proverbs 22:6 (KJV)

"Do not waste time arguing over godless ideas and old wives' tales. Instead, train yourself to be godly." 1 Timothy 4:7 (NLT)

Word of the Day

Train – A work out to improve your mental, physical or professional wellbeing. To study and sharpen your tools. To cultivate your abilities for an intended goal or desire.

Quotes

"The great end of education is to discipline rather than to furnish the mind; to train it to the use of its own powers, rather than fill it with the accumulation of others." Tryon Edwards

"If you train your brain to focus on the positive aspects of your life and what you are grateful for, you will be able to handle all of trials and tribulations that life throws at you." Pam Malow-Isham

"Love was bestowed on the world by God, in order to train the soul for God." Friedrich Ruckert

Questions

"What are some of the characteristics of God you would like to inherit? What about His strength? His goodness? His wisdom? His patience? His faithfulness? His peace? God wants to impart all of those things and more to us as we are ready to receive them. God wants to share Himself with us. He wants to train us up to be like Him." Stormie Omartian

Declarations

I **train** my mind to look for, pick up on, and dwell on what is good. I get excited over the smallest pleasures. I **train** myself to appreciate what is right in front of me. I no longer take me, my surroundings, job, home, family, or God for granted. I have **trained** myself to be, and live gratefully. I **train** to support my minds vision of beauty.

By setting aside time to study, and meditate on God's word, I **train** myself to hear God talking to me. And then He **trains** me to be more like Christ. I am **training** to be more generous, and loving. I see with my heart and focus on what God wants for me. I **train** myself to be happy no matter what crazy circumstances are going on around me.

I **train** myself to like fresh fruits, and vegetables at every meal, and for snacks. My lifestyle of **training** my body with daily exercise has really paid off, and boy do I feel jazzed and ready to go. I give it my all, and **train** for the gold medal in life. I like being strong, agile, and motivated to **train** daily. **Training** is fun. I love being accountable.

I **train** my ears to listen and understand when someone is speaking to me. I **train** my mouth to speak kind words that build me and others up. I am gentle to the people around me. I **train** my arms to embrace the lonely with extra hugs. I **train** my fingers, so they don't point judgment at me, or others. I **train** my stomach to digest God's wisdom and expel grace. I **train** my feet to walk the path of peace.

I **train** my heart to be open to love, vulnerable, and eager to forgive. I **train** my eyes to see beauty in everyone. I **train** myself to walk on the authentic path. I **train** my legs to jump at the great opportunities in front of me. I am a live wire as I give it my all, and **train** one more time for a race. I collaborate well with others. I act on wise advice as I **train** with my friends. We **train** well as we support each other.

116:
Rest
April 25

Bible Verses

"But now the Lord my God has given me rest on every side; there is neither adversary nor evil occurrence." 1 Kings 5:4 (NKJV)

"You will rest safe and secure, filled with hope and emptied of worry." Job 11:18 (CEV)

Word of the Day

Rest – Enjoying some downtime. Sleep in peace. To pause, be quiet and enjoy the peace. To abstain from work and worry. A tranquil state.

Quotes

"Talk not to me of the wisdom of women; I know my own sex well; the wisest of us all are but little less foolish than the rest." Mary, Queen of Scots

"Absence of occupations is not rest; a mind quite vacant is a mind distressed." William Cowper

Pam's Perspective

I was raised Seventh Day Adventist. From Friday night sundown to Saturday night sundown we could not do any work, play, or watch TV. We went to church, and nothing more. I hated it. When I moved out, I worked seven days a week. I worked until I got sick, so I reevaluated my life. Now I value the benefit of a Sabbath rest but am not compelled to be legalistic about the day, or times. I make rest a priority, and if I feel like taking a nap, I do it with no guilt. It feels great!

Questions

Do I value myself enough to set aside times of rest? Do I rest well at night? If not, what can I do to ensure I get a good night's sleep?

Declarations

God's glorious Spirit **rests** on me. I give myself permission to **rest** and relax. I walk in humility as I trust God, and do His will. Today is a great day to **rest**. As I sit to **rest**, I notice all the beautiful things. I am caring and kind as I pet my dog while we **rest** together.

I **rest** assured in myself, knowing I have what it takes to do a great job. I am thoughtful and considerate. I welcome moments when I am required to **rest**. I find my reason why I want to succeed. I use my downtime to replenish and strengthen my body, and mind.

I **rest** my cares on God for He cares for me. I turn every worry over to God and **rest** on His unfailing promises. It is OK for me not to know everything. I **rest** sure knowing God has my best interests in mind. I act from a place of love. I am humble enough to turn my dreams over to God, and **rest** confidently, knowing that everything will turn out for the highest good for everyone concerned.

It is OK to have a break and **rest**. I don't have to work seven days a week. I take a short **rest** from my computer, get up, stretch, and take a walk. After I have **rested**, I get to work and accomplish great things. I use my talents to make a difference in someone's life. I have all the time I need to accomplish all my assignments before I **rest**.

I remain at **rest** during troubled times putting my faith in God. I exercise patience, as I trust God, and **rest** in His peace. I appreciate this wonderful life when I **rest**. I set aside a day of **rest** to rejuvenate my mind, body, and spirit. God is always working on my behalf.

As I trust and lay down tonight, God **rests** my body and restores my soul. I develop a calm presence. Sweet peace is mine as I **rest** in sleep. I have nice dreams of the victories to come. I **rest** well at night.

117:
Rich
April 26

Bible Verses
"Be not afraid when one becomes rich, when the glory of his house increases." Psalm 49:16 (RSV)

"With me are riches and honor, enduring wealth and prosperity." Proverbs 8:18 (NIV)

Word of the Day
Rich – Possessing ample material goods. Having the wherewithal to do as you please. Opulence. Prosperity.

Quotes
"Ideas once planted in the brain fructify, and bear their harvest more or less bountiful and rich as they are fertilized by thought." Cyrus Augustus Bartol

"The only way for a rich man to be healthy is, by exercise and abstinence, to live as if he were poor." Sir William Temple

Pam's Perspective
Inner peace is my greatest riches. That is what I strived for years to achieve. As I gave up the struggle and surrendered to God, I received peace. I foolishly fell back into striving after a few years and started working for approval again. Thank God He reminded me that I could abide in the richness of peace when I remember I am His beloved. I continue to let go and let God. As I release fear, I gain peace.

Questions
How many ways do I feel rich today? What are some riches right in front of me that I take for granted? Can I be content with what I have right now while still working toward riches? Can I help someone else become rich?

Declarations

I now feel **rich**, **rich**, **rich**. In fact, I am abundantly **rich**, monetarily, physically, emotionally, socially, mentally, and spiritually as well. Multiple opportunities are **richly** rolling my way. I remember that everything is doable because I am **richly** satisfied with my work.

I attach myself to God and have peace. For God is my gold, silver, and **riches**. I am thrilled to see all the **riches** God is bringing me right now. I am a generous giver, and I like to share my **riches**. I always have more than enough money. I am faithful at saving money, so my **riches** grow. I serve my community with joy in my heart and give unconditionally. I am **rich** in friendships.

I am **rich** with wonderful, caring, loving friends who support and encourage me to be my best. I say thank you for the abundance. There is a gold mine within me. I am **rich** in peace. I am extremely **rich** with contentment, completely satisfied with what I have.

I am **richly** rewarded for all I do. My inner wealth attracts increasing prosperity each day. I am reaching my **rich** goals. I magnetize **rich** people with my poise and smile. I make and earn a lot of **riches**.

I nurture myself by eating lots of vegetables. I feel great pleasure from the **rich** health, and strength of my body. I am a healthy vessel through which good energy flows. All my activity **richly** rewards my health. I allow myself the pleasure of being trim and strong.

All my **riches** reproduce. My universe is full of **riches**, peace, and love. I love creating the positive thoughts that fuel my **rich** life. I accelerate my earning capacity by continuing to take classes, so I can learn, and grow **richer**. I have a **rich** spiritual life from which I draw my strength. God is in my corner, so I am extremely **rich**.

118:
Poor
April 27

Bible Verses
"[God] is not partial to princes, nor does He regard the rich more than the poor, for they all are the work of His hands." Job 34:19 (AMP)

"This poor man cried, and the Lord heard him, and saved him out of all his troubles." Psalm 34:6 (KJV)

Word of the Day
Poor – Lacking material belongings, or money. Scarcity mentality.

Quotes
"It is not the man who has little, but he who desires more, that is poor."
Seneca

"He hath a poor spirit who is not planted above petty wrongs." Owen Feltham

"It is the mind that maketh good or ill, that maketh wretch or happy, rich or poor: for some, that hath abundance at his will, hath not enough, but wants in greatest store; and other, that hath little, asks no more, but in that little is both rich and wife. For wisdom is most riches." Edmund Spenser

Pam's Perspective
I grew up poor, living in a trailer park with my Dad not around and my Mother on welfare. I was picked on because we didn't always have nice things to wear. I had to change my inner dialogue, so I no longer saw myself as poor, to be rich.

Questions
Why would I feel poor surrounded by abundance? Is there a way for me to barter some of the services that I need? Do I really need all the stuff I have? Have I given myself permission to earn a good living?

Declarations

I am generous and give wisely to those who are **poor** and in need. I listen to God and give to who, and what resonates with my heart. I am content with what God has given me. I like myself, have hope, and believe all is well, regardless of how **poor**, or rich I am. I could never be **poor** because the Eternal One wholly loves me.

I am **poor** at giving up. I greet everyone with a loving smile and a warm embrace. I speak words that empower **poor** people to live up to their God-given potential. I shower hope on the **poor** in spirit and give inspiration to all. I am **poor** at giving up when others need help.

The more I give to help the **poor**; the more God abundantly blesses me, so I have more to give. I cannot out give God. God inspires me to be a blessing to everyone I meet and richly rewards all my efforts.

We all deserve to be loved and valued. I show equal respect, and validation for everyone, regardless of their social standing. I look for the silver lining in every cloud. Both rich, and **poor** people are fun to be around. I display love, peace, hope, and charity in all I do.

I habitually save for my future to prevent being **poor**. I balance my work and play. I love life. I am comfortable with the riches I have. I cheerfully open my eyes, heart, and hands to stand up for the **poor**.

I am not afraid of what people think of me. I am at ease with the imperfections of my body. I stay away from foods with **poor** nutritional value. I crave the healthy foods that my body needs.

I am glad I don't dwell on any **poor** decisions I made in the past. I move forward with pleasure as I decide what success looks like for me. I apply knowledge to the best of my ability and live life large.

119:
Character
April 28

Bible Verses
"An honorable man makes honorable plans; his honorable character gives him security." Isaiah 32:8 (NET)

"Light exposes the true character of everything." Ephesians 5:13 (GW)

Word of the Day
Character –Being of good judgment. A trustworthy person. Integrity.

Quotes
"People seem not to see that their opinion of the world is also a confession of character." Ralph Waldo Emerson

"Thoughts lead on to purposes; purposes go forth in action; actions form habits; habits decide character; and character fixes our destiny." Tyron Edwards

Pam's Perspective
When I was twelve, I was hanging around a girl that was seventeen, and we decided to run away from home together. We went to Meijer to pick up a few things for the trip and got caught shoplifting. I was crying and devastated. They called my mom, and she said, "Send her to jail." The police asked how my home life was and I told them. When my mother finally did pick me up, she had a couple of her friends with her so she could shame me. The girl I was with spent the night in jail and got probation. Fortunately for me, they never pressed charges. I have never stolen anything since then. It scared me straight; I didn't want to go to jail.

Questions
Do I ask myself questions to inspect my character? Will I decide to be a person of impeccable character? What does that look like for me?

Declarations

I am honest, of good **character**, and have the backbone to do the right thing. I treat everyone with respect, dignity and accept his or her differences. I am accountable for what I say, and how I say it, so I speak kindly to everyone. I never take my **character** for granted. Because I look; I find joy. I rejoice in everyone's uniqueness and special gifts. I am grateful for people of **character** to model.

I develop my inner moral compass by reading God's Word, and doing what is right at the proper time. I have a Godly **character**, and leadership is now evident as I listen to the Holy Spirit. I ask God to mold my **character** into the best me I possibly can be. I am endowed with confidence and **character**. I respond well to the tests of my **character**. I love the freedom that good **character** provides.

Helping people is fun. I am loyal to my friends, and family. I build a good reputation, and **character** by my consistent actions. Integrity is my way of life. I respect authority and stand firm on my convictions. My thankful heart manifests in my words, actions, and **character**.

I am a person of self-mastery who represents **character**, and moral discipline. I alone determine the type of **character** I will embody, and mannerisms of the person I choose to become. I use self-control, and self-discipline so I can form good habits. I set a good example of what a person of **character** looks like so others can follow my lead.

My **character** speaks volumes about myself. I have the ability to choose the type of **character** I want to experience. I am true to myself while living the perception I want others to have of me. I have great resources with my friends. We help each other out. I realize the people I chum with have a constructive or destructive influence on my **character**. So I surround myself with people of sterling **character**.

120:
Zeal
April 29

Bible Verses
"For I bear them witness that they have a zeal for God, but not according to knowledge." Romans 10:2 (ESV)

"Even so you, since you are zealous for spiritual gifts, let it be for the edification of the church that you seek to excel." 1 Corinthians 14:12 (NKJV)

Word of the Day
Zeal – Having a strong intensity toward something. A passion for life. Having the eagerness to get a job done with zest.

Quotes
"Kindness has converted more sinners than zeal, eloquence, or learning." Frederick William Faber

"Zeal is very blind or badly regulated when it encroaches upon the rights of others." Pasquier Quesnel

"Experience shows that success is due less to ability than to zeal. The winner is he who gives himself to his work, body, and soul." Charles Buxton

"Had I but served my God with half the zeal I served my king, he would not in mine age have left me naked to mine enemies." Shakespeare, Henry VIII

"Never let your zeal outrun your charity. The former is but human; the latter is divine." Hosea Ballou

Questions
How do I feel about zealous people? How will I use my zeal for good? What things can I put in place to keep my zeal for life from waning?

Declarations

With **zeal,** I promote my optimistic attitude and my positive way of being. My **zeal** for showing kindness has a ripple effect that cascades abundantly, overflowing to the people around me. I am filled with **zeal** as I relish over all of my accomplishments this past year.

I show **zeal** at work and surpass my employer's expectations. I am **zealous** for life, and it shows in my bank account. My **zeal** for reading is a habit I formed to gain wisdom. There are more than enough creative solutions filling my mind to take on any, and every challenge that comes my way. I am **zealous** to learn new things.

My **zeal** for working out has paid off, as I am now slim, trim, fit, and healthy. I keep getting stronger. I get great results because I am **zealous** about changing up my workout to make it more fun.

I am **zealous** about infecting people with great thoughts to produce a good mindset. The more I spread my joy, the more I have. My **zeal** for life transforms the apathetic, invigorates the lethargic, and inspires the depressed. Everyone feels happier in my presence and more content with their lives when they leave. They become **zealous** for change and take action to make their dreams come true.

My **zeal** for travel inspires others to become more adventuresome. I visit someplace new each year. I take the greatest vacations. My **zeal** attracts the nicest friends. I am fascinated by new experiences and exotic places. I attract great service and receive the best discounts.

The **zeal** of God has consumed me with love, and delight as I bask in His favor, and goodness towards me. I love my life and live from my heart. Thanksgiving is on my lips for my wonderful life. I am the recipient of many blessings, and **zealous** to share them with others.

121:
Idleness
April 30

Bible Verses
"Up with thee, idleness, go to school with the ant, and learn the lesson of her ways!" Proverbs 6:6 (KNOX)

"Laziness leads to a sagging roof; idleness leads to a leaky house." Ecclesiastes 10:18 (NLT)

Word of the Day
Idleness – Lacking goals and ambition. Being slothful and lethargic. Doing nothing. Being able to rest your mind and body.

Quotes
"It seems to me that all of the evil in life comes from idleness, boredom, and psychic emptiness, but all of that is inevitable when you become accustomed to living at others expense." Anton Pavlovich Chekhov

"It is impossible to enjoy idling thoroughly unless one has plenty of work to do. There is no fun in doing nothing when you have nothing to do. Wasting time is merely an occupation then, and a most exhausting one. Idleness, like kisses, to be sweet must be stolen." Jerome K. Jerome

Pam's Perspective
I like to keep busy, but when I realized you could find rejuvenation in idleness, I stopped thinking less of myself for doing nothing. Sometimes I need to chill out.

Questions
How do I view idleness? Do I have too much idleness in my life now or not enough? Why is that? How can I use my idleness to stimulate my creativity? How can I use my idleness to my benefit?

Declarations

My life is filled with the exhilaration of taking on new challenges. It is also filled with **idleness**. I love my days off, cuddled up with a great book. I keep a good balance of work and play to keep my creative juices flowing. I know overworking, and burnout is counter-productive, so when I work, I work really hard. I also take time for **idleness** and relaxation to rejuvenate my mind, body, and spirit.

When it is time to return to work, I throw off **idleness**, flip the switch, and I am supercharged with stamina. I am a powerhouse of possibilities igniting my workplace with leading edge ideas. When I am giving it my all at work, I am totally focused. I take the industrious path. **Idleness** is far from my hands, so I work hard.

Because I work hard when I work, I do not feel guilty at all when I set aside time for **idleness**. There is no joy if all I do is work, so I make sure I take care of my health by enjoying every moment of **idleness**. When I am relaxing in **idleness**, I feel content to enjoy the moment. I make the world a better place while I am here.

I have dominion over my faculties, and I choose what is best for me at any given time, either work or **idleness**. I do not waste my **idle** time interfering in people's affairs by asking meddlesome questions. I concentrate on noticing where I need help and improve myself. I let them work on themselves for I know change is an inside job.

Peace dwells in my soul as I enjoy the **idleness** of prayer. I am not concerned about bothering God with **idleness** because I am never a bother. I am always welcome and lovingly received, no matter if I am industrious, or **idle**. God created us to work, and to enjoy **idleness**, so I take pleasure in both. I am grateful for my **idle** time off. In the **idleness** of the night, I rest assured that all is well.

122:
Action
May 1

Bible Verses

"Get up! It's your duty to take action. We are with you, so be strong and take action." Ezra 10:4 (NOG)

"Dear children, let us not love with words or speech but with actions and in truth." 1 John 3:18 (NIV)

Word of the Day

Action – The power to get something done. Being in motion, not stagnant. An industrious person's deeds. Exercising choices and following through.

Quotes

"Take action to create the feelings versus waiting for the feelings to take action. One is proactive; the other is reactive." Tiffany Peterson

"A superior man is modest in his speech, but exceeds in his actions." Confucius

Pam's Perspective

I used to date someone that was all talk. I would tell him talk is cheap; actions speak louder than words, show me. He never did, and so he did not last long as a reliable friend. I realized a person's actions show who they truly are, and what they care about, no matter what they are saying from their mouth.

Questions

"What has been some of your biggest fears, anxieties, and worries that – now that you look back on it – were overblown? What was the result once you got past those fears? Where in your life are you letting fear, doubt or worry stop you from taking the necessary actions for happiness and success?" T. Harv Eker

Declarations

My **actions** prove that I am a go-getter who is a very capable, and trustworthy person. I am experienced at being good at keeping my word. I invoke my genius as I read great literature, and take **action**.

The **actions** I take to increase my knowledge are paying off. I am highly sought after for consultations, motivational speeches, and paid very well. My **action** at Toastmasters was worth the effort.

By the **actions** I take today, I continue to increase my wealth. It is no one else's responsibility to support me, but myself. I exert **actions** that expand my wealth. I give myself the license to get paid well for my endeavors. There is more than enough money to go around.

I enjoy listening to pleasant, uplifting music and viewing nature. I rejuvenate myself by my healthy **actions**, and stimulating thoughts. I design my life in a clear-cut way by filling my mind with positive principles. I fill my body with good healthy food, the right quantity of **action** to keep me strong, and the proper amount of sleep.

I am responsible for the **actions** I take, and the **actions** I do not take. I am quick to take **action** on great ideas. I continue taking **actions** to reach my goals. I am smart about my **actions,** so I do a good job.

I tell myself that I can take courageous **actions** despite any fears. I take **action** daily on the things that are important to me. I take **action** to connect with the people I am closest to. Family is very important.

My **actions** precede me because I make the most of every minute of every day. I genuinely like myself because I take all the **actions** that are expected with the future I am committed to living into. No **action** is necessary to find myself smiling, nor is a reason needed.

123:
See
May 2

Bible Verses
"I would have been without hope if I had not believed that I would see the loving-kindness of the Lord in the land of the living." Psalm 27:13 (NLV)

"Those who have a pure heart are happy, because they will see God." Matthew 5:8 (NLV)

Word of the Day
See – To identify with your eyes. To survey your surroundings. To observe and appraise a situation. To envision things.

Quotes
"I never expect to see a perfect work from an imperfect man." Alexander Hamilton

"If we would see others as they see themselves, our shyness would soon become compassion." Robert Brault

"Those who by faith see the invisible God, make no account of present losses and crosses." Samuel Rutherford

"O wad some power the giftee gie us, to see oursel's as ithers see us!" (Sottish dialect – Poem: To A Louse) Robert Burns (1759-1796) (Oh would some power the gift give us, to see ourselves as others see us.)

"Christ sees our victory before we begin." Pam Malow-Isham

Questions
Do I see the qualities of my friends and coworkers or their faults? How do I see myself? What's the best thing I "see" in my life today?

Declarations

I give thanks that I can **see** perfectly. I **see** God in every face; I **see** innocence in every person. I **see** with my brilliant eyes that I am free to **see** with love. I **see** past evil-doing with my loving-kindness.

I am encompassed with joy, and totally secure. People can **see** my inner contentedness is not dependent upon outside circumstances. I live in the now, and **see** each moment as a new adventure. I choose to **see** my elegance and self-sufficiency. I **see** my eyes are getting clearer, and brighter each day. I **see** myself with the eyes love.

Maintaining my focal point is natural to me. I **see** out of both eyes with clarity the fantastic life I am creating. I **see** my success first in my mind, and then in the material form. I am a visionary and **see** plainly my perfect aim. I **see** people helping me. I **see** happy people coming out of the woodwork to support and promote my business.

God gives me perfect vision, and it is safe for me to **see** what I need to **see** about myself so I can mature. I am now able to **see** my own importance and good looks. I have the clear-cut vision of God to **see** myself the way He does. I have great eyesight and healthy eyes.

I **see** clearly the open way that God has made for me. God **sees** me as wonderfully made, always forgiven, eternally His, extremely beautiful, and funny to watch. I choose to enjoy my life. I like to see the beauty around my home. I exude integrity. I am keenly aware of Divine favor resting on me, my children, family, and home.

I have been given free will to choose what I want to **see**, and what kind of life I want to experience. I **see** blessings chasing me down. I **see** good fortune coming from the north, south, east, and west. I **see** myself as strong, successful, happy, healthy, generous, and rich.

124:
Miss
May 3

Bible Verses

"Desire without knowledge is not good— how much more will hasty feet miss the way!" Proverbs 19:2 (NIV)

"See that no one misses God's loving-favor. Do not let wrong thoughts about others get started among you. If you do, many people will be turned to a life of sin." Hebrews 12:15 (NLV)

Word of the Day

Miss – To error in judgment or overlook something you could have done. To reach an unintended aim or drop the ball. A lapse in awareness.

Quotes

"One may as much miss the mark by aiming too high as too low." Proverb

"Preparation will never miss a favorable circumstance." Pam Malow-Isham

"Do not disdain the small. The whole of life - even the hard - is made up of the minute parts, and if I miss the infinitesimals, I miss the whole." Ann Voskamp

Pam's Perspective

Being in a hurry, I would miss the gifts right in front of me. Taking the time to slow down to pay attention to little details, has enriched my life, and brought me much joy, and satisfaction. Now I never miss an opportunity to smile.

Questions

What have I missed out on by being impatient? What will I miss if I continue on my current path? What opportunity did I miss because I wasn't prepared? What will I be open to and not miss today?

Declarations

I learn from successful people, so I **miss** the likelihood of failure. I am perceptive. I am passionate about enjoying every moment. I seize every opportunity that comes my way, so I won't **miss** a trick.

I make sure I **miss** being too hurried, so I don't **miss** the simple pleasures that surround my daily life. I never **miss** seeing beauty. Favorable circumstances continue to come my way as I notice them.

I prefer to **miss** time surfing the Internet so I can spend quality time with my family, friends, and God. When I **miss** my quiet time with the Almighty, I **miss** the guidance I receive from a faithful Friend.

I love arriving early for appointments, giving myself plenty of time to get where I need to be. I **miss** the embarrassment of walking in late by always arriving early. I am a shining example of punctuality.

I honor every commitment I make. I have a wealth consciousness, so I pass the malls, **miss** the sales, and save for the future. I have a couple years' wages in the bank. I **miss** late payments by paying my bills early. I **miss** bad investments by being cautious, and thorough.

Life is an exciting adventure as I meet new friends, and cherish old ones. When I **miss** a friend, I make sure I pick up the phone and give them a call or a written note. I am thankful for my hands, and my ability to write thank-you notes, and words of encouragement.

I find it easy to live in peace as I **miss** out on the chaos. I **miss** boredom by being curious and spending time engaged in activities that satisfy me. I never **miss** an opportunity to laugh and play games with my children or friends. People **miss** me when I am not around because I am the kind of person who is a lot of fun.

125:
Share
May 4

Bible Verses

"Sing to the Lord, all the earth! Share the news of his saving work every single day!" 1 Chronicles 16:23 (CEB)

"But do not forget to do good and to share, for with such sacrifices God is well pleased." Hebrews 13:16 (NKJV)

Word of the Day

Share – To give without compensation a portion of your time, knowledge or assets. Benefit from a financial investment. To deliver a blessings.

Quotes

"If liberty and equality, as is thought by some, are chiefly to be found in democracy, they will be best attained when all persons alike share in government to the utmost." Aristotle

"Light is the task when many share the toil." Homer – Iliad. Bk. XII. L. 493

"All who joy would win must share it. Happiness was born a twin." Lord Byron

Pam's Perspective

I have to remind myself to share my thoughts, feelings, possessions, time, and kind deeds because it did not come naturally to me. It is in sharing that I reap the most happiness. Being stingy does not feel good, and blocks the flow of God's gifts. The more I share, the more I have to share, and the more I want to share.

Questions

Why do I find it easy to share compliments, credits, and rewards? What can I share today? How have I shared my gifts with the world?

Declarations

I **share** smiles with everyone I see. I **share** hugs and positive words with my friends. I like to **share**; it's fun. There is always more than enough to **share**. I frequently **share** laughter, joy, and excitement.

I take time to listen to others with an open mind as they **share** ideas. I encourage people to **share** with each other. I **share** the credit and the rewards of my work. Because I am so likable, people **share** cool ideas, and opportunities with me. I **share** possibility thoughts today.

I **share** the love of the Lord with everyone I meet. I feel privileged to be able to **share** my life with God and reap the benefits. Today I intend to dream big, **share** big, and enjoy little details. I find it easy to be courteous, and peaceful. I choose to **share** my joy today.

I **share** the responsibility of chores with my mate. I like to help out. I **share** respect, and admiration for my mate's good qualities. I **share** memories with my family as we hang out together in unity. I teach my children the joy of **sharing**, and the gifts of happiness it brings.

I **share** the obligation of improving my community by **sharing** one small act of kindness at a time. I discover new joys when I volunteer for worthy causes. I have a cheerful, **sharing** spirit that welcomes all.

I feel content releasing the excess stuff around my house so I can **share** it with someone who would enjoy it more. The more I **share** with people, the more I get. I **share** comfort, and assistance readily.

I project confidence as I **share** my gifts with the world. I **share** my story and inspire people to take action on their dreams. I help people in spite of any fears of rejection. I feel self-assured as I **share** my knowledge, and invest in the well-being, and health of others.

126:
Retain
May 5

Bible Verses
"If you forgive the sins of any, they are forgiven them; if you retain the sins of any, they are retained." John 20:23 (NKJV)

"Retain the standard of sound words which you have heard from me, in the faith and love which are in Christ Jesus." 2 Timothy 1:13 (NASB)

Word of the Day
Retain – To absorb knowledge and have total recall of it. To keep. To procure and cherish. Preserve. To hire or contract.

Quotes
"Retain your faith by continuing to see with the eye of faith. If you can't see it, you can't have it. You can only have it if you see it." Lester Sumrall

"The cask will long retain the flavor of that with which it was first filled." Horace

Pam's Perspective
Trying to retain permission from different authors to use their quotes was quite the chore. I think I am honoring someone by quoting them. Out of fear and lack, some people let their ego get in the way, and therefore are not in my book. I had bought two books from one author, one paper, and one kindle version. Because the quote I wanted to use was in the kindle version I had purchased, she said I could not quote her unless I also bought a paper copy. I was not going to lie and say I had, so I did not quote her. I do not think one quote will make, or break a book.

Questions
What is the most important thing for me to retain? Why? Have I retained enough assets to live comfortably? Why do I retain the best friends?

Declarations

I **retain** a good attitude. I **retain** my sense of balance and wellbeing as I move through the day. I dare to ask for what I want. I **retain** what I desire because I trust in the Lord. I have it made in the shade.

I **retain** my intimate connection with God. I am thankful that I don't have to work to **retain** His favor. I am forever His child and always loved. God's power is working wonders in my life today. I **retain** the previous miracles that have appeared, and I expect to **retain** more.

I **retain** a clean mind because I read, and focus on what is pure, and lovely. I **retain** everything I read with my great memory. I **retain** great vision, and can easily recall what I see. I **retain** what I hear, so I make sure that I am listening to positive things that will benefit me.

I value my time. I **retain** a humble attitude as I give of my time to be of service. I **retain** more when I give things away. I **retain** my self-respect by saying no to things I do not want to do. I am lighthearted and easy to get along with. I **retain** old friends and attract new ones.

I remember to keep my cool and **retain** my composure when someone does something I don't like. I **retain** my peace. I am blessed with patience. I play full out when it is time to play, and **retain** my competitive edge while having fun. I show up prepared, and ready to go. I **retain** good habits that hedge against apathy and foster a positive outcome. Everything is possible for me to **retain** today.

Most of my fears and insecurities are just a false belief appearing real, so I **retain** my confidence by repeating positive declarations. I am the master of balance and poise. In spite of appearances, I will believe for the impossible, and **retain** the miraculous. I think of my vision as an already accomplished fact. I **retain** my unstop-ability.

127:
Reply
May 6

Bible Verses
"A person finds joy in giving an apt reply— and how good is a timely word!"
Proverbs 15:23 (NIV)

"For I will give you the right words and such wisdom that none of your opponents will be able to reply or refute you!" Luke 21:15 (NLT)

Word of the Day
Reply – To acknowledge someone's question with a response. To have a reaction or comeback for something said. A verbal declaration.

Quotes
"The impromptu reply is precisely the touchstone of the man of wit." Moliere

"Silence is true wisdom's best reply." Euripides

"Silence is less injurious than a weak reply." Charles Caleb Colton

Pam's Perspective
I pause before I reply so my words are thought out, and kind. I recently found out my love language is words of affirmation. Go figure; I write a book full of affirmations. Of course, I married someone who speaks a different love language who can be impatient, and hasty in his reply. It takes time if that is not your love language to learn it, and communicate in a nice way. It doesn't happen overnight. Patience, forgiveness, and trust are keys to a happy marriage.

Questions
How do I respond when someone replies in a sarcastic tone? Do I pause and give careful thought before I reply? Is my reply true and kind?

Declarations

I am abundant with bright smiles. I always think before I **reply**. I am kind and considerate of every **reply** I give away. People say I am a contribution to my friends. I am patient and wait when people take their time to **reply**. I **reply** in truth when asked a question.

When someone gives me a snide **reply** I smile, and send them a little prayer before I **reply** with kind words because I see they are hurting inside. I can love someone even if I do not like how they **reply**.

I **reply** yes to God, and serve Him with gladness in my heart. I thank God for His infinite wisdom giving me the most appropriate **reply** at the very moment I need it. God always sends the **reply** to my prayers at just the right time. He **replies** because I am loved.

I say yes, and go beyond the call of duty when asked if I will **reply** with help. I **reply** to difficult situations with a positive attitude and a can-do spirit. I emit feelings of joy and abundance. I am honest in my **reply** and bold in what I want to get across. I believe in myself.

I like developing habits of mastery, and good ethics. It is OK to **reply** with an unpopular answer. I am professional, and cordial with every **reply** I make. It is as simple as ABC to **reply** with kind words.

I get to choose how I will **reply** in any, and every situation, so I stay alert about how I am **replying** in words and deeds. I take a deep breath before I **reply** so I can focus on the best possible answer.

My life is phenomenal because I follow my passions and dreams. I am rewarded with abundance. I love asking myself questions and coming up with brilliant **replies**. I trust my inner guidance. I am gifted, and a genius beyond description. Just listen to my **replies**.

128:
Prayer
May 7

Bible Verses

"And all things you ask in prayer, believing, you will receive." Matthew 21:22 (NASB)

"Therefore, confess your sins to one another, and pray for one another so that you may be healed. The effective prayer of a righteous man can accomplish much." James 5:16 (NASB)

Word of the Day

Prayer – The act of talking to God through thoughts, words or actions. Giving thanks to God. Communicating with your heart to God's heart.

Quotes

"The time of business does not differ with me from the time of prayer; and in the noise and clatter of my kitchen, while several persons are at the same time calling for different things, I possess God in as great tranquility as if I were on my knees at the sacrament." Brother Lawrence

"In souls filled with love, the desire to please God is a constant prayer." John Wesley

Pam's Perspective

I started Praying Hands around Flint to pray for our city in the fall of eighty-nine. I was excited to see people from different denominations coming together in unity to see how we could help our city. We impacted our community for good.

Questions

Do I believe in the power of prayer? Do I pray before I have to make important decisions in my life? Why do I set aside time for prayer?

Declarations

I live in a state of continual **prayer** as I commune with God throughout my day. I stand amazed at the awesomeness of my Creator. I rejoice knowing God hears my **prayers** and answers my **prayers** at the perfect time. I have a robust faith in my God.

Prayer cures ailments and eases an anxious mind. All my **prayers** have a blessing built into it for someone. As I **pray**, I forgive quickly, and often. My healing is revealed when I **pray**. I trust God. My **prayers** work wonders. I lay hands on the sick, and they recover.

I appreciate the fact that I can **pray** to the Creator of the Universe, and I will not be turned away. Nothing is too small or too big for the God who loves to hear my **prayers**. I release all doubts now as I do my part, and **pray.** God will answer my **prayers** in His perfect time.

I have the patience for my **prayers** to be answered. I love leaning into God with my **prayers** as He covers me with His benevolence. I am a reflection of love, and forever grateful that I am His child. He has been a great Daddy to me. I do not have to do anything for His love except accept it. I like to **pray**. My God makes house calls.

I **pray** bold **prayers**. Miracles happen when I **pray** the **prayer** of faith. My **prayer** life enhances my relationship with the Eternal One. Jesus is my friend. As I **pray,** I listen with open ears to hear God imparting His wisdom to my life. **Prayer** restores my soul as I **pray** in the Spirit. My **prayers** move mountains and heal the sick.

I offer **prayer** to my friends. I like attending spiritual support groups. We **pray** for each other's needs and inspire each other in a variety of ways. There is power in group **prayer**. I am happy knowing people are **praying** for me. I am a **prayer** warrior.

129:
Confidence
May 8

Bible Verses

"It is better to take refuge in the Lord than to put confidence in man." Psalm 118:8 (RSV)

"Finally, let's draw near to the throne of favor with confidence so that we can receive mercy and find grace when we need help." Hebrews 4:16 (CEB)

Word of the Day

Confidence – A strong assurance and boldness in oneself. Havinnng a certainty in another person or thing. The faith and courage to believe God.

Quotes

"Confidence in the goodness of another is good proof of one's own goodness." Michel de Montaigne

"Difficulties are God's errands, and when we are sent upon them, we should esteem it a proof of God's confidence - as compliment from God." Henry Beecher

"Does he deserve thy confidence, who bullies all – who all annoys; who cares not where he gives offense, who cares not what his rage destroys?" Thomas Stott

"If once you forfeit the confidence of your fellow-citizens, you can never regain their respect and esteem." Abraham Lincoln

"Confidence is the best beauty secret." Pam Malow-Isham

Questions

What have I built my confidence on? What can I do today to increase my confidence? Why do I appreciate people with confidence?

Declarations

I fake **confidence** until I embody it. I have spunk and charm. I look people in the eye, so they know they are speaking to someone with **confidence**. I am **confident** enough to let someone else get the credit for what I did. God knows and will reward me accordingly.

Because God is on my side, I stay in a state of total **self-confidence**. I am fearless and self-assured. I try new things in new ways. I possess keen desire to succeed while radiating joyous feelings. People are eager to back my projects because of my great **confidence.**

My **confidence** puts me out front. Because I have the **confidence** to speak up for myself, I get what I want. My **confidence** takes me great places. I remember my wins and follow my excitement. I build **self-confidence** by my actions. I like being a big picture thinker.

I tap into an infinite reservoir of **confidence**, and courage as I go for the gold. I trust myself to do a superb job. I am more than **confident** as I think about my strengths. By achieving the goals I set for myself, I build even more **confidence**. I was created to do great exploits for God's glory. I instill **confidence** in others by my inner strength.

I let go of every negative thought and think new thoughts of hope, **confidence**, and poise. I have the **confidence** to stand up for myself, and the things I hold as sacred. I stretch myself to the limits. With **confidence**, I instinctively transform every experience into joy.

I naturally have well-founded **confidence** and personal charisma. I am beautiful with unlimited **confidence**, and belief in myself. I am well-groomed and stylish. I like the **confidence** I am creating as I set aside time to study. I am dazzling, brilliant, creative, highly productive, and oozing out **confidence** as I exhibit a successful life.

130:
Uncertainty
May 9

Bible Verses
"Charge them that are rich in this world, that they be not high-minded, nor trust in uncertain riches, but in the living God, who giveth us richly all things to enjoy." 1 Timothy 6:17 (KJV)

"But the wisdom from above is first pure, then peaceable, gentle, open to reason, full of mercy and good fruits, without uncertainty or insincerity." James 3:17 (RSV)

Word of the Day
Uncertainty – Not being sure of the future. Worry and unease about something. A lack of confidence. A gamble.

Quotes
"Truth is confirmed by inspection and delay; falsehood avails itself of haste and uncertainty." Tacitus

"Uncertainty and expectation are the joys of life. Security is an insipid thing." William Congreve

"The greatest loss of time is delay and expectation, which depends upon the future. We let go the present, which we have in our power, and look forward to that which depends upon chance-and so quit a certainty for an uncertainty." Seneca

"Have peace while embracing uncertainty by trusting God." Pam Malow-Isham

Questions
How do I react in the face of uncertainty? Has it stopped me in the past? Will I allow it to stop me in the future? Can I be at peace with uncertainty?

Declarations

I experience the Divine in everything, especially myself. When I am **uncertain** what direction to take, I stop, pray, and ask for guidance. I am exactly where I am meant to be. I have ears that hear what God is telling me today. I embrace **uncertainty** as I put my trust in God.

Uncertainty is the spice of life. I am respected as a go-getter and a leader in my field. I keep all the agreements I make, regardless of the **uncertainty** of the future. My word is my bond. I burn excuses and plow ahead. I always try one more time and never give up.

I relax into **uncertainty**, rather than struggling my way through life. I always have more than enough. I save, so I have a surplus for an **uncertain** future. **Uncertainty** does not bother me. I am brave.

Part of the **uncertainty** of my health is up to me. As I exercise, eat healthy food, and take supplements, I have a better chance at feeling vivacious, and full of energy. My thoughts focus on feeling good.

Relationships totter between **uncertainty**, and stable. I am always free to take the high or the low road, so I consistently take the high road that is offense free and unburdened. I express gratitude for the opportunity to have rewarding relationships in **uncertain** times.

I would rather live in the **uncertainty** of the possibility of getting my feelings hurt than being alone, and lonely. I open myself up to new friends. I am friendly, so I make friends easily. I like being connected with a community of people who inspire me to be my best.

I enjoy every **uncertain** moment, as it may be my last. I stay calm during **uncertainty** because I know everything will turn out OK. I rest in peace during this **uncertain** era knowing God is in control.

131:
Rude
May 10

Bible Verses
"Answering before listening is both stupid and rude." Proverbs 18:13 (MSG)

"Expel a mocker, and watch the wrangling go with him; rivalry and rude remarks will also stop." Proverbs 22:10 (VOICE)

Word of the Day
Rude - Someone that is disrespectful and insulting. Vulgar and uncivil. Arrogant. Inexperienced and rough.

Quotes
"The earliest form in which romances appear is that of a rude kind of verse." Thomas Bulfinch

"Men, even when alone, lighten their labors by song, however rude it may be." Quintilian

"Lack of thought is no excuse for being rude." Pam Malow-Isham

Pam's Perspective
Traveling around the world is great fun, but if you don't read up on others customs, you will unknowingly be rude and offend the people you want to help. I saw some Americans throw hard candy to kids that landed on the ground. Our tour guide stopped the trolley, went over and picked up the candy, and handed it to the children. He said you throw food to a dog, but never to children.

Questions
How do I respond to rudeness? Do I ever catch myself being rude? If so, why is that? Why do I let rude comments roll off my back?

Declarations

My gentle nature attracts the nicest people into my life. I am worthy to be heard. Standing up for myself is not **rude**. I count. When a person is **rude** to me, I smile and realize they are just unhappy. I respond with love and patience. I choose not to be **rude** at all times.

I trust when I step up to the plate I will hit a home run, despite **rude** comments. I trust my competency as I discover my own potential. I deserve to live a great life. I am respectful, so I ignore **rudeness**.

It is a pleasure to be of service, even to **rude** people because they can't steal my joy. My joy comes from within. My enthusiasm blows **rude** people away. They do not stick with me long because they know they cannot affect me with their **rudeness**. I am extremely powerful. I am full of happiness as I blow off **rudeness**.

I give **rude** people the right to take up space. A **rude** enemy always looks bigger than he really is. Jesus is my ever-present help in times of irritation. I have a forgiving spirit. I deserve kind treatment, and so do others. I even tend to leave **rude** waitresses a tip. We all have a rotten day now and then. I have a passion for seeing the best in the **rudest** people. I am a disciplined person of grace with a great smile.

I am smart. I think, and act my way to success as I journal my **rude**, and kind thoughts. I live in the awareness of who I am becoming and focus on that. It would be **rude** to think I know it all, so I give myself permission to go on an inquiry trip. Research is fun.

I ask for forgiveness if I let a **rude** wisecrack or gesture slip out. I keep my tongue in check. I am in harmony with nature and not **rude** to people or animals. I like being kind. Because of my pure thoughts, I reflect a sweet nature. I live in a grand world that is fun to play in.

132:
Appreciate
May 11

Bible Verses
"A mocker does not appreciate a warning. He will not go to wise people."
Proverbs 15:12 (GW)

*"Learn to appreciate and give dignity to your body, not abusing it, as is
so common among those who know nothing of God." 1 Thessalonians 4:4
(MSG)*

Word of the Day
Appreciate - To recognize the worth of life and everything in it. To give
thanks for what you see, hear or receive. To hold in high esteem.

Quotes
*"It contributes greatly towards a man's moral and intellectual health, to be
brought into habits of companionship with individuals unlike himself, who
care little for his pursuits, and whose sphere and abilities he must go out of
himself to appreciate." Nathaniel Hawthorne*

*"In order to appreciate a great man, we must know his surroundings. We
must understand the scope of the drama in which he played – the part he
acted – and we must also know his audience." Robert Green Ingersoll*

*"We ask you to the extent of your ability to appreciate this man and his
deed, in spite of the difference between you and him. Who cares whether he
belonged to your clique, or party, or sect, or not?" Henry David Thoreau*

"Living in bliss is the ability to appreciate all." Pam Malow-Isham

Questions
Do I appreciate the hard lessons? What have I taken for granted that I
need to appreciate? Whom do I appreciate? What do I appreciate?

Declarations

Appreciation is always a win-win, so I give and receive it freely. The more I **appreciate** people, the more they **appreciate** me. I activate my **appreciation** muscles by staying present and noticing the small things. I **appreciate** how fantastic I am. My friends **appreciate** me.

I **appreciate** all the wonderful people who are in my life now. I am grateful for the privilege of making a positive contribution to the world, simply by doing my work with a joyous attitude. I speak kindly to everyone I meet **appreciating** our uniqueness and beauty.

I **appreciate** everything I have achieved in my life, and who I am. I **appreciate** all the lessons I have learned from the mistakes I have made in the past. They give me new insights on how to accomplish my next goals. I **appreciate** my wonderful life and all the trials in it!

I remember to **appreciate** the people around me. I **appreciate** the way I communicate with my partner. I listen with an open heart. When I notice my partner has done something nice for me, no matter how big or small, I tell him or her that I **appreciate** it.

It feels so good to wake up in the morning **appreciating** what I already have. I have an **appreciative** heart that is ever expanding in its capacity to show, and give love. I **appreciate** all the treasures that surround me. I express **appreciation** for the big, and little things. I believe in myself. The more I **appreciate** what I have, the more I will have to **appreciate**. I **appreciate** my willingness to review.

I make a list of God's past faithfulness towards me. There is always one more reason to give thanks and be **appreciative**. I symbolize the way an **appreciative** person would live and act. I **appreciate** long hugs. I am enthusiastic about my future **appreciating** the next quest.

133:
Safe
May 12

Bible Verses
"The name of the Lord is a fortified tower; the righteous run to it and are safe." Proverbs 18:10 (NIV)

"The fear of man brings a snare, but whoever leans on, trusts in, and puts his confidence in the Lord is safe and set on high." Proverbs 29:25 (AMP)

Word of the Day
Safe - Sheltered from violence, mischief, and foul play. Protected from harm. Not adventuresome, cautious and guarded.

Quotes
"Where the press is free and every man able to read, all is safe." Thomas Jefferson

"There is nothing so strong or safe in an emergency of life as simple truth." Charles Dickens

"Where an excess of power prevails, property of no sort is duly respected. No man is safe in his opinions, his person, his faculties, or his possessions." James Madison

"Being safe is an illusion we yearn to materialize. No matter how safe we may think we are, tragedies come to us all sooner or later. The answer is to turn all our cares over to God, be fearless, and trust no matter what, we will come through the other side with a greater revelation of God's love." Pam Malow-Isham

Questions
Is it necessary for me to feel safe before I take action? Why or why not? Do feel like I live in a safe world? Have I set up safety measures for myself and family? What are my thoughts on safety? How can I elevate fear?

Declarations

It is **safe** to dream again knowing that all things are possible when I believe. I feel **safe** to be myself. I feel **safe** practicing self-acceptance as I allow myself the freedom to sing, dance, praise, and love. I feel **safe** thinking for myself. I choose to love and enjoy myself.

Filling my mind with inspirational messages, and declaring good affirmations, is a **safe** way to keep from depression. It is **safe** to work with the powers of my mind. I remember it is **safe** to love and be loved. I feel **safe** expressing my feelings with my friends.

Being on the court, playing full out, and giving it my all, is a **safe** way to get ahead. Risking taking a chance on my dreams is a **safe** way to keep mediocrity at bay. Passionately working toward my goals is how I stay **safe** from getting hung up by discouragement.

I keep my home, and car **safe** with a first aid kit, fire extinguisher, and emergency supplies. I plan ahead and take responsibility for keeping myself **safe** when I go out. I leave my valuables in a **safe** place. I park in well-lit places at night. I travel in groups and let people know where I am going. I stay aware of my surroundings. I have a backup plan, just in case, so I always have a feeling of **safety**.

I give generously, save wisely, and feel **safe** that God will keep me from lack. I feel **safe** passing my abundance around. I am thankful for the **safe** roof over my head, and all the lovely things in my home.

I feel **safe** today, and tomorrow will take care of itself. I am **safe** going cool places and having fun. I am **safe** because God is always with me. God is concerned with every aspect of my life and wants only the best for me. God willingly loves me and keeps me **safe** day, and night. Goodness hovers over me keeping me **safe** as I sleep.

134:
Vulnerable
May 13

Bible Verses
"Do not cheat poor people just because they are vulnerable or use shady tactics in court to crush those already suffering:" Proverbs 22:22 (VOICE)

"Speak out on behalf of the voiceless, and for the rights of all who are vulnerable." Proverbs 31:8 (CEB)

Word of the Day
Vulnerable - Allowing yourself to be accessible and unguarded. Exposed to danger. Free from walls and barriers. Truthful.

Quotes
"To share your weakness is to make yourself vulnerable; to make yourself vulnerable is to show your strength." Criss Jami

"Being vulnerable opens doors of unprecedented joy." Pam Malow-Isham

Pam's Perspective
When I was fifteen, I fell head over heels in love with a man that was twenty-six. He put me up on a pedestal and treated me like gold. Six months later he turned abusive and crazy. It then turned into a rollercoaster romance for the next six months. I made a vow to myself when we broke up for the last time that I would never let anyone get that close to me again. I kept that promise until January 2000 when I realized why I was still single. It was because I wouldn't let anyone get close. So then I let my guard down and opened myself up to being vulnerable.

Questions
How has being vulnerable helped me? Do I make a habit of being vulnerable with my feelings? Whom will I be vulnerable with today?

Declarations

I make a conscious choice to embrace my **vulnerability** and live the authentic lifestyle. Although I have been hurt in the past, I choose to be prudent, and **vulnerable**. Therefore I can love with no holding back, giving fully to the experience of loving, and being loved.

I am transparently **vulnerable** which opens up new lines of communication. I am thankful for my mouth so I can speak what is on my heart. I am able to recognize when I need to forgive and let go. I am smart enough not to hold a grudge. I am forgiving.

I direct my passions to serve my highest good. When I become **vulnerable** and admit that I need help, God is right there meeting my every need. The more exposed, and **vulnerable** I am, the more people open up to me. As I freely give, I freely receive. I live a triumphantly **vulnerable** life. I practice being **vulnerable**, and free.

I push past the fear of being **vulnerable**, or scared, and just be myself. I am grateful for all the friends, and love that comes my way. People are inspired by my **vulnerability** and moved to become **vulnerable** themselves. I attract loyal, **vulnerable** associates.

I am confident as I admit my faults, and weaknesses, knowing they have no power to rule over me when I verbalize my **vulnerable** tendencies. I face my challenges head-on, and transform my insecurity into courage. I become who God has created me to be.

Jesus became **vulnerable** for me, so I can be a powerful witness for Him. My heart overflows with appreciation when I think about what God has done for me. I am **vulnerable** to God. My life is evidence of what it is like to be Spirit-led and joyful. I live as though I am eternally loved. I am brave enough to be **vulnerable** today.

135:
Satisfied
May 14

Bible Verses

"You will eat, you will be satisfied, and you will bless the Lord your God in the wonderful land that he's given you." Deuteronomy 8:10 (CEB)

"From the fruit of his words a man shall be satisfied with good, and the work of a man's hands shall come back to him [as a harvest]." Proverbs 12:14 (AMP)

Word of the Day

Satisfied - Happy and fulfilled. Gratified. Self-pleased.

Quotes

"To be satisfied with a little is the greatest wisdom; and he that increaseth his riches, increaseth his cares; but a contented mind is a hidden treasure, and trouble findeth it not." William Melmoth

"The recipe for perpetual ignorance is: Be satisfied with your opinions and content with your knowledge." Elbert Hubbard

"Being satisfied with life is as easy as making a decision." Pam Malow-Isham

"No one is satisfied with his fortune or dissatisfied with his wit." Antoinette Deshoulieres

"Rest satisfied with doing well, and leave others to talk of you as they please." Pythagoras

Questions

Do I know what it takes for me to be satisfied with my life right now? Am I satisfied from within or from external stimuli? Is that working for me?

Declarations

Being fully **satisfied** with my life the way it is right now enables me to soar ahead of the crowd to achieve even greater success than I thought was possible. Exuberantly skipping toward my goals is a fun way of moving forward. I am **satisfied** with what I have, yet I still enjoy laboring for the greater things that God has for me.

I have the ability to visualize and realize my dream as fulfilled, and **satisfied**. I am **satisfied** with my work because I have done it to the best of my ability, and have done a great job. I focus on desirable images, visualizing my goals **satisfied**. I continue to amaze myself.

I prioritize my health by taking supplements, eating raw food, and keeping my body moving. I feel **satisfied** with lowering my sugar intake. I feel **satisfied** when I have a healthy treat. I love the way I take care of myself. I look in the mirror and say, 'I love you.'

I am **satisfied** with what is so. What I have is what I have. I forgive myself for not being perfect. I am **satisfied** with where I live, even if it is not flawless or ideal. I keep my place uncluttered, and clean. I simplify my life and choose to be **satisfied** with what I own.

Creatively pursuing my purpose has **satisfied** the longing of what I am I here to do. I follow my heart. I now feel **satisfied** with who I am, and who I will become. I am unique and special. Giggles are a part of my daily life. I am **satisfied** with joy. I am comfortable in my own skin, **satisfied** with the way I look, and the way I live my life.

God **satisfied** all the longings of my soul. God **satisfied** the empty place in my heart by filling it with His love. Although I am **satisfied** with the former things of God, I know there is more. So I listen to hear a fresh word, look to see miracles, and expect larger blessings.

136:
Wish
May 15

Bible Verses
"Then you will have hope for the future, and your wishes will come true."
Proverbs 23:18 (NCV)

"Wish good for those who harm you; wish them well and do not curse them."
Romans 12:14 (NCV)

Word of the Day
Wish - The hope that what you desire will come to pass. A yearning.

Quotes
"True instruction is this: to learn to wish that each thing should come to pass as it does. And how does it come to pass? As the Disposer has disposed it. Now He has disposed that there should be summer and winter, and plenty and dearth, and vice and virtue, and all such opposites, for the harmony of the whole." Epictetus

"Be not angry that you cannot make others as you wish them to be since you cannot make yourself as you wish to be." Thomas à Kempis

"The words wish and hope, indicate a lack of trust in the Higher Power, and it is disrespectful." Carol Woods

"Nothing is so easy as to deceive one's self; for what we wish, that we readily believe." Demosthenes

"Wishes turn into substance when you have faith." Pam Malow-Isham

Questions
What do I wish for? Do I wish for solutions or do I create them? Why will I turn my wishes into actions, and fulfilled realities?

Declarations

I can have as many **wishes** as my heart desires. There is no limit to how many **wishes** I can **wish** for. I put energy toward what I **wish** for. What I **wish** for matters. I am wonderfully **wishful.** My **wishes** come to me frequently with great speed because I believe.

I have a willingness to see things in a new light. I anticipate what I **wish** for. I use every opportunity to move forward towards my **wishes**. I never waste my time **wishing** when I could be taking action. I am the only one who can stop me, so I become unstoppable.

I remember that abundance is my birthright as a child of God. I sense a feeling of inner happiness coursing through my veins as I visualize my **wishes**. Good is my outcome. My guardian angel is always near, so I have nothing to fear. I relax and turn all my **wishes** over to God knowing they will be answered in record time. I pass on **wishing** harm to my enemies and pile on the blessings.

Even though sometimes I **wish** I was a kid again and could stay that way forever; I know that is just a silly fantasy. I am thankful for the opportunity to grow up and **wish** for bigger, and better things. I am happy being a responsible adult making my **wishes** a reality.

I have fun playing the **wishing** game. I love seeing people's **wishes** granted. I invite my friends to play along, and we **wish** for the craziest things. We laugh as we talk about our **wishes**, and how we are going to react when they come true. I only **wish** well for others.

Even if I have a few pounds to lose, I never **wish** I were anyone but me. I am pleased as punch with myself just the way I am. I use the gifts that God has given me. I **wish** everyone could see the beauty that lies within them. I can change the world, one **wish** at a time.

137:
Peace
May 16

Bible Verses

"I will lie down and sleep in peace, for you alone, O Lord, make me dwell in safety." Psalm 4:8 (NIV)

"When a man's ways please the Lord, He makes even his enemies to be at peace with him." Proverbs 16:7 (NKJV)

Word of the Day

Peace – Having a calm and tranquil mind. Free from chaos and strife.

Quotes

"He that neither coveteth to please men, nor feareth to displease them, shall enjoy much peace." Thomas à Kempis

"Lord, make me an instrument of your peace; where there is hatred, let me sow love; where there is injury, pardon; where there is doubt, faith; where there is despair, hope; where there is darkness, light; and where there is sadness, joy. O divine Master, grant that I may not so much seek to be consoled as to console, to be understood as to understand, to be loved as to love. For it is in giving that we receive, it is in pardoning that we are pardoned, and it is in dying that we are born to eternal life. Amen" Anonymous

Pam's Perspective

Peace is a state of mind that you can carry with you 24/7. Staying peaceful is not always easy, but it is always possible. Trust God, and release all your worries.

Questions

Where do I find the most peace? Do I surround myself with peaceful people? With a peaceful environment? Why do I make peace a priority?

Declarations

I am at **peace** with my spirit, mind, and body. **Peace** is my natural state of mind. I reject irrelevant thoughts, and distractions so I can concentrate on what I need to get done. I allow my positive voice on the inside to rule my world. I am the master of my **peaceful** mind.

I have the power, and ability to be a **peacemaker**. I consistently give thought to what is really important to me, and what my values are. I grow in **peace** as I live in love. I discover **peace** within me as I put my trust in God. My success increases every day in every way.

When I practice becoming unconditionally friendly, **peace** just consistently shows up. Great joy is mine as I live in an authentic, **peaceful** way. My thoughts constantly focus on living healthy and staying **peaceful**. **Peace** divinely guides me all day long.

I allow **peace** to rule my life. I love **peace** and stay totally at ease during difficult times. I am thought of as a **peacemaker** wherever I go. I am relaxed, patient, **peaceful**, and balanced. My enthusiasm arises from my joyous, and **peaceful** center. I live surrounded in **peace**. I am OK just the way I am, no matter what others think.

God's **peace** heals all my wounds and quiets the chaos in my head. I am grateful for God's wonderful blessings; His **peace** that passes all understanding, and His love. As I take deep breaths, God fills my lungs with **peace**. I breathe out all stressful emotions and go free. I continue to experience joy, **peace**, and serenity all day long.

My aim to be **peaceful** is working. My vision is aligning with the Almighty. I have deep, unshakable faith in what I am doing. I feel secure and **peaceful**. I say **peace**, be still, to all the storms that come my way. **Peace** miracles pop up on a regular basis.

138:
Turbulence
May 17

Bible Verses
"Therefore we are unafraid, even if the earth gives way, even if the mountains tumble into the depths of the sea, even if its waters rage and foam, and mountains shake at its turbulence. (Selah)." Psalm 46:3-4 (CJB)

"I am completely confident and incredibly proud of you. Even in all this turbulence I am at peace—I am overflowing with joy." 2 Corinthians 7:4 (VOICE)

Word of the Day
Turbulence – Circumstances that are annoying or disturbing. Chaos.

Quotes
"Many a calm river begins as a turbulent waterfall, yet none hurtles and foams all the way to the sea." Mikhail Lermontov

"Such for wise purposes it is presumed, is the turbulence of human passions in party disputes, when victory more than truth is the palm contended for, that the post of honor is a private station." George Washington

Pam's Perspective
The turbulence of growing up in a house where I felt like I had to walk on eggshells to avoid getting yelled at was tough. I was to be seen, not heard and made to believe that my opinion did not matter. Through the turbulence, I learned to be resourceful, and self-sufficient. Now I am bold and handy at fixing things.

Questions
Do I allow the turbulence of this world to affect my well-being? What will I do to stay calm in the midst of turbulence?

Declarations

I shift my mind from **turbulence** to serenity by changing what I focus on. I control my thoughts and train my mind to meditate on what is holy. I read my affirmations repeatedly. I feel them with impact. I picture them vividly. All **turbulence** is pushed aside.

I claim the peace of God now. I have present, ongoing results that show the world how God blesses me in the midst of **turbulence**. In my heart, I am in love with God, and He me. I am reminded again that my sins are forgiven, and I am free from my **turbulent** past.

I celebrate the **turbulence** in life. I am not afraid of **turbulence** in my workplace because God is my source. I can easily afford things, even in a **turbulent** economy. I always have enough to meet every need I have. There is always something glorious coming my way. I am conservative in my spending and generous in my giving.

I make a frontal attack against the **turbulence** in my life by my outlandish prayers. I repent of the **turbulence** I have caused people. I ask for forgiveness. God moves on my behalf for reconciliation. Negative attitudes from people do not hold me back. I forgive.

Praise reports are on my lips as there is nothing but blue skies and smooth sailing from here on out. I have a propensity to look for the good in everything, even during **turbulence**. I embrace **turbulence**; it is my friend. I am thankful for what I learn from **turbulence**.

I have found myself laughing at **turbulence**, knowing I can conquer any **turbulence** that comes my way. I respond to **turbulence** when it arises with a calm mind. I have the power to embrace tranquility. I have the power to cause or reduce **turbulence** when I walk into a room. I create an atmosphere of peace, and serenity wherever I go.

139:
Sleep
May 18

Bible Verses
"In peace I will both lie down and sleep; for thou alone, O Lord, makest me dwell in safety." Psalm 3:5 (RSV)

"It is vain for you to rise up early, to take rest late, and to eat the bread of [anxious] toil--for He gives [blessings] to His beloved in sleep." Psalm 127:2 (AMP)

Word of the Day
Sleep – To doze off and be unaware. To slumber or cease activity. To be unaware of one's surroundings.

Quotes
"It is better to sleep on things beforehand than lie awake about them afterwards." Baltasar Gracian

"Silence is the sleep that nourishes wisdom." Francis Bacon

Pam's Perspective
I could get by on a couple hours sleep when I was young. Now I value my sleep. I have trained myself to fall asleep as soon as my head hits the pillow by telling myself, starting with my feet, and working my way up to my head, my feet are relaxed now and ready to sleep. On the rare occasion that I can't sleep, I get up, and read, or do something else instead of lying in bed feeling frustrated.

Questions
Have I trained myself to fall asleep quickly? How has that served me? What steps will I put in place to ensure peaceful night's sleep? Why do I relinquish the stress of the day, and fall to sleep easily?

Declarations

I **sleep** like a baby. I feel so secure and peaceful as I know I am resting in God's powerful arms keeping me safe at night as I **sleep**. I relax knowing God has me covered. I go to bed early, so I get enough **sleep** to feel rested. When I wake up, I am glad I **slept** well.

I write in my gratitude journal before retiring to bed, counting my blessings, and contemplating God's kindness towards me. I am glad that I can fall **asleep** without external assistance. I fall **asleep** fast.

I drink a cup of chamomile tea before I go to bed to help me **sleep**. I think up new inventions and creative ideas as I **sleep**. I go to **sleep** thinking about the kind of person I want to be. When I **sleep,** I envision being full of vigor and vitality, able to create vast wealth. The world needs my talents, so I get enough **sleep** to stay sharp.

When I **sleep,** I dream of things to come. I **sleep** well and always get enough to keep me healthy, and feeling great. My dreams are pleasant and restful. I **sleep** taking comfort in knowing the Lord.

I ask myself a question and then go to **sleep** knowing the answer will be there in the morning. I stay calm, let go, relax, and breathe in deep. It is easy for me to **sleep** now. I am worthy of a good night's **sleep**. I trust everything will swing in my favor as I **sleep** in peace.

I now surrender to **sleep**, feeling totally supported by the creator of the Universe. **Sleep** comes naturally to me. I move mountains as I **sleep**, and awake feeling totally confident, strong, and mighty.

I am pleased that I get to escape in my **sleep** from the worries of the day. I train myself to quickly go to **sleep**, and rest soundly with self-hypnosis. I grant myself the precious benefits of **sleeping** now.

140:
Awake
May 19

Bible Verses
"My eyes are awake through the night watches, that I may meditate on Your word." Psalm 119:148 (NKJV)

"Jesus died for us so that, whether we are awake or asleep, we will live together with him." 1 Thessalonians 5:10 (CEB)

Word of the Day
Awake – To be conscious of what is going on. Alive, attentive and aware in this moment. Observant of surroundings.

Quotes
"If you're awake, you are blessed. Life is a priceless gift, appreciate every minute of it." Kim Serafini

"Living the awake life requires trusting God, listening to His still small voice, and acting in spite of fear. When I awake to the reality of God's love for me, I become transformed into a powerful soul that is compelled to share His love with others. Choosing to stay awake is a process I enjoy." Pam Malow-Isham

"Hope is the dream of a man awake." French Proverb

"Life is a waste of wearisome hours which seldom the rose of enjoyment adorns, and the heart that is soonest awake to the flowers is always the first to be touch'd by the thorns." Thomas Moore

Questions
What greatness will I awake within me today? Do I stay awake late at night? What steps will I take to awaken more confidence in myself? Will I make it a daily practice? What can do to become a high performer?

Declarations

I **awake** each morning with a smile on my face, and a song in my heart. The first thing I do when I **awake** is say, thank you God for another beautiful day to share your love. I **awake** happy to be me.

As I **awake** the dreams inside of me, I visualize them coming true. I **awake** the genius within me as I see solutions, and new possibilities for growth and advancement, everywhere I go. I am willing to **awake** to success, so I go the extra mile, and do what it takes.

New answers **awake** within me as I ask God for guidance. I receive a collection of brilliant ideas. I **wake** up to realize who I am in Christ. I am in partnership with Him to advance the goodness of God. My protector is always **awake**, keeping me safe. I bear God's glory and likeness. I **awake** to love, joy, mercy, and hope.

My health **awakes** within me as I eat fresh fruits and vegetables. My muscles **awake** with strength and power as I exercise them. I **awake** to joy. I condition my mind to be **awake** to all the good around me.

I encourage myself to **awake** the drive within me that I need to accomplish my goals. I am safe. Success is mine as I **awake** the miracle of my mind to think only on divine thoughts, and the good I want to see come about. I live **awake,** being present every moment.

I choose to help other people become **awake** to their greatness by being an encourager. I always have something nice to say. It is easy to give compliments and praise people. I give more than I receive.

I practice opening my heart to people and leading with love. I live my life **awake** to all the unlimited potential that is out there. I see myself as I can be. I **wake** up inspired to conquer the world.

141:
Order
May 20

Bible Verses
"Whoever offers praise glorifies Me; And to him who orders his conduct aright I will show the salvation of God." Psalm 50:23 (NKJV)

"Let all things be done decently and in order." 1 Corinthians 14:40 (NKJV)

Word of the Day
Order – A directive to do something. To keep the law of the land. To line up groups of things, catalog or alphabetize. Things sorted out.

Quotes
"Order is sanity of the mind, the health of the body, the peace of the city, the security of the state. As the beams to a house, as the bones to the microcosm of man, so is order to all things." Robert Southey

"The Christian religion alone contemplates the conjugal union in the order of nature; it is the only religion which presents woman to man as a companion; every other abandons her to him as a slave. To religion alone do European women owe the liberty they enjoy." Bernardin de Saint-Pierre

"Whenever I prepare for a journey I prepare as though for death. Should I never return, all is in order." Katherine Mansfield

"The greatest part of a writer's time is spent in reading in order to write: a man will turn over half a library to make one book." Samuel Johnson

Questions
Do I seek an orderly life? How well do I respond to orders? How well do I give orders? How will I order my day to make the most of it? Is there a part of my life that I need to put in order? If so, what am I waiting for?

Declarations

I obey God's **orders** to the best of my abilities. I remember to listen to the still small voice of the Holy Spirit. I like discipline. I rejoice as God **orders** my steps. My home is **orderly**, organized, neat, and clean. I **order** my day, so I have time for reflection, work, and play.

I put in **order** the details of how I want my day to go the night before. I arrange my objectives in **order** of their importance. I follow my plan in **order** to reach my goals. I give myself an **order** to take action to improve my life. I trust Providence that I will succeed. I have an **orderly** mind, and I like being an **orderly** person.

People will follow **orders** from someone they trust. I elicit criticism from associates in **order** to improve myself and our environment. I recognize the exclusive gifts of my employees. I provide space in **order** for my employees to shine. On a regular basis, I provide positive feedback to support my employees in **order** for them to know I care. I anticipate the concerns and actions of those I lead and prepare for them in **order** to serve them effectively.

I **order** healthy food when eating out. I love moving my body in **order** to stay flexible and stable. My mood is enhanced as I put my life in **order**. I **order** my thoughts before I speak, so I am kind.

I arrange my bills in the **order** I will pay off fist to get, and stay, debt free. I align my finances in **order** and put aside a healthy retirement, and a bundle to leave for an inheritance. All my legal papers are in **order**, so my family is well taken care of no matter what happens.

I eagerly expect plenty. I issue an **order** for lack and negativity to leave, and for prosperity and plenty to come. I choose to be happy living an **orderly** life as I celebrate all the simple pleasures in it.

Disorder
May 21

Bible Verses
"We exhort you, brothers, admonish the disorderly, encourage the faint-hearted, support the weak, be patient toward all." 1 Thessalonians 5:14 (WEB)

"For where there is envy and selfish ambition, there will also be disorder and wickedness of every kind." James 3:16 (NRSV)

Word of the Day
Disorder –Chaos. Messy. Unsettled. Turmoil. Infirmity.

Quotes
"Idleness is an inlet to disorder and makes way for licentiousness. People who have nothing to do are quickly tired of their own company." Jeremy Collier

"War begets quiet, quiet idleness, idleness disorder, disorder ruin; likewise ruin order, order virtue, virtue glory, and good fortune." Sir Walter Raleigh

"There is a universal balance throughout nature, and everything finds its level. There is order where there appears disorder, and no stream runs in one direction, without a counter stream to restore the equilibrium." Frederick Marryatt

"Every governmental institution has been a standing testimony to the harmonic destiny of society, a standing proof that the life of man is destined for peace and amity, instead of disorder and contention." Henry James

"Many physical disorders stems from negative thinking." Pam Malow-Isham

Questions
How does disorder make me feel? Do I put up with the disorder in my home? What is the best way for me to address any disorder in my life?

Declarations

I eradicate **disorder** in my house by daily picking up after myself and putting things where they belong. I take care of my mail as soon as it comes in, so I don't accumulate piles of **disorder**. I leave things better than I find it. I consistently finish every undertaking I start.

I am whole and complete just because I say so. I give myself a break when I am too busy to deal with **disorder** and realize it will get done eventually. What I say is sacred, so I forgive myself for the **disorder** I have caused. I refuse to feel guilty about my **disorderly** mess.

I forgive my messy friends when they are **disorderly**. I poke fun at our **disorderliness**. We strengthen our relationship because of our tolerance, and acceptance. I am empathetic with **disorderly** people. I maintain my joy in the midst of **disorder** by keeping my peace.

I am led forth in peace and joy as I follow God's plan for my life. I am open to alternatives to help me fix any **disorder** in my life. I stand for what is right as I give my attention to the areas that bear fruit. I smile even though my world is **disorderly**, and not perfect.

I place a high value on myself because I make wise choices. I release my genius by dispensing of any **disorder**. I give my negative, **disorderly** thoughts over to God. I banish **disorder** as I take the time to reevaluate, and reset my goals several times each year. God helps me despite my **disorder**, so I plunge ahead. I am unstoppable.

Disorder and clutter are afraid of me. I have the authority to take charge of my life, and I like it. Even when I mess up, I spring into action to remove any **disorder**. I admit when I need a hand with the **disorder**. I don't take casually the things I need to take care of, so I act. I am thankful for the freedom to be who God called me to be.

143:
Promise
May 22

Bible Verses
"For the promise is for you and for your children, and for all who are far off, as many as the Lord our God will call." Acts 2:39 (HCSB)

"And this is the promise that He Himself made to us: eternal life." 1 John 2:25 (HCSB)

Word of the Day
Promise – A guarantee of your word. An earnest pledge. Contract. A strong hope or possibility for good to come about.

Quotes
"God never made a promise that was too good to be true." Unknown

"God made promises, not metaphors, so we can claim them." Pam Malow-Isham

"Our Lord has written the promise of resurrection, not in books alone, but in every leaf in springtime." Martin Luther

Pam's Perspective
I had so many promises broken as a kid; I had a hard time believing anyone. I am amazed how many people make a promise to do something, and then don't keep their word, like it doesn't matter. It does matter, because if you can't keep your word, no one will respect, or believe you, and it will be your own fault.

Questions
Have I ever make a promise, knowing I could not keep it? Do I avoid making promises to avoid responsibility? What promise will I keep today?

Declarations

I look at my schedule to see if I can realistically make a **promise** first before I commit. I value myself. I follow through on my **promises,** so I keep my self-respect and build my confidence. My friends know I value them. I communicate that by keeping the **promises**, I make.

I value my own word and keep my **promises**. I am a guardian of my **promises**, so I make sure I am able to keep it. That way I don't disrespect them or myself. I honor people, so I don't put other things ahead of the **promises** I have made to them. I can be trusted.

Little **promises** are just as important as the big ones. I am clear on the expectations of my **promises**, on the results I am to deliver, and actions I am to take. I set a firm deadline to when my **promise** will be fulfilled. I like being accountable and keeping my **promises**.

I recommit to disregarded **promises**. I am a super dependable person who has a brain for business. I follow through on the **promises** I make no matter how hard they are to complete.

I get all my business agreements and **promises** in writing, so there are no misinterpretations of what is expected from either party. I hold people liable for the **promises** they make to me. Because I am thoughtful, I maintain eye contact when talking with someone.

I **promise** to be honest with myself. When I see that I cannot keep a **promise**, I immediately contact the person and let them know what has happened, and why. People respect my humanity.

God has made 7,000 **promises** in His word, and it is up to me to claim them. God always keeps His **promises**. God's **promises** are carried out through me because I believe. I am **promise** defender.

144:
Surprise
May 23

Bible Verses
"Look among the nations, and see! Be surprised and full of wonder! For I am doing something in your days that you would not believe if you were told." Habakkuk 1:5 (NLV)

"Do not be surprised, my brothers and sisters, if the world hates you." 1 John 3:13 (NIV)

Word of the Day
Surprise – An unanticipated event. A startling occurrence. To be amazed.

Quotes
"Novelty, surprise, change of scene, refresh the artist, - "break up the tiresome old roof of heaven into new forms." Ralph Waldo Emerson

"A sudden, bold, and unexpected question, doth many times surprise a man, and lay him open." Francis Bacon

"Expect nothing at all and accept as a joyful surprise whatever good you find in matrimony." Mrs. Frank Leslie

Pam's Perspective
My biggest surprise and mystery is why everybody doesn't love me. I think I am marvelous! People who I want to love and help, ignore me or refuse my help. I can't change them, but I can pray for them. One day, they might like me, or not.

Questions
What is a surprise that my mate would love that I could give? How do I react to surprises? How will I surprise myself with my accomplishments?

Declarations

Cheerful **surprises** appear before me as I smile throughout my day. I love **surprises**. I **surprise** myself with how much I get done once I set my intentions, and get to work. I have unlimited potential, and today is a great day to release it. I am **surprised** that not everyone looks for the positive when that is the happiest, easiest way to live.

Everywhere I look is a new **surprise**, if I just take the time to look. God **surprises** me with new mercies and favors every day. I am eager and open to the next happy **surprise** that is on the way.

I **surprise** people who have hurt me with forgiveness. God has been merciful to me, so I show mercy and forgiveness, just because I can. **Surprisingly**, nothing anyone can do will steal my joy. I **surprise** people with my happiness, and my ability to come through every challenge. I am a delightful **surprise** when I show up.

My faith gains momentum as I have the courage to believe, and create based on my word alone. I am happy because I say I am. I **surprise** myself with creativity and cleverness. The **surprise** of love and kindness directed at me from above overwhelms me. I go out in the sunshine and get **surprised** by the beauty right around me.

Surprised by additional compensation is a regular occurrence because of my fabulous abilities. I focus on advancement. I am outrageously **surprised** at the connections I make. I meet the wisest people as my network of friends continues to increase.

I **surprise** my mate with unexpected kisses. I **surprise** my friends with smiles and gifts. I remember to play like a kid. People are **surprised** at my ability to find amusement in the littlest of things. I **surprise** a waitress by my generous tip and make his or her day.

145:
Mind
May 24

Bible Verses

"I keep the Lord in mind always. Because He is at my right hand, I will not be shaken." Psalm 16:8 (HCSB)

"For who has known the Lord's mind, that he may instruct Him? But we have the mind of Christ." 1 Corinthians 2:16 (HCSB)

Word of the Day

Mind – The unseen part of the brain by which thoughts, perception, intellect, judgment, and imagination comes from.

Quotes

"When you begin to THINK AND GROW RICH, you will observe that riches begin with a state of mind, with definiteness of purpose, with little or no hard work." Napoleon Hill

"The face is the mirror of the mind, and eyes without speaking confess the secrets of the heart." St. Jerome

"Where the mind goes, the man follows." Joyce Meyer

Pam's Perspective

My mind is my most important asset. It is up to me to program and manage it, for it is where I derive all my pleasure, peace, and contentment from. I am the ruler of my mind, and I choose not to let the chaos of the world to upset me.

Questions

What do I allow my mind to dwell on? Am I conscious of what I am thinking? What is the best way for me to train my mind today?

Declarations

God has given me a brilliant **mind**. I enhance my **mind** by learning new subjects. I get excited about all the new avenues that are opening up for me. I like to read biographies about great people. I tell my **mind** how I am going to act today. I tell my **mind** to be thoughtful and respectful, one hundred percent of the time.

I expect to receive the revelation of God in my **mind**. I preoccupy my **mind** with the Word of God. I tune into God as I pursue wisdom. I think like Christ and set my **mind** on what is above. God has given me an observant **mind** that is sound, full of wisdom, wonder, and creativity. I use the power of my **mind** to think my way to success. I have a genius **mind,** and I get wiser every day.

I open my **mind** to new ideas, knowledge, and insights. I exercise my **mind** by doing brain games of all kinds. Playing games is fun. I am always up for a challenge, and the ability to expand my **mind** and thinking skills. I exercise my **mind** and my body every day.

I keep my **mind** healthy and focused on what is good. I have a clever **mind**. I take responsibility for the words that come out of my mouth. I keep my **mind** sharp, watch what I say, and think before I respond. My words are powerfully pleasant, sweet, and refreshing.

I face what I need to face, head on, and tackle it with ease until it is resolved. I am alert and radiant. I fill my **mind** with thoughts of passion, plenty, purity, peace, potential, purpose, and possibility.

I have a creative **mind** that finds new ways to have fun and laugh every day. I am cloaked with gladness as I cultivate curiosity and wonder. I remember to take myself lightly. My **mind** embraces new experiences with glee. I have a good **mind,** and I think for myself.

146:
Realities
May 25

Bible Verses
"This is what we speak, not in words taught us by human wisdom but in words taught by the Spirit, explaining spiritual realities with Spirit-taught words." 1 Corinthians 2:13 (NIV)

"The One who testifies to these realities makes this promise: The Anointed One: Yes. I am coming soon. To which we say, 'Amen. Come, Lord Jesus.'" Revelation 22:20 (VOICE)

Word of the Day
Realities – Facts. The way things are. Living in the real world. Genuine.

Quotes
"The greatest achievement was at first and for a time a dream. The oak sleeps in the acorn, the bird waits in the egg, and the highest vision of the soul a waking angel stirs. Dreams are the seedlings of realities." James Allen

"You can create realities that are peaceful, abundant and happy just by practicing being that way every morning. Repetition works wonders." Pam Malow-Isham

"Show is not substance; realities govern wise men." William Penn

Pam's Perspective
I lived in a dismal reality before I came to know the love of Christ. I was fearful, hurting and melancholy. Experiencing unconditional love freed my spirit.

Questions
Am I happy with the realities I have created thus far in my life? Why or why not? Am I going to create any new realities this year?

Declarations

I wake up full of enthusiasm for the day ahead of me. My powerful conversations predict my marvelous **realities**. I listen, so people feel heard, and understood. Because I have a philosophy of winning, my **reality** is I win. I have the heart of a lion. I am intense and vibrant.

I set up my **realities** of success. I generate good emotions. I like being happy. I believe I can create the life I desire, so I go forward with speedy actions, doing just that. The way I live says more than the things I say, so I build integrity and hard work into my **realities**.

God is in motion in my life designing **realities** that prosper me and work out in my favor. I participate with gladness in co-creating a loving **reality**. I express my beliefs with my words and deeds. I balance my spiritual, emotional, physical, and mental **realities**.

I have the fantastic **realities** I envision. I love by choice. I trust God's kindness to shine on me and illuminate my **reality**. I have the keys to the vault of abundance, and I open the door of prosperity now. I have elegant furnishings in my home. My house and car are paid off in full. I provide my family with a nice place to live.

I have intelligent values. My **realities** of health, fitness, and mental stamina are advantageous to feeling great. I radiate peace in my body and get in perfect shape. My heart and lungs are healthy. I eat good food and pick the healthiest snacks when given a choice. My **reality** of emitting good vibes brings about positive emotions.

I love the **reality** of growing networks of positive people to associate with. I am radically good to the people around me, generating the **reality** of an abundance of friends. I think about what will make the most difference for the people around me, and then act on it.

147:
Triumph
May 26

Bible Verses

"Yes, the Lord is for me; he will help me. I will look in triumph at those who hate me." Psalm 118:7 (NLT)

"But thanks be to God, who always leads us in triumph in Christ, and through us spreads and makes evident everywhere the sweet fragrance of the knowledge of Him." 2 Corinthians 2:14 (AMP)

Word of the Day

Triumph – Extreme jubilation because of one's achievement. Conquer.

Quotes

"Give pleasure. Lose no chance in giving pleasure. For that is the ceaseless and anonymous triumph of a truly loving spirit." Henry Drummond

"The harder the conflict, the more glorious the triumph." Thomas Paine

"Every great and commanding moment in the annals of the world is the triumph of some enthusiasm." Ralph Waldo Emerson

"Brave men rejoice in adversity, just as brave soldiers triumph in war." Seneca

Pam's Perspective

I have triumphed over depression, addiction, and poverty because I have been diligent with persistently reprograming my mind with positive thoughts.

Questions

Do I treat myself well when I triumph? Do I share my triumphs with my buddies? Why will I triumph today in all my endeavors?

Declarations

I have been created to **triumph** over anything and everything that comes my way. I am the designer of my destiny. I remember past **triumphs** and realize I can do it again. I am up to any test that comes my way. No matter how many times I fall, I rise **triumphant**.

Today I feel more **triumphant** and prepared because I have done what is on hand to do. I am a professional. I polish my people skills and broaden my circle of friends. I get the job done with excellence, and on time. I am an enthusiastic mentor. I declare my victory every day. My ideas spark **triumph**. I am in tune with the positive. I enrich people around me by encouraging them to take **triumphant** steps.

I warrant my **triumph** by the thoughts I think, the words I speak, and what I do. I step into a state of empowerment by thinking enthusiastic, **triumphant** thoughts. I affirm **triumph** in my daily life. I think about who I am going to be in order to be **triumphant** and become that person. I have a say in my **triumphant** experience.

My colleagues celebrate with me over my latest **triumph**. I get the applause. We like to help each other out. I delegate readily and follow up consistently. I am grateful for the car I have, as my dream car gets closer to manifesting. I am **triumphant** at managing money.

I **triumph** in the face of adversity. I take actions to make a difference. I come from a **triumphant** stance. I feel my power growing with every **triumphant** thought. I am **triumphant** and full of strength.

I **triumph** over my insecurity as I receive boldness from God. My loving father likes to see my **triumph**. I am always **triumphant** because I serve a **triumphant** God. I have allowed God to lead my steps. There is nothing too big that God and I can't **triumph** over.

148:
Defeat
May 27

Bible Verses

"The Lord saved me from death; he stopped my tears and kept me from defeat." Psalm 116:8 (GNT)

"For every child of God defeats this evil world, and we achieve this victory through our faith." 1 John 5:4 (NLT)

Word of the Day

Defeat – To conquer a thing or person. Unsuccessful. A Setback.

Quotes

"The general of a large army may be defeated, but you cannot defeat the determined will of a peasant." Confucius

"Not in the clamor of the crowded street, not in the shouts and plaudits of the throng, but in ourselves, are triumph and defeat." Henry Wadsworth Longfellow

"The defenders of slavery had sown the seeds of their own defeat. They dug the pit in which they fell." Robert Green Ingersoll

Pam's Perspective

I tried to defeat someone that was bent on making my life unhappy. The angrier I got, the worse it got. But when I let the anger go, and didn't let it bother me, the person became disinterested and stopped. I defeat the hatemongers with love. I smile, help, and hug the person who at times, I would like to punch.

Questions

Have I let past defeats affect my well-being or my current state? What is the biggest thing I have defeated? What will I defeat today?

Declarations

I am enthusiastic about life. I know there is nothing that can **defeat** God; therefore, there isn't anything that can **defeat** me. I laugh in the face of **defeat**. The smart choices I make today get me what I want.

I enjoy having a warm and trustworthy telephone manner. I **defeat** every objection by finding out what is their wrong core assumption. **Defeat** works in my favor and can be easily reversed. I am a value to the marketplace because I have survived **defeat**. I'm incredible!

I vault my company to new levels of performance and blow the competition away. I **defeat** every obstacle that comes my way. I differentiate myself by the value I bring, and the results I produce. I learn new insights and better ways to perform from every **defeat**.

I am thankful for previous **defeats**, and all the knowledge I have learned from them. I have a posture of strength and victory. I drink extra water to **defeat** sugar cravings and hunger pangs. I **defeat** lethargy by staying active and keeping fit. I control what I do.

I venture on with a grin in the face of possible **defeat**. I expand and enlarge my life. I am **defeat** resistant. I immediately **defeat** any negative thought with a positive one. God's love spills over in all areas of my life **defeating** negativity. I latch onto every promise God has for me. I always have a seat at the Kings table. He knows me by name and smiles when He thinks about me, despite my **defeats**.

I give myself permission to recover from my past **defeats** by creating a compelling vision of the fabulous future that I can live into. I am aware of my intuitive thoughts that bring about my highest good. I have an inner feeling of self-worth and value. Making mistakes does not **defeat** me because I change for the better. I am **defeat** proof.

149:
Worry
May 28

Bible Verses
"But whoever listens to me will live without worry and will be free from the dread of disaster." Proverbs 1:33 (GW)

"Don't concern yourself about what you will eat or drink, and quit worrying about these things." Luke 12:29 (GW)

Word of the Day
Worry – To contemplate over uncertain things that could happen but probably will not. To fear the future. To doubt God.

Quotes
"You can never worry your way to enlightenment." Terri Guillemets

"There are two days of the week upon which and about which I never worry. One of these days is yesterday: yesterday with all its cares and frets, with all its pains and aches... And the other day I do not worry about is tomorrow... Its sun will rise in roseate splendor, or behind the mask of weeping clouds, but it will rise. Until then the same love and patience that hold yesterday and hold tomorrow, shine with tender promise into the heart of today." Robert Jones Burdette

Pam's Perspective
Worry consumed me for years until I started the let go, let God, game. I take my worry, let God have it, and go about having a great day. After all, He is God and can handle any worry that I could ever come up with. So I release it and go free.

Questions
How has worry impacted me? What has worry cost me? Do I worry more than I trust? Have I allowed worry to affect me? Can I live worry-free?

Declarations

I turn my **worry** over to God as I place this day in His hands. This is a new day with unlimited possibilities. I set my intentions, and leave **worry** behind. I take a quantum leap towards my goals and get more done, because I have pushed **worry** aside, and made room for fun.

There is nothing to fear or **worry** about, so I move ahead with joy. It is nice to know that I have plenty of time to get everything done that I need to get done. I cultivate positive relationships that benefit both parties. My friends remind me that **worry** is a waste of time.

I know words that create disharmony and doubt, leave me confused and filled with **worry,** so I leave them out of my vocabulary. I am healed and restored as I speak words that produce the good life. I neutralize any **worry** by speaking God's word over my life.

I can be counted on to get rid of **worry**. I go for a walk with a friend, and our **worries** evaporate. I have an uplifting mindset. I am aware of who makes me happy, and who doesn't. I don't **worry** about what other people say about me because I am OK. I stay in touch with my mentors, and visionaries who inspire me to live a **worry**-free life.

My emotional responses come from a calm, **worry**-free mind. It is automatic for me to be thankful. I craft the results of a prosperous, happy future where things go my way. I rain optimism on the **worry** parade with my mental resilience. Receiving favor is normal for me.

I make a checklist, so I don't have to **worry** about what I need to get done. Then I feel motivated when I check things off my list. I practice positive self-care by getting a massage and leaving all my **worries** on the table. As I meditate, I turn all my **worry** over to God. I affirm the presence of peace resides in me, and I am **worry** free.

150:
Calmness
May 29

Bible Verses

"By long forbearance and calmness of spirit a judge or ruler is persuaded, and soft speech breaks down the most bonelike resistance." Proverbs 25:15 (AMP)

"For this is what Adonai Elohim, the Holy One of Isra'el, says: 'Returning and resting is what will save you; calmness and confidence will make you strong — but you want none of this!'" Isaiah 30:15 (CJB)

Word of the Day

Calmness – The state of being calm and peaceful. Tranquility.

Quotes

"Ye do well to remember that habitual affectionate communion with God, asking Him for all good which is needed, praising Him for all that is received, and trusting Him for future supplies, prevents anxious cares, inspires peace, calmness, and composure, and furnishes a delight surpassing all finite comprehension." James H. Aughey

"Calmness stems from a peaceful center." Pam Malow-Isham

"Calmness is not always the attribute of innocence." Lord Byron

"Avoid all haste; calmness is an essential ingredient of politeness." Alphonse Karr

"Power is so characteristically calm, that calmness in itself has the aspect of power, and forbearance implies strength." Edward G. Bulwer-Lytton

Questions

What areas of my life do I need calmness? Do people relate to me as a calm person? How can I cultivate more calmness in my life?

Declarations

There is a **calmness** about me that comes from the Lord. Nothing can phase my **calm** center. I have a **calm** mind because I take the time to meditate. I fill my day with **calmness** and joy. I care about people, and they feel it, by the **calmness** of my speech. My love and **calmness** help ease the pain of a worried friend or family member.

I gather up information and make well-informed decisions on living healthy. My health is my responsibility, so I stay **calm**. I actively participate in the healing process by incorporating **calmness** and love into my day. I have **calmness** of spirit as I walk in humility.

I am familiar with how **calmness** helps me stay grounded. I stay **calm** while revealing my feelings to my family, even when things don't go my way. With **calmness**, I defuse every tense situation.

I am great at getting things done in a **calm** manner. With **calmness**, I envision my goals realized. I am adept at persuading others to accept my ideas. It is sensible to stay **calm** while investing in my future. By **calmness**, I fill myself with an awareness of abundance.

I affirm my goals each day in **calmness**, knowing they are coming to pass at just the right time. I am cleared for greatness. I have a healthy **calm** mind. With **calmness**, I have confidence that I will be able to figure out any problem that comes my way. I feel **calm** and safe. Now is the time for me to demonstrate my divine legacy.

I encourage **calmness** in my home. I pray for my enemies and send **calmness** their way. My **calmness** makes me a better listener, kinder, and more tolerant. I act lovingly and remember to forgive myself when I am not **calm**. I grow sweeter every day. I continue to improve my ability to stay **calm** and peaceful in this hectic world.

151:
Perspective
May 30

Bible Verses
"*Look up, and be alert to what is going on around Christ—that's where the action is. See things from his perspective.*" Colossians 3:2 (MSG)

"*Now you are coming to him as to a living stone. Even though this stone was rejected by humans, from God's perspective it is chosen, valuable.*" 1 Peter 2:4 (CEB)

Word of the Day
Perspective – How someone chooses to see things. Viewpoint or mindset.

Quotes
"*My perspective causes me pain or pleasure, depending on how I chose to perceive events or someone's actions. Changing your perspective changes everything. If we take the time to see things from the other person's perspective, empathy will arise, and our judgments will diminish. From God's perspective, everyone is lovable.*" Pam Malow-Isham

"*Meditation is the soul's perspective glass, whereby, in her long remove, she discerneth God, as if He were nearer at hand.*" Owen Feltham

"*Our senses deceive us; we begin life with delusion. Our senses deceive us with respect to distance, shape, and color. That which afar off seems oval turns out to be circular, modified by the perspective of distance; That which appears a speck, upon near approach becomes a vast body. To the earlier ages, the stars presented the delusion of small lamps hung in space.*" Frederick William Robertson

Questions
Why is my perspective so important to my positive outcome? What is my perspective on my health? My social life? My spiritual life? My finances?

Declarations

Looking at people from God's **perspective**, I see them through eyes of love. I am intoxicated with joy as I happily share God's love to the world with my positive **perspective**. I grin for no reason at all.

I think about my **perspectives**, and how I came to believe in them. I am honest about my **perspectives**, and how they define my life. I gravitate toward people with a good attitude. I realize that some people have had a negative impact on my **perspective**, and some a positive. I have learned from them both and will continue to grow.

I ask others what their **perspective** is, and listen graciously. It is OK to shift my mind if I find new information that makes more sense. It is good to challenge my **perspectives**, and reevaluate what I believe.

When I have the **perspective** that I don't like something in someone, I need to take a step back and look at myself. Often, it is something in me that I have not yet dealt with. I release the need for judgment.

I remember to have a caring, and generous **perspective**. My life dramatically changes, as I show support and love to the people around me. They feel uplifted, and so do I. My friendly **perspective** looks for more opportunities to bless those who cross my path.

When I see things from another person's **perspective**, it is amazing how many times mine changes. Everyone has issues they are dealing with. Both of our **perspectives** are valuable and worth listening too. Having a **perspective** of accepting our humanity is beneficial.

I appreciate my extraordinary ability to see the sunny **perspective** of every situation. I walk in streams of plenty as I live in the light of the Lord. I am thankful for each and every gift I freely receive.

152:
Optimism
May 31

Bible Verses

"The Lord is my strength and my shield; my heart trusts in him, and I am helped. My heart leaps for joy, and I will give thanks to him in song." Psalm 28:7 (NIV)

"Know this—I am most emphatic here, friends—this great Message I delivered to you is not mere human optimism. I didn't receive it through the traditions, and I wasn't taught it in some school. I got it straight from God, received the Message directly from Jesus Christ." Galatians 1:11-12 (MSG)

Word of the Day

Optimism – Having a positive point of view. Confident idealism. Happy.

Quotes

"It is the hopeful, buoyant, cheerful attitude of mind that wins. Optimism is a success builder; pessimism an achievement killer." Orison Swett Marden

"When I look in the glass I see that every line in my face means pessimism, but in spite of my face – that is my experience – I remain an optimist." Richard Jefferies

"Optimism – the doctrine or belief that everything is beautiful, including what is ugly." Ambrose Bierce

Pam's Perspective

At seventeen I was given the Optimist Creed, the poem, Promise Yourself, by Christian D. Larson. I loved it, and continue to live by it still today.

Questions

Is optimism my first choice on how I respond? How is optimism enhancing my life? Why do I make optimism a priority in my life?

Declarations

I choose to look at the world through the illumination of **optimism**. In the morning, I awake feeling **optimistic** and remind myself of the many blessings I have. I **optimistically** expect miracles today. I am a joy to be around because I am genuinely grateful, and **optimistic**.

Optimism is the way to health and happiness. My mental habit of **optimism** energizes my mind, body, and spirit. I am thankful for the setbacks I have had, for they allow me to appreciate the good times even more. I am driven to improve myself as I focus on **optimism**.

I affirm out load my goals each day to remind myself of where I am going, and why. My **optimistic** declarations keep me feeling happy, motivated, and raring to go. I always look at what's right in my life.

Although I believe for an **optimistic** future, I turn the outcome over to God and trust that He has my best interest in mind. I balance my **optimism** with reality, so I calculate the risks and make sound decisions. I am sensible, objective, and keep a close grip on reality.

It is normal for me to think negative, and **optimistic** thoughts. I accept that I am human, and deal with my problems head-on. I impact the thoughts of others with my **optimism**. When I consider the possibility of being negative, or **optimistic**, **optimism** wins every time. I am a light to the world when I am kind and **optimistic**.

I am unique, **optimistic**, and think outside of the box. I shape my environment for good. Positive things always happen to me. My joyful energy is welcoming. I love allowing my **optimism** to operate freely as I make service a methodical part of my life. My **optimistic** long-term thinking inspires generations to come. My **optimism** pay's it forward. I am **optimistic**, happy, and enthusiastic by design.

153:
Begin
June 1

Bible Verses
"Leave your simple ways behind, and begin to live; learn to use good judgment." Proverbs 9:6 (NLT)

"Great is his faithfulness; his mercies begin afresh each morning." Lamentations 3:23 (NLT)

Word of the Day
Begin – To take a first step toward the desired goal. Spring forth. Initiate.

Quotes
"Always begin with love. You'll never go wrong. Your communication will be filled with grace and compassion and kindness. Think this is a tough one? Okay, then imagine that everyone you meet will be dead the next day. That will change the way you look at them. And, you'll feel a shift take place in your heart. Communicate from THAT place." Mary Jane Mapes

"Where self ends, God begins." Rebecca Barlow Jordan

"It is easier not to begin to go wrong than it is to turn back and do better after beginning." President James Garfield

Pam's Perspective
When I began speaking great declarations over my life, I didn't believe what I was saying. But with repetition and conviction, I began to see it was working. My transformation has been slow, steady, amazing, and totally worth it.

Questions
Is there a project that I need to begin? What new habit will I begin today?

Declarations

I **begin** smiling as soon as I wake up. I **begin** each day by saying thank you God for your mercy that **begins** anew each morning. When I **begin** my morning with prayer, it goes very well. I **begin** to trust God for aid and watch Him come through. I **begin** acting like I believe God will answer my prayers. I **begin** now to be Spirit-led.

I **begin** every endeavor with a positive attitude and joyful expectancy. I feel God's guidance **beginning** to bubble up inside, showing me the loving way to act. As I **begin** to listen to the voice of God and step out in faith, His words **begin** to become crystal clear. I will accomplish my work not by my power, but by His Spirit.

I can **begin** today to create something rich, and beautiful. I **begin** giving love, money, help, encouragement, support, inspiration, good deeds, and hugs before I need them. I **begin** saving money, so I always feel rich. I am conscious of my saving, and spending habits.

My future is bright and exploding with possibilities. I **begin** each project on a positive note. I **begin** on time. I don't have to know how I will accomplish a goal, or finance it, I just have to **begin**, and the wherewithal will come at just the right time. It always does.

I **begin** to decide what I want, write it down, and then take action. New ideas come as I **begin** to write. I remember why I am going where I am going. I finish what I **begin**. I see solutions as I **begin** to face problems. I **begin** enjoying every moment from here on out.

Because I **begin** acting like the person I would like to become, before long, I am that person. I **begin** changing myself to be the best I can possibly be so people will want to follow my example. I **begin** now to hold myself to a higher standard and go the extra mile.

154:
End
June 2

Bible Verses

"And though you started with little, you will end with much." Job 8:7 (NLT)

"But in the end, the holy people of the Most High will be given the kingdom, and they will rule forever and ever." Daniel 7:18 (NLT)

Word of the Day

End – The stopping point. To finish. Cease. Halt. Demise. To break off.

Quotes

"The end of law is not to abolish or restrain, but to preserve and enlarge freedom. For in all the states of created beings, capable of laws, where there is no law, there is no freedom." John Locke

"To contemplation's sober eye, such is the race of man, and they that creep, and they that fly, shall end where they began." Thomas Gray – Ode on the Spring

Pam's Perspective

I had a dog named Happy. When it was time to end her life it was very difficult because she had a rash, was filled with big tumors, and I couldn't stand to see her suffer any longer. I had rescued her from the shelter. She had been abused, but the time spent with us to the end of her life was filled with lots of love. I can relate to Happy. The first part of my life was afflicted, but now I feel lots of love and know I will have lived a positive life, dedicated to service, and helping people to the end.

Questions

What is the best way for me to end my workday? What is the best way for me to end a conversation? Am I prepared for death? How do I want people to think about me in the end? Will I end with regrets or smiling?

Declarations

At the **end** of the day, I write in my gratitude journal. I am thankful for many things. Somehow, things always work out for me in the **end**. God is with me to the **end,** guiding me every step of the way. I feel secure in God as I immerse myself in His wisdom. Because I reach out to help people around me, I **end** up being blessed myself.

I rejoice for I will win in the **end**. I choose to challenge myself to create the best life, instead of just **ending** up with a mediocre life. I **end** the negative chatter in my head by daily declaring positive affirmations over my life. My thoughts and actions **end** up partnering together, so I **end** up with a beautiful masterpiece.

If someone is complaining, I **end** up turning the conversation to something positive. I am a game changer. I ask questions so that people **end** up talking about themselves. I love to listen. I **end** conversations with family and friends with, "I love you."

At the **end** of a job interview, I lay the groundwork for follow up. I ask how I did. Then I ask to be moved to the head of the line. I stand out. I push through to the **end**, seeing my glorious outcome surpass everyone's expectations. I **end** each sale with a thank you. At the **end** of a project, I celebrate my victory. My dreams **end** fulfilled.

I **end** things that are unproductive and do things that move me toward my goals. I plan for success, and **end** up on top. God promotes me at the perfect time, and I **end** up in the winner's circle.

I breakthrough and **end** every hindrance that could get in my way of success. I put an **end** to procrastination, and always do what I need to do when I need to do it. I live each day to the fullest, so at the **end** of my life, I can leave a legacy of good works, with no regrets.

155:
Seek
June 3

Bible Verses
"But seek first the kingdom of God and His righteousness, and all these things shall be added to you." Matthew 6:33 (NKJV)

"For everyone who asks receives, and he who seeks finds, and to him who knocks it will be opened." Matthew 7:8 (NASB)

Word of the Day
Seek – To look about carefully. Investigate diligently. Petition.

Quotes
"The fountain of content must spring up in the mind, and he who has so little knowledge of human nature as to seek happiness by changing anything but his own disposition will waste his life in fruitless efforts." Samuel Johnson

"Joy has not cost. Do what you love. Do what makes your heart sing. And never do it for the money. Don't go to work to make money; go to work to spread joy. Seek ye first the kingdom of Heaven, and the Maserati will get here when it's supposed to." Marianne Williamson

"A great man does not seek applause or place; he seeks for truth; he seeks the road to happiness, and what he ascertains, he gives to others." Robert Green Ingersoll

"When you seek to give more compliments and praise than you obtain, bright will be your countenance, and joy will fill your day." Pam Malow-Isham

Questions
What am I seeking for? How will I know when I find it? Is what I'm seeking lining up with my values? Why do I seek to learn more today?

Declarations

I **seek** to show, and share the love I have received. I **seek** and share what is good, to encourage a happy and healthy life. It feels absolutely fabulous knowing I am free from condemnation. I do not have to **seek** approval from God because He freely accepts me.

Love permeates my whole being. I **seek** to live my life like I believe God really loves me. God wants to infuse me with joy. When I **seek** Him, I burst out with the joy of the Lord, and boy do I feel great!

I **seek** out opportunities to bless people. God's favor rests upon me to serve those close at hand. I **seek** to reciprocate good deeds. I reap a great harvest of friends as I go about **seeking** to help those around me. Being kind comes naturally to me, and I love the way it makes me feel. I **seek** out the richness of loving, warm companions.

Because I **seek** to get clarity on my goals, I zoom in and get them done super-fast. Achieving excellence is how I operate. I congratulate myself for **seeking** to work on a specific goal, a little each day. I maintain persistence, with follow-through, as I **seek** to fulfill my goals. I **seek** to do my best, give my best, and be my best.

I **seek** out a prosperous life. I add Miracle Grow to my bank account and watch it bloom in abundance. I notice all the support I have around me. I tap into my inner strength and accomplish amazing things. I **seek** to find good in every endeavor I experience.

I face myself squarely and **seek** to deal with the good, bad, and ugly. I **seek** to accept myself just the way I am. I am uniquely wonderful. I **seek** to keep learning, loving and laughing. I **seek** to live in the real world. I **seek** to get over myself and become more authentic. I **seek** to surround myself with smart people. I **seek** the truth and find it.

156:
Find
June 4

Bible Verses

"So shalt thou find favour and good understanding in the sight of God and man." Proverbs 3:4 (KJV)

"I love those loving me, and those seeking me earnestly do find me." Proverbs 8:17 (YLT)

Word of the Day

Find – To attain what you are looking for. To get what you want. Attain.

Quotes

"Pleasure is spread through the earth in stray gifts, to be claimed by whoever shall find." William Wordsworth

"You cannot teach a man anything; you can only help him find it within himself." Galileo Galilei

"All we want in Christ we shall find in Christ. If we want little, we shall find little. If we want much we shall find much; and if in utter helplessness we cast our all on Christ, He will be to us the whole treasury of God." Bishop H. Whipple

Pam's Perspective

In August of eighty-nine, I went to Phoenix AZ to find the will of God for my life. I got up early, climbed a mountain, watched the sunrise, prayed, and heard nothing. I was disappointed. But I did find as I went home and back to work, that God was with me all along. I didn't need a mountaintop experience to find God.

Questions

What good can I find to do today? How will I find myself next year?

Declarations

By reprogramming my conscious mind, I **find** golden nuggets of wisdom from the great things I read. I **find** time for the things that are really important to me. I **find** that the mindset of optimism is the best way to live. I am crystal clear about what I want, so I **find** it.

I can identify, and **find** many of the reasons for any illnesses. I can **find** ways for my body to heal. I **find** the more I move, the more energy I have. Exercise is normal, natural, and fun. I **find** I enjoy the process of making sound decisions, and creating healthy habits.

I **find** stray tokens of pleasure whenever I stop to enjoy them. I **find** that even on the rotten days, I can choose to be at peace, or suffer in misery. I **find** am sensitive to how I view the world. I am happy to **find** I have a choice in enhancing my well-being. I choose to **find** joy in the little things. I appreciate this wonderful experience of life.

I **find** self-competition is the best way for me to spur myself on. I stay in an open state of mind. By shedding any limiting beliefs, I **find** clarity of purpose. I like **finding** stability and being honest.

I first **find** ways I can be of service before asking to be served. I **find** activities that I am passionate about where I can be of assistance. I **find** ways to love the unlovable. I **find** it delightful to learn new things. I **find** life worth living. I **find** positive people to be around who encourage me to be my best. I **find** new friends wherever I go.

I **find** nothing is too big for God in whom I **find** my strength. I **find** the more thankful I am, the more I have to be thankful for. I **find** it easy to laugh and have fun. I **find** that God can use me when I am willing. I **find** I am a work in progress. I **find** acceptance within and feel the seal of approval from God's throne. I feel worthy and loved.

157:
Obstacle
June 5

Bible Verses

"So get going. And as you go, know this: with integrity you will overcome all obstacles; even if you run, you will not stumble." Proverbs 4:12 (VOICE)

"He reveals profound mysteries beyond man's understanding. He knows all hidden things, for he is light, and darkness is no obstacle to him." Daniel 2:22 (TLB)

Word of the Day

Obstacle – A bump in the road or a stumbling block. A blockage.

Quote

"Obstacles cause growth, and show what you are made of." Pam Malow-Isham

Pam's Perspective

I had a cast on my leg in June of two-thousand when we took the kids to Toronto. While being loaded from a wheelchair to the bus, a driver jammed my left thumb backward. The next day at home I had an appointment with the orthopedic doctor for my leg. I showed him my thumb, and he cast my left arm. I cried. Being a massage therapist, I had to look for other work. I got a job through the census bureau until my casts were off, and I could massage again. I threw my right leg over on the passenger's seat and used my left leg to drive. I had a bag I with all the census material, and a walker I used to hop up people's stairs. I didn't let an obstacle like a cast on my left arm and right leg stop me from supporting myself.

Questions

What is the biggest obstacle I face today? How do I react when obstacles arise? How do I view obstacles? Is that view serving me? If not, why not? How can I take the next obstacle, and turn it into a success story?

Declarations

I enjoy meeting new friends as I travel around the world. My smile breaks down any language **obstacles** that could occur. I love a good challenge. I confront every **obstacle** by the power of the Holy Spirit. Color, ethnicity, or religious differences are no **obstacle** to love.

I see every **obstacle** as the ability to improve myself and grow stronger. I am fearless, refined, and polished. I am savvy about recognizing **obstacles** for what they are growth instruments. I have grit and stamina to overpower every **obstacle** and seize the day.

When I encounter an **obstacle**, I look within and see where I might have doubted myself. I then remember my past successes, and I encourage myself with positive declarations. By reframing my **obstacles**, I become more resilient. I am thankful for my powerful brain that is full of wisdom. I joyfully meet every **obstacle** head on.

Big **obstacles** are no big deal to me because my God is greater than any **obstacle**, and it is an easy fix for Him. I easily jump through hurdles, run through **obstacle** courses, and forge ahead gloriously. I dare to win today and kick every **obstacle** out of my way.

I am aware of my spiritual connection, and what causes me to sense inner peace, and happiness, despite insurmountable **obstacles**. I consistently move forward toward my target and overthrow every **obstacle**. When I connect to the Holy Spirit, **obstacles** vanish, and miracles show up. I create my best life ever, despite **obstacles.**

Since I know that **obstacles** are a part of life, I don't get upset when they do come along. They are just another tiny bump in the road as I drive down victory lane. I am more than a conqueror in this life. I gain experience and confidence with every **obstacle** I overcome.

158:
Path
June 6

Bible Verses
"Thy word is a lamp unto my feet, and a light unto my path." Psalm 119:105 (ASV)

"Consider well the path of your feet, and let all your ways be established and ordered a right." Proverbs 4:26 (AMP)

Word of the Day
Path – A direction to take. Walkway or passage. Trail. Roadway.

Quotes
"The path of precept is long, that of example short and effectual." Seneca

"Every closet has its mosquito; every gap has its bush, every bean has its black, every grain has its bran, every man has a fool in his sleeve, every path hath a puddle, every day hath its night, every light hath its shadow." Haitian Proverb

Pam's Perspective
I saw a contest, and I had a feeling if I entered it, I would win. So I did, and I won the opportunity to meet, and work with some really nice people. They paid my airfare, lodging, meals, gave me a stipend for the week, and some cool gear. I spent a week in July of two-thousand and thirteen cleaning up the Verde River in Arizona and creating paths for people to access the river with their kayaks. It was a lot of fun, and I would do it again if given a chance. Enhancing the environment wherever you are is always the right path to take.

Questions
Do I get excited in the morning about the path I am on? Is the path I am on right for me? If not, why not? Is there a new path I could take?

Declarations

I wake up motivated, ready to take on the world because I am on the right **path**. I do the things I love while taking the rare **path**. I miss the obstacles that lead me off my **path** by focusing on my objectives. I begin by tackling the difficult first in order to get it out of my way.

I breathe in the beauty all around me. I build my cardio endurance by doing 30 minutes of exercise daily, walking down the healthy **path**. I am grateful for my happy feet that carry me down the thanksgiving **path**. I always have time to stop and admire God's handiwork. My **path** to health is filled with joy and lots of action.

Earning money comes easily to me as I prance down the prosperity **path**. I am connected to the Source of all things. I feel on top of my game as I easily dissolve every hindrance that is in my **path**. Mercy follows me, and grace leads me on the **path** of righteousness.

I stroll down the **path** to my goals without apprehension. There is plenty of time to complete the **path** before me. My internal teacher shows me that the **path** of love, and acceptance, is the best **path**. I am on a pleasant **path** paved with peace, praise, and celebration.

I have the freedom to pursue right relationships with others on the kindness **path**. I am benevolent, and inviting on the unity **path** as I make new friends, and cherish old ones. Jesus guides my **path**. Even if I get scared, I do what feels right. I have an unshakable center.

God is in a good mood today, shining warmhearted affection on me, lighting my **path**. I take the initiative to study, decide what I believe, and what **path** to take. I awaken to faith in God as I stay open-minded on my **path** to wisdom. I am respectful of people's choices. I choose a good **path** that leads others to see their light within.

159:
Change
June 7

Bible Verses
"And he said: "I tell you the truth, unless you change and become like little children, you will never enter the kingdom of heaven." Matthew 18:3 (NIV)

"God never changes his mind when he gives gifts or when he calls someone." Romans 11:29 (GW)

Word of the Day
Change – To transform into something else. Switch or reversal. To switch around. Reverse.

Quotes
"There is no misfortune or unhappiness or ill luck we cannot change into some measure of success and contentment, by the force of thought and the persistency of faith in the goodness of God and the belief that we are God's heirs." Ella Wheeler Wilcox

"Everyone thinks of changing humanity, and nobody thinks of changing himself." Leo Tolstoy

"The universe is change; our life is what our thoughts make it." Marcus Aurelius

Pam's Perspective
With the constant change in the world around me, the only constant thing I have found is Christ. The more I change to be like Him, the happier I become.

Questions
How do I feel about change? How often do I change? What is the most important thing for me to change now? What change will I make today?

Declarations

I am open to **change**. I reevaluate and reset my goals to stay on track throughout the year. I **change** my destiny by intentionally deciding to create something great. Minor setbacks are easily overcome as I **change**, and set new goals. My life feels like a grand adventure.

I break the agreements I had about playing small, and **change** them so I can play in the big arena. I am on the court, having fun, giving it my all. I like having smart goals. **Change** is easy for me. I set specific, measurable, achievable, relevant, and time-bound goals.

The more I learn, grow, and **change**, the more confidence I have. I have an abundance of great ideas. I like **change** because that is how I progress. I become a better problem solver as I **change** to be more positive. I **change** to be flexible, and easy to get along with. I allow myself to feel uncomfortable, so I am motivated to **change** faster.

I **change** the negative chatter in my mind by the mental rehearsal of positive thoughts, so I **change** the way my brain works. I am brainy and intuitive. I apply what I learn, and create new emotions to go with my **changed** plans. I **change** to leave room for the new, and uncommon. I believe in my potential and **change** for the better.

I **change** my health by what I physically do. I stay in action daily while having fun. I love living a healthy lifestyle. I **change** the way I act and create different circumstances that enhance my life as I age.

I accept others as they are, even if they don't want to **change**. I focus on how I can **change** and don't worry about **changing** others. I visualize my **changed** self the way I want to be. I picture a bright **changed** future where I am on top. I start right now to **change** what I can. I keep rewarding myself for the **changes** I continue to make.

160:
Unchanging
June 8

Bible Verses

"Who has prepared and done this, calling forth and guiding the destinies of the generations [of the nations] from the beginning? I, the Lord - the first [existing before history began] and with the last [an ever-present, unchanging God] - I am He." Isaiah 41:4 (AMP)

"So God has given us two unchanging things: His promise and His oath. These prove that it is impossible for God to lie. As a result, we who come to God for refuge might be encouraged to seize that hope that is set before us." Hebrews 6:18 (VOICE)

Word of the Day

Unchanging – Not able to change. Eternal. Unfailing

Quotes

"There is what I call the American idea... This idea demands, as the proximate organization thereof, a democracy,-that is, a government of all the people, by all the people, for all the people; of course a government of the principles of eternal justice, the unchanging law of God; for shortness sake I will call the idea of Freedom." Theodore Parker. Speech at the N. E. Anti-slavery Convention. 1850

"Our hope is not hung upon such untwisted thread as "I imagine so," or "It is likely;" but the cable, the strong rope of our fastened anchor, is the oath and promise of Him who is eternal verity: our salvation is fastened with God's own hand and Christ's own strength to the strong stake of God's unchanging nature." Samuel Rutherford's Letters 1637

Questions

Are there any unchanging values I have acquired? Do I believe in God's unchanging love for me? What unchanging thing has changed for me?

Declarations

My **unchanging** dream of making the world a better place to live will never die. I commit to **unchanging** excellence in all I do. I look for the **unchanging** patterns that help me to be the most efficient in reaching my goals. I write down and keep track of my behaviors and how I feel. I like being mature enough to seek out help often.

I am **unchanging** in my determination to go the distance. I attract positive help and attention. I have a great support team whom I am accountable to. They keep me motivated and moving forward. With **unchanging** resolve, I become the best I can possibly be.

I hold onto the **unchanging** hand of God and trust that I am shielded from harm. God's word is **unchanging** and still holds the same power and wisdom as when it was first inspired; therefore I rely on it completely. My **unchanging** belief in a loving Presence watching over me allows me to feel secure. I dwell in safety.

Being well grounded in the revelation of the Eternal One, I do great exploits. God's **unchanging** promises never fail me. I marvel at the vastness of the mercy and blessings that I continue to receive.

I can change my mind and change myself as many times as I want. I think for myself. I am aware of the thinking that brings me up and the thoughts that bring me down. Even though my thoughts may waver, my belief in God is **unchanging**. He is my fortress.

I have an **unchanging** mind about the importance of personal growth and development, so I review my purpose, study great books, listen to inspiring messages, learn from wise people and meditate on truth. I **unchangingly** demonstrate love, kindness, joy, peace, and acceptance wherever I go. I am a light to the world.

161:
Cheer
June 9

Bible Verses
"Worry weighs a person down; an encouraging word cheers a person up."
Proverbs 12:25 (NLT)

"Doth anyone suffer evil among you? Let him pray; is any of good cheer? Let him sing psalms." James 5:13 (YLT)

Word of the Day
Cheer – Spreading happiness and delight. To clap for joy. To shout. To inspire someone and perk them up.

Quotes
"A poet is a nightingale, who sits in darkness and sings to cheer its own solitude with sweet sounds." Percy Bysshe Shelley

"If, as I have been assured by many, my book have proved a comfort, and have been able to cheer in the hour of darkness, that is indeed an ample reward, and is the utmost I have ever hoped." Sir John Lubbock

"Let us be of cheer, remembering that the misfortunes hardest to bear are those which never come." James Russell Lowell

Pam's Perspective
By acting cheery, I cheer myself up. I am my own cheer master because I like to feel good. Then I use my cheer to infect everyone around me.

Questions
What makes my life cheerful? Do I hang around cheery people? Do I look for reasons to be cheerful? How can I spread cheer to everyone near me?

Declarations

I spread **cheer** wherever I go. Smiling comes easily to me. I maintain the habit of being **cheerful**. I **cheer** people up with my kind words of encouragement. It is the easiest thing to do and costs me nothing.

Though trials and trouble may come my way, I believe, and trust God's promises, knowing, He has my back. I find when I spend my energy helping others I become **cheerful** and content with my life. There are people who has it worse off than I. I look around and count my blessings for all the things I have to be **cheerful** about.

I have a jolly disposition and enjoy being a propagator of **cheer**. I'm filled with **cheer** and good looks because God lives in me. The Lord is working miracles in my life now. I am very connected to Yahweh.

I **cheer** myself up by putting on happy music. I sing at the top of my lungs just for the fun of it. I breathe in **cheer** and exhale out anxiety. I like being mindful of how I feel. I think greater than how I am feeling at this moment. I have a **cheerful** temperament. I am safe.

I am staying healthy and living joyfully. My brain releases happy endorphins from my **cheerful** thoughts. I can accomplish anything I set my mind to with ease. I have a prosperity consciousness.

I look at images that **cheer** me up. I am surrounded by fascination and awe. I am grateful as I remember past miracles and former victories. I remember how it feels to be **cheerful**, and then act that way now. I smile more than anyone else because I am full of **cheer**.

I am found to be **cheery**, no matter what may occur. I am full of **cheer**, goodwill, peace, compassion, wisdom, and love. I entwine **cheer** in my day. I love being optimistic and dispersing **cheer**.

162:
Gloom
June 10

Bible Verses
"He uncovers mysteries hidden in darkness; he brings light to the deepest gloom." Job 12:22 (NLT)

"If you offer your food to the hungry and satisfy the needs of the afflicted, then your light shall rise in the darkness and your gloom be like the noonday." Isaiah 58:10 (NET)

Word of the Day
Gloom – Feeling downhearted and discouraged. Unhappiness.

Quotes
"To bear adversity with meek submission to the will of God; to endure chastisement with all long-suffering and joyfulness; to appear cheerful amid surrounding gloom, hopeful amidst desponding circumstances, happy in God when there is nothing else to make us happy; he who does this has indeed made great advances in the divine life." John Angel James

"The friend in my adversity I shall always cherish most. I can better trust those who helped to relieve the gloom of my dark hours than those who are so ready to enjoy with me the sunshine of my prosperity." Ulysses S. Grant

Pam's Perspective
When I read I could create my own joy that did not depend on anything outside of myself, I flourished. I crowded out all the gloom with positivity, and you can too.

Questions
When I feel gloomy, do I allow myself to wallow in it all day? Why or why not? Why do I need this lesson in gloom today?

Declarations

I don't listen to the **gloom** and doom of the news. I don't read of the tragedies in the newspaper. Instead, I set my eyes on the pleasant things around me, and read uplifting literature. It is easy to lift myself out of **gloom** by singing and putting a smile on my face.

Journaling every day helps me to shed light on how I am feeling, and organize my thoughts. It is good to get all my thoughts down on paper, even the **gloomy** ones. It is OK to cry once in a while.

I recognize the things that fill me with **gloom**, and I refrain from those things. I am aware of what I need to change to release **gloom** from my surroundings. Exercise chases the **gloom** away, so I get up and move. Going for a walk is great therapy, and my pets love it too.

My goal when I meet someone who is **gloomy** is to turn their frown upside down, and their despair into hope. I am diplomatic when I walk away from negative people who want to stay that way. I send them a blessing of peace. The closer I get to God, the more accepting I am of others. I just allow people to be **gloomy** if they want to be.

I do the things that serve me well and help me stay in joy. I cancel **gloom** with my cheerful expectancy. I choose joy. I know things are going to turn around for me sooner, than later. I feel safe because I trust God. I have an unlimited power source that cares for me. God has redeemed me from **gloom** and filled my heart with rejoicing.

My natural instinct is to love myself, so I release negative, **gloomy** thoughts. I let go of doubts. I make a miracle out of this ordinary life. I change my **gloomy** language into positive declarations that inspire and cheer me up. Today I am full of hope. I am the master of my destiny. I use my potential to do something amazing with my life.

163:
Become
June 11

Bible Verses

"Walk with the wise and become wise, for a companion of fools suffers harm." Proverbs 13:20 (NIV)

"God made him who had no sin to be sin for us, so that in him we might become the righteousness of God." 2 Corinthians 5:21 (NIV)

Word of the Day

Become – To be transformed into something else or someone else. To shift.

Quotes

"We never know the love of the parent till we become parents ourselves. When we first bend over the cradle of our own child, God throws back the temple door, and reveals to us the sacredness and mystery of a father's and a mother's love to ourselves." Henry Ward Beecher

"Christ never called anyone to be small, but he calls small folks to become kings and priest unto God." Rev. T. P. Frost

Pam's Perspective

I am grateful I can decide to become whatever I choose. My options are endless. When I believe in myself, and take action, miracles happen. I can become a world changer or a bum on a street corner. The decision is mine. I have become all the things I have set out to become by focusing on my vision, and perseverance. I will continue to evolve and become something different as time goes on.

Questions

Am I pleased with what I have become? Why or why not? What do I want to become in the future? What steps do I have to take to reach this goal?

Declarations

I accept myself for who I have **become**. I have suffered loss, been hurt, abandoned, yet I have overcome many struggles. I **become** stronger and more resilient with every trial I go through. I am up for the challenge to **become** the finest I can be. I have come a long way baby, and the best is yet to come. I **become** the best me ever.

In an effortless way, I **become** wealthy physically, mentally, and spiritually. I have a glorious future ahead of me. My assets **become** multiplied with interest. People love handing me money. I **become** rich by tithing and giving things away. Every day I choose to **become** more thankful for all the remarkable gifts I receive.

I **become** fit and healthy by eating smaller portions and exercising. I love eating carrots, celery, and other healthy snacks. I turn on health and turn off disease. I look forward to getting up and moving so I can **become** toned. My body naturally loves to walk in nature. I **become** more creative by incorporating play into my daily life.

I **become** a person of integrity by keeping my word, and doing what I say I will do, even when I don't feel like it. I spur myself to think outside the box, so I **become** innovative. As I ask myself powerful questions, I **become** brilliant. I **become** a leader by serving others.

My habits **become** me. I **become** lovable by forgiving, and accepting people. By loving and serving others, I **become** someone God can use. Encouraging others invigorates me to **become** more positive.

My true self is forever connected to the Divine. I **become** more like Christ as I walk in love. I am never alone. I **become** joyful when spreading the good news, and helping others. When I minister to others with the intent of being a contribution, I **become** fulfilled.

164:
Choice
June 12

Bible Verses
"Today I have given you the choice between life and death, between blessings and curses. Now I call on heaven and earth to witness the choice you make. Oh, that you would choose life so that you and your descendants might live!" Deuteronomy 30:19 (NLT)

"Wise choices will watch over you. Understanding will keep you safe." Proverbs 2:11 (NLT)

Word of the Day
Choice – To make a decision. To pick something. To choose.

Quotes
"Of the blessings set before you make your choice, and be content." Samuel Johnson

"It may be infinitely worse to refuse to forgive than to murder, because the latter may be an impulse of a moment of heat, whereas the former is a cold and deliberate choice of the heart." George Macdonald

Pam's Perspective
Being offered a choice between two restaurants is as easy as any other choice we have to make. The hardest thing is putting off the decision to some undetermined time when I could possibly have a better option. Now is the only time I have so I make a choice and live with it. I am always relieved when I do.

Questions
When I make a choice, do I give it careful consideration? Am I happy with the choices I have made about my life? Why or why not?

Declarations

I am glad for the freedom of **choice**. I alone am in charge of my life. Every day I make wiser **choices** than the day before. I start each day with the **choice** to become a person of excellence. I enjoy **choosing** to bless the world using my expertise. I **choose** sensibly.

I give myself permission to **choose**. I believe in my **choices**. I know love is a **choice**, so I **choose** to let love filter through me. The **choice** to forgive is always a good one. My **choice** to declare positive things over my life has paid off with increased confidence and power.

My **choice** to mentor children has unending eternal rewards. My **choice** to associate with the people I admire has enriched my life. I have intelligent friends who contribute to our community. We encourage each other to **choose** carefully. I like being accountable.

Unexpected increases pour into my bank account as my wealth grows. Being wealthy is a **choice**, so I save my money, make wise investments, and stay out of debt. The **choice** to grow up can be a difficult one. But that **choice** gives me influence, and poise.

The wisest **choice** I ever made was to surrender to the Holy Spirit. I have the freedom of **choice** to pursue God in my own way. Being Spirit led inspires me to make **choices** that are for my highest good.

I live in harmony with nature, and save the environment with my **choice** to go green. The **choice** to go for walks in nature connects me to my Creator. The **choice** to plant flowers and trees has enhanced the beauty of my community. I like **choosing** organic produce. My **choice** to eat wholesome has bolstered my strength and stamina. I am pleased with the **choices** I make. Happiness is a **choice**, so I create it and share it with others. I always think of worthy things.

165:
Stand
June 13

Bible Verses
"So stand up and do not be moved. Wear a belt of truth around your body. Wear a piece of iron over your chest which is being right with God." Ephesians 6:14 (NLT)

"Meanwhile, God's holy people passionately and faithfully stand their ground." Revelation 13:10 (MSG)

Word of the Day
Stand – The position of being upright and still. To take a stance on a specific belief. Having conviction of purpose and single-mindedness.

Quotes
"Prejudices, preconceived opinions and beliefs always stand in the way of true wisdom." Ralph Waldo Trine

"I find the great thing in this world is not so much where we stand, as in what direction we are moving: To reach the port of heaven, we must sail sometimes with the wind and sometimes against it – but we must sail, and not drift, nor lie at anchor." Oliver Wendell Holmes, Sr.

"The world will not, cannot, must not, stand still because a few slow and satisfied people have fallen into a groove and are dazed at the thought of essaying any other method of life." Ella Wheeler Wilcox

Questions
What do I stand for and what is it costing me? Do I stand up for my beliefs or go with the crowd? Who will I stand up for today? Who stands up for me? When I am standing in line, do I count my blessings or complain? What am I not willing to stand for any longer?

Declarations

I have eager expectations of the good that is coming my way. I **stand** when I have done everything I could, I **stand** secure in my trust of God. God knows me by name and **stands** by my side. I **stand** in the face of troubles and watch the Lord bring me through unharmed.

The revelation of God's love is revealed through me as I **stand** up to help others. I **stand** up for those who can't **stand** up for themselves. I do what I do as an act of love. I take my service to a higher level. I **stand** straight and confident as I magnify goodness and grace.

Standing with my friends, we elevate our community. I find great happiness in my daily activities. I avoid Facebook when I am in the presence of friends. I **stand** around accomplished people and become their friend. I will not **stand** for anything less than success.

I contribute to my vitality by what I eat. I have boundless moxie. I **stand** up straight and tall. My **standing** desk keeps me in top form. I like being independent, **standing** on my own two feet. I like being responsible; it feels great. I am an expert in my field and do **outstanding** work. My spectacular memory keeps me on track.

I respect people who take a **stand** for the things they believe in, even if it differs from me. Variety is the spice of life. I have friends from all walks of life. I admire people who **stand** up for their selves. I **stand** for and defend the principles that I hold as sacred like peace, honesty, kindness, equality, compassion, generosity, and charity.

I **stand** in the sweet spot of God's favor as He directs tenderness toward me. As I **stand** and step out of the boat, I become bold. I **stand** up to my obstacles and overcome them. I **stand** out in the crowd with my bright smile. I **stand** on the firm foundation of love.

166:
Sit
June 14

Bible Verses
"You will open the eyes of the blind. You will free the captives from prison, releasing those who sit in dark dungeons." Isaiah 42:7 (NLT)

"To those who win the victory I will give the right to sit beside me on my throne, just as I have been victorious and now sit by my Father on his throne." Revelation 3:21 (GNT)

Word of the Day
Sit – To be seated on something supportive of one's weight. To remain still, to halt standing. To give your feet a rest.

Quotes
"Bless my soul, when I sit down and think over the things which I once feared might possibly descend upon me, I laugh! Where are those feared things now? I don't know – have almost forgotten that I ever feared them."
William Walker Atkinson

"How vain it is to sit down to write when you have not stood up to live."
Henry David Thoreau

"Even if you are on the right track, you will get run over if you just sit there."
Will Rogers

"After dinner sit awhile; after supper walk a mile." Proverb

Questions
When I sit at my desk, do I have a specific purpose on how much work I will get done? What place of honor will I sit at in the future?

Declarations

I **sit** with a smile on my face as I cultivate gratitude by thinking about all my blessings. I **sit** and write in my gratitude journal to remind myself how great my life really is. Happy days are here to stay. As I **sit** in the quiet and meditate on God's Word, great truths are revealed to me on how to live a joy-filled life. I **sit** in awe.

No matter whom I **sit** next to, I enjoy the moment and make a new friend. I give myself permission to take a pause and **sit** down once in a while. What a joy it is to **sit** with my friends as we laugh out loud.

I develop habits that are so powerful; people **sit** in amazement. I **sit** in a place of honor. I **sit** with the wise leaders of my time. After I **sit** and visualize my great outcome, I proceed to see that it comes to pass. I never **sit** on my hands and wait for something to happen. I get up and take immediate, determined action to get things done.

I excite my spouse when I walk in the door. We enjoy each other as we **sit**, and hold hands. It is fun to share family time together as we **sit**, and play games. We spend time together, so we stay together.

When I **sit** down to eat, I give thanks for what I am about to receive. I eat nutrient-dense foods that are organically grown. I push away seconds and thirds. **Sitting**, and holding in my stomach in, is a great way to increase my core strength. Lifting my legs and arms while I **sit** and watch TV is easy to do. I enjoy **sitting** and doing chair yoga to maintain my muscle tone. I exercise even while **sitting** down.

I **sit** in the front row, so I don't miss a thing. I **sit** with style. I **sit** in a place where I am treated like a royal messenger of the King of Kings. I **sit** up straight with my head held high, knowing I am a winner. I **sit** surrounded by positive vibrations that are encased in love.

167:
Forgive
June 15

Bible Verses
"For You, Lord, are kind and ready to forgive, rich in faithful love to all who call on You." Psalm 86:5 (HCSB)

"But if you don't forgive men their trespasses, neither will your Father forgive your trespasses." Matthew 6:15 (WEB)

Word of the Day
Forgive – To release all hurts, real or imagined. To let go of blame.

Quotes
"He that cannot forgive others breaks the bridge over which he must pass himself; for every man has need to be forgiven." Edward Herbert

"A wise man will make haste to forgive, because he knows the true value of time, and will not suffer it to pass away in unnecessary pain." Samuel Johnson

"The noblest vengeance is to forgive." Proverb

Pam's Perspective
Choosing to forgive the person who destroyed our four wedding videos before we even got a chance to watch them was difficult. Because that person was mad and not even at me, he destroyed them. I never got to see the people wishing us well, and comments on how to make our marriage last. I never even got a sorry. But carrying around bitterness was harder than forgiveness, so I let it go, and forgave.

Questions
What does forgiveness look like to me? Is there anyone who I feel has hurt me or offended me? Am I willing to forgive them and go free?

Declarations

Just because I **forgive** someone does not mean I condone what was done, said, or that I forget what happened. It simply means that I am a strong person who is powerful enough to **forgive**. I like feeling free, and light. I **forgive** and release any mental stress I might have.

I release negative thoughts about others as I **forgive** them. I **forgive** everyone, including myself. I accept people for who they are, and I **forgive** them entirely. All that has made me mad, I **forgive**. Things past, present, and future I **forgive**. I **forgive** everybody who has ever hurt me and can possibly need **forgiveness**. I am very generous.

I release all resentments, hurts, and grudges. I accept, and realize, life is not fair. I absolutely **forgive** myself and walk in freedom. I am free, and all others are free. I heal myself as I offer **forgiveness**, and grow spiritually, and mentally. I give myself the gift of **forgiveness**.

I only have one father. Being mad at him for not being perfect, will not change him. I **forgive** my father now. I **forgive** my mother, for I know she did the best she could, with what she had to work with. I have a **forgiveness** lifestyle. I continue to **forgive** on a daily basis.

I ask for **forgiveness**. I live in harmony with all different types of people. I allow people to changes on their own time. I have a benevolent spirit and **forgive** easily. I am thankful when people **forgive** me for the mistakes I make. I accept **forgiveness** from people who offer it. I choose to walk in **forgiveness**.

My life is built on trust in God. I love being **forgiven**. I am grateful that the Almighty **forgave** me. I walk in the liberty that God has given me. My debts have been canceled. I remember to live like I am **forgiven**. I allow myself the freedom to live in joy, peace, and love.

168:
Blame
June 16

Bible Verses
"The person who lives free of blame, does what is right, and speaks the truth sincerely." Psalm 15:2 (CEB)

"Some people ruin themselves by their own stupid actions and then blame the Lord." Proverbs 19:3 (GNT)

Word of the Day
Blame – To complain about and attack verbally. To condemn.

Quotes
"They whose guilt within their bosoms lie, imagine every eye beholds their blame." William Shakespeare

"When you blame others, you give up your power to change." Dr. Robert Anthony

"That man has great tranquility of heart who cares neither for praise nor for blame." Thomas à Kempis

"I like to praise and reward loudly, to blame quietly." Catherine the Great

"In other men we faults can spy, and blame the mote that dims their eye; each little speck and blemish find, to our own stronger errors blind." John Gay

Questions
Do I blame my parents for how I turned out? Do I blame the economy for the state of my finances? Do I blame my genes for my body shape or health? Do I blame my God for the evil that is happening in the world? Do I believe blaming anyone for anything will help me in any way?

Declarations

I enjoy being in charge of my life living **blame** free. I have no need to **blame** anyone, for I alone am the creator of my destiny. I shatter the feeling of being a victim as I am liable for all the decisions I make. No one owes me anything. I work hard and earn my own way. I choose to be happy no matter what happens to me, or around me.

I overcome self-judgment and quit **blaming** myself for the mistakes I have made in the past. I determined to be kind as I release all **blame**. I am able to receive love, acceptance, and a variety of gifts. I believe in myself and know I can overcome any obstacle that comes my way. **Blame** has never helped me, so I unshackle myself and let it go.

I tear down walls and reinvent myself as a **blame**-free person. The more I love and care for myself, the less I **blame** myself, or others. I discover how great I really am. I have choices, and control over my body. I have the courage to accept responsibility for all my choices. I have options for being healthy. I live exempt from **blame**.

By trying to assign **blame**, I waste my time and solve nothing. I choose to stay optimistic and fearless as I move through life. I have good intentions about the good I want to do in this world free from **blame**. I speak positive, uplifting words that are willed for my good. I become more heroic as I free myself from **blame** and shame.

By dropping the attachment I have to a problem, and turning it over to God, I receive a supernatural downpour of grace. When I admit that I have created my own problems, and quit playing the **blame** game, I take back my power. I love learning new lessons. I allow space for compassion to flow through me as I see my neighbor without any **blame**. Letting **blame** go allows me to see with loving eyes. I live a stress-free life that is **blame** free, and full of joy.

169:
Transcend
June 17

Bible Verses

"But this beautiful treasure is contained in us—cracked pots made of earth and clay—so that the transcendent character of this power will be clearly seen as coming from God and not from us." 2 Corinthians 4:7 (VOICE)

"Don't worry over anything whatever; tell God every detail of your needs in earnest and thankful prayer, and the peace of God which transcends human understanding, will keep constant guard over your hearts and minds as they rest in Christ Jesus." Philippians 4:6-7 (PHILLIPS)

Word of the Day

Transcend – To transform into something better. To improve upon.

Quotes

"Socrates taught for 40 years, Plato for 50, Aristotle for 40, and Jesus for only 3. Yet the influence of Christ's 3-year ministry infinitely transcends the impact left by the combined 130 years of teaching from these men who were among the greatest philosophers of all antiquity." Author Unknown

"Positive declarations will transcend a nice life into an enthusiastic adventure that is filled with passion, vision, and drive." Pam Malow-Isham

"The great minds, the great works transcend all limitations of time, of language, and of race, and the scholar can never feel initiated into the company of the elect until he can approach all of life's problems from the cosmopolitan standpoint." William Osler

Questions

Can I transcend petty grievances and allow love to rule my day? How will I transcend anger? What problem will I transcend today?

Declarations

I **transcend** my neighborhood by making friends with my neighbors, knowing their names, and making an effort to connect. I **transcend** my life by connecting with positive people who have the desire to improve. I align with people to **transcend** my accountability.

In spite of my mood, or circumstance, I **transcend** to get things done on time, with the highest quality of service. I am a persuasive leader who leads by example. I **transcend** petty talk about what is going wrong with the world and encourage people to look for solutions.

I release all the gripes and complaints I have and **transcend** to allow forgiveness in. I dump grievances and embrace love. As I **transcend** bitterness, I am filled with compassion and understanding. I grow from my mistakes and **transcend** to become a better person.

God **transcends** all my expectations and covers me with affluence. I am wealthy on all levels. I **transcend** my day by reflecting on the positive aspects. As I expand my awareness, I **transcend** to my true self. I am modest as I **transcend** my ego, and release arrogance.

I drive outside the noisy city to take a walk in the peaceful woods, and my mood **transcends** immediately. Looking at the puffy white clouds brings a smile to my face, and puts a song in my heart. I am determined to **transcend** the past, have a great day, and do well.

My positive self-image **transcends** any insecurity I used to have. I hone my power and shape my life into a beautiful masterpiece. I am a powerhouse of possibilities transforming my world. I am beautiful. I give myself permission to **transcend** my thought life. I think like God. I affirm the answers I need are in route and will arrive right on time. I **transcend** from average to brilliant.

170:
Overcome
June 18

Bible Verses

"Listen! I have given you authority, so that you can walk on snakes and scorpions and overcome all the power of the enemy, and nothing will hurt you." Luke 10:19 (GNT)

"Do not be overcome by evil, but overcome evil with good." Romans 12:21 (AMP)

Word of the Day

Overcome – To come out on top. To beat an opponent. Triumph over.

Quotes

"Success is to be measured not so much by the position that one has reached in life as by the obstacles which he has overcome." Booker T. Washington

"Overcome first in your mind, and the body will follow." Pam Malow-Isham

"I will seize fate by the throat; it shall certainly never wholly overcome me." Ludwig van Beethoven

"A nail is driven out by another nail. Habit is overcome by habit." Desiderius Erasmus

"No individual can develop into the largest manhood or womanhood without the education that comes from struggling to overcome difficulties.'" Orison Swett Marden

Questions

What have I overcome in the past? How have past difficulties made me stronger and more resilient? What will I overcome today?

Declarations

I **overcome** any and every problem that comes my way. I am more than a conqueror. Today I **overcome** fear with faith, bitterness with forgiveness, and apathy with enthusiasm. I earn good money and **overcome** poverty because I work hard, tithe, and give generously.

I find my voice and **overcome** the fear of public speaking by joining Toastmasters, rehearsing my talks, believing in my message, and just going for it. I grow more confident with time. I am a champion. I **overcome** and outshine my competition with my bold behavior.

I **overcome** boredom by taking massive action immediately. I **overcome** negative thinking by infusing my brain with positive thoughts, and God's word. I **overcome** procrastination by doing what needs to be done right away. I thrive on action. I **overcome** my failures by learning from them and trying something new.

I **overcome** sickness by eating healthy, exercising, and believing in God who created me, lives in me, and is able to heal me. I allow myself to feel Gods love filling every cell of my being with vibrant health. I **overcome** bad habits by creating new life-enriching habits.

I **overcome** sadness by singing happy songs and dancing freely around. I **overcome** loneliness by being friendly, joining groups, and volunteering for things I believe in. I realize no one is going to come knocking on my door to ask if we can be friends. I have to put forth effort at being likable, kind, positive, trustworthy, and cheerful.

I **overcome** my indifference by caring about people and getting involved in helping them. I release the need to feel superior to anyone as I perform random acts of kindness. I **overcome** gloom by smiling at everyone I meet. Today I can **overcome** anything!

171:
Exercise
June 19

Bible Verses
"But if they cannot exercise self-control, let them marry. For it is better to marry than to burn with passion." 1 Corinthians 7:9 (NKJV)

"But solid food belongs to those who are of full age, that is, those who by reason of use have their senses exercised to discern both good and evil." Hebrews 5:14 (NKJV)

Word of the Day
Exercise – Moving your body for fun or work. Putting forth effort.

Quotes
"Old minds are like old horses; you must exercise them if you wish to keep them in working order." John Adams

"Lack of activity destroys the good condition of every human being, while movement and methodical physical exercise save it and preserve it." Plato

"If a man does not exercise his arm he develops no biceps muscle; and if a man does not exercise his soul, he acquires no muscle in his soul, no strength of character, no vigor of moral fiber, nor beauty of spiritual growth." Henry Drummond

Pam's Perspective
Realizing the form of exercise I do does not matter as long as I do it was a game changer for me. I can have fun while exercising without the drudgery of a gym.

Questions
Do I exercise my mind, body, and spirit? What exercise will I do today?

Declarations

I place a high value on my health, the way I look, and the way I feel. I always find creative ways to **exercise**. I give myself the gift of energy and strength by **exercising**. I have great posture. I **exercise** a lot of willpower and stamina. I believe I am a winner and act like it.

I visualize myself at the perfect weight as I do the **exercises** I need to do to reach my goal. I am energized. I feel great as I **exercise** both self-restraint and discipline. I am aware of what I need to change. I alone am in charge of what I eat, and how much **exercise** I get. I become skinny by the way I **exercise** control as I eat.

I am thankful for my clear complexion and pretty face. By **exercising** I gain a brighter outlook on my life. I **exercise** my lungs and breathe in life, and healing. I enjoy learning new **exercise** games. I find the perfect **exercise** to match my personality while having fun.

I accept that I have to **exercise** to stay able-bodied, so I make movement a high priority in my day. I have fun while I am **exercising** with my friends. I love to play active games. I consistently **exercise** my body two to three times a week.

I honor God in my body by **exercising** and enjoy all the benefits that it has on my life. As I **exercise** my body, I **exercise** my spirit and feel righteous. When I don't feel like **exercising**, I do it anyway, because once I get going, I am glad I did. I **exercise** jumping for joy.

I **exercise** my power to make wise decisions. I get extra brainpower by **exercising**. Health and prosperity are surrounding me now as I choose to embrace them with **exercise**. Positive affirmations have paid great dividends in building my confidence, and resolve. I let go of all self-limiting ideas. I stay fit and agile while **exercising.**

172:
Goal
June 20

Bible Verses

"I press toward the goal for the prize of the upward call of God in Christ Jesus." Philippians 3:14 (NKJV)

"But the goal of our instruction is love from a pure heart and a good conscience and a sincere faith." 1 Timothy 1:5 (NASB)

Word of the Day

Goal – Having something to work toward. To hit the mark. Objective.

Quotes

"Just as a master musician may cause the most beautiful strains of music to pour forth from the strings of a violin, so may you arouse the genius which lies asleep in your brain, and cause it to drive you upward to whatever goal you may wish to achieve." Napoleon Hill

"Goals are the DNA of your success." Richard Gaylord Briley

"If you want to live a happy life, tie it to a goal, not to people or things." Albert Einstein

"There is everything in keeping the mind saturated with one's aim until it becomes a life habit, in setting the life currents on all of the forces within us towards the goal of our ambition. This will after a while create a sort of tide which will tend to float things our way." Orison Swett Marden

Questions

Do I have short-term, mid-range, and long-term goals written down? If not, why not? Why do I find achieving goals easy for me?

Declarations

I am a **goal** setter. I like making plans for my fantastic future. I write my **goals** down, so they are always before me. When I review my **goals** in the morning, I make the most of my day. I visualize the best outcome, quickly, and easily as I set **goals** that are achievable for me.

I love being assured of myself as I work toward my **goals**. I set dates and times for all my **goals** to be completed. I take big leaps of faith toward my **goals**. I am filled with appreciation for life. I continue to amaze myself with all the **goals** that I have achieved thus far.

I concentrate on my **goals** and let other people work on their **goals**. The pursuit of my big **goals** is paved with the completion of many little **goals**. I take care of myself by reaching my **goals**. My **goals** are perfect for me. I give it my all and get my **goals** accomplished.

God gives me the solutions I need to reach each **goal**. I am flexible as I attain my **goals**. I release the know-how and the outcome to God and enjoy the process. I am the exception that God chooses to bless. My **goals** are accelerated with grace as favor comes my way.

I am filled up with warm feelings as I see my **goals** in sight. I spend time brainstorming on the most important **goals** in my life. I write a personal mission statement that reflects the **goals** on my list. I state my **goals** in positive declarations. With the clear picture of my **goals** before me, I can plan out what to do next. I finish what I start.

Brilliant surprises come my way as I give myself permission to succeed. I am worthy of attaining every **goal** I set. Because I express gratefulness to the people around me, they appreciate me and want to see me attain my **goals**. New doors fling open as I am matched with the connections I need to reach my **goals** at the right time.

173:
Ask
June 21

Bible Verses
"You haven't done this before. Ask, using my name, and you will receive, and you will have abundant joy." John 16:24 (NLT)

"Now this is the confidence that we have in Him, that if we ask anything according to His will, He hears us." 1 John 5:14 (NKJV)

Word of the Day
Ask – To address someone for instruction or knowledge. Questioning.

Quotes
"Great thoughts and a pure heart- that, is what we should ask of God." Johann Wolfgang von Goethe

"We are not only to ask Him and invoke Him, but to command Him and to use Him, and fully expect His almighty efficiency to accomplish the work for which He sent us. Just as the laws of electricity, when properly understood, place at our command the forces of electricity, so, when we yield to the laws of the Spirit's operation, we may command the Spirit's operation and fully count upon His mighty working infinite power." Albert B. Simpson

"Hope against hope and ask till ye receive." James Montgomery

Pam's Perspective
Until I gave myself permission to ask for what I wanted, I settled for what I got.

Questions
What am I asking for? Do I expect things, actions, or gifts from people or God that I have not asked for? Why do I ask? Am I asking the right way?

Declarations

I **ask** for the favor of God to descend around my work, home and family. I am able to **ask** and express my feelings in a healthy, positive way. I **ask** people to believe in themselves and quit second-guessing their brilliance. I **ask** for forgiveness when I have wronged someone, intentionally, or unintentionally. I **ask** God for grace.

I **ask** for what I want. When I need a hug, another cup of coffee, or a friend to talk to, I **ask**. I know people can't read my mind, so if I want something, I **ask** for it. I know the worst thing that can happen is they will say "no" and I am no worse off than I was before I **asked**. I am able to be open with people while **asking** for assistance.

Today I welcome new adventures with love and gratitude. I love **asking** all kinds of questions and finding out all kinds of cool stuff. I exercise my right to **ask** for the best things. I **ask** boldly.

I am not afraid to **ask** for support. I **ask** God to show me His heart so I can be more lovable. I **ask** for wisdom, guidance, cooperation, friendship, and assistance. I **ask**, and my cup fills up and runs over. My joy spills out to people who don't even **ask** for it.

I am confident to **ask** for exactly what I want. I **ask** my boss for a raise. There are always perks and bonuses headed my way. I am in control of my finances, so I am a fearless **asker**. I **ask** for discounts and upgrades. I am shown partiality wherever I go because I am a King's Kid. A special delivery of abundance is on the way for me.

It is natural for me to **ask** my mate for simple pleasures. I am brave enough to **ask** for my share and kind enough to help others. I am an example to others on how to **ask**, and live a fulfilled life. I **ask**, and I receive. I always have an abundant supply because I **ask** for it.

174:
Answer
June 22

Bible Verses

*"A gentle answer turns away wrath, but a harsh word stirs up anger."
Proverbs 15:1 (NIV)*

*"Everything you say should be kind and well thought out so that you know
how to answer everyone." Colossians 4:6 (NOG)*

Work of the Day

Answer – To acknowledge someone and come back with information.

Quotes

*"Go and tell Jesus everything, is the divine command; but do not tell Him
what answer to give in return." J. Parker*

*"A man may fulfill the object of his existence by asking a question he
cannot answer, and attempting a task he cannot achieve." Oliver Wendell
Holmes, Sr.*

"All men, well questioned, answer well." Plato

*"Hear one man before you answer; hear several before you decide." J.
Damhouder*

Pam's Perspective

*Being young I thought I had all the answers and older people were dumb. I
see now how little I knew and how much more I have to learn. I just smile
now when I see younger people acting like I used to. I plan to keep learning
until I die.*

Questions

Where is the best place to look for answers? Why do I need the answer?
What is God saying to me? What am I doing about it?

Declarations

I know the **answers** to my questions are on the way, even before I ask. I know the One with all the **answers**. I ask brilliant questions and get brilliant **answers**. When asked, I **answer** with wisdom. When called upon, I give myself permission to **answer** correctly.

I like to study. Because I am humble, I realize I don't know all the **answers,** but I can find them out. I like being knowledgeable. I search the Internet for more **answers**. I like researching and learning new things. I put forth effort in finding the right **answers**. I befriend smart people. I like to give people breaks, so I **answer** with respect.

I realize the need for community. The **answer** for loneliness is being friendly, joining groups and volunteering. When feeling forlorn, I allow friends to cheer me up. When playing games, I give people credit for their good **answers**. I am gracious, resourceful and patient.

If I don't know the **answer** when I am in a class, I am smart enough to say so. Then I wait for the correct **answer**. I am reliable, confident and always give an honest **answer**. I **answer** my phone with a smile on my face. When **answering** a question, I think before I respond.

I find the **answers** when I go within myself. I remember the **answers** to the questions. My heart recognizes the right **answer**. I honor my core values. I believe all **answers** are within my reach. I ask a question before I go to sleep and when I arise, I have the **answer**.

I **answer** the call of God on my life. Jesus is the **answer** and my ever-present friend, helper, confidant, advisor, healer, lover, and Lord. I **answer** with faith and conviction about my faith in God. God in me provides the right **answer** now. I am thankful that God **answers** my prayers. In His perfect timing, I receive all the **answers** I need.

175:
Passionate
June 23

Bible Verses
"God proves to be good to the man who passionately waits, to the woman who diligently seeks." Lamentations 3:25 (MSG)

"And now, isn't it wonderful all the ways in which this distress has goaded you closer to God? You're more alive, more concerned, more sensitive, more reverent, more human, more passionate, and more responsible." 2 Corinthians 7:11 (MSG)

Word of the Day
Passionate – Romantic and loving. Enthusiastic about a goal. Zealous.

Quotes
"As Iron is eaten away by rust, so the envious are consumed by their own passion." Antisthenes

"What is enthusiasm but a passionate belief in what seems to be a high and holy aim – an unselfish devotion to some noble cause – a consecration of heart and mind and soul to the attainment of a great object?" Orison Swett Marden

Pam's Perspective
If I decide before I start a project that it is going to be boring, it always is. If I decide I am going to be passionate, and enjoy something before I start, no matter how hard it is, I do my work with a smile. When you can be passionately thankful for every breath you breathe, step you take, touch you feel, sight you see, fragrance you smell, and deed you do, you will be joyfully blessed, and happy, all your days.

Questions
What am I passionate about? Am I channeling my passion in the right direction? Do I connect with other passionate people to work with?

Declarations

I am **passionate** about feeling great, so I always look at the sunny side of life. I **passionately** work to upgrade my life and add more enjoyment to it. Each and every day I focus on the things that I am **passionate** about. I can easily improve myself by being **passionate**. I associate with like-minded, **passionate** people who are pleasant.

I infect people with my **passion** and awaken their keen interest. I feel safe loving myself **passionately**. I marvel at all the **passion** and beauty around me. I have such a hot, juicy, **passionate** relationship with my mate that we inspire others to live with a **passion** too.

I remove distractions so I can stay **passionately** focused on what I am doing. My intense drive to achieve my goals fuels my **passion**. My enthusiasm attracts other **passionate** people to do business with. I discipline myself to follow my plans as I prioritize my day.

I only speak about what I want. I am **passionate** about bringing life to every area of my existence. I am **passionately** thankful for all the thousands of blessings I receive, the seen, and the unseen.

I **passionately** restrict my actions, so I get what I want. I achieve what is desirable to me. I put everything in place in order to be successful. My **passion** motivates me to constant improvement. I use my **passion** for good as I make a positive impact on humanity.

God is **passionate** about saturating me with His love, and I am **passionate** about sharing His love with others. I get jazzed as my **passion** for doing good and helping people thrive, expands. I am **passionate** about pouring love on every person I meet and bringing joy into every situation. I am **passionate** about spreading humor to my friends, and family. I live in a **passionately** happy world.

176:
Dull
June 24

Bible Verses

"Behold, the Lord's hand is not shortened at all, that it cannot save, nor His ear dull with deafness that it cannot hear." Isaiah 59:1 (AMP)

"For this people's heart has grown dull, and their ears are hard of hearing, and they have shut their eyes; so that they might not look with their eyes, and listen with their ears, and understand with their heart and turn— and I would heal them." Matthew 13:15 (ESV)

Word of the Day

Dull – Drab or flat in color. Tiresome and uninteresting. Shallow and self-absorbed. Simpleminded.

Quotes

"Poets are never young in one sense. Their delicate ear hears the far-off whispers of eternity, which coarser souls must travel towards for scores of years before their dull sense is touched by them. A moment's insight is sometimes worth a life's experience." Oliver Wendell Holmes Sr.

"I find we are growing serious, and then we are in greater danger of being dull." William Congreve

"Anger makes dull men witty, but it keeps them poor." Francis Bacon

"Nothing is dull when you are curious." Pam Malow-Isham

Questions

Do I ever consider myself dull? Do I think of life as dull? What does dull look like to me? Do I ever get stuck in a dull routine? Do I ever take the time to get to know people who I perceive as dull? If not, why not?

Declarations

I jump at **dull** opportunities and turn them into great adventures. I become exactly what I decide to be, even if it is **dull** to some people. A supernatural pathway of plenty comes rushing to overtake any **dull** results. I open my doors and windows to welcome it all in. I laugh at the **dull** defeatist as I zoom past them with massive success.

I spice up a **dull** menu with something hot. I love trying new foods. I don't consider vegetables **dull**, but life-giving, and delicious. My vision about my beautiful body determines what I eat, and how much I eat. I am grateful for my strong legs. **Dull** shoes are better than no shoes. I appreciate my arms so I can hug the **dull** ones.

I get rid of the **dull** things in my home that I no longer need. Letting go is easy now. I release the angel of blessing over my life in prayer. I never have a **dull** time because I am engaged in the present moment, savoring every delicious second of my existence. I am enthusiastic about learning **dull** subjects because I find everything interesting. I love watching Ted Talks and being inspired.

I rejoice as the **dull** of winter bursts into spring with all the delicate flowers. When I am feeling down, and **dull**, I remember that God thinks I am fantastic. Because of His gentleness toward me, I accept that I am beautiful and worthy of love. I allow God's healing word to work in me. I have decided to be well, and live well. Prayer is the first thing I do, not a **dull** last resort. I trust in the Lord to see me through every storm. I am energized right now with love.

I bring a spark in me to light up every **dull** room I walk into. **Dull** faces are turned into smiles with my shining face. Even my **dull** jokes get a chuckle. My life is anything but **dull** because I have the DNA of a champion. I choose victory today over a **dull** existence.

177:
Fight
June 25

Bible Verses
"Avoiding a fight is a mark of honor; only fools insist on quarreling."
Proverbs 20:3 (NLT)

"I have fought the good fight, I have finished the race, and I have remained
faithful." 2 Timothy 4:7 (NLT)

Word of the Day
Fight – To dispute, scuffle, scrap or clash over. War. Conflict

Quotes
"Men will wrangle for religion; write for it; fight for it; die for it; anything
but live for it." Charles Caleb Colton

"Who has a harder fight than he who is striving to overcome himself?"
Thomas à Kempis

"If there be no enemy, no fight; if no fight, no victory; if no victory, no
crown." Mr. Savanar

Pam's Perspective
When my husband gets mad and wants to fight, I refuse to allow him, or
anyone else to ruin my day. There is no sense trying to reason with someone
who will not listen. It will just frustrate you both. You cannot fight with
someone who does not want to fight. So I choose to laugh, go for a walk, or
just be silent and talk later after he has cooled off.

Questions
Who do I fight? What do I fight for and why? What would my life be
like if I chose not to fight? Is all the fighting really worth my effort?

Declarations

I am fearless and self-assured, empowered with Divine strength as I **fight** on. I know no matter what battle comes my way; I am not alone, for God **fights** for me. I **fight** for the things I believe in like truth, love, honor, goodwill, joy, and beauty. I **fight** for my success.

I am socially responsible and **fight** for what is right. I can also easily learn to keep my peace and be still. I consider people's reactions, but they never victimize me. I interpret wisely before I decide to **fight**, because I live as a peacemaker. I show kindness to my enemies.

I **fight** for the underdog and lift up the downtrodden with actions of mercy and premeditated service. I practice loving my neighbor, even the ones that are quite different from me. I let go of any anger that I may be carrying so I won't start a **fight**. I am an ambassador of love.

Some **fights** are worth winning. My family is worth **fighting** for. I **fight** to keep my marriage growing in love and passion. I **fight** to keep my children safe and **fight** for their education. I **fight** for my health. I charge past any insecurity and **fight** to conquer it.

I love being authentic. I surround myself with inspiring people who are a joy to be near. I **fight** for equality among the genders. Some things are just worth **fighting** for. Easy **fights** don't exist, so I stay prepared. I **fight** to keep going and never give up. I am a victor.

I **fight** and defeat every negative thought that tries to enter my mind. I capitalize on my strengths. I **fight** for the change I want to see in me. I continue to get better as I focus on my positive traits. I laugh as I **fight** the good **fight** of faith because I am a winner. I **fight** to keep a great reputation and honor myself. I **fight** to have the habit of mastery. I am grateful to live and **fight** another day.

178:
Surrender
June 26

Bible Verses
"Behold, they may gather together and stir up strife, but it is not from Me. Whoever stirs up strife against you shall fall and surrender to you." Isaiah 54:15 (AMP)

"Nor must you surrender any part of yourselves to sin to be used for wicked purposes. Instead, give yourselves to God, as those who have been brought from death to life, and surrender your whole being to him to be used for righteous purposes." Romans 6:13 (GNT)

Word of the Day
Surrender – To release and let go of. To hand over control to another.

Quotes
"The greatness of a man's power is the measure of his surrender." William Booth

"Through surrender, those feelings of emptiness caused by constant striving, pushing and trying to attain something better than "here now" become pleasantly filled with Divine goodness. The deeper the let go, the more abundance, inner peace and joy will come rushing into your life." Jafree Ozwald

Pam's Perspective
After years of building up walls to protect me from being hurt, the concept of surrender was foreign. When I did decide to surrender to God, my burdens lifted. I find when I continue to surrender to His will, I stay in peace.

Questions
Do I surrender my body to the activities that keep it strong and in good working order? What and to whom am I surrendering to?

Declarations

I now **surrender** to the highest power in the universe, the alpha, and omega, the beginning, and end, the great I Am. The Lord is here and lives in me. I **surrender** to the Existing One who is everywhere.

My greatest prayer is that of an attitude of **surrender** and asking God to pour out His high voltage grace over me. I believe in a good God who really has my best interest at heart. I **surrender** to that God. The One who never fails, or forgets, and always protects me.

Surrendering to God can only enhance my life. When I **surrender** to the highest authority to lead my life, I am divinely guided in all my days. I **surrender** to uncertainty, putting my faith in God to work everything out for my good. I **surrender** to everlasting love.

I share my joy and enthusiasm for life as I **surrender** to the moment. I love being helpful in spreading cheer. I **surrender** to my greatness. I am very capable, trustworthy, and intelligent. I release dependence from others that I could easily take care of myself. I am realistic about my qualities, and my limitations. I enjoy being mature and responsible, not **surrendering** to apathy, or slothfulness.

By allowing God to take control of my existence, I **surrender** and tear down old thought patterns that no longer serve me. When I fall down to **surrender** to His will, I am unshackled and released to stand tall, thrive, and live in freedom. I am footloose and fancy-free.

The Ancient of Days has known from the beginning that I am lovable and He will forever care for me. As I **surrender** my mind to the omniscient Source, I am infused with the mind of Christ. The God of the universe **surrenders** His love to me voluntarily, without hindrance. Thank you, is my hearts reply, as I **surrender** to Him.

179:
Positive
June 27

Bible Verses

"Jesus Christ, the Son of God, whom Silvanus, Timothy and I have preached to you, is himself no doubtful quantity; he is the divine "yes." Every promise of God finds its affirmative in him, and through him can be said the final amen, to the glory of God. We owe our position in Christ to this God of positive promise: it is he who has consecrated us to this special work, he who has given us the living guarantee of the Spirit in our hearts." 2 Corinthians 1:19-22 (PHILLIPS)

Word of the Day

Positive – Affirmative and sure. Efficacious and successful.

Quotes

"Positive happiness is constitutional and incapable of increase; misery is artificial, and generally proceeds from our folly." Oliver Goldsmith

"Whenever I observe something in my reality that I don't like or that conflicts with my positive intentions, I do my best to look for any shred of hope for improvement and focus on that. I keep observing with a positive bias, always asking, "What's good about this?" As I observe my present reality, I'm literally trying to bend it in the direction of my intentions. I look for any reasonable excuse that the momentum of a situation is positive and improving in the direction of my intentions. I accept the situation as it is, so there's no denial, but I'm imagining it getting better at the same time. So even though this particular point may not be what I want, I imagine it as part of a line that's sloping towards my goal. I observe the position but visualize it with a positive velocity." Steve Pavlina

Questions

How many positive things are happening in my life? Do I take the time to appreciate them? Have I written down my positive qualities? Do I look for the positive in others? Why do I dwell on the positive?

Declarations

Through my **positive** actions, I can make a **positive** difference in my community, helping one person at a time. I am the **positive** gift that helps people smile. I am a joy to be around. My **positive** energy changes the mood of the people around me. I am a **positive** person.

The **positive** benefit from eating healthy sustains my high energy level. I accentuate the **positive** traits in my personality with celebration. I honor myself by the **positive** way I talk about myself. I miraculously manifest my dreams because of my **positive** mindset.

I am **positively** resilient and have overcome a multitude of trials. I open the banks of heaven and gratefully receive a **positive** overflow of riches of every kind. I feel **positively** taken care of, day and night. I am open to new **positive** ideas because change is easy for me.

My **positive** intent to love mean-spirited people has made me a better person. Being kind is a **positive** phenomenon. I am very valuable and **positively** liked. I love creating **positive** memories with my friends as we conquer every adversity that comes our way. I can make a **positive** change in my family. I do **positive** things for my children, and my children's children, that leaves a lasting legacy.

I allow the **positive** benefits of God's kingdom to rule in my life. I am **positive** that I am highly treasured in God's eyes. He loves to pull out all the stops to help me succeed. Nothing can compare to the abounding joy I continually receive from the wellspring.

I am **positive** enough to cheer myself up. I look for ways I can share my **positive** enthusiasm. Reading **positive** books inspires me to be assertive. I take the initiative to make a **positive** difference in my life. I am a **positive** soul with a bright light. I have a **positive** end.

180:
Negative
June 28

Bible Verses

"So the men Moses sent to scout out the land, and who returned and incited the entire community to complain about him by spreading a negative report about the land - those men who spread the negative report about the land were struck down by the Lord." Numbers 14:36-37 (HCSB)

Word of the Day

Negative – Adverse, pessimistic, cynical and bad. Having unfavorable results. Neutralizing. Counterproductive.

Quotes

"There was a positive side to every negative tragedy I have been through. When I look for the lesson, I mature and evolve, instead of wallowing in self-pity. I improve my mood, health, wealth and friendships by being positive. Being positive and having a positive impact on people is a habit that can be cultivated by choice. Take charge of your life and eliminate the negative." Pam Malow-Isham

"Positive anything is better than negative nothing." Elbert Hubbard

Pam's Perspective

Years ago my best friend was very negative. She was bent on seeing the negative side of everything. I invested five years trying to improve her attitude. The only thing that happened was mine became worse. I could not change someone who did not want to change, but I could protect myself from her negativity by moving on.

Questions

How can I be proactive with the negative that is going on around me? Do I first see the negative or the positive in any given situation? Why is that? Why do I avoid negative thoughts, words, or deeds?

Declarations

I focus on the good aspects of people to avoid the **negative**. I am finding new ways to grow. I am grateful for the **negative** people who teach me patience and tolerance. **Negative** is not bad; it's just **negative**. I accept things as they are, the **negative** with the positive.

I learn from my **negative** experiences and gain value. Life is always giving me instructions. I happily allow the natural learning process in me to take place. I retain what I need to retain, **negativity** and all.

Although it is almost impossible, I try to stay away from **negative** people. I think and communicate from the positive and leave the **negative** alone. I set a good example on how to turn the **negative** experiences into a positive one. I choose to attract the nicest friends.

I recognize my **negativity** and failures, as well as my strong points and successes. I acknowledge my **negative** ways, so I can grow up, and change my ways. I can achieve anything I want. Without the **negative**, I would not appreciate all my magnificent blessings.

I exude positive vibrations in the world that have a boomerang effect on my wellbeing. I give myself permission to release **negative** thought patterns that have held me back. My smile melts the **negative** tendency of being a victim. I discharge all **negativity** now.

God's Word has transformed my life with a clear delineation about leaving the **negative** behind and accentuating the positive. I let go of the **negative** frivolous things that used to consume me. I feel comfortable in my own skin, so I shed **negative** thoughts. I have more energy and stamina since I have eliminated my **negative** thinking. I have pep in my step, fire in my belly, and a worthy goal that I am working towards. I positively feel energized, and wealthy!

181:
Care
June 29

Bible Verses

"The righteous cares about justice for the poor, but the wicked have no such concern." Proverbs 29:7 (NIV)

"I care very little if I am judged by you or by any human court; indeed, I do not even judge myself." 1 Corinthians 4:3 (NIV)

Word of the Day

Care – To be responsible for. Guardianship. To watch over. To value something or someone. Thoughtfulness and consideration.

Quotes

"The care of human life and happiness, and not their destruction, is the first and only object of good government." Thomas Jefferson

"Care and diligence bring luck." Proverb

"The more care should we take, to keep the simple, scriptural account continually in our eye: pure love reigning alone in the heart and life." John Wesley

Pam's Perspective

When I was laid up and bedridden the first three months of my broken leg, I was overwhelmed by the great care I received from Gary. We had only been dating two months when he emptied my bedpan, cooked, cleaned, did laundry for me, and never complained once. I decided to marry Gary since I saw how much he cared.

Questions

What do I care for? Who do I care for? How well do I take care of myself? How many ways can I show that I care for myself and my family?

Declarations

I **care** about the people in my life. I do what I can to help them out as much as I can. Friends are great medicine, so I get regular doses of **caring** conversations, social engagements, and sharing of deep feelings and thoughts. I cultivate supportive, **caring** friendships, and expand my social circle. I love spontaneously and **care** generously.

I know that God **cares** for me, loves me, and directs my steps. God **cares** enough to keep me out of harm's way. I **care** for myself by setting aside "me" time. I honor God by honoring myself. I make choices that are honest and **caring**. **Self-care** is of utmost importance to my wellbeing, so I schedule an edifying routine that benefits me.

I am incredible. I pay **careful** attention to the thoughts I think, and the words I speak. I take great **care** of my body with the foods I eat, and the exercise I get. I pursue the creative outlets I **care** about. I **care** about myself to get enough sleep. As soon as my head hits the pillow, I am out. I sleep soundly and dream of future successes.

I don't **care** to talk about what I can do; I just do it. I take risks to gain the things I **care** about. I **care** about getting organized, so I use my time efficiently. I am emotionally equipped for taking **care** of my life and handling every problem that comes my way. I **care** about my neighborhood. I recycle and **care** enough to become a good steward of the environment, safeguarding it for future generations.

I love people and **care** about them, even when I don't agree with their point of view. Everyone **cares** about their point of view, and would not intentionally believe theirs was stupid. Therefore when I listen and respect people's opinions, it shows I **care**. As I slow down and relax, I have a mind that accesses wisdom and common sense. I **care** about the best way to reply, so I listen to the Holy Spirit.

182:
Neglect
June 30

Bible Verses
"Do not neglect hospitality, because through it some have entertained angels without knowing it." Hebrews 13:2 (NET)

"And do not neglect to do good and to share what you have, for God is pleased with such sacrifices." Hebrews 13:16 (NET)

Word of the Day
Neglect – To forget about. To be unconcerned for or indifferent. Dismiss.

Quotes
"We should not be so taken up in the search for truth, as to neglect the needful duties of active life; for it is only action that gives a true value and commendation to virtue." Marcus Tullius Cicero

"Perpetual devotion to what a man calls his business is only to be sustained by perpetual neglect of many other things." Robert Louis Stevenson

"If I neglect myself, I lose self-respect. Then my ability to give to others declines; so I take care of myself first, so I can continue to serve others." Pam Malow-Isham

"A little neglect may breed great mischief." Ebenezer Cobham Brewer

"He that thinks he can afford to be negligent is not far from being poor." Samuel Johnson

Questions
Is there anyone who neglects to treat me with respect that I put up with? Why is that? Have I done anything lately to neglect myself? What would benefit by me neglecting it? What have I neglected to do for too long?

Declarations

I **neglect** feeling rushed because I always make enough time in my schedule to get things done. I never **neglect** to arrive on time. I do a lot of worthwhile things while **neglecting** useless distractions. I work hard and reap the rewards others **neglected** to pick up.

Watching, or **neglecting** the news will not change it, so I **neglect** the negativity of the news media that promotes fear. **Neglecting** sarcasm is one of the kindest things I can do. Even when I have **neglected** to recognize God at work in my life, He is still there.

When someone **neglects** to be courteous, I never take offense. When I am angry and want to **neglect** my manners, I stop before I say a hurtful statement. I remember to keep my mouth shut and turn it over to God. Soon my mood changes, and I am glad I held my peace. I never hold a grudge. Forgiveness feels so right, so I **neglect** anger.

I am family centered as I work at strengthening our bond without **neglecting** my work. I am overjoyed that I do not **neglect** to take the time to listen to my friends and spend time with them to improve our relationships. I pay careful attention not to pass by someone without **neglecting** to say a kind word. Being kind is so easy to do.

I have the healthiest lungs because I don't **neglect** fun activities that keep me moving. I observe what is best for me. I appreciate the peace and serenity of my life while inserting moderate movement. I can take the stairs and feel strong, so I **neglect** the elevator.

Curiosity is a gift I emphasize. I instigate creativity. I watch over my thoughts, never **neglecting** the importance of them. I keep my brain active by learning new things and asking a lot of questions. I have a beginner's mind, examining things others **neglect** to think about.

183:
Warrior
July 1

Bible Verses
"As arrows are in the hand of a warrior, so are the children of one's youth."
Psalm 127:4 (AMP)

"But the Lord stands beside me like a great warrior. Before him my persecutors will stumble. They cannot defeat me. They will fail and be thoroughly humiliated. Their dishonor will never be forgotten." Jeremiah 20:11 (NLT)

Word of the Day
Warrior –A fearless individual. An excellent fighter. Soldier.

Quotes
"Warrior pose battles inner weakness and wins focus. You see that there is no war within you. You're on your own side, and you are your own strength." Terri Guillemets

"It is said the warrior's is the twofold way of pen and sword, and he should have a taste for both ways." Miyamoto Musashi

"The warrior who cultivates his mind polishes his arms." Duc de Boufflers

Pam's Perspective
When I was in my twenties, I studied Tang So Do Karate. I yearn to be a warrior for love, like Wonder Woman. Simplicity in promoting love works best. Being a broken warrior, who ministers despite my deficiencies, has expanded my love.

Questions
Who is my favorite warrior/superhero that I would like as a mentor? Why is that? What is stopping me from being more like that person?

Declarations

I am a **warrior** aglow with God's goodness. I lead with love. Being a peace **warrior**, I encourage cooperation and togetherness. I am a **warrior** illuminated by love. I am up for sharpening my skills as a benevolent **warrior**. Nothing stops me. I don't back down, for I am fearless in the face of hard times. God's **warrior** Spirit lives in me.

The time for me to embrace my significance is now. God is on my side, so I am a brave **warrior**. I live faithfully hearing the voice of the Lord and obeying. I activate my **warrior** power by calling on the Almighty for help. I am a **warrior** in the army of God, conquering fear, discouragement, and doubt. Victory is the outcome for me.

I am a mighty **warrior**. I am in control and have fine-tuned my **warrior** ways. I am diligent in study and have outlined the assignment for my day. I take action, do the work, and win the **war**. I am flexible as I follow my plans that are headed for success. I am a dynamic **warrior** defeating all my enemies, prevailing until the end.

I know I have to do some training and fight some battles to be the best **warrior** I can be. Truth and honor are my armor. I am a **warrior** of light as I master the art of telling my story, and making a positive difference. I am a philanthropic **warrior** as I nurture the self-esteem of others by the optimism I share. I let Spirit lead, and speak through me, as I embolden everyone I encounter. I am a gifted **warrior**.

Now is the opportunity for me to apprehend my divine inheritance. I am a King's kid. A **warrior** of love and forgiveness, spreading light and good news everywhere I go. I get on board with what God is doing. With the backing of the Almighty, I slay downheartedness, distress, and infuse each opportunity with opulence, peace, and glory. I am the **warrior** of light, joy, harmony, and generosity.

184:
Opponent
July 2

Bible Verses

"I'll give you words and wisdom that none of your opponents will be able to counter or contradict." Luke 21:15 (CEB)

"And let your instruction be sound and fit and wise and wholesome, vigorous and irrefutable and above censure, so that the opponent may be put to shame, finding nothing discrediting or evil to say about us." Titus 2:8 (AMP)

Word of the Day

Opponent – Someone who challenges you. An enemy or rival.

Quotes

"The best thing to give to your enemy is forgiveness; to an opponent, tolerance; to a friend, your heart; to your child, a good example; to a father, deference; to your mother, conduct that will make her proud of you; to yourself, respect; to all men, charity." Clara Lucas Balfour

"Give way to your opponent; thus will you gain the crown of victory." Ovid

"Every dictator is an enemy of freedom, an opponent of law." Demosthenes

Pam's Perspective

My biggest opponent has always been myself. Conquering my negative self-talk with affirmations has given me confidence and a happy outlook on life.

Questions

Do I see people that have different viewpoints than I as an opponent, or a friend? Who is my real opponent? What am I fighting for? Could I turn a current opponent into a colleague? What am I waiting for?

Declarations

The effort my **opponent** puts forth challenges me to do my best, so I rise to a new level of ability. God's Word is the best equalizer against any **opponent**. I dodge the bullet, evade the onslaught of negativity, and stick it out to defeat every **opponent** I face.

I am a savvy negotiator against any **opponent**. With divine backing, I hold my ground. We don't have to see each other as **opponents**. I see my **opponent** as resembling me and know we can benefit from helping each other, rather than **opposing** each other. I am thankful for the chance to spar with my **opponent** to stimulate advancement.

I am a winner, and I act like one. I explore new creative avenues to beat my **opponent** because I know God has made me very artistic. My fierce **opponent** turns into a loyal friend. I shake hands with my **opponent**, congratulating them for making me work for the win.

I choose to look at my **opponent** with compassionate eyes. My only **opponent** is my apathy. I am totally capable of realizing my dreams in the face of any **opponent**. **Opponents** fear me. I have a knack for getting things done and doing things right.

I take time to be silent and go within, so I can face the real **opponent**, me. I am a model for people to follow. I ignore the complaints of my pessimistic **opponent**. I set boundaries so my negativity **opponent** can't thrive. I utilize my energy by spreading goodwill.

The faithfulness of Jesus gives me hope to make peace with my **opponent**. I allow God's banner of love to fly over my heart. I delight to do God's will. I lay aside every hindrance from every **opponent**, and fix my eyes on Christ. I am grateful to be part of the family of God. I like sharing laughs and hugs with my family.

185:
Restraint
July 3

Bible Verses
"Blow the trumpet in Zion; set apart a fast [a day of restraint and humility]; call a solemn assembly." Joel 2:15 (AMP)

"Isn't this the fast I choose: releasing wicked restraints, untying the ropes of a yoke, setting free the mistreated, and breaking every yoke?" Isaiah 58:6 (CEB)

Word of the Day
Restraint –Repressing urges. Self-discipline. Self-government. Restriction.

Quotes
"Most evil is perverted good. For instance, extravagance is generosity carried to excess. Revenge is sometimes a sense of justice which has put no restraint upon itself. Woman's worst fault is perverted self-sacrifice." Frederick W. Robertson

"There is always a limit to self-indulgence, none to restraint." Mahatma Gandhi

Pam's Perspective
I am still a work in progress. As soon as I conquer one bad habit, I find another one that needs restraint. I used to think 'If I use restraint in this one area, I will be free in all other areas that I need restraint.' Unfortunately, I have not found that to be true. I have also perceived that if I am not diligent, I can fall back into old familiar patterns that do not serve me. Some things are easy to restrain, and some not. Recognizing my frailty improves my compassion for others who struggle.

Questions
What restraints do I have? What restraint do I need? Could it be good to place a restraint on some of my desires? What would my life be like if I lifted the restraint on my creativity? What cool thing could I invent today?

Declarations

I place a **restraint** on my lips, so I do not speak evil of anyone. I recognize we are all human. I am free from bondage and the **restraint** of being a people pleaser. I am a God pleaser. I empathize with others. I had **restraints** in the past, but there is joy in the now.

The **restraints** that used to hold me down are gone by the power of Grace. I have no habits that **restrain**, or entice me in any harmful way. I place God in control of my life and put my trust in Him. I gladly follow the **restraints** placed in my heart because I know God only wants the best for me. His love makes me feel safe and secure.

By putting **restraints** on my apathetic self, I work out when I don't feel like it. I always do just the right amount of exercise to stay in shape. I do what is best for my body. The **restraint** I use to turn down dessert has left me feeling more healthy and in control.

I am continually discovering new things. There are no **restraints** on what I can accomplish. I give myself permission to say no to the things that do not interest me. I am responsible for walking in the revelation I have been given through the Holy Spirit, whatever **restraint** that is. I am thankful for Godly **restraints** on me.

I lift the **restraints** off my imagination, and I design in detail my life and make it a great one. I declare I can handle every task that comes my way. I stay happy, so I make every moment count. I am a success magnet, and there are no **restraints** on how much I can earn.

I gracefully step through open doors with no **restraints**. I break the **restraints** of shyness and conformity and leave nothing unsaid to my loved ones. They know how much I care. I can live **restraint** free with love, as I pursue my dreams. My life is phenomenal.

186:
Liberty
July 4

Bible Verses
"Now the Lord is the Spirit, and where the Spirit of the Lord is, there is liberty." 2 Corinthians 3:17 (NKJV)

"But the one who looks into the perfect law of liberty and continues to do it, not being a forgetful hearer but a doer who acts, this one will be blessed in what he does." James 1:25 (LEB)

Word of the Day
Liberty – Freedom to be what you want to be. Choice. Opportunity.

Quotes
"We hold these truths to be self-evident: that all men are created equal; that they are endowed by their Creator with certain unalienable rights; that among these are life, liberty, and the pursuit of happiness." Thomas Jefferson

"Is life so dear or peace so sweet as to be purchased at the price of chains and slavery? Forbid it, Almighty God! I know not what course others may take, but as for me, give me liberty, or give me death!" Patrick Henry

"Education is a better safeguard of liberty than a standing army." Edward Everett

"He that would make his own liberty secure must guard even his enemy from oppression; for if he violates this duty, he establishes a precedent that will reach to himself." Thomas Paine

Questions
Why do I forget about the liberty that I already have? What would my life be like if I used that liberty? What liberty will I walk in today?

Declarations

I take back the **liberty** that was stolen from me. I have the **liberty** to hold my ground and stand up for myself. I pardon people who have hurt me. I walk in **liberty** as I free myself from any silly resentment.

My confidence skyrockets off the charts as I free myself from negative thinking, and walk in optimistic **liberty**. I have the **liberty** to think pleasant thoughts. I like operating at my best. I have the **liberty** to choose wisely, and to act well. I am made of the right stuff.

I have the **liberty** to spread complements to those around me. I declare I am greeted with smiles, warm embraces, and hopeful words. I allow others and myself the **liberty** to grow and evolve. I am laid back. I grant everyone the **liberty** to be themselves.

I am grateful for the opportunity to live in a country that cares about **liberty** and justice for all. I appreciate the **liberty** of freedom of speech and being unrestrictive in what I can say. I exercise my **liberty**, reason, and will to choose sensibly. The **liberty** to assemble peaceably and the power of the written word is invaluable.

Liberty grows in me as I educate myself. I enjoy the **liberty** I have to do what is right. I love what I do. I am thankful for the **liberty** to become the best person I possibly can become, and the freedom to make it happen. I live responsibly. I make a big impact on my world.

I have the **liberty** to only say yes to the things that fire me up. I walk in a state of **liberty** that is so enticing and joyful that people want the **liberty** that I have. My **liberty** comes from Christ. I love the **liberty** of being able to worship God in the way that I choose. The spirit of **liberty** living inside me brings power to overcome any challenge. I manifest my dreams as I choose **liberty**, and walk in freedom.

187:
Vice
July 5

Bible Verses

"Some of humankind hated the light. They scampered hurriedly back into the darkness where vices thrive and wickedness flourishes." John 3:20 (VOICE)

"(I use an everyday illustration because human nature grasps truth more readily that way.) In the past you voluntarily gave your bodies to the service of vice and wickedness—for the purpose of becoming wicked. So, now, give yourselves to the service of righteousness—for the purpose of becoming really good." Romans 6:19 (PHILLIPS)

Word of the Day

Vice – A human weakness that one gives themselves over to.

Quotes

"For as faintness is a disease of the body, so is vice a sickness of the mind. Wherefore, since we judge those that have corporal infirmities to be rather worthy of compassion than of hatred, much more are they to be pitied, and not abhorred, whose minds are oppressed with wickedness, the greatest malady that may be." Anicius Manlius Severinus Boethius

"Virtue has a veil, vice a mask." Victor Hugo

"Adorn thyself with simplicity and with indifference towards the things which lie between virtue and vice. Love mankind. Follow God. The poet says that Law rules all. And it is enough to remember that law rules all." Marcus Aurelius

Questions

How has vice helped me in the past? Is there a vice I need to release? What would my life be like vice free? When will that be possible?

Declarations

I overcome the struggle of my **vices** by surrendering to God. I drink from the unlimited source of purity and light, and thirst no more. God leads me to conquer every **vice** and keeps me in perfect health.

Even though I was infatuated with a **vice** for a while, and allowed it to rule, I now claim my authority over it. I am grateful that my **vice** did not overpower me. I will survive and make the most of my life.

I take an inventory of myself. I realize I am fallible and capable of giving in to **vice**, so I cut people slack who have not overcome their **vices**. God gives me the strength to stay on the over-comers path.

I prime my mind with thoughts from above. I write down and set goals that will help me conquer every **vice** I no longer need. I break out of my comfort zone and do the uncomfortable things I need to do, in order to overthrow every **vice**, fear, and self-doubt that I have.

I rise above every **vice** that would try to hold me down. I feel very content, so I have no need for any **vice** to numb my satisfaction. I appreciate all the leverage and power I have not giving into **vice**.

I gain certainty by shedding limiting beliefs about my **vice**. Sweet radiance is on my countenance as I sing for joy, overcoming every **vice** that no longer serves me. I declare I have a forgiving heart and a kind spirit. I know God hears every unspoken need and sends the answer. I say thank you for an unmerited favor, and saving grace.

I hang around disciplined people. I take off my **vice** mask and strive to impersonate Jesus. I restore the clarity of my purpose and the reason for my mission when I meditate on my values, instead of my **vices**. Love heals all things and frees me from every **vice**.

188:
Virtue
July 6

Bible Verses

"He loves virtue and equity; the Eternal's love fills the whole earth." Psalm 33:5 (VOICE)

"Yea, and for this very cause adding on your part all diligence, in your faith supply virtue; and in your virtue knowledge;" 2 Peter 1:5 (ASV)

Word of the Day

Virtue – Morality. Temperance. Integrity. Having a good character, kindness, generosity, incorruptibility, and love.

Quotes

"Kindness is the sunshine in which virtue grows." Robert Green Ingersoll

"Certainly virtue is like precious odors, most fragrant when they are incensed, or crushed: for prosperity doth best discover vice, but adversity doth best discover virtue." Sir Francis Bacon

"Virtue is indeed its own reward, and it alone shines far and wide, regardless of fortune; nor is it elevated by any power, or desires to become famous by the applause of the crowd, having no desire of outward help, nor any deed of praise." Claudianus

"I hope I shall possess firmness and virtue enough to maintain what I consider the most enviable of all titles, the character of an honest man." George Washington

Questions

What virtue do I hold dear? Who is the most virtuous person I know? What virtue do I need to nourish and cultivate today? What does a person of virtue look like to me? Do I model that person? Why or why not?

Declarations

I invite God's presence to penetrate every fiber of my being. I am focused as I choose all the **virtues** that I aspire to, so I may emulate them. I have the power of God on my side to help me walk in **virtue**.

I mirror mercy to remind others of God's grace. I make good on the promises I make to myself. With repetition, I reconstruct my inner thought life to fabricate the outer life of **virtue** that I want to live. I promote accountability, doing what I say I will do, on time.

I walk in love as I stay on task. I ask myself what I need to know as I pattern after the **virtue** of wisdom and wonder. I am economical with my resources. I shrewdly negotiate the best deals as I play with the **virtue** of assertiveness, fairness, and flexibility. I like being rich.

I work on myself, contemplating the **virtues** I want to enhance while supporting others to work on themselves. I am grateful for my friends that model the **virtue** of loyalty, patience, and tolerance. I have much to learn. I inspire honesty and good works. My list of **virtues** continues to grow as I develop courage, graciousness, modesty, eloquence, reverence, generosity, joy, and strength.

Cleanliness and order serve me well. As I simplify my life, it frees me from unimportant clutter. Orderliness and patience are **virtues** I like. Temperance makes daily life tranquil. I indulge myself in gratitude. With fortitude, I work on the **virtues** most important to me now. My guts, persistence, passion, and reliability define me.

I practice the **virtue** of authenticity and caring as I go through my day. Tenacity is a **virtue** I use to create a better self-image by thinking the way God thinks. I create new **virtues** and habits that aid me. I lead with meekness, empathy, bravery, and enthusiasm.

Help

July 7

Bible Verses

"Our help is in the name of the Lord, Who made heaven and earth." Psalm 124:8 (ESV)

"For I, the Lord your God, will hold your right hand, saying to you, 'Fear not, I will help you." Isaiah 41:13 (NKJV)

Word of the Day

Help – To benefit someone with or without expecting compensation. To offer relief, guidance or advice to someone.

Quotes

"Self-help books, CD's and seminars are completely worthless without a strong commitment to both internalize and put into action what you've learned." Michael Althsuler

"Be not afraid of life. Believe that life is worth living and your belief will help create the fact." William James

Pam's Perspective

When I help people, I help myself feel good too. I would rather give than receive. Receiving help is a lesson that was hard for me to learn. Help is always available if I swallow my pride and ask for it. I was used to being the person who helped others, but when I broke my leg in three places, I learned the gift of how to receive.

Questions

Who will I help today? Why will I do it regardless if I get paid or not? How can I help myself feel better about myself? Is there anything stopping me from helping myself become successful? If so, what can I do about it?

Declarations

I **help** raise the bar of my thinking with my daily declarations. After I have been **helped**, I can **help** others. I always feel better when I **help** someone. I **help** people believe in themselves by my words of praise. Giving compliments is easy, **helps** people feel good, and is free. I **help** myself by believing in my ability to do a great job.

People love me because of my optimism **helping** to light their way. I **help** inspire people to dream big again. My strong excitement about life **helps** invigorate the enthusiasm of others. I love giving my best, **helping** out wherever I can. Instead of sitting around waiting for **help**, I can **help** myself thrive by getting busy, and take action.

I **help** myself stay healthy by my wise food choices. I prefer fresh fruit over sugar. I cooperate with my body and give it enough rest and relaxation to **help** it heal properly. I **help** myself smile.

I enhance my community by volunteering to **help**, and by making it a more beautiful place to inhabit. I **help** the earth by planting trees, flowers, and shrubs. I **help** pick up litter wherever I am, doing my part of teaching people to respect where they live.

I **help** out at home. I **help** out around my church. I **help** contribute financially, spiritually, and verbally with all my kind words and deeds. I believe in the spiritual gift of **helps**. I am a great **helper**. I **help** myself to all the promises of God, trusting they are true, and seeing them come to pass in front of me. I **help** people laugh.

Whenever I get disappointed, I pray for **help**, and God's Spirit lifts mine to a peaceful place. God showers me with blessings and favor as I receive a gully-washer of **help** from Him. I **help** spread the love and joy of God wherever I go. I am happy, bright, and free.

190:

Harm
July 8

Bible Verses
"Cease from anger, and forsake wrath; do not fret—it only causes harm."
Psalm 37:8 (NKJV)

"Strive not with a man without cause, if he have done thee no harm."
Proverbs 3:30 (DARBY)

Word of the Day
Harm – To do violence against someone or something. Sabotage.

Quotes
"Life is thickly sown with thorns; I know no other remedy than to pass rapidly over them. The longer we dwell on our misfortunes, the greater is their power to harm us." Voltaire

"He harms himself who does harm to another, and the evil plan is most harmful to the planner." Hesiod

Pam's Perspective
I have harmed myself more than all the abusers, tormentors and mean people combined, by reliving it in my head. Most of my life I spent putting myself down for not living up to the unrealistic expectations I had for myself. Living in denial of my shortcomings, I harmed myself by numbing out with external substances. Then I put myself down for that. Learning to love myself has been the greatest gift I could ever give myself. I no longer am addicted to substances that harm.

Questions
Is there anyone who has harmed me that I need to forgive? Is there anyone I need to make restitution to for any harm I may have caused?

Declarations

I assimilate the most nutritious vegetables at every meal. I eat whole, organic, fresh food. Rarely, do I **harm** my body by overeating, but when I do, I give myself a break and decide to make wiser choices in the future. I recognize the habits that promote health and do more of them. I recognize the habits that **harm** me and choose to avoid them.

I am careful about what I put before my eyes, so I don't **harm** myself by the negativity of the news. Fear immobilizes and **harms** me, so I shake it off and turn up the volume of my affirmations. I do not allow thoughts that are **harmful** to dwell in my righteous mind.

I absolve resentment and anger for I know they do me **harm**. I mend broken relationships and restore peace. I am free from any pain or **harm**. There is no **harm** in listening to people with different ideas than mine. I stay open, so I can understand where they are coming from. I would rather feel the **harm** of being betrayed by a friend than to close myself off and hide from the people around me.

When I hide my shame, I **harm** myself. I repent, renounce and say no more to the **harmful** connection I have with guilt and shame. I break that connection now, in Jesus name. God chose to bring me out of the **harm** of guilt, and reward me with clout. When the enemy tries to **harm** me with **harmful** accusations like, 'you're no good', or 'you're not enough,' I laugh, and remind myself, I am God's child. He smiles and tells me my future is safe with Him.

I release toxic, **harmful** memories and put my focus on Christ. I have no worries. Nothing I've ever done can cause God to **harm** me. Nor do I have to **harm** me, or try to earn my way. God loves me even when I can't feel it. I am divinely sheltered from **harm**. When I accept that I am weak without Him, He makes me powerful.

191:
Up
July 9

Bible Verses

"So I will thank you as long as I live. I will lift up my hands to pray in your name." Psalm 63:4 (GW)

"Yes, speak up for the poor and helpless, and see that they get justice." Proverbs 31:9 (NLT)

Word of the Day

Up – A place that is above something else. Heavenward. To raise. To elevate or increase.

Quotes

"Dream up the impossible to walk in the miraculous." Pam Malow-Isham

"I know of no one who has done more for humanity than Jesus. In fact, there is nothing wrong with Christianity…The trouble is with Christians. You do not begin to live up to your own teachings." Mahatma Gandhi

Pam's Perspective

My weight has gone up and down. I have tried every diet imaginable and lost hundreds of pounds, only to gain them back. Having hypothyroidism does not help either. Losing the emotional baggage through counseling, making better food choices, doing some form of exercise, and working on this book while declaring positive things over my life has enabled me to manage my weight. Being comfortable in my own skin, regardless of my size, is worth its weight in gold.

Questions

Who do I look up to? Can I get that person to mentor me? If not, what traits about that person can I copy? What do I think about when I look up?

Declarations

I count my blessings as I rise **up** early and make the most of my day. I start **up** with a positive attitude. I jazz **up** my wardrobe with a smile. Drinking pure water is a great pick-me-**up**. I juice **up** with fresh fruit and veggies in the morning. I eat **up** my vegetables first.

I push **up** the intensity of my workout to maximize my desired results. I build **up** my body by lifting weights. Doing **sit-ups** help strengthen my core. I love working out with my friends. I am thankful for the people who encourage me and pump me **up**. I love feeling sturdy, stout, and strong. I sit **up** straight and tall.

I **uphold** my values and create practices that support them. I look **up** for help and give thanks. I lift **up** the people around me by my kind words, prayers, and actions. I easily step **up** the volunteering in my community. I readily start **up** new groups to promote unity.

I never give **up**, or give in, concerning the progress of my dreams. I show **up** and show off my expert skills. By being creative, I imagine **up** the coolest inventions. I am **up** for any challenge and ready to go.

I pick **up** good habits. I zip **up** my lip when I want to make a rude comment. Just because someone blows **up** in front of me does not mean I have to react. I hold **up** a banner of love. I listen **up** on how I can bring harmony to the situation. There is always space for peace.

I drive **up** to my beautiful home that is paid off. My furniture and decor are of the highest quality and in the best taste. I embrace my success. I love being grown **up** as I create my own destiny. I face **up** to my shortcomings and determine to change them. I listen **up** when new opportunities come my way. I am **up** for the next great adventure. I send my praise **up** to the One who makes it all happen.

192:
Down
July 10

Bible Verses

"Yet, you desire truth and sincerity. Deep down inside me you teach me wisdom." Psalm 51:6 (GW)

"But after Christ offered one sacrifice for sins, forever, he sat down at the right side of God." Hebrews 10:12 (NCV)

Word of the Day

Down – At the bottom. Lower than something else. Underneath.

Quotes

"Make it a rule, and pray to God to help you to keep it, never, if possible, to lie down at night without being able to say: "I have made one human being at least a little wiser, or a little happier, or at least a little better this day." Charles Kingsley

"The decision to become more successful boils down to the desire for greater freedom." Gary Ryan Blair

Pam's Perspective

Being down in the dumps does not have an upside. I have lived with depression on and off for most of my life. Getting down on myself for being down, doesn't help. I have to force myself to get up and go to church, dances, events, and the gym, or I would just stay home. When I get out and interact with people, or do service work, I always feel better. Being in a supportive community lifts me up.

Questions

Do I get down on the floor and stretch? How often? Do I ever look down on anyone? Why will I help someone who is down and out? What do I reach for when I get down? Who helps me out when I am down?

Declarations

I allow God to tear **down** the walls around my heart and fill it with love. I align myself with the reality of what is going on in heaven and live it **down** here on earth. The Lord is present and lives in my midst. I have a faith I am proud to hand **down** to future generations.

When someone tries to talk **down** to me, I smile and remind them we are equal as human beings. I crash **down** barriers of prejudice and break **down** walls of outdated mindsets. I step **down** off my high horse, humble myself, and admit when I have made a mistake.

I get **down** to business when it is time to work. I shoot **down** negative thoughts that try to creep in. I cast **down** perfection and shut down bias. I promote teamwork. I am always in high demand. When I slow **down**, I can see the good fortune in front of me.

When I fall **down** and don't think I can go any further, I tell myself, 'just one more time; you can do it, just one more time,' and yes I can keep going. When I am feeling **down**, I pick myself up by counting my blessings. I lie **down** at night after doing excellent work all day and know that I have done all that needs to be done **down** here.

I bow **down** to a perfect God who then sets me on high. There is a spot **down** deep in my heart that only God can fill. I now receive God's touch **down** in my heart. I am singled out for special consideration from God, and nothing can get me **down**.

I have fun when I boogie **down** on the dance floor. I throw **down** my shyness, swing **down** my dread, and let my freak flag shake away any sadness. My exuberance for life tears **down** my insecurities. I love my uniqueness, and my ability to smash **down** fear. I let **down** my guard, and open up to new playmates. I love making new pals.

193:
Sacred
July 11

Bible Verses
"Do not give that which is holy (the sacred thing) to the dogs, and do not throw your pearls before hogs, lest they trample upon them with their feet and turn and tear you in pieces." Matthew 7:6 (AMP)

"Greet all the brethren with a sacred kiss." 1 Thessalonians 5:26 (AMP)

Word of the Day
Sacred – Cherished and blessed. Sanctified. Anointed. Godlike.

Quotes
"The sacred rights of mankind are not to be rummaged for among old parchments or musty records. They are written, as with a sunbeam, in the whole volume of human nature, by the hand of the divinity itself; and can never be erased or obscured by mortal power." Alexander Hamilton

"Surely there is grandeur in knowing that in the realm of thought, at least, you are without a chain; that you have the right to explore all heights and depth; that there are no walls nor fences, nor prohibited places, nor sacred corners in all the vast expanse of thought." Robert Green Ingersoll

"Your own mind is a sacred enclosure into which nothing harmful can enter except by your permission. Your own mind has the power to transmute every external phenomenon to its own purposes. If happiness arises from cheerfulness, kindliness, and rectitude (and who will deny it?), what possible combination of circumstances is going to make you unhappy so long as the machine remains in order?" Arnold Bennett

Questions
Do I view my world and everything in it as sacred? Why am I sacred?

Declarations

I am a **sacred** receptacle anointed by God for good works. My life is a **sacred** ministry of showing God's love. I am very appreciative as I look up to God and thank Him for helping me bring the **sacred** to earth. I am available to God as He moves through this **sacred** vessel and uses me to be a blessing. People realize I have been with Jesus.

I enjoy the **sacred** time I set aside to talk to my Creator. I surrender to the unknown without going through an analytical process. I know God will always see me through every **sacred** detail. I move from survival mode to **sacred** creation. God is able to do lavishly above all I can ask, or think. I look for the silver lining in every situation.

I have a **sacred** mindset. I elevate my conscious as I read the **sacred** scriptures, and meditate on what is holy. I learn from within. I have the privilege of making **sacred** decisions and controlling my destiny. I have a spirit of **sacred** expectancy behind every decision I make.

Every step I take is on **sacred** ground. I step aside and get out of my own way. My **sacred** ears are open to hearing what the Spirit is saying to me. I open my **sacred** mouth to bless the **sacred** people around me. I am grateful for all the **sacred** aspects of my life. I keep my word and hold it as **sacred**. I bring my **sacred** vision to life.

I elongate this **sacred** moment in prayer, so I don't rush past it. I relish every **sacred** occasion. I enjoy finding ways to serve my **sacred** community. I make food for the sick, and go visit them. I take the time to show I care. I say a **sacred** prayer for healing and restoration.

I help with the little-**sacred** things I do, making a big difference in the lives of many. I see everyone as **sacred** and special. I bless my **sacred** pet with love. I'm God's **sacred** gift, made for His enjoyment.

Profane
July 12

Bible Verses
"You shall not swear falsely by My name, so as to profane the name of your God; I am the Lord." Leviticus 19:12 (NASB)

"Do we not all have one father? Has not one God created us? Why do we deal treacherously each against his brother so as to profane the covenant of our fathers?" Malachi 2:10 (NASB)

Word of the Day
Profane – Being abusive to oneself or someone else. Disrespectful.

Quotes
"Scriptures, n. The sacred books of our holy religion, as distinguished from the false and profane writings on which all other faiths are based." Ambrose Bierce

"The foolish and wicked practice of profane cursing and swearing is a vice so mean and low that every person of sense and character detests and despises it." George Washington

Pam's Perspective
Surviving the profane act of rape, more than once was not easy. I did nothing to cause or deserve it, but it happened. I wish I would have had the courage to report them, but I was young and insecure. Keeping quiet prolonged my pain, and they probably went on to rape, or hurt others. God's grace, admitting it happened, and counseling, helped me heal. Time, love, and forgiveness, heals all wounds.

Questions
Do I use profane language? What must I do to keep my mind from the profane? Have I ever looked at a person as profane? Do I act profanely?

Declarations

I train myself to look for the good and avoid the **profane**, without denying its existence. We all have a **profane** side to us, and when we own up to that part of ourselves, it no longer has power over us. I make a conscious shift to shun the **profanity** of all the bad news in the world, so I can focus on the beautiful sacred things around me.

I am responsible for what I listen to and what I see, either **profane** or holy. I am discerning with what I watch on TV, theater, or on the internet. I also know I cannot un-see something once I have seen it, or take something back once I have said it, so I am vigilant not to put anything **profane** before my eyes, or utter **profanity** from my lips.

I regard even the most **profane** individual as sacred because they are a child of God. People in the gutter need love too. When I acknowledge the **profane** in my own life, it is easier to forgive the **profane** in others. I recognize I am divine, and so are everyone else. God loves us all; even the ones we think are the most **profane**. God has a sense of humor and laughs at our judgmental attitude.

I purge my house of any **profane** clutter. I like to share and donate to charities. I am respectful of the environment. I think greater than the **profane** conditions in the world. I live in the present, and choose to release all the **profane** from my past. I no longer need it. God continues to free me from the **profane,** destructive things that happened to me. Everywhere I walk, sit, or stand is holy ground.

When I hear outright **profanity**, or see **profane** behavior, God still wants me to forgive, and pray for my enemies. It feels good to be kind, and release the **profanity** of hate, judgment, and bitterness. Healing occurs when I show love. I choose to live out the principles of God and walk in the light of love, mercy, peace, and grace.

195:
Enough
July 13

Bible Verses
"God is magnificent; he can never be praised enough. There are no boundaries to his greatness." Psalm 14:3 (MSG)

"If you find honey, eat just enough— too much of it, and you will vomit." Proverbs 25:16 (NIV)

Word of the Day
Enough – Ample amount. Bountiful quantity. Plentiful.

Quotes
"Secret #1 – You're good enough as you are. Secret #2 – If you genuinely don't think you're good enough, please refer back to secret #1." Tim Brownson

"No man is rich enough to buy back his past." Oscar Wilde

"Man is fond of counting his troubles, but he does not count his joys. If he counted them up as he ought to, he would see that every lot has enough happiness provided for it." Fyodor Dostoevsky

"He who wants little always has enough." Zimmerman

Pam's Perspective
God sees you as enough, just the way you are. No matter how long it takes, do what you must, and don't give up until you feel the truth that you are enough.

Questions
What does enough look like to me? When will I have enough? How will I know when I have enough? If I am not enough today, when will I be?

Declarations

I always have **enough** of whatever I need because I live in a world of abundance where everything is unfolding perfectly. I am diligent **enough** with my positive thoughts and declarations that I stay assured of a favorable outcome. I am successful **enough** today.

God is wise **enough** to handle all my problems, and answer every question I could ever think of. I am smart **enough** to give all my concerns over to the Omniscient one. I receive the precise answer at the right time. I am spiritual **enough** to know I don't have to work for God's approval. I pray **enough** to keep troubles away.

I eat just **enough** to fill the void, without stuffing myself. I eat plenty of fruits and vegetables. I drink **enough** water to get in eight glasses a day. I am disciplined **enough** to exercise, and stay active. I show myself **enough** appreciation to keep going when times get tough.

I am talented **enough** to keep a great job. I am resourceful **enough** to make something, out of nothing. I always find a way. I am prepared **enough** when asked a question and informed **enough** to know that I do not know it all. I will thrive on learning new things this year.

I am humble **enough** to admit when I make a mistake. I am curious **enough** to keep asking questions. I am enlightened **enough** not to let sarcasm affect me. I am strong **enough** to offer mercy. I am gracious **enough** to forgive. I care **enough** to love the so-called unlovable.

I am cute **enough** to turn heads when I walk by. I am pleasant **enough** to have a lot of supportive friends. I am generous **enough** to my children. I am nutty **enough** to get a laugh and have fun wherever I go. I am aloof **enough** to create mystique. I am attentive **enough** to do what is right. I am special **enough**, always.

196:
Excessive
July 14

Bible Verses

"So do not be excessively righteous or excessively wise; otherwise you might be disappointed. Do not be excessively wicked and do not be a fool; otherwise you might die before your time." Ecclesiastes 7:16-17 (NET)

"Don't drink wine excessively. The drunken path is a reckless path. It leads nowhere. Instead, let God fill you with the Holy Spirit." Ephesians 5:18 (VOICE)

Word of the Day

Excessive – Extravagant and more than enough. Superabundant.

Quotes

"The desire of power in excess caused the angels to fall; the desire of knowledge in excess caused man to fall; but in charity there is no excess; neither can angel or man come in danger by it." Francis Bacon

"The excessive increase of anything causes a reaction in the opposite direction." Plato

"One is never more on trial than in the moment of excessive good fortune." Lew Wallace

Pam's Perspective

Excessive worry over my choices and future was a total waste of time. I no longer listen to the voice that tells me to worry. Everything has worked out fine.

Questions

Have I been excessive with my spending? How can I be excessively happy? Is there such a thing? Am I excessive with my need to fit in?

Declarations

I spend **excessive** time in the healing power of the great outdoors. I include walking in my daily regimen. I inhale the **excessive** beauty all around me. By not spending **excessive** time indoors, I balance my exercise, and delight myself with nature, no matter what kind of weather is going on. I am **excessive** about enjoying life, being happy, staying active, and living carefree. I can conquer the world.

I am **excessively** blessed and highly favored. God has proven His **excessive** love for me time and time again. I have received **excessive** joy. I celebrate being forgiven, well-liked, and chosen for greatness. I am **excessively** settled and secure, no matter what life throws at me.

I concentrate on the present moment, so I am not spending **excessive** time thinking about the past, or the future. I am grateful for this day. I create an environment of **excessive** peace around me at all times. No one can steal my joy. I generate **excessive** joy with Holy Spirit.

My positive thinking is **excessively** bigger than the memory of any defeat. I show **excessive** kindness to myself as I release self-judgment and doubt. I am **excessively** smarter than I think I am. I am **excessively** happier than I used to be because I smile more.

I perform **excessively** well under pressure. I conceive of the ideal work conditions and make it happen. I am **excessive** about reinventing myself. I keep asking myself better questions. I oblige myself to think outside the box, being **excessive** with my creativity.

I am **excessive** in showing compassion, and goodwill. As I connect to the **excessively** loving Source, I continue to express gratitude. I am grateful that I have been pardoned, and set free from **excessive** condemnation. I am **excessively** loved by God just the way I am.

197:
Direction
July 15

Bible Verses
"Point your kids in the right direction— when they're old they won't be lost." Proverbs 22:6 (MSG)

"Have you ever seen a massive ship sailing effortlessly across the water? Despite its immense size and the fact that it is propelled by mighty winds, a small rudder directs the ship in any direction the pilot chooses." James 3:4 (VOICE)

Word of the Day
Direction – The path to an objective. An aim or intention to hit. Trajectory.

Quotes
"The direction of the mind is more important than its progress." Joseph Joubert

"God does not guide those who want to run their own life. He only guides those who admit their need of His direction and rely on His wisdom." Winkie Pratney

"We should school ourselves rather in the direction of wide intelligence than of great learning." Democritus

Pam's Perspective
Every time I over commit and try to head in several different directions, I stress out and become unproductive. When I refocus on my big goal, say no to the unimportant, and change my direction, I accomplish great things.

Questions
Do I take the direction of the easy path, or the hard one? How many times have I changed the direction of my life? Am I heading in the best direction to reach my goals right now? Do I seek God for direction?

Declarations

I yield to God in all my ways, and He steers me in the right **direction**. I can see clearly and distinctly the divine plan for my life, and the **direction** I should take. There are no obstacles in my way.

As I aid myself to think outside the box, I see various **directions** I can take. I challenge my mind, so I have the best **direction**. I point my thoughts in **directions** that are pleasing and lovely. I am in the driver's seat. I manage my mind, so it goes in the **direction** I choose.

I take the time to think about my thoughts and reactions that are responsible for my current state. If I am moving in the best possible **direction**, I keep it up. If not, I turn around and head the other way.

Living my dreams and owning my power gets me pumped up. I get out of the way and let God take the helm of my life. I give the green light of hope to my dreams and run in the **direction** to fulfill them.

I like writing the **direction** of my life story. I travel on the highway of love, moving in an upward **direction** toward my positive end. I am resourceful and believe in myself. I keep putting one foot in front of the other. I keep moving in a decisive **direction**.

As I put healthy, nutritious things in my body, I thrive. I incorporate brain-boosting foods like walnuts and spinach into my diet. I choose a healthy **direction** for my eating habits and enjoy the benefits.

I create an accountability group for myself that keeps me moving in a positive **direction**. Getting coached will reinforce the **direction** I need to take. I seek godly input from my mentors. I open myself up to **directions** that reach my goals. Changing **direction** can be fun. I like having lots of options. I move in a successful **direction**.

Journey
July 16

Bible Verses

"The priest answered them, 'Go in peace. Your journey has the Lord's approval.'" Judges 18:6 (NIV)

"The Lord will protect you on your journeys— whether going or coming— from now until forever from now." Psalm 121:8 (CEB)

Word of the Day

Journey – An adventure from point A to B. A voyage to a far-off place.

Quotes

"We are not provided with wisdom; we must discover it for ourselves, after a journey through the wilderness which no one else can take for us an effort which no one can spare us." Marcel Proust

"Hope is like the sun, which, as we journey toward it, casts the shadow of our burden behind us." Samuel Smiles

"Prayer and provender never hinder a journey." Proverb

Pam's Perspective

When I started the journey of writing this book, I had no idea it would be years, and thousands of hours later, but it is a journey I do not regret. Even if it would have taken me twice as long, it was worth it for the growth I have received.

Questions

Am I enjoying my journey? Do I stop and take time to reflect on my journey? Does my journey have a purpose? What is the funniest journey I have ever gone on? What was the hardest journey, and what did I learn?

Declarations

Risk taking can be an exciting **journey** of exploration. I can go on an inventive **journey** to find creative ways of making a living. I am willing to get paid very well for my extraordinary talents. I claim my financial breakthrough now. I am on an abundance **journey**. I trust my instincts to notice why I am on this **journey** in the first place.

My industrious work ethic moves me to the top of my field. I grow wiser on my educational **journey**. I make learning fun on my **journey**. I enlarge my scope of right seeing and thinking. I focus on the good stuff in my **journey**. There is beauty everywhere I look.

I see myself as healthy, whole, and stunning. My **journey** to health has taught me many things. I can restart my healing **journey** now. I have an insatiable zest for life. Because I take care of myself on this **journey**, I have a reserve of extra energy to help others. I am the owner of a strong body, a brilliant mind, and impeccable character.

I enjoy the **journey** and see my plans completed. I am poised for success. I squeeze out more pleasure from every experience and **journey** I take. I see within me the acceptance I desire. I live in a friendly place. I frequently connect with the right people on my **journey**. Keeping in touch with my friends enhances my **journey**.

I stay in an atmosphere of abundant gratitude on my **journey**. I am thankful for this wonderful **journey** of life. I am willing to let things go that no longer support me on this **journey**. God gives me the gift of freedom of choice. There is no **journey** too tough for me. God passionately rejoices over me as we continue our **journey** together. My faithful companion is always with me on my **journey**. Sudden bursts of favor and blessings are sprinkled in front of me, and around me, expanding my health, happiness, and wealth.

199:
Thoughts
July 17

Bible Verses

"Above all, be careful what you think because your thoughts control your life." Proverbs 4:23 (ERV)

"For my thoughts are not your thoughts, neither are your ways my ways," declares the Lord. "As the heavens are higher than the earth, so are my ways higher than your ways and my thoughts than your thoughts." Isaiah 55:8-9 (NIV)

Word of the Day

Thoughts – Contemplation. Judgment. Reflection. Thinking.

Quotes

"The best remedy for evil thoughts is to have the mind occupied with pure and ennobling thoughts. The mind cannot be a vacuum. It must be filled, if not with the good, with that which is evil. Let not the stream of your life be a murmuring stream." John H. Aughey

"You are today where your thoughts have brought you; you will be tomorrow where your thoughts take you." James Lane Allen

"I have often thought if the minds of men were laid open, we should see but little difference between that of the wise man and that of the fool." Joseph Addison

"I have always thought the actions of men the best interpreters of their thoughts." John Locke

Questions

How conscious am I about the thoughts I think? Do I ever dwell on unproductive thoughts? Am I willing to change my thoughts?

Declarations

I am the master of my **thoughts**. I alone can control my **thoughts** and create the destiny of my dreams. I choose my **thoughts** carefully and decisively. Today my **thoughts** are God-centered and positive.

When a **thought** leaps into my mind, does not mean I have to dwell on it. If it is something good, I say, "Yes." If not, I discard it and put my attention on what is good. As I silence my **thoughts** and spend time in stillness, I shift my mood. I find that sliver of hope to go on and I run with it. My pure **thoughts** produce positive effects.

I have cheerful **thoughts** and attract cheerful people. My **thoughts** are infused with heavenly wisdom. I clean house and throw out any negative **thoughts**, and stinking thinking. Being tidy and organized is fun. I create new habits that reinforce the good I want to see.

I pay the price to reach my goals by the **thoughts** I choose to think, and the actions I take. By focusing my **thoughts** on the good that is going on in my life, I stay positive. My divine **thoughts** motivate me to seek out ways to be of service rather than to be served.

I train my **thoughts** to improve my health emotionally, physically, and spiritually. I work with a life coach to help me overcome any hitches in the road or any limiting beliefs. I like having someone that is cheering me on and encouraging me to be my best. I declare positive **thoughts** over my life to nudge out the negativity that tries to press in. I open many doors with my beautiful smile.

My **thoughts** are holy. My **thoughts** are God inspired and creatively infused by the Holy Spirit. God's love for me is unending. God's **thoughts** toward me are always pleasant, filled with mercy, and grace. I receive a double portion of favor today and land on top.

200:
Deeds
July 18

Bible Verses

"Let them praise Yahweh for his loving kindness, for his wonderful deeds to the children of men!" Psalm 107:8 (WEB)

"I remember the days long past; I meditate on all your deeds; I contemplate your handiwork." Psalm 143:5 (CEB)

Word of the Day

Deeds – The effort one takes or the way someone responds with their actions. An activity, task, or undertaking.

Quotes

"It is our own past which has made us what we are. We are the children of our own deeds. Conduct has created character; acts have grown into habits, each year has pressed into us a deeper moral print; the lives we have led have left us such as we are today." Rev. Dr. John Bacchus Dykes

"No matter what a man's aims, or resolutions, or professions, may be, it is by one's deeds that he is to be judged, both by God and man." Henry Ward Beecher

"My deeds are a revelation of what resides in my heart." Pam Malow-Isham

"We should believe only in deeds; words go for nothing everywhere." Rojas

"Our deeds determine us, as much as we determine our deeds." George Eliot

Questions

What deeds am I most proud of? Why is that? How many charitable deeds have I done this week? Why are my deeds matching my words?

Declarations

My charitable **deeds** are an everyday occurrence. It is very rewarding volunteering for charity events. I meet the nicest people. I am philanthropic with my humanitarian **deeds** done in secret. I always have enough time to help out with kind, neighborly **deeds**.

I exercise my good judgment, do benevolent **deeds**, and grasp all opportunities available. I allow peace to harmonize my interactions and relationships. I do charitable **deeds** without having to be recognized. I have a readiness of mind to do compassionate **deeds**.

When I have the chance to do a good **deed**, I do it, even if I don't feel like it, because I know down the road, I may be needing some help, and there will be someone helping me with a good **deed**. I continue to reap what I sow, so my considerate **deeds** are ever present.

I look for the beauty in everyone. I surround myself with people who are kind, generous, and who do thoughtful **deeds**. I am a great coach who lifts people up. I work hard and deliver my best. I am willing to do good-hearted **deeds**. I love what I do.

I go through whatever I need in order to be in the will of God. I check my motives to make sure my **deeds** are Christ-centered and gracious. I give from a pure heart. I remember how much I have been forgiven, and all the kind **deeds** that have been done for me. I grow more thankful as I continue to reflect on past **deeds** received.

God transfers over to me the **deed** of His kingdom because I am a child of the King. I never want for anything. I write my own ticket and get paid what I ask. Opulence is mine. I praise God for His marvelous **deeds** towards me. God always delivers on His promises. I glorify God by my loving **deeds**, kind words, and good character.

201:
Believe
July 19

Bible Verses

"Therefore I tell you, whatever you ask in prayer, believe that you have received it, and it will be yours." Mark 11:24 (RSV)

"For God so loved the world that he gave his one and only Son, that whoever believes in him shall not perish but have eternal life." John 3:16 (NIV)

Word of the Day

Believe – To accept as trustworthy, honest and credible. Confidence. To have faith in and hold as true. Presume.

Quotes

"I believe the first test of a truly great man is in his humility." John Ruskin

"Why, sometimes I've believed as many as six impossible things before breakfast." (Alice's Adventures in Wonderland) Lewis Carroll

"If I am ashamed of what I believe, then I better rethink what I believe." Bruce Garner

Pam's Perspective

When you believe in yourself, you honor God, because you are created in His image. He believes in you enough to send His son to take your place on the cross. God sees Jesus in you. When you cut yourself down, you are hurting God and yourself. Look in the mirror and say, "I love you. I see Jesus in you!"

Questions

What are some of the things I believe in? How have I come to believe this is my truth? Do I ever question what I believe? If not, why not?

Declarations

I **believe** anything I set my mind to; I can achieve. Because I **believe**, I am going to see great things happen on my behalf, and through my hands. I am what I say I **believe**. I **believe** I am all that, and a bag of chips. I train myself to **believe** the best is always coming my way. My **belief** in my partner draws us closer together every day.

I **believe** opportunities are around every corner. I **believe** I walk in divine health. I **believe** I get better with age. I invest in myself and eat organic. I **believe** I can stay healthy, fit, and full of life for as long as I have breath. I **believe** in being optimistic. I **believe** in drinking lots of pure water, so I stay well hydrated and full of energy.

I will know and understand the exceeding greatness of God's kindness towards me because I **believe**. I **believe** I can come back from every setback, and conquer every challenge. I strengthen my **belief** muscles by reading God's word, speaking of past victories, and acting courageously. I **believe** in me. I **believe** what I say. I do make a difference. I **believe** I can attract truthful business partners.

I **believe** God is on my side and wants me to succeed, so I am shown abundant favor wherever I go. I **believe** God loves me. Everything I can dream of is doable with God's help because I **believe**. All things are possible. I **believe** at this moment that I will receive a brand new touch from heaven. Miracles are happening for me now.

I receive instruction from God as I take the time to listen. I **believe** I can hear the voice of the Lord. The Holy Spirit is in my life. I **believe** God, and miracles happen. I am bold about my faith. I allow the power of God to flow through me when I pray, and people get healed. I **believe** supernatural occurrences are normal. I **believe** my laugh can ignite happiness, and joy can come from simple things.

202:
Get
July 20

Bible Verses
"Get up and walk throughout the land, for I will give it to you." Genesis 13:17 (NET)

"You shall dwell with us, and the land will be before you. Live and trade in it, and get possessions in it." Genesis 34:10 (WEB)

Word of the Day
Get – To obtain something by effort. To access, apprehend or secure.

Quotes
"Do not take life too seriously. You will never get out of it alive." Elbert Hubbard

"You cannot get things from God until you know God will give them to you. You cannot just say, 'Thy will be done.' That's not faith." Lester Sumrall

"When you get into a tight place, and everything goes against you, till it seems as though you could not hang on a minute longer, never give up then, for that is just the place and time that the tide will turn." Harriet Beecher Stowe

"Climb the mountains and get their good tidings." John Muir

Pam's Perspective
I get excited, because I get whatever I visualize, believe, plan, and work for. I get what I declare, so I declare great things.

Questions
How do I get happy? How do I get motivated? Who do I get excited about seeing and why? Why will I go out and get what I want today?

Declarations

I **get** excited about all the opportunities in front of me. I know what I have to do because I have written it out the night before. I **get** up and **get** going in the morning. Because I **get** up early, I make the most of my day. I **get** to show off my stuff and make my own way.

I appreciate all I **get** to do, be, and have. I **get** to believe in myself and be great. I **get** to choose to have a loving life, full of happiness. I have high energy to **get** things done. I **get** to expand my awareness. I **get** to learn something new while **getting** smarter every day.

I rock! I **get** healthy by eating wholesome foods, and taking extra supplements. I **get** enough water to stay well-hydrated. I **get** strong by lifting weights. I **get** confident with declarations. I **get** adequate rest for my body. I know how much sleep I need to feel my best.

Because I give a lot of love, I **get** a lot of love and merriment in return. I am playful. I **get** glad by helping my neighbors. I **get** happier as the day goes on. I **get** cheerful because of my friends.

I **get** the most out of my co-workers because I know how to give compliments. I **get** brazen enough to ask for a raise. I **get** what I ask for. I **get** so involved in projects that I lose track of time. I **get** ahead today. I utilize every moment to **get** the most out of it. I look for places of agreement in order to **get** along with the critical ones.

I **get** God's attention when I pray. I **get** to break the patterns that have held me down. I **get** to move beyond my limitations, and into freedom. I **get** to prepare, train, and then win. I look within and **get** courage and guidance. I **get** to perform on God's behalf to celebrate His greatness. I identify myself with the fortunate, and **get** the best deals. I **get** an extra favor. My life **gets** more fabulous every day.

203:
Everything
July 21

Bible Verses
"Everything that lives and moves will be your food. Just as I gave you the green grasses, I now give you everything." Genesis 9:3 (CEB)

"Everything is lawful, but not everything is beneficial. Everything is lawful, but not everything builds others up." 1 Corinthians 10:23 (NET)

"Do everything without grumbling or arguing." Philippians 2:14 (NET)

Word of the Day
Everything – All encompassing. The whole entire thing.

Quotes
"Everything has bottom-line consequences; therefore, everything counts."
Gary Ryan Blair

"Be content with your lot; one cannot be first in everything." Aesop

"How you do anything is how you do everything." Cheri Huber

"God is all love; it is He who made everything, and He loves everything He has made." Henry Brooke

"As in everything practice makes perfect, so by awakening within ourselves the love of God, we shall attain to a high degree of love." Rev. Francis Spirago

Questions
Can I control everything? Do I try? Do I pray about everything? Will I rejoice in everything today, and give thanks? Will I give everything over to God today? Do I strive for excellence in everything I do?

Declarations

I add spice to my life by getting excited about **everything**. I regard myself highly, just the way I am. I automatically think positively about **everything**, because of the way I have programmed my mind. I keep getting better at **everything**. I love **everything** about me.

I enjoy looking at the splendor of **everything**. I am kind to animals, and **every** living **thing**. **Everything** has a purpose and a reason for being. I value **everything** in my life, and the lessons I have learned.

I am willing to accept responsibility for **everything** I say. What I say matters. I choose to be a channel of grace and loving-kindness. I realize that I create **everything** in my world with the words I utter from my mouth. I change my language to what is beneficial.

I realize I cannot do **everything**, so I learn to delegate. The things that I do perform, I do very well. I organize **everything**, so I know where it is, and how to find it. I make lists and create plans for my future. When I check **everything** off my list, I create a new list.

I am granted **everything** I need, and **everything** is awesome. I have the ability to see **everything** working out for my good. **Everything** is multiplying in my favor. In **everything**, I do the best I can, with what I have. I feel satisfied with the way I invest and save my money. God is backing me in **everything** I do for He is ever present.

I am curious to search out **everything** pertaining to the Holy Spirit in order to be confident and settled in what I believe. I question **everything**. I live with an open heart. I surrender **everything** and turn it over to God. I am immovable in my decision to trust God with the results. I relax, and let go. I demonstrate the love of Christ in **everything** I do. With God on my side, **everything** is possible.

204:
Nothing
July 22

Bible Verses
"Those who love your law are completely secure; nothing causes them to stumble." Psalm 119:165 (NET)

"What exists now is what will be, and what has been done is what will be done; there is nothing truly new on earth." Ecclesiastes 1:9 (NET)

Word of the Day
Nothing – Empty, meaningless, zero. Insignificant. Irrelevant. An unimportant act. Worthless or useless.

Quotes
"There is nothing either good or bad but thinking makes it so." William Shakespeare

"There is nothing more remarkable in the life of Socrates than that he found time in his old age to learn to dance and play on instruments, and thought it was time well spent." Michel de Montaigne

"Nothing matters much, but everything matters a little." Elbert Hubbard

Pam's Perspective
When I come from nothing but kindness and being a gift, I make room for miracles to happen. I become someone's lucky break.

Questions
If a disaster hit, and I was left with nothing, how would I react? Have I let nothing tangible, or little fears get me down? If so, why? Is there nothing worth dying for, or living for? Why, or why not?

Declarations

I am relieved that **nothing** can diverge me from the love of God. **Nothing** above and **nothing** below can keep us apart. **Nothing** I ever do, or **nothing** I have done, can keep us apart. There is **nothing** I have to work toward or **nothing** I have to do, in order to prove my love to God. He knows I love Him, and **nothing** else matters.

I leave **nothing** up to chance, so I plan out my days, months, years, and life. I leave the results up to God because I know He wants the best for me, but He still wants me to make plans. I do **nothing** by accident. I am assured of success, and **nothing** but victory ahead.

Nothing gets me down. I let **nothing** negative dwell in my mind. I am a wise keeper of my thoughts. **Nothing** vile is allowed to stay in my mind for I eradicate it immediately. I put **nothing** corrupt before my eyes. I alone am responsible for what I watch, so I gaze upon the beauty of nature. I keep healthy, happy, and wholesome thoughts.

Nothing has control over me. I put **nothing** toxic in my body, on my body, or around my body. My body is the temple of the Holy Spirit, so I honor it. I allow **nothing** bad to come out of my mouth.

I am so full of life that **nothing** hinders me. Obstacles that waylay some people are **nothing** for me. I thrive on surprises. I am passionate about my mission to spread love and compassion to the people around me. **Nothing** is more important than the love I share.

Nothing about people disarms me anymore. I see people in a naïve, unassuming way. I contemplate their good traits. I seek out ways to be a blessing and a friend. I am honest and loyal to my friendships. **Nothing** good gets by me, for I am observant. **Nothing** like noticing little miracles, that some people take for granted, to make my day.

205:
Right
July 23

Bible Verses

"He was handed over to die because of our sins, and he was raised to life to make us right with God." Romans 21:2 (NLT)

"So let us not grow tired of doing what is right, for in due time we will reap, if we do not give up." Galatians 6:9 (MOUNCE)

Word of the Day

Right – Having to do with being fair, just and honest. Morally correct.

Quotes

"Work joyfully and peacefully, knowing that right thoughts and right efforts will inevitably bring about right results." James Lane Allen

"The main purpose of life is to live rightly, think rightly, act rightly. The soul must languish when we give all our thought to the body." Mahatma Gandhi

"Anybody can become angry – that is easy, but to be angry with the right person and to the right degree and at the right time and for the right purpose, and in the right way – that is not within everybody's power and is not easy." Aristotle

"Narrow minds think nothing right that is above their own capacity." Francois De La Rochefoucauld

"Being compassionate feels better than being right. I am on the right path when I do good things and care about all humanity." Pam Malow-Isham

Questions

Why does it matter to me who is right, or who is wrong? What is the right way to live? Why do I think that? Am I sure I am right?

Declarations

I do the **right** thing, at the **right** time, for the **right** reason. I am on the **right** track. I finish at just the **right** time. **Right** now is the **right** time to get in shape, and stay in shape. I eat the **right** food. With perseverance, I get it **right**. I like taking the **right** actions.

I consistently seek to do what is **right** before God, and my fellow man. I have contentment, and peace of mind, because I think, say, and do what is **right**. I do what is **right** before I get the **right** results. I have the **right** to rule as a child of God. God sees me as **righteous**.

I give up the **right**, to be **right**, about false beliefs I have had in the past; therefore, I can create empowering beliefs for my future. I am **right** to pause before I speak. I am open to **right** thoughts, and new ideas. I interpret things the **right** way. I am made of the **right** stuff.

Nothing can compare with the peace of being **right** with God. It is always the **right** time to pray. Yes, is the **right** response when I hear God knocking at my heart's door. I am safe **right** now. **Right** now, God is here with me. I listen to what He says and then obey.

Being sympathetic, and forgiving, keeps me **right** on target for love. I select the **right** friends. Because I have the desire to get things **right**, I pray before I act. I apply the wisdom that I have learned, at the **right** time, in the **right** way. I influence the **right** people.

I have the **right**, and freedom to succeed. I am **right** for the job, so I earn a lot. I secure the **right** amount of funding for my projects. I choose the **right** business associates by asking the **right** questions. I appreciate my **right** brain rational. I do things **right** the first time. I am on the leading edge in the **right** field. I have the instincts for the **right** opportunities. I am on the **right** path to be successful.

206:
Wrong
July 24

Bible Verses

"Forget about the wrong things people do to you. Don't try to get even. Love your neighbor as yourself. I am the Lord." Leviticus 19:18 (ERV)

"See that no one pays back wrong for wrong, but at all times make it your aim to do good to one another and to all people." 1 Thessalonians 5:15 (GNT)

Word of the Day

Wrong – A mistake or error in judgment. Inaccurate. Faulty. Abusive, criminal, or corrupt behavior.

Quotes

"Dreaming about a thing in order to do it properly is right, but dreaming about it when we should be doing it is wrong." Oswald Chambers

"No one can take advantage from a wrong committed by himself." Latin Maxim

"The best woman does no evil, does much good, and goes out of her way to inspire and encourage those who have been doing wrong to new aspirations and endeavors." Ella Wheeler Wilcox

"It is better to suffer wrong than to do it, and happier to be sometimes cheated than not to trust." Samuel Johnson

"When I view something or someone as wrong because I don't take the time to learn about it or them, then I am the one who is wrong." Pam Malow-Isham

Questions

Do I have any wrong beliefs about myself? Is there a wrong I need to make right? How often do I admit that I am wrong?

Declarations

There is nothing **wrong** with me that God can't fix. God's created me just the way I am, and I am precious in His sight. We make a great team. God sees nothing **wrong** with my appearance. God does not make **wrong** people, but some people choose **wrong** actions.

I wait for God's perfect timing. I observe miracles taking place, even if my prayer is said in the **wrong** way. I am **wrong** when I give up and doubt God, so I tell myself to keep on believing, and just trust.

I have the unstoppable endurance for clearing up the **wrongs** I have made, and confessing when I do **wrong**. I am charitable to myself when I am **wrong,** so I vow to do better next time. I realize my humanity, and my **wrong** behavior is forgivable. When I am **wrong** about myself, I inundate myself with mercy, grace, and love.

I am kind to myself and think kind thoughts. I appreciate life, and I am glad to be here, even if I eat the **wrong** food. Taking care of my diet, and eating healthily gives me a new lease on life. Eating the **wrong** kinds of food like sugar, and junk food, does not serve me well, so I choose to stop it. I love eating spinach, and greens.

I feel good about the skills I have, but I would be **wrong** if there is no room for improvement. I readily admit when I am **wrong**. I shift from a **wrong** attitude into a joyful existence by declaring it so. I affirm the presence of peace wherever I am. Even when I do something unintentionally **wrong**; God turns it around for good.

God's faithful love watches over me, even when I think **wrong** about Him. I am found worthy of love. I am embraced with kindness. There is nothing **wrong** with me in God's eyes. I see myself the way God sees me, as perfect, totally lovable, fun, and a joy to watch.

207:
Much
July 25

Bible Verses

"Do not associate with those who drink too much wine, with those who eat too much meat." Proverbs 23:20 (NOG)

"He that is faithful in that which is least is faithful also in much: and he that is unjust in the least is unjust also in much." Luke 16:10 (KJV)

Word of the Day

Much – Having plenty. More than enough. An ample supply.

Quotes

"You got more than you see! Little in the hands of Jesus makes much." Pastor Berniece Matejcek

"If we take simply what we have and use it as God commands it will do much good; for Moses had a rod in his hand, but with this, he did great wonders." Rev. J. R. Miller, D. D.

"When you so believe a truth as to put it to bed and smother it with the bolster of neglect, it is much the same as if you did not believe at all. An official belief is very much akin to infidelity. Some persons never question a doctrine." Charles Spurgeon

"Kind words do not cost much; they never blister the tongue nor lips... Kind words make other people good-natured." Blaise Pascal

Questions

How much more can I learn about my current occupation? How much love can I take in today? How much love can I give away? How much would my life change if I were fearless? What would I accomplish?

Declarations

I always have so **much** to be thankful for, that I spend my days, and nights, counting my blessings. There is so **much** to explore when I travel. I stay amazed at all of God's marvelous creation. Everywhere I look I see beauty. I make a list of all the cool places I want to visit. My bucket list keeps getting bigger because there is so **much** to see.

As **much** as I might want to escape the consequences of my actions, I know I am the only one responsible for how I act. **Much** of the time, I am full of bliss. I laugh **much**, and frequently. There is **much** for me to do while I am here, so I spend my time wisely. I have **much** enjoyment hanging out, playing games with my children.

I drink **much** water, to stay well-hydrated. Because I push **much** of the junk food away, I stay slim and sexy. I love fresh juice. The vegetables I eat provide **much** of the nutrients that my body craves. It feels nice to have a lot of energy, and **much** more strength than I used to. With **much** work, and effort, I have crafted out a wonderful life. I enjoy being transformed into a healthy, vibrant human being.

I feel so **much** joy because I am accepted, loved, and cared for by the Holy Spirit. I get happier every day. I have discovered the key to my happiness: loving God and loving people. I have **much** joy to give today. I give **much** more than I take. I willingly forgive **much**, and often. I overflow with gratitude because I have received so **much**.

I am emotionally secure, have a sound mind, and dwell in safety. I get **much** done, with time to spare. I invest, save, and tithe **much**. I don't have to ask how **much** something costs. I always have **much** more than enough, because I spend, and save, in balance with my income, that is always expanding. I think **much** about the promises of God. God guards my wealth and multiplies it profusely.

208:
Decline
July 26

Bible Verses

"Get wisdom, get understanding: forget it not; neither decline from the words of my mouth." Proverbs 4:5 (KJV)

"'Behold, I will make the shadow cast by the declining sun on the dial of Ahaz turn back ten steps.' So the sun turned back on the dial the ten steps by which it had declined." Isaiah 38:8 (RSV)

Word of the Day

Decline – To turn down the offer. To decay or fall apart. Downgrade.

Quotes

"Choose to decline in negative thought so you can rise in wisdom, optimism, love, and friendship. It is always our choice how we think, act and respond to life." Pam Malow-Isham

"The decline of literature indicates the decline of a nation. The two keep pace in their downward tendency." Johann Wolfgang von Goethe

"Tolerance does not mark the progress of a religion. It is the fatal sign of its decline." Isidore van Cleef

"Greater completion marks the progress of art, absolute completion usually its decline." John Ruskin

Questions

Do I need to decline to spend, so I can save for my vacation? What frivolous activity can I decline, so I can complete a difficult task I have been putting off? Is there a habit I need to decline? Will I decline from looking at my phone, so I can spend quality time with the people I love?

Declarations

I do activities that spark my interest, bring me joy, and **decline** all the rest. I am respectful, and courteous when I **decline** an invitation. I **decline** the notion of giving up because I am a winner. When I get a chance to hang around people who complain, I **decline**.

The **decline** of my negative thinking results in my positive attitude. We are all human, and God **declines** from playing favorites. He loves us with all, our oddities, and quirks. As I **decline** from bigotry, I am able to relate to all people everywhere, with love, and kindness.

I **decline** the drama of aloofness and welcome charity. When I am tempted to watch TV, I **decline**, so I can read great books, and gather much wisdom. My sage advice is in high demand. I **decline** the trap of comparison and enjoy being totally free, and full of life.

I am diligent with daily exercise, so my body does not **decline**. My level of body fat continues to **decline** as I persevere with exercise. I easily cross the finish line and claim the gold. I get more muscular and firm as the days go by. I have strong hips to carry me around. I love eating things that are good for me, so I **decline** the sugar.

God's love for me never **declines**. When my doctor gives me a negative report, I **decline** to accept it. God's Spirit inside me, heals every **declining** cell in my body. The Holy Spirit provides the good health I desire. God's ability to keep His promises has not **declined**.

When someone says life is hard, I **decline** to believe it. I **decline** to miss my mastermind group. I keep my eyes, and ears, open for improvement. I talk about all the good that has come my way. I associate with high achievers who know how to get things done. I am not in the **declining** business, but the increasing business.

209:
Give
July 27

Bible Verses

"Lord, you give me all that I need. You support me. You give me my share."
Psalm 16:5 (ERV)

"Give, and it will be given to you: good measure, pressed down, shaken together, and running over will be put into your bosom. For with the same measure that you use, it will be measured back to you." Luke 6:38 (NKJV)

Word of the Day

Give – To deliver a gift. To convey a message. To share or produce.

Quotes

"Give light, and the darkness will disappear of itself." Desiderius Erasmus

"Give me a place to stand, and with a lever, I will move the world."
Archimedes

"Everybody needs beauty as well as bread, places to play in and pray in, where nature may heal and give strength to body and soul." John Muir

"Give yourself entirely to those around you. Be generous with your blessings. A kind gesture can reach a wound that only compassion can heal." Steve Maraboli

Pam's Perspective

I cannot give to every person, cause, or organization that asks. So when I give, I ask, why I am giving, so I can check my motives, and give from a pure heart.

Questions

Do I give with expectations or open-handedly? Is my giving abundant, or sparse? What will I give away today? To whom will I give, and why?

Declarations

I am enthusiastic about **giving** encouragement to those around me. I **give** a smile to everyone I see. I **give** a silent prayer, and blessing, to people who pass me by. I **give** my partner the opportunity to voice his/her concerns, dreams, likes, or dislikes, in our relationship.

I open my hands wide to **give** freely. God has **given** me much to share. I love feeling free from greed, and hoarding. I am a cheerful **giver**. I often pack up things to **give** to Goodwill. I **give** of my time to help those in my community. I **give** to show thanks for what I have been **given**. It is my pleasure to **give** without restrictions.

I **give** of my finances to great causes. I **give** a tithe to the church. I **give** extra offerings because I can. I can't out **give** God. My business is booming. I am unharmed by the economy. My income continues to increase. I have sound investments and money in the bank.

I **give** thanks to God, and praise His name for all He has done for me. I **give** friendship to the lonely. I am admirable, frank, and **give** respect where it is due. I **give** unconditional love, intentionally, to those around me. I **give** laughter, without reserve, to spread my joy.

I **give** myself a break when I mess up. I **give** myself a pat on the back when I deserve it. I **give** myself time to recharge my battery. What I **give**, returns to me multiplied, and running over. I **give** so others can receive a blessing from me. I find satisfaction in **giving**.

I surrender to the unknown, feeling totally supported, as I **give** God the reigns of my life. I **give** my attention to awe and wonder. Life is fascinating. There is always something I can **give** if I take the time to look. I am a superstar. I can **give** lessons, at things I am good at. I **give** gleefully, without reserve. I **give** peace, with my presence.

210:
Take
July 28

Bible Verses
"Love each other with genuine affection, and take delight in honoring each other." Romans 12:10 (NLT)

"God saved you by his grace when you believed. And you can't take credit for this; it is a gift from God." Ephesians 2:8 (NLT)

Word of the Day
Take – To gain control of. To pick up. To buy or consume. Endure.

Quotes
"Take care of the pence; for the pounds will take care of themselves. Take care of the minutes, for the hours will take care of themselves." Philip Stanhope

"To take a walk is to vegetate; to saunter is to live… To saunter is to enjoy life; it is to indulge the flight of fancy." Honore de Balzac

"Give thyself more diligently to reflection: know thyself: take counsel with the Godhead; without God put thine hand into nothing." Epictetus

"Could a greater miracle take place than for us to look through each other's eyes for an instant?" Henry David Thoreau

Pam's Perspective
I used to take every free thing that was offered to me. Not because I needed it, but because I had a lack mentality. Now I only take the free things that I can use.

Questions
Do I see myself as a giver or taker? Who do I take from? What will I take?

Declarations

I **take** hold of the promises of God, believing they are true. I **take** action, knowing God will give me strength. I **take** a stand for what is right. I **take** delight in being a shining light, to reveal God's love.

I **take** responsibility for everything that is happening in my life, the good, and the less desirable. I **take** my ambition to the next level. I **take** the consistent action to reach the top. I **take** risks, to achieve my goals. I **take** pride in my work and do it with excellence. I **take** back my power. I **take** advantage of all the opportunities in front of me.

I listen to great messages and **take** the time to comprehend them. Then I **take** the best points and incorporate them into my life. I **take** my thoughts to a higher level, dwelling on the good. I **take** the time to think before I respond, so I can be known as a wise individual.

I **take** the path less traveled and see the wonders along the way. I **take** time to play, have fun, and inhale all the beauty around me. I **take** a rest and restore my soul. I **take** laughter, and joy to the extreme. I **take** charge of my life and indulge in every precious moment. I **take** possession of my dreams and see them fulfilled.

I choose to **take** action steps to create a healthy body. I **take** pleasure in exercising. I **take** nothing for granted. I pay attention to what I eat. I **take** an apple with me for a snack. I **take** gratification in my ability to stay healthy. I **take** as many vacations as I can.

I **take** on being the kind of person who respects others. **I take** charge of a difficult situation and turn things around. I **take** the time to give the people around me, a compliment or give them a nod. It **takes** no effort to smile, so I keep one on my face. I am happy, and I believe that every **undertaking** I **take**, will come out positively great.

211:
Load
July 29

Bible Verses
"Bless the Lord, who daily loads us with benefits." Psalm 68:19 (NKJV)

"For My way of carrying a load is easy and My load is not heavy." Matthew 11:30 (NLV)

Word of the Day
Load – Weight. To pile on top of. Baggage. An affliction. Trouble.

Quotes
"Sympathy is two hearts tugging at one load, bent beneath one sorrow." Charles Henry Parkhurst

"We may have troubles, but our hearts need not be troubled since the Trouble-Sharer is with us to divide the load." M. T.

"Poverty is the only load which is the heavier, the more loved ones there are to assist in bearing it." Jean Paul Richter

"The ass will carry his load but not a double load; ride not a free horse to death." Miguel De Cervantes. Don Quixote Ch. lxxi.

"This portable quality of good humor seasons all the parts and occurrences we meet with in such a manner, that there are no moments lost: but they all pass with so much satisfaction, that the heaviest of loads, (when it is a load), that of time, is never felt by us." Sir Richard Steele

Questions
Do I load myself down with worries? Do I try to load too many things on my calendars? What load will I give over to God, and leave there?

Declarations

I **load** my soul with wisdom, by reading Proverbs over, and over again. I **load** my spirit with thanksgiving, as I dwell on all the wonderful things God has done for me. God pushes over my heavy **loads** and breaks down my burdens, so I can handle anything.

I let go of the **load** of wanting things to be perfect, and different from the way they are, and I accept the realities of life. I drop the **load** of trying to change people. I **load** up on tolerance and patience.

I **load** my grocery cart with the fresh vegetables that are in season. I **load** my plate with delicious fruits and vegetables. I **load** my body with nutritious food. I have a great immune system that I **load** up with vitamins and supplements. I **load** my lungs with fresh air.

I am responsible for the **load** I choose to carry, so I consciously decide what to pick up, and what to put down. When a **load** is too heavy to bear, I turn it over to God, and He carries it for me.

I am comfortable making a lot of money. I have my own funds. I **load** my vision board full of dreams, goals, and things that are yet to come. I believe in my ability to get ahead. I have a **load** of optimism.

I **load** my lips with praise and gratitude. I **load** my mind with positive thoughts. I **load** my speech with mercy. I **load** my heart with love. I **load** my memory with the happy thoughts of the gifts of times past. I cram a **load** of fun, and laughter, into every day.

I help my friends get a **load** off their mind, by listening. We all need a friend to support us when we get **loaded** down. I place a heaping **load** of love over all my relationships and sprinkle them with joy. I **load** myself with courage, as I take on the next big challenge.

212:
Unload
July 30

Bible Verses
"Then I will go to God's altar with nothing to hide. I will go to God, my rapture; I will sing praises to You and play my strings, unloading my cares, unleashing my joys, to You, God, my God." Psalm 43:4 (VOICE)

"When your merchandise was unloaded from the seas, you satisfied many peoples. You enriched the kings of the earth with your abundant wealth and goods." Ezekiel 27:33 (HCSB)

Word of the Day
Unload – To unpack or empty something. Unburden.

Quotes
"When your ship comes in, make sure you are willing to unload it." Dr. Robert Anthony

"Chrysanthemums from gilded argosy unload their gaudy scentless merchandise." Oscar Wilde

Pam's Perspective
I feel better when I release my anger, by taking deep breaths than when I unload it on the person who I feel deserves my wrath. Learning to keep quiet, and hold my tongue, has saved me a lot of friendships, and hardships. When I approach someone with a calm spirit and talk in a kind manner, it is a lot easier to work out our differences, than if I come at them yelling, trying to get my point across.

Questions
What negative thoughts, behaviors, attitudes, and habits can I unload? What new God inspired thoughts, behaviors, and habits can I pick up?

Declarations

I **unload** the old guilt in my life, turn it over to God, and pick up His peace that passes understanding. I know that I am not under any condemnation from God but under grace. I **unload** all skepticism and put my trust in a loving God. I am grounded in calmness.

I **unload** depressing thoughts and replace them with the positive. I raise the bar of my thinking. I listen to happy music and sing like no one is listening. By **unloading** false beliefs like, I am too old, or young, to start a project, I intentionally accomplish great feats.

I **unload** old habits that no longer serve me and commit to creating new, life-enriching, habits that renew, regenerate, and strengthen me. I **unload** the thought that life owes me. Now is the time for me to take charge of my life, and **unload** lethargy. I jump into action.

I like getting to know fun, dedicated people, who know how to get what they want. I **unload** disinterest and become fascinated with people. I **unload** loneliness, by going out, and making new friends.

I **unload** old beliefs that I'm not good enough, smart enough, strong enough, pretty enough, or competent enough. I **unload** self-doubt and hesitancy. I create new God generated beliefs that enliven, empower, enrich, inspire and invigorate me. I love feeling full of power, toughness, courage, and charm. My magnetism compels people to help me fulfill my dreams, so I can **unload** my creativity.

I rally my inner determination, and God's power, to design my life the way He intended it to be. I **unload** procrastination, and take up a "get it done now" philosophy! I can do anything I set my mind to. As I **unload** fear, I allow the Almighty to work in me, through me, and around me. Love is who I am, and who I'll stay.

213:
Discipline
July 31

Bible Verses
"Blessed is the one you discipline, Lord, the one you teach from your law." Psalm 94:12 (NIV)

"Listen to advice and accept discipline so that you may be wise the rest of your life." Proverbs 19:20 (GW)

Word of the Day
Discipline – The ability to use self-control and restraint when faced with a goal or a problem. To correct or educate.

Quotes
"No evil propensity of the human heart is so powerful that it may not be subdued by discipline." Seneca

"But the genius of good-nature is perhaps as rare as any other form of genius. Cheerfulness in most cheerful people is the rich and satisfying result of strenuous discipline; and to attain this, as to attain other blessings, the proverb holds good of 'no pains, no gains; no sweat, so sweet.'" Edwin Percy Whipple

"The surest test of discipline is its absence." Clara Barton

"Self-reliance is a noble and manly quality of the character, and he who exercises it in small matters schools himself by that discipline for its exercise in matters of more momentous importance." W. Rathbone

Questions
Will I discipline myself to create a happy, fulfilling life? Do I consider discipline a friend, or foe? Where do I need the most discipline? Where do I need less discipline? Why will I discipline myself to reach my goals?

Declarations

I am blessed with confidence, because of my **discipline**. I **discipline** my body through exercise, enjoying the strength, stamina, and energy I receive. I am **disciplined** with my self-care, and up-keep. I have good looks, an attractive body, and a friendly personality.

I **discipline** my taste buds to enjoy fruit, over candy, and vegetables, over junk food. I can even **discipline** myself to fast from certain food groups, to give my body time to heal, and reset itself. My health is in my hands, and how I **discipline** myself determines my vitality.

Discipline is how I honor God, and myself. I like being **disciplined**. I **discipline** my tongue to keep quiet when I want to lash out. I say a quick prayer and then release it. Everyone who knows me thinks of me as a **disciplined** person of integrity. I activate my genius as I **discipline** my mind, by listening to inspirational speakers and reading great books. I am always learning, so I stay on top.

I continue to show up, keep it real, and be **disciplined** in all I do. As I **discipline** myself to put things away immediately, I enjoy a clutter-free environment. I love my beautiful, clean house. Regardless of whether I like, or dislike a task, I am **disciplined** enough to do it.

Being **disciplined** to save money has allowed me to feel very rich because I always have money when I need it. I am financially free because my income is determined by me. I am a **disciplined** saver.

I **discipline** my heart to be open and receptive to God and hear His intuitive leads. I practice the **discipline** of declaring great truths of how God sees me as beautiful, victorious, healed, blessed, wealthy, more than a conqueror, powerful, and a highly favored child of God. I inspire others to live a **disciplined** life and reap great rewards.

214:
Undisciplined
August 1

Bible Verses
"To discipline a child produces wisdom, but a mother is disgraced by an undisciplined child." Proverbs 29:15 (NLT)

"For you yourselves know how you ought to follow our example because we did not act in an undisciplined manner among you." 2 Thessalonians 3:7 (NASB)

Word of the Day
Undisciplined – Not being able to control one's thoughts, words or actions. Unrestrained. Untrained.

Quotes
"The man of imagination who is untrained (unlearned, uneducated, undisciplined) has wings and no feet." Joseph Joubert

"A handful of men, inured to war, proceed, as it were, to certain victory, while on the contrary, numerous armies of raw and undisciplined troops are, but multitudes of men dragged to the slaughter." Publius Flavius Vegetius Renatus

Pam's Perspective
Being undisciplined with your thoughts will cause you grief. It takes steadfast tenacity, and patience, to be the authority over your thoughts. But since that is where we derive most of our pleasure or pain, it is worth mastering. Repetition is how to train yourself in anything. So make sure you are repeating the right stuff.

Questions
Do I judge people for being undisciplined? Have I ever been undisciplined in the same area I am judging others? What undisciplined practice do I want to release today? What action can I take to create a new discipline?

Declarations

Even though there are times when I'm **undisciplined**, I am still a good person, with lots of value. When I am **undisciplined**, and fall, I keep getting up one more time. I focus on my goals. I eliminate the unnecessary stress of being **undisciplined**, by taking action.

I never let people with **undisciplined** minds affect my attitude. I am the master of my thoughts, and my reactions display my maturity. I choose to be happy right now. I fill my **undisciplined** mind with positive thoughts, and I learn something new every single day.

I can be **undisciplined** and still get a lot accomplished. Just because I don't do what the time management gurus suggest, does not mean I am not productive. I believe in myself, and get the job done. My **undisciplined** style has the advantage of keeping me from boredom.

My life is working out perfectly now that I am not as **undisciplined** as I used to be. I take care of myself by doing some form of exercise that is fun for me. I play a lot of active games. Every step I take is working towards the betterment of my good health, and vitality.

Being **undisciplined** with my breathing shortens my breath and endurance, so I practice taking deep inhalations of clean, fresh air. I learn fast from my mistakes and move on. I take time to relax. I stay in perfect health, by visualizing peace throughout my body.

When I am **undisciplined** with my eating, I give myself empathy. I stop judging myself, and others, that I see are being **undisciplined**. We all overeat once in a while, and being **undisciplined** does not make us bad. I eat healthy most of the time. God gives me self-restraint and does not see me as **undisciplined**. God sees me as equipped. I can do all things because He gives me strength.

215:
Faith
August 2

Bible Verses
"Now faith is the assurance of things hoped for, the conviction of things not seen. For by it the men of old received divine approval. By faith we understand that the world was created by the word of God, so that what is seen was made out of things which do not appear." Hebrews 11:1-3 (RSV)

Word of the Day
Faith – An inner confidence. A belief in God to keep His word.

Quotes
"Faith is the link that unites human feebleness to the divine strength and makes the impossible possible." Rev. C. W. L. Christian

"Faith never looks at circumstances nor surroundings, but keeps a steadfast gaze on Christ." Mattie Perry

"Faith expects from God what is beyond all expectation." Andrew Murray

Pam's Perspective
In August of nineteen eighty-nine, my mother drove me to the airport in Detroit. She was running late picking me up. On the way her car overheated started sputtering, steam was arising under the hood, and the gauge was over to Hot. Faith emerged in me, I touched the car, and I said, 'Oh no you don't, In the name of Jesus, cool down and work right now!' Immediately the car stopped sputtering, cooled down, and the gauge went back to C. I made my flight on time.

Questions
What does faith mean to me? Do I have complete faith in God? Why or why not? Do I have complete faith in myself? Why or why not?

Declarations

I am bold as a lion. I act as a person of great **faith**. I put myself entirely into the arms of a loving Father who has **faith** in me. I come alive as I allow the life of heaven to fill my body, soul, and spirit. I am very grateful that I don't have to work to earn my **faith**, for it is a free gift from God. I enjoy living every moment in God's presence.

I am full of **faith**, and hope. I have deep, unshakable **faith** in God. My super-excellent victory is here. I have **faith** in myself to follow through on keeping my word. I know, no matter how impossible the situation seems, God knows the way out, and has me covered.

My unbreakable **faith** keeps me strong during tough times. As I seek the kingdom of God, He reveals to me great ideas. I have **faith** God will provide for my needs. I am agreeable to do His will. With pure determination, my unwavering **faith** has kept me safe from distress.

Faith can unite the impossible. I have the right to share the views of my **faith**. I talk with kind words and keep an open mind as I listen to others share their **faith**. I leave the judgments to God. As I reflect on our differences, I create an opening for love. I have **faith** in love.

I pray the prayer of **faith**, and people get healed. My **faith** in God continues to grow. I have **faith** that miracles are all around me. My **faith** expands as I open my mind. The power of **faith** in my life is evidence that God is real. I am a mighty miracle to behold.

I learn to be comfortable speaking in front of people. I am a master at being focused, and eloquent. I have poise, **faith**, and charm. I have **faith** that I can get my point across to impart wisdom, and inspiration to my audience. I direct the power of my mind to keep my **faith** alive. I have **faith** that my words are beneficial.

216:
Doubt
August 3

Bible Verses
"How happy are those who have no doubts about me!" Matthew 11:6 (GNT)

"He said to Thomas, 'Put your finger into My hands. Put your hand into My side. Do not doubt, believe!'" John 20:27 (NIV)

"Have loving-kindness for those who doubt." Jude 1:22 (NLV)

Word of the Day
Doubt – Having questions, fear, and distrust. Skepticism. Curiosity.

Quotes
"Never run before God's guidance. If there is the slightest doubt, then He is not guiding. Whenever there is doubt - don't." Oswald Chambers

"Modest doubt is called the beacon of the wise." William Shakespeare

"It is beyond a doubt that all our knowledge begins with experience." Immanuel Kant

Pam's Perspective
Being lied to resulted in me doubting everyone. Unfortunately, it also caused me to be suspicious, and cynical. That was a lonely way to live. When I trust, instead of doubt, I opened myself up to connections and togetherness. I have found I can doubt, while still being open to learning, or making new friends.

Questions
Do I have doubts about myself? What are my biggest doubts? Do I let doubts worry me? Do I have doubts about my future? Do I doubt God?

Declarations

When **doubts** try to creep in, I realize it and press on anyway. I never **doubt** my intuition, even when things look difficult to do. I know where my help comes from. God never lets me down. I build a strong resolve, by conquering my **doubts**. I can overcome anything.

I anticipate when I might have **doubts**, and I ask for help from friends. I receive support, and encouragement from people who care about me. I am on a championship team. Whenever I am plagued with **self-doubt**, I remember all that I have achieved in the past. I amaze myself with all I get done. I thrive despite my **doubts**.

Love is revealed to me, in spite of my **doubts**, and frees me from all anxiety. I **doubt** there is anyone who can steal my joy because I choose not to **doubt** or let others affect me. I respond with a smile. I accept people's uniqueness because God delights in our differences.

There is nothing wrong with **doubting** things now and then. I have learned from my **doubts**, and what triggers them. Every day I declare I am courageous, smart, decisive, dependable, and strong.

I face **doubters** head-on when they tell me I can't complete a project they think is impossible. I laugh in the face of **doubt** and believe I can do all things, through the One who gives me strength. I **doubt** there is anything that I can't accomplish, once I set my mind to it.

It is good to **doubt**, question, and study for myself. I love to learn new things. God is not intimidated by my **doubts** about Him or His ways; therefore I can feel confident to share all my **doubts** with Him. God is much grander than all my **doubts**, and fears. I can trust God to steer me in the right direction. God even uses **doubters** like me, to share His love, with **doubters** who don't identify with Him yet.

217:
Inside
August 4

Bible Verses

"I praise the Lord because he taught me well. Even at night he put his instructions deep inside my mind." Psalm 16:7 (ERV)

"That is why we never give up. Our physical body is becoming older and weaker, but our spirit inside us is made new every day." 2 Corinthians 4:16 (ERV)

Word of the Day

Inside – The interior part of something. The core or center. The inner portion of my being.

Quotes

"The visible world is but man turned inside out that he may be revealed to himself. All that sensibly exists is but the mind's furniture." Henry James

"There are powers inside of you which, if you could discover and use, would make of you everything you ever dreamed or imagined you could become." Orison Swett Marden

Pam's Perspective

My biggest battles have been inside myself. Being inside my head, with all my fears, was a scary place to be. Until I learned to be with my thoughts, and question their validity, I allowed them to have power over me. When I realized my fears were an illusion, and I could challenge them, I created a whole new powerful reality to live into. Healing my inside, changed my outside.

Questions

Do I like to work inside, or outside? What inside of me do I need to work on? Do I go inside to look for answers, or do I look to others for advice?

Declarations

I am beautiful **inside,** and out. I take care to nourish my **insides** with the highest quality of food. I have great resolve **inside** of me to stick with a healthy diet. When I walk **inside** the gym, I am there to exercise and strengthen my muscles. I push myself a little harder, and feel the burn, in a good way. My **inside** coach keeps me going.

I take measures to put healthy material **inside** my mind. I treasure the Word **inside** me that I have memorized, and can easily recall. I am on the **inside** circle of Divine blessings. My guardian angels are with me, watching over all I do. They help pick me up when I fall.

My life is a reflection of what is going on **inside** of me, so I am very conscientious of what I am reading and watching. I choose wisely those things that benefit my soul. When I feel anxiety **inside**, I pray and find peace from God. I am comfortable **inside** my own skin.

I am willing to be real, open up, and speak my truth. I give myself credit for all the wonderful things I have accomplished. I am nice on the **inside** and kind to myself. I am aware **inside** that I am so much more than what people see. I am special to God. I am good enough, just the way I am, and I have nothing to prove to anyone else. I care more about who I am deep **inside** than who others think I am.

I am tolerant of others when **inside** I want to scream. I am fair and polite. I give allowances, and breaks, because **inside**, I know I need them too. It feels great to smile, be kind, and show compassion.

The love of God **inside** me shines through to everyone I meet. I surrender to the Light **inside** me, to heal every thought, and calm my mind. I resonate with love. My peace comes from the **inside**. I am willing to be quiet **inside** and listen to what God is telling me.

218:
Outside
August 5

Bible Verses
"So on the outside you look as though you have God's approval, but inside you are full of hypocrisy and lawlessness." Matthew 23:28 (GW)

"That is why you are no longer foreigners and outsiders but citizens together with God's people and members of God's family." Ephesians 2:19 (GW)

Word of the Day
Outside – The exterior part of something. Furthest away from the core.

Quotes
"Outside circumstances cannot affect a calm mind." Pam Malow-Isham

"Man is no better than a leaf driven by the wind until he has completely mastered his great lonely duties… He owns a great house, a wonderful house, but it is shut up, and he lives outside with his fellow cattle; the inside is wholly unknown to him, and he has lived outside so long that he is afraid of the inside. Think, my good brothers and sisters, of the great high serene world in which you might live, move, and have your being." Rev. John Pulsford

"Education is our only political safety. Outside of this ark all is deluge." Horace Mann

"A man should have duties outside of himself; without them, he is a mere balloon, inflated with thin egotism and drifting nowhere." Thomas Bailey Aldrich

Questions
Why do I let outside forces influence me? Do I enjoy being outside, or do I prefer to stay indoors? How often do I go outside for a walk?

Declarations

Nothing **outside**, anywhere in the world can affect my inner peace for more than a minute. I am self-reliant and peaceful. I think for myself and make my own decisions. I know the entire universe is **outside**, conspiring in my favor, to bring blessings my way.

By removing any **outside** limitations I placed on myself, I easily achieve the miraculous. I build unstoppable courage from my experiences because I can pick myself up when I fall. I allow my mistakes to educate, and mold me, into a better person on the inside, and **outside**. I am oblivious to the **outside** negativity around me.

The **outside** of my house is just as neat as the inside. I serve my family well. I give myself to the task of being good and doing good things for others. I love going **outside**, working in the yard, and soaking up the sun. Breathing in the **outside** air feels like a sigh of relief. I learn from my children the value of fun as we play **outside**.

I am easy to talk to, and fun to be around. I am happy to share the credit with the people **outside**, who help things come together for my business. I enjoy having a warm, and trustworthy phone voice. I desire to do my best and work for the best. I find reasons to win.

On the **outside** chance that things don't go as planned, I always have a backup plan. I like being prepared. I release the need to become emotionally attached to any outcome. I live **outside** the box of apathy and inside the realm of possibilities. I am powerful.

Phenomenal, happy days are the norm for me. **Outside** resources are drawn to me in a variety of ways. God's goodness has no end. Help is everywhere. People **outside** of my sphere of influence notice my poise and are drawn to help me succeed. I am forever blessed.

219:
Use
August 6

Bible Verses
"Knowing how to charm a snake is of no use if you let the snake bite first."
Ecclesiastes 10:11 (GNT)

"He also said to them, 'Pay attention to what you hear! The same rules you use to judge others will be used by God to judge you—but with even greater severity'." Mark 4:24 (GNT)

Word of the Day
Use – To benefit from. To utilize something for a specific need or aim.

Quotes
"The advantage of living is not measured by length, but by use; some men have lived long, and lived little; attend to it while you are in it." Michel de Montaigne

"It is not enough to have a good mind; the main thing is to use it well." René Descartes

"The use of riches is better than their possession." Fernando de Rojas

Pam's Perspective
I find a use for things other people throw out. I use several layers of old newspapers as a barrier to prevent weeds from growing, and then put mulch on top. It is natural, decomposes, and works better than any fabric or plastic.

Questions
Why is it important to use my talents today? How can I use my gifts to have fun, make money, and help my community? Do I have a use for all the things in my home? If not, why am I hanging on to them?

Declarations

I **use** my talents to the best of my ability. I **use** my mind to steer me in the most positive direction. I **use** my thoughts to keep me focused on my goals. I am full of gifts I **use** to benefit me, and my family.

I **use** God's word to direct my steps. I **use** my prayers to touch the heart of God. I **use** my lips to sing praise and give thanks. I lift my arms to worship the Almighty. I **use** my voice to share good news.

I repeat the process of reading the Bible, to grow closer to God. With gratefulness, I **use** the inspired ideas that are divinely bestowed upon me. I **use** my free time to listen to God, so I hear truth spoken to me in my heart. I **use** kind words to boost the people around me.

I **use** my hands to help the people in my area. I **use** my wisdom to teach the ones who want to learn. I love giving back, just for the fun of it. I **use** my smarts to inspire my children. I find **use** in things others consider as trash. I am very creative in the way I **use** things.

I **use** my spare time to get last minute details done. I dazzle my fans. I **use** my connections to help people network together, so everyone benefits. I **use** my imagination to rise to greater abundance.

I am accountable for how I take care of, or **use** the environment. I am conscious about recycling and giving things a second life, instead of filling up the landfills. My small effort makes an important impact.

I **use** my friendly hello to open up conversations. I **use** my smile to open doors. I **use** my laughter to bring a smile. I **use** my wit to excite laughter and good feelings. I bring joy to everyone I meet. When others think I might be all **used** up, I jump back in the race and end up on top. I am the comeback kid. I love **using** my skills to win.

220:
Useless
August 7

Bible Verses
"Without the help of the Lord it is useless to build a home or to guard a city."
Psalm 127:1 (CEV)

"Keep away from worthless and useless talk. It only leads people farther away from God." 2 Timothy 2:16 (CEV)

Word of the Day
Useless – Not good for anything. Hopeless or pointless. Not of value.

Quotes
"For a few brief days the orchards are white with blossoms. They soon turn to fruit, or else float away, useless and wasted, upon the idle breeze. So will it be with present feelings. They must be deepened into decision, or be entirely dissipated by delay." Theodore L. Cuyler

"Half the sorrows of women would be averted if they could repress the speech they know to be useless, -nay, the speech they have resolved not to utter." George Elliot

"Useless laws weaken the necessary laws." Charles de Montesquieu

"No one is useless in this world who lightens the burden of it to anyone else." Charles Dickens

"Nothing that has ever lived is lost; nothing is useless not a sigh, a joy, or a sorrow which has not served its purpose." Madame De Gasparin

Questions
Why is being negative a useless waste of my time? What is one useless activity that I do? Could I give it up? Will I? When?

Declarations:

It is absolutely **useless** to try to get me down because I always wake up on the right side of the bed. When I think maybe something I have done is **useless**, suddenly, something unexpected happens, and an apparently impossible benefit comes to pass. I feel safe inside as I release **useless** thoughts about lack, and meditate on abundance.

I don't permit people to be sarcastic, negative, or derogatory toward me because that would be allowing them to treat me as **useless**. I love myself, even if others don't. Sarcasm is **useless**. I always treat myself with the utmost respect. I respect others as I exchange kindness for meanness. I will walk in love, releasing **useless** bigotry.

I find it **useless** to give up because God continues to encourage me. I am confident and make friends quickly. I choose my friends wisely. Life is too short to spend **useless** time with the critical ones.

I take steps to keep **useless** weight off my body by having lots of fun while I exercise. I can always learn a new game because I love to play. I throw out **useless** sugary snacks and fill my refrigerator with fresh fruits, and vegetables. My immune system functions great because I eat a lot of raw food. Eating healthily is the way I thrive.

I trust God to **use** me. I stop dreading **useless** circumstances and no longer procrastinate. I take action knowing I have my act together. My durability and determination shine as I follow my path, and steer clear of **useless** rabbit trails that take me around in circles.

I marvel at all the wonders around me. I fill so-called **useless** days by visiting an elderly relative, writing a thank-you letter, or donating blood. There is always something kind I can do. I reap great rewards and find nothing **useless** about charity.

221:
Respect
August 8

Bible Verses
"Stand up in the presence of the aged, show respect for the elderly and revere your God. I am the Lord." Leviticus 19:32 (NIV)

"Show proper respect to everyone, love the family of believers, fear God, and honor the emperor." 1 Peter 2:17 (NIV)

Word of the Day
Respect – Receiving or giving consideration, recognition or high regard. Being courteous and reverent towards someone.

Quotes
"Esteem cannot be where there is no confidence, and there can be no confidence where there is no respect. The pure cannot have respect for the vicious, and the vicious have no respect for each other" Henry Giles

"Respect reproduces respect." Pam Malow-Isham

"Earnestness commands the respect of mankind." John Hall

Pam's Perspective
The times where I have demanded respect, it never came. I can only earn respect. I can rant, and rave, because I deserve respect, to no avail. I am grateful I no longer seek evidence of my value outside of myself. Grasping the enormity of self-respect was very liberating. Now if someone does not show me respect, I am unfazed.

Questions
Do I respect my work? Do I respect myself? Do I respect my mate? How many ways do I show respect to others? How do I like to receive respect?

Declarations

I **respect** myself. I **respect** my values, thoughts, ideas, and actions. I feel good. I like being the **respectable** person that I am. I **respect** myself enough to say no when my heart tells me no is the right answer. God has given me the power to stand up for myself.

I **respect** the authority of my leaders. Even if the person that is in power is someone I didn't vote for, I still **respect** and pray for him or her. God has all things in control and can see what I cannot.

I love **respecting** the environment, by planting beautiful flowers, and trees. I make the world a more beautiful place to live. Getting in nature is calming to my soul, and **respectful** of my spirit. I **respect** every living creature. I love taking pictures of animals playing.

I have self-control, **self-respect**, and confidence in my decisions. By **respecting** people's opinions, and accepting their individuality, I have acquired a lot of great friends. I am valuable and deserving of mutual **respect**, and honor. I am trustworthy, and down to earth.

People **respect** me for being myself, and for standing up for the things I believe in. I show **respect** by my kind words, and edification of others. I am fascinated by other people's stories. Listening shows **respect** and is the best way to make and keep friends. I am identified as **respectful**. I open doors for people. I show **respect** by offering my seat to people older than I, with a smile on my face.

I **respect** people's beliefs, even if it is different than mine. God loves all His beautiful children, no matter how misguided we are. I share my faith with love, and **respect**, to reveal God's heart, not judgment. Arguing about religious beliefs never converted anyone. I show **respect** by the grace I gift to others. Love works wonders.

222:
Disrespectful
August 9

Bible Verses

"Never show disrespect for God or curse a leader of your people." Exodus 22:28 (GW)

"They shouldn't speak disrespectfully about anyone, but they should be peaceful, kind, and show complete courtesy toward everyone." Titus 3:2 (CEB)

Word of the Day

Disrespectful –Dishonor and irreverence. Devoid of respect.

Quote

"Violent gestures or quick movements inspire involuntary disrespect." Balzac

Pam's Perspective

A few years back a friend emailed me telling me of all her troubles and ended it asking for prayers, and if I felt inclined to take up an offering for her, that would be great. When I emailed her back that I was praying for her but did not know where she expected me to take up an offering for her at, and my husband and I were not inclined to give her money, she got offended. She told me where I could stick my prayers, how stingy, cold-hearted, greedy, and uncaring we were, and how shameful we should be for not giving her money. She did not ask for a certain amount; we were supposed to guess the magical number and mail her a check. I loaned her money in the past, and because she thought she needed it more, and we had plenty, she didn't repay. Prayer and forgiveness are what I offer her now.

Questions

Whom have I been disrespectful to? Do I need to apologize? How do I react when disrespected? Is there anyone I need to forgive who has been disrespectful to me? Why do I find it easy to forgive, and let go?

Declarations

When someone is **disrespectful** to me, either on purpose, or by accident, I smile, take a deep breath, and thank them for sharing. I do not take it personally because I know they are **disrespectful** to themselves by acting that way, and they are probably hurting inside. I send prayers their way, as I walk in kindness and forgiveness.

I am esteemed for my truthfulness. I can show care for someone, while holding them responsible, without being **disrespectful**. I teach people how to be respectful by my words, and actions. I honor my elders and value their wisdom. Even if I don't agree with them, I still can listen and agree to disagree, without being **disrespectful**.

Being **disrespectful** is rude, so I say please, and thank you a lot. I am a courteous driver, and let people in. I stay calm while driving, even during traffic jams when people become **disrespectful**. These moments give me time to count my blessings and sing praises to God. I value my car by keeping it clean, not **disrespecting** it by leaving it dirty, filled with clothes, wrappers, or trash.

I have a strong backbone that stands up to **disrespectful** people. Showing love to people who **disrespect** my faith is the easiest way to win them over. I walk with a pep in my step, and my head held high. I do not worry about those who are **disrespectful**, because my respect, and confidence, comes from God, who is within me.

I get the ball rolling, and am the first to forgive when someone has been **disrespectful**. I choose not to let **disrespectful** people get me down. I am unique, rare, and special. God has faith in me. I am grateful that when I have been **disrespectful** to God, He did not discard me. No amount of **disrespect** can change His love towards me. His love knows no limits, and His mercy no end.

223:
Compassion
August 10

Bible Verses
"The Lord is good to everyone. He showers compassion on all his creation."
Psalm 145:9 (NLT)

"Once again you will have compassion on us. You will trample our sins under your feet and throw them into the depths of the ocean!" Micah 7:19 (NLT)

Word of the Day
Compassion – Showing kindness and mercy to someone without judgment. Benevolence.

Quotes
"How far you go in life depends on your being tender with the young, compassionate with the aged, sympathetic with the striving and tolerant of the weak and the strong. Because someday in your life you will have been all of these." George Washington Carver

"People may excite in themselves a glow of compassion, not by toasting their feet at the fire, and saying: 'Lord, teach me compassion,' but by going and seeking an object that requires compassion." Henry Ward Beecher

Pam's Perspective
Compassion arises from a heart full of love. When I ease the suffering of another, or when I share my own suffering experience, I open myself up to receive Christ's love. I show myself compassion by eating healthy and taking the time to exercise.

Questions
What does compassion look like to me? How do I feel when someone shows me compassion? Do I offer compassion freely?

Declarations

I have **compassion** for others by respecting their rights, freedom, race, beliefs, and choices. I honor their uniqueness. I remind myself that the person next to me is just like me, seeking happiness, trying to fend off suffering, has known sadness, and seeks to fill their needs as I do. I cherish the gift of friendship. God's **compassion** emerges from my loving heart to treat people like Jesus would.

God's **compassion** for me fills my heart with joy. Thus I share His love with others. I practice **compassion** to those who are rude, by trying to understand what they are going through. I love being kind. I find ways to extend **compassion** to those who are in need.

Life is beautiful when I lead with **compassion**. I foster **compassion** easily in my social circles, simply by recognizing the commonalities we all have. I like sending out get well and thank you cards. I have meaningful relationships as we grant **compassion** to each other.

I am happy because I practice giving **compassion** to the people around me. Talking bad about someone doesn't help him, or her. I actively pursue peace. I upgrade my **compassion** as I walk my talk. I realize that life is not fair, so I don't get upset when I am not treated fairly. I am **compassionate** anyway and prevail nevertheless.

I treat myself with **compassion** by the foods I eat, the things I read, the exercise I get, and the good thoughts I think about myself. Setting aside time for a hot bath is a great way to be **compassionate** to myself. I release my brilliance to shine on the world today.

I am fair to everyone, even-tempered, and **compassionate**, yet I have room to grow. I start now blooming to my full potential. God is still working on me and reveals His **compassion** to me more each day.

224:
Cruel
August 11

Bible Verses
"Good people take good care of their animals, but the wicked know only how to be cruel." Proverbs 12:10 (ERV)

"Wrath is cruel, and anger is overwhelming; but who is able to stand before jealousy?" Proverbs 27:4 (WEB)

Word of the Day
Cruel – purposefully being mean, barbaric or rude. Revengeful. Evil.

Quotes
"Do you believe our creator would allow us to have a worthwhile desire and then not give us the ability to achieve it? That would be a cruel mockery." Richard Bliss Brooke

"The belief of a cruel God makes a cruel man." Thomas Paine

"He who is cruel to animals becomes hard also in his dealings with men. We can judge the heart of a man by his treatment of animals." Immanuel Kant

"What a cruel thing is war; to separate and destroy families and friends, and mar the purest joys and happiness God granted us in this world; to fill our hearts with hatred instead of love for our neighbors." Robert E. Lee

"Scoff not at the natural defects of any which are not in their power to amend. It is cruel to beat a cripple with his own crutches!" Thomas Fuller

Questions
When was the last time someone was cruel to me? When was the last time I was cruel to someone? Why is being cruel so foreign to me?

Declarations

I have vibrant health, and emotional stability, because I am not **cruel** to my body. I release all that does not serve me. I get up and get moving, to invigorate my toned, sensual body. Feeding my body junk food is **cruel**, so I invest in organic produce and take the time to fix it. I am driven, and ready to send healing to this **cruel** world.

Even though I was silly doubting God was in control, and thinking He was **cruel**, He loved me unconditionally anyway. I do not serve a **cruel** God. The God I serve never gives up on me. The love of God melts the **cruel** tendencies in me and fills me with goodness.

I encourage friends to stay away from people who enjoy being **cruel**. I forgive people who have been **cruel** to me. I treat **cruel** people with compassion. My smiling face warms **cruel** hearts. I pray for **cruel** people because they are hurting inside, and crying out for help.

Cruelty is not an option for me. I have a caring, and tactful approach when it comes to evaluations. I notice the nice things that people don›t see, and appreciate the beauty of every living being. I am broad-minded, and a valuable contributor to the people around me.

Volunteering at the humane society shows precious animals that not all people are **cruel**. Pets are God's little love messengers. They are never **cruel**, always accepting, and fun to be around. If we all do our part and show a little love, the world can be an exceptional place to live. I help shelters that comfort people from the **cruelty** of others.

I forgive myself for the times I have been **cruel** with the way I talk to myself. I immediately recognize and change my vocabulary, so I speak life, health, and abundance to my mind, body, soul, and spirit. I am kind to myself and appreciate everything I have been through.

225:
Early
August 12

Bible Verses
"[Very] early the next morning, while it was still dark, Jesus woke [got up] and left the house. He went to a lonely [isolated; deserted] place, where he prayed." Mark 1:35 (EXB)

"So be patient, brethren, [as you wait] till the coming of the Lord. See how the farmer waits expectantly for the precious harvest from the land. [See how] he keeps up his patient [vigil] over it until it receives the early and late rains." James 5:7 (AMP)

Word of the Day
Early – Arriving before expected. Prompt. The first part of the day. Sooner than an anticipated. Ahead of schedule.

Quotes
"Early to bed and early to rise makes a man healthy, wealthy and wise." Benjamin Franklin

"They are much to be pitied who have not been taught to feel, in some degree, as you do; who have not, at least, been given a taste for nature early in life. They lose a great deal." Jane Austen

"The early bird catches the worm." William Camden

"Early tragedy is no excuse for cynicism and apathy." Pam Malow-Isham

Questions
What is my perception of people who arrive early? How do I perceive early risers? Why am I always early for appointments? When I arrive early, how do I feel? Do I get up early, and start my day with prayer?

Declarations

Seeking God **early,** and often, imparts discernment, and balance in my life. I love being an **early** bird. I greet each day with a smile. I get up **early** and enjoy my time thanking God for another beautiful day of life. I seek **early** inspiration, so I start my day on the right track.

Just because I might have developed unhealthy eating habits at an **early** age, does not mean I have to suffer health problems the rest of my life. I let go of non-supportive behaviors. I invigorate my body by doing stretches in the **early** morning. I am in good health, and in great shape. I energize myself with my **early** exercise. I often lay down **early** to rest or take a nap. Power naps are the best.

I remember in the **early** morning to moisturize my skin, to keep it soft. I am aware of what makes my body feel good. I am always changing for the better, getting healthier every day. As I yield to God, I become the powerhouse He created me to be. I am valiant.

Early in my life, I could feel the pull of the Holy Spirit enticing me with love. I teach my children in their **early** years about God's grace. I am a good parent who participates in rearing them up to be productive citizens. I am **early** to give praise, comfort, and support.

Early I inspire the people around me to become the best they can be. I attract emotionally healthy people to hang out with who arrive **early,** or on time. I believe in my own self-care. I am joyous, pleasant, and fun. I arise **early** to have breakfast with my friends.

I get the **early** bonuses. I free myself from stress by leaving **early** for appointments, to give myself plenty of time. I enjoy my freedom. I am sophisticated, and attract abundance **early,** and easily. I produce great results, enjoy my life, and am comfortable being **early**.

226:
Late
August 13

Bible Verses

"It is useless for you to work so hard from early morning until late at night, anxiously working for food to eat; for God gives rest to his loved ones." Psalm 127:2 (NLT)

"The vision will still happen at the appointed time. It hurries toward its goal. It won't be a lie. If it's delayed, wait for it. It will certainly happen. It won't be late." Habakkuk 2:3 (GW)

Word of the Day

Late – Not showing up on time. Tardy. After sunset. Deceased or old.

Quotes

"You can never do a kindness too soon, for you never know how soon it will be too late." Ralph Waldo Emerson

"Better three hours too soon than a minute too late." William Shakespeare

"To men grown old, or who are growing old, it is too late! Ah, nothing is too late till the tired heart shall cease to palpitate." Henry Wadsworth Longfellow

"It is never too late to give up our prejudices." Henry David Thoreau

"It is never too late for God to come through with a miracle. He is still in the miracle-working business." Pam Malow-Isham

Questions

What is my perception of people who are late? Why am I never late for appointments? Why is it never too late to make a difference?

Declarations

I stay **late**, work hard, and make the most of my day. I have a well-defined strategy for reaching my goals. I establish credibility before it is too **late**. I accept the responsibilities that I care about. I leave in plenty of time to get to my destination, regardless of the traffic, so I am never **late**. I live a fulfilling life. It is never too **late** to start over.

I choose not to be **late** in correspondence, so I set aside time each week to take care of letters, notes, bills, emails, thank you, and birthday cards. Nothing gets by me. I get positive results with my work that is never handed in **late**. I stay on top of my resources. I find it easy to manage my finances, so I don't have **late** payments.

I praise God from the early morning, till **late** in the evening. As I stay up **late** and look at the stars and moon, I plot my course for the next day. I sparkle with stardust and moonbeams. I surrender to Love. I radiate friendliness wherever I go. It is never too **late** to seek after God. I am not too **late** to reaffirm my commitment to Him.

I believe God for miracles, even if I think it's too **late**. God crushes and breaks down the walls of my fear, and disbelief. Even in trying circumstances, I am at total peace, because God is never **late** in coming through with the perfect answer for me, right when I need it.

I trust in Divine guidance, even when I think God's **late**. God is not afraid of my doubts. I am His beloved. I believe God when others say it is too late; He heals my body. I walk by faith and believe for the best. I abide in a world where miracles are a daily occurrence.

At every age, it is never too **late** to set a new goal or dream a new dream. Time is my friend. I start fresh each day. I am spontaneous with my wit, and laughter. I create a purely positive state of living.

227:
Rules
August 14

Bible Verses
"Get out the message—God Rules! He put the world on a firm foundation; He treats everyone fair and square." Psalm 96:10 (MSG)

"Whoever enters an athletic competition wins the prize only when playing by the rules." 2 Timothy 2:5 (GW)

Word of the Day
Rules – The policy or order of things. The law or guidelines set before us by God, parents or government that determines the best way to live.

Quotes
"The ideas I stand for are not mine. I borrowed them from Socrates. I swiped them from Chesterfield. I stole them from Jesus. And I put them in a book. If you don't like their rules, whose would you use?" Dale Carnegie

"But like any wisdom too well said or too well known, the rules of success are frequently esteemed too simple to be effective, too trite to be true. This, despite fossil imprints of them found in both Testaments of the Bible, attesting to their early discovery and long use by those who fathered all human prosperity." Richard Gaylord Briley

Pam's Perspective
I used to believe there were some rules we were to follow in order to lead a fulfilling life. I have come to the conclusion that we make up our own imaginary rules, and it is up to us to choose to have a fulfilling life, or not.

Questions
What rules do I follow? Why am I liberated by the rules I follow? Why do I like following rules? Are there any rules I dismiss? Or need to dismiss?

Declarations

I choose to live by the **rules** of God that are put here for my benefit. I am thankful for guidelines, and **rules** to follow. Regardless if others follow the **rules**, I am true to my higher self. As I follow the **rules**, I feel well-grounded, being committed to excellence, and integrity.

I make up my own **rules** about how I want to live and conduct myself that are best for me. I have **rules** about eating, drinking, working, playing, and sleeping. We all have **rules**, and it is up to us if we are going to keep them. I follow **rules** that align with my heart.

I celebrate the **rules** of friendship as I attract support. I have creative, loving friends. I like being around people with well-defined goals, and **rules**. You know where you stand, and what is expected of you, so there aren't any surprises, or unmet, unknown expectations.

I **rule** over my mindset, so it stays positive. I forgive, one more time. I honor my body and follow the **rules** of healthy eating, and exercise. I am the effect of my good health and sexy body. I love feeling whole. I am a mirror of God's beauty and restoration.

I am a victorious warrior who **rules** over my own life. I read the **rules**, so I know how to play the game, or operate the machinery. It would be silly to try to change the **rules** just to suit me. I break the **rules** of following the crowds and blaze a trail of excellence.

The issue of authority is settled. God **rules**, and is in charge of me. God is still God, and I am not. I receive the assets, and wisdom of heaven because I obey God's **rules**. I receive prosperity in every dimension of my life. Jesus is my brother in arms. I am well connected. I am meant to be a sent one who smiles, while I **rule** over defeat, shatter failure, rise to the top, and proclaim the good news.

Rebellion
August 15

Bible Verses

"Return, rebellious children, and I will heal your rebellion. 'Here we are; we come to you, for you are the Lord our God.'" Jeremiah 3:22 (CEB)

"Every person who practices sin commits an act of rebellion, and sin is rebellion." 1 John 3:4 (CEB)

Word of the Day

Rebellion – Being defiant against the controlling powers. Insurrection.

Quotes

"If particular care and attention is not paid to the ladies, we are determined to foment a rebellion, and will not hold ourselves bound by any laws in which we have no voice or representation." Abigail Adams

"Originality is independence, not rebellion; it is sincerity, not antagonism." George Henry Lewes

"War begins where reason ends. The thing worse than rebellion is the thing that causes rebellion." Frederick Douglass

"Rebellion to tyrants is obedience to God." Benjamin Franklin

"Resolved, that the women of this nation in 1876, have greater cause for discontent, rebellion, and revolution than the men of 1776." Susan B. Anthony

Questions

What does rebellion look like to me? How do I deal with rebellion? Is there rebellion in my life that I need to deal with?

Declarations

The tone and delivery of what I ask my children helps to determine whether or not I experience their **rebellion** or respect. I am fearless in the face of any hurt. I stand my ground and move forward in love. I include my children in creating a solution for their **rebellion**. I put our agreement on paper to solidify it and make it real. I look beyond **rebellion** to see what is really going on. I am insightful.

I was made a winner of my **rebellious** nature by turning it over to God. I forgive the unforgivable and soar above harm. Reconciliation is my game. I choose to respond with grace because I have a sufficiency of peace. I love being versatile, and vibrant. I transform **rebellion** because I model kindness, courtesy, respect, and patience.

I may seem **rebellious** as I choose to stand up at my desk and work, instead of sitting down. If you call being healthy and taking charge of your life **rebellion**, so be it. I rejoice in the shape I have. I am open to conversations about physical fitness, health, and longevity.

When my body wants to **rebel**, and binge on sugar, I give myself a pep talk and stay on the healthy path. I can be anything I choose to be. I love myself as I speak to my inner **rebellious** child, and remind myself of my worth. I am unique and express myself freely.

I value my life and my opinions. I can respect myself, and allow others to have their own point of view. We can agree to disagree, and remain friends without a **rebellion**. Diversity is great.

I rearrange my life to enjoy the simple pleasures. It is easy to let go. I free myself from unwanted baggage and the **rebellion** of wanting to hang on to everything. I think about how I can help people with all the things I have, and what I can do next. I am a generous giver.

229:
Circumstance
August 16

Bible Verses
"Those who trust in the Lord are steady as Mount Zion, unmoved by any circumstance." Psalm 125:1 (TLB)

"Arise [from the depression and prostration in which circumstances have kept you—rise to a new life]! Shine (be radiant with the glory of the Lord), for your light has come, and the glory of the Lord has risen upon you!" Isaiah 60:1 (AMP)

Word of the Day
Circumstance – The cause of what is going on now. Coincidence. The manifestation of events that happen by chance or on purpose.

Quotes
"What's causing your suffering and pain is not the circumstance you are in, but your thoughts about the circumstances you're in." Sonia Ricotti

"Circumstances are the rulers of the weak; they are but instruments of the wise." Samuel Lover

"Character, not circumstances, makes the man." Booker T. Washington

Pam's Perspective
I do everything in my power to create favorable circumstances, but life is not fair. I used to get upset, blame God, and everyone else for trying times. Not anymore. I say, oh well, let's try something new. NOTHING can affect my grateful heart!

Questions
Do I let the circumstances of life affect my mood? Why or why not? What makes me content? Why will I choose to be happy in any circumstance?

Declarations

I am willing to be flexible and evolve, as **circumstances** change. I take a fresh inventory of where I am, and where I am not, without condemnation. Then, I deal with what I need to deal with. I get help when I need it. Life reaches out, and helps me, as I help others. I rejoice in every **circumstance** because I know the giver of life.

I give attention to what my body is telling me. I have learned how to be content in any **circumstance**. I allow the breath of God to move in my body so I grow healthier. I maintain a youthful appearance. I never let **circumstances** interfere with my workouts or self-care.

Just because my **circumstances** may look dim, doesn't mean that I give up. I commit to being productive. I believe everything will be for my greater good. God's presence comforts me, gives me strength, and courage, no matter what the **circumstances** are. I trust my creator. I focus on the God that is bigger than my **circumstances**.

I give thanks in all **circumstances**. There is always something to be grateful for. I like being in action, fulfilling my dreams. I am optimistic in every **circumstance**. I am happy to participate in other people's miracles. It is fun being around me in any **circumstance**.

I create **circumstances** that generate opportunities. I overflow with new possibilities as I turn within for guidance. I fill myself with the awareness of abundance. I save for the future and create a reserve. I allow myself to grow up and become a mature, valuable citizen.

I am enough, and what I do is enough, in every **circumstance**. The world moves over for me because I know where I am going, and I don't let **circumstances** stand in my way. I am set apart for great things. Every morning I declare I am going to have a great day.

230:
Intent
August 17

Bible Verses
"The Lord advises those who fear him. He reveals to them the intent of his promise." Psalm 25:14 (GW)

"For the word of God is living and effectual, and more piercing than any two-edged sword; and reaching unto the division of the soul and the spirit, of the joints also and the marrow, and is a discerner of the thoughts and intents of the heart." Hebrews 4:12 (DRA)

Word of the Day
Intent – What a person resolves, plans or wills to do. A decisive act.

Quotes
"Some are so intent upon acquiring the superfluities of life that they sacrifice its necessaries in this foolish pursuit." Oliver Goldsmith

"My failures have been errors in judgment, not of intent." Ulysses S. Grant

"As small letters hurt the sight, so do small matters him that is too much intent upon them: they vex and stir up anger, which gets an evil habit in him in reference to greater affairs." Plutarch

Pam's Perspective
Our intent shapes our existence for either good or bad. My intent with this book is to empower people to walk in their divine authority and live victoriously.

Questions
How has my intent affected my outcome? Is my intent to look good, or make a difference? What good intent will I put into action today?

Declarations

I set my **intentions** for the day, and then release them to God knowing everything will work out perfectly. I am a highly blessed, and favored kid. Because of the **intent** I have to praise God for all things, I live in a continual state of gratitude, and bliss.

I am affluent. My **intent** to do everything with excellence gets me noticed. I educate myself about money and investments. My **intent** to attract wealth works so well that I live in abundance. I am aware of more. I work with the **intent** to prosper. I plant positive thoughts in my brain with the **intent** that they will produce a great harvest.

I offer a grin to someone who is frowning, with the **intent** to pick him, or her up. I roar with laughter, as it is my **intent** to feel good. My smiles are contagious and may cause an epidemic of joy. I co-create my abundantly cheerful life with God's help. I like being me.

My first **intent** is to smile, as I welcome people into my circle of friends. I am generous with my **intent** to listen, so I can help people feel heard, and understood. I humble myself before God. I am here to offer support and be a blessing. My **intent** is to show grace to the lovable, and the unlovable, and allow God to move through me.

All my **intent** is useless if I do not put into practice what I **intend** to do. My body craves the nutrients it receives from eating vegetables, and fruit, and they taste so good. I have a wonderful life. My **intent** is to stay healthy. With exercise, I keep my stamina up to par.

Happy, prosperous people are naturally drawn to me. I have a great sense of humor and take things lightly. My **intent** to have fun, and make people laugh is ongoing. There is not a day that passes that my spouse and I do not laugh. We are a jovial couple.

231:
Overlook
August 18

Bible Verses

"A person's wisdom yields patience; it is to one's glory to overlook an offense." Proverbs 19:11 (NIV)

"Because God is not unjust or unfair He won't overlook the work you have done or the love you have carried to each other in His name while doing His work, as you are still doing." Hebrews 6:10 (VOICE)

Word of the Day

Overlook – To look past faults and forgive. To pardon or excuse.

Quotes

"The art of being wise is the art of knowing what to overlook." William James

"After all, one knows one's weak points so well, that it's rather bewildering to have the critics overlook them and invent others." Edith Wharton

"Much, however, of what we call evil is really good in disguises, and we should not quarrel rashly with adversities not yet understood, nor overlook the mercies often bound up in them." Sir John Lubbock

Pam's Perspective

I have overlooked the sociopathic tendencies of certain family members, praying they would change. They haven't, but I have stopped being manipulated by them.

Questions

Can I overlook someone's faults without condemning them? What do I overlook? What should I overlook? Am I overlooking something that I need to address? Am I overlooking something I should confront?

Declarations

Since my present mood is sunny, I **overlook** grumpy people. I feel from a loving space, and **overlook** snide remarks from hurting people. I am filled with light and have kind feelings toward my fellow man while **overlooking** any deficiency they may have.

I laugh as I almost **overlooked** the birds flying around, singing joyfully, with not a care in the world. I can be like the birds, and trust that God will take care of me like He takes care of them. I am glad God has not **overlooked** me but takes delight in caring for me.

I **overlook** my preconceived judgments about how difficult a task might be, and plunge full speed ahead, getting it done quickly. I focus on learning while **overlooking** my inadequacies. I can win, and carry on, no matter what. I **overlook** the negative and focus on the positive. I am able to face any obstacle or problem and solve it.

I bring glory to God because I **overlook** people's idiosyncrasies, and see the beauty inside of them. I help people draw out their latent talents, and hidden fortitude, by believing in them. I encourage them to dream big, so they can **overlook** their blunders, and build on their abilities. We all have gifts in us that we can develop.

I **overlook** desserts for the better, healthier choices of fresh fruits. I crave veggies for snacks. I draw on my inner resources. I allow myself to feel secure. I look in the mirror without **overlooking** my imperfections and tell myself that I am beautiful and lovable.

Instead of **overlooking** my faults, I choose to put consistent effort into improving myself. I put faith in what I say about myself. I like bettering myself. I show up and leave nothing **overlooked**. I take charge of my life and make the most out of it every single day.

232:
Look
August 19

Bible Verses
"Look at those who are honest and good, for a wonderful future awaits those who love peace." Psalm 37:37 (NLT)

"Always look happy and cheerful." Ecclesiastes 9:8 (GNT)

Word of the Day
Look – To see or put your attention towards. To stare or behold. To perceive with your own eyes. Observe.

Quotes
"A gentle word, a kind look, a good-natured smile can work wonders and accomplish miracles." Professor William Wells

"'Look unto Me' and not 'you will be saved,' but 'you are saved.' The very thing we look for, we shall find if we will concentrate on Him." Oswald Chambers

"It is not fitting, when one is in God's service, to have a gloomy face or a chilling look." Francis of Assisi

Pam's Perspective
I look to God for guidance as I go about sharing His love. I look with love past the superficial and accept people for who they are. I look with generosity to see what I can share. I look to see the beauty in everything. I look for the blessing behind every problem. I look for the lesson after every mistake.

Questions
When I look at my family what, do I see? When I look at my neighbors, what do I see? When I look at myself, what do I see?

Declarations

I **look** with caring eyes. I **look** at the image of God in every person I encounter, even the ones that act like the devil. I **look** to understand, not criticize. I **look** with empathy. I **look** at things from a different angle, so I can change what is so for me. I **look** with kindness.

I love, and approve of myself, with all my imperfections. I am highly favored and **looking** good. Every morning I **look** at myself in the mirror with loving eyes and tell myself positive statements to reinforce my great **outlook** on life. I like the way I **look**. I take a second **look** and notice my inner and outer beauty. I **look** fabulous.

I am a pleasure to be near. My sphere of leverage continues to grow, as I **look** for new companions. I **look** for cheerful people to be with. I **look** for connections. I **look** for an inspiring mentor and coach. I **look** to meet new friends, as I spice up my social life.

I alone am in charge of what I **look** at, so I make sure it is of benefit to my mind, body, soul, and spirit. I have a serious dedication to my personal development. I **look** for wisdom in the simple things. I love to **look** for and read educational books. I muse over good words.

I **look** to God for answers. He gives me a right now word for today. I have a secure connection with the Divine. I **look** for answers from within. I **look** at all the good that is in front of me. I am grateful for my eyes to **look** at things with wonder. I always **look** for something to feel good about. **Lookout**, I found it. I **look** at myself with love.

I **look** at my life and create the life I want. I am willing to **look** foolish, in order to learn something new. I eagerly **look** ahead expecting possibilities, because my life is brimming with joy. As I **look**, I find my purpose. I **look** forward to my next great adventure.

233:
Today
August 20

Bible Verses

"I am teaching you today—yes, you— so you will trust in the Lord."
Proverbs 22:19 (NLT)

"For God says, "At just the right time, I heard you. On the day of salvation, I helped you." Indeed, the "right time" is now. Today is the day of salvation."
2 Corinthians 6:2 (NLT)

Word of the Day

Today – Pertaining to the present moment right now. Current time.

Quotes

"A man should never be ashamed to own he has been in the wrong, which is merely admitting that he is wiser today than he was yesterday." Proverb

"Tomorrow's church will be what I am today." Bruce Garner

"Our cares are all today, our joys are all today; and in one little word, our life, what is it but - Today." Martin Farquhar Tupper

Pam's Perspective

Since the things I do today creates my future, I start my day by asking what good can I do today. I remember that today is a gift. When I prioritize my day, I get a lot more done than when I don't have things written down.

Questions

Do I see today as a gift or drudgery? What is the best use of my time today? How can I make the most of today to enhance my future? Will I pray today? Will I add laughter, fun, and adventure to my day?

Declarations

Today I take immediate action on my, to-do list. I excite the positive. I dream big, audacious dreams **today**. I do the most important task first. I unleash my greatness to perform at the top of my game **today**.

I live approved of by God. My community benefits from my charity **today**. I believe God for miracles **today**. I love watching them come about. God is constantly working in the background, on my behalf **today**. Even when I can't see it; I know He has it all handled.

I am overflowing with love, joy, and vitality **today**. I have so many opportunities **today** knocking at my doors that are seeking me out. It is all within my reach **today**. I can accomplish anything my heart desires. I do things **today**, so I will not have regrets next year.

I have power over my thoughts, and words **today**. Everything is doable. I have fun creating new goals **today**. My acclaim spreads as I help my community unite, and work peacefully together.

I am thankful that I hear God's voice and walk in victory **today**. I eat healthily **today** and every day. I have an amazing body that looks fabulous. I enjoy all kinds of movement and activities. I see how beautiful I really am **today**. I feel better with each passing hour.

I am rejoicing **today** because of how I spent my time last month. I am very selective about how I spend my time, and whom I spend my time with. I make the most out of every moment **today**. I focus on what I can do of value **today** and then enjoy my productivity.

Today is a great day to be alive. **Today** is a great day to praise God for all my blessings. I live a life of service. **Today**, I will be kind, and generous, just for the fun of it. I am Spirit's representative of love.

234:
Acceptance
August 21

Bible Verses
"He will make his appeal to God, and God will grant acceptance; he will see God's face and shout with joy, knowing God has restored his right standing." Job 33:26 (VOICE)

"For if one man's offence meant that men should be slaves to death all their lives, it is a far greater thing that through another man, Jesus Christ, men by their acceptance of his more than sufficient grace and righteousness, should live all their lives like kings!" Romans 5:17 (PHILLIPS)

Word of the Day
Acceptance – Feeling loved and accepted the way you are. Recognizing what is. Acknowledging the facts the way they are.

Quotes
"The first thing a kindness deserves is acceptance; the next, transmission." George MacDonald

"What is new finds better acceptance than what is good or great." Denham

Pam's Perspective
The acceptance I give myself is by far the most important. When I can really accept, and love myself, then I can do the same for others, but not before. People feel your acceptance or lack thereof and respond accordingly. Fortunately, God's acceptance of us is unconditional love, given freely, without any strings.

Questions
What does acceptance look like to me? How do I show acceptance to the people around me? Have I accepted myself with all my humanity?

Declarations

I am full of **acceptance** for myself. By **accepting** myself for who I am, and who I am not, I can then change myself for the better. It is nice to receive **acceptance** from others, but I am the only one who can validate, and **accept** myself. I **accept** worthy compliments.

I choose to **accept** people, be calm, and live in the moment. I create an atmosphere of **acceptance** around me. I listen to other people's points of view. I train myself to tune in, and really hear how people want to be **accepted**. I am the one who people think of as **accepting**.

I remember that God loves and **accepts** everyone unconditionally, and I can choose to do the same. When I do, I shine forth Gods light to the world, and His love is shown through me by my **acceptance** of others, and myself. I am always nice to the people around me. I offer support, and love, whenever I can. I enjoy making new friends, and building strong relationships, by **accepting** our differences.

My **acceptance** into the winners club is automatic. I am brave and emulate the people I want to be like. I have great brainpower, and wisdom, because I continue to improve, by **accepting** my genius. I have precision in my thoughts and actions, so I enjoy optimal health. I **accept** that I will continue to advance as long as I have a life.

By **accepting** that I am not chained to my own aptitude, I can create a mindset that is unstoppable. My growth mindset is focused on gaining knowledge, and learning something new. I like myself.

I like working hard for the things I get. I **accept** that there is no free lunch, so I get off my seat, and get into action. The **acceptance** of myself has made me well-off. The will of God for my life is to be responsible, honorable, **accepting**, and compassionate.

235:
Ignorance
August 22

Bible Verses
"Smart people keep quiet about what they know, but stupid people advertise their ignorance." Proverbs 12:23 (GNT)

"For this is the will of God, that by doing good you may put to silence the ignorance of foolish men." 1 Peter 2:15 (NKJV)

Word of the Day
Ignorance – Blindness to one's inadequacies. Deficient in judgment.

Quotes
"Ignorance and bungling with love are better than wisdom and skill without." Henry David Thoreau

"Humility and knowledge in poor clothes excel pride and ignorance in costly attire." William Penn

"The greater the ignorance, the greater the dogmatism." Sir William Osler

Pam's Perspective
Never let your ignorance of how to do a project, or how to achieve your dreams, stop you. Once you decide on what you want, the 'how to' takes care of itself. In 2008 I did not know how to start a community garden or a children's garden. I was told I didn't possess enough time, talent, or know how to do it. In March 2009 I was honored with a Community Hero Award trophy for completing it.

Questions
How can I disband ignorance from my life? Am I as ignorant about my shortcomings as I pretend to be? What will it take for me to improve?

Declarations

By being patient, I overlook the **ignorance** of others. I deliberately study, and consciously think positive thoughts to keep **ignorance** at bay. Boredom never occurs to me because I enjoy working on my goals. I am a great judge of character and have good judgment.

I recognize and tell the truth about my **ignorance** of a subject. I know I do not know everything, so I look for the wisest person who is competent on that topic and ask for their advice. I am wise to ask.

God sees me as capable, and gives me a robe of favor, despite my **ignorance**. By studying God's Word, I am infused with wisdom to discern what is right, from wrong. I search out and find new revelations on how to lead an excellent life. I live my vision full out.

I forgive the people who have hurt my feelings out of **ignorance**. I am grateful for the people who have overlooked my **ignorance**, because I know I have been rude. I remember to be full of grace.

I practice seeing everyone as a person of value and bless them. I remember I can be **ignorant** at times too, so I offer mercy. I am conscious of keeping an open mind, so I can learn new things. I ignore the **ignorance** of people who tell me I can't.

God imparts the perfect solution to me for every problem that comes my way. I receive added spunk to complete my task, even when I am **ignorant** of the know-how. I display **ignorance** with charm.

My **ignorance** ignites curiosity in me to go on a discovery trip. I gladly remain connected to the Almighty as I stay open and eager to learn about my **ignorance**. I have lots to read, learn, and understand. I elevate my self-esteem by feeling strong, happy, and competent.

236:
Wisdom
August 23

Bible Verses
"But true wisdom and power are found in God; counsel and understanding are his." Job 12:13 (NLT)

"If you need wisdom, ask our generous God, and he will give it to you. He will not rebuke you for asking." James 1:5 (NLT)

Word of the Day
Wisdom – The skill to comprehend great truths, act on them and relay them to others. The understanding to think clearly. Tactfulness when relating to people. Savvy; smart.

Quotes
"The most manifest sign of wisdom is continued cheerfulness." Michel de Montaigne

"A proverb is the wit of one and the wisdom of many." Lord John Russell

"Music is a higher revelation than all wisdom and philosophy." Ludwig van Beethoven

"True wisdom is always simple, never complicated." Pam Malow-Isham

"God is a light that is never darkened: an unwearied life that cannot die; a fountain always flowing; a garden of life; a seminary of wisdom; a radical beginning of all goodness." Alanus de Rupe

Questions
If I had the wisest person on earth sitting next to me, what would I ask her? How can I apply this wisdom? How can I increase my wisdom?

Declarations

Declaring good things over my life has had a profound effect. I am full of **wisdom.** Everything I need to know is revealed to me as I listen to God. If I am meant to know something, He will show me.

I am a genius as I implement my **wisdom**. God's power, strength, peace, **wisdom**, and joy are mine. His love fills my heart and unveils to me better ways to serve mankind. I remember I am **wise**.

When I look for understanding to solve my problems, a new idea is revealed, and I see the solution as God dispels any confusion in my mind, and replaces it with **wisdom**. I represent the Mighty One. God empowers my ministry with foresight, honor, and **wisdom**.

I am inquisitive about life and continue to expand my horizons, as I expand my **wisdom**. I am well-rounded and well-grounded. I gain **wisdom** from assessing and contemplating the past. I discuss things with my mentor to glean nuggets of **wisdom**. I associate with **wise** people. I have conversations that matter. People know I care.

Because the creator of the universe lives within me, I am greater than he who lives in this world. The realization that in the depths of my being dwells God's power, and **wisdom**, gives me confidence, and assurance to press on. I am sought out for my **wisdom**.

I am always ready to receive divine **wisdom** as I take the time to listen to God. I rejoice today for the **wisdom** I am attaining as I stimulate my mind with God's word. I have all I need in Christ.

I have absolute trust in God's **wisdom** for me. I know I will be able to succeed in any circumstance, for God continually presents me with all necessary **wisdom**, in the right way, and at the right time.

237:
Ordinary
August 24

Bible Verses
"It is true that I am an ordinary, weak human being, but I don't use human plans and methods to win my battles." 1 Corinthians 10:3 (TLB)

"God chose what the world considers ordinary and what it despises—what it considers to be nothing—in order to destroy what it considers to be something." 1 Corinthians 1:28 (GW)

Word of the Day
Ordinary – Familiar or routine; generic, dull or modest.

Quotes
"The great lesson from the true mystics is that the sacred is in the ordinary that it is to be found in one's daily life, in one's neighbors, friends, and family, in one's backyard." Abraham H. Maslow

"There never has been a great and beautiful character, which has not become so by filling well the ordinary and smaller offices appointed of God." Horace Bushnell

"The greater intellect one has, the more originality one finds in men. Ordinary persons find no difference between men." Blaise Pascal

Pam's Perspective
I take my ordinary smile everywhere I go. Seeing people smile back at me, brightens my day. Ordinary gestures can bring light to every situation.

Questions
Do I find joy in the ordinary? Do I get bored with the ordinary? How may I find miracles in the ordinary? Do I consider myself ordinary?

Declarations

I enjoy every second of every day. I generate feelings of joy, harmony, and peace from my **ordinary** life. I am the image and likeness of God. My spirit is ageless, and there is nothing **ordinary** about me. As I do what is right, and good, my **ordinary** life reaps a great harvest. I am at home with my progress and success.

I am a precious jewel in the eyes of God, who thinks I am much more than **ordinary**, but a priceless gem. I am well cared for. All of God's power is within this **ordinary** vessel, to do great exploits. The kingdom of Heaven is being acted out as I listen to God, and obey.

I enjoy perfect health. My favorite **ordinary** drink is lots of pure water every day. I can begin right now to create a beautiful **ordinary** life, filled with bliss, and contentment. I am grateful that I can be used to spread joy, and happiness in **ordinary** ways. I am beautiful.

I stimulate excitement with my **ordinary** laughter. My natural self-expression leads people to appreciate what they already have, in their **ordinary** life. **Ordinary** moments turn into lasting beautiful memories. There is breathtaking beauty all around me when I look.

I approach every situation from a win-win perspective. I say yes to teamwork and fun. **Ordinary** jobs turn into great adventures. There is nothing **ordinary** about my work because I do a great job. My **ordinary** deeds surpass my coworkers. I pay attention to the details. I declare I have what it takes, no matter how **ordinary** I am.

Taking vacations all over the world are entertaining, and a great learning experience. I find different cultures fascinating. There is no such thing as an **ordinary** individual. We are all special. Discovery is enlightening. I am fortunate I don't take the **ordinary** for granted.

238:
Extraordinary
August 25

Bible Verses
"Although your former state was ordinary, your future will be extraordinary." Job 8:7 (CEB)

"And God did unusual and extraordinary miracles by the hands of Paul." Acts 19:11 (AMP)

Word of the Day
Extraordinary – Being incredible and marvelous. Amazing and rare.

Quotes
"One machine can do the work of fifty ordinary men. No machine can do the work of one extraordinary man." Elbert Hubbard

"Those that God used in the past were just ordinary people with an extraordinary Master. They were not all champions of great faith, but little people who saw their own need, and put their small faith in a great God." Winkie Pratney

"Perfection consists not in doing extraordinary things, but in doing ordinary things extraordinarily well. Neglect nothing; the most trivial action may be performed to God." Angelique Arnauld

Pam's Perspective
When I see everything as extraordinary, my life is filled with wonder. I look for miracles and revelation. As I act extraordinary, I become extraordinary.

Questions
What if I looked at everything and everyone as extraordinary? How could my life change? Is it possible for me to live an extraordinary life?

Declarations

I ask God for the **extraordinary**, and He gives it to me in abundance. Great is God's affection for me, and **extraordinary** His favor on my behalf. I have the seal of God's approval on me, so I embrace my life of plenty. Jesus is at the center of my **extraordinary** life.

I work for **extraordinary** people. I get **extraordinary** reviews. I have the **extraordinary** confidence to do a great job, at whatever I need to do. Excellent, and **extraordinary** is the way my work is perceived. Nothing is too hard for me to accomplish with my **extraordinary** gifts. Today is the best day of my life. I have a lifetime commitment to staying active, fit, educated, and **extraordinarily** joyful.

I like eating **extraordinarily** healthy food. Every cell in my body is full of life. My enthusiasm for trying new foods opens up **extraordinary** flavors and delicacies for me. I will taste anything once to see if I like it. Exotic food is **extraordinary** and delicious.

I appreciate all my **extraordinary** relationships. I automatically attract others who are honest, sincere, and who value my beliefs, as I value theirs. I have **extraordinary** friends. People listen to what I have to say. I am so magnetic and compelling that people see me as **extraordinary**. My beliefs complement my **extraordinary** life.

I achieve **extraordinary** goals. I hire **extraordinary** experts who coach me to reach farther and become even more **extraordinary**. I am on fire, as I do ordinary things, in an **extraordinary** way.

My sense of identity is rooted in God's **extraordinary** love for me. God is my Father whether I measure up, or not. He runs to embrace me, even before I even ask. His **extraordinary** mercy knows no end. I am forever grateful for all the good I continue to receive.

239:
Practice
August 26

Bible Verses
"But everybody who hears these words of mine and doesn't put them into practice will be like a fool who built a house on sand." Matthew 7:26 (CEB)

"But he said, 'Happy rather are those who hear God's word and put it into practice.'" Luke 11:28 (CEB)

Word of the Day
Practice – The training, preparation, and repetition needed to acquire a skill. Undertake or follow through.

Quotes
"The practice of making big agreements and keeping them is just that - a practice." Brian Klemmer

"Of all parts of wisdom the practice is the best." T. Thompson

Pam's Perspective
It always amazed me when people would come into the dance studio, and expect to become a good dancer or learn a wedding dance in just a couple lessons. People would not expect other things to come that easy, but somehow, dance was the exception they thought. Can you become a concert pianist in two lessons, would be my reply. You have to practice a lot, to be good at something. Some of us need more practice than others at dancing, personal restraint, forgiveness, being kind, compassionate, or loving. What I practice shows what I value.

Questions
What do I practice the most? How is that affecting me? Am I conscious of my practices? Do I practice what I need? Why do I have the best practices?

Declarations

I **practice** what I preach. I love speaking about good things. The **practice** of patience is a daily occurrence for me. I choose to **practice** forgiveness, and mercy every day. I am a consistent winner, and I **practice** winning. I **practice** smiling and thinking happy thoughts.

Audiences love me, as I **practice** speaking in front of them. I execute my memorization **practice** correctly to wow the crowds. The way I get good at anything I do is by consistent, dedicated **practice**. I set aside time to **practice**, so I guarantee the mastery of my craft.

I make the time to **practice** the things that are important to me. I **practice** keeping my word, and being a person of integrity. I reinforce positive behavior as I **practice** laughing for no reason at all. I **practice** sending out thoughtful notes, thank you cards, and cheering people up. **Practicing** consideration pays dividends.

I remember to pray for people I disagree with as I **practice** clemency. I **practice** praying and listening to my Creator throughout my day. God's manifold wisdom is revealed to me as I **practice** yielding to Him. I tell God how I really feel, and trust He understands.

I love feeling generous because I **practice** giving. I **practice** putting money away for my future. I buy locally while thinking globally. My **practice** of tithing, and giving to charities, feels good to me. I always have plenty to share. I love to be hospitable, and philanthropic.

I am relentless in my **practice** of taking care of myself first, so I can easily take care of others. I **practice** the golden rule. I **practice** counting my mate's positive qualities. I **practice** giving my mate well-deserved foot rubs. My **practice** of taking the time to listen improves my relationships. I **practice** gratitude and kindness.

240:
Refrain
August 27

Bible Verses

"Refrain from anger, and forsake wrath. Do not fret—it leads only to evil."
Psalm 37:8 (NRSV)

"For he that will love life, and see good days, let him refrain his tongue from evil, and his lips that they speak no guile." 1 Peter 3:10 (KJV)

Word of the Day

Refrain –To resist from doing or saying something. To avoid temptation.

Quotes

"If refraining from prayer altogether can be considered snobbish and ungrateful, praying without gratitude is as Francis 'Cray Love' Chan puts it, 'serving leftovers to God'" Kate Braestrup

"No man ever believes with a true and saving faith, unless God inclines his heart: and no man, when God does incline his heart, can refrain from believing." Blaise Pascal

"When will talkers refrain from evil speaking? When listeners refrain from evil hearing." Julius Charles Hare

"We who have escaped cannot refrain from singing without the walls of the dungeon, in the hope that some within may hear and take heart." Spurgeon

"When I choose to refrain from gossip and welcome only good news, my circle of friends and influence grows." Pam Malow-Isham

Questions

What will I refrain from today? What have I refrained from in the past?

Declarations

I am courageous as I **refrain** from following the crowds. I blaze a new trail. I enjoy all the luxuries of my life and **refrain** from taking them for granted. Because I always expect positive results, I see them arrive. I **refrain** from doubt. I create a life I love by **refraining** from negativity. I am motivated to see my dreams come true.

I **refrain** from shirking responsibility and accept that I have created what is currently in my life, no matter what it is. I blossom, and **refrain** from blame, or playing the victim game. I come from a place of integrity, influence, and power. I recognize my strengths.

I eat only the healthiest foods and **refrain** from wasted calories. I easily, and joyfully maintain my perfect weight. I enjoy stretching in the morning, increasing mobility, staying alert, flexible and strong.

I speak uplifting words and **refrain** from profanity or trash talk. I **refrain** from gossip and walk away from people who do. I stand up for people who are being slandered and tell the good news. My way of acting is friendly, generous, and noble. I **refrain** from talking adversely. I see the best in everyone, as I see the best in myself. I **refrain** from passing judgments and live with love in my heart.

God sees, and loves me, even when I mess up, or abandon Him. He is always there with open arms and never **refrains** from blessing me. I am appreciative of His gentle ways as I run back to His side.

I have a positive relationship with my heavenly Father. Great is my love for God, and even greater is His love for me. I **refrain** from hiding my light because I glow brightly. I have come to know the presence, and peace of God in my everyday life. I am a partaker in God's promises and **refrain** from taking them for granted.

241:
Moving
August 28

Bible Verses
"The righteous keep moving forward, and those with clean hands become stronger and stronger." Job 17:9 (NLT)

"Let heaven and earth praise Him, the seas and everything moving in them." Psalm 69:35 (TLV)

Word of the Day
Moving – Being mobile and unfixed. Evolving. Arousing strong feelings.

Quotes
"The happiness and peace attained by those satisfied by the nectar of spiritual tranquility is not attained by greedy persons restlessly moving here and there." Chanakya

"God cannot steer a vehicle that is not moving." Dottie D. Caldwell, MA, LPC

"The important work of moving the world forward does not wait to be done by perfect men." George Eliot

Pam's Perspective
I remind myself to keep moving. I get up from my desk, run up, and down the stairs, stretch, or go for a walk. I get stiff sitting, so every half hour, or so, I move. Doing balance exercises while watching TV, doing squats at the sink, leg lifts at the stove, or arm circles at the refrigerator keeps me moving in a healthy direction.

Questions
Do I keep moving to avoid something I need to deal with? If so, why? Am I moving in the direction of my goals? Am I moving closer to God?

Declarations

Moving with purpose, I get things done, so people can count on me. Every day I am **moving** forward in the pursuit of my dreams. I am seen as brave, as I am **moving** toward my next goal. I can have a fabulous life right now while **moving** toward a gratifying future.

Limitless excitement is mine as I ignite a flame of passion in people, **moving** them from despair, to renewed hope, and a greater vision for their life. As I am **moving** along, I pick up a lot of great friends. I start with love, and kindness while **moving** toward understanding.

Dancing around, and **moving** with joy in my heart is a great way to get some exercise, have fun, and stay fit. I love **moving** onward. I have a happy mind, **moving** from one positive thought to another.

Moving towards God is always a great idea. He is the best pilot for me. I am **moving** my mind to a place of tranquility, by slowing down, taking deep breaths, and thinking about great things.

Moving triumphantly past old hurts by offering forgiveness, frees me to live the victorious life. I continue **moving** upwards, and onwards. **Moving** beyond negative thinking is the way I live. Because I am thankful for every moment of my life, I enjoy true contentment. I am a champion today, filled with good thoughts.

Confidently **moving** ahead of the crowd by my excellent work is the norm for me. I lead with humility, and compassion while **moving** away from authoritarianism. I stay open for correction, and input.

I am in control, and I like it. I am **moving** from glory to glory as I open my anointed mouth to declare how I want my life to be. I speak into existence the quality of the life I want to live.

242:
Staying
August 29

Bible Verses
"What a gift life is to those who stay the course! You've heard, of course, of Job's staying power, and you know how God brought it all together for him at the end. That's because God cares, cares right down to the last detail." James 5:11 (MSG)

"Meanwhile, the saints stand passionately patient, keeping God's commands, staying faithful to Jesus." Revelation 14:12 (MSG)

Word of the Day
Staying – To wait, stall or postpone while dwelling in the same position. To stick in one spot.

Quotes
"In every furnace, there is One like the Son of Man. In every flood of high waters He stands beside us – staying the heart with promises, instilling words of faith and hope, recalling the blessed past, pointing to the radiant future, hushing fear, as once He stilled the dismay of His disciples on the lake." Rev. F. B. Meyer

"God wants to give us staying qualities. He wants to put into us something that will make us stand when other people fall." Rev. James Pennington

Pam's Perspective
Staying optimistic only happens with consistent effort. Staying healthy doesn't happen by hoping, and praying; it happens by staying active, and eating healthy. Staying grateful is the best way to live a happy and contented life.

Questions
Am I staying on the path toward my goals? Am I staying faithful to my dreams? Am I staying the course? What will I be staying dedicated to?

Declarations

Staying calm is natural for me. I know the right thing to do, and I do it. I release all my anxiety and turn it over to a caring God. **Staying** close to God keeps me at peace, and gives me the wisdom to meet the day. I gain peace of mind by meditating on His word.

Staying on the mountaintop gives me a great view of where I have been, and where I am going. I am **staying** the course to achieve my dreams and goals. I make long-term plans to improve my life while **staying** curious. I have rational thinking that always serves me well. **Staying** generous, and thankful is my accustomed way to live.

Staying healthy is very important in my life, so I watch what I eat. I am **staying** alert and in top condition. **Staying** determined to feel great; I exercise daily. I am **staying** active and having fun.

I like to ask questions and think for myself. **Staying** open-minded is a good thing for building positive relationships. I find it fascinating to hear different opinions. I appreciate people's devotion to their beliefs, regardless if it is different from mine. I like **staying** tolerant.

I am **staying** free from shame, and condemnation because I have accepted Christ's fantastic forgiveness and His reassuring love. I cannot earn favor with God. It has already been given to me and is automatic. My goal is to become as kind and forgiving as Christ.

Staying present, and enjoying each moment, helps me to be happy. I am **staying** joyful today by choice. I keep **staying** cheerful, and a joy to be around. My burning desire to help people realize how great life is, gives me **staying** power to keep encouraging everyone. I like giving long hugs, **staying** close to the ones I love. I am grateful I am **staying** physically fit. I am lovely, loved, and highly regarded.

243:
Selfish
August 30

Bible Verses

"Don't act out of selfish ambition or be conceited. Instead, humbly think of others as being better than yourselves." Philippians 2:3 (GW)

"People whose lives are based on selfishness think about selfish things, but people whose lives are based on the Spirit think about things that are related to the Spirit." Romans 8:5 (CEB)

Word of the Day

Selfish – A narcissistic, greedy and self-seeking individual.

Quotes

"Prayer cannot be selfish – ceases to be prayer when it is prompted by selfishness; for it is the inbreathing of the Holy Ghost. It is the desire for things according to the will of God." John Hill Aughey

"Mediocrity is the height of selfishness, and excuses are simply another way of being dishonest." Brian Klemmer

"What a cage is to the wild beast, law is to the selfish man." Herbert Spencer

"Since we are selfish by nature, we must cultivate generosity, kindness, and philanthropy." Pam Malow-Isham

Questions

How do I feel when someone acts selfishly in front of me? Have I ever acted the same way? What does selfish look like to me? Do I consider myself selfish? Why can I be selfish, and kind at the same time?

Declarations

Selfishness is neither good nor bad. It just depends on how I look at it. There is someone who needs my care, including me. I am my number one priority, and I am **selfish** about making sure I am well cared for. When I am full of love, I easily love the people around me. Although making daily positive declarations may seem **selfish**, it is the most productive way to start my day and stay in a great mood.

I pledge to be **selfish** in looking after myself first. I guard my energy deliberately. I am a strong, secure person who is not afraid of being **selfish**. I am **selfish** enough to eat healthy, no matter who is around. I can be **selfish**, while still giving freely of my time, energy, and money. I am never **selfish** with the compliments, or atta-boys.

When I wake up, I have a childlike expectancy of all the good things that will come my way. I am **selfish** with my time that I set aside for me. I enjoy my workouts and stay in great physical shape. Walking, baseball, football, tennis, biking, yoga, ballroom dancing, downhill skiing, and hitting the gym, are sure ways to bring a smile. I am **selfish** enough to do the activities I love and leave the rest alone.

I become a world changer when I give up being **selfish** and focus on others. I become charitable with ease. When I aim my attention at being a blessing, rather than being blessed, I feel more satisfied than if I were **selfish**, thinking only of myself. I like being helpful.

When I am responsible for getting my own needs met, be they physical, mental, social, or spiritual, I can then take care of others. I realize I need God. The solution to every problem I have is on its way because I trust God. He was not **selfish** with His only son but gave him freely to me. I cannot be **selfish** in keeping His love all to myself. I choose to share His abundant love, and joy with the world.

244:
Selfless
August 31

Bible Verses
"Christ arrives right on time to make this happen. He didn't, and doesn't, wait for us to get ready. He presented himself for this sacrificial death when we were far too weak and rebellious to do anything to get ourselves ready. And even if we hadn't been so weak, we wouldn't have known what to do anyway. We can understand someone dying for a person worth dying for, and we can understand how someone good and noble could inspire us to selfless sacrifice. But God put his love on the line for us by offering his Son in sacrificial death while we were of no use whatever to him." Romans 5:6-8 (MSG)

Word of the Day
Selfless – Being charitable, generous and loving. Living open-handed and looking out for others.

Quotes
"The belief that unhappiness is selfless and happiness is selfish is misguided. It's more selfless to act happy. It takes energy, generosity, and discipline to be unfailingly lighthearted, yet everyone takes the happy person for granted. No one is careful of his feelings or tries to keep his spirits high. He seems self-sufficient; he becomes a cushion for others. And because happiness seems unforced, that person usually gets no credit." Gretchen Rubin

"Jesus was selfless for me; I can be selfless for him. As I humble myself, and serve my fellow man, and consider their interests, I reveal compassion and the love of Christ. By helping my neighbors, it invests me in my community, and gives me a sense of belonging, and togetherness." Pam Malow-Isham

Questions
What selfless act will I perform today? What selfless person is my role model? How has being selfless enhanced my life?

Declarations

I am God's ambassador of love, bliss, and hospitality. My **selfless** ways promote happiness, and encouragement. I know no good turn goes unnoticed, and I do a lot of them. I practice being kind, and **selfless**, by opening doors, giving up my seat, giving small gifts, or saying a compliment. My **selfless** devotion to doing the right thing, and showing mercy, has timeless rewards, and great feelings.

The **selfless** act of drinking lots of pure water keeps me well hydrated and feeling great. I like being **selfless** as I take the time to cook healthy meals for my family. It preserves our health and pays us with renewed vigor, and stamina. We grow closer every day as we enjoy meals together, and serve each other **selflessly**.

When I look beyond my own problems and act **selflessly**, I broaden my horizons and expand my world. I find more ways to be **selfless** as I bring happiness to others. People seek out my counsel and emulate my **selfless** life. My choice of picking a **selfless** mentor is something I take seriously. I am in charge of the results I produce.

I have the capacity to engage in **selfless** acts of service whenever I choose. I also know I cannot be all things to all people, so I choose my service wisely. I am courageous as I share God's **selfless** love. I remember the times when God came through for me. I am **selfless** as I share the love of Christ with everyone, just for the joy of giving, even to the mean, ungrateful people with frowns on their faces.

Because I **selflessly** give of myself, people are drawn to me. I enjoy telling stories of friends who act **selflessly**. The **selfless** act of acknowledging the brilliance of others has endeared a lot of people to me. It is so easy to do, and I do it well. I see all my relationships as sacred. I do mundane things in spectacular, **selfless** ways.

245:
More
September 1

Bible Verses
"You put more joy in my heart than when their grain and new wine increase." Psalm 4:7 (GW)

"But I will always have hope. I will praise you more and more." Psalm 71:14 (GW)

Word of the Day
More – An expanded or enhanced amount. Supplementary. Extra.

Quotes
"The more you give, the more you will be able to give; the more you receive, the more you will be willing to receive; and the more you pray, the more you can pray." Kate Braestrup

"Never promise more than you can perform." Publilius Syrus

"In every walk with nature one receives far more than he seeks." John Muir

"When you think from a place of more, you get more." Pam Malow-Isham

Pam's Perspective
More is always an option, no matter what. You can get more strife, and heartache, or you can get more love, peace, and abundance. Because I expect more, I get it.

Questions
Is there more work I could do to reach my dreams? What more do I want? Why? Is there more I could do to increase my happiness? How much more can I give? Can I do more to improve my health?

Declarations

I have **more** patience today than I had yesterday. I practice **more** ways to show kindness. The **more** I practice, the better I get. I am **more** than enough. The **more** I learn about the nature of love, the **more** I want to know. I am **more** authentic today in all I do and say.

There is always **more** than enough for me. I am supply conscious. I feel **more** hopeful, knowing God is in control. There is **more** waiting to be provided to me from the one with infinite resources. The **more** I give, the **more** I receive. I donate **more** than I did last year.

I am **more** than enough. There is **more** balance, and peace in my life, now that I trust God. I am loved **more** than ever before. God has **more** grace than I can use up. The **more** I profess and think about all the good I want to see show up in my life, the **more** it does.

I have **more** energy than ever before. I am **more** health conscious today because I am aware of the benefits of feeling good. And yes, I do feel good! I have **more** power, and strength with each new day. **More** health, vitality, and vigor are mine now as I practice eating healthy, and moving **more**. I have **more** fun every day. I appreciate **more** quality, over **more** quantity. I am a **more** magnet.

I create **more** value, with less effort. I am confident in what I am creating. **More** opportunities show up for me, so I always have a lot of choices. I have **more** testimonials about my great service that continue to come in. I have **more** business than my competitors.

I laugh **more** today than yesterday. I think **more** about what I can give, rather than what I can get. I implement **more** doing, and less talking. I achieve **more** with fewer hours than most. I am the kind of person that people move over for. **More** is always an option.

246:
Less
September 2

Bible Verses
"Riches taken by false ways become less and less, but riches grow for the one who gathers by hard work." Proverbs 13:11 (NLV)

"Don't let anyone think less of you because you are young. Be an example to all believers in what you say, in the way you live, in your love, your faith, and your purity." 1 Timothy 4:12 (NLT)

Word of the Day
Less – A declining amount. Lacking or reduced. Incomplete.

Quotes
"The less time I spend berating and judging myself for not measuring up to my high expectations and instead spend the time telling myself positive affirmations, the better my life and relationships go, and the better I feel." Pam Malow-Isham

"The less people know, the more they yell." Seth Godin

"The more a man judges, the less one loves." Honore de Balzac

"There is nothing we can do to make God love us more, there is nothing we can do to make God love us less." Philip Yancey

"Have more than thou showest, speak less than thou knowest, lend less than thou owest." Shakespeare

Questions
Is there less I need to do today? Do I have a less mentality? Do I ever view myself as less than? Do I need to eat less of any certain kind of food? Why is having less a good thing? How can I worry less?

Declarations

I spend **less** time texting, and more time being present with the person I am with. I remind myself that I was created for **less** drama and more greatness. I love getting massages, so I carry **less** stress.

I do **less** complaining and more complimenting. The **less** I hang on to hurts, the lighter I become. The **less** negative things I talk about, the better I feel. The **less** violence I put before my eyes, the kinder I become. The **less** news I read, the calmer I stay. Relaxing feels great!

I feel better when I eat **less** processed food. I eat **less** sugar than I used to. I treat myself well. The **less** weight I carry, the lighter I feel. The **less** I sit, the stronger I become. The **less** caffeine I have, the easier I fall asleep. I am **less** worried about impressing people, and more determined to serve God. I take pleasure in being grateful.

I spend **less** time in the city, and more time in nature. I take in all the lovely sights of the outdoors, from the shape of a rock, to the grandeur of the night sky; appreciating everything in my field of vision. God has made a beautiful world for me to enjoy. I talk **less** and listen more. I am familiar with what the Holy Spirit says.

I study, and reflect, as I forget **less**, and remember more. I have an exceptional brain. I get things done more effectively, in **less** time, because I am resourceful. I fear **less** and become speedy in reaching my goals. I give up my **less** than enough thinking because I live on easy street. I spend **less** than I make. I am content with **less**.

The **less** I concentrate on myself, the more friends I have. I pray to be a vessel of excellence. The **less** I worry, the freer I become. **Less** is more. The **less** I criticize, the nicer I am. God has **less** rules than I think. He wants me to hate **less**, and love more freely, and often.

247:
Design
September 3

Bible Verses

"An idea well-expressed is like a design of gold, set in silver." Proverbs 25:11 (GNT)

"We have also received an inheritance in Christ. We were destined by the plan of God, who accomplishes everything according to his design." Ephesians 1:11 (CEB)

Word of the Day

Design – To draw something. To think something up. Invent.

Quotes

"Two persons who have chosen each other out of all the species with a design to be each-other's mutual comfort and entertainment have, in that action, bound themselves to be good-humored, affable, discreet, forgiving, patient, and joyful; with respect to each other's frailties and perfections, to the end of their lives." Joseph Addison

"When any great design thou dost intend, think on the means, the manner, and the end." Sir John Denham

Pam's Perspective

Let your imagination run wild. I did not realize I could design a beautiful flower garden until I did it. It is amazing what you can design if you just give it a try. I dream of things I want to achieve, and places I want to go. I succeed by design.

Questions

How can I design a purpose that gets me excited about getting up in the morning? Will I design a productive, happy life? Will I design my future?

Declarations

I determine what truly drives me, and sets me on fire. I then **design** my life accordingly. I am someone rare and specially made that way by God's **design**. I am in perfect rapport with the Creator of life.

I **design** alone time with the Holy Spirit to be renewed. I **design** my prayer time and make it a priority in my day. I **design** a sacred place to be alone with the Almighty. I feel loved with every ounce of my being. I **design** a serene garden as I look at the beauty of nature.

I **design** time for breaks in my day to get up, move, and stretch. I **design** my training program at home to do some form of cardio, flexibility and strengthening exercises. I **design** my workouts to mix up my muscle groups, so I stay adaptable. I **design** a way for me to track my progress in a notebook, journal, or an app. I **design** my grocery list around my healthy eating habits. It is my birthright to be healthy, fit, and totally fulfilled. God **designed** me for greatness.

I **design** my day the way I want it to go the night before. By writing down, in order of importance, I get everything done. I **design** big dreams. I love being artistic, **designing** new things. I infuse my room with aromatherapy to help in the **design** process.

I am the **designer** of my destiny. The way I creatively finance my endeavors is inspiring. I attract money like a magnet. I **design** a great savings plan for my money. I attract the most generous people in my life. We **design** fun ways to interact, and share ideas.

I choose to enjoy this beautiful day, even if it doesn't work out the way I **designed** it to. I **design** programs to inspire people to pull themselves out of mediocrity, and into abundance. I am a great mentor, by **design**. I **design** a dazzling future that gets me excited.

248:
Destiny
September 4

Bible Verses
"You, Lord, are my portion, my cup; you control my destiny." Psalm 16:5 (CEB)

"You guide me with your counsel, leading me to a glorious destiny." Psalm 73:24 (NLT)

Word of the Day
Destiny – The way your future will turn out. God's will for your life.

Quotes
"Women is equally interested and responsible with man in the final settlement of this problem of self-government; therefore let none stand idle spectators now. When every hour is big with destiny and each delay but complicates our difficulties, it is high time for the daughters of the Revolution in solemn council to unseal the last will and testament of the fathers, lay hold of their birthright of freedom and keep it a sacred trust for all coming generations." Susan B. Anthony

"A person often meets his destiny on the road he took to avoid it." Jean de La Fontaine

"Destiny is no matter of chance. It is a matter of choice. It is not a thing to be waited for; it is a thing to be achieved." William Jennings Bryan

Pam's Perspective
I used to think my destiny was fixed and predetermined. Glad I got that wrong.

Questions
Do I have my destiny planned out? Have I involved others in helping me? Have I prayed about my destiny? What do I want my destiny to look like?

Declarations

I am a seeker of wisdom, and unlimited resources are coming my way. I am excited about the uniquely rewarding **destiny** that I am creating. I am grateful for the successes I am generating. I choose a **destiny** where things happen for the highest good of all involved.

I am happy to be engaged with every part of my **destiny**. I am passionate about my **destiny** and willing to take risks. I am elated by all the support I receive from family, friends, and tribe, in order to see my **destiny** come to realization. I recognize I can't do it alone, so I welcome help. My **destiny** is secure. God is my source.

Declaring my positive affirmations every morning reinforces my fantastic attitude, and in turn, influences my **destiny**. I always feel physically great, and ready to go. I love being relentless. I choose to listen to God's voice within, who steers me towards my perfect **destiny**. Great is the Holy Spirit's affection for me.

I keep working to see my **destiny** come true. I put myself out there, working on my **destiny**. God gives me the strength to take a leap of faith to fulfill my **destiny**. I am constantly improving. My leadership skill helps my company design the best products, and services.

I am set apart for a special purpose and a remarkable **destiny**. I know how to possess my own vessel. I am a responsible grownup. The **destiny** I am devoted to is bigger than the status quo. I have an accountability partner that keeps me in line with my **destiny**.

I like creating my **destiny** each day, and choosing how I want it to go. I never settle for mediocrity when the sky's the limit. I have tremendous concentration, so I focus on what is relevant, and worth my time. I am learning how to control myself, and reach my **destiny**.

249:
Power
September 5

Bible Verses

"Some trust in their war chariots and others in their horses, but we trust in the power of the Lord our God." Psalm 20:7 (GNT)

"Behold, I have given you authority to tread on serpents and scorpions, and over all the power of the enemy, and nothing will injure you." Luke 10:19 (NASB)

Word of the Day

Power – Authority, and dominion to perform something. Strength.

Quotes

"Never stand begging for that which you have the power to earn." Miguel de Cervantes

"One spark of fire can do more to prove the power of powder than a whole library written on the subject." Billy Sunday

"Nothing can add more power to your life than concentrating all of your energies on a limited set of targets." Nido Qubein

Pam's Perspective

Having the power not to worry about what others think is liberating. The power I feel when I do not react when someone is rude or tries to start a fight is immense. As I practice using restraint over my words, and actions, I increase my power.

Questions

Do I use my positional power to unite people together, or tear them apart? How do I attain power? Will I use my power to create a wonderful life? Have I asked for supernatural power? Why do I use my power for good?

Declarations

I have the **power** to overcome any adversity that comes my way. I am more than a conqueror! I take the imaginary limits off God and see His **power** work through me. I am clothed with **power** and grace! I daily infuse my mind with positive thoughts and wisdom.

I know my words have the **power** to encourage, and uplift people, or tear them down. So I choose the high road before I speak, and use my **power** to praise people. I **powerfully** listen when others speak. I always have the **power** to say "NO" if that is what I want and need to say. I am very respectful of my time, and how I spend it.

I am a **powerful** person who loves to move my **powerful** body. I step into my **superpower** with my action. I show up as a person of **power**, and depth. I have the **power** to finish every task I start. I use my **power** to visualize the positive outcome I desire deliberately.

I now use God's **power** to lift my thinking away from problems, and into the miraculous. I always have the **power** to be kind, even if I don't feel like it. I have the influential **power** for all to see that nothing is going to stop me from reaching my dream. I am a passionate person who owns my **power** and reaches my goals.

I act like a person of **power**, and influence. Because I sit in a position of **power**, I check my ego at the door and serve with decency. I have a **powerful** impact on everyone around me. I am full of **power**, and wisdom. I see God's goodness in amazingly **powerful** ways.

I know with God's **power**, anything is possible. I see miracles happening in my life on a daily basis. My **power** source comes from the Lord. I am a **powerhouse** of possibilities. I align my **power** thoughts with God to become a co-creator of my wonderful life.

250:
Powerless
September 6

Bible Verses

"Those who exploit the powerless anger their maker, while those who are kind to the poor honor God." Proverbs 14:31 (CEB)

"He invigorates the exhausted, he gives strength to the powerless." Isaiah 40:29 (CJB)

Word of the Day

Powerless – Ineffective to perform. Defenseless. Vulnerable. Frail.

Quotes

"The "words" of God and the "Word" of God stand together; to separate them is to render both powerless." Oswald Chambers

"Time, whose tooth gnaws away everything else, is powerless against truth." Thomas Huxley

"Talents to strike the eye of posterity should be concentrated. Rays, powerless while they are scattered, burn in a point." Robert Eldridge Aris Wilmott

Pam's Perspective

Feeling powerless is a learned response to adversity. I suffered from it for many years. Gaining the knowledge that I could actually stand up for myself, and make my own way, was exhilarating. I chose to learn how to help myself, and build up my confidence. Now I know nothing can make me powerless, except my thoughts.

Questions

What does powerless look like to me? Do I ever render myself powerless with my thoughts? Why do I find admitting I am powerless invigorating?

Declarations

When I admit that I am **powerless**, and need God's help, I am able to release all my fears, so they no longer stop me. The more I let go, the more potential I have. I quit pretending I am **powerless.** I stand in Christ's authority. I take command of my ability and lead the way God wants me to. I no longer cower, but stand tall in God's might.

I love being in charge of what I put in my body. Fruits and vegetables are my first choice. Because I am diligent about my workouts, I become strong. I have a mighty metabolism that keeps me from feeling **powerless**. Healthy cells naturally regenerate in my body. I have a positive future, and a healthy lifestyle, so I am no longer **powerless** over any sugar cravings, or negative habits.

Sickness is ancient history because God is my healer. I am no longer **powerless** over disease. I accept my healing now. Pain dissolves as I allow the Holy Spirit to replace my **powerlessness** with soundness.

I am creative in my work. I make a commitment to myself to be financially responsible, so I never have to feel **powerless** to debt, or having someone else support me. I earn my own living. I make a decision to save for the future, and not spend more than I make.

I no longer feel **powerless** in my life, but in control. For the next 24 hours, I will notice all my choices. I am ready, and willing to create a way of being that is courageous, active, and dynamic. I like being mature, and resourceful, rather than being a victim, and **powerless**.

I lift myself up from feeling **powerless** to being fierce, by learning something new each day. I am equipped for every good work. I create even greater competence in everything I do, so I don't feel **powerless**. I am addicted to the positive feelings of being optimistic.

251:
Labor
September 7

Bible Verses
"You will enjoy the fruit of your labor. How joyful and prosperous you will be!" Psalm 128:2 (NLT)

"Now he who plants and he who waters are one, and each one will receive his own reward according to his own labor." 1 Corinthians 3:8 (NKJV)

Word of the Day
Labor – Being industrious. Employment for wages. Struggle. Chores.

Quotes
"Poorly paid labor is inefficient labor, the world over." Henry George

"Without labor, nothing prospers." Proverb

"Labor, all labor, is noble and holy." Mrs. Frances Sargent Osgood

"Labor is the law of happiness." Abel Stevens

Pam's Perspective
Ninth through twelfth grade I worked as a custodian at my high school. Forty hours a week during the summer, and fifteen hours a week during the school year. Plus I babysat on the weekends. Hard labor made me appreciate the clothes, shoes, and supplies I bought for school. I bought my first car with my own money at sixteen. It was a Vega, and it burned more oil than gas, but it was all mine.

Questions
What do I think about labor? What do I labor at? How well do I perform my labor? How could I improve my labor? Why do I enjoy my labor?

Declarations

I have fun as I **labor** doing what I love. I have great opportunities ahead of me. I take classes to enhance my skills, and up my game. I am highly paid for the **labor** I perform. Because I **labor** to give birth to new ideas, I improve my life and the lives of others.

I enjoy **laboring** in my garden because I receive such healthy, and delicious rewards. Every day my **labor** gets easier and easier. It is therapeutic to pull weeds, talk to my plants, and play in the dirt.

I get a kick out of **laboring** to help my friends see the sunny side of life. Even though at times I have to **labor** to love the difficult people in my life, I do it willingly. I have a lot of smiles and love to share. I profit in life by my **labors** of helping the helpless and being kind.

I sing, as I **labor** serving my spouse, showing respect, and love. My family thinks I am great. I am conservative with my criticism and generous with my endorsements. I never consider ministering to my family **labor**, but a pleasure. I have much to be thankful for.

I have a cozy home. The **labor** of keeping my home tidy, and well organized, is well worth the effort. I like being clutter free. I use Feng Shui to make the spaces in my home flow with serenity, and abundance. All my appliances are in good working order. The **labor** of painting with the perfect colors to express my uniqueness is fun.

I am grateful and humbled as I **labor** to serve such a benevolent God. Knowing that the Master of the universe watches over me, gives me peace. I am passionate about the **labor** of telling everyone how much Jesus loves them. My heart stays in the right place, and I know to whom I belong. The love of God flows from my heart. I am a blessing to my spouse, family, friends, and community.

252:
Fun
September 8

Bible Verses

"So I recommend having fun, because there is nothing better for people in this world than to eat, drink, and enjoy life. That way they will experience some happiness along with all the hard work God gives them under the sun." Ecclesiastes 8:15 (NLT)

"Never make light of the king, even in your thoughts. And don't make fun of the powerful, even in your own bedroom. For a little bird might deliver your message and tell them what you said." Ecclesiastes 10:20 (NLT)

Word of the Day

Fun – Cheerful diversion. Pleasurable celebration. Good humor. Having an enjoyable time while playing or at work. Merriment.

Quotes

"If fun is good, truth is still better, and love most of all." W. M. Thackeray

"Life can be crazy, but with good friends, it's just fun." Amy Gage

Pam's Perspective

I don't understand serious people who go around frowning all the time. I like to have fun and make my life into a game that I enjoy playing. No matter what I am doing, or who I am with, I choose to make it fun. Life is too short not to have fun, and enjoy yourself. God loves to see his children play, and have fun, and so I do.

Questions

Do I engage in activities that are fun for me? How much time do I set aside each week for fun? Do I hang around fun people? What is my favorite, fun thing to do? Do I do it? Why do I make everything fun?

Declarations

Today is a **fun**-filled day where happy surprises come my way. I have a **fun** spirit that rejoices as I play, and celebrate this juicy life. I help people feel good about themselves. My positive energy is **fun** to be around. I want good things for everyone, including myself. I have **fun** being an encourager. I jump for joy, just for the **fun** of it.

I fuel the **fun** in my work environment to increase productivity. Resources are abundant around me. I surrender to all the good that is coming my way. My path is paved with **fun**, as I enjoy today's gifts. I increase my influence, and leadership by increasing my **fun**.

Traveling around the world is **fun**. I give myself permission to play and have **fun**. I look for joy everywhere I go and make having **fun** a priority. I lighten up, consistently doing something **fun**, that I enjoy.

I choose to be successful today while I am having **fun**, doing what I love. I have **fun** giving things away, and freeing up space for the new. I am objective, beautiful, and **fun**. I appreciate the way I look and my **fun** life. I have **fun** friends, and we love to laugh it up at sporting events, concerts, theme parties, or restaurants.

I was created for laughter, joy, and **fun**. Serving God, and others are **fun** and brings me more joy than focusing on myself. I can have **fun**, and be spiritual too. I am thankful that God has a great sense of humor, and likes to have **fun**. I am influenced by the Holy Spirit.

Everything can be **fun** if I think it is. I am mindful of the **fun** I have had in the past. Learning new games is **fun**, and stretches my mind. I can have **fun** by myself, or with friends. I get excited about having **fun** and making new friends. I explore my artistic side by painting, sketching, or photography. I welcome **fun** to come my way.

253:
Turn
September 9

Bible Verses

"All the ends of the earth shall remember and turn unto Jehovah, and all the families of the nations shall worship before thee." Psalm 22:27 (DARBY)

"Turn my heart to your decrees, and not to selfish gain." Psalm 119:36 (NRSV)

Word of the Day

Turn – To shift something. To twist or bend.

Quotes

"It is our own fault if our greatest trials do not turn out to be our greatest advantages." Dean Stanley

"Never give up. Never ever give up. Why? Because just when you are about to give up is when things are about to turn around in a grand way. Hold on. Great things are waiting for you around the corner." Sonia Ricotti

"They say hard work spotlights the character of people. Some turn up their sleeves, some turn up their nose, and some don't turn up at all." Byron Dorgan

Pam's Perspective

When I had my broken leg and was off work for eight months, my church brought over several boxes of food, which really helped out. Being self-employed, if I didn't work, I didn't eat. Now, in turn, I help with our food pantry at the church. I know how it feels to be off work, and am glad I can assist others in their time of need.

Questions

Where do I turn for guidance? When will it be my turn to win? How can I turn problems into opportunities? Do I turn within for strength?

Declarations

I use every second of my life, and **turn** it into something good. It is my **turn** to have it all. I **turn** up at the right time, to meet the right people. I **turn** on the charm. I **turn** my plans over to God, and they **turn** out great. I **turn** to my heart to heaven and receive wisdom.

I **turn** away from haughtiness and focus on being of service. That is where I find my real joy. I love being in harmony with the flow of God's goodness. I live in a worry-free zone as I **turn** from doubt, to trust. As I **turn** to the Lord, all my needs are met, plus some.

I **turn** my eyes away from raunchy TV shows and **turn** the channel. I **turn** toward what is pleasant. I use good manners, take **turns**, and share. I acknowledge when my partner sees me doing something they don't like. I can admit when I am wrong and **turn** around. I **turn** to love. Communication is key to our great relationship.

I make my day count. I **turn** doubt into undefeatable faith, by speaking aloud my declarations, and God's Word over my life. As I **turn** to the light of God, I am healed. I **turn** my focus to the good. I **turn** my fears over to God, and in return receive strength, courage, direction, and peace. I take **turns** and participate in acts of kindness.

I **turn** from excuses and resolve to get things done. Every favorable circumstance comes my way. I **turn** disappointments into learning experiences. I **turn** offense into another opportunity to forgive and show God's love. I **turn** my ears, mind, and heart, toward heaven.

I **turn** up the volume of my stereo as I dance for joy. I like taking walks outside, **turning** around, and looking at all the beauty that God has created for me to enjoy. Love **turns** towards me. I take nothing for granted. The birds **turn** to sing me a happy song.

254:
Stagnant
September 10

Bible Verses

"A good person's mouth is a clear fountain of wisdom; a foul mouth is a stagnant swamp." Proverbs 10:31 (MSG)

"My people are guilty of two evils: They have abandoned Me, the spring of living waters; And instead, they have settled for dead and stagnant water from cracked, leaky cisterns of their own making." Jeremiah 2:13 (VOICE)

Word of the Day

Stagnant – Something that is dormant. Idle or static. No moving.

Quotes

"Iron rusts from disuse; stagnant water loses its purity, and in cold weather becomes frozen; even so does inaction sap the vigors of the mind." Leonardo da Vinci

"To be filled with Christ is not only to be filled with the Divine life in every part, but it is to be filled every moment. It is to take Him into the successive instants of our conscious existence and to abide in His fullness. For this is not a reservoir, but a spring. It is a life which is continual, active and ever passing on with an outflow as necessary as its inflow, and if we do not perpetually draw the fresh supply from the living fountain, we shall either grow stagnant or empty. It is, therefore, not so much a perpetual fullness as a perpetual filling." A.B. Simpson

"A stagnant life is a waste of opportunities. Why would you want to wallow in stagnation when you can choose to live passionately?" Pam Malow-Isham

Questions

When I see an area of my life that is stagnant, what do I do? Do I ever feel stagnant in my spiritual life? What am I doing to prevent stagnation?

Declarations

I think like a genius. I keep my brain from getting **stagnant**, by learning new things. I break free from **stagnant** thoughts as I stimulate growth in my mind, by meditating on good things. I am always moving in a forward direction toward my goals. I take action when I feel I have been in the **stagnant** mode for too long. I direct love toward myself and nourish my mind with happy thoughts.

Although I try to help **stagnant** people, I do not allow them to drag me down. We each have to choose our own way. I am a straight shooter and tell it like it is. **Stagnation** is a choice we can change. I can love my **stagnant** friends, without spending all my time with them. I seek out new friends that have an improvement mindset.

I realize that at times everyone feels **stagnant**. The key is not to stay there or beat myself up for being there in the first place. I set new goals that excite me to dream, so I leave **stagnation** behind. I spend time contemplating my purpose in life, and how I envision it in the future. I look ahead and visualize the best coming my way.

I make good decisions about what, and when I eat. I get healthier every day. I feel in control when I am aligned, balanced, and strong. I have a toned physique. I exercise so my muscles don't grow **stagnant**, and weak. I am in tune with the workings of my body, and what it needs. I radiate peace in my body, so I stay in perfect health.

I am diligent about the time I spend with God, so my spiritual life does not grow **stagnant**. I have more than just an intellectual knowledge of God. We have an intimate relationship that benefits us both. I stay open to what God is doing in my community. God resurrects new things in me to share with others. I am thankful God is not **stagnant** with blessing me. I continue to stay amazed.

255:
Hope
September 11

Bible Verses

"But those who hope in the Lord will renew their strength. They will soar on wings like eagles; they will run and not grow weary, they will walk and not be faint." Isaiah 40:31 (NIV)

"For I know the plans I have for you," says the Lord. "They are plans for good and not for disaster, to give you a future and a hope." Jeremiah 29:11 (NLT)

Word of the Day

Hope – Having an optimistic expectancy. Faith that your dreams will come true. Anticipate.

Quotes

"All things are possible to him who believes; they are less difficult to him who hopes, more easy to him who loves and still more easy to him who perseveres in the practice of these virtues." Brother Lawrence

"He that lives in hope dances without music." Proverb

"In the presence of God, fear grows dim, and hope glows bright." Rebecca Barlow Jordan

Pam's Perspective

As long as I have hope in my heart, nothing is impossible. I keep hoping for the best, and it always shows up. Funny how that works.

Questions

What is my greatest hope? Have I acted on my hopes? Who do I put my hope in? Do I put all my hopes in God's hands? Why or why not?

Declarations

Hope springs from my heart every morning as I spend time with God. I hold on with **hope** to my vision, and see it come alive. I grow beyond any limiting beliefs as my **hope** grows. I sanction my will to match God's will, which is always expressing love, and **hope**.

I count my blessings and **hope** for more. I spend time with **hopeful** people. God weaves people in, and out of my path, to share **hope**. I practice being compassionate, friendly, happy, and **hopeful**.

Each day I have more **hope** and proficiency in my ability to defeat any problem and overcome any obstacle. I always **hope** for the best, and I get it. I realize God is in charge, I am not, and my **hope** is in Him. As I worship God and enjoy His presence cleansing me, and setting me free from the grime of the world, I am filled with **hope**.

Because of my strong **hope** that my body will heal itself, and stay healthy, it does. I release all disbelief and turn to **hope**. I relax, and breathe in **hope** for a brighter day, as I trust God. I live in a state of extreme bliss. Flexing my **hope** muscles strengthens my faith.

I easily share my story of **hope**. I have much to share. My **hope** to face the day improves my mood. People want to hear what I have to say. I am an encourager who speaks with **hope**. I expect God to give me words full of wisdom, and **hope**. **Hope** can bring freedom to the people around me. God can do things that I can only **hope** for.

I am a seeker of unlimited **hope**. I have **hope**, and I will never give up! I place my **hope** in God. I am always supported by my **hopeful** friends. I am sent by God to do the work of my Father. I allow God's **hope** to multiply within me now. I have ever increasing **hope** in my ability to win. I matter, and make a big difference in the world.

256:
Hopeless
September 12

Bible Verses
"All of them are giving out of their spare change. But she from her hopeless poverty has given everything she had, even what she needed to live on."
Mark 12:44 (CEB)

"God promised Abraham a lot of descendants. And when it all seemed hopeless, Abraham still had faith in God and became the ancestor of many nations." Romans 4:18 (CEV)

Word of the Day
Hopeless – A dejected, despondent attitude. Forlorn. Menacing.

Quotes
"Yet the Pharisee is the failure of the ages through his one great ghastly success of old. The history of the human race shows no one to be more terribly, eternally, and hopelessly in the wrong than he; while even materially considered, history proves no man's mission to have been greater success through defeat than Christ's." Anna Agnes McGinley

"No labor is hopeless." Joseph Roux

Pam's Perspective
Feeling hopeless, not knowing how to stop the repeated sexual assaults as a child was common for me. I felt like it was my fault, I must be really bad because there had to be something wrong with me in order for this to happen. The hopelessness stayed through most of my childhood, but I am proof there is hope after tragedy.

Questions
If I feel hopeless, what do I do? Who do I turn to? How do I recover?

Declarations

On the rare occasion that I do feel **hopeless**, I don't beat myself up.
I know it is a part of life. I feel sorrow, and allow myself time to cry,
mourn, shout, and be human. Then I talk kindly to my hurt self
and tell myself that I will be OK. When I feel **hopeless**, I encourage
myself in the Lord. I confidently trust God to take care of me.

Even if today seems **hopeless**, I know in my heart, that tomorrow,
things will turn around for my good. I know this too shall pass.
I refuse to let the disappointments in life get me down. I am
aware of the good things that are a part of my life. I appreciate my
endurance.

I decided to devote some of my time to restore hope to the
hopeless. I value my time here on earth. When life looks **hopeless**,
and I think that God has forgotten me, I remember He hasn't. I
stay in the present moment and enjoy the real world. I decided to
look for the gift in every circumstance. I have a promising future.

No one is ever a **hopeless** cause. There is goodness in everyone. As
I look with compassion, I can see we all are hurting inside, yelling
"love me." I am a **hopeless** romantic because I believe in love. The
essence of the Divine is always with me, even when I feel **hopeless**.

When I feel anxious, or **hopeless**, I pamper myself and give myself
a break. I take a hot bath, and let **hopelessness** go down the drain.
I treat myself kindly. I get a massage and leave my **hopelessness** on
the table. I look in the mirror and tell myself how beautiful I am.

I am open to the **hopelessly** mysterious, uncertain, hereafter. Even
though I don't know what lies ahead of me, I will continue to do
my best. I find a way to win, no matter what. I love discovering new
resources in me. I walk under the window of heaven's blessings.

257:
Dominate
September 13

Bible Verses
"All things are lawful for me, but not all things are helpful. All things are lawful for me, but I will not be dominated by anything." 1 Corinthians 6:12 (ESV)

"At one time you yourselves used to live according to such desires, when your life was dominated by them. But now you must get rid of all these things: anger, passion, and hateful feelings. No insults or obscene talk must ever come from your lips." Colossians 3:7-8 (GNT)

Word of the Day
Dominate – To prevail over, influence or dictate. Hover over.

Quotes
"The mind comes, finally, to take on the nature of the influences which dominate it. Understand this truth, and you will know why it is essential for you to encourage the positive emotions as dominating forces of your mind, and discourage – and eliminate negative emotions. A mind dominated by positive emotions, becomes a favorable abode for the state of mind know as faith." Napoleon Hill

"Dominate your thoughts, and you will dominate your life." Pam Malow-Isham

Pam's Perspective
Living with people who would dominate, and bully me in a variety of ways, toughened me. I learned to stand up for the underdog, especially if it was me.

Questions
Do I dominate anyone? Do I allow anyone to dominate me? How can I dominate in my field? Am I selective about what dominates my mind?

Declarations

I stand tall with confidence and become the person who **dominates** my life in all areas. I have unlimited ability to achieve anything I set my mind to. I choose to **dominate** my willpower and self-control. I love feeling strong. By deciding to work out at least 10 minutes at a time, I end up getting my whole routine done by the end of the day.

I **dominate** the marketplace. People are eager to do business with me. My bank account is overflowing. I **dominate** my business, and do the best I can, with what I have. I never take "no" for an answer. I follow up and follow through. I have a surplus of referrals. As I train my brain to learn a new task, my genius is **dominate**. I look people in the eye and convey my determination to succeed.

People feel a sense of calm as they walk into my home because I let peace **dominate** my dwelling. I aggressively **dominate** my thoughts with positive affirmations. It feels good to be nice to myself. I focus on good things. I have my dream car and enjoy keeping it clean.

I give others the green light to **dominate** the conversation, so I can learn from them, and make them feel special. I show mercy to people who try to hide their insecurities, by being **dominate** and trying to bully people. We all need love. I easily overlook flaws. I can be **dominate** while being gentle, and showing compassion. I like to emulate my heroes. I pick the precise thoughts to **dominate** my mind to produce perfect results. I am generous to a lot of people.

I cheerfully **dominate** the remote control of my mind to watch happy, healthy, programs. I sing for no reason and smile on purpose. I redefine who I want my identity to be. I keep training like a winner. I see myself **dominating** the steps I need to achieve my goals. I allow God to **dominate** my life with His presence of peace.

258:
Submission
September 14

Bible Verses
"Remember that [by submission] you magnify God's work, of which men have sung." Job 26:24 (AMP)

"Through the proven character of this service they will glorify God because of the submission of your confession to the gospel of Christ and the generosity of your participation toward them and toward everyone." 2 Corinthians 9:13 (LEB)

Word of the Day
Submission – To surrender. To give in or yield. Humility. Obedience.

Quotes
"There is an immeasurable distance between submission to the cross and acceptance of it." Charlotte Elizabeth Tonna

"Leadership is an act of submission to God. To be a leader means listening to all kinds of people and situations. Out of that listening, we are hoping to discern the mind of God as best we can. This is the price of leadership – it's an act of sacrifice. So leadership is part and parcel of the work of submission to God." Richard Foster

Pam's Perspective
Growing up I thought, if I lived a life in submission to God, my life would be boring, dogmatic, fanatical, and full of thou shall not's. Nothing could be further from the truth. Now I have more fun, am free to live without condemnation, feel loved all the time, sing for no reason, and peace permeates my soul.

Questions
What does submission look like to me? Is my submission to the Lord complete? Are there areas of my life that I need to give to Him?

Declarations

God is always looking out for me. I yield with appreciation, and **submission** to the Highest One, who brings me great satisfaction. I follow my heart as I put my faith, and **submission** in Christ.

I have an intellect that is accessible to everything. I sit each morning quietly in **submission**, making my request known to God. I turn everything over to the Sovereign One and then go about my day worry free, knowing the answer, or help is on the way.

I never put myself in harm's way, or compromise my integrity. I can be **submissive**, without giving my power away. I **submit** to create even greater competence in everything I do. My **submission** to education makes me wise. I live in an atmosphere of creativity, abundance, and serenity. I focus on the bountiful rewards to come.

Structure is a good thing. I lead with quality, evoking trust, and **submission**. I remove all limitations I had placed on my mind which were never there at all. I release all imagined barriers. I believe in the person I am capable of becoming. I give up having to know it all. I can be in charge while being in **submission** to a higher authority.

What God is, I am. Just as Christ lived in **submission** to the Father, so do I. There is joy in my heart, and hope for my future. I live in **submission** to a higher cause of loving God and loving people. I turn my attention to the peace within me as I see the chaos that is happening in the world. I thankfully **submit** to the Prince of Peace.

I live as simply as possible. Being spiritually minded, and living in **submission** to God gives me the confidence to know that He hears, and answers my prayers. I am grateful God is still in control and is working everything out for my benefit. I feel loved and cared for.

259:
Indulge
September 15

Bible Verses
"Death and life are in the power of the tongue, and they who indulge in it shall eat the fruit of it [for death or life]." Proverbs 18:21 (AMP)

"But you must not indulge in this charade. Instead, among you, the greatest must become like the youngest and the leader must become a true servant." Luke 22:26 (VOICE)

Word of the Day
Indulge – To succumb to the wants of self-pleasure. Pamper or spoil.

Quotes
"Let us with caution indulge the supposition that morality can be maintained without religion... Reason and experience both forbid us to expect that national morality can prevail in exclusion of religious principle." George Washington

"An over-indulgence of anything, even something as pure as water, can intoxicate." Criss Jami

Pam's Perspective
When I indulge in sugar, I am left wanting, never satisfied. When I indulge in worshiping God, for even 5 minutes, I am filled up, and satisfied for the whole day. I am allowed to indulge in anything I want, but not everything is beneficial to me. God loves me regardless of what I indulge in. When I am led by the Spirit, instead of the flesh, I indulge in things that edify my body, instead of tear it down.

Questions
What is the best way to indulge my dreams? How can I indulge in rich, healthy living? What truth will I indulge in? What fun can I indulge in?

Declarations

I **indulge** in the frivolous pleasures of watching a sunset or gazing at stars. I give up being self-conscious and **indulge** in liking myself the way I am. I practice saying constructive declarations to reinforce my positive beliefs. I **indulge** in visualizing my dreams coming true.

Taking time out for me is a healthy requirement that I **indulge** in. I frequently **indulge** in the luxury of a hot relaxing bath, with candles, Epson salt, essential oils, and soft music. I say yes to relaxation! A place of freedom resides in me that I can always retreat to, as I **indulge** in quiet time. I come back stronger, and more capable of being my best as I recharge. I am good to myself on purpose.

I **indulge** in helping out my community. Volunteering is fun, and a great way to **indulge** my philanthropic side. I meet the nicest people who share similar values. The more I help, the better I feel. I always have enough time for myself, family, work, church, and charities.

I gladly receive coaching from my mentor. I work for the best in my field. I **indulge** in taking short breaks during the day, so I can come back, be laser-focused, and get twice as much done.

God takes delight that I **indulge** in telling Him my every concern, and question. When I stop trying to figure everything out and allow God to be in charge, things go smoothly. There is always a godly solution waiting to be revealed to me. Great is God's love for me.

I permit myself to **indulge** in a little chocolate now and then, guilt-free. I **indulge** in play when I have been working too hard. I choose to keep my spirits high, by **indulging** in joyous thoughts. The Holy Spirit laughs with me. It is good to **indulge** in laughter with my friends. I find humor in the smallest things. Oh yes, life is very good.

260:
Abstain
September 16

Bible Verses
"Now food will not improve our relationship with God — we will be neither poorer if we abstain nor richer if we eat." 1 Corinthians 8:8 (CJB)

"Dear friends, I urge you as strangers and temporary residents to abstain from fleshly desires that war against you." 1 Peter 2:11 (HCSB)

Word of the Day
Abstain – To pass on something. To deny an impulse or desire.

Quotes
"Blessed is the man who, having nothing to say, abstains from giving wordy evidence of the fact." George Eliot

"When you doubt, abstain." Zoroaster

"Remember that it is not enough to abstain from lying by word of mouth; for the worst lies are often conveyed by a false look, smile or act." Abraham Cahan

"Though a man cannot abstain from being weak, he may from being vicious." Joseph Addison

Pam's Perspective
When I abstain from watching the news, reading the newspaper, and surfing social media, I stay in a tranquil state. It is so easy for me to get sucked into the negativity, with all the drama of the day, so I to turn it off to stay peaceful.

Questions
What do I need to abstain from? What is the cost of not abstaining from sugar? Why is it easy to abstain from negativity?

Declarations

I **abstain** from stockpiling a lot of stuff. Simplicity is my motto. I live a meaningful life full of inspiration, and purpose. I am sensible. I **abstain** from a complicated life. I have one that is easy, and carefree.

I **abstain** from gossip, and negative talk. I choose to speak only good things that always serves my highest good, and enriches the people around me. Or I **abstain** from speaking and say nothing. I **abstain** from being pessimistic because optimism encourages health.

I am consciously aware of what is best for my body, and I **abstain** from what is not. When I choose to fast and **abstain** from certain foods for a set amount of time, I cleanse my body and my mind. I become healthy, as I shed toxins, by drinking lots of pure water.

My unlimited mercy draws people to me like a magnet. I decide to listen and **abstain** from daydreaming. I **abstain** from taking offense or being judgmental. I walk in love. When I **abstain** from the media and focus on relationships, my life is enriched one hundred fold.

I **abstain** from procrastination by putting down on paper exactly how much time I spend doing each task during a twenty-four hour period. Then can see how much I actually get done, and it motivates me to become a top producer in my field. I never **abstain** from getting started on a new project because I love a challenge. I keep myself in a ready state, so I am prepared for every opportunity.

I find it fun, and rewarding when I spend time going within. I listen to my higher self. I **abstain** from feeling guilty about when, or how often I worship God. We have a continual communion. Wherever I go, God is with me, and I am with Him. I get spiritual in my own way and don't worry if it meets anyone else's approval but God's.

261:
Perfection
September 17

Bible Verses
"I have seen a limit to all perfection, yet Your commandment is boundless."
Psalm 119:96 (TLV)

"In this [union and communion with Him] love is brought to completion and attains perfection with us, that we may have confidence for the day of judgment [with assurance and boldness to face Him], because as He is, so are we in this world." 1 John 4:17 (AMP)

Word of the Day
Perfection – Superiority of character. Wholeness. Maturity.

Quotes
"We are part of a vast Universe that is carefully orchestrated with the most Divine Perfection. Once we are tuned into this perfection that is already here now, our lives emulate a divine synchronicity everywhere we are." Jafree Ozwald and Margot Zaher

"That is true perfection of man to find out his imperfections." Augustine of Hippo

"Perfection is not a human trait." Victor Hugo

Pam's Perspective
Trying to reach perfection was a losing game. When I no longer expected perfection from myself, I could relax, risk more, try new things, and enjoy my life.

Questions
What does perfection look like to me? Do I expect perfection from myself? Do I expect perfection from others? Is perfection an illusion?

Declarations

I release the need for **perfection** and deal with what I have been given. I learn from every experience I go through. The better I feel about myself, the less I beat myself up for not being **perfect**.

I give myself a break, realizing I am not God, nor will I ever be God. Although His **perfection** works mightily through me, and I accomplish fantastic feats, I humbly acknowledge my humanness.

I can strive for **perfection** by doing a first-rate job. I am satisfied with what I get done, even though it is far from **perfect**. As long as I do my best, I sleep in peace. I set myself free from **perfection**.

I deserve **perfect** health, so I continue to take care of myself, and listen to what my body needs. I eat whole, organic, fresh food. I will **perfect** my eating, the way God planned for us from the beginning.

I see clearly the **perfection** around me. I have clarity of mind. Right now is a **perfect** time for a massage. I glorify my body by treating it kindly. I respect myself as I honor this **perfect** temple of the Holy Spirit. I am good enough. I decide to be happy right now.

I integrate what I have learned from my coach into my life. I am a slice of **perfection**. Everything is accomplished simply to **perfection** through me as I trust God. Being authentic about committing to, and working towards impeccability, is a positive phenomenon.

I enjoy being human, even though I am not **perfect**. Today is the **perfect** time to express my brilliance and compassion. I am worthy of feeling **perfectly** happy and fulfilled. I release all criticism from the **perfectionist** in me. It is soothing to know that God sees the **perfection** of Jesus in me. I am a miracle worker for God.

262:
Imperfection
September 18

Bible Verses

"You are absolutely beautiful, my darling, with no imperfection in you."
Song of Solomon 4:7 (HCSB)

"Rather, the payment that freed you was the precious blood of Christ, the lamb with no defects or imperfections." 1 Peter 1:19 (GW)

Word of the Day

Imperfection – Something with a blemish or stain. Shortcoming.

Quotes

"Endeavor to be always patient of the faults and imperfections of others for thou has many faults and imperfections of thine own that require forbearance. If thou are not able to make thyself that which thou wishest to be, how canst thou expect to mold another in conformity to thy will?"
Thomas à Kempis

"No human face is exactly the same in its lines on each side, no leaf perfect in its lobes, no branch in its symmetry. All admit irregularity as they imply change; and to banish imperfection is to destroy expression, to check exertion, to paralyze vitality. All things are literally better, lovelier, and more beloved for the imperfections which have been divinely appointed, that the law of human life may be Effort, and the law of human judgment, Mercy." John Ruskin

Pam's Perspective

I become beautiful, and approachable when I accept the imperfections in myself because then I can accept them in others also. I look for the beauty in imperfection.

Questions

Do I accept others imperfections? Do I accept my own imperfections?

Declarations

I don't use my **imperfections** as a human being, as an excuse not to do what is right, or noble. Nor do I use my **imperfections** as the reason for failure, or living below what I am capable of becoming. I realize I have **imperfections**, just like everyone else. I work on improving my **imperfections**, and inadequacies every day.

I embrace my **imperfections**, quirks, and all. I love myself just the way I am. I tap into my **imperfect**, creative side that likes to have fun. I look forward to failing **imperfectly**. I have the grace for making adjustments, and modifications in myself.

I am in the perfect flow to see my dreams fulfilled. I dare to believe that I can achieve success, in spite of my **imperfections**. I am unique, special, and **imperfect**; just ask me, and I will tell you. I reaffirm and confess to myself, and to the world that I was born for success.

I improve my confidence by facing my **imperfections**. When I accept my **imperfections**, I let go of the undue stress that I used to put on myself. I am free to be me. I also encourage others to accept their **imperfections** as I accepted mine. Life is too short for stressing out.

God's purposes are not hindered by anyone's **imperfections**. God's perfect plan is facilitated by this **imperfect** vessel. I serve a kind, and merciful God. I am overwhelmed when I think about how God sees my dark thoughts, and every **imperfection**, and still loves me.

God is for me today. I come boldly into the presence of God, and I find peace and contentment. I embrace my **imperfect** self with love. My beliefs enhance my life. Whether I believe it or not, God loves all **imperfect** people. God's perfect plan for me is to feel loved. I have access to the Divine anytime, no matter how **imperfect** I may be.

263:
Joy
September 19

Bible Verses
"My spirit finds its joy in God, my Savior." Luke 1:47 (GW)

"Oh, what joy for those whose disobedience is forgiven, whose sins are put out of sight." Romans 4:7 (NLT)

Word of the Day
Joy – Bliss, glee, and humor are arising from within and bubbling over. The feeling you have when you are happy.

Quotes
"Once you are resonating with thoughts filled with joy, gratitude, and appreciation for what you do have, then whatever you want to create seems to just fall into your lap!" Jafree Ozwald

"The fullness of joy is to behold God in everything. God is the ground, the substance, the teaching, the teacher, the purpose, and the reward for which every soul labors." Julian of Norwich

"Joy is love exalted; peace is love in repose; long-suffering is love enduring; gentleness is love in society; goodness is love in action; faith is love on the battlefield; meekness is love in school; and temperance is love in training." Unknown

"God's joy can't be destroyed by anything or anyone." Pam Malow-Isham

Questions
Do I count it all joy when trials come? What does joy look like to me? How do I create joy? Where do I find my joy? How do I share my joy?

Declarations

Joy, wisdom, and the peace of God prevail continually in my mind. God's **joy** fills my soul. I am full of integrity, thoughtfulness, and **joy**. God's nature is a continual **joy**. I can generate great **joy**, and happiness, right now, by smiling and thinking **joyfully**. Thoughts of **joy** bring me more success. I practice **joyful** living every day.

I bring **joy** into my life by playing and making life fun. With every breath, I breathe in **joy**. I get off the merry-go-round of the crazy life and stop, so **joy** can show up. I turn down noise, so I can hear **joy**. I allow **joy** to permeate my entire being. When I am still, **joy** arrives. I find **joy** in the little pleasures of life. **Joy** is my natural state.

I create waves of **joy** when people come into my presence. Laughter is a constant buddy that bubbles up inside me. I cannot hide my **joy**, nor do I want to. I love bringing **joy** with me everywhere I go. I choose to share my **joy** with the world. **Joy** is my true experience.

I know I am my own source of **joy**, so I am never bored. I absolutely love myself. I look for **joy** everywhere I go and make having fun a priority. I actively pursue people, and events, that brings me great **joy**. I take responsibility for creating my own **joy** and entertainment.

I allow no one to steal my **joy**. If people want to be miserable, that is their choice. I choose **joy**. I have the power to keep my **joy**, no matter what. I live a satisfying life by being **joyfully** optimistic.

I have much to contribute. I am generous with my things and **joyously** give from a state of abundance. With earnest intent, I am committed to living **joyfully**. I look forward to each new **joy**-filled hour with anticipation. Because my thoughts concentrate on **joy**, I live in **joy**. My life gets more **joyous** the more **joy** I care to share.

264:
Sorrow
September 20

Bible Verses

"The blessing of the Lord makes rich, and he adds no sorrow with it."
Proverbs 10:22 (RSV)

"And God shall wipe away all tears from their eyes; and there shall be no more death, neither sorrow, nor crying, neither shall there be any more pain: for the former things are passed away." Revelation 21:4 (KJV)

Word of the Day

Sorrow – The pain and misery of mourning. Tribulation and distress.

Quotes

"Bion seeing a prince weep and tearing his hair for sorrow, asked if baldness would cure his grief." Jeremy Taylor

"If we could read the secret history of our enemies we should find in each man's life sorrow and suffering enough to disarm all hostility." Henry Wadsworth Longfellow

"The error of one moment may become the sorrow of a whole life." Benjamin Elliott Nicholls

Pam's Perspective

I tried drinking my sorrows away, but the only thing I got was a hangover. Facing my problems, and dealing with them was a much better solution.

Questions

What have I learned from times of sorrow? How can I help others who are sorrowful? Why did I need this lesson in sorrow?

Declarations

I will not allow past or present **sorrow** to keep me from my future joy. I go through what I have to go through and come out on top. **Sorrow** cannot define me, so I make the most of each day. I don't try to control what I am not responsible for. **Sorrow** is what I make of it.

Even though there are times when I create my own **sorrow**, God still loves me. God's presence is with me through every **sorrow** and eases my pain. I give myself permission to grieve, and feel **sorrow**. I am heroic as I face every **sorrow**. This too will pass. I am thankful that **sorrow** does not last long. As I see myself the way God sees me, the **sorrow** passes. God's word enlightens my mind with peace.

I respect all living creatures, especially the little vulnerable ones. I free my pets from the **sorrow** of abuse, and starvation. My way of acting is with love and tenderness. In return, my pet turns my **sorrows** into joy. I have a positive attitude despite the **sorrow** that is around me. I don't allow my feelings to dictate what truth is. I take care of what I can take care of, and leave the rest to God.

As I overlook other's offenses, I rid myself of undue **sorrow**. I comfort friends who are **sorrowful** with my generous support. I am a precious gift to be around. I offer sympathy to those who are **sorrowful.** I am thankful for my compassionate, loyal friends who stick by me in times of **sorrow**. We make a great team.

When I focus on the beauty of life, instead of **sorrow**, I enjoy my life much more. I break out of my comfort zone and face the real **sorrow** in my life. I can heal anything I am willing to face. My healer is God. I walk with the courage of the Lord. I practice the principles of Proverbs, so I get wiser every day as I learn to be more like Christ. Because I change the **sorrowful** way I think, I change my reality.

265:
Good
September 21

Bible Verses
"And God saw the light, that it was good: and God divided the light from the darkness." Genesis 1:4 (KJV)

"Now we know that all things work together for good for those who love God, who are called according to His purpose." Romans 8:28 (TLV)

Word of the Day
Good – Something pleasant. Favorable. Useful. Beneficial. A person of integrity and honor. Kindhearted.

Quotes
"If I wish to be a power in the world for good, we must cling to the good only; see only good; hear only good; know only good; think only good. Then we shall be strong and steadfast and have good judgement to know always just what word to say to each person we meet." Emma Curtis Hopkins

"A good pilot proves himself in a tempest; a good soldier on the battlefield; a good Christian in adversity." St. Cyprian

Pam's Perspective
I had good grandparents who we lived with until I was five. They showed me how to be godly, fruitful, and jovial. They taught me how to take charge, and be reliable. When I think about good things, share good things, and do good deeds, I feel good. The good I do today lays the groundwork for my future blessings.

Questions
Do I recognize good things before bad? Are my thoughts focused on what is good or what irritates me? How much good can I do today?

Declarations

I am an extremely **good** person. I unleash my unlimited potential for **good** now. I enhance the world by the **good** services I perform each day. I look for the **good** in others. There is always something **good** I can find when I take the time to listen to our similarities, instead of our opposing views. I like doing **good** on purpose.

Good things are chasing me down, so I stop, so they can catch up. I set challenging deadlines that drive me to deliver the **goods**. I am **good** enough to make the grade. I believe in my **good** abilities, and skills. I have purposeful **good** self-talk that builds my confidence.

I have a **good-looking** body to go along with my gracious heart. I visualize my **good** health coming to pass. I love the **good** feelings I get from working out. I am committed to **good** health. I eat **good** food and look **good**. I have devoted **good** friends who cheer me on the **good** path. We laugh, have fun, and are **good** for each other.

Abundant **good** is available to me, and I am ready to receive it. The **good** I do in my community has an impact on future generations. I make work my play. I am a **good** leader who communicates with ease. I am always up for a **good** adventure. It is **good** to be alive.

I decide to think on **good** things, so I enjoy my life even more. I repeat **good** thoughts as needed. I have been made well and set apart for **good** works. I am a reflection of God's **goodness**.

I have a **good** time watching the sunset. It is **good** for me to be in nature. I feel relaxed as I stroll along, and relish the beauty around me. I know that when I pray, answers will come at the right time, and in the right way. Nothing can prevent the **good** that God has for me. I serve a **good** God, full of loving-kindness, mercy, and grace.

266:
Bad
September 22

Bible Verses
"So the servants brought in everyone they could find, good and bad alike, and the banquet hall was filled with guests." Matthew 22:10 (NLT)

"Do not let anyone fool you. Bad people can make those who want to live good become bad." 1 Corinthians 15:33 (NLV)

Word of the Day
Bad – Something that is imperfect. Having a foul temperament. Corrupt.

Quotes
"No man is wholly bad, and in all lives some moments come when the vision presents itself of a worthier and happier life which might be lived. What is needed is courage to make the start, for, while life lasts, it is never too late." E. C. Burke

"The bad fortune of the good turns their faces up to heaven; the good fortune of the bad bows their heads down to the earth." Saadi

"It is far better to live alone than to die in bad company." L. W. Lightly

Pam's Perspective
Some things that I thought were bad, like eating seafood, I now enjoy. Some people who I used to think were bad, are now my friends, because I got to know them. When my fixed way of looking at something, or someone was bad, it left me no room for anything, but bad thoughts. Now I look for the good and find it.

Questions
What do I consider is bad? Why? How do I respond to bad situations? Why do I always expect the best outcomes, instead of bad ones?

Declarations

I am happy for the privilege of being able to choose how I want to act, feel, and respond to any **bad** situation. I reach out and share my truth of how **bad** I am feeling. Isolation is never a good response to **bad** feelings, so I call on my friends, and they always help.

We all have a **bad** day sometimes. As I share my **bad** days along with my good, I reveal my humanity. My true friends are always there for me on the **bad** days to give me encouragement, and a shoulder to lean on. It is ok for me to accept my good and **bad** parts.

I am honest about my **bad** traits and do not put on airs. I take the time to work on my **bad** habits. I create new ones that empower me and replace the **bad** ones. I can easily fix my flaws by concentrating on the good I want to be and then acting that way. I disperse my **bad** thoughts by replacing them with what is noble, and good.

Every moment is a gift I can use for good, or **bad**. Just because I made a **bad** decision in my past, does not mean I am a **bad** person. I learn from my **bad** choices and commit to constant improvement. As I look to God, instead of my **bad** circumstance, my mood lifts, and I'm healed. I remember I am God's favorite child, not a **bad** kid.

When I start to feel **bad**, I get up and start moving. I never feel **bad** when I dance. Just going for a walk changes my mood. God is with me through every **bad** situation and brings me peace. Unexpected blessings are on the way. I reap where I have not planted.

God does not look at me as a **bad** person. He loves me just the way I am. I renounce the **bad** thoughts that tell me I am not good enough to approach God. I am a priceless gemstone in His eyes. I will never be too **bad** for God to withhold His love from me. I am eternally His.

Never
September 23

Bible Verses
"Never eat too much, even if you are very hungry." Proverbs 23:2 (ERV)

"Love never gives up on people. It never stops trusting, never loses hope, and never quits." 1 Corinthians 13:7 (ERV)

Word of the Day
Never – Not going to happen by any means or at any time.

Quotes
"No one cares to speak to an unwilling listener. An arrow never lodges in a stone: often it recoils upon the sender of it." St. Jerome

"I have never met a man so ignorant that I couldn't learn something from him." Galileo Galilei

"The man who labours well need never despair of anything at all… By attention and by toil all things are attained." Menander

Pam's Perspective
The things I have judged people for has come back to haunt me. I thought I would never act like so and so, only to find myself acting that way. Some things I have said I would never do, like bungee jumping, I did. Some places I thought I would never go, I have gone. Some things I thought I would never own, I now have. Some people who I said I would never forgive, I forgave.

Question
"What have you given the world it never possessed before you came?" Billy Sunday

Declarations

I am ecstatic that God's love **never** runs away from me, it chases me down. I **never** worry about being alone, because God is ever present. I **never** worry about what people think, because my approval comes from within. I am very gifted. I am grateful for the time I spend with my loved ones. My family **never** says a bad word about me.

I **never** run from a challenge. I always keep the end goal in front of me, so I focus on the rewards, instead of the challenges. I remember to try one more time. I **never** expect anything from anyone, and then when I do receive something, it is a great blessing. I like being self-sufficient. I operate from my creative core and am **never** limited by my past mistakes. I **never** give up on me, my family, or my goals.

I **never** take an elevator when there is only one flight of stairs to climb. I **never** overeat, or binge on junk food. I am conscious of what I eat. I treat myself with the love and respect I deserve. Every day I stretch, get up, and move. I am **never** complacent.

I **never** charge more than I can pay off every month. I **never** want for anything, because I serve a very generous God. I **never** ignore a whisper from the Holy Spirit telling me to pause or wait. I **never** stop learning about my finances, and the different ways for me to invest my resources. My bank account continues to increase.

I **never** do anything against my will. I make wise choices about my time. I **never** listen to negative reports. I am **never** a complainer or faultfinder of others. Because I **never** hold a grudge, and freely forgive, I stay healthy, happy, and at peace. I **never** fixate on the negative aspects of someone. I aim to find the good in everyone. I tune myself to the positive things of what is going right in my mind, body, spirit, and physical surroundings. I **never** quit dreaming.

268:
Always
September 24

Bible Verses
"The Lord will rule forever and always." Exodus 15:18 (CEB)

"This is God, our God, forever and always! He is the one who will lead us even to the very end." Psalm 48:14 (CEB)

Word of the Day
Always – Perpetually with us. Eternally. Habitually. Evermore.

Quotes
"And I can always give thanks because an all-powerful God always has all these things - all things - always under control." Ann Voskamp

"They never taste who always drink. They always talk who never think." Prior

"Conquering or conquered, in plenty or want, happy or unhappy, sorrowful or gay, he always sings; and one would say that the song is his natural expression." Thomas Crofton

"If you always trust God, you will live with a peaceful center that cannot be shaken during troublesome times." Pam Malow-Isham

Pam's Perspective
During reactionary times I remind myself that I am never always right, wrong, good, or anything else, and neither is anyone else. Every person is dualistic.

Questions
What is something that I always do? Do I think I am always right? How can I improve today? Why do I always focus on the good?

Declarations

I **always** give thanks for all that I am experiencing, even when it is not **always** perfect. I **always** think positive and have a great outlook on life. I **always** follow the invites from God. I **always** have faith in a fantastic future. Synchronistic appointments **always** appear.

I **always** think before I speak. I **always** have good news to share, because I serve a great God. I live in perfect harmony with people, animals, and the planet. I **always** work to serve my highest good. I **always** believe in myself. I **always** brighten the world with my light.

I **always** make a difference no matter where I am. I live on purpose, and **always** enrich the lives of the people around me. I **always** look for the best in people. The good I do for others **always** returns to me multiplied. I **always** have a surplus, because I **always** help out. I have a generous heart. There is **always** plenty for all, so I share.

I **always** take definitive action toward my goals. I **always** see myself as healthy, and fit. I **always** enjoy eating raw food. I take an apple as a snack. I **always** look for healthy recipes to cook. I **always** like cooking healthy meals. I **always** love having a toned body.

I am superior to my circumstance. I **always** ask myself, what is the gift that I can get from this adversity. Trials are **always** apart of life and an opportunity for growth. I have a positive team of friends that **always** stand beside me. Things **always** work out great for me.

God is **always** beside me, cheering me on. I **always** seek God's Kingdom first, and everything I need is **always** brought my way. Love **always** wins. I **always** take the time to pray as I seek to know Him better. I immerse my brain with God's truth. I am **always** a wisdom magnet. God's love is **always** more than enough for me.

269:
Humanity
September 25

Bible Verses

"So God did just that. He created humanity in His image, created them male and female." Genesis 1:27 (VOICE)

"How precious is your unfailing love, O God! All humanity finds shelter in the shadow of your wings." Psalm 36:7 (NLT)

Word of the Day

Humanity – Male or female human beings. Citizens of the world.

Quotes

"You must not lose faith in humanity. Humanity is an ocean; if a few drops of the ocean are dirty, the ocean does not become dirty." Mahatma Gandhi

"It is a law of our humanity, that man must know both good and evil. No great principle ever triumphed but through much evil. There never was a principle but what triumphed through much evil; no man ever progressed to greatness and goodness but through great mistakes." Frederick W. Robertson

"Jesus was the living Word of His message to mankind. God spoke through Him and by Him those words which spell Love in the language of humanity, - sacrifice, selflessness; tenderness, sympathy – all the words born of that rich pregnancy of Love which fructified at the coming of an Incarnate God among mankind. This is the God we want." Anna Agnes McGinley

"As messed up as humanity is, there is good to be found." Pam Malow-Isham

Questions

What do I like about my humanity? What can I do to help humanity get along with each other? Why do I find humanity so fascinating?

Declarations

My intensity makes a difference and is a benefit to **humanity**. I ask myself how I can be of service to the people around me, and then I take action. I speak into people's potential to encourage them to grow. I love sharing beneficial content with **humanity** to expand goodwill. I love to serve **humanity** with my creative ideas.

I am thankful that God has not given up on **humanity**. God uses me to reach out to **humanity** to show His extravagant love. I practice listening, understanding, and being supportive. People know I care about them, and I know people care about me. I am forever blessed.

I help **humanity** with my gifts because I make something really great out of my life. I treat everyone I meet with courteous regard, just like I want to be treated. I speak my truth with kindness and respect. My quality thoughts create books to further **humanity**.

My acceptance of my own **humanity**, as 'more than enough,' allows me to be the dynamic individual that I am. I make room for quiet time, and contemplation so I can accept all **humanity**, and not just people like me. I am pleased God loves all **humanity,** not just a few.

God understands **humanity** with all its quirks and chooses to pursue us anyway tenaciously. I choose to participate in restoring hope to **humanity** with my positive attitude. I agree to work for all **humanity** with sincerity, and love. God encourages all **humanity**.

God's image is imprinted on all **humanity**. I recognize that we are all important, and interdependent on each other. Isolation is not an option. I take actions to benefit myself, and **humanity**. It is a win, win game that I play. There is more than enough for all **humanity**. The more I help **humanity** and consider others, the better I feel.

270:
Word
September 26

Bible Verses
"Others, like seed sown on good soil, hear the word, accept it, and produce a crop -some thirty, some sixty, some a hundred times what was sown." Mark 4:20 (NIV)

"In the beginning was the Word and the Word was with God and the Word was God." John 1:1 (CEB)

Word of the Day
Word – A way to communicate by verbal or written form. Decree. A statement from someone. A commitment to someone.

Quotes
"The solution to your pollution is to apply the Word of God." Dr. Clarice Fluitt

"Jesus Christ was the manifestation of the word of Truth. He was that word. If we cling close to the word of Truth how can He be taken from us? We are one with Him in God." Emma Curtis Hopkins

"False words are not only evil in themselves, but they infect the soul with evil." Socrates

Pam's Perspective
People see if my words match my actions. Either I keep my word, or I do not. There is no in-between, or excuse, that will take the place of me keeping my word.

Questions
How cautious am I about the words I use? Do I ever say words that I regret? Why is breaking my word not an option for me?

Declarations

I know that life and death are in the power of my **words**. I bless the people who have prophesied good **words** over me. God speaks to me through His **Word**. I prophesy the **Word** of God over myself.

My **word** is my bond. I keep my **word** and do what I say I am going to do. People know they can count on me. I am careful to only give my **word** to jobs I can do, and in a timely manner. Kind **words** are always the norm for me. I aim to help people with my **words**.

I love learning new **words** and expanding my vocabulary. I discipline myself to learn new **words** each week. I radically change my career by the thoughts I think, and the **words** I say. By repeating joyful **words** to myself, I enhance my mood and grow happier.

As I stay receptive to the Holy Spirit, things are revealed in the spirit realm, as well as in the natural realm, that I have not known before. The favor of God opens doors for me that no one can shut. My **words** produce big results and have a powerful impact. I allow the spirit of wisdom and revelation to create my experiences.

I have a powerful **word** to share with others. I am a unique gift to the world. God's **Word** resides in and works through me. I use my **words** to influence, and heal the people around me. I am selective about the **words** I use. I am careful not to cause harm, or humiliation with my **words**. My **words** repair, and improve the broken-hearted.

I am the mirror of my thought life. I use gentle, courteous **words** when I talk to myself. I stop bullying myself and use the power of my **words** to reinforce my positive side. My **words** matter. I choose **words** that promote harmony, kindness, and generosity. I speak my **words** with humility, and conscious thought, to promote peace.

271:
Plan
September 27

Bible Verses

"May he give you the desire of your heart and make all your plans succeed."
Psalm 20:4 (NIV)

"Ask the Lord to bless your plans, and you will be successful in carrying them out." Proverbs 16:3 (GNT)

Word of the Day

Plan – A blueprint or draft of your intention. A way of organizing your thoughts about how you want your future to look. To prepare beforehand.

Quotes

"God is not against His people's success; He plans for it." Richard Gaylord Briley

"The man who makes everything that leads to happiness depend upon himself, and not upon other men, has adopted the very best plan for living happily." Plato

"You can never plan the future by the past." Edmund Burke, Jan. 19, 1791

Pam's Perspective

As a teenager, I would get so frustrated with my mother because she had to write all her plans down. I would say, "Can't you remember anything." Now here I am just like her and have to write everything down. I have turned into my mother! I didn't plan on that. Sooner or later, it happens to us all. We act like our parents.

Questions

Do I have detailed plans for my life in writing? Do I plan out my day the day before? How often do I look at my plans? How well do I stick to my plans? Why are my plans successful? What is my next big plan?

Declarations

I am very conscious of the **plans** I make, and with whom I make them. I set aside time to **plan** my day, so I know what I have to do. I stick to my **plan** and tackle first things first. Because I **plan** on being productive today, I am. I like seeing my **plans** come to pass.

Although I am strict in keeping the **plans** I make, I am also flexible, and open when I need to be. I get busy launching my **plans**. If my **plan** fails, I roll with the punches. I make new **plans** and start all over again. I reap the rewards of my brazing, daring **plans**.

God gets a kick out of the **plans** I make. I pray about my **plans**, give them over to the Lord, and then I get started. I begin now, to change my life for the better. I **plan** on divine favor coming my way. I **plan** to honor my life's call. I **plan** to stay healthy, active, and flexible.

I think about how I want my future to look, and then make **plans** to create it. I am passionate about my **plans**. I am conscious of my important role in the grand scheme of things. I gravitate towards things that excite me, make me feel good, and furthers my **plans**.

I visualize my **plans** coming to fruition. I focus on what I love. When things don't go as **planned,** I simply brush myself off and refocus. I **plan** on learning from my mistakes and growing wiser. I respect the **plans** I make. Since I **plan** my life out to be fabulous, it is.

I am very creative with the **plans** I make to help my family. I lay the foundation for a high-quality life. I **plan** on having fun and enjoying my life. Joy is in my heart now. People notice my confidence and want to help complete my **plans**. I relax into the feeling that everything is OK with the **plans** I have made. I lay my head on my pillow at night knowing God is watching over all my **plans**.

272:
Settle
September 28

Bible Verses
"Occupy the land and settle in it, because I am giving it to you." Numbers 33:53 (GNT)

"If you and your neighbor have a difference of opinion, settle it between yourselves and do not reveal any secrets." Proverbs 25:9 (GNT)

Word of the Day
Settle – To choose. Establish in mind. Fix thoughts on.

Quotes
"Men are never so likely to settle a question rightly as when they discuss it freely." Thomas Babington Macaulay

"Settle for excellence to fend off mediocrity." Pam Malow-Isham

"It is better to debate a question without settling it than to settle a question without debating it." Joseph Joubert

Pam's Perspective
I had a long list of qualifications I wanted in a mate, had it written down on paper and was not settling for less. When I would show someone, they would laugh and say my expectations were too high. I would say 'I am happy with myself so why should I settle.' That is why I waited until I was thirty-eight before I got married. Gary met every qualification except one on my list; he doesn't dance.

Questions
Do I ever settle for less because it is convenient? Why would I settle when I can have the best? What have I settled for that I need to toss?

Declarations

I **settle** for getting things done instead of procrastinating about when and what to do. My eloquent steady actions **settle** me on top of the rest. I realize what has stopped me in the past, so I make a plan to overcome it. I **settle** for being on top instead of **settling** for crumbs. I have a noble character, a loving spirit a **settled** mind.

I **settle** my mind on the fact that God validates me and is ever near. I am free to live unshackled. I **settle** my hope in God's generosity. I show people the light in me more often than the dark. I **settle** my mind on the peace within me instead of the chaos in the world.

I operate far better when I am strengthening my body and eating healthy. I like improving my physical and mental wellness. I know **settling** for poor health is not a choice for me, so I am diligent with my self-care. I unplug for an hour so I can read, meditate and **settle** my thoughts on what is holy and worthy of my attention.

I have **settled** my faith in God that He will work everything out for my good. I **settle** my feet on the solid rock of Christ. God has **settled** his kindness on me. I decide to love God and to love people.

The best is yet to come so **settling** for less is not an option. I am responsible with my spending. I don't **settle** for used items unless that is what I want because I have saved enough to get what I want. The universe is a bountiful environment with plenty of everything.

I operate on all cylinders, not **settling** for complacency. I become the kind of person that positively impacts large numbers of people. I **settle** for being a propagator of cheer. Jesus is my companion and loves it when I pray for my enemies and do good things for them. I **settle** for being kind, considerate, trustworthy and lovable.

273:
Procrastination
September 29

Bible Verses

"A lazy person craves food and there is none, but the appetite of hard-working people is satisfied" Proverbs 13:4 (NOG)

"Jesus said, 'No procrastination. No backward looks. You can't put God's kingdom off till tomorrow. Seize the day.'" Luke 9:62 (MSG)

Word of the Day

Procrastination – Postponing what needs to be done. Hesitancy. Indecision and reluctance to do something.

Quotes

"Working is one of the most dangerous forms of procrastination." Gretchen Rubin

"Procrastination is the thief of time." Edward Young

Pam's Perspective

I procrastinated finishing this book because I am dyslexic and writing is very difficult for me. I am not a wordy person. Sometimes I would only get one line done and then draw a blank, have to walk away and come back. I would ponder how I could say this or that throughout my day. I have revised this book six times. I am glad I procrastinated publishing because this is much better than my first version and I have grown considerably as a person. Putting myself down because I procrastinated never helped me, so I used the time to stimulate my creativity.

Questions

Do I allow procrastination to drag me down? Do I procrastinate on purpose? Why do I make the most of my time and take prompt action?

Declarations

I gain victory in the area of **procrastination** by making a detailed list and then promptly acting upon it. I focus on now. I appreciate all I have done in the past and all I will do in the future, but right now is all I have. I am wise about the use of my time and what I get done.

Instead of **procrastinating** when I don't know how to do something, I ask for help. People love to lend a hand to someone who appreciates them. I incorporate some professional know how, in order to get organized, so I don't **procrastinate** on things that don't excite me. I do what I can to fend off **procrastination**.

I **procrastinate** when outside on sunny days. I give my body a treat by soaking up the sun and breathing in fresh air. I smile as I give thanks for all my wonderful blessings. I have been known to **procrastinate** getting up after a twenty-minute nap on Sunday.

I **procrastinate** from leaving a gathering too quickly when there are so many interesting people I could get to know. I make quick connections wherever I go. I hang out with people who emit zeal and courage. I gather coaching as I surround myself with winners.

I **procrastinate** getting up from my quiet time with the Lord because that is where I find my strength. I am happy with what God is doing in my life right now. I honor myself by being disciplined. I preach myself a little sermon to get me moving in a positive direction.

I recognize that I can be a **procrastinator.** I progress in my own time. I choose to give myself mercy when I **procrastinate** on purpose. I ask myself 'what is this **procrastination** costing me' and 'what am I getting out of it in return'? I have more than enough time to spare to accomplish what I want, so I can say goodbye to **procrastination**.

274:
Hurry
September 30

Bible Verses
"I hurry to keep your commandments— I never put it off!" Psalm 119:60 (CEB)

"The plans of the diligent end up in profit, but those who hurry end up with loss." Proverbs 21:5 (CEB)

Word of the Day
Hurry – To rush, quicken or run. Accelerate or hustle. To act swiftly.

Quotes
"The mind which concentrates itself upon the one idea, I must do this thing, does it eventually, no matter what obstacles intervene. The mind which says, 'The procession is so long ahead of me it is useless for me to try to hurry; I must just jog along' – that is the mind which never gets beyond the jogging pace. The procession is always ahead." Ella Wheeler Wilcox

"If I have uttered a single irritating word, may the winds take it up and hurry it off immediately!" Horace

"He sows hurry and reaps indigestion." Robert Louis Stevenson

Pam's Perspective
I accomplish more in half the time when I go slow and am not in a hurry. Rushing has caused me more accidents than if I would have taken my time. So I relax, take a deep breath, stay calm, and slow down, so I don't make mistakes.

Questions
Do I really need to hurry as much as I do? Do I accomplish more or less by hurrying? What if I chose slow and steady instead of fast and hurried?

Declarations

I **hurry** away from chaos to create a new paradigm in which to live, play and fully express myself. I have the capacity to operate from a place of wisdom. I live my life in the overflow of wonder, gratitude, and joy. I **hurry** to give hugs, blessings, smiles, and compliments.

I am always in a **hurry** to make amends with people whom I have offended. Although I never purposely try to hurt anyone, sometimes people take things the wrong way. I **hurry** to forgive people who get under my skin. I am inspired to do the right thing at the right time.

I am never too much in a **hurry** to ignore the importance of what matters most in my life. My relationships matter. I pay attention to what is going on with my partner and give an ear when he or she wants to talk. I need people around me to help enrich my life.

When I am in a **hurry** to get somewhere, I pause for a moment and breathe. I think about where I am going and why. I have plenty of time to drive, so I don't **hurry** aimlessly. I am conscious and aware of my surroundings at all times. **Hurry** is not the only option for me.

Because I am in a **hurry** to correct what is not working in my life, I confront it now. I do not wait for someone else to solve my problems; I solve them myself. I gladly take charge and rehabilitate my thinking, so I focus on solutions. I am never too **hurried** to pray for direction. I **hurry** to talk to God and then wait for the perfect answers. I am grateful to have an ever-present friend I can talk to.

I am kindhearted and in a **hurry** to show it. I **hurry** off to the gym to work out. I think of myself as a thin, healthy person, regardless of my weight. I love myself purely. As I **hurry** toward my goals, I learn to enjoy the ride. I can do things well without being in a **hurry**.

275:
Cease
October 1

Bible Verses
"As long as the earth exists, seedtime and harvest, cold and hot, summer and autumn, day and night will not cease." Genesis 8:22 (CEB)

"Cast out the scorner, and contention shall go out; yea, strife and reproach shall cease." Proverbs 22:10 (KJV)

Word of the Day
Cease – To halt or quit. To close or finish. To call something off.

Quotes
"When a thing ceases to be a subject of controversy it ceases to be a subject of interest." William Hazlitt

"Cease to inquire what the future has in store, and take as a gift whatever the day brings forth." Horace

"Remove the cause, and the effect will cease." Waldorf

Pam's Perspective
When I cease to look for common ground with another, I stop God from using me. When I cease to presume my way of thinking is the only right way to think, I then can allow the Holy Spirit to instruct me in the sacred way of loving kindness. We must cease staying in our comfortable groups where everyone thinks the same, believe God and start sharing the good news of Christ.

Questions
What would happen if I would cease to worry? Can I cease getting upset? Will I? Why is it easy for me to cease unsavory habits?

Declarations

I **cease** feeling inadequate because I am a powerful phenomenon that produces incredible results. I **cease** finding fault with myself when I mess up. I am the one whom God loves completely. With prayer, I dissolve any negative emotions that could do me harm.

I **cease** procrastinating on the things I need to do. I start right now with one small step that moves me toward the direction of my goals. I **cease** speculating on how things could have been and put my attention on how wonderful my life really is. I make a positive shift to **cease** all strife. I act for the long term and **cease** with fantasy.

I let go of the need to control my surroundings as I **cease** to worry. Meditation helps me **cease** any fear I may have. As I breathe deeply and surrender to God and the unknown, I relax and feel content. The life of God powerfully flows through me **ceasing** all anxiety.

I **cease** being stagnant because my desire to be in peak shape motivates me to keep active and continue working out no matter how I feel. My cravings for sugar have **ceased** because I **cease** to eat it. I **cease** my thirst by drinking a lot of water and staying hydrated.

God never **ceases** to bless me. I write my own plan. I fix my eyes on my priorities and **cease** spending time on unimportant tasks. I **cease** feeling down. I go within to find the guidance I need. God's wisdom never **ceases** to amaze me. I stand in awe of God's great love for me.

I never **cease** to be curious because I love learning new things. I take the necessary steps to make the most of my day. I **cease** putting off what I can easily do right now. I find myself smiling at my productivity. I **cease** being bored because I am creative. Every day I declare I am courageous, smart, decisive, dependable and strong.

276:
Continuous
October 2

Bible Verses
"What a Day that will be! No more cold nights—in fact, no more nights! The Day is coming—the timing is God's—when it will be continuous day. Every evening will be a fresh morning." Zechariah 14:6-7 (MSG)

"I am continuously thanking my God for you when I think about the grace God has offered you in Jesus the Anointed." 1 Corinthians 1:4 (VOICE)

Word of the Day
Continuous – Something that repeats or loops. Endless. An ongoing process that does not stop.

Quotes
"Talent! There's no such thing as talent. What they call talent is nothing but the capacity for doing continuous hard work in the right way." Winslow Homer

"The habit of common and continuous speech is a symptom of mental deficiency. It proceeds from not knowing what is going on in other people's minds." Walter Bagehot

Pam's Perspective
During the summer I walk in my garden daily, and I continually pull weeds. There is not a time that I go out that I don't see a weed that has popped up overnight. If only my flowers and vegetables could be as hardy as the weeds. I also must be continuous with my declarations to keep the negative thought weeds out.

Questions
What have I continuously fed my mind? What do my continuous actions say about me? Why is it good to continuously monitor my thoughts?

Declarations

I am **continually** expanding as a positive person. I have **continuous** hope that everything will turn out in my favor. I have abundant energy and fervor for life. People **continue** to believe in me and are excited to help me out. I graciously receive compliments.

I am **continuously** asking intellectually challenging questions as I search out the truth. I have a lot of clarity and freedom in my life. I am **continuously** going beyond what has stopped me in the past to create new empowering experiences. I get my expected results.

I bring **continuous** color into my world. Bright and happy are my days. I permanently change my life by **continuous** positive actions. Since I am **continuous** with my positive affirmations, my bad days are few and far between. My word is law. My **continuous** good mood is created by my smile, thoughts, words, and actions.

I know that as I **continually** offer prayers of thanksgiving to God, He showers me with more abundance. I **continually** light up the world with my smile. I **continually** reveal God's love as I do good works and give hugs and money from a grateful heart.

I **continuously** do the right thing. I pay attention to each moment of my life. I **continually** work on bringing people together in unity. We have more in common than we think. God loves us all the same. As I **continue** to put God first, He teaches me how to serve my neighbor.

I belong to God, and I **continuously** give thanks throughout the day for my fulfilling life. I am proud of what I have accomplished in the past, and I plan to get better **continually**. When I set aside time for Christ in my day, it goes very well. I can master anything I set my mind to. I love being most likely to succeed as I **continue** to grow.

277:
Ruin
October 3

Bible Verses
"Those who are wise store up knowledge, but the mouth of a stubborn fool invites ruin." Proverbs 10:14 (NOG)

"With his talk a godless person can ruin his neighbor, but righteous people are rescued by knowledge." Proverbs 11:9 (NOG)

Word of the Day
Ruin – To shatter and deplete something. Wreak havoc on. Defeat.

Quotes
"Imagination frames events unknown, in wild, fantastic shapes of hideous ruin, and what it fears, creates." Hannah More

"What each man feared would happen to himself, did not trouble him when he saw that it would ruin another." Virgil

"Ingratitude ruins the chance for happiness and success." Pam Malow-Isham

Pam's Perspective
There was a time when I wanted to ruin the people who hurt me. The more I plotted and wallowed in anger and bitterness, the worse I felt. When I finally realized I was giving my power away to the people who hurt me, and they were going about their life unscathed, unaware of my hatred is when I decided to release it and let it go. Instead of seeing myself as ruined, I see myself as free.

Questions
What is one action that will ruin my healthy lifestyle? How can I ruin complacency? Why won't I let a negative thought ruin my day?

Declarations

By continuing to learn and grow, I keep myself from **ruin**. I am virtually guaranteed big consistent wins because I persist. I break out in laughter as some silly negative person tries to **ruin** my day. I am invincible to rude comments. I am a person of significance.

Divine luminosity appears just at the perfect moment to thwart off any **ruin**. I marvel at the goodness of God. God trusts me to bring His visions about. I love being soft-hearted and open to all God has for me. No one can **ruin** my faith because it comes from within.

Because I enjoy eating healthy fruits and vegetables I have **ruined** my desire for junk food. I am fit and fun-loving. I love my beautiful, clean, well-organized kitchen. I am thankful that I have healthy food in my refrigerator. I eat it before it gets **ruined** or spoiled.

I am **ruined** for the mundane and boredom of everyday living. I rise above mediocrity and soar above the crowd. I have no need to escape my reality because Christ is in the center of my life, leading me on to greatness. I am rooted in love. Nothing can **ruin** my spirit.

When my dark, rebellious side comes to the surface and tries to **ruin** and sabotage my hard work, I face my fears. I realize I can **ruin** my life or I can celebrate my life, so enjoy my existence. Nothing can **ruin** my positive attitude. I am aboveboard in all my undertakings. I confess the blessings of influence and power of God over my life.

I focus thoughts of light toward what some might consider **ruin** and see the miraculous take place. I see the big picture. I am a visionary who loves to see **ruined** things repurposed. I like being creative. I rescript my **ruin** story into a victory story. I am **ruined** for the ordinary as I walk in the supernatural. God is good all the time.

278:
Amend
October 4

Bible Verses
"Fools mock at making amends for sin, but goodwill is found among the upright." Proverbs 14:9 (NIV)

"Thus says the Lord of hosts, the God of Israel, amend your ways and your doings, and I will let you dwell in this place." Jeremiah 7:3 (RSV)

Word of the Day
Amend – To enhance and upgrade. To fix, help or clean up. Reform.

Quotes
"We are to bear with those we cannot amend and to be content with offering them to God. This is true resignation. And since He has borne our infirmities, we may well bear those of each other for His sake." John Wesley

"Gladly we desire to make other men perfect, but we will not amend our own fault; we will that other men be straightly corrected, and we ourselves will not be corrected." Thomas à Kempis

"The duty of man is the same in respect to his own nature as in respect to the nature of all other things, namely not to follow it bit to amend it." John Stuart Mill

Pam's Perspective
Since I am the only one who can amend my ways, I don't look to others to do it for me. I amend what is necessary and what will advance my growth.

Questions
What is the most important thing I need to amend? What is stopping me?

Declarations

I am loved by God no matter if I make **amends** with Him or not. He chases after me with passion, speed, and determination. God has my best interests in mind. When I do admit that I need God, He is there with open arms ready to accept my **amends**. Being aware of my oneness with God has **amended** my thoughts. We are a great team.

When I ask for help, I always get it. The Holy Spirit is never late. I **amend** the knowledge of God in my head and the presence of God in my heart. I walk in love, as I am humble enough to admit when I need to make **amends** and then do so. I find my security in God.

I **amend** my eating habits to what my body needs. I have a super-fast metabolism and a lot of energy. I stay healthy and active. I appreciate all the things I have learned as I have **amended** my study habits to enhance my skills. I am thankful I can discover new ideas.

I **amend** my perception and realize what is really important in my life. I release all hurts now. I choose to extend forgiveness and look past peoples faults. I love making **amends** as I walk in love. I make **amends** quickly, so people with great attitudes join my team.

I choose to make **amends** for the mistakes I have made in the past. I am responsible for acting rashly. I am vigilant about self-monitoring my ego and my self-righteous ways. I realize I can be judgmental, so I **amend** my thoughts and attitude to accept diversity lovingly.

I show up for my miracle. Everything I need is right in front of me. I **amend** my investments by increasing my savings. I stop spending what I don't have and wait until I can pay cash. God multiplies His favor over me as I increase in wisdom, friendships, joy, and money. I **amend** my face to add a smile, brighten my day and share my cheer.

279:
Say
October 5

Bible Verses

"God said to Moses, "I Am Who I Am. So say to the Israelites, 'I Am has sent me to you.'" Exodus 3:14 (CEB)

"Let all those that seek thee rejoice and be glad in thee: and let such as love thy salvation say continually, let God be magnified." Psalm70:4 (KJV)

"You will have to live with the consequences of everything you say." Proverbs 18:20 (CEB)

Word of the Day

Say – To talk out loud. To make known with your voice. To verbalize.

Quotes

"When you have nothing to say, say nothing: a weak defense strengthens your opponent, and silence is less injurious than a weak reply." Charles Colton

"Men who have much to say use the fewest words." H. W. Shaw

"God is not who you think He is; He is who He says He is." Dr. Clarice Fluitt

Pam's Perspective

Giving myself permission to have a say in how I want my life to go is major in creating a fulfilling life. By having a say, I produce a life of substance and am no longer a victim of circumstances. Realizing I have a say and acting on it is key.

Questions

Do I think carefully before I say something? Do I ever say something and then regret it? Why does what I say make a difference?

Declarations

What I **say** is sacred. I am righteous because God **says** I am. I am responsible for what I **say** all the time. My words create my fabulous reality, so I am very conscious of what I **say**. There are no limits to what I **say** I can create. I am worthy of the best because I **say**.

God **says** nice things about me. God **says** I am His child and he loves me no matter what. My faith is sealed, and I can trust God. I devote myself to God and **say** I am a child of the King. I have nothing to fear. I believe what God **says** and that settles it.

I am bold enough to have my **say**. I am bright enough to **say** nice things to myself. I **say** I am kind and a pleasure to be around. I get happy by helping people. Being of service brings a smile to my face.

I manage what I **say**. I think about what I am **saying** before I **say** it. The cost of not being present is too great to throw away, so I stay in the now. I am consistent with who I am, with what I **say**. What you see is what you get. I am authentic, so no one can **say** I am a phony.

I have the courage to create my world based on what I **say** alone. I enjoy meeting with my mastermind group that **says** I am great. I am conscious of my relationships, and I work on improving them. Pure creation comes from what I **say**. With nothing, I am happy.

I am on the court, in action, and shaking things up with what I **say** and how I **say** it. Every word I **say** is baited on steroids and draws abundance my way. Everything I **say** works for me. I get what I **say**.

Today I choose to be delightful and **say** what is on my mind in a kind and courteous manner. I give my thoughts a voice because what I have to **say** matters. I am a vessel that **says** loving things.

280:
Evidence
October 6

Bible Verses

"I will sing forever about the evidence of your mercy, O Lord. I will tell about your faithfulness to every generation." Psalm 89:1 (GW)

"The evidence of the Spirit's presence is given to each person for the common good of everyone." 1 Corinthians 12:7 (GW)

Word of the Day

Evidence –The data or confirmation that something is true or false.

Quotes

"Facts are stubborn things; and whatever may be our wishes, our inclinations, or the dictates of our passions, they cannot alter the state of facts and evidence." John Adams

"There is no evidence that after the Holy Spirit once came, he ever left the world. He is here now, ready to help you to overcome." Billy Sunday

Pam's Perspective

My husband took me on an Alaskan cruise a few years ago. While in Skagway we stopped in a jewelry store so he could purchase some gold nuggets for investment. He saw a beautiful pear-shaped emerald and decided to have it mounted on a gold nugget for a necklace for me. I was shocked, bewildered, and happy. That evening with my head turned, so he did not know, I cried myself to sleep with happy tears. I was so very grateful that he loves me, and the evidence was shown with his gift.

Questions

What evidence points to good friendships? Do I need evidence to prove my worth? Why? Is there evidence that I have faith?

Declarations

The **evidence** that God loved me first overwhelms me with gratitude. I have access to a higher reality that I can tap into any time I want just by praying. I am ravished by the love of God, and I can feel it. There is more than sufficient **evidence** that God is real and loves me enough to send His son to die in my place.

The **evidence** that God exists makes me want to sing for joy. I am eternally connected to the Most High. I praise God for the **evidence** of His great mercy towards me. I am thankful that I have a helper from above. My abounding joy is **evident** as I bring the gladness of heaven to those around me. The **evidence** of beauty is everywhere.

I look for **evidence** of success in the past, so I can focus on achieving even more success in the future. I am a product of my thoughts, and my life is the **evidence** of those thoughts. I have access to unlimited wisdom. I generate what I choose whenever I choose. Multitudes listen to me because I am enlightened and led by the Holy Spirit.

The **evidence** of my workouts is showing in my growing strength and endurance. Adventure is in my blood. I explore new interests, so I can evolve. The **evidence** is apparent in the bold steps I take to get ahead that I am a winner. **Evidence** shows, I do what is fair.

I seek wise counsel about investing, and the **evidence** shows up in my overflowing bank account. I spend money on the people I choose to bless and surprise. I appreciate my ability to tip well and help out. **Evidence** proves that I can enhance my wealth by being generous.

Now is my time to produce the **evidence** of living a highly favored life. I believe in miracles, regardless of any **evidence**. I act like it is already accomplished and then watch my miracle show up.

281:
Adequate
October 7

Bible Verses
"Not that we are adequate in ourselves to consider anything as coming from us, but our adequacy comes from God." 2 Corinthians 3:5 (MOUNCE)

"For what [adequate] thanksgiving can we render to God for you for all the gladness and delight which we enjoy for your sakes before our God?"
1 Thessalonians 3:9 (AMP)

Word of the Day
Adequate – Decent enough to get by. Tolerable or average. Passable.

Quotes
"Whatever else it should or should not be, he warns us; education must be an inoculation against the poisons of life and an adequate equipment in knowledge and skill for meeting the chances of life." Havelock Ellis

"No pen can give an adequate description of the all-pervading corruption produced by slavery." Harriet Ann Jacobs

Pam's Perspective
I did not have an adequate perception of God growing up. I saw Him as a mean old man ready to punish me at any moment. Unfortunately, many Christians around me at the time reinforced that belief. But the Holy Spirit revealed to me love, mercy, peace, grace, kindness, joy, and hope. Oh, that we would be led by Love rather than traditions. God is more than adequate to meet our every need.

Questions
Do I have adequate finances? Do I have adequate knowledge? Why should I settle for adequate when I am extraordinary?

Declarations

I am clear on what success is for me so I can realize it. I am more than **adequate** for any challenge that comes my way. I **adequately** create a vision so powerful that it pulls me forward and pushes me up. I revitalize myself by revisiting my dreams and goals.

I am completely forthright in my business dealings. I build a reserve in every area of my life, so I always have an **adequate** supply. I add value just for the joy of it. People love working with me.

I have the **adequate** wisdom to be successful. I acknowledge myself for my accomplishments. My **adequate** knowledge has taught me I have a lot more to learn. I am a team player who amplifies success.

I refuse to accept **adequate** work from myself when I am capable of so much more. I go the extra mile and do everything with excellence. I also expect more than **adequate** work from the people I employ, hire and mentor. Doing half-hearted labor is unacceptable to me. Everything I do, I do it as unto the Lord as I respect our bond.

My **adequate** exercise routine keeps me healthy and in great shape. I have more than **adequate** power over my will. Stability and poise is the way I roll. I display reverence for my body, mind, and spirit.

My brain is **adequate** enough to find solutions. I am smarter than I realize. I am ready and willing to be a leader. I am grateful for my **adequate** gifts and my extraordinary life. I think like a top producer.

My life is thriving. I am thankful that the God I serve is more than just **adequate**. Nothing is impossible. With God on my side, I am more than **adequate** to handle any and every circumstance that comes my way. I am thankful for my miraculous life.

282:
Inadequate
October 8

Bible Verses
"I was unsure of how to go about this, and felt totally inadequate—I was scared to death, if you want the truth of it—and so nothing I said could have impressed you or anyone else. But the Message came through anyway. God's Spirit and God's power did it, which made it clear that your life of faith is a response to God's power, not to some fancy mental or emotional footwork by me or anyone else." 1 Corinthians 2:3-5 (MSG)

Word of the Day
Inadequate – Not perfect or acceptable; unsatisfactory or rundown.

Quote
"The dogmas of the quiet past are inadequate to the stormy present. The occasion is piled high with difficulty, and we must rise with the occasion. As our case is new, so we must think anew and act anew." Abraham Lincoln

Pam's Perspective
I taught Ballroom Dancing at Arthur Murray Dance Studio in the 80's. When I first started, I was totally inadequate for the job with no experience in dance and little confidence. I asked the owner, 'you train me, and I will train your students.' They agreed, and I just had to know one more step than my students did to be the expert. It took me two years to build up enough confidence to teach a group lesson. I eventually competed in dance competitions similar to Dancing with the Stars. As with most things in my life I have felt totally inadequate to do the job but somehow mustered up enough courage to try, and it always works out.

Questions
Do I see myself as inadequate? Do I see others as inadequate? Can I accept people's inadequacies? Will I be happy despite my inadequacies?

Declarations

I have a zest for life, and I am glad to be here. I play big in the world despite any **inadequacies** that I may have. I rise above my own **inadequate** feelings and look at all the good I have done. I clear my head of all **inadequate** thoughts and dwell on the possibilities.

I encourage people who feel **inadequate**. We all have unique gifts to share. Sometimes I feel **inadequate** when it comes to being open, so I hang around a diverse group of advisers. I am grateful for what I have gleaned from them because they increase my understanding.

Learning brings joy, excitement, and challenge to my life. I am addicted to educating myself on new things. I tell the truth about my **inadequacy** of a subject because I always have room to grow.

I keep calm and stay cool-headed when an **inadequate** driver cuts me off. I am in control of my emotions at all times. I enjoy giving them a break. Some people may be **inadequate** at restraining their anger. I feel relaxed and in control behind the wheel. I always feel safe as my angels are watching, carefully steering me along.

Even though my words are **inadequate** to describe how great God is, I give it my best shot. God saw that we were **inadequate** without Him so He made a way for us through Jesus Christ and the Holy Spirit. We will always be **inadequate** compared to perfection, but always loved and welcomed. I am very grateful for grace.

I speed up my happiness by smiling a lot and often. I am **inadequate** at staying down or being grumpy. I broadcast the good news about how great I feel to everyone around me. People like me and my positive attitude. Because I am **inadequate** at going it alone, I gather a group of supportive friends to make life more enjoyable and fun.

283:
Confusion
October 9

Bible Verses
"Fill their faces with confusion, that they may seek thy name, O Jehovah."
Psalm 83:16 (ASV)

"For God is not a God of confusion, but of peace...." 1 Corinthians 14:33
(ASV)

Word of the Day
Confusion –Easily distracted. Lacking focus, order, or calmness.

Quotes
*"I had begun to see without emotion, and to hear without confusion, when
a light breeze, of which the freshness communicated a new sensation of
pleasure, wafted its perfumes to me, and excited in me a kind of additional
self-love." Thomas Cogswell Upham*

*"Truth is ever to be found in simplicity, and not in the multiplicity and
confusion of things." Sir Isaac Newton*

Pam's Perspective
*Confusion plagued me for years because I am an introvert. I used to think
I was weird because I didn't talk a lot like my twin sister. People would
ask me what I was thinking, and my mind would be totally blank when I
would say nothing. I envied people who could talk for hours. I was confused
why it was so difficult for me to carry on a conversation. I can ponder over
something and come up with all kinds of responses, but put on the spot; I
can't think of much. I thought I was damaged until I realized that was how
God made me, and He doesn't create junk.*

Questions
What is the best way for me to dispel confusion? Do I get confused often?

Declarations

I have the power of the Holy Spirit in me. I link up with God and harness peace. Since I know that God is not the author of **confusion**, I say **confusion** 'go,' and it has to leave. I gain certainty from **confusion** by meditating on God's Word. I have clarity from within.

Sometimes all I need to do to get **confusing** thoughts out of my head is to write them down. I do not worry if my spelling is perfect. I do the work of journaling. I am honest with myself and what I am feeling. I can **confuse** people with my wisdom. I come up with genius ideas by spending 20 minutes a day writing in a journal.

I see value in asking questions when I am **confused**. Sometimes, just walking away and coming back is all I need for the answer to appear. When I am in a state of **confusion,** I slow down and breathe deeply and tell myself to cool it. I keep silent, so I can listen to the answers. Then I receive a solution out of the blue; it always comes.

I am sure of myself. Every day I declare that I am more than a **confusing** thought. Just because **confusing** thoughts enter my brain does not mean I have to dwell on them. I do something. I get up and exercise so I can focus clearly and send **confusion** running.

I give myself a break when **confusion** crops up and realize I will be OK. I trust the process of believing in myself and recognizing that I have all I need within me to get the job done. **Confusion** does not have a hold on me. I release **confusion** and abide with certainty.

When I decide to get a job done, I do it well. I clearly speak when I talk, so there is no **confusion** about what I expect. I expect excellence because that is what I give. I put things in order and keep a clean desk to keep **confusion** at bay. I know where things are.

284:
Surety
October 10

Bible Verses
"He who is surety for a stranger will suffer, but one who hates being surety is secure." Proverbs 11:15 (NKJV)

"It is senseless to give a pledge, to become surety for a neighbor." Proverbs 17:18 (NRSV)

Word of the Day
Surety – Confidence. Guaranteeing someone's debt. Responsible party. Putting up bail money.

Quotes
"If there is any person more to be pitied than a spendthrift, it is he who willingly becomes the surety of a spendthrift." St. Athanasius

"Abstinence is the surety of temperance." Plato

Pam's Perspective
I let a dear friend borrow some money, and after two installments she stopped making payments. When asked why she stopped, she stated she needed the money more than I because I had a lot of money and didn't need it as she did, or so she thought. Two years later I received the money from another source. It was a hard lesson to learn because I love her so much and was surprised with her entitlement mentality. I have learned to keep a friend, never let them borrow money.

Questions
Have I bailed anyone out of a tight spot? Did it work out? What do I put my surety in? Have I ever been surety for another person? If so, what guarantee do I have of repayment? Why am I financially responsible?

Declarations

I am thankful that Jesus is the **surety** for me and I can trust that He always guides my every move. I don't have to try to work my way into God's good graces because I am already there. My **surety** is secure with Him. God keeps His word and hears my prayers.

Through Christ, I have **surety** that all of God's promises are true. I stand in faith knowing that God is able to keep His word. As I declare God's promises over my life, I have the ultimate **surety**.

God is my **surety** and takes care of me. There is no ceiling on what I can accomplish, so with **surety**, I accomplish great things. I remove any limitations I have placed in my mind and realized, I am more than enough. I love to share what I have because there is plenty for all.

I refuse to pay interest on credit cards that are a **surety** to debt. I gain victory over my spending by waiting before I make any large purchase until I have carefully thought it over. I make a list before I go to the store and buy only by what is on my list. I am in control of my finances. I am **sure** I have what it takes to succeed.

Glory to God, I am free from the chains of debt. No one has to be financial **surety** for me. I write my own ticket. I save at least ten percent of all I make. I tithe at least ten percent and give additional offerings. I love being able to help people and various causes. I am a disciplined saver and know how to say 'no thank you.'

Being **sure** and steady as I go, I astound myself at my achievements. I am the one whom the Holy Spirit works through. The **surety** of God's love for me gives me peace of mind and confidence to face the day. Knowing I don't have to prove my worth to anyone is priceless. I give myself fully to God, and He fully gives me everlasting joy.

285:
Few
October 11

Bible Verses

"Teach us to number our days and recognize how few they are; help us to spend them as we should." Psalm 90:12 (TLB)

"The man of few words and settled mind is wise; therefore, even a fool is thought to be wise when he is silent. It pays him to keep his mouth shut." Proverbs 17:27-28 (TLB)

Word of the Day

Few – A tiny supply. Lacking volume or quantity. Less than a bunch. A small amount.

Quotes

"Wealth consists not in having great possessions, but in having few wants." Epictetus

"Love all, trust a few, do wrong to none." William Shakespeare

"How many observe Christ's birthday! How few, His precepts. O 'tis easier to keep holidays than commandments." Benjamin Franklin

Pam's Perspective

I have found a few loyal friends are much better than a ton of acquaintances. True friendships are worth cultivating. It is comforting knowing I can count on a few to lift me up, help me out or just hang out. Having a few good friends is priceless!

Questions

Can I be content with a few things? What few things will I remember? Are there a few habits I need to change? What few things will I let go of today?

Declarations

My spunk and determination is an encouragement for a **few**. I hold myself out to be a positive phenomenon that gallantly changes my world. I practice a **few** simple disciplines today that will positively affect my tomorrow. I stay fully engaged in everything I do.

I have **few** wants because I am content with what I have. I am fun to be around and very charismatic. I believe in my self-worth. **Few** things upset me because I easily brush off negativity. I love a **few** challenges. I am proud of myself because I help a **few** people smile.

My **few** powerful statements really get my point across effectively. I have **few** distractions because I eliminate energy drains. I stay in a place of peace when I am faced with stress. I am committed to seeking out reliable advice from a **few** reliable mentors.

I have **few** words to say because I carefully consider them before I speak. With **few** words, I turn people to the ministry of reconciliation instead of offense. I am a hope propagator and live in the light. A **few** people are encouraged to be happy because of me.

Few people can keep up with me because I am very industrious. I work despite difficulties and finish what I start. God is my partner, and we are unstoppable. I say a **few** prayers and God comes through again. I stay open to the conversations of heaven as I worship God. My worries are far and **few** between.

I have **few** cares when clouds roll in, as they sometimes do. I trust God who is with me always and never lets me down. I know that **few** resources in the hands of God are more than enough to meet any challenge I could ever face. I walk in faith and do the **few** things I know how to do. Who I am is a blessing to the world today.

286:
Many
October 12

Bible Verses
"He does things too marvelous for people to understand. He does too many miracles to count!" Job 9:10 (ERV)

"You will lie down unafraid, and many will look to you for help." Job 11:19 (TLB)

Word of the Day
Many – More than one or a few. Bountiful in number. Plentiful.

Quotes
"He of whom many are afraid ought to fear many." Sir Francis Bacon

"A single sunbeam is enough to drive away many shadows." Francis of Assisi

"The wonderful secret about our problems, by the way, is this: Unlike a question which has but one answer, problems have many answers." Richard Gaylord Briley

"Fortune gives too much too many, enough to none." Martial

"Our Lord has many weak children in his family, many dull pupils in his schools, many raw soldiers in his army, many lame sheep in his flock. Yet he bears with them all, and casts none away. Happy is that Christian who has learned to do likewise with his brethren." John Charles Ryle

Questions
How many gifts do I have? How many dreams can I come up with? How many things can I give away today? How many smiles can I share? How many ways can I be a blessing to someone today?

Declarations

Many esteem me for my cheerful countenance and my loving ways. I am enthusiastic about **many** things. People care about me because of the contribution I am to them. I have **many** friends that love and support me in **many** ways. **Many** imitate my positive attitude.

I have **many** options for my dream home. The sky is the limit. I draw out all the things that are important to me. There are **many** suitable places for me to put down my roots and make a positive difference. My ever-expanding vision pulls me forth, one step at a time. I invest in my **many** passions and keep my dreams alive.

My health is getting better and better. There are **many** ways that I continue to improve my physical body by walking and keeping movement apart of my daily life. I have a great heart and healthy liver. I do **many** actions that support my disciplined life.

I am very grateful for my **many** blessings and all the things I have. It is incredible how **many** channels God uses to pour out His favor on me. I am open to receiving them all. It is impossible to count how **many** ways God shows me His love. I continue to stay amazed.

God loves taking care of me. He speaks to me in **many** forms as I keep my heart open. No matter what the situation is, I choose to stay upbeat. Though **many** negative thoughts may enter my mind, I choose to dismiss them and fill my mind with **many** godly ideas.

Many are my victories and few my defeats, but I learn from them all. I use everything to my advantage. I am very thankful for **many** things. God uses me in the midst of my **many** messes and creates a marvelous masterpiece that impresses the world. I am someone's miracle when I use the **many** talents that God has given me.

287:
Attract
October 13

Bible Verses

"And he remarked, 'That is what I meant when I said that no one can come to me unless the Father attracts him to me.'" John 6:65 (TLB)

"And when I am lifted up from the earth, I will attract all people toward Me." John 12:32 (NLV)

Word of the Day

Attract – To elicit help. To evoke something to come close. To call forth.

Quotes

"Our thoughts have the power to attract wealth, health and happiness, or poverty, sickness, and sadness. We are created in the image of God and have the potential to do great things. So choose carefully what thoughts you intend to focus on today and dismiss the rest." Pam Malow-Isham

"Faith is not a notion, but a real strong essential hunger, an attracting or magnetic desire of Christ, which as it proceeds from a seed of the divine nature in us, so it attracts and unites with its like." William Law

"What if you gave someone a gift, and they neglected to thank you for it – would you be likely to give them another? Life is the same way. In order to attract more of the blessings that life has to offer, you must truly appreciate what you already have." Ralph Marston

"We do not attract what we want, but what we are." James Lane Allen

Questions

Do I attract the things I desire? If not, why not? Do I focus on what I want to attract? Why do I attract the best experiences? Why am I so attractive?

Declarations

Every time I visualize my desired outcome, I **attract** it. My internal magnet **attracts** what my heart desires. I welcome everything that I **attract**, even the occasional adversity; because that is where I learn my greatest lessons. I believe in my inner strength and endurance.

I like taking long walks to bask in the healing energy of the sun. I tune into nature and tune into God. He speaks through His creation in many glorious ways. I **attract** health into my veins, joy into my heart, strength into my bones, and wisdom into my brain. I **attract** everything that my spirit, soul, and body need. Nothing is left out.

When I know the outcome of the goals I want to **attract**, I follow steps to acquire them. I come from a state of abundance, so I **attract** more abundance. I clear a place to **attract** the perfect accessories for my home and office. It is OK to **attract** riches as I use them for good. I worship God, not things and put Him first in all I do.

Accountability is the way I **attract** responsible people. I am conscious of the way I talk, so I **attract** the best. By becoming excellent in my field, I **attract** the perfect customers that stay loyal for years. I **attract** the perfect opportunities that are divinely appointed at the right time. I am **attractive** in countless ways.

My kind gestures **attract** pleasant responses. I like to offer help. I only **attract** loyal, loving friends. I come from an attitude of 'how can I serve,' not 'what's in it for me.' Every day I become a kinder, happier person because I choose to be. I **attract** happiness.

I **attract** enjoyable experiences. I inspire others to let go and be playful. We are here to **attract** laughter and love. What we give out, we **attract**. My cup overflows with love, peace, and joy.

288:
Repel
October 14

Bible Verses

"Jehovah suffereth not the soul of the righteous [man] to famish; but he repelleth the craving of the wicked." Proverbs 10:3 (DARBY)

"And blessed (happy—with life-joy and satisfaction in God's favor and salvation, apart from outward conditions—and to be envied) is he who takes no offense in Me and who is not hurt or resentful or annoyed or repelled or made to stumble [whatever may occur]." Luke 7:23 (AMP)

Word of the Day

Repel – To cast aside and keep at bay. To offend someine with your words or actions. To irritate, annoy or offend.

Quotes

"Laughter repels sadness and people who complain." Pam Malow-Isham

"There's something like radar inside the human heart that senses the displeasure of others. Displeasure and ingratitude are like a repellant to human relationships." Francis Frangipane

"Oh! If there is one law above the rest, written in wisdom – if there is a word that I would trace as with a pen of fire upon the unsunned temper of a child - If there is anything that keeps the mind open to angel visits, and repels the ministry of ill, -'tis human love! God has made nothing worthy of contempt. The smallest pebble in the well of truth has its peculiar meaning, and will stand when man's best monuments have passed away." Nathaniel P. Willis

Questions

Do I ever repel people who are different than I? Do I get to know people who at first I am repelled by? What negative can I repel today?

Declarations

There is no one who can **repel** God from loving me. It's a done deal. God liberally enwraps me with His glorious peace. People see the brightness of God shining through me **repelling** the darkness.

Because I choose to walk in forgiveness, I **repel** all feelings of hurt and offense. I **repel** sadness with my cheery attitude. I can easily **repel** thoughts or stories about how someone has done me wrong. We all make mistakes. I am stronger than any hurt I've encountered.

I am very lovable because I **repel** judgment, condemnation, and comparison. I skip for joy as I **repel** misery and negativity. I let go of small annoyances that really don't matter. I **repel** counterproductive thinking and make exceptional choices about what enters my mind.

I **repel** people who tell me something can't be done because I know all things are possible with the God I serve. I **repel** down the mountain of fear and conquer every challenge that comes my way.

I **repel** sickness by my healthy eating. I am diligent with my workouts and putting myself first. I do what is best for my family and me. I have a chiseled body and a smart mind. I **repel** sugar and eat my vegetables. I **repel** apathy by never giving up.

I **repel** poverty and accept my authority as a child of the King who has unlimited resources. I can have it all because I work hard for what I get. I am a source for good and fully engaged in my life.

I am an agent of light. God **repels** all my enemies. Jesus has won the victory, so I have nothing to fear. I am already victorious right now. I **repel** indifference and lethargy. I take by force the kingdom of heaven, spreading joy, reconciliation, and love everywhere I go.

289:
Employee
October 15

Bible Verses
"Then he said, "Do you understand what I have done to you? You address me as 'Teacher' and 'Master,' and rightly so. That is what I am. So if I, the Master and Teacher, washed your feet, you must now wash each other's feet. I've laid down a pattern for you. What I've done, you do. I'm only pointing out the obvious. A servant is not ranked above his master; an employee doesn't give orders to the employer. If you understand what I'm telling you, act like it—and live a blessed life." John 13:12-17 (MSG)

Word of the Day
Employee – Someone that receives wages for working for someone else. A person for hire. Apprentice.

Quote
"Well trained employees are the lifeblood of any successful business defined by a livable wage, health care, and a pension." Gary Isham

Pam's Perspective
In 1990 I worked as a custodian at my church for one year and then quit. Two years later, Ray Barr, a board member asked me what it would take to get me to come back. I said if my wage was doubled, I got full medical benefits; I could set my hours to work around my massage clients and only work twenty hours a week. I got the job. He told the board that I could do more in twenty hours than the former couldn't do in forty hours. Being a good employee paid off. I worked there for three more years until my massage business was thoroughly established.

Questions
What kind of employee am I? Do I give my employer an honest day's work? What would make me a better employee? What about the best?

Declarations

I am the best **employee** my company has ever seen. Everything I do is unto the Lord, so I do a great job. I am the kind of **employee** that is an asset to my company. I arrive on time and work my full shift.

Everyone knows the lazy **employee** that tries to shirk their work and do as little as possible. I do not back up to my paycheck. I give God and my employer my best while I am here on earth. I get the bonus because I am the **employee** that produces great results.

My co-workers vote for me to be **employee** of the year because they know who goes exceedingly beyond what is expected of them. I have a great working relationship with every **employee**. I am glad to work with **employees** who do their work well while smiling.

I draw boundaries before I know I will have a problem with a negative **employee**. I govern my reactions and choose harmony. I leave no stone unturned when it comes to getting along. I dissolve walls of strife by trying to understand where the **employee** is coming from. I rethink how I feel about people who I disagree with.

I am a respectful **employee** that enjoys being kind. Respect is always being granted to me. I expect people to respond nicely to me and they do. I am the **employee** that is a pleasure to have. The Most High appoints me for fame and glory as I trust in Him.

I am the **employee** who gets promoted for my great ideas. I am not a mindless **employee**, but one with an intuitive mind. I like being the trusted one. I am the industrious **employee.** I am useful as I consider every angle and then speak my mind. My ingenious insights draw out clever people that help me succeed, who are glad to do it. I market my talents shamelessly. I am the **employee** everyone wants.

290:
Boss
October 16

Bible Verses
"If your boss is angry at you, don't quit! A quiet spirit can overcome even great mistakes." Ecclesiastes 10:4 (NLT)

"If your sinful old self is the boss over your mind, it leads to death. But if the Holy Spirit is the boss over your mind, it leads to life and peace." Romans 8:6 (NLV)

Word of the Day
Boss –A leader or administrator. Business owner. An important person.

Quotes
"The only time some people work like a horse is when the boss rides them." Gabriel Heatter

"I do not like a man who thinks he is boss… I do not like a man who thinks he has got authority and that the woman belongs to him-that wants for his wife a slave. I would not have a slave for my wife. I would not want the love of a woman that is not great enough, grand enough, and splendid enough to be free. I will never give to any woman my heart upon whom I afterwards would put chains." R. Ingersoll

Pam's Perspective
Everyone is their own boss whether they work for themselves or someone else. We all work in front of Jesus. We are the boss of ourselves and accountable for the type of work we put out, either good or unsatisfactory.

Questions
Am I the kind of boss who people want to work for? Am I the kind of boss who leads by example? What do my employees say about me?

Declarations

I am my own **boss,** and I set my standards high. No one has to tell me to work hard because everything I do is in dedication to God. God is an awesome **boss**. I can feel His strength and insight guiding my way. When I submit to God as my **boss**, I am in good hands.

My **boss** gives me raises and promotions when they are due. I work in the perfect place, attracting the perfect **boss** to work for. I have control over my work and what kind of work I put out. First-rate quality is what I am about. I delight in honoring my **boss** for all the things he or she does right. I can always find something good.

I am a skillful **boss** who loves what I do. I warrant the best service from the people I **boss**. Being competent and kind comes naturally to me. My exemplary communication skills are second to none. As my employees' communicate to me, I am the **boss** who listens.

I release any wealth-building limitations I could have. I prosper in everything I put my hands too. I choose kind ways to **boss** the people under me. I am right on track for a record-breaking year.

I expand my business this year. My business thrives and is known for its charitable deeds because of the kind of **boss** I am. I do a bang-up job for my customers, and they appreciate my excellent service.

People say I am a great **boss**. I am straightforward and tell the truth with tact. I state what I want clearly and concisely, so there are no misinterpretations. I am a servant **boss** who people love to follow.

Every day I become a nicer, more dependable **boss**. I am a **boss** who has worth, talents, and wisdom. People treat me like a VIP. I am the **boss** who demonstrates the best practices of a disciplined life.

291:
Standard
October 17

Bible Verses
"Until we all reach the unity of faith and knowledge of God's Son. God's goal is for us to become mature adults—to be fully grown, measured by the standard of the fullness of Christ." Ephesians 4:13 (CEB)

"Some of the brothers traveling by have made me very happy by telling me that your life stays clean and true and that you are living by the standards of the Gospel." 3 John 1:3 (TLB)

Word of the Day
Standard – The principles a person lives by. Usual. Common.

Quotes
"Hold yourself responsible for a higher standard than anybody else expects of you. Demand more of yourself than anybody expects of you. Keep your own standard high. Never excuse yourself to yourself. Never pity yourself. Be a hard master to yourself, but lenient to everybody else." Henry Ward Beecher

"The great aim of your life should be to keep your powers up to the highest possible standard, to so conserve your energies, guard your health that you can make every occasion a great occasion." Orison Swett Marden

Pam's Perspective
Optimism is my standard approach to everything, and how I raised myself from being a victim to someone who overcomes and thrives.

Questions
Do I judge people with higher standards than I judge myself? What standards do I set for myself? Can I raise my standards? Will I?

Declarations

I acknowledge myself for the high **standards** I live by. No one tells me what my **standards** are. I am the only one who gets to choose that. I stop struggling and invite peace to stay. It really can be easy when I trust and obey God's leading. I am secure in Christ. Smooth sailing from here on out is the **standard** I use to reach my goals.

My life is fantastic because of my **standard** routine of exercising, eating healthily, and trusting God. I am great at every age, a beautiful gem. I ignore the number of my age and focus on staying healthy. I eat a wide variety of vegetables to broaden my taste buds.

It is **standard** for me to get upgrades when I fly. I can fly first class. Vacations are fun. I love seeing sights and meeting new friends. I have a rich and satisfying life. Miraculous is the **standard** of my life.

My **standard** way of operating is to be flexible and willing to see all sides of every story. I have unprecedented favor with the people I meet. I receive a flash of inspiration to motivate any crowd when I talk about having high **standards**. I easily prove my point.

I am grateful for my work. I remember to say thank you, often. My **standard** of giving expands each year. The more generous I am, the more I have to give. I keep attracting more and more wealth. It is **standard** for me to stay in the presence of highly motivated people.

The Bible is the best **standard** for me to follow. I choose to love God, love my neighbors and love myself. I get more loveable every day. I set an excellent **standard** for people to follow. I am fortunate to have such caring friends. My loving family supports me in numerous ways. It is **standard** for me to receive unexpected gifts in the mail. My **standard** attitude is one of kindness, grace, mercy, and charity.

292:
Great
October 18

Bible Verses
"You have given me your salvation as my shield. Your right hand, O Lord, supports me; your gentleness has made me great." Psalm 18:35 (TLB)

"For you are great and do great miracles. You alone are God." Psalm 86:10 (TLB)

Word of the Day
Great – Ample in volume. Vast. Noteworthy. Praiseworthy.

Quotes
"The great man is the one who does not lose his child's heart." Mencius

"Jesus Christ said great things so simply." Blaise Pascal

"God sees that you are worth a great deal or He would not have paid such an enormous price for you." Rev. Bud Robinson

"Great men and great women have rarely had great fathers and mothers." Benjamin Jowett, M.A.

Pam's Perspective
I believe every person has greatness in them. We are all capable of accomplishing great feats. The only problem is most don't recognize it, including me at times. That is one reason why I wrote this book, to help us realize it. If I can help one other person feel great, then this book is a success. So go out and do great things.

Questions
How great is my God? What great thing can I accomplish today? How great is my dream? Why do I believe great things will come my way?

Declarations

I set the tone for how my day will go, and I say it is going to be a **great** day! I have **great** character. I affirm a **great** vision for myself that is ever unfolding. I am a **great** person serving an infinitely **great** God. I make the most of the time I have and obtain **great** outcomes. I manifest **great** works as I put my whole heart into what I am doing.

The **great** cloud of witnesses are cheering me on to victory. I am surrounded by the benevolence of a **great** and generous God. God has made Himself known to me, and I am eternally grateful. God prepares me for the next **great** victory as I read His word and walk in faith. It all works out beautifully for me in a calm environment.

I have a **great** memory and a sound mind. I understand more today than the day before. It's a snap to attract **great** opportunities because of the **great** thoughts I think. Removing limiting beliefs comes easily to me. I have **great** self-control and find it easy to stay on target.

People around me think that I am **great** because of my humble attitude, warm smile and **great** self-confidence. I draw **great** lifelong friends into my circle, and we enhance each other's lives. I choose to have all the **great** things I desire. I am a **great** treasure to my family.

I am a **great** cook. I naturally pick the healthiest things for my family to eat that provides the **greatest** nutrients. I enjoy being fit. I claim **great** things for myself and my household. I step into more self-love by stretching and toning my beautiful body and boy do I feel **great**!

I broadcast **great** words of wisdom to those who will listen. I am the gift that gets **great** applause as I utter truths from above. I continue to do **greater** works because of who lives within me. Today I intend to live with passion as I take full responsibility for my **great** success.

293:
Contribution
October 19

Bible Verses

"Tell the people of Israel to bring me their sacred offerings. Accept the contributions from all whose hearts are moved to offer them." Exodus 25:2 (NLT)

"Their contributions were more than enough to complete the whole project." Exodus 36:7 (NLT)

Word of the Day

Contribution – A gift that is given to a charity, person or group. Donation.

Quotes

"Never respect men merely for riches, but rather for their philanthropy; we don't value the sun for its height, but for its use." Unknown Author

"Tis always best to tell the truth. At every crisis, I recommend this as a chief contribution to security in life." Menander

"The noblest contribution which any man can make for the benefit of posterity is that of a good character." John Winthrop

Pam's Perspective

When I think about the people who have made the biggest contribution to my life, it is the people who did little things like give an encouraging word or doing a kind deed. We can all be a contribution to someone.

Questions

Am I a contribution to my family? Am I a contribution to my community? Who is a contribution to me? What has been my biggest contribution to the world so far? What contribution will I make today?

Declarations

I love being a **contribution** to the people around me. I **contribute** what I have and do not worry about what I have no control over. Helping people is fun. I position myself to be able to serve others.

I can talk myself into being a **contribution** to people who have different beliefs than I. We are all human. It is wonderful to watch people's hard shells melt away as my soothing words are a **contribution**. I am comfortable being a **contribution**.

I am a **contribution** to myself by the way I eat, sleep and exercise. I love eating raw food. I spread awareness about the benefits of clean eating and the **contribution** that it makes to my health.

By **contributing** abundantly, I strike it rich in the goldmine of my heart. As I lovingly **contribute** to my family, I feel greatly rewarded. I am not motivated by anything external. My motivation comes from within. Being a **contribution** brings me joy and a sense of purpose.

I like to study and figure things out. I like educating myself on the things that motivate me the most. I live on my own terms and **contribute** to whom I choose. My clear goals remind me to keep pushing on. I work through difficulties while being a **contribution**.

I am a valuable **contributor** to the people I work with. I encourage my teammates to focus on solutions. I notice people who do excellent work and remember to thank them for their **contribution**.

I train myself to act immediately and stop questioning myself. I have more than enough brains to do a great job. My positive **contribution** to the world speaks for itself. I leave the world better than I found it. My **contribution** leaves a legacy for future generations to enjoy.

294:
Demand
October 20

Bible Verses
"If the military demand that you carry their gear for a mile, carry it two."
Matthew 5:41 (TLB)

"I demand that you love each other as much as I love you." John 15:12
(TLB)

Word of the Day
Demand – To address someone from an authoritative position. To
entreat zealously. To assume that you are justified to request a thing.

Quotes
*"How absurd men are! They never use the liberties they have, they demand
those they do not have. They have freedom of thought, they demand freedom
of speech."* Soren Kierkegaard

*"The universe doesn't give you what you want in your mind; it gives you
what you demand with your actions. In essence, you don't get what you
WANT, you get what you ARE."* Steve Maraboli

*"When desperate ills demand a speedy cure, distrust is cowardice, and
prudence folly."* Dr. Samuel Johnson

*"There is a demand in these days for men who can make wrong conduct
appear right."* Terence

Questions
Have I ever demanded my rights while not giving others theirs? What
type of demands do I place on my family, friends, co-workers or
employees? Why do I demand more from myself than others?

Declarations

I **demand** that I have a daily dose of laughter and fun. I deserve to enjoy my life, so I do. I nurture myself with the time I set aside for relaxation and reflection. By **demanding** playtime, I get more done.

I re-energize my life with happy moments that **demand** participation. I play the game of life and win big. I schedule time off and regular vacations. God **demands** we rest regularly.

God listens to my **demands** and answers my prayers. I freely give my heart to God because that is what He **demands**. I am rewarded with peace, love, and eternal assurance. Love **demands** trust. I serve a compassionate God. I can **demand** a breakthrough right now.

I **demand** more from myself than from anyone else and more than I thought I was capable of giving. I proactively work on my mind to increase my knowledge and understanding. I can focus on **demand. I** make great use of my public library. I **demand** excellence from myself. I like believing in myself and making a difference.

I use self-control over my spending, so I am not overburdened by the **demands** of debt. I choose wisely. I do my research and buy a home in my budget. I **demand** of myself to save for the future and invest wisely. I establish an emergency fund, so I am not caught off guard when they arise. I make sure my insurance covers my needs.

I **demand** myself to dream big. I **demand** myself to keep a positive attitude, so I never let discouragement get me down. I desire to become the best person I possibly can be. My profitability rises as I increase my skills. I am in high **demand** with an overflow of referrals. I view everyone as equals and **demand** fairness and honesty. Because I **demand** accountability, I earn respect.

295:
Afraid
October 21

Bible Verses
"Because I was afraid of something awful, and it arrived; what I dreaded came to me." Job 3:25 (CEB)

"Overhearing what they said, Jesus told him, 'don't be afraid; just believe.'" Mark 5:36 (NIV)

Word of the Day
Afraid – Anxious about the future. Cowardly or timid. Fearful.

Quotes
"God is not afraid of your questions or complaints." Pam Malow-Isham

"Resolved, never to do anything which I should be afraid to do if it were the last hour of my life." Jonathan Edwards

"He will never have true friends who is afraid of making enemies." W. Hazlitt

Pam's Perspective
I was always afraid of heights. I never climbed trees as a kid. I would stand on a chair and get dizzy. When I turned thirty, I decided I was tired of living afraid and decided to start challenging myself. I took up downhill skiing. I remember the first time I went half-way up the bunny hill, and that was high enough for me. I almost hyperventilated when I got on the chairlift but I survived. Like most of my fears when I face them, they vanish or at least become manageable.

Questions
Am I afraid of what people think? Am I afraid of success? Am I afraid of failure? What am I afraid of? Why? What can I do to overcome fear?

Declarations

I am the person others are **afraid** to be. I know my importance, and I make a difference. I practice being strong, bold and fearless. I stop acting **afraid** and trust God. I act with imagination and flair, getting the life I desire. I am not **afraid** of a little or a lot of hard work.

When I look at all the people who are **afraid** of what is happening in the world, I remember to pray. I have put my confidence in God. I am not **afraid** of circumstances because God is greater than anything that comes. I stay available to all the miracles that God has for me.

I walk tall into any room and am not **afraid** to talk to anyone. People find it easy to converse with me. I like making new friends. I always feel welcome wherever I go because I recognize the greatness in others. I am not **afraid** to ask for advice or a helping hand.

My body heals itself because I have a healthy immune system. I get up and move to break my static energy. Physical activity shifts my mood from being **afraid** to being chipper. I rule my mental state, and I choose not to live **afraid,** but to live confident and assured.

I surrender my body weight to God and release any stuck feelings. I find peace in this present moment. I am not **afraid** to get honest with myself. I get real with my fears and surrender them to God. I can be **afraid,** admit my weaknesses and still move forward with a smile.

I intentionally do things that I am **afraid** of so I can challenge myself again and again. I can think for myself. Instead of being **afraid** of making the wrong decisions and procrastinating, I make decisions fast. I find out soon enough if I was right or not and move on from there. I conquer everything that I am **afraid** of and every fear that comes my way by acting brave. I am victorious and worthwhile.

296:
Daring
October 22

Bible Verse
"My imprisonment has instilled courage in most of our brothers and sisters, so they are trusting God more and have been even more daring as they speak the good news without fear." Philippians 1:14 (VOICE)

Word of the Day
Daring – Adventuresome. A high-spirited person. Valiant. Brave. Having the audacity to act in spite of your fears.

Quotes
"Fear made her bold. Under a show of daring great fear is concealed." Lucan

"The wise and active conquer difficulties by daring to attempt them; sloth and folly shiver and shrink at sight of toil and hazard, and make the impossibility they fear." Nicholas Rowe

Pam's Perspective
My sister-in-law Janet and I decided to be daring and jump out of a perfectly good airplane in August of 1998. We wanted to jump into the new century fearless. We trained all day to do a static line jump and leap out at 3,000 feet, but near the end of the day, they changed us to do a tandem jump at 13,000 feet. We then got to freefall for 10,000 feet at a rate of about 120 miles an hour for about fifty seconds before the parachute opened and we floated down to the earth were we landed ungracefully. Facing one of my greatest fears and surviving was exhilarating! I am glad we did it, and I would recommend everyone to face their fears.

Questions
Am I daring to reach my full potential? Do I see myself as daring? How can I be more daring? What daring act will I perform today?

Declarations

I am **daring** enough to speak the word of God over my life. I **dare** to believe that God will keep His vows to me. I experience an internal shift when I am **daring** enough to rely on God's strength to guide my way. **Daring** victories are mine as I step out in faith.

My choice to do the right thing affects other people. I **dare** to be brave today. I am **daring** to reach all of my career, personal, and spiritual goals. I am prosperous because of my productive activity. I **dare** to release the good, so I accept the best that is on the way.

I love **daring** to act like a healthy person. I love feeling my muscles get stronger and stronger as I work out with weights. I get around other **daring** people who motivate me to keep moving. I **dare** to do what God wants me to do with my life. I am a shining light.

I am **daring** to live my life with ease. Simplicity is my motto. God uses me to bring happiness to my friends. I say yes to God. We are a great team. I like believing God for the impossible and watching it come to a realization. I am **daring** to be courageous. I **dare** to win.

I am **daring** more and more to be like Christ. The more love I show people, the more love is shown to me. **Daring** to take a chance on love pays off with happiness galore. I feel secure in my own skin. I **dare** to improve the atmosphere of the places I inhabit.

I am **daring** to try things that others won't, so I can stay on the leading edge. I have a reputation of integrity and excellence. I **dare** to disrupt conventional thinking by asking lots of great questions. It is fun being a risk-taker and a trailblazer. I am a history maker. I am the kind of person who always goes the extra mile. My **daring** personality inspires people to live life in a courageous way.

297:
Prepare
October 23

Bible Verses

"Prepare your work outside, get everything ready for you in the field; and after that build your house." Proverbs 24:27 (NRSV)

"Therefore prepare your minds for action; discipline yourselves; set all your hope on the grace that Jesus Christ will bring you when he is revealed." 1 Peter 1:13 (NRSV)

Word of the Day

Prepare – To plan, develop or strengthen. To set the stage for success. To anticipate and develop your ideas.

Quotes

"We shall say that whatever we prepare for we shall get." David Starr Jordan

"It is thrifty to prepare today for the wants of tomorrow." Aesop

"If you long for a beautiful character, claim it, assume it, stick to it with all possible tenacity, and you not only prepare the mind to receive it, but you also increase the power of the mind to attract it." Unknown - The Children's Friend

Pam's Perspective

I had to prepare for months before I won my first speech contest. If I had not prepared, I would not have won. I ask myself how I can best prepare for whatever I am facing and then go about doing the work, so I am ready for anything.

Questions

What is the best way for me to prepare for my future? Do I prepare for emergencies? How do I prepare for my day, week, month, and year?

Declarations

I **prepare** for my activities by planning ahead. By doing the steps of writing out my goals and visualizing them coming to pass, I **prepare** for their arrival. I like being ahead of the game, so I always **prepare** for any obstacles. I am a forward thinker who lives **prepared.**

I love to study and **prepare** for whatever my future holds. Reading is fun as I soak up insights. I give myself the gift of confidence by being **prepared**. I have done my homework, and it shows. I stay up on the latest trends and do a bang-up job. I am **prepared** to work my plan without fail. I always deliver my best because I stay **prepared.**

I **prepare** for emergencies before they happen so I am not caught off guard. I fix my appliances as soon as they break. I **prepare** an escape route in case of a fire. I have **prepared** a reserve of cash for accidents. I **prepare** my investments to be diversified and spread around.

I create personal boundaries so I can have the time I need to **prepare**. I reduce stress by taking the time to **prepare** for all meetings. Just because some people do not **prepare** does not give me license to slack off. I am above that. I do what's right even if it is not easy. I am willing to provide added value to every group I am involved with.

I am **prepared** for my next great adventure. I make a habit of learning new things, so I am **prepared** to talk about a variety of subjects. I don't know what boring is because I am fascinated by everything under the sun. I have much knowledge to learn.

People appreciate my gifts as I **prepare** to share them with the world. I decide what I am going to do and I do it, no matter what. I can take little actions toward my goals, and those little actions keep adding up to big wins. I have **prepared** myself for success.

298:
Pretending
October 24

Bible Verses
"Love should be shown without pretending. Hate evil, and hold on to what is good." Romans 12:9 (CEB)

"They will go on pretending to be devoted to God, but they will refuse to let that "devotion" change the way they live. Stay away from these people!" 2 Timothy 3:5 (ERV)

Word of the Day
Pretending – Playing a role. Imagining. Concealing the truth. Bluffing.

Quotes
"There's a cost for everything. There's no free lunch. Every benefit has a corresponding cost or something you must give up. There's a price to acknowledging that you have choices (as there are different consequences for pretending that you don't.)" Brian Klemmer

"We ought to slip over many thoughts that pass through our minds, and pretend not to see them." Marquise De Sevigne

Pam's Perspective
I was in the Miss Flint Beauty Pageant in nineteen eighty-three and the following year the Miss Michigan Beauty Pageant. I pretended like I was confident. I was scared to death, but pretending helped give me the nerve to walk across the stage and strut my stuff. I didn't win, but they were great experiences.

Questions
What have I been pretending about? What has it cost me? Why does being real in relationships far outweigh pretending and get better results?

Declarations

I start my day saying 'Lord work in me today and use me for your good.' I stop **pretending** to be helpless when I am more than capable of managing my own problems. They are just springboards for greater success. **Pretending** that what I say doesn't matter is irresponsible. I am obligated for every word I say or don't say.

I stop **pretending** that eating sugary snacks are not hurting me when I feel unhealthy after I eat them. I know the truth, and I am honest with myself. **Pretending** I like eating fruits and vegetables instead of junk food has had a very positive impact on my health. And it turns out I do like eating healthy foods after all.

I adore **pretending** that all my dreams are coming true. I laugh in the face of challenges **pretending** to be bigger than I can handle. I can manage them all. By taking consistent action in my life, I get things done. I easily control any impulse or negative thought.

I love playing games with children, **pretending** that we can conquer the world. It stimulates our imagination muscles. Plus it is fun and draws us closer together. A win, win for both of us. I **pretend** to be happy, so generous laughter bubbles up as I spread my joy.

Pretending that I am perfect is a waste of time. It feels great to be myself, without **pretending** to have it all together. I am fine being me. God created me in His image to be a light and share His love. God loves me enough to die for me, so I don't **pretend** to be God.

God is in a good mood towards me today. I like being real with God. It does me no good to **pretend** to my Creator. It is reassuring to know that wherever I go, God goes with me. Talk about a sense of security. I **pretend** to be fearless as I walk with courage today.

299:
Accountability
October 25

Bible Verses
"I can guarantee this truth: The people living now will be held accountable for all these things." Matthew 23:36 (GW)

"For whoever keeps the whole law but fails in one point has become accountable for all of it." James 2:10 (ESV)

Word of the Day
Accountability – A person who takes full responsibility for their actions. Answering to another person or higher power.

Quotes
"A body of men holding themselves accountable to nobody ought not to be trusted by anybody." Thomas Paine

"If you don't hold yourself 100% accountable for every thought you think, word you speak and action you take, you are living in denial and playing the blame or victim game." Pam Malow-Isham

"Some favorite expressions of small children: "It's not my fault... They made me do it... I forgot." Some favorite expressions of adults: "It's not my job... No one told me... It couldn't be helped." True freedom begins and ends with personal accountability." Dan Zadra

"We shall be held accountable not only for what we do but also for what we do not do." Rev. Milford H. Lyon

Questions
How high do I value accountability? What does accountability look like to me? Who will I choose to be my accountability partner?

Declarations

I alone am **accountable** for my life. I hold myself to a higher standard. I know anything I refuse to deal with will continue to happen, so I choose to handle things right away. **Accountability** for my actions keeps me honorable. I set a good example to follow.

I am **accountable** for my life and enjoy getting things done in a timely manner. By publicly stating my goals, I motivate myself to follow through. I bring my goals out in the open for the world to see because I am **accountable** for my words. I am specific and concise.

We are all connected and can be a contribution to each other by holding each other **accountable**. One way I motivate myself is to have someone I am **accountable** to for my actions, either in person, over the phone, by text, or email. I set deadlines and timelines.

I frequently evaluate my work. I attract people that are reliable who believe in **accountability**. We are committed to being authentic and are determined to be **accountable** for all the actions we take or don't take. I elevate my self-esteem by being **accountable**.

I am happy because I do the things that keep me healthy. My health coach maintains my **accountability** to living well. I stay in top shape; even if it is just to do a couple extra squats or leg lifts while doing dishes, arm circles while watching TV or run up the stairs one more time. I easily make movement a part of my daily life.

I choose to do the right thing. By being **accountable,** I inspire others to take charge of their lives. I am brave and **accountable**. I create a lifestyle of **accountability** that improves the decisions I make. I ask my teammates to hold me **accountable** and not give up on me. I have **accountability** partners to me keep me focused on my goals.

300:
Treachery
October 26

Bible Verses
"You destroy those who tell lies; the Lord abhors a man of bloodshed and treachery." Psalm 5:6 (HCSB)

"For let him who wants to enjoy life and see good days [good—whether apparent or not] keep his tongue free from evil and his lips from guile (treachery, deceit)." 1 Peter 3:10 (AMP)

Word of the Day
Treachery – Dishonesty. Scams. A traitor who acts like a friend.

Quotes
"It is not possible to sound a lasting power upon injustice, perjury, and treachery." Demosthenes

"Tricks and treachery are the practice of fools, that don't have brains enough to be honest." Benjamin Franklin

Pam's Perspective
Treachery is a part of life. I had the treachery of watching my best friend date my boyfriend. Then my first true love was extremely jealous. I found him cheating, but he wanted to put his guilt on me. A few years later I had a fiancé who I found out was already married and had five kids! I learned to select better friends, never date anyone who was jealous or secretive, and to pick myself up and try again.

Questions
Have I ever been involved in treachery? If so, did I make restitution? What has been my response when treachery has happened to me? Do I hold a grudge or let it go? Why is my choice of friends so important?

Declarations

I have faith to trust the people around me until proven otherwise. The **treachery** of spying on people is not how I operate. I focus on the work I have to do and allow others to do their work. If needed, I distance myself from people who are bent on **treachery** and evil.

When the heartbreak of **treachery** happens in my life, I talk to my loving heavenly Father. I walk in forgiveness and pray for peace. I allow no root of bitterness to germinate in my spirit. I realize this is another opportunity for growth. I easily overcome every **treachery** and past hurt by turning it over to God. I choose to walk in love.

When I look at superstars who fall to **treachery** and scandal in the media, I remember, I could be **treacherous** except for God's grace. I have no time for gossip. I am willing to be guided by His Spirit and molded into His likeness. I tap into positive energy and stay there.

I am tactful when it comes to giving instructions to my children, so they don't rebel and turn to **treachery**. I am glad for the exceptional communication we now have. I daily pray for them that they would be happy, peaceful, trustworthy, loyal, satisfied and very successful.

I make sure I take care of myself and own up to my responsibilities. I set loving boundaries to keep myself away from the **treachery** of overeating. I manage to keep my weight off by being true to myself. I do something today to produce the results I want in the future.

I evaluate the effectiveness of my self-talk. Am I being **treacherous** to myself or edifying myself? I realize the consequence of **treachery** of talking down to myself is a poor self-image. I forgive myself for negative thinking. I continue to empower myself by remembering all my great qualities and abilities. I get better looking each day.

301:
Single
October 27

Bible Verses
"The light of the body is the eye: if therefore thine eye be single, thy whole body shall be full of light." Matthew 6:22 (KJV)

"Who of you by worrying can add a single hour to your life?" Luke 12:25 (NIV)

Word of the Day
Single – A person that is alone and not married. Separate from the whole group. A specific piece. Distinguished apart.

Quotes
"The devil has not armies enough at his command to capture one single saint of God who dares to trust Him in the face of everything." Rev. J. H. Norris

"Love is composed of a single soul inhabiting two bodies." Aristotle

"Every single word we speak radiates either positive or negative energy. What kind of energy are you sending forth?" Pam Malow-Isham

"All the darkness in the world cannot extinguish the light of a single candle." St. Francis of Assisi

Pam's Perspective
A single grain of sand in my shoes can cause a blister. A single negative thought dwelt upon can cause fear, anger and harmful actions to yourself or others.

Questions
Do I have a single purpose in life? What single thing can I do to enhance my life? Do I single out positive traits and enhance them? If I had a singleness of purpose, what could I get done this week, month, or year?

Declarations

I have a **single**-minded focus on what I want and what I have to do to get it. Every **single** thing I do matters. I do more than I say I am going to do, just because that is who I am. I pay attention to every **single** detail. I take nothing for granted for all things are precious.

I make my life festive and fun as I celebrate the fact that not a **single** thing can keep God's great love from benefiting me. The Holy Spirit comes through for me every **single** time. I feel energized from above and **singled** out for blessings. I am thankful for every **single** thing.

I sustain a still mind with **singleness** of purpose to love God and share His love. I make every **single** action I take count. I create a wonderful life of meaning. I could believe every **single** report of all the miracles and wonders around the world that God is performing. He is still in the miracle-working business for my family and me.

No matter if I am **single** or married, I choose to be happy. No **single** person completes me. I am complete in God. I alone create my joy or misery. I **single** out every emotion and decide if it can stay or go. I am the master of my emotions at all times and in all circumstances.

I get back up every **single** time I fall down. I know God is faithful, so when I feel defeated and the world seems like it is caving in on me, I step forward and praise God whom my help comes from. My sure-fire way to cheer myself up is to praise God every **single** time.

I am familiar with the Word of God. Every **single** word encourages me to keep the faith. Every **single** day I grow in my ability to persist. I **single**-handedly choose to carry out deliberate acts of service. I am a social person that likes to **single** out kindness and generosity. God has **singled** me out for glory and given me permission to succeed.

302:
Both
October 28

Bible Verses

"He will bless them that fear the Lord, both small and great." Psalm 115:13 (KJV)

"Does a spring of water bubble out with both fresh water and bitter water?" James 3:11 (NLT)

Word of the Day

Both – Having this and that. Not having to choose between two items.

Quotes

"A closely related reason for not operating from a place of responsibility is held by many Christians. I see this because I'm a born-again Christian. Their paradigm of either/ or encompasses the idea that either I am responsible or God is. That "box" means that if I'm going to be responsible, I must deny that God is all-powerful. This reasoning sounds humanistic, so a fundamentalist believer would reject it. Or if I let God be all-powerful, then I'm the victim because it's "God's will." Unfortunately, this is where many Christians are. They blame the devil or God, so they don't have to be responsible. In my humble opinion, this is hogwash. God is all-powerful, and we are responsible. It's not either/or; it's both." Brian Klemmer

"We can worship our past or change the future, but not both." Richard Gaylord Briley

Pam's Perspective

I am both a sinner and a saint at the same time. God created me this way. He knows I will mess up and still sees me as a saint. He loves both sides of me.

Questions

Do I use both sides of my brain? Do look at both sides of every story?

Declarations

I feel **both** safe and supported. I feel the strength in **both** my legs getting stronger, the more I use them. I love my body. I ensure that I get **both** the exercise and the rest I need to feel good. I eat **both** fruits and vegetables. I value **both** consistency and persistence.

I have **both** the courage and ability to succeed in life. I spend **both** my time and money on great causes. There is always enough. I am rich. I am **both** a courteous driver and a law-abiding citizen. I like getting **both** an idea off the ground and turning a business around.

Both the love and correction from my parents were beneficial. I practice having good manners. I say **both** please and thank you. I like to share. I love to help **both** the elderly and the young. **Both** young and old are fun to be around and learn from.

I am **both** wise in some areas of my life and naive in others. I practice **both** listening and responding. I stay in peace. **Both** sides of the story are worth paying attention to before making a decision. I go outside and enjoy **both** the sunshine and the rain.

I send **both** handwritten birthday cards and thank you notes. People enjoy the personal touch. I maintain a practice of **both** visioning and gratitude. I am **both** enthusiastic and full of energy. I ask **both** what I can do to help, and how may I be of service.

I am here **both** to please God and be pleased by God. I enjoy **both** the material and spiritual worlds. I stay in balance in **both**. I **both** believe and pray for miracles. I have been known to get mad and glad, **both** in the same hour. I **both** forgive and release hurts. I attract **both** favor and aid sent my way. I am **both** a saint and a sinner, a leader, and a servant, as I celebrate the dichotomy of life.

303:
Whole
October 29

Bible Verses
"The whole city celebrates a good man's success—and also the godless man's death." Proverbs 11:10 (TLB)

"And how does a man benefit if he gains the whole world and loses his soul in the process?" Mark 8:36 (TLB)

Word of the Day
Whole – Perfect the way something is. All inclusive. In one piece. Absolute. Healthy on all levels, not sickly or weak. Comprehensive.

Quotes
"God created us whole. Unfortunately, a lot of us don't realize we are created in His image and not in the image of a down-and-outer. Allow the Holy Spirit to fill your whole mind with how God sees you." Pam Malow-Isham

"A woman should be like a single flower, not a whole bouquet." Anna Held

"An early-morning walk is a blessing for the whole day." Henry David Thoreau

"Sunday clears away the rust of the whole week." Joseph Addison

"Do your work with your whole heart, and you will succeed – there's so little competition." Elbert Hubbard

Questions
Do I sit out the whole song, or do I get up and dance? Why is it worth looking at the whole picture before coming to conclusions? Do I take care of my whole being; body, mind, and spirit? If not, why not?

Declarations

The **whole** of my life is a blessing to others. I appreciate the person I am as I continue to grow into someone even better. I am **whole** and complete just the way I am. I am exactly who I have constructed myself to be. I say sweet things to myself, my **whole** life through.

I have embraced God as my source, so I am **whole**. All my needs are met. I change my **whole** job around by being grateful. I practice my religion where ever I go. God is eager to work with me for the common good of all. I show the **whole** world the love of Christ.

I unleash the **whole** of my greatness and become the person I was created to be. I follow my passion **wholeheartedly**. I use my **whole** mind to think well, examine my assumptions and what I believe.

I stop, look at the **whole** picture, and appreciate everything I have accomplished so far. I embrace the **whole** of my life, both the good and the bad. I learn from both. I take advantage of the naughty and nice parts of me. Denying I have faults would only keep me separate from my **whole** self. I stay balanced. I can be **whole** and not perfect.

I have the discipline to focus my **whole** attention on someone that is talking. I try to step into the other person's shoes so I can experience their **whole** thought process. I use my **whole** energy to get to know them. I do this out of love and respect to show I care. I like hanging out with **whole**, authentic people because we challenge each other.

The **whole** Godhead, Father, Son, and Holy Spirit are working in my favor. I **wholly** devote myself to being loved by the Trinity. I do the things that are in my heart to do. My **whole** life is perfect, just the way it is and so am I. I am valuable, **whole** and respectable. I choose to be happy and productive throughout my **whole** life.

304:
Part
October 30

Bible Verses
"You made all the delicate, inner parts of my body and knit them together in my mother's womb." Psalm 139:13 (TLB)

"Honor the Lord with your wealth and with the first and best part of all your income." Proverbs 3:9 (GW)

Word of the Day
Part – An individual ingredient of a particular thing. A separate item that is a segment of a whole piece. Partial.

Quotes
"But even the Word of God does not build faith within us unless it becomes part of our spiritual person. There have been men who quoted the Bible and lived like the devil. It's not how much you know about the Bible, but how much of God's Word becomes a part of you." Lester Sumrall

"If you don't do your part, don't blame God." Billy Sunday

"No society can surely be flourishing and happy, of which the far greater part of the members are poor and miserable." Adam Smith

"Each of God's saints is sent into the world to prove some part of the divine character." Spurgeon

"We create the greater part of our miseries if we are honest." Pam Malow-Isham

Questions
How many parts have I divided my life into? Is there any part that I have neglected? What can I do to balance all the parts of my life?

Declarations

I manifest every particular **part** of my dreams. I bring out the **part** of me that is the little child and play with wild abandon. I enjoy every single **part** of my life no matter what is going on. Every **part** of my body is healthy and working perfectly. I smell nice and look clean. I invest **part** of my day in prayer, **part** in exercise, **part** in meditation, **part** in reading and study, **part** at work, **part** in play, and **part** in sleep. I allow God's all-consuming love to fill every **part** of my life.

I take **part** in designing my multi-faceted life. I work on the **part** of me that is needing a boost. It is OK to see a therapist for the **part** of me that I feel is out of control. Asking for help is a smart thing to do. I accept every **part** of me. Every **part** of me is wonderfully made.

I have the foresight to learn about every **part** of my investments. I save **part** of what I earn. I always gain by living openhanded. I am aware of the **part** of me that wants to give, the **part** that wants to save and the **part** that wants to keep it all to myself. There is symmetry in how I live as I put all **parts** of my life on God's altar.

When I start a project, I finish every single **part**. I go to town on the **part** of me that wants to procrastinate and give it a swift kick. I easily manage the **parts** of me that are lazy. The **part** of me that wants to be the boss, I give the responsibility to. The **part** of me that wants to be the employee, I give the repetitive things too. I am happy with both **parts** of my character and give them both time.

I go from glory to glory as I move through each **part** of my life. I have the courage to do my **part** to improve my community. I take **part** in helping out. I am **part** of a thriving group of people who support and comfort each other during good and bad times. I do my **part** in keeping the environment clean, beautiful, and protected.

305:
Aimless
October 31

Bible Verses
"God's Message: Cursed is the strong one who depends on mere humans, who thinks he can make it on muscle alone and sets God aside as dead weight. He's like a tumbleweed on the prairie, out of touch with the good earth. He lives rootless and aimless in a land where nothing grows." Jeremiah 17:5-6 (MSG)

Word of the Day
Aimless – Not having a destination in mind. Flighty. Indecisive. Having no thought. Undirected.

Quotes
"The hand of God never tires, nor are its movements aimless. It makes all things subservient to its designs, and, at every turn, disappoints the calculations of man, causing the most insignificant events to expand to the mightiest consequences, while those that have the appearance of mountains vanish into nothing." John Lanahan

"Aimlessly hoping never accomplished anything. If you want your dreams to come true, you must visualize them, be excited about them, work for them and don't give up until you have realized them. The journey is needed for true enjoyment and satisfaction in life." Pam Malow-Isham

"The true adventurer goes forth aimless and uncalculating to meet and greet unknown fate." O. Henry

Questions
"Where are you going? Where does your path lead? You can never know the future, yet wandering aimlessly is unlikely to be the source of a fulfilling life." Jonathan Lockwood Huie

Declarations

I begin each morning with a specific purpose in mind of what I want to get done, so I do not spend my day **aimlessly**. One of the first things I do is smile and drink a large glass of water. I **aimlessly** stretch and wake up my muscles. I will enjoy this beautiful day.

Sometimes I **aimlessly** pick a place in God's word, and He speaks to me. I am never **aimless** about my spiritual practice but set aside a specific allotment of time, so I can hear the new thing God is telling me. As I spend time on my devotions, I get a download of wisdom.

The seemingly **aimless** jobs like doing the dishes and cleaning my house are easy and delightful. I am thankful for beautiful dishes to eat on, a chair and a table to eat at and a safe place to live. **Aimlessly** going around my home and being thankful improves my mood. I am thankful I am sheltered from the elements and my needs are met.

While I am on a plateau, I do not feel **aimless** because that can be the time of greatest growth. The ups and downs in life, although they may seem **aimless** at the time, provide me the ability to learn from the opposition. I move forward with resolve to enjoy my life.

Doing acts of kindness in an **aimless** fashion is always acceptable. I am open to the many synchronicities of good coming my way. I go forth with peace and happiness today spreading my joy. I can have an outrageously great time during troubled times, no matter what.

I am very diligent. I am not **aimless** when it comes to fulfilling my dreams but take continuous focused action to achieve them. Money flows easily to me because of the value I provide. I have specific plans, so I don't wander around **aimless**. I am responsible for every solitary part of my life. Being **aimless** is not an option.

306:
Aim
November 1

Bible Verses
"So let us then definitely aim for and eagerly pursue what makes for harmony and for mutual up building (edification and development) of one another." Romans 14:19 (AMP)

"For we take thought beforehand and aim to be honest and absolutely above suspicion, not only in the sight of the Lord but also in the sight of men." 2 Corinthians 8:21 (AMP)

Word of the Day
Aim – To focus on a target. To move in a certain direction. To concentrate your energies on a specific purpose.

Quotes
"If the highest aim of a captain were to preserve his ship, he would keep it in port forever." Thomas Aquinas

"We aim above the mark to hit the mark." Ralph Waldo Emerson

"The true philosopher's aim must ever be, fit audience let me find, though few." Augustus William Hare

"The aim of argument, or of discussion, should not be victory, but progress." Joseph Joubert

"Miracles happen when your aim is love." Pam Malow-Isham

Questions
What do I aim to accomplish? Do I aim to get my point across and that is it, or am I open to seeing the other person's point of view?

Declarations

I allow God to mold me into the person I am ordained to be. Even my subtlest actions **aim** to make a large difference in the long run. I **aim** to be a healing force in my community, so I encourage everyone I meet. I allow my passions to come out. I **aim** to be like my heroes.

I **aim** at eradicating my thinking of negative thoughts, so I saturate my mind with what is pleasant and of a good report. I am willing to make the changes I need in order to heal myself from any disorder. Confessing the positive over my life **aims** me in the right direction. It brightens my day and gives me some great things to ponder on.

I **aim** high and surpass my expectations. I fly into difficulties with ease as I **aim** to accomplish my goals. Because I have taken measurable steps to reach my goals, my **aim** is right on the mark. By holding myself accountable, I **aim** to assure my success.

My **aim** for being close to God pays me with His presence, joy, strength, and peace. God **aims** for me to prosper and be healthy, so I **aim** to eat healthily and manage my finances wisely. I invent healthy outlets for my frustrations, hurts, and trials that **aim** at well-being. I love eating healthy food while spending time outside in nature.

My **aim** is always to do well and show kindness to everyone I meet. When I see injustices in the world, I **aim** to help. I go over the top in my giving, **aiming** to be a blessing. I put my money into action.

I **aim** to treat myself with loving kindness today. I take the day off and just relax. I make a choice today to write in my gratitude journal and reflect on my many blessings. I buy myself some flowers. I soak in a hot tub and allow all my stress and tension to melt away. I use essential oils. I **aim** for bliss. I hit with accuracy what I **aim** for.

307:
Messenger
November 2

Bible Verses

"A wicked messenger falls into trouble, but a trustworthy courier brings healing." Proverbs 13:17 (HCSB)

"Very truly, I tell you, servants are not greater than their master, nor are messengers greater than the one who sent them." John 13:16 (NRSV)

Word of the Day

Messenger – A courier or transporter. A person who reports news or info.

Quotes

"Not only must the message be correctly delivered, but the messenger himself must be such as to recommend it to acceptance. If there must be 'truth of doctrine,' there must also be 'innocency of life.'" Joseph Barber Lightfoot

"The messenger may come in many forms; be alert." Carol Woods

"A babe in the house is a well-spring of pleasure, a messenger of peace and love, a resting place for innocence on earth, a link between angels and men." Martin Farquhar Tupper

Pam's Perspective

Pets are God's little love messengers. They are never cruel, always happy to see you, accepting, and fun to be around. Our world would be a happier place if we took on their loving qualities and greeted everyone with wags and kisses.

Questions

What type of messenger am I going to be today? Am I open to messengers who look or act differently than I? Will I listen to their message?

Declarations

I am a **messenger** of peace and tranquility. Harmony flows into a room when I walk in. Affirmations are my first thoughts. I enjoy all the opportunities I have to serve and be a **messenger** of hope. I share the **message** of peace and love as I travel around the world.

Being a **messenger** of health is rewarding. Encouraging people to eat nourishing foods and exercise often is a recipe for wholeness. I am a delicious dish serving up the **message** of wisdom and love.

I am a heart-centered **messenger** offering great value in everything I do. I am far better than I realize. I creatively think outside the box. I fan the fire of curiosity as I always seek to learn something new. I can be a **messenger** of invention as I spark creativity and insights.

I am the perfect **messenger** to be a voice in my community for good, even if it is just to one other person. My neighbors love me. Every culture adds value to the world. My welcoming **message** finds every race beautiful to look at and a blessing to be around. I have a noble **message** that shares the mercy and goodness of God.

I never let someone distract me from hearing a **message** from God. I love being led by the Holy Spirit. I know His voice and feel His presence. I have extra love to share. I am God's **messenger** here on earth, so I share good news everywhere I go. Being a **messenger** of light, I illuminate people with the shining truth of God's love.

I am a **messenger** of prosperity. I honor myself for walking against the grain and going for my dreams, living in the top one percent. I give from a very pure heart. I like to celebrate my life of abundance. God has a vested interest in me and loves to see me succeed. My **message** is abundance, grace, peace, hope, tolerance, and joy.

308:
Authority
November 3

Bible Verses

"But so that you may know that the Son of Man has authority on earth to forgive sins" then He said to the paralytic, "Get up, pick up your bed and go home." Matthew 9:6 (NASB)

"These are the miraculous signs that will accompany believers: Thy will use the power and authority of my name to force demons out of people. They will speak new languages. They will pick up snakes, and if they drink any deadly poison, it will not hurt them. They will place their hands on the sick and cure them." Mark 16:17-18 (GW)

Word of the Day

Authority – The person in a leadership position. A judge or person of influence. The one with the clout to make decisions. Divine right.

Quotes

"Obedience to lawful authority is the foundation of manly character." Robert E. Lee

"When we consistently suppress and distrust our intuitive knowingness, looking instead for authority, validation, and approval from others, we give our personal power away." Shakti Gawain

"Jesus gave us the authority to use His Name and live as victors, not defeated ants. Believe in that name and be set free. Recognize that we are authorized to walk in divine authority and watch the miraculous happen." Pam Malow-Isham

Questions

How do I relate to authority? Do I ever get defensive if I disagree with the authority of a boss or a leader? Do I follow the authority of God?

Declarations

I install an **authoritarian** mindset and steady resolve to do what is right. I lead myself, so I can earn the **authority** to lead others. Yes, I am human and fallible. I apply controls to restrain myself from me. I adhere to **authority** as I value the laws of the land and obey them.

I absolutely believe that I can be the trusted **authority** and have the right to claim it. I am unlimited. Because I am a person of **authority**, I guard my heart, head, and ego. I humbly serve the people under or over my **authority**. I am the **authority** figure that people seek out.

I have great colleges that put their faith in my **authority**. I revolutionize our company culture with creativity. Using my **authority** to bring about leadership development in my office pays off with employee success. We work together well as a team.

I pray for the **authority** figures of my country, regardless if they are the ones I voted for. God is still on the throne and whoever is in office is under His **authority**. I remember that this too shall pass. **Authority** figures come and go, so there is no need to stress out.

I keep gratitude as the cornerstone of my life. I gladly submit to the **authority** of God. God has given me **authority** over sickness in my body, and I command it to leave. I have been given **authority** to speak God's word and get results. I walk in divine health as I allow God to permeate every cell of my body making it whole. God's word is life changing, and His promises are not subject to how I feel.

My **authority** on inspiring people is infamous. I know **authority** when I see it, and I follow the rules. I have the **authority** to live in peace during troubled times because I trust God. When I walk into a room, I have the **authority** to make a positive difference, and I do.

309:
Ideal
November 4

Bible Verses
"Yes, all have sinned; all fall short of God's glorious ideal;" Romans 3:23 (TLB)

"And above all these [put on] love and enfold yourselves with the bond of perfect-ness [which binds everything together completely in ideal harmony]." Colossians 3:14 (AMP)

Word of the Day
Ideal – The perception of flawlessness. Perfect specimen. Optimal.

Quotes
"For even those who have renounced Christianity and attack it, in their inmost being still follow the Christian ideal, for hitherto neither their subtlety nor the ardour of their hearts has been able to create a higher ideal of man and of virtue than the ideal given by Christ of old." Fyodor Dostoyevsky

"The vision that you glorify in your mind, the ideal that you enthrone in your heart – this you will build your life by, and this you will become." James L. Allen

"Greatness in the arts is only obtained at the cost of a kind of adventure. The conquered ideal is the prize of audacity. He who risks nothing gets nothing. The genius is a hero." Victor Hugo

Pam's Perspective
Jesus Christ was the ideal human and the ideal role model for me to follow.

Questions
What does my ideal day look like? What does my ideal life look like? What does my ideal mate look like? Will I relinquish what is not ideal?

Declarations

I live the **ideal** life that I have designed. I bring color into my world in a variety of ways that are **ideal** for creativity. What is available to me is unlimited. My life is heroic. It is never too late for me to start something new. Today is a glorious day for me to live my **ideal** life.

I show the **ideal** way to respond, by showing mercy and being silent when anger is directed my way. I follow in Christ's footsteps. Even though the future is very seductive, I live in the present, enjoying the now. I participate in every part of my life, faulty and **ideal**.

I believe in my **ideal** future coming together. My life is guided by beliefs I choose. Even if life doesn't turn out **ideal** as I would like, it is still worth living. I try new **ideals** and risk being different. God has put me in the **ideal** family for maximum growth, even if it looks like He made a mistake. I imitate Christ as I serve my flawed family.

I plant a vegetable garden and reap the **ideal** foods that are organic and chemical free. There are many ways for me to lose weight and keep it off. I have the **ideal** plan for doing it. By exercising, eating healthy and drinking lots of water, I have the **ideal** body.

Smiling is the **ideal** way to make friends. I have **ideal** relationships because of the boundaries I set up in the beginning to curtail any prospect of conflict in the future. I know I don't have to say yes to every invitation. I consider doing less or sometimes more. Saying no is **ideal** at times. I am free to be me and do what I believe is **ideal.**

I take the necessary steps to turn my **ideal** plan into a reality. I create ways to make money that are **ideal**. What I share is **ideal** for others. There are numerous ways I can reach my goals, so I consider alternatives that are **ideal**. I get perfect reviews that are **ideal**.

310:
Real
November 5

Bible Verses
"Keep these thoughts ever in mind; let them penetrate deep within your heart, for they will mean real life for you and radiant health." Proverbs 4:21-22 (TLB)

"Beware! Don't always be wishing for what you don't have. For real life and real living are not related to how rich we are." Luke 12:15 (TLB)

Word of the Day
Real – Absolute proof of existence. Certain; Legitimate. Irrefutable.

Quotes
"'I am the Almighty God' - El-Shaddai, the Father-Mother God. The one thing for which we are all being disciplined to know that God is real. As soon as God becomes real, other people become shadows. Nothing that other saints do or say can ever perturb the one who is built on God." Oswald Chambers

"Desire a thing, pray for a thing, and take what you ask for and it will be made real to you." Rev. F. W. Cox

Pam's Perspective
Being real takes guts. It is much easier to be superficial. To have real friends I have to open myself up to ridicule and the possibility of rejection. I have to admit my flaws and hope the other person accepts me anyway. Only by being vulnerable can I enjoy the pleasures of true friendship. Real people attract real friends.

Questions
What is the best way for me to be real and honor my higher self? Am I aware of my real feelings and how to express them? How do I respond to people who act phony? Am I brave enough to be real?

Declarations

I like being **real** without putting on any pretenses. I am the **real** deal. People are attracted to me because they know a **real** person when they see one. I am easy to get along with. I am wiser because of the valuable lessons I learned from **real** mistakes I made in the past. I get great pleasure and healthy rewards by eating **real** food.

I serve the **real** God who is in charge of the universe, yet has time for me. I am **really** special in God's eyes. I renew my pledge to God and feel **real** peace. God stays true to me, ever loving me back. The Holy Spirit makes no **real** distinction about who He blesses or heals.

I live in the **real** world and accept responsibility for what I create. I give **real** service with a humble heart. I am courageous enough to embrace change. I get **real** and say what is on my mind while being nice about it. I am **realistic** about my strengths and weaknesses. I am methodical in coming up with **real** solutions to every problem.

People feel appreciated and listened to from me being **real**. I walk the walk by doing what I say I am going to do. I acknowledge that I am a very valuable person who thinks **really** great thoughts. I am **really** brilliant. I spark conversations that inspire **real** action.

I am grateful for my **real** friends who don't put on facades or try to be something they are not. My **real** way of working out is going for a walk. I tear off the veil of trying to look good and just be myself. There is nothing I need to hide. What you see is what you get.

I have **real** satisfaction with every facet of my life. I am one of a kind, a **real** sight to behold. My **real** values bless my family, friends, and community. I am always truthful, thoughtful and a **real** winner. I notice all the **real** blessings I have and share them with others.

311:
Ought
November 6

Bible Verses
"Everyone who lives ought to be wise; it is as good as receiving an inheritance." Ecclesiastes 7:11 (GNT)

"For the Holy Spirit will teach you in that very hour and moment what [you] ought to say." Luke 12:12 (AMP)

Word of the Day
Ought – Anxiety about thoughts. Concern over responsibility. An obligation or duty.

Quotes
"Each mind ought sometimes to be diverted that it may return to better thinking." Phaedrus (Plato)

"We ought not to give the fine flour to the devil, and the bran to God." Proverb

"One of the best ways to develop mental repetition is simply to picture the way you ought to behave. See yourself as a winner (not a loser) in everything you do." Dr. Ron Jenson

Pam's Perspective
When my mind starts thinking I ought to do this or that, I stop and realize it could be an old pattern trying to sneak back and bite me. Who am I trying to impress? I don't have to do anything at all. I can choose to do something if I like.

Questions
Do I think about if I ought to be putting this before my eyes? What ought I to focus on? What ought I to think about myself? What ought I to do?

Declarations

I think about happy things in the midst of trials. I know what I
ought to dwell on, so I make a conscious choice to think about
what is exquisite. Throughout my lifetime I **ought** to continue to
grow as a person. I view the complexity of the world from different
angles. I **ought** to give everyone respect and a chance to prove
themselves.

By thinking I **ought** to do something, I cause myself undo suffering
and grief. But if I do what is right in from of me, it is easy, and things
work out. I accomplish more than others, in a shorter amount of
time, because I am efficient. Only I can fulfill the special purpose I
was put here for, so I do what I **ought** to do in order to achieve it.

When I get the thought that I **ought** to call a friend, I pick up
the phone and follow through. I value the friendship we have and
give it the attention I **ought**. I ask provocative questions, and we
stay engaged. People **ought** to be friendly, longsuffering, and able
to get along, so I do what I **ought** to bring unity and grace to all
situations.

I pat myself on the back for doing everything I **ought** to do. I don't
worry about the opinions of other people who think I **ought** to do
this or that. I listen to and follow my heart. God never steers me
where I **ought** not to go. I **ought** to be truly comfortable in my own
skin, so I feel great. I have the freedom to think positive about myself
and how I look. I look fabulous. I like being a winner. God thinks I
ought to be myself, and that is enough to make Him happy.

I live an inspired life. I overcome any prosperity building limitations
and become the wealthy person I **ought** to be. I realize I **ought**
to learn my lessons the first time, so I don't have to repeat them. I
release all that is unnecessary, so I can perfect my success. Today is
the day I choose to break down every barrier that stands in my way.

312:
Vocation
November 7

Bible Verses

"Everyone has his own vocation, in which he has been called; let him keep to it." 1 Corinthians 7:20 (KNOX)

"I therefore, a prisoner in the Lord, beseech you that you walk worthy of the vocation in which you are called." Ephesians 4:1 (DRA)

Word of the Day

Vocation – A job or trade. A career or craft that one does to make a living. The undertaking of a heavenly mission. The desire to fulfill an inclination or longing.

Quotes

"Your real vocation is your life, and work is a part of it. It is a significant part of it - but still just a part. If you don't take charge of this mind-set, you will not succeed authentically. You'll either burn out or fizzle." Dr. Ron Jenson

"We are apt to mistake our vocation by looking out of the way for occasions to exercise great and rare virtues, and by stepping over those ordinary ones which lie directly in the road before us." Hannah More

"The test of a vocation is the love of the drudgery it involves." Logan Pearsall Smith

"The ultimate vocation of every finite, rational being is thus absolute unity, constant identity, perfect harmony with himself." Johann Gottlieb Fichte

Questions

Why does my vocation matter? Am I good at my vocation? Would I be better suited for another vocation? If so, what will I do about it?

Declarations

I am truly blessed and fortunate to have found the **vocation** I love. I say yes to good work. My **vocation** comes easily to me and is a joy to perform. It is a privilege to work hard and perform a needed service.

I am honored and feel secure with the knowledge of my **vocation** that I do a great job. I am passionate about the **vocation** I chose. My coworkers think highly of me. I get along well with the people I work with. I practice patience, persistence, and perseverance.

I ask God to bless my **vocation** and or give me something better. I dedicate my **vocation** to God who in returns endorses me with His approval. God is in the driver's seat of my life. I find mentors who help me further my **vocation**. My high **vocation** is to serve God and share His love. I put meaningful action behind my prayers.

I use what God gives me to honor Him. I am relentless in doing well. My **vocation** of bringing benevolence and a sense of belonging to my group of friends gives us a reason to celebrate. I accept imperfection in others and see their beauty. Uniqueness is common.

I enjoy my **vocation.** I get more progressive every day. I am unreasonable when it comes to tolerating incomplete work. I take pride in my work. I expect the best results in my **vocation**, and I get it. I am the covert force within my successful organization. My **vocation is** rewarded because I share the credit and compliments.

My love of doing well is evident in my **vocation**. Excellence is commonplace in my performance. I am highly compensated for the duties I perform. I am a total game changer who rocks this world. I am worthy of a high wage. My wealth increases daily. I speed up the frequency of the bonuses I get by turning my play into my **vocation**.

313:
Strong
November 8

Bible Verses

"Be strong and of good courage, do not fear or be in dread of them: for it is the Lord your God who goes with you; he will not fail you or forsake you." Deuteronomy 31:6 (RSV)

"Finally, my brethren, be strong in the Lord and in the power of His might." Ephesians 6:10 (NKJV)

Word of the Day

Strong – An able-bodied person full of strength. Athletic and well-built. Mighty in mental capacities and intelligence. Competent and tough.

Quotes

"Who is strong? He that can conquer his bad habits." Benjamin Franklin

"Let anyone get into a quiet state for a few minutes each morning, and then will to be self-possessed and cheerful all through the day. Will to be strong against any besetting weakness, and he will soon be surprised at the new power he has gained." Erastus Whitford Hopkins

"To believe is to be happy; to doubt is to be wretched… To believe is to be strong. Doubt, cramps energy. Belief is power. Only so far as a man believes strongly, mightily, can he act cheerfully, or do anything that is worth the doing." Frederick W. Robertson

"Remember when the judgment is weak the prejudice is strong." Kane O'Hara

Questions

When will I realize how strong I really am? Is my thinking strong enough to combat the negative world? If not, why? Will I make my body strong?

Declarations

I have a **strong** sense of gratitude for everything in my life. I am a **strong** and knowledgeable person. I maintain a **strong** will to make the most of my life. I make an inventory of my dreams, strengths skills, tools, and resources. I use my ingenuity to my advantage.

I am **strong** when I admit my weaknesses and set boundaries for myself accordingly. I am mentally **strong** enough to balance my emotions and think about what is going on. I do the right thing every time. I give serious attention to my **strongest** desires.

I have given my heart to God. I am **strong** with His might and authority. I am unmoved by what people say or do. I serve a **strong** God who is bigger than any problem I could ever have. I act on the call of God on my life. By faith, I live **strong** and face every fear.

I am **strong** enough not to get distracted by the turmoil in the world. I focus on what is happening right in front of me. Because of my **strong** integrity, I have the ability to delay gratification. I **strongly** believe I can have a joyous life. I create my own happiness.

By taking the time to exercise my muscles, I make them **strong**. I use my time wisely. Movement is a part of my daily life. I have a **strong** goal that I am playing for. I play positive tapes in my head to keep my mind **strong**. I have **strong** willpower to stick to a healthy diet. My **strong** body gets **stronger** with every weight I lift. I keep going.

My **strong** mental fortitude is one of my greatest assets. I naturally transform every experience into a breakthrough. I grow **stronger** with every trial and use them as a springboard to greatness. I value my **strong** sense of flexibility. I keep an open mind. I am great. Bravery comes naturally to me. I manifest a happy, fulfilling life.

314:
Sensitive
November 9

Bible Verses
"And I will give them one heart [a new heart] and I will put a new spirit within them; and I will take the stony [unnaturally hardened] heart out of their flesh, and will give them a heart of flesh [sensitive and responsive to the touch of their God]." Ezekiel 11:19 (AMP)

"Be sensitive to each other's needs — don't think yourselves better than others, but make humble people your friends. Don't be conceited." Romans 12:16 (CJB)

Word of the Day
Sensitive – Being keenly aware of one's senses. Emotional or nervous.

Quotes
"Our God is not made of stone. His heart is the most sensitive and tender of all. No act goes unnoticed, no matter how insignificant or small. A cup of cold water is enough to put tears in the eyes of God. God celebrates our feeble expressions of gratitude." Richard J. Foster

"The heart of silver falls ever into the hands of brass. The sensitive herb is eaten as grass by the swine. Fate will have it so." Ouida

Pam's Perspective
I have always been sensitive. I can cry with a thought or by seeing a commercial. Tears just flow. I cry when I am happy or sad. That is just how God created me. I do know that being sensitive to the Holy Spirit produces wisdom.

Questions
How do I react to sensitive people? Do I view a sensitive person as weak? Am I open to being sensitive? Why can I be sensitive and caring?

Declarations

I allow myself to be **sensitive** and be OK with it. My **sensitivity** shows by all I do and say. I feel secure because I am **sensitive** to the Holy Spirit's voice. **Sensitive** children are happy around me and feel safe. I give the **sensitive** grace and mercy I have received to others.

My friends see me as **sensitive** and charitable. I have the ability to be **sensitive** to the hurting, inspiring to the disadvantaged, yet stern to the slacker. I have a powerful conviction that keeps me going.

I am **sensitive** to my body's needs, so I am conscious about what I eat. I know vegetables and herbs are medicines that are beneficial for the cells in my body to heal. I increase my brain power by the foods I eat. I use essential oils to lift my spirits and heal my wounds.

I value my time, so I am s**ensitive** and set limits with whom I share it. My **sensitive** friends are glad I can keep a secret. I give my friends a reassuring glance to encourage them and let them know I care.

I thrive on kindness. I am **sensitive** to impatient people who do not realize how wonderful this very moment is. I am patient in every situation. Everything I do reflects the goodness of God.

My **sensitive** side empathizes with the ones who are hurting. I easily cheer up the people around me and become more **sensitive** to their needs. I honor my tribe by giving and receiving love.

My community loves me. I am **sensitive** to all people groups, stand up for injustice, and believe we are all created equal in the eyes of God. We all have a right to exist. I accept my frailty and love myself completely. I remember my worth. I make use of my **sensitive** side by making my world positive and a better place to live.

315:
Protection
November 10

Bible Verses
"My God is my rock, in whom I find protection. He is my shield, the power that saves me, and my place of safety. He is my refuge, my savior, the one who saves me from violence." 2 Samuel 22:3 (NLT)

"He will cover you with his feathers. He will shelter you with his wings. His faithful promises are your armor and protection." Psalm 91:4 (NLT)

Word of the Day
Protection – Being safeguarded from being hurt. A shelter. Self-defense.

Quotes
"I declare to you that woman must not depend upon the protection of man, but must be taught to protect herself, and there I take my stand." Susan B. Anthony

"The brave alone know how to forgive; valor inspires awe, and promises protection; the height of true valor is to dare to do your duty on all occasions." William Hardcastle Browne

Pam's Perspective
I grew up believing the fairytale that I was a princess, and I needed a prince charming to rescue me, and we would live happily ever after. My prince would be my protection from all harm and would support me in every way. I spent too much time waiting for someone to save me instead of saving myself from the delusion of helplessness. God and my brain is my best protection from any harm.

Questions
What kind of protection do I use to safeguard against negativity? Why would I fear anything if God is my protection?

Declarations

I am safe and secure no matter where I am for God is my **protection** and my security. I pray a **protective** hedge around my family and children. I am thankful that I can place my confidence in God knowing I can call on Him at any time for the ultimate **protection**. I am always in the presence of God. Where I am is holy.

God is mindful of my sorrows and cares for me when I foolishly want to place a wall of **protection** around my heart. God heals and restores my soul. He says 'trust me.' Then God fills the part of my heart that is longing for meaning and purpose. Knowing I am His beloved gives me the **protection** I need to love again and again.

I am thankful for the **protection** of my guardian angels that watch over me and keep me from harm. I am **protected** at night when I fall asleep. I know that I am safe in God's precious arms. I am covered with the **protection** of God's love. I stay **protected** day and night.

My positive mindset is the **protection** I need to stay in a good mood. The light of Christ radiates **protection** opposing the negativity and evil around me. I don't allow life to weigh me down because I have been anointed to bring deliverance and healing to the oppressed.

Continual growth is the best **protection** against boredom. I achieve what I set my mind to. I have bold expectations. Everything I dream about is doable. I predict interesting times that shift in my favor.

God's **protection** over my finances affords me the ability to bless a lot of people. I press into the laws of prosperity, and I am overtaken with abundance. All my bills are paid, and I am debt free. Hard work is the best **protection** against poverty. The little things that I do matter. I receive approval and **protection** from every direction.

316:
Battle
November 11

Bible Verses
"When you fight against your enemies, I will send my great power before you. I will help you defeat all your enemies. The people who are against you will become confused in battle and run away." Exodus 23:27 (ERV)

"When the Philistine came forward to meet David, David ran quickly toward the battle line to meet the Philistine." 1 Samuel 17:48 (AMP)

Word of the Day
Battle –A scrimmage between two sides. To combat someone.

Quotes
"Be kind, for everyone you meet is fighting a harder battle." Ian Maclaren

"In battle, the greatest cowards are in the greatest danger; boldness is the best defense." Sallust

"Never go into battle with your mouth closed. Speak the Word of God." Tamara Taylor

"Courage in danger is half the battle." Plautus

Pam's Perspective
The battle to stay positive in this negative world will only be won with diligence. I remind myself to smile all the time. By being proactive, I keep myself happy.

Questions
Who is my biggest battle against? Do I prepare for my battles with prayer? What battle will I win today? What battle will I concede?

Declarations

I am a champion who prepares before every **battle** with prayer. I jump into the **battlefield** of life with a purpose in my heart, a dream in my head, and a strong spirit of determination to come out on top.

With firm footing, I get ready for **battle** by standing in integrity and peace. I lift up the shield of faith, put on the helmet of salvation, and wield the word of God, which is an indispensable weapon, declaring triumph over my life. Over insurmountable odds, I come out ahead.

I win the **battle** against insecurity by getting proficient in my area of expertise. I focus on building up myself first to be a godly person. I have heavenly sight. I see past the walls of fear, doubt, and unbelief as I **battle** to live a holy life. There is a purpose in going through every trial. God has already won the **battle**.

I pick my **battles** wisely. Since most **battles** are trivial, I keep my distance. I focus on what really matters to me and let others fight their own **battles**. God's mercy is a shelter for me in every **battle**.

In times of **battle**, I receive an abundance of grace. I make distinct choices to forgive those who are mean instead of going to **battle** with them. I forgive so the **battle** of strife, bitterness, and offense will not influence me. God has transformed my attitude. I choose to forsake gossip, so I win the **battle** of spreading rumors. I make mistakes too, so how I behave matters. There is life in my words.

I run toward the **battlefields** with courage in my heart. I believe I am capable, with God's help, to come away victorious from every **battle**. He is renewing my mind with hope. I am the victor over the **battle** of my mind. Because I make positive confessions over my mind, body, and life, I win the **battle** of negativity before it creeps in.

317:
Ahead
November 12

Bible Verses
"Nathan replied to the king, 'Go ahead and do whatever you have in mind, for the Lord is with you.'" 2 Samuel 7:3 (NLT)

"You will succeed in whatever you choose to do, and light will shine on the road ahead of you." Job 22:28 (NLT)

Word of the Day
Ahead – Preceding in order or at the head. In the foreground. Foremost. To lead off or start first.

Quotes
"I leave this rule for others when I'm dead, be always sure you're right - then go ahead!" David Crockett

"All great discoveries are made by men whose feelings run ahead of their thinking's." Charles H. Parkhurst

"The life ahead can only be glorious if you learn to live in total harmony with the Lord." Sathya Sai Baba

"When we are sure that we are on the right road there is no need to plan our journey too far ahead. No need to burden ourselves with doubts and fears as to the obstacles that may bar our progress. We cannot take more than one step at a time." Orison Swett Marden

Questions
How do I get ahead in life? How do I get ahead of my competitors? Have I planned ahead for my retirement? If not, when would be a good time to start? Have I planned ahead for fun? What am I looking ahead to?

Declarations

I am open to the lessons that teach me how to get **ahead**. I run full speed **ahead** to the fulfillment of my goals. I am **ahead** of the game because I listen to God. God knows **ahead** of time what I think, how I will behave and still loves me regardless of my screw ups.

Every time I am kind, it spreads positive energy **ahead**, through the world, and then circles back to me. I take a few minutes each day to try something new. I go **ahead** and lead the way for others to follow.

I save **ahead** of time before I need it. I have a good name that demonstrates my honor **ahead** of me. I get **ahead** financially by first believing I can. I resolve to make sound financial decisions and be honest about my spending and saving habits. I discern now is time to get my act together and take authority over all areas of my life.

As I look **ahead** to where I want to go, I stay focused on my vision. I am enthusiastic about my life. Happiness is with me wherever I go. I plan for exercise **ahead** of eating so I can stay strong and fit. I am comfortable taking care of myself and living life on my own terms.

I speak about the good that is coming my way **ahead** of time. I allow myself to move **ahead** of the norm, rise above the crowd and come out on top. I let all the advantages of being a child of God appear before me now. I am accessible to the good that is **ahead** of me. When I arrive **ahead** of schedule, upgrades are the norm.

I act happy and shine with hope. I live joyfully. I praise God **ahead** of time because just as He has helped me in the past, He will help me again. The victory is mine because God has won the conflict for me **ahead** of time. My blessing is in my obedience and trust. I see the big picture and enjoy all the pleasures of being alive.

318:
Behind
November 13

Bible Verses

"Let go of anger and leave rage behind! Don't get upset-it will only lead to evil." Psalm 37:8 (CEB)

"Love others well, and don't hide behind a mask; love authentically. Despise evil; pursue what is good as if your life depends on it." Romans 12:9 (VOICE)

Word of the Day

Behind – In the back of something. Rearward. Trailing; tail end.

Quotes

"What lies behind us and what lies ahead of us are tiny matters compared to what lives within us." Henry Stanley Haskins

"Every man has a bag hanging before him, in which he puts his neighbor's faults, and another behind him in which he stows his own." William Shakespeare

"When you release the negative stories and experiences that are behind you, it makes room for love to move in. It is as easy as a decision. God is patiently waiting for your reply." Pam Malow-Isham

"Christ with me, Christ before me, Christ behind me, Christ in me, Christ beneath me, Christ above me, Christ on my right, Christ on my left, Christ where I lie, Christ where I sit, Christ where I arise. Christ in the heart of every man who thinks of me, Christ in the mouth of every man who speaks of me, Christ in every eye that sees me, Christ in every ear that hears me." Saint Patrick

Questions

Do I gain anything by looking behind? Do I ask God to get behind my plans? Why is the worst behind me and my best ahead?

Declarations

God works **behind** the scenes orchestrating multiple blessings in my favor. I cast my cares **behind** me now and rely on God to pull me through. There is a miracle **behind** every mishap. I put confusion **behind** me. Today I reap great rewards from former tragedies.

I do not look **behind** me at what used to be. I have a clear vision of what I want to be, do and have. I am in charge of my business. I focus on my priorities and accomplish mighty works. The boss marvels at what I get done. I leave the competition **behind**.

My way of acting is ahead of the norm as I place **behind** me judgment and condemnation. I enjoy walking in liberty. As I leave **behind** the blame game, it opens up vast opportunities to move forward. I get **behind** positive people. Peace flows **behind** me.

I like to recycle, reuse and go green. I treasure this beautiful planet Earth. **Behind** every gardener is a beautiful garden. I scatter compost **behind** the plants and see my flowers flourish. I throw trinkets of kindness around. I love getting **behind** worthy causes.

I get **behind** my friends and give them a hand. I love to play with children. I give the gift of undivided attention. I see clearly with both eyes to notice the person in front of or **behind** me. I see **behind** the mask of hurting people and show them love. There is someone longing to be noticed and treasured **behind** every broken person.

As I think on the Word of God, I leave **behind** useless thoughts. I am in touch with the greatest power in the universe. I stand **behind** what I believe. I am convinced things will go my way. When I speak life into my body, it heals quickly. God gets **behind** me and does the miraculous in my life. I accept an overflow of health and energy.

319:
Former
November 14

Bible Verses

"Do not say, 'Why were the former days better than these?' For it is not from wisdom that you ask this." Ecclesiastes 7:10 (NRSV)

"Remember not the former things, nor consider the things of old. Behold, I am doing a new thing; now it springs forth, do you not perceive it? I will make a way in the wilderness and rivers in the desert." Isaiah 43:18-19 (ESV)

Word of the Day

Former – Something that happened before the present time. Old. Ancient. Once upon a time.

Quotes

"Not to know what has been transacted in former times is to be always a child. If no use is made of the labors of past ages, the world must remain always in the infancy of knowledge." Marcus Tullius Cicero

"One should speak well and act honourably: the one is an excellence of the head, the other of the heart, and both arise from nobility of soul. Words are the shadows of deeds; the former are feminine, the latter masculine. It is more important to be renowned than to convey renown. Speech is easy, action hard. Actions are the stuff of life, words its frippery. Eminent deeds endure, striking words pass away. Actions are the fruit of thought; if this is wise, they are effective." Baltasar Gracian

Questions

What is the best way for me to make the most of my former victories? What is a former gift that I am thankful for? Do I have any former talents that I need to breathe new life into? Do I have a former friend that I need to connect with? What former thing do I need to release?

Declarations

The **former** days are gone, and I am entirely focused on the good in front of me. The time for me to embrace my significance is now. **Former** ailments have reminded me of the importance of taking care of myself. **Former** stumbling blocks have made me wiser.

Former regrets have made me accept responsibility for my actions. **Former** habits and thought patterns that no longer serve me are now released. I break free from **former** hereditary patterns that used to trap me. I start fresh from unlimited possibilities. All things are new and viable. **Former** insecurities are gone as I embrace courage, confidence, and well-being. I am a rare beautiful multi-faceted gem.

Former resentments have taught me the necessity of forgiveness. My kindness proves that the power within me is greater than the power of suspicion. I reject the **former** voice that told me I am not good enough. **Former** disappointments remind me that life is not fair. So what. I listen to the Holy Spirit telling me I am loved.

Former times of being bullied have made me more compassionate and respectful of others feelings. **Former** loneliness is replaced by trustworthy friends. **Former** intolerance is replaced by acceptance. I am thankful that my **former** indifference has turned into gratitude since I noticed how fortunate I am to be alive today.

Former obstacles are unimportant. I am getting better in every area of my life. **Former** hardships have made me stronger. **Former** defeats have improved my perseverance. **Former** handicaps have made me humbler. **Former** failures have made me more resilient. I see what I want as already accomplished. **Former** ambitions are revived as I dream big again. I go within and create the pictures I want to see by designing my intentions to be unstoppable.

320:
Present
November 15

Bible Verses
"Let such people understand that what we say by letter when absent, we will also do when present." 2 Corinthians 10:11 (NRSV)

"Grace to you and peace from God the Father of our Lord Jesus Christ, who gave Himself for our sins to rescue us from this present evil age, according to the will of our God and Father." Galatians 1:3-4 (HCSB)

Word of the Day
Present – This instant. Commencing now. Immediate time; even now.

Quotes
"We should not fret for what is past, nor should we be anxious about the future; men of discernment deal only with the present moment." Chanakya

"Enjoy the present day, trusting very little to the morrow." Horace

"Life is divided into three terms – that which was, which is and which will be. Let us learn from the past to profit by the present, and from the present, to live better in the future." Author Unknown

Pam's Perspective
I remind myself to stay present for I easily get distracted. Multitasking is a waste of my energy. I can only focus on one thing at a time. Being grateful for what I have in the present moment contributes to my overall happiness and well-being.

Questions
Do I fantasize about how I think something should be instead of enjoying the present moment? Why is the present the most important time?

Declarations

I am willing to stay in the **present** moment when I want to wander off. I realize my mind is a powerful tool that I can use for my demise or my betterment. When negative thoughts wander into my brain, I stay **present,** so I can derail them. The world is my servant.

I enjoy this **present** moment no matter what is going on. I focus on loving God, others and myself. To breathe and be alive is a beautiful thing. I am able to receive good things from God right now on this **present** day. An infinite wave of possibilities **presently** arrives to bless me. Everything I touch flourishes. I am filled with contentment as I appreciate this **present** time. Money flows effortlessly to me.

I am the sum total of all my actions. I enjoy myself in the **present** while setting big, fun goals for the future. I am a courageous soul who likes to be bold. I like taking care of the little details in order to elevate my strengths. There is no time like the **present** to get things done. I watch what I say because I get what I profess.

God is **present**, not far off. As I recognize all the gifts in front of me, I become more grateful. This **present** time is the right time to receive my healing inside my body and mind. God is always working in the **present** and loves our communion. I remember to come back to the **present** moment when I start to worry about the future. I put my trust in God and release all fear now. Everything I touch flourishes.

I am filled with contentment as I appreciate this **present** time. I am continually being offered the best opportunities as I enjoy my **present** occupation. I break new ground and outperform my peers. I get to choose what kind of life I will live, so I predestine good favor my way. I receive blessings almost too big to contain in the **present**. Things always work out for my benefit as I live in the **present**.

321:
Shrink
November 16

Bible Verses
"My son, do not despise or shrink from the chastening of the Lord [His correction by punishment or by subjection to suffering or trial]; neither be weary of or impatient about or loathe or abhor His reproof." Proverbs 3:11 (AMP)

"But my righteous one will live by faith. My soul takes no pleasure in anyone who shrinks back. But we are not among those who shrink back and so are lost, but among those who have faith and so are saved." Hebrews 10:38-39 (NRSV)

Word of the Day
Shrink – To diminish in size. To become less than before; shrivel. To deflate in posture or stance.

Quote
"I love the man who can smile in trouble, that can gather strength from distress, and grow brave by reflection. 'Tis the business of little minds to shrink, but he whose heart is firm, and whose conscience approves his conduct, will pursue his principles unto death." Thomas Paine

Pam's Perspective
It is OK for me to shrink some of my responsibilities when I feel exhausted. In nineteen ninety-two I was diagnosed with chronic fatigue syndrome and fibromyalgia. So when I am tired now, I rest without guilt. I have tried every medical and natural remedy I could find. It may seem insignificant, but the thing that has helped me the most is my positive thinking. Just by smiling, I feel better.

Questions
When I am confronted, do I stand up for myself or do I shrink away from confrontation? How does that serve me? Do I shrink from responsibilities?

Declarations

I clean my house with a happy, glorious attitude. I never **shrink** back from work but treat everything as a sacred job and a joy to do. Because I am industrious, I **shrink** from unemployment. My work is holy. When I **shrink** from being self-centered and ask for help, I get it. I run hard after wisdom as an act of love so I can support my family. I **shrink** from ego and go get a job, no matter what.

I get around people who encourage me to be more than I think I am capable of being. I **shrink** away from negative people. I **shrink** back from complaining and comparing other people to myself. I choose to see with happy eyes. God has great things planned ahead for me.

I **shrink** my debt. I invest in my future and give back to others. I live in the land of plenty where poverty **shrinks** and wealth abounds. I am thankful for the abundance. I love being intentional in my generous giving. I am thankful for the responsibility God has given to me. I opt into God's favor by asking for it. I never **shrink** back.

My waist **shrinks** to the perfect size for me as I continue to eat healthily. I am happy and able-bodied as I **shrink** from watching TV and get up and move. I am honest with myself and never **shrink** away from what I need to face. I like being mature. As my limitations **shrink**, my capabilities increase. I get better every day.

I flat out enjoy my life, and I like myself. I put my trust in God, and my fears **shrink** out of sight. As I accentuate what is beneficial, and **shrink** away from anxiety, my life becomes delightful. I have an ongoing relationship with Christ that continues to reinforce how much He loves me. My doubts **shrink** in His presence. My knowledge grows as my ignorance **shrinks**. I **shrink** my ego to give humility a boost. I remain pliable in the hands of a loving God.

322:
Stretch
November 17

Bible Verses
"He asked you to preserve his life, and you granted his request. The days of his life stretch on forever." Psalm 21:4 (NLT)

"I am the one who made the earth and created people to live on it. With my hands I stretched out the heavens. All the stars are at my command." Isaiah 45:12 (NLT)

Word of the Day
Stretch – The lengthening of one's muscles. The expansion of one's mind.

Quotes
"To stretch my hand and touch Him, though he be far away; to raise my eyes and see him through darkness as through day; to lift my voice and call Him – this is to pray!" Samuel W. Duffield

"Everyone has his allotted time upon earth: a brief and irretrievable space is given to all: but it is virtue's work alone to stretch the narrow space by noble deeds." Virgil

Pam's Perspective
God wants us to keep stretching our mind, body, and circle of influence. We were not created as fixed objects but as magnificent beings that can explore and invent. Stretch yourself today to step out of your comfort zone and try something new.

Questions
Do I stretch when I get up or just when I feel sore? Would I benefit if I stretched my body more? What about stretching my mind? Will I? How can I stretch my imagination and give God room to move in me?

Declarations

I love getting up in the morning, taking the time to **stretch**. I increase the blood flow to my muscles as I **stretch**. Because **stretching** is so important to improve the elasticity in my connective tissue, I decide to make it a daily habit. As I elongate my muscles, I become more agile. **Stretching** helps to improve my range of motion, my ability to perform well and become better balanced. I like being adjustable.

I **stretch** my awareness as I exist in a state of awe and wonder that God Almighty, who created heaven and earth, chose me to live in and work through. God **stretches** the time I spend with Him. I am a mountain dissolver as I **stretch** my faith. God's abounding grace **stretches** over me like a shield. I **stretch** my conviction as I dare to believe for the impossible. I am an observer of the miraculous.

As I **stretch** my thinking to look at things through the light of Christ, I enlarge my world. I adapt easily to change. I use my passions for good. I continue to **stretch** my goals and look for new opportunities. I leave nothing behind. I **stretch** my big dreams even bigger. I am an explorer of truth steadily **stretching** my mind to learn.

I intentionally succeed at the things I try. I **stretch** my vocabulary to learn new words and increase my knowledge. I **stretch** myself as I read books that are from a different genre than what I am used to or like. When I permit myself to **stretch** past my comfort zone, it is wonderful how much is revealed to the eager student.

I **stretch** past old familiar ways of doing life that does not work any longer and proclaim my greatness. I **stretch** my eyes open to see all that is around me. I am enthusiastic. People see me as an example of how to live joyously. I like spreading joy and laughter. I **stretch** my circle of friends as I walk in acceptance. I love being social.

323:
Clarity
November 18

Bible Verses
"The Eternal's directions are correct, giving satisfaction to the heart. God's commandments are clear, lending clarity to the eyes." Psalm 19:8 (VOICE)

"These people are not ignorant about what can be known of God, because He has shown it to them with great clarity." Romans 1:19 (VOICE)

Word of the Day
Clarity – To comprehend. Seeing with certainty. Transparency. Clear.

Quotes
"To the degree there is clarity, the mind does not distinguish between an actual experience and one that has been vividly imagined." Richard Bliss Brooke

"Clarity is the good faith of philosophers." Luc de Clapiers

"The best way to succeed is to have a specific Intent, a clear Vision, a plan of Action, and the ability to maintain Clarity. Those are the Four Pillars of Success. It never fails!" Steve Maraboli

Pam's Perspective
I had 20/20 vision until I reached forty-six. It is frustrating as my clarity has diminished with time. I am very grateful for reading glasses. Like my vision changing, so must I, or I will not have the clarity I need in the future.

Questions
Do I ask God to show me clarity on how to best live? Do I have clarity of thinking? Do I have clarity of goals and purpose? How would my life be if I lived in the clarity of God's love and acceptance of me?

Declarations

I am more than what I am living now, so I receive **clarity** from God to guide my way. I am overjoyed that God cares for someone like me. I never have more **clarity** than when I am in God's presence. I am acceptable in God's eyes. I see with **clarity**. I notice the details.

I meditate and decide with **clarity** what I want. I make it a priority to envision the things I want to accomplish and how I am going to do it. I get **clarity** on my goals by sitting down and putting them on paper. My perseverance gives me **clarity** on how to do a good job.

My **clarity** of fitness is evident because of my healthy lifestyle. The **clarity** of my good judgment in food choices is revealed by what I eat. I take action today in view of the **clarity** of my plans. I eat small portions and enjoy every morsel of nutrition that I ingest.

I live in an extraordinary state because of the **clarity** of my beliefs. I am free to be myself. My **clarity** of thoughts allows me to perceive things others do not understand. The **clarity** of my attention brings people close to me because they feel heard. I am a great listener.

Because I have **clarity** about what my strengths are, I continue to develop them and increase my effectiveness. I deliberately glance in the mirror and talk to myself. The **clarity** of my declarations is spot on. I change my inner voice with my positive affirmations. I spend time throughout my day declaring I am enough. I am comfortable being myself around others. I am a winner, and I act like one.

I learn from the best. I communicate with **clarity**. I ask specifically for what I want. I trust that I will be helped. I get what I ask for because of the **clarity** of my questions. I am a problem solver. I am enriched with worth, power, confidence, strength, and **clarity**.

324:
Reflection
November 19

Bible Verses

"My mouth will overflow with wisdom; the reflections of my heart will guide you to understand the nature of life." Psalm 49:3 (VOICE)

"I, wisdom dwell [with] prudence, and find the knowledge [which cometh] of reflection." Proverbs 8:12 (DARBY)

Word of the Day

Reflection – To ponder. Contemplation of an idea. Thinking.

Quotes

"What self-control doesn't mean is mindless self-sacrifice or knee-jerk self-denial. On the contrary, it represents an affirmation of self, for it requires not the negation of instinct but its integration into a more complete form of character - one that takes account of more than just immediate pleasures and pains. The self-control I'm talking about means acting in keeping with your highest level of reflection." Daniel Akst

"For the provident there are no mischances and for the careful no narrow escapes. We must not put off thought till we are up to the chin in mire. Mature reflection can get over the most formidable difficulty." Baltasar Gracian

Pam's Perspective

When I take time to get alone with my thoughts and reflect how my life is going, I recognize where I need to improve. Then I can take action and course correct.

Questions

What do I think of the reflection I see in the mirror? How much time do I set aside for reflection? Why is it necessary to take time for reflection?

Declarations

I am a **reflection** of God's eternal light and goodness. I surrender myself voluntarily to God. My **reflection** shows that I have unbroken fellowship with the Almighty. The kingdom of God is in my midst **reflecting** peace. I am a **reflection** of His unending grace.

I enjoy the time I take for **reflection**. I have plenty of time. What I hear from heaven is the activity I perform. What comes out of my mouth is a **reflection** of what is in my heart, so I think carefully before I speak. I allow what God is telling me to manifest.

My friends are a **reflection** of the type of person I am, so I choose them wisely. My friends are true-blue. God wants me to be the best that I can be, and serve Him joyfully. I am aware of Jesus living in me, and I am hilariously happy. I **reflect** an appreciation for everything.

I see the **reflection** of the unconditional love of God in my pet's eyes. I am like them, eternally grateful for being chosen, loved, protected, well taken care of and well fed. My love **reflects** back to my pet in an infinite circle of affection, friendship, delight, and devotion.

I am attentive to what I put before my eyes, so my **reflection** does not become tainted. I meditate on God's Word because I love wisdom. The **reflection** of the fruit of the spirit is evident in my life; love, joy, peace, patience, kindness, goodness, faithfulness, gentleness and self-control. I have a forgiveness lifestyle.

I have a beautiful face and a warming smile that **reflects** my cheery personality. I am anointed with gladness and expect good things to come my way. I believe in a sovereign God who loves me unconditionally. His **reflection** shows up in the most unique places, like the people who help carry my groceries or open my doors.

325:
Expand
November 20

Bible Verses
"I bless God every chance I get; my lungs expand with his praise." Psalm 34:1 (MSG)

"I will chase after Your commandments because You will expand my understanding." Psalm 119:32 (VOICE)

Word of the Day
Expand – To amplify and multiply something. To verbalize and elaborate on a subject. To embellish or beef up.

Quotes
"Our life is short, but to expand that span to vast eternity, is virtue's work." Shakespeare

"As my love expands, so does my contentment." Pam Malow-Isham

"The mind attaches itself by idleness and habit to whatever is easy or pleasant. This habit always places bounds to our knowledge, and no one has yet taken the pains to enlarge and expand his mind to the full extent of its capacities." Francois de La Rochefoucauld

"Now I lay me down to sleep, I pray that love my soul will keep. My body rest, my love expand to every soul in every land. God bless.... Amen." Kate Braestrup

Questions
What would my life look like if I allowed my abundance to expand? What would my life look like if I allowed my love to expand? Will I expand my capacity to explore new ideas, concepts, and lands this next year?

Declarations

As I become more accepting of people, my circle of friends **expands**. I see from God's point of view and **expand** my horizons. I **expand** my sight to see with loving eyes. I **expand** my tolerance and patience for other human beings as I **expand** my ability to love.

By **expanding** my interests, I become versatile. I love to **expand** my mind as I read something new every day. I **expand** my knowledge and **expand** my possibilities for advancement. I **expand** past my parents and make them proud. I trust that I will be spiritually strong and humble. I accept what is and **expand** upon the good.

I **expand** my appreciation for life by **expanding** the things I am pleased about. I am an active participant in my life as I **expand** my goals. I enjoy picking a tomato off the vine and eating it fresh. I **expand** my vitality by eating raw, locally grown produce.

I live in the overflow of **expanding** good cheer. Every day I become a better person to be around. I accept my humanness and flaws and still feel lovable. Even if my waist **expands**, I am still beautiful. I am filled with virtue. I can choose to be content and gratified, right now.

My wealth **expands** as my love **expands**. I have a higher vision that **expands** and pulls me forward. I **expand** my business by paying close attention to customer service. My referrals continue to **expand**. My purpose **expands** every day. I am willing to **expand** the type of work I do in order to attract more opportunities for employment.

Wherever I go favorable treatment **expands** in my direction. Getting gifts and upgrades are normal for me. I feel adored by God. I give myself permission to **expand** my success. I am free to express my truth and pursue a joy-filled life. My blessings continue to **expand**.

326:
Preserve
November 21

Bible Verses

"What you say can preserve life or destroy it; so you must accept the consequences of your words." Proverbs 18:21 (GNT)

"Do your best to preserve the unity which the Spirit gives by means of the peace that binds you together." Ephesians 4:3 (GNT)

Word of the Day

Preserve – To perpetuate the integrity of something. To safeguard or shield from damage. To uphold incorruptibility.

Quotes

"One way to recollect the mind easily in the time of prayer, and preserve it more in tranquility, is not to let it wander too far at other times. You should keep it strictly in the presence of God; and being accustomed to think of Him often, you will find it easy to keep your mind calm in the time of prayer, or at least to recall it from its wanderings." Brother Lawrence

"Best of all is it to preserve everything in a pure, still heart, and let there be for every pulse a thanksgiving, and for every breath a song." Konrad von Gesner

Pam's Perspective

I thought about preserving my youthful look by going to a plastic surgeon a couple years ago. When he looked at me and said, "There is nothing wrong with your face except you've had too many birthdays!" I laughed and went home.

Questions

What would be the best way to preserve my health? How can I preserve my wealth? What am I doing to preserve my friendships? Is it working?

Declarations

I **preserve** my integrity by keeping my word. I meditate regularly to **preserve** my peace and remain calm during difficult times. I am valuable. I **preserve** a great attitude by thinking happy thoughts.

As I move closer to God, I **preserve** our time together and release all fear. I feel safe and secure now. Moving freely from glory to joy, I embrace my life. I live by the promises of God and **preserve** my victory. I am motivated to be a faithful witness for God.

I **preserve** my wealth to leave an inheritance for my children's children. I **preserve** the memory of past achievements to encourage myself when I feel dismayed. Inner wealth is mine. I enroll people to **preserve** my vision and create new ones. I remain successful.

I am a happy soul. I am deserving of having great relationships and honest friends. I am loyal and trustworthy. I **preserve** my friendships by staying in touch. I look for the good in everyone. I infect people with laughter and joy. I smile often. I am safeguarded throughout eternity, as I trust a faithful God to **preserve** my soul.

I **preserve** my immune system by taking daily vitamin supplements. I **preserve** my stamina by deliberately exercising. I choose to take the stairs. I stay well hydrated by drinking lots of pure water. I do a yearly cleanse. I **preserve** my health by being conscious of what I eat, how much I eat, and how often. I have abundant self-control. I **preserve** my beauty from the inside out by radiating love.

I **preserve** my destiny by declaring I am competent. I trust that God's faithful to grow the seeds I plant and **preserve** them. I have been blessed to become a blessing. It is obvious how grateful I am. I **preserve** my character by doing what I say I am going to do.

327:
Mission
November 22

Bible Verses
"For a long time now—to this very day—you have not deserted your brothers but have carried out the mission the Lord your God gave you." Joshua 22:3 (NIV)

"I, even I, have spoken; yes, I have called him. I will bring him, and he will succeed in his mission." Isaiah 48:15 (NIV)

Word of the Day
Mission – An assignment of great worth. A calling from within. Goal.

Quotes
"A small body of determined spirits fired by an unquenchable faith in their mission can alter the course of history." Mahatma Gandhi

"Every mission constitutes a pledge of duty. Every man is bound to consecrate his every faculty to its fulfillment. He will derive his rule of action from the profound conviction of that duty." Giuseppe Mazzini

Pam's Perspective
My mission is to encourage and help people realize their greatness and potential. That motivates me and gives me a passion for keeping going. No matter where I am I can encourage someone and make their day, and that makes mine. I get my inspiration from the Bible and listening to audiobooks from a variety of genres. I also love watching Ted Talks. I find them fascinating, and they stir the creativity in me. No matter how old I get, I want to keep learning and exploring.

Questions
Do I have a mission statement? Who do I need to ask for help in finishing my current mission? What is my mission here on earth?

Declarations

I sit down and write a **mission** statement for my life that aligns with my current beliefs and values. I release the old **mission** and pick up the new. I decide what is important to me and incorporate it into my **mission** statement. I have a meaningful **mission** here on earth.

All my needs are divinely met as I see my **mission** come true. What I do not have for my **mission**, God provides. I walk in cooperation with the Holy Spirit. God directs my steps and leads to the perfect **mission**. I am on the right path to realize my **mission** and fulfill my calling. I align with heaven and abundance comes my way.

I have been given the **mission** of loving God, loving my neighbor and loving myself. It is not a **mission** that I take lightly. I enhance myself by allowing God's presence to flow through me. I work in unity with my neighbors. People see a revelation of God working in my life. My way of being is calm and poised. The **mission** of loving myself is one I do humbly, thoughtfully, and with care.

The **mission** I have on delivering positive encouragement to others keeps me motivated and optimistic. I seize every opportunity I have to carry out my **mission**. I am a go-getter with a positive attitude.

I have the creativity and ability to accomplish my **mission** in record time. I willingly surrender all to God to fulfill the **mission** to which I am called. I am confident I will succeed as I see my **mission** unfold.

I have a **mission** to reveal to people how great they really are. My **mission** of love and inclusion embraces all humanity just like God does. I see what is right with people. I expound on and emphasize their many assets. My **mission** to cheer people up is ongoing. I like to have fun and bless people. My **mission** continues to evolve.

328:
Victory
November 23

Bible Verses

"The Lord is my strength and my song; he has given me victory. This is my God, and I will praise him—my father's God, and I will exalt him!" Exodus 15:2 (NLT)

"But thanks be to God, who gives us the victory through our Lord Jesus Christ." 1 Corinthians 15:57 (NASB)

Word of the Day

Victory – The achievement of winning in life despite conflict or hurdles. Defeating your enemies. Attaining the prize.

Quotes

"A defeat to a brave man is only a victory deferred." James Ellis

"Victory follows me, and all things follow victory." George De Scuderi

"The struggle alone pleases us, not the victory." Blaise Pascal

"Every moment of resistance to temptation is a victory." Frederick William Faber

Pam's Perspective

Having the victory of completing a goal is rewarding. Being handed something for nothing feels void and does not give the satisfaction of victory like working and conquering difficulties. Challenging trials makes the success sweeter.

Questions

Do I ever consider something a victory even if I have not won? Do I celebrate every victory? How will I live in victory today?

Declarations

I live in **victory** because the Lord is on my side. I cast off all feelings of mediocrity, unleash my power to succeed and call forth **victory**. The same God who was with Daniel in the lion's den is with me now bringing **victory** my way. I am willing to receive abundance.

I plan out the **victory** steps I need to achieve my desired results. People, situations or feelings do not intimidate me. I am more than enough. I am a **victor**. I conquer every difficulty that may come my way. Even when I fall down and mess up, I have **victory** in Christ.

I release my full potential and manifest **victory** in every area of my life. I am an advocate for my dreams. I claim the **victory** now over negative thoughts and pulverize them with happy thoughts. I give myself the freedom to laugh out loud and speak up when I need to.

I gain **victory** over my weight by exercising and being conscious of what I eat. **Victory** is easy when I choose raw fruits and vegetables. I am really proud of myself. I give myself the gift of respect. I gain **victory** over my cravings one minute at a time. I focus on what I can do right, and the **victory** follows. I get contentment from the Lord.

I live a **victorious** life! I am a winner, love doing a great job and do not stop until **victory** arrives. I will persist and not give up until I succeed. I stir up the passion in me to take on new adventurers, climb new mountains and come out **victorious**. And so it is.

Victory is mine. I am very courageous as I take advantage of **victorious** circumstances. I am the **victory** breed that is fearless. Jesus Christ won the **victory** over death and resides within me. God's presence in me is the same as was with Christ. We are one. I don't have to wait for the **victory** because I already have it.

329:
Own
November 24

Bible Verses

"Do not say to yourself, 'My power and the might of my own hand have gotten me this wealth.'" Deuteronomy 8:17 (NRSV)

"All one's ways may be pure in one's own eyes, but the Lord weighs the spirit." Proverbs 16:2 (NRSV)

Word of the Day

Own – The material property that one has paid for. Dominate. Rule. To be accountable for one's actions. To take full charge of a given situation.

Quotes

"I love you the more in that I believe you have liked me for my own sake and for nothing else." John Keats

"I will work in my own way, according to the light that is in me." Lydia Maria Child

"This above all; to thine own self be true." William Shakespeare

"God has put man's life into his own keeping. He is to be the architect of his own character. The here of his own statue. The arbiter of his own destiny." Rev. Charles S. Macfarland, Ph. D.

"As I own my mistakes, I own my potential. Admitting my failures gives me power over them. Then they can't have dominance over me." Pam Malow-Isham

Questions

What kind of example am I setting? Do I own my mistakes and failures or just successes? Do my possessions own me? What will I own up to today?

Declarations

Even when I am reluctant, I **own** up to what I have created thus far in my life. I alone am responsible for my mess or success. I **own** every decision I have made and will make. Growing up, being responsible and **owning** my birthright is a powerful place to stand.

The affluence of heaven saturates my mind as I **own** my power. I **own** my thoughts and decide what I will meditate on. I guard my **own** heart and protect it from offense. I **own** my competency. My mind is in top form, working well, and **owning** my talent.

I enjoy being endorsed by God as I turn **ownership** of my heart over to Him. Creative bursts of inspiration surge through my body as I create my **own** disciplines that improve my health and life. I **own** my exercise program and take it to the next level. I just show up and **own** my strength. It is fun to play. I choose to live triumphantly.

I **own** my house free and clear. I **own** the nicest furnishings in my home. I use Feng Shui to decorate and arrange my home in the most pleasant, welcoming way. I realize colors affect my mood. I add plants to bring life inside. I feel motivated, energetic, and balanced when I walk in the door. As I remove clutter, I remove negativity.

My life is luscious. I love sharing positive energy. I **own** my importance and recognize God created me to win. I am a successful facilitator of my **own** happiness. I am blessed beyond measure. I stay happy and healthy. I assume **ownership** of my world.

I **own** the fact that I am beautiful, unique, and smart. I love myself. I **own** the room when I walk in, and everyone wants to be around me. I ooze wisdom, harmony, and contentment. I am a free thinker who is not afraid to study, find things out, and **own** my brilliance.

330:
Borrow
November 25

Bible Verses

"The rich rule over the poor. The one who borrows is a slave to the one who lends." Proverbs 22:7 (ERV)

"Now if there is a willingness to help, give within your means. That's perfectly acceptable. No one expects you to go without or borrow to give." 2 Corinthians 8:12 (VOICE)

Word of the Day

Borrow – To loan. To use for a short period of time. Rent.

Quotes

"Unfaithfulness in the keeping of an appointment is an act of clear dishonesty. You may as well borrow a person's money as his time." Horace Mann

"I not only use all the brains I have, but all I can borrow, and I have borrowed a lot since I read it to you first." Woodrow Wilson

Pam's Perspective

On October seventeen, nineteen ninety-two, I flipped ten times my Nissan 360ZX that I had wanted since I was twelve years old. I was knocked unconscious and when I came to my head was under the passenger's dash, and my legs were straddled between the T-tops. The Jaws of Life was used to free me. After the time off work, physical therapy and medical bills, I had to file bankruptcy in ninety-six. I felt totally humiliated that I had gotten to that point. I have managed to stay debt free and built my credit back up. Now I don't spend what I don't have.

Questions

Do I return things in a better condition? Why borrow when I can lend?

Declarations

I pay my bills on time and never **borrow** more than I can afford. **Borrowing** money to live beyond my means is a foolish way to live. I am fully capable of being patient and waiting until I have saved enough money to purchase whatever I desire so I don't **borrow**.

I always return things that I **borrow** in a better condition than before I got it. I am trustworthy and always in control of all my actions and affairs. I am thankful that I don't have to **borrow** money to live. I always have more than enough. I am disciplined in my saving.

I look for and find bargains galore and things on sale. I do not have to pay retail. Wholesale is the way I go. Cash is king, and I can always get a great deal. I store up for a rainy day, so I do not have to **borrow** from anyone. Having a surplus allows me to feel confident.

If on the rare occasion I would allow someone to borrow money from me, it would not be very much. I get everything in writing, with clear dates on when the **borrowed** money is to be repaid. There is a specific deadline for each payment. If the **borrower** asks for more money, I say no. I need an emergency fund, so I do not let people **borrow** from it. I am thankful I am debt free.

My investments are increasing daily. I have power over my finances, and I love being on top. I have a conservative budget. I associate with wealthy people and **borrow** their ideas. I love rich people. I **borrow** thoughts and reinvent them into my own masterpiece.

I am glad that I am a part of what God is doing here on earth. I **borrow** God's wisdom to manage my money and affairs. I praise God as my revenues continue to rise. My business is booming. I am very wealthy and appreciate all the many gifts I have received.

331:
Disapproval
November 26

Bible Verses
"So Zacchaeus hurriedly climbed down and gladly welcomed him. But the bystanders muttered their disapproval, saying, 'Now he has gone to stay with a real sinner.'" Luke 19:6-7 (PHILLIPS)

"But refuse and avoid irreverent legends (profane and impure and godless fictions, mere grandmothers' tales) and silly myths, and express your disapproval of them. Train yourself toward godliness (piety), [keeping yourself spiritually fit]." 1 Timothy 4:7 (AMP)

Word of the Day
Disapproval – Criticism. The dissatisfaction showed by someone who does not approve of your actions.

Quotes
"Nothing should so much diminish the satisfaction which we feel with ourselves as seeing that we disapprove at one time of that which we approve of at another." La Rochefoucauld

"Most of our fellow-subjects are guided either by the prejudice of education or by a deference to the judgment of those who perhaps in their own hearts disapprove the opinions which they industriously spread among the multitude." Joseph Addison

"Disapproval of self is the worst disease imaginable." Pam Malow-Isham

Questions
What do I do when I have disapproval for someone? Have I ever disapproved of myself? How do I react when I feel the disapproval of a loved one? Does disapproval of people matter to me?

Declarations

I know I am always approved of by God, so I do not worry about the **disapproval** of people. I am grateful others **disapproval** does not affect me. Joy fills my heart as I bask in unending grace. I partake in the greatest thrill in the world, accepting and sharing God's love.

There is nothing wrong with me that the Holy Spirit and I cannot fix. I release all **disapproving** thoughts I have had about myself and go free. I serve God with my whole being, trusting and believing in His Word. God uses me to spread the good news to the world.

I am aware that my **disapproval** of the evil around me can make me cynical. Instead of listening to the **disapproval** of the various news reports, and the disasters around the world, I focus on the good things that are happening in my community. The **disapproval** from arrogant people will not prevent my prayers for them.

I associate with respectable people who do not **disapprove** of their wealth. I live open-handedly and do what I enjoy most. I prophesy blessings over my children and see their **disapproval** of things flee. I allow marvelous moments to happen despite anyone's **disapproval.**

I listen inside to what resonates with me and do not worry about the **disapproval** of others. I stay true to myself. Having the **disapproval** of others does not change my beliefs. I move in the direction my heart takes me. I take action without attachment to the outcome.

I shake the earth with my powerful message. I have the authority to make my message known, regardless of anyone's **disapproval**. Everywhere I go, I represent the creator of the universe. God's word abides in me. God does not see **disapproval** in me, only perfection because He sees Christ residing in me. How fortunate am I!

332:
Thanksgiving
November 27

Bible Verses
"I will praise God's name in song and glorify him with thanksgiving." Psalm 69:30 (NIV)

"For everything God created is good, and nothing is to be rejected if it is received with thanksgiving." 1 Timothy 4:4 (NIV)

Word of the Day
Thanksgiving – Appreciativeness for all the blessings we receive. Recognizing grace and saying so. Verbally giving thanks. A special day set aside to be grateful to God for His many gifts.

Quotes
"Thanksgiving eradicates greed, anger, and depression. When thanksgiving is the first thing on your lips instead of the last, your life will be filled with joy and contentment." Pam Malow-Isham

"The lawfulness of the action which thou desirest to undertake, let thy devotion recommend it to divine blessing. If it be lawful thou shalt perceive thy heart encouraged by thy prayer; if unlawful thou shalt find thy prayer discouraged by thy heart. That action is not warrantable which either blushes to beg a blessing, or having succeeded, dares not present a thanksgiving." Francis Quarles

"Pride slays thanksgiving, but a humble mind is the soil out of which thanks naturally grow. A proud man is seldom a grateful man, for he never thinks he gets as much as he deserves." Henry Ward Beecher

Questions
Is thanksgiving my first response to life's circumstances? How can I make thanksgiving a part of my daily life? Do I associate with thankful people?

Declarations

I will give **thanks** to God for the good times and the bad times. I get up each morning, look in the mirror, and say 'thank you God for allowing me to serve you one more day.' My heart stays full of **thanksgiving** for my health, family, friends, and possessions.

Thanksgiving is on my lips as I admire this incredibly beautiful day. I am **thankful** for the sunshine and rain. I am **thankful** for laughter and tears. I stay in exceptionally great spirits as I find more things to be **thankful** for. I am **thankful** I have a guardian angel watching over me, keeping me safe. I love participating in what God is doing.

The practice I have of **thanksgiving** benefits me in thousands of seen and unseen ways. My **thankful** heart is a blessing to my spouse. Even when I am down and cannot see God's purpose in my current situation, I will offer a sacrifice of **thanksgiving** to the Eternal One.

As I focus on the abundance of joy in my heart, **thanksgiving** is the natural response. **Thank you** God, that what you have done before, You will do for me, and more. I continue to grow ever more **thankful** with each passing day. The overflow of **thankfulness** is poured out on the people around me. I am **thankful** for inventors.

I am blessed by sharing **thankfulness** with others. I like hanging around people that are happy and **thankful**. As I deliver **thanks** to people, I bring out the best in them. It is nice to be noticed and **thanked**. I attract the best experiences just because I give **thanks**.

My family, friends and I celebrate with **thanksgiving** and laughter the **Thanksgiving** Day holiday. Being **thankful** is common with me. I voluntarily express my **thanksgiving** to God. I bless my body with **thanksgiving**, nice thoughts, good food and lots of water.

333:
Halt
November 28

Bible Verses
"And Elijah came unto all the people, and said, how long halt ye between two opinions? If the Lord be God, follow him: but if Baal, then follow him. And the people answered him not a word." 1 Kings 18:21 (KJV)

"And He came up and touched the coffin; and the bearers came to a halt. And He said, 'Young man, I say to you, arise!'" Luke 7:14 (NASB)

Word of the Week
Halt – To freeze movement. To let up motion. To standstill. Stop.

Quotes
"If people were to halt before they spoke, and consider, 'is what I am about to say beneficial?' the world would be a quieter place." Pam Malow-Isham

"The halt of toils exhausted caravan, comes sweet with music to thy wearied ear; rise with its anthems to a holier sphere!" Oliver Wendell Holmes

"In the house or harvest-field, halt and lame and blind he healed, when he walked in Galilee." Henry Wadsworth Longfellow

Pam's Perspective
After seeing a woman with the skin ripped off her arm from her elbow to her breast I halted at the top of the 171-foot tower in Las Vegas thinking, I have to dance tonight in a Ballroom competition, I need my arms. I met fear and jumped.

Questions
How can I halt a cold or keep it at bay? How often do I halt to give thanks? How can I halt negativity in my environment?

Declarations

My robust body likes to eat for nutrition, so I stay fit as a fiddle. I find it easier to turn away sweets and **halt** the sugar when I make a choice live healthily. I am thankful for vegetables. I walk in divine health, so I **halt** the behaviors that take away from my vitality.

Jehovah is proud of me for believing in the impossible. I get more dynamic each day. I **halt** the negative thoughts that try to creep in. I turn them around to focus on what is positive. I zoom past little challenges that try to **halt** me from reaching my goals. I **halt** to pick up trash when I see it lying around no matter where I am at.

I **halt** and look things up when I am unsure. Google is a beautiful thing. I promote wellbeing within myself by what I read. I create an encouraging workplace and enjoy the people I work with.

With anticipation, people **halt** to listen to what I have to say. I **halt** when someone does a good job and compliment them immediately. I **halt** and intentionally do things that show people I care and respect them. Being considerate comes naturally to me. **Halting** to notice the little things that mean a lot to people is worth the time.

I **halt** my spending so I can live debt free with a large bank account. I am blessed by all the victories I have achieved. I will **halt**, count my blessings and give thanks. I **halt** to think about good times and bad. They have shaped me into the perceptive person I am today.

I am absolutely thrilled about my dreams and **halt** to ponder them. God **halts** to listen when I pray. God's word is a powerful tool to **halt** and defeat any enemy that comes my way. I **halt** and use what I have proven to be true. God's word can break any bondage and set every captive free. I am grateful that God **halts** to watch over me.

334:
Advance
November 29

Bible Verses
"Leave your old, foolish ways and live! Advance along the path of understanding." Proverbs 9:6 (ERV)

"Furthermore, because we are united with Christ, we have received an inheritance from God, for he chose us in advance, and he makes everything work out according to his plan." Ephesians 1:11 (NLT)

Word of the Week
Advance –Upgrade. To speed up. To rise up the ladder of success.

Quotes
"In time of war we must be speedy in execution, and advance to honor through the path of danger." Silius Italicus

"It is reasonable to have perfection in our eye that we may always advance toward it, though we know it can never be reached." Samuel Johnson

Pam's Perspective
In Two-thousand and three I visualized in advance, winning an all-expense paid trip for two to Thailand. I wrote it on paper exactly how I envisioned it. I felt the excitement with tears in my eyes how I would feel when they drew my name. I told everyone I was winning that trip. My husband didn't believe me, thought it was rigged and thought I was crazy, but when they drew my name, he came running down the aisle after me. Even though Gary doubted, I took him with me.

Questions
Do I look at all the facts in advance of making a decision? How do I see myself advancing? What goal will I advance today?

Declarations

I visualize in **advance**, the perfect result I want to see. I have high self-esteem. I know I am going to have a great day in **advance** because I say so. When someone does something upsetting, I am ready because I practice forgiveness and mercy in **advance**.

I **advance** my purpose by keeping my commitments. When obstacles get in my way, I **advance** head-on, without hesitation. I choose to take the steps necessary to **advance** my career. I like working hard. Discernment is always available in abundance to me. I **advance** my job with ease as the perfect connections manifest at the right time.

I am grateful in **advance** for receiving my very good fortune. I **advance** the variety of ways I receive income by staying open-minded. I believe I can **advance** up the ladder of success with ease. As I give **advanced** service, I receive abundant compensation.

I **advance** on accomplishing my bucket list as I dare to be adventuresome and do more things. I **advance** my perception of different cultures as I travel around the world. All of God's people are beautiful and a joy to be around. I find everything intriguing and everyone appealing. I **advance** my joy by sharing it with others.

I love to **advance** my knowledge and learn new things. As I **advance** in age and wisdom, I make new friends and stay sharp. I **advance** my brain with memorizing facts, playing games and mediation. I **advance** diversity in my studies and see my mind expand.

Angels **advance** ahead of me, to make my way safe. God knew me in **advance** and called me His friend. I pray in **advance** and go forth in power. I permeate love. I am surrounded by the power of the love of the Lord. The love of God is the solution I seek. Love is my ministry.

335:
Prosperity
November 30

Bible Verses
"The Lord will give you prosperity in the land he swore to your ancestors to give you, blessing you with many children, numerous livestock, and abundant crops." Deuteronomy 28:11 (NLT)

"Whoever pursues righteousness and love finds life, prosperity and honor." Proverbs 21:21 (NIV)

Word of the Day
Prosperity – Having more than enough money to meet your needs and plenty left over. Being well off finacially. Wealth.

Quotes
"There is in every woman's heart a spark of heavenly fire which lies dormant in the broad daylight of prosperity, but which kindles up and beams and blazes in the dark hour of adversity." Washington Irving

"The misfortune of the wise is better than the prosperity of the fool." Epicurus

"The more people you help, the 'richer' you become, mentally, emotionally, spiritually, and definitely financially." T. Harv Eker

"Education is an ornament in prosperity and a refuge in adversity." Aristotle

"A prosperity mindset will magnetize wealth." Pam Malow-Isham

Questions
What does prosperity look like to me? Do I consider myself to be a prosperous person? Why or why not? How can I best use the prosperity that I have been given? How can I acquire more prosperity?

Declarations

I exist as a **prosperous** expression of creativity. I am a King's kid, and an heir to all the good God has for me. Instant happy feelings flow through me now as I allow **prosperity** to arrive. God is my immediate source of **prosperity** and gives me His infinite supply.

My Beloved loves me truly and continues to bless me with **prosperity**. I was created to be **prosperous,** and I am deserving of upgrades. I magnetize wealth-building projects. I look to find the **prosperity** of God at my doorstep. **Prosperity** comes easily to me.

Prosperity has afforded me the ability to do great things to bless my church and community. **Prosperity** is positive thinking put into action. I am dependable, honest and generous in my giving.

Giving feels really rewarding and something I take great pleasure in. **Prosperity** looks for new opportunities to blossom through me. I do something productive every day to allow my **prosperity** to grow.

I saturate my thoughts with affluent ideas. When I choose thoughts of **prosperity**, I experience **prosperity**. I live knowing **prosperity** is chasing me down. I slow down so it can catch me. **Prosperity** is my friend. I am humbled by my **prosperity** and do not let it go to my head. I feel accomplished when I fall asleep. I allow myself to dream sweet dreams and wake up feeling energized and ready to go.

I have a **prosperity** mindset and everything I set my hands to **prosper.** I clear any thoughts of not having enough and replace them with **prosperity** thoughts of riches pouring in. I take gigantic leaps of faith. As I elevate my thinking, my **prosperity** grows. My mind is certain about the wealthy person I am. I share my gifts freely. I am a powerhouse of generosity. Today I am **prosperity** personified.

336:
Poverty
December 1

Bible Verses

"He will listen to the prayers of those in poverty. He will not ignore them."
Psalm 102:17 (ERV)

"There is profit in hard work, but mere talk leads to poverty." Proverbs
14:23 (CEB)

Word of the Day

Poverty – Being in debt. A shortage of funds. Impoverished.

Quotes

"Being grateful eliminates the poverty in your mind." Pam Malow-Isham

"He who is not capable of enduring poverty is not capable of being free."
Victor Hugo

"We are not limited by money but by the poverty of our dreams." Doug
Wead

"Poverty is want of much but avarice of everything." Publius Syrus

Pam's Perspective

I grew up instilled with a poverty mindset. All I heard was we can't afford
that. I'm not made of money. Do you think money grows on trees? Only rich
people get to do that or go there. It took me years to eradicate those poverty
thoughts. But with repetition and perseverance, I no longer have a broke
mentality.

Questions

Out of the several forms of poverty are there any I attract? Am I diligent
at keeping poverty at bay? Why or why not? How do I view poverty?

Declarations

I refuse to let my dreams die. I realize that I can be happy in **poverty** as well as in plenty, so the plenty arrives. I have a "why" that is bigger than the "I can't." I am fearless, no matter what the circumstance because I know the God who has conquered **poverty**.

I have a giving heart, just like Jesus. Just because I may have been born into **poverty** does not mean I have to say there. I have the power to succeed. God has the riches on a thousand hills, and I am His kid. God's Spirit has freed me from the slavery of **poverty**.

I choose my own fate and **poverty** is not a part of it. Everything I desire is doable, as I walk down the first-class road. I am a tool in the hand of God to create multiple miracles. Breaking the financial **poverty** cycle is a miracle I am fortunate to be a part of. I lean into my abundance as I seek after wisdom like a hidden treasure.

I release all **poverty** thoughts. I was made with explosive potential. I cling to the promises of God. My riches come from within. No matter my state, I will choose to be content. I deflect the chains of **poverty** by speaking God's Word and proclaiming my positive declarations. There is always something good to think about.

Poverty is not welcome in my home. I love my family, and my family loves me. I am disciplined with my savings, and investments, so **poverty** stays away. I have a wealthy way of being that keeps **poverty** at a distance. I do not have a **poverty** spirit, but a rich one.

I am grateful for all the blessings God has bestowed on me and tithing is a natural part of my worship to Him. It keeps **poverty** at arm's length. I give because I enjoy giving. I love being spiritual, and rich too. My optimistic outlook comes from Christ.

337:
Slow
December 2

Bible Verses

"He who is slow to anger is better than the mighty, he who rules his [own] spirit than he who takes a city." Proverbs 16:32 (AMP)

"Understand [this], my beloved brethren. Let every man be quick to hear [a ready listener], slow to speak, slow to take offense and to get angry." James 1:19 (AMP)

Word of the Day

Slow – Lethargic and lagging energy. Drawn out. Not fast.

Quotes

"Life is like unto a long journey with a heavy burden. Let thy step be slow and steady, that thou stumble not. Persuade thyself that imperfection and inconvenience are the lot of natural mortals, and there will be no room for discontent, neither for despair" Tokugawa Leyasu

"Let no one be slow to seek wisdom when he is young nor weary in search thereof when he is grown old. For no age is too early or too late for the health of the soul." Epicurus

Pam's Perspective

Getting behind a slow driver used to aggravate me. I was in such a rush that I would miss the scenery. As I took on playing the game, life is easy, I slowed down, and now I enjoy everything. Even traffic jams can't get me upset. It gives me time to count my blessings and pray for my country and the people next to me.

Questions

Do I slow down and smell the flowers? When things go slower than I like, how do I react? Why is it good to go slow at times?

Declarations

I am **slow** to come to conclusions, as I like to get both sides of the story before I make a decision. I permit myself to listen and to **slow** down and wait until the other person is finished talking. I take great care of my relationships to be as attentive and respectful as possible.

My silent strength is revealed when someone lashes out at me, and I am **slow** to respond. I am **slow** to anger, or judge, and quick to release any offenses. As I **slow** my thoughts and get them on paper, I can then easily speak the words I want to say with clarity. I am thankful for my gratitude journal so I can pen my ideas.

Even if my investments are **slow** growing, they are still on the upward incline. I like saving money. I will do what others will not do. I go **slow** and appreciate the time it takes to get something done. I realize when things are going **slower** than I would like, I have the opportunity to learn more patience. It is fun to see my goals achieved, even if it is **slowly**. I can enjoy being **slow**.

I **slow** down and take advantage of the wisdom of the elders in my community. We are hitting it off because I take notice. They have a lot to share, and I have a lot to learn. **Slow** can be a hidden gem. When my body communicates to me, I **slow** down and listen.

God is never **slow**, even when I get impatient. God is always faithful. There is a time to go **slow,** and wait in faith for God to come through, so **slow** I go. **Slow** and easy going is my motto.

It feels great to take a deep, **slow** breath, and relax. By taking things **slowly**, I have created inner confidence by trusting in God. I am grateful for the answers. I **slow** down enough to recognize and be grateful for all the amazing surprises and miracles that arrive.

338:
Fast
December 3

Bible Verses
"The stingy try to get rich fast, unaware that loss will come to them."
Proverbs 28:22 (CEB)

"Prove all things; hold fast that which is good." 1 Thessalonians 5:21 (KJV)

Word of the Day
Fast – Expedient in getting something done. Accelerated speed. To happen swiftly. Steadfast or firm.

Quotes
"Hold fast to the Bible. To the influence of this Book we are indebted for all the progress made in true civilization and to this we must look as our guide in the future." Ulysses S. Grant

"A man must often exercise or fast or take physic, or be sick." Sir W. Temple

"Never think that God's delays are God's denials. Hold on; hold fast; hold out. Patience is genius." Buffon

Pam's Perspective
I used to be fast at passing judgment. Now I am fast to forgive and accept people with all their quirks and ideas that are different than mine. I can agree to disagree. Life passes by so fast that holding petty grievances are a waste of time.

Questions
How has going fast helped me? How has going fast hurt me? Do I ever go so fast that I forget about the journey? How fast am I to pass judgment? How fast am I to forgive? How fast am I to make amends?

Declarations

I take command of my destiny and move **fast** to reach my goals. I think **fast** on my feet, and people are enthralled with my wit. I have style, charisma, and charm. I have the power and ability to increase my self-esteem. I can have twice as much confidence anytime I want by taking action. I am **fast** to remember how great I really am.

I am glad I created a reading habit. I am **fast** to comprehend what I read. Learning is fun. I see enormous changes in me. I gain excellent ideas. I pick up information **fast**. People like me because they can see I accept myself when I act intelligent and when I act foolishly.

I hold **fast** to my passions, goals, and dreams. They are **fast** at coming true. I reach them in record time. I allocate my time wisely as I go **fast** through the day with ease. I am **fast** to smile. I am **fast** to program my subconscious mind by speaking positive affirmations.

I am **fast** to say I am sorry. I recognize when I am wrong and admit it. I am **fast** to make amends. I am intuitive and know what is right or wrong, so I am **fast** to act on it. I am **fast** at trying new challenges.

I live in the overflow of God's grace and favor, and I am **fast** to share it. I am **fast** to pray for people who need healing of their mind, body, spirit, or finances, and God is **fast** to respond. I am **fast** to sense the anointing of the Holy Spirit on me. God has me on His mind and is **fast** to send support my way. God's love spills over to bless me.

I like earning a good living and am happy with my income. I like making plans and am **fast** to make course corrections when needed. I am **fast** at being patient, tolerant, and kind to the people around me. I take an active approach to keeping my love alive. I like to try new adventures. Bring them on. I am determined to win **fast**.

339:
Myself
December 4

Bible Verses

"Then the angel of God called again to Abraham from heaven. 'I, the Lord, have sworn by myself that because you have obeyed me and not withheld even your beloved son from me, I will bless you with incredible blessings and multiply your descendants into countless thousands and millions, like the stars above you in the sky, and like the sands along the seashore. They will conquer their enemies." Genesis 22:15-17 (TLB)

Word of the Day

Myself – The person I claim to be. My personality. My true self.

Quotes

"I am still determined to be cheerful and to be happy, in whatever situation I may be; for I have also learnt, from experience, that the greater part of our happiness or misery depends upon our dispositions, and not upon our circumstances. We carry the seeds of the one or the other about with us, in our minds, wheresoever we go." Martha Washington

"I know that I have the ability to achieve the object of my Definite Purpose in life, therefore, I DEMAND of myself persistent, continuous action toward its attainment, and I here and now promise to render such action." Napoleon Hill

Pam's Perspective

When I only focus on myself I feel shallow and empty, but when I devote myself to helping others and being of service, I have a purpose and feel fulfilled and happy.

Questions

How do I treat myself? How do I talk to myself? How do I think about myself? How do I care for myself? How will I respect myself today?

Declarations

I love **myself** precisely the way I am with all my flaws and faults.
I am in control of my body and find it marvelous. I feed **myself**
nutrient-rich foods that enhance my wellbeing. I give **myself** the
exercise it needs to stay strong and limber. I like pampering **myself**.
I am sacred, and I reward **myself** with haircuts, hot relaxing baths,
facials, pedicures, manicures, waxing, massages, and spa days.

I am unreasonable in holding **myself** accountable. The market price
for **my** indispensable service continues to rise. I have limitless favor
in **my** field. I hold **myself** to a superior standard, so I only put out
superior work. People are happy to pay me top dollar for **my** work.

I trust **myself** to pick the perfect mentor for me. I listen to **myself**
when I feel a check in my spirit. I educate **myself**, so I know **my**
rights. I hold **myself** in high esteem, therefore, so do other people.

I respect **myself** by saving every week more than I spend, so I
increase **my** wealth. I put **myself** in authority over the management
of **my** finances. I earn a great living, pay **my** own way, and praise
myself for being frugal. I love **myself** enough to take care of myself
and my family financially. I praise **myself** for what I do right.

I coach **myself** to try new things. I like listening to others speak
more than **myself**. I find **myself** delighted by others. People are
fun. I stress less about **myself** when I am helping others and paying
it forward. I laugh at **myself** and see the humor in all of life.

I am a promoter for **myself**. I feel good about **myself** being clean
and well-groomed. Right now is the best time for me to create **my**
ideal life. I allow **myself** to take pleasure in the small things. I like
myself. I am devoted to living **my** joy-filled life, passionately.

340:
Yourself
December 5

Bible Verses

"To worry yourself to death with resentment would be a foolish, senseless thing to do." Job 5:2 (GNT)

"For the whole Law is summed up in one commandment: Love your neighbor as you love yourself." Galatians 5:14 (GNT)

Word of the Day

Yourself – The person you are most of the time. Your true self.

Quotes

"Since you're the only person on the planet who hears every word you think or say, you have a tremendous opportunity to influence yourself." Mary Jane Mapes

"You may find your worst enemy or best friend in yourself." Unknown

"Faith in yourself isn't a result of success. It's the cause of it." Steve Pavlina

"When working for others, sink yourself out of sight; seek their interest. Make yourself necessary to those who employ you by industry, fidelity and scrupulous integrity. Selfishness is fatal." Henry Ward Beecher

"If you want to ask a lot from yourself, it helps to give a lot to yourself." Gretchen Rubin

"Like yourself and the whole world becomes beautiful." Pam Malow-Isham

Questions

What do you like about yourself? What can you improve about yourself? When did you last treat yourself to something really delightful?

Declarations

You are happy with **yourself** and how you conduct **your** life. People listen with an open mind to what **you** have to say. **You** think clearly and express **yourself** with confidence. **You** like being considerate and helpful. **You** find **yourself** being patient while waiting in line.

Watching **yourself** in the mirror as you declare **your** greatness adds to **your** confidence. **You** like **yourself,** and **you** feel strong. **You** are nice to **yourself.** **You** feel absolutely fantastic. **You** are free to love **yourself** and move forward with intensity, dignity, and grace.

You take time for **your** family and friends. **You** question **yourself** and **your** actions. **You** have a great memory. **You** have tools all around **you,** and **you** can use them to help **yourself.** **You** give **yourself** permission to cut up, be happy, and have fun. **You** grant **yourself** time to walk outside, get some fresh air, and enjoy nature.

You are concise about the intentions **you** set for **yourself,** so straight is your path. **You** make big changes easily to achieve the dreams **you** set for **yourself.** Challenging **yourself** makes life interesting. **You** are thankful for options. By setting **your** mind to something, it gets done. **You** always find a way to win. **You** do what is important first.

You indulge **yourself** in some reading and quiet time. **You** surround **yourself** with easy going, fun people. **You** are given to hospitality and generosity. **You** are ageless and an inspiration to millions. **You** are good looking and confident. **You** are glad **you** are not alone.

You find **yourself** going from glory to glory, motivating everyone you meet. **You** treat **yourself** with kindness and respect as you feel God's presence enriching **your** life. **You** find **yourself** being more like Christ. **You** have no regrets. **You** excel at the game of life.

341:
Life
December 6

Bible Verses
"You will show me the way of life, granting me the joy of your presence and the pleasures of living with you forever." Psalm 16:11 (NLT)

Jesus told her, "I am the resurrection and the life. Anyone who believes in me will live, even after dying." John 11:25 (NLT)

Word of the Day
Life – The time we are alive on this planet. Having vitality. Enthusiasm.

Quotes
"Giddy' up is my way of saying life is meant to be enjoyed. Savor every moment. We are bombarded with negative all day long. Let's remind ourselves about how dang cool life really is." Joe Morton

"Healing was a way of life for Jesus. It should be a way of life for all of us, also." Joan Hunter

"To love life is to love God. Harder and more blessed than all else is to love this life in one's sufferings, in undeserved sufferings." Leo Tolstoy

Pam's Perspective
Most of my life I walked around feeling like I was waiting for my life to start before I could be great. News flash, it started, and I am already great! Now I enjoy every moment and never wait to laugh, have fun, help a friend, or take a risk.

Questions
Am I living the life of my dreams? If not, what would that life look like? What actions can I take to enhance my life? Who will I share my life with?

Declarations

My **life** is great! I enjoy **life** with its many riches and rewards. I have everything I need to live a satisfying **life**. Rather than impressing others, I design a **lifestyle** that demonstrates my core values.

I strengthen my immune system by adding fresh vegetables, spices, and herbs to my meals. I squeeze every bit of juice out of **life** and enjoy tasting all the flavors. I walk barefoot in the grass and get grounded to mother earth. I garden, play in the dirt, and grow my own food. Eating healthy improves my **life** in countless ways.

I believe in my dreams. I breathe **life** into the projects I take on. I enjoy the good **life** where things swiftly go my way. I live a **life** of excellence that I construct. I live a comfortable **life**. I alone answer to the consequences of the choices I have made in my **life**.

Life is rewarding and full of excitement! I have a special reverence for **life**. I spend my **life** supporting worthwhile projects. I share my talents with the world. I try new things along **life's** journey.

Because my inner dialog is positive, it enhances my **life**, and it stays that way with my confident declarations. **Life** works for me. Being optimistic is natural for me. I consciously choose what I want to think about. I am infused with the joy of **life** coursing through my veins. I make the time to relax and appreciate my upbeat **life**.

I love my **life**! I invest in experiences that create lasting memories for my family and me. Meeting new people improves my **life**. I have really cool friends. I deserve all the good things **life** has to offer me. All is well with my **life**, family, health, career, and finances. I love the **life** I live and am grateful to I live a **life** I love. I get cool gifts from God that I didn't even ask for, like sunshine, and rainbows.

Death
December 7

Bible Verses
"But God raised Him up. He allowed Him to be set free from the pain of death. Death could not hold its power over Him." Acts 2:24 (NLV)

"He will wipe every tear from their eyes. There will be no more death' or mourning or crying or pain, for the old order of things has passed away." Revelation 21:4 (NIV)

Word of the Day
Death – To cease being alive. No longer in the land of the living.

Quotes
"Life is worth living through every grain of it, from the foundations to the last edge of the cornerstone, death." William Ernest Henley

"Wherefore, O judges, be of good cheer about death, and know of a certainty that no evil can happen to a good man, either in life or after death." Sir John Lubbock

Pam's Perspective
When I was young, I was terrified of death because I believed if I had one bad thought and had not repented before I died, I would go straight to hell. When I believed in a mean God, I was mean to others and myself. Now I fear nothing. I realize God did not come to condemn the world but to save it. He was chasing me down and loving me while I hated and rejected Him. Death has lost its sting.

Questions
Do I have a fear of death? What are my thoughts on death? Do I have my papers in order in case of my death? If not, why not? Do I have my funeral planned out? Will I have any regrets at my death?

Declarations

I fear not **death**, because I know to be absent from this body is to be present with my Lord. **Death** comes to every living thing. With every breath, I draw closer to **death**. Everyone I know and love is going to see **death**. I have a limited time here on earth. That is the way God designed it. Therefore, I make the most out of every day.

I turn a deaf ear to the negative chatter in my head. I say **death** to negativity. I get more loving to myself and others with time. As I look in the mirror at myself, I smile because I am undefeatable.

Laughing just because I can, and rejoicing to be alive is a wonderful thing. I stop reading all those predictions I find in the newspapers about gloom, doom, and **death**. I remind myself of the faithfulness of God as I make a list of past challenges I overcame. I am light and free, sensing I will never be separate from God who resides in me.

Since I never know when **death** will arrive for me, my family, or friends, I stay in touch. I call, write, and visit as often as I can. I say **death** to the lone ranger. I need companionship. As I give myself to loving others, I fulfill my greatest purpose, sharing the love.

I am chosen by God to dissolve barriers of separation. Instead of wishing **death** to my enemies, I pray blessings over their head. My greatest lessons come from people who irritate me the most. I put to **death** the pride in my heart and forgive even when it is hard.

Underlining joy abides within me laughing at **death**. Nothing can separate me from the love of God, not even **death**. There is a season of **death** and life. Everything is perfect in God's eyes, even **death**. Until my **death**, as long as I have breath, I will enjoy every moment, be thankful for everything, and praise God for it all.

343:
Experience
December 8

Bible Verses

"You have let me experience the joys of life and the exquisite pleasures of your own eternal presence." Psalm 16:11 (TLB)

"Fear-of-God is a school in skilled living— first you learn humility, then you experience glory." Proverbs 15:33 (MSG)

Word of the Day

Experience – Personal wisdom on how to do or how something is done. Drawing knowledge from past exposures to something. A good understanding of one's observations.

Quotes

"For the truth behind the universe is that God is Father, Son, and Spirit, and the one unflinching purpose of the blessed Trinity is that we would come to taste and feel, to know and experience, the very trinitarian life itself." C. Baxter Kruger

"No man's knowledge here can go beyond his experience." John Locke

"The experiences of others can give us powerful insights and keep us from calamities, but will never teach us anything if we are not open to learning them. That is why it is important for us to broaden our horizons and keep a beginners mindset." Pam Malow-Isham

"Knowing what all experience goes to show, no mud can soil us but the mud we throw." Lowell

Questions

Do I create experiences that lift me up or bring me down? What good can I take from every experience? Do I relish the experience of being alive?

Declarations

I have a raw willingness to **experience** every aspect of my life. I am willing to look foolish, take chances, and **experience** difficulties in order to be a master of my craft. I appear assertive. I **experience** productivity as I use my creative imagination to make work easier.

I am **experiencing** the power of love and forgiveness every day. I am grateful that God is accessible to me 24/7. I **experience** God's grace, even when I don't live up to the standards I set for myself. The relief I **experience** when I give up being perfect is like a breath of fresh air. I am grateful for all my **experiences**, good and bad.

I **experience** the presence of serenity when I walk in nature. From every **experience**, I gain wisdom. I practice what I say I believe. By being thankful for everything I have, I **experience** contentment. I conform to the identity of the Almighty. I **experience** mercy as I give mercy. By helping others, I **experience** happiness. I receive things that are unexplainably good. I **experience** a calm, comfortable life.

I **experience** a change in my thinking because of what I have chosen to meditate on. What is the **experience** I will have when someone is mean to me? I can dwell on it and **experience** anger and grief, or I can let it go and **experience** freedom. It is always my choice.

The tenderness I **experience** from my mate is a gift. I **experience** being well taken care of and well thought of. People relate to me as a person of significance. I have gratitude in my heart just to be alive.

I attract the next great **experience** to me by always being ready for it. I get a move on to see who I can help. I love to **experience** being someone's blessing. I affect people on the planet in a grand way as I show how to cherish the **experiences** of peace, joy, love, and bliss.

344:
Inexperience
December 9

Bible Verses
"*Saul answered David, 'You can't go and fight this Philistine. You're too young and inexperienced—and he's been at this fighting business since before you were born.'*" *1 Samuel 17:33 (MSG)*

"*The council was caught by surprise by the confidence with which Peter and John spoke. After all, they understood that these apostles were uneducated and inexperienced. They also recognized that they had been followers of Jesus.*" *Acts 4:13 (CEB)*

Word of the Day
Inexperience – Ignorance. The absences of experience. Inferior.

Quotes
"*Prejudice and self-sufficiency naturally proceed from inexperience of the world, and ignorance of mankind.*" *Joseph Addison*

"*The heart is forever inexperienced.*" *Henry David Thoreau*

Pam's Perspective
I have never let inexperience stop me from accomplishing a goal. Everyone is inexperienced in the beginning, and we will stay that way if we never try new things. When I first started my goal setting girlfriend group, I had no idea what we would do or what I would come up with, but I knew I yearned for connections. Insights and inspiration come when you are willing to try new things.

Questions
Do I judge someone that is inexperienced and act arrogant, or do I give them a break and be kind? Where have I let inexperience stop me?

Declarations

Regardless of my **inexperience**, I am still worthy of a fulfilling career. I understand there is a price to be paid for accomplishing something worthwhile, so I give it my all, despite my **inexperience**.

I might be **inexperienced** in dating, but I know what I like. I have a long list of qualifications I want in a mate, and I will not settle until God brings that person along. We volunteer at the same places.

Although I am **inexperienced** in some things, I can use my head and figure it out. I am realistic about the steps I need to take and the amount of work entailed to complete every project. Then because of my **inexperience**, I add more time knowing it will take longer.

My **inexperience** serves me well as I ignore people who want to pick a fight. I obey my conscious and keep quiet when the **inexperience** of a self- righteous person judges me. My well-chosen behavior of tolerance is an asset. I ignore their **inexperience**. I make allowances for the **inexperience** of others. I am a facilitator of love and peace.

Despite my **inexperience**, I plunge ahead and don't allow anything stop me. I turn everything to my advantage today. I set deadlines for my action plan. As my **inexperience** diminishes, I reap great rewards. I hear the beautiful sound of my associates, well done!

God uses my **inexperience** to confound the wise. I stand in front of the crowd in defiance of my **inexperience** and wow my audience. God's ways are childlike and simple. His methods are true. The mistakes from my **inexperience** in the past has taught me many valuable lessons. I am grateful I do not have to relearn them. Once is enough, thank you very much. I remind myself of my brilliance. Even with my **inexperience**, I am a leader in my community.

345:
Win
December 10

Bible Verses
"Don't you realize that in a race everyone runs, but only one person gets the prize? So run to win!" 1 Corinthians 9:24 (NLT)

"Those who win the victory will receive this from me: I will be their God, and they will be my children." Revelation 21:7 (GNT)

Word of the Day
Win –To come in first place. To triumph over obstacles. To achieve goals.

Quotes
"We need more of the courage that dares and the courage that does, that recognizes right and pursues it, that owns a duty and discharges it, that sees a wrong and rights it, a right and aids it. There are many of us who do great acts, but because we wait for great opportunities life passes and the acts of duty and brotherly love are not done at all. Life is made up of infinitesimals. Small attentions, kind looks, and helpful words. Come what many, my brethren, in the moil and toilsome way of life, hold fast to this love. We win by tenderness. We conquer by forgiveness." Brother Whipple

"We win by tenderness. We conquer by forgiveness." Frederick W. Robertson

Pam's Perspective
My husband and I took up kayaking and were on the Pine River a lot. We all won because we were on the river having fun, enjoying the wildlife.

Questions
How do I go about winning the game of life? Do I think of myself as a winner? If not, why not? Why is winning important to me?

Declarations

I play to **win**. I think of a happy place, in the **winner's** circle, and the wonderful feeling of accomplishment that I receive. I give my mind time to percolate creative ideas on the best possible action to take to **win**. I put problems on the back burner and focus on **winning**.

I psyche myself up by saying I am going to **win**, so I do. I am bold. I know actions follow thoughts, so after I think about how wonderful it is to **win**; I get busy making it happen. I take my gifts to a whole new level by sharpening my skills and believing I can **win**.

Winning is always available to me. I take colossal action to achieve my **win**. I love to come in first. I am a **winner**. I collaborate with other **winners** to benefit us both. I **win** my teammate's corporation by giving them credit. **Win, win** is the game I like to play.

Out of peacefulness, I can **win** every conflict that comes my way. I don't care if I **win** an argument, only if I **win** a friend. Love is my top priority. I am versatile with my dialogue because I read a variety of topics. I love to help others **win** and feel good about themselves. I **win** friends by being friendly. I **win** happiness by sharing.

As my pet **wins** my heart, I **win** the prize of a forever friend. It is a **win, win** for both of us. God reveals His tenderness to me through the affection of my pet. Both love and are always happy to see me.

God loves me and wants me to **win** today. I trust in the Lord, so I dismantle all fear with my faith. I am grateful for past **wins**. I like to **win**. I am surrounded by an atmosphere of plenty. I **win** confidence in myself by taking action. I lead the way to victory. I am a **winner** who faces my problems with a can-do attitude. I enjoy **winning**. By practicing mindfulness, I am a **winner** who comes out on top.

346:
Lose
December 11

Bible Verses
"Those who want to save their lives will lose them. But those who lose their lives for me will find them." Matthew 16:25 (GW)

"So don't lose your confidence. It will bring you a great reward." Hebrews 10:35 (GW)

Word of the Day
Lose – To displace an object. To have something stolen. To suffer loss.

Quotes
"Our doubts are traitors and make us lose the good we oft might win by fearing to attempt." William Shakespeare

"You must lose a fly before you can catch a trout." English Proverb

"Whoso neglects learning in his youth, loses the past and is dead for the future." Euripides

Pam's Perspective
I was the ugly duckling and the kid everyone picked on. When I was in third grade, the two most popular girls in the school came up to me on the playground. One told me to bend down and tie her shoe that she had just unlaced or she was going to kick my butt. I did it because I didn't want to lose in a fight. But I lost my self-respect. It took me years to build it back up. Now I don't allow anyone to bully me. I have confidence now by standing up for myself and my beliefs.

Questions
What is the best way for me to lose weight? What is the easiest way to lose strife? What is the simplest way to lose a bad attitude?

Declarations

I make plenty of mistakes and **lose** sometimes, but I never quit trying. I don't let outside circumstances throw me off center. I have **lost** plenty and survived in the past. I **lose** the failure notion and give it my all. Everything I try is obtainable. I never **lose** hope.

I function at an optimal pace, so I do not **lose** my stride. I feel good walking with purpose. I **lose** weight, keep it off, and stay healthy. I **lose** being dehydrated by drinking lots of water. Drinking vegetable juice restores my vigor. I am perfectly made. Improving is the norm for me. Discipline, self-control, and will-power; that describes me.

I remind people frequently how much I love them, so they don't **lose** heart. I **lose** the electronics and stay present with whom I am with. I like being empathetic. I **lose** having to talk when I can listen.

I develop a good, healthy thought regimen. I catch myself when I have a negative thought and **lose** it right away. I bring my attention back to the moment. I concentrate on the positive. I remember all the trials God has brought me through, so I do not **lose** the lesson.

I **lose** the notion that I will be a success overnight because I know all good things take energy and time to accomplish. I can't **lose** because I am someone's hero. I **lose** the bad attitude forever, so I rise to victory. I **lose** defeat. I **lose** my inhibitions and just be myself.

God has given me a lovely life to live. I am a spark of hope when people **lose** their spunk. I love cheering them back up. I **lose** my sense of entitlement and put others first. I **lose** placing the blame on other people when I am the only one responsible for my actions and my station in life. I **lose** fear and say the things I have been afraid to say. I say I love you often. I am composed, certain, and courageous.

347:
Initiate
December 12

Bible Verse
"We do this by keeping our eyes on Jesus, the champion who initiates and perfects our faith. Because of the joy awaiting him, he endured the cross, disregarding its shame. Now he is seated in the place of honor beside God's throne." Hebrews 12:2 (NLT)

Word of the Day
Initiate – To commence doing something from the start. To introduce a new way of thinking or acting. To start. To install.

Quotes
"We will initiate social change for the betterment of the planet by starting in our own family and community." Gary Isham

"Providence would only initiate mankind into the useful knowledge of her treasures, leaving the rest to employ our industry that we might not live like idle loiterers." Sir Thomas More

"Initiate a smile and watch happiness grow." Pam Malow-Isham

Pam's Perspective
It takes guts to initiate something. I rarely feel like initiating anything, but I do anyway. Initiating a conversation is the first step to creating a friend. Initiating movement is how to lead a dance so your partner can follow you. Initiating is the hardest part of any task. Once you get moving, things naturally occur.

Questions
Am I in the habit of initiating a conversation with someone I don't know? Am I the first to initiate friendship? What good will I initiate today?

Declarations

I have boundless enthusiasm as I **initiate** my day with laughter. I inherit the good I **initiate**. Before I **initiate** work on my desires, I **initiate** a prayer to get God's approval. I see victory clearly as God enables me to be glorious. I belong to the miracle of the day club. When someone does something to upset me, I **initiate** forgiveness.

People are impacted in a grand way by my big dream becoming a reality. I use my ambition to **initiate** my goals. I **initiate** the three most important objectives I need to reach my goals, and then I get busy. I **initiate** setting aside time, so I can accomplish my plan.

The way I **initiate** new visions inspires the complacent to get moving. I manifest the qualities of God flowing through me as I **initiate** charity. When I walk into a room, I am the first to **initiate** a conversation. I **initiate** goodwill in my community by my volunteer work. I am naturally easy to get along with, so I have an abundance of friends. I **initiate** my memory by commanding it to remember. I have a sound mind. I give myself time to get what I **initiate**.

I **initiate** good fortune by declaring blessings and being a blessing. My way of being generous is contagious. I **initiate** saving money before an emergency happens. I allocate enough resources in my budget to keep things repaired. I brainstorm to **initiate** grand ideas. As I **initiate** love and optimism, I get happier every day.

God first **initiated** His love for me, and He has not changed His mind. I **initiate** confidence by declaring what God says about me. I am loved beyond measure, a child of God, a king's kid, a citizen of heaven, set free, delivered, righteous, chosen, redeemed, worthy, forgiven, holy, victorious, and unblemished. Knowing this, I **initiate** boldness to take on every challenge that comes my way.

348:
Conclude
December 13

Bible Verses
"So I conclude that, first, there is nothing better for a man than to be happy and to enjoy himself as long as he can." Ecclesiastes 3:12 (TLB)

"Therefore we conclude that a man is justified by faith without the deeds of the law." Romans 3:28 (KJV)

Word of the Day
Conclude – To complete a task, performance or thought. To terminate talking. To fulfill an obligation. To make up one's mind.

Quotes
"What you can show using physics, forces this universe to continue to exist. As long as you're using general relativity and quantum mechanics you are forced to conclude that God exists." Frank Tipler

"In the morning, prayer is the key that opens to us the treasure of God's mercies and blessings; in the evening, it is the key that shuts us up under his protection and safeguard. Prayer, as the first, second, and the third element of the Christian life, should open, prolong, and conclude each day." Henry Ward Beecher

Pam's Perspective
If I conclude that all my beliefs are true, then I never ask questions or inquire about them. Continual inquiries and study wards off faulty thinking and actions.

Questions
Have I ever concluded something too soon because I thought it was hard? How will I conclude my day? How will I conclude my life?

Declarations

I **conclude** that God is for me and wants the very best for me. There is nothing wrong with me if I am sad once in a while. Life is both up and down, so I have decided not to take myself so seriously. I can **conclude** to either enjoy my life or be miserable. I choose joy.

I **conclude** we all deserve to be loved and cared for, no exceptions. I can **conclude** to be a realist and honest with myself while also being happy. I encourage people so they can realize they are not alone in hard times. I am gifted with understanding. I listen to both sides of a story before I reach a **conclusion**. I make an impact on my friends.

As I have an open heart, the secrets of God are revealed to me. I have **concluded** that it is better to serve God and sense His presence than to wander around aimlessly. His mind-boggling joy makes life relevant. I embrace all the adventures that are coming my way.

Even though sometimes I want instant gratification, I **conclude** that patience pays off. I **conclude** that every action I take, no matter how big or small, is getting me closer to reaching my goals. Even if it takes me five or ten years to **conclude** it, it will be worth it.

I will be remembered long after I am gone. When I **conclude** my life, I will have left a legacy of compassion and good deeds. I glorify God in my life. There is great festivity in heaven when they look at me. God has already **concluded** that I will spend eternity with Him.

As I look within I **conclude**, I still have a ways to go. I **conclude** to abolish any deep standing resignation and practice diligence. I am grateful for God's involvement in my experiences. As I look around, I **conclude** there is more for me to do, so I get busy. In **conclusion**, I welcome wealth, wisdom, and a renewed sense of wonder.

349:
Dishonor
December 14

Bible Verses

"You must not dishonor God or curse any of your rulers." Exodus 22:28 (NLT)

"Instead of shame and dishonor, you will enjoy a double share of honor. You will possess a double portion of prosperity in your land, and everlasting joy will be yours." Isaiah 61:7 (NLT)

Word of the Day

Dishonor – To reproach, slight or outrage someone. To degrade something of value. Blemish, scorn.

Quotes

"If you be affronted, it is better in a foreign country to pass it by in silence and with a jest, though with some dishonor, than to endeavor revenge... If you can keep reason above passion, that and watchfulness will be your best defendants." Sir Isaac Newton

"Ridicule dishonors more than dishonor." Francois de La Rochefoucauld

"For some reason, we think of doubt and worry as small sins. But when a Christian displays unbelief, anxiety, or an inability to cope with life, he is saying to the world, "My God cannot be trusted," and that kind of disrespect makes one guilty of a fundamental error, the heinous sin of dishonoring God. That is no small sin." John MacArthur

"The greatest dishonor is ingratitude." Pam Malow-Isham

Questions

Do I ever dishonor someone by not listening to them? Are there ways that I am dishonoring myself? If so, what will I do about it?

Declarations

I value my mind, so I do not **dishonor** it by filling it with worry, chaos, and filth. I fill my mind with God's Word. I set the tone for love and peace in my thinking, talking and in all my actions.

I take things lightly so if someone says something to **dishonor** me I can choose to let it go. Holding onto an offense does not serve me well, so I release all hurts. I keep my cool when people talk down to me. I realize it is just their insecurities being manifested as they **dishonor** themselves by acting superior. I cannot control how another person thinks or acts, but I can control how I will respond.

When I am tempted to **dishonor** someone by judging them because they are different than me, I remind myself that God loves all His children the same. I see through considerate eyes. I choose not to **dishonor** anyone with my words, so I speak with loving-kindness.

I show up for my friends, so I do not **dishonor** them, even when I do not feel like it because I am a person of my word. I celebrate the successes of my friends when I hear of their good fortune.

God loves me, even if I **dishonor** Him by doubting He is in control, or when I take things for granted. I have nothing to fear and much to gain by putting my hope in God, so I rejoice in His certain promises.

If I **dishonor** myself by overeating, I forgive myself and propose to do better. I drink a large glass of water before meals, so I don't eat too much. I chew slowly and mindfully, enjoying every morsel. I choose not to **dishonor** myself by playing small and acting like I don't know what to do. I choose to believe God for the miraculous now. I have access to God's power and knowledge within me through prayer at any time. Nothing is too hard for me and God.

350:
Honor
December 15

Bible Verses

"Honor your father and mother,' and 'love your neighbor as yourself.'."
Matthew 19:19 (NIV)

"Now to the King eternal, immortal, invisible, the only God, be honor and glory forever and ever. Amen." 1 Timothy 1:17 (NIV)

Word of the Day
Honor – goodness in principles and deeds. Trustworthy. To cherish.

Quotes
"There are three classes of men; lovers of wisdom, lovers of honor, and lovers of gain." Plato

"When the will defies fear, when the heart applauds the brain, when duty throws the gauntlet down to fate, when honor scorns to compromise with death – that is heroism. The abolitionists were heroes. He loves his country best who strives to make it best." Robert Green Ingersoll

Pam's Perspective
I heard when I prayed, Honor your Father, not because he was a good dad, he wasn't, but because it is the right thing to do. Even though my dad was abusive, didn't send me cards or presents for any birthdays or holidays and was rarely there, I am glad I listened and took care of him for the last two years of his life. It was difficult but also a gift that I cherish. I have no regrets.

Questions
Do I live a life that is honorable? Do I honor my commitments? Why or why not? Do I honor my parents? What or who do I honor and why?

Declarations

I **honor** God with my life and aim to share His love with the world. I see positive traits in people and **honor** their uniqueness. The Holy Spirit inspires me for good works. I am kind to everyone I meet. I accommodate those with whom I disagree. I **honor** everyone.

My friends are important to me. Since none of my friends can make decisions for me, I have to **honor** myself by making wise choices. I savor the experience of being loved, respected and **honored** by my friends. We **honor** each other while enjoying our differences.

I cultivate the love within me as I **honor** and see myself as a person of importance. By **honoring** my body with exercise, I feel energized, and ready to take on the world. I put food into my body that I can be proud of. I **honor** myself with patience, respect, and movement.

I **honor** my word and follow through with what I say I am going to do. **Honor** and integrity are what I am all about. I am an **honorable** person with great values. I **honor** others and myself by being joyful.

I respect and **honor** my mate by caring about what is important to him or her. I always work to settle any squabble in the best possible way. I am the first to say 'I am sorry.' I **honor** my mate's point of view and listen with open ears. I **honor** our vows and stay loyal. I **honor** our commitment together. I have great tolerance and faith.

I **honor** my parents, even if I think they do not deserve it. They did try their best. My parents are unique, and I can learn from their experiences when I keep an open mind. It is ok that they are not flawless. Their parents were also flawed. I can **honor** them without feeling inferior. I **honor** my elders, show respect, and grow wiser from their wisdom. I enjoy a long life of **honor** and satisfaction.

351:
Failure
December 16

Bible Verses
"If you forgive the failures of others, your heavenly Father will also forgive you." Matthew 6:14 (GW)

"We have been ransomed through his Son's blood, and we have forgiveness for our failures based on his overflowing grace." Ephesians 1:7 (CEB)

Word of the Day
Failure – The deterioration of one's dreams or goals. The frustration of not accomplishing what you set out to do. A temporary defeat.

Quotes
"We have forty million reasons for failure, but not a single excuse." Rudyard Kipling

"Failure is not permanent, and neither is success." Michael Althsuler

"Indecision and delays are the parents of failure." George Canning

"The greatest insights are extracted from failure." Pam Malow-Isham

Pam's Perspective
I have been a failure at a lot of things I have tried. We all have been at one time or another if we are honest and admitted it. That's how I learn and grow, so I discover the gift and move on. Without failure, success would be uninspiring.

Questions
How do I respond when a failure occurs? What have I learned from my past failures? Do I ever take failure personally? Do I laugh at failure?

Declarations

I have been a **failure** many times in my life, and I am sure I will **fail** again. **Failure** is a part of life I now look forward to in order to learn a new lesson. Learning from every **failure,** I become wise. I never give up if I have a **failure**. It is just a tiny speed bump in the road.

I forgive myself for every **failure** I have made. I allow myself the time I need to heal after a **failure**. When I soak in a hot tub, I release all my **failures**. Then I pull the plug and watch it go down the drain. I admit my **failures** and move on. I love myself despite my **failures**.

I approve of myself because of the **failures** I have endured. God lifts me from **failure** to great triumphs. I am not afraid of **failure** because it allows me to grow. With strong confidence in myself, I reach my desired results. I make the most of every opportunity. I forgive everyone for his or her **failures,** just as Christ has forgiven me.

Greater good comes from my **failures** when I share them with others so they can see how they can rise above **failures** too. I release steam when I talk about my **failure** to a trustworthy person. I have noble friends. I belong to a group of radical **failures** who support and encourage each other. We go to King Jesus for our answers.

My **failure** to hit a target only slows me down. Nothing is impossible for me. I figure out a way to overcome every **failure,** no matter how big or small. I follow through with what I need to do. I recognize myself as a mighty force for good despite my **failures**.

I accomplish much. I read about **failures** who have overcome immense challenges. Because I have been given divine solutions, I have no need to repeat past **failures**. I am glad I listened. God sees past my **failures** and recognizes me as His favorite child.

352:
Success
December 17

Bible Verses
*"David had success in all his undertakings; for the Lord was with him." 1
Samuel 18:14 (NRSV)*

*"Plans go wrong for lack of advice; many advisers bring success." Proverbs
15:22 (NLT)*

Word of the Day
Success – The achievement of one's desires. Good fortune. Winning.

Quotes
*"The great high-road of human welfare lies along the old highway of
steadfast well-doing; and they who are the most persistent, and work in the
truest spirit, will invariably be the most successful; success tread on the heels
of every right effort." Samuel Smiles*

*"Success is being happy with your accomplishments, peace in your
mind, loving yourself, and living out your well-defined purpose." Pam
Malow-Isham*

*"Success in life is a matter, not so much of talent or opportunity as of
concentration and perseverance." Charles W. Wendte*

Pam's Perspective
*Having a fear of success, it was much easier to slack off, sleep in, and read or
watch TV. But succeeding feels better than any excuse I could have made.*

Questions
What does success look like for me? How will I know when I reach
success? What have I let stop me from achieving success?

Declarations

God has given me the authority to be a **success**. I am a person whom God uses and favors with **success** in all my undertakings. I use my **success** to bless the people around me. I continue in my magnificent fascination of changing the world one person at a time as I inspire them to become **successful**. I like being my best and acting nice.

I look for scriptures to declare that is pertaining to what I am petitioning God for, so **success** is sure. My body is a holy temple where God dwells. Miracles occur when I am near because I allow God to use me. I embody **success** to those around me.

By achieving financial **success**, I am able to store up a reserve to survive disastrous times, and help others. I restore a **successful** balance to my home from the years that the locust has eaten. I spread my wealth around. I am at ease with who I am.

I gleefully focus my mind on **success** now. I choose to do what it takes to be a **success**. With the help of my **successful** mastermind group, we energize each other to reach our goals. I easily handle hard times. I give myself permission to be a smashing **success**.

My passionate thoughts drive my **success**. I not only look like a **success**, I am one. My best hasn't even happened yet. I am disciplined and structured in my game plan for **success**. I am completely open and available to take in a plethora of **success** today.

God is rolling up His sleeves now on my behalf to make me a **success**. I dwell in an atmosphere of love and plenty. I receive the best gifts from a variety of sources. I know what to do to foster **successful** opportunities. I praise God in advance of my **success** because He always comes through for me. I love being **successful**.

353:
New
December 18

Bible Verses
"His great love is new every morning. Lord, how faithful you are!"
Lamentations 3:23 (NIRV)

"Anyone who believes in Christ is a new creation. The old is gone! The new has come!" 2 Corinthians 5:17 (NIRV)

Word of the Day
New – The beginning of an idea, design or product. Different, unique and original. Something that has never been done before.

Quotes
"New opinions are always suspected, and usually opposed, without any other reason but because they are not already common." John Locke

"Every Christian out to be, in his human measure, a new incarnation of the Christ, so that people will say, "He interprets Christ to me. He comforts me in my sorrows as Christ Himself would if He were to come and sit down beside me"." Rev. J. R. Miller, D. D.

"Thinking positive thoughts will give you a new point of view, elevate your disposition and improve your health." Pam Malow-Isham

"Back of all this demand for new and better things, there is one quality which one must possess to win, and that is DEFINITENESS OF PURPOSE, the knowledge of what one wants, and a burning DESIRE to possess it." Napoleon Hill

Questions
What are some new dreams, goals, adventures, ideas, challenges or habits that I can take on in this New Year? Will I look at myself in a new light?

Declarations

I rejoice this **new** day to look at everything in a **new** way. I have a **new** lease on life. I am an ambassador of freedom. I embrace **new** dreams that before seemed impossible, but now I see things in a **new** light. **New** revelation is continually being revealed to me as I study God's word. I keep searching for **new** and better ways to live.

I pray **new** powerful prayers. I encourage myself to go within to find the **new** answers I need. I look forward to what each **new** hour brings. I am devoted to God's purposes, and He is devoted to inspiring me with **new** ideas, inventions, and ways of being.

I create **new** ways to play. I make **new** friends as I take the time to get to know **new** people. Everybody is special, and in my life for a reason: to teach me a **new** lesson. And boy do I have a few more lessons to learn. I get out of my own way and respond to people with the love of Christ. I am willing to take the next **new** step.

I release all doubts and negative self-talk that I have inflicted on myself and affirm a **new** language of love and possibilities. My **new** way of being that is kinder toward myself, and others is rewarding.

I creatively find **new** ways to press on, flourish and prosper as I grow up and mature. **New** beginnings are always possible. I begin a **new** way of thinking and acting. The strong liking I have for **new** positive books creates my **new** enthusiastic, can do, attitude.

I am done with dried up religion and dead works. I answer to a **new** higher calling. The Spirit of God invades me with a **new** life. **New** God-inspired plans infuse my thinking as I seek to follow Him in a **new** manner. **New** hope springs up in my heart as I embrace His affection for me. This is a **new** day with unlimited options.

354:
Old
December 19

Bible Verses

"I have been young, and now am old, yet I have not seen the righteous forsaken or their children begging bread." Psalm 37:25 (NRSV)

"In old age they still produce fruit; they are always green and full of sap." Psalm 92:14 (NRSA)

Word of the Day

Old – Geriatric and getting on in years. Elderly or mature. Something that is antiquated and unstylish. Dated.

Quotes

"The young man knows the rules, but the old man knows the exceptions." Oliver Wendell Holmes, Sr.

"When grace is joined with wrinkles, it is adorable. There is an unspeakable dawn in happy old age." Victor Hugo

Pam's Perspective

For some reason, I had in my mind that twenty-five was old. On my twenty-fifth birthday, I woke up and saw crow's feet around my eyes that I didn't see the night before. Then I found my first gray hair and started bawling. Now I am twice as old and feel much younger. The older I get, the less I care about appearances and what others think of me. There is a freedom, and confidence that comes with age that is priceless to the recipients who embrace their maturity with joy.

Questions

What old habit, thought or attitude will I release today? Do I consider myself old or do I still have something to contribute? If so, how?

Declarations

I clean out the clutter and throw out or donate **old** items that are no longer needed, so I can make room for the new. I like creating open spaces. Even **old** things that are still in use sometimes have to go. I find new uses for **old** items as I recycle and repurpose **old** things.

My **old** friends are very important to me. I appreciate **old** friends, and I take time to show it. My kindness to others pays dividends. No matter how **old** I get, I don't cower down when it comes to a trial. I rise to every challenge head on like an **old** warrior.

Holding onto **old** resentments, hurts, and misunderstandings do not serve me well, so I let them go. I send **old** wounds to heaven. I move on and return to a peaceful place. I treat people well. I allow forgiveness and healing to flow as I live without regret.

The **older** I get, the wiser I get. I search out **older** people to gain their wisdom. I enjoy reading **old** stories of great people who conquered their fears and made an impact on society. I trust the discernment of my heart as I get **older** and hear God's voice more clearly.

God breaks every chain and bondage from my **old** life. I release **old** negative thought patterns telling me I am not good enough because I know that I am. I simply decide to accept the backing of the Holy Spirit on my behalf and claim my birthright. I am strong and bright. The same God of **old** is still in the miracle-working business for me.

I am as **old** or young as I feel. I am liberated and set free. I always stay active, feeling great at every age. I enjoy what I have been given today, an opportunity to make a difference in the world. No matter how **old** I get, I am still a child of God and a wonderful expression of the divine, living, and working through me. I make a difference.

355:
Creative
December 20

Bible Verses
"Live creatively, friends. If someone falls into sin, forgivingly restore him, saving your critical comments for yourself. You might be needing forgiveness before the days out." Galatians 6:1 (MSG)

"Each of you must take responsibility for doing the creative best you can with your own life." Galatians 6:5 (MSG)

Word of the Day
Creative – Having the ability to be inventive. Artistic. Visionary.

Quotes
"Genius is essentially creative; it bears the stamp of the individual who possesses it." Madame de Stael

"Through the instrumentality of our thought forces we have creative power, not merely in a figurative sense, but creative power in reality. Everything in the material universe about us, everything the universe has ever known, had its origin first in thought." Ralph Waldo Trine

"Live in the very soul of expectation of better things, in the conviction that something large, grand, and beautiful will await you if your efforts are intelligent, if your mind is kept in a creative condition and you struggle upward to your goal. Live in the conviction that you are eternally progressing, advancing toward something higher, better, in every atom of your being." Orison Swett Marden

Questions
Do I regard myself as a creative person? Why or why not? Do I hang around creative people? What inspires me to be creative? What is the most creative thing I have done? What creative thing will I do today?

Declarations

I am a **creative** thinker who **creates** new ways to inspire others and myself. I can help mankind with my **creativity**. I take **creative** action to reach my goals. Every day my **creative** juices are overflowing with new concepts. I can do anything I set my **creative** mind to.

God's **creative** power is working through me to be a blessing to others. I am infinitely **creative** as I think up the most innovative things. My **creative** ideas continue to amaze me. I feel fortunate to have an intimate connection with Divine **creativity**. I love feeling **creative**. My authority and **creativity** are bestowed from above.

I discover **creative** ways to get moving and exercise that are fun. I am **creative** in my entertainment wherever I go. I **create** new ways to show I care. I accumulate opportunities to stay **creative**. God backs me with **creativity**. I work smart. I am calm, capable and **creative**.

I spur on random acts of kindness with my **creativity**. I am grateful when I think about all my **creative** friends. Every day I get more **creative** in keeping my promises. I actively stay in the driver's seat and get things done so I can have and live a **creative** life.

I am a highly **creative** genius. The questions my **creative** mind thinks up to stimulate conversations with people is exhilarating. I flow with **creativity** throughout my day. I visualize the way I want my life to be and **create** it. I become who God identifies me to be.

I **creatively** secure new sources of income that freely come to me in a landslide of abundance. I improve my work by being open to **creative** ideas. I make plans for success as I **create** products that reap profits. **Creative** people are attracted to me, and we spur each other on to **create** bigger and better goals. I do everything with excellence.

356:
Distinction
December 21

Bible Verses
"For there is no distinction of the Jew and the Greek: for the same is Lord over all, rich unto all that call upon him." Romans 10:12 (DRA)

"But there are distinctions of gifts, but the same Spirit; and there are distinctions of services, and the same Lord; and there are distinctions of operations, but the same God who operates all things in all." 1 Corinthians 12:4-6 (DARBY)

Word of the Day
Distinction – The contrast between things. Set apart. Exception. Prestige.

Quotes
"Joy increases and suffering decreases as one masters the distinction between events and one's feelings about those events." Jonathan Lockwood Huie

"The real difference between men, is energy. A strong will, a settled purpose, an invincible determination can accomplish almost anything; and in this lies the great distinction between great men and little men." Thomas Fuller

Pam's Perspective
In 1997 I started taking classes through Landmark Education and went through their curriculum for living. It was the most life-transforming class I have ever taken. I experienced the language phenomenon "distinction" and "ways of being." My view of life changed and I was no longer a victim. Instead of reacting to all my problems I was able to create a life I loved! Because I could see the limiting beliefs that held me back mentally and spiritually, I grew closer to God.

Questions
How may I become a person of distinction? What do I manifest?

Declarations

I live powerfully into the **distinctions** I choose. I ask myself, 'who am I becoming'? I operate from my best self by living into the **distinction** of being a person of integrity. Because I have the ability to be affluent, caring, cheerful, fair, hospitable, dependable, realistic and so much more; I have become someone of **distinction.**

I walk in the **distinction** of trust knowing God is taking care of me. I **distinctively** pick words that motivate me and live by those words. I hear God speaking words of encouragement to me. I live out the **distinction** of being a loving and generous person. I speak **distinctive** words that create life, freedom, and wealth.

I give myself permission to be powerful and live into the **distinction** of victory. I see in the **distinction** of light, beauty, and acceptance. I put aside personal prejudice and open my ears as I hear in the **distinction** of truth and wisdom. I am an encourager. I live in the **distinction** of tolerance allowing people to be who they are.

The **distinction** of receiving God's love is extreme joy to me. Because of my jovial disposition, I have the **distinction** of being lighthearted and animated. I live in the **distinction** of forgiveness and unity. I stop talking, remove distractions and listen to the **distinction** of receptiveness and understanding. I am the **distinction** of love.

I taste the **distinction** between bitter and sweet. I excitedly try new food. I will try anything once. I embrace the simple life and release the struggle as I play in the **distinction** of laughter, merriment, and fun. I like giving long hugs. I frolic in the **distinction** of love and togetherness. I make no **distinction** about the people I serve, love, or help. I empower people with the **distinctive** words I speak. I am glad to see my dreams come true. I am a person of **distinction**!

357:
Charity
December 22

Bible Verses
"Be generous: Invest in acts of charity. Charity yields high returns."
Ecclesiastes 11:1 (MSG)

"And let everything you do be done in a spirit of charity." 1 Corinthians
16:14 (KNOX)

Word of the Day
Charity – Giving a helping hand to someone who has less than you.
Having a philanthropic heart. Being kindhearted and generous.

Quotes
"Love attracts Charity, Anger attracts Violence, Peace attracts Tranquility,
Judgment attracts Blame, Laughter attracts Health, Strife attracts fighting,
Contribution attracts Increase, Exploration attracts Wisdom, and Fear
attracts Anxiety. What are you committed to attracting? Whatever is
showing up for you is a clue." Pam Malow-Isham

"Studies show that, quite to the contrary, happier people are more likely to
help other people, they're more interested in social problems, they do more
volunteer work, and they contribute more to charity. They're less preoccupied
with their personal problems. By contrast, less-happy people are more apt to
be defensive, isolated, and self-absorbed, and unfortunately, their negative
moods are catching (technical name: emotional contagion). Just as eating
your dinner doesn't help starving children in India, being blue yourself
doesn't help unhappy people become happier." Gretchen Rubin

Questions
Is charity my first response or an after-thought? How many charitable
causes do I support? What act of charity will I perform today?

Declarations

I start my **charity** at home and give the most to the people closest to me. My thoughts of **charity** reflect from my face and eyes. I know God loves a cheerful giver and shines His favor on me because of the kind deeds I do every day. I train myself to be **charitable**.

I free myself from selfishness by giving of my prayers, finances, and time. I speak from a place of **charity** and a welcoming heart. I connect with people wherever they are and listen. I am always noticing new ways to spread **charity**, hope, love, and peace.

Since I have been blessed with so much in abundance, I always have more than enough to give liberally to the **charity** of my choice. I take advantage of all the **charitable** opportunities in front of me. The **charity** I give is unconditional. I love to give anonymously.

I like sharing the resources I have. I actively get involved in **charity** work and make it part of my lifestyle. It is rewarding to be generous with my time, volunteering to help people in my community. I get more joy from helping people than the ones receiving my **charity**.

I accept the responsibility of being a **charitable** person. I help older people with their lawn work, cleaning, cooking, or other **charitable** acts I can do. I search out ways to improve just one other person's life with my **charity**. Divine approval is mine as I reap enormous rewards of internal peace and happiness from the **charity** I render.

At **charity** events, I meet the nicest people with the biggest hearts and dazzling smiles. I am devoted to good works and **charity**. I plan for **charity**. I share my good feelings about **charity** with everyone I meet. I make the right use out of the gifts that I have been given. Serving people is my natural way of expressing love and **charity**.

358:
Hindrance
December 23

Bible Verses
"But he turned and said to Peter, 'Get behind me, Satan! You are a hindrance to me. For you are not setting your mind on the things of God, but on the things of man.'" Matthew 16:23 (ESV)

"He proclaimed the kingdom of God and taught about the Lord Jesus Christ—with all boldness and without hindrance!" Acts 28:31 (NIV)

Word of the Day
Hindrance – A handicap or drawback. A restriction against. Distraction. Someone who is a interference or deterrent.

Quotes
"Trials, temptations, disappointments - all these are helps instead of hindrances, if one uses them rightly. They not only test the fiber of character but strengthen it. Every conquering temptation represents a new fund of moral energy. Every trial endured, if weathered in the right spirit, makes a soul nobler and stronger than it was before." James Buckham

"I only seek in my old age to perfect that which I had not before thoroughly learned in my youth, because my sins were a hindrance to me." Saint Patrick

"The real democratic American idea is, not that every man shall be on a level with every other man, but that every man shall have liberty to be what God made him, without hindrance." Henry Ward Beecher

Questions
Do I look at the hindrances I face and use them as an excuse for failure or fuel for success? Will I help someone else overcome a hindrance? What hindrance will I destroy today to reach my goals?

Declarations

I rely on God who pulls me through every **hindrance.** I take the time to stop, pray, and ask what this **hindrance** is revealing to me. I bring a touch of spirituality with me, everywhere I go, like kindness and patience. I clear my mind and come from a loving space to see the best possible options because when I look for something, I find it.

I make a list of the things that are a **hindrance** in my life, so I know where I stand. Then I find the solution on how to remove the **hindrance** quickly and with ease. Because I recognize the **hindrance** that is keeping me from obtaining a goal, I am not defeated by my own self-deception. I admit my faults and enjoy growing.

I realize I can always improve my life, so I look for ways to do so. I release the **hindrance** of every fear that tries to come my way. I face criticism and rejection head-on. I learn from every **hindrance.**

I think proactively by cultivating my mind with new information, so the **hindrance** of an automatic routine won't make me complacent. I adapt quickly to change so the **hindrance** of getting stuck in a rut won't happen to me. Nothing is a **hindrance** to me today.

I look fantastic! I remove tempting sweets from my view that are a **hindrance** to my health. My muscles are getting stronger every day as I remove all excuses that would **hinder** my workouts. I perform best when I am eating whole foods. I enjoy taking small incremental steps toward healthy living which produces a physically fit me.

I am optimistic and open to creating miracles in my life now despite **hindrances**. I see only a bright future that is **hindrance** free. I keep **hindrances** at bay by building up my knowledge, enthusiasm, self-esteem, and confidence. I invest in myself because I am worth it.

359:
Usual
December 24

Bible Verses
"I don't want to take too much of your time, so I ask that you listen with your usual courtesy to our brief statement of the facts." Acts 24:4 (CEB)

"And [then] he prayed again and the heavens supplied rain and the land produced its crops [as usual]." James 5:18 (AMP)

Word of the Day
Usual – Expected outcome. Routine; familiar; average; traditional.

Quotes
"In the usual progress of things, the necessities of a nation in every stage of its existence will be found at least equal to its resources." Alexander Hamilton

"The foolish man wonders at the unusual, but the wise man at usual." Ralph Waldo Emerson

"Self-deception is so far from impossible that it is one of the most ordinary phenomena with which we are acquainted. Nothing is more usual than for a man to impute his actions to honorable motives, when it is nearly demonstrable that they flowed from some corrupt and contemptible force." William Godwin

Pam's Perspective
There is nothing usual about anyone's life when we look with wonderment.

Questions
What does my usual day look like? What is my usual way to handle a problem? What is my usual way to celebrate? Do I have a usual workout program in order to stay fit? What can I do to spice it up?

Declarations

I do **usual** things extraordinarily well. I help people see the beauty around them. I am a joy magnet. I am thankful for positive mentors who encourage me to propagate my **usual** gifts into currency.

It is **usual** for me to ace every job interview and land the one I want. The **usual** and customary vacations are nice once in a while to recharge and invigorate my soul. My **usual** vacation pay continues to increase along with my time off. I search the **usual** websites for the top vacation destinations and find the coolest places to visit.

My **usual** disposition is easy-going, fun, and accepting. I applaud my uniqueness. I give my **usual** smile and hug as I greet my friends and laughter always follows. I believe I can make a contribution to the people around me just by being my **usual** bubbly, inspiring self.

I am known by God. I take my **usual** time to study, meditate, and reflect on my best friend in the universe. What a joy to know Christ is smiling on me and enjoying our time together. I always feel safe. Our **usual** alone time improves our relationship and intimacy. My **usual** walk in the garden is breathtaking as I view all the beauty.

Usual fruits and vegetables find their way onto my plate as I relish all the nutrition they give me. I give thanks for their gifts. My **usual** day consists of stretching and toning my muscles. It is **usual** for me to jump at opportunities for self-improvement and enhancement.

I look at my tasks, and as **usual**, pick the hard ones first to get them out of the way. I am grateful to my colleagues. I am a great helper at work. The quality of my **usual** work far exceeds the expectations of my boss. Regular recognition is the norm for me. It is **usual** for me to receive unexpected gifts and multiple checks in the mail.

360:
Miracle
December 25

Bible Verse
"God did extraordinary miracles through Paul." Acts 19:11 (NIV)

Word of the Day
Miracle – An unexpected occurrence. Wonderment; awe. Surprise.

Quote
"Faith doesn't make sense; that's why it makes miracles." John Di Lemme

Pam's Perspective
Two weeks before Christmas in eighty-nine, I decided with some friends to have a Christmas dinner for the homeless. We called it Miracle Christmas because it would be a miracle if we pulled it off. The Mayor of Flint reneged on the location two days before the dinner, so the Salvation Army allowed us to use their facility. They never allowed anyone, even members to rent it out and we got it for free. We went around for two weeks getting donations of all kinds. I had no idea what it took to cook for large numbers of people, but Christmas eve morning, Joe Ambrose showed up and said, I am here to cook. He cooked straight through Christmas day. He read something in the paper and just showed up. We fed over 400 people, gave them all food and presents to take home, had the place decorated to the max, Santa showed up for the kids and carolers sang during dinner. It went so well the Salvation Army invited us back the following year. The fifth-year Joe got sick, and the week before Christmas Phil Fahrenbruch, the executive chef of the Bavarian Inn in Frankenmuth volunteered and brought his entire crew to cook. He cooked for five years until his kids came along, then Joe came back to cook. I organized Miracle Christmas for thirteen years, and every year it was a miracle!

Questions
Do I believe in miracles? Do I expect miracles? What was my last miracle?

Declarations

I believe and know that **miracles** are possible. I keep my heart open to hear from God as I feel His **miracle** presence in me. I see **miracles** take place in my life and in the lives of the people around me.

I start my day from a tranquil place. I forgive my enemies and watch the **miracles** flow. By releasing all resentments and hurts, I receive the **miracle** of peace. I see my **miracle** manifest today. Praise God, He does not change and is still in the **miracle** running business.

There is nothing too hard for God who always meets my needs. I am thankful for the **miracle**-working God who never lets me down. I receive practical **miracles** and little **miracles** too. I talk to God and know He listens and answers my prayers in **miraculous** ways.

I see common **miracles** that others take for granted. I walk in faith, and I expect supernatural **miracles** to occur on a regular basis. I expect greatness from myself because I am a **miracle** too. I live in an atmosphere where **miracles** naturally happen daily in my life. People's hope is renewed as I talk about my **miracle** engaging God. I inspire my community by sharing the **miracles** I have received.

When I believe, no **miracle** is impossible. Every need, God fulfills. I ask Jehovah-Rapha, the God who heals, to perform a **miracle** in me. I can say to any sickness, leave, and it will. I profess **miracles** over my life now. I am blissfully happy because I believe in **miracles**.

God is the author of **miracles**, and it is His good pleasure to perform them whenever He pleases. I am filled with joy as I recognize **miracles** in my own backyard. I am glad for God's intervention on my behalf. The Lord is faithful and makes me look good. Every part of my being is consumed with love, peace, joy, and **miracles**.

361:
Rejoice
December 26

Bible Verses
"This is the day the Lord has made. We will rejoice and be glad in it." Psalm 118:24 (NLT)

"Rejoice in the Lord always. Again I will say, rejoice!" Philippians 4:4 (NKJV)

Word of the Day
Rejoice – To celebrate and enjoy life. To exude joy and laughter.

Quote
"We need a larger joy. We need a joy that will not only rejoice in the gifts of God, but will rejoice in God Himself and find in Him our portion and our boundless and everlasting delight. We need a joy that will not only rejoice in the sunshine but in the hour of darkness and apparent desertion, when men misunderstand us, when circumstances are against us and when even God seems to have forgotten us. We need a joy that will not only rejoice in all things but rejoice evermore. We need a joy that even when we do not feel the joy will "count it all joy" and rejoice by faith." A.B. Simpson

Pam's Perspective
When I sing praises to God, my spirit is renewed, body healed, and my mind becomes peaceful. I rejoice even when I don't feel like it because I always feel better after I have. There is something about rejoicing in the midst of the storm that brings strength and courage to face every adversity. I have been healed of headaches, neck and back pain while singing joyfully to the Lord. Rejoice away your sickness.

Questions
Is rejoicing apart of my life? What do I have to rejoice about? How do I feel when I rejoice? Why can I find it easy to rejoice in every situation?

Declarations

God's peace, harmony, and joy flow through me now as I **rejoice** in being alive. I am optimistic about making decisions that pertain to my life. I **rejoice** as I act on them and see my dreams come true. I **rejoice** to be intelligent and able to make a great living.

I choose to **rejoice** and count my blessings every day, even when I don't feel like it, or am feeling down and blue. Then I am **rejoicing** because I feel glad I did. I look and act like the champion God created me to be. I **rejoice** that Jesus is revealed to and through me.

I **rejoice** having the privilege to worship God. I step over the imaginary chicken line and share my faith with a friend. I **rejoice** because I have lots to share about God's miraculous provision and healing. I feel the lavishness of God's mercy watching over me.

I have a table filled with plenty before me. I am a person of substance because I **rejoice**. I am happy, joyous, and free. God is pleased with me, and nothing can separate me from His love. I **rejoice** that I have eternal life. I **rejoice** that I am not a slave to sin but a servant of the Lord. I think cheery thoughts and **rejoice** because I serve a good Master. I am grateful God loves me.

People are drawn by my passion as I **rejoice** for no reason. I practice the discipline of **rejoicing**, knowing that God continues to guard me with a host of angels. I live a happy life with a **rejoicing** attitude. The enemy is defeated, and I stand with Christ in the winner's circle.

God wants the very best for me now, and I connect with His power. No matter what trial I go through I will **rejoice** and declare I am His. I **rejoice** because my name is recorded in heaven. I **rejoice** because the same Spirit that raised Christ from the dead resides in me.

362:
Sad
December 27

Bible Verses
"Why am I discouraged? Why is my heart so sad? I will put my hope in God! I will praise him again— my Savior and my God!" Psalm 42:11 (NLT)

"Be happy with those who are happy. Be sad with those who are sad." Romans 12:15 (NLV)

Word of the Day
Sad – To be melancholy or down in the dumps. Grieved. Heavyhearted.

Quotes
"For all sad words of tongue and pen, the saddest are these, 'It might have been.'" John Greenleaf Whittier

"Sad is the ungrateful person who can't appreciate what he already has. He will not experience bliss until he embraces gratitude." Pam Malow-Isham

"Sad is his lot, who, once at least in his life, has not been a poet." Lamartine

"This is one of the sad conditions of life, that experience is not transmissible. No man will learn from the suffering of another; he must suffer himself." James H. Aughey

Pam's Perspective
You never know what someone is going through. At one time I isolated myself when I was sad, which made me sadder. I did not realize the value of community.

Questions
When I get sad, what do I do? Who do I turn to when I get sad?

Declarations

I am glad for the **sad** times in my life because it makes the happy ones that much more joyous. I could sit with my **sad** thoughts and review my life. I wonder what the **sad** thoughts have cost me. I am grateful for friends who lift my spirits when I am **sad** or just sit with me, not say a word and hold my hand. I sing despite being **sad**.

God has not promised me a rose garden with continuous sunshine. There are times when I will be **sad**. I know the rain comes and the thorns of a rose will prick me, but it is still worth it to smell the flowers along the way and relish every season of my beautiful life.

Although I get **sad** and I feel hurt when a dear friend leaves my life, or a beloved pet passes on, I refuse to buy into the lie of closing my heart off so I won't get hurt again. Because that is even a **sadder**, lonelier state, so I open my heart wide to love again and again. I am grateful for children's laughter. While being **sad**, I can go for a walk, play a game, watch a comedy, get a coffee, or take a hot bath.

When I am **sad**, I ask myself if there is anything I can do to be a positive influence on someone else. Then I go help that person feel valued. By helping others, I get the flow of good energy moving again. I focus on being a blessing to others instead of wallowing in my **sadness**. I acknowledge my **sad** feelings so I can deal with them.

There is a time to be **sad**, and I am OK with that. I feel no judgment from God about my **sadness**. God's inexhaustible love covers me when I am **sad** and happy. His restorative power untangles my messes and gives me the victory. I cannot deny my emotions, even if they are **sad**. Trusting God is my best defense against worry, fear, anxiety, frustration, and **sadness**. I remember how to create joy. **Sadness** may endure for a night, but joy comes in the morning!

363:
Wonder
December 28

Bible Verses

"People were overcome with wonder, saying, 'He does everything well! He even makes the deaf to hear and gives speech to those who can't speak.'" Mark 7:37 (CEB)

"And God confirmed the message by giving signs and wonders and various miracles and gifts of the Holy Spirit whenever he chose." Hebrews 2:4 (NLT)

Word of the Day

Wonder – To be filled with questioning and investigation. Astonishment. Fascination. To be surprised.

Quotes

"Wonder is the feeling of a philosopher, and philosophy begins in wonder." Plato

"People travel to wonder at the height of mountains, at the huge waves of the sea, at the long courses of rivers, at the vast compass of the ocean, at the circular motion of the stars; and they pass by themselves without wondering." Saint Augustine

"Living in a state of wonder is how miracles happen and creativity blossoms." Pam Malow-Isham

"All things are wonder since the world began; the world's a riddle, and the meaning's man." Barton Holyday

Questions

Do I wonder how my life will turn out? What am I doing to enhance it? What wonders will I marvel at, admire, and appreciate today?

Declarations

I embrace every little detail of my life with a sense of joy, awe, and **wonder**. I am inspired by God on high. I enjoy this delicious experience of life with all the **wonders** in it. There is so much promise in life as I **wonder** about all the possibilities that lie ahead of me. I am open to seeing things in a **wonderful** new light.

I **wonder** why I am God's reward. He could have chosen anyone in the universe, and he chose me to be His friend, companion, and conductor of **wonder**. Blessed am I. With a grateful heart I receive Christ's steadfast love. Yes, I feel God's **wonderful** presence with me wherever I am. Oh how **wonderful,** I am loved and well thought of!

The Father gets a grin permeating across His face when He looks at me **wondering** what I will do next. God didn't need me; He wanted me, and still does. He extends His **wonderful** hand of favor to me.

My **wondrous** world of joy is here now. I release the magic of effortless accomplishment as my dreams appear. I act confident as I **wonder** how God is going to come through for me again. I spring up with inspiration and burst forth with **wonderful** ideas.

I appreciate my **wonderful** self. Being released from condemnation is a **wonderful** thing. **Wonder** is where miracles happen. What a **wonderful** season I am in as I realize I am surrounded by grace.

I **wonder** how I could have been so blind to all of the **wonders** that are right in front of me. It is remarkable how much I used to take for granted that I now am amazed by. God is working **wonders** and miracles in my life now. I am flabbergasted by just how cool and **wonderful** my life continues to be. I treasure all the little pleasures I experience. I am absolutely delighted with my **wonderful** life.

364:
Expectation
December 29

Bible Verses

"For surely there is a latter end [a future and a reward], and your hope and expectation shall not be cut off." Proverbs 23:18 (AMP)

"And they exceeded our expectations: They gave themselves first of all to the Lord, and then by the will of God also to us." 2 Corinthians 8:5 (NIV)

Word of the Day

Expectation – The possibility of. Hopes. Chance. Likelihood.

Quotes

"We are to speak the gospel to men in the authority of God, and with the exaptation of its power, and we are to claim the Holy Ghost to accompany the words and give efficacy to our testimony." A.B. Simpson

"Expectation is the fastest way to miracles." Pam Malow-Isham

"Father, I lay down my unmet expectations. I give them to You. I thank You for my children. I have had unrealistic expectations for my children. Father, I lay my unrealistic expectations for my spouse on Your altar. Also, I lay my unmet expectations for my parents on Your altar. Father, more importantly, I lay my unrealistic expectations for myself on Your altar. Nobody, including myself, will ever be able to live up to the high expectations that I have set. I release all my expectations to You. I lay them on your altar. Father, I want to meet only Your expectations. Thank You for showing me how to do that, in Jesus' name. Amen." Joan Hunter (Power to Heal)

Questions

What is my expectation of God and how is that serving me? What is my expectation of about myself? What are my expectations of others?

Declarations

Every day I wake up with a sense of **expectancy** knowing that something good is about to happen to me. I live a life of **expectancy** and optimism. My **expectations** meet with success. Each day is a continuous **expectation** and revelation of God's goodness to me.

I am realistic about the **expectations** I put on myself, so I do not **expect** perfection. My **expectations** are flexible that I put on others as I cannot change them. I always have the **expectations** of a winner.

I cannot **expect** to stay healthy if I eat and drink nutrient deficient foods. Although I take a variety of supplements and extra fiber, I **expect** to get most of my nourishment from the fruits and vegetables I eat. I am proud of myself for the little things I do right. I **expect** to walk in divine health. I throw myself parties with happy people.

The **expectations** I have for work continue to expand as I advance in my career. I **expect** to work with and for very intelligent people. I choose rightly. I provide value to a lot of people. I **expect** to get the bonuses, benefits, and extra vacation days. I **expect** to think above average and reap exceptional results. I attract wealth into my life because of my gigantic unattached **expectations**.

My words have the power to create my **expectations,** so I am deliberate about what I say. I am good enough right now. I know that the perfection of God is at work in all areas of my life and the good that I am **expecting** is already happening or on the way.

I act cheerful. I have extra-large **expectations** about what God is going to do for me. My great spirit of **expectancy** is in line with God. No matter what is the outcome of my **expectations**, I still choose to be happy and carefree. My contentment comes from within.

365:
Ignore
December 30

Bible Verses

"Fools show their anger at once, but the prudent ignore an insult." Proverbs 12:16 (NRSV)

"If you ignore criticism, you will end in poverty and disgrace; if you accept correction, you will be honored." Proverbs 13:18 (NLT)

Word of the Day

Ignore – To intentionally avoid or omit. To pay no attention to.

Quotes

"One learns to ignore criticism by first learning to ignore applause." Robert Brault

"Trust me that as I ignore all law to help the slave, so will I ignore it all to protect an enslaved woman." Susan B. Anthony

"Men of ill judgment oft ignore the good that lies within their hands, till they have lost it." Sophocles

"When you ignore negativity, you recognize impeccability." Pam Malow-Isham

Pam's Perspective

Ignoring my problems never made them go away. They just intensified. As hard as facing a problem is, it is much better than letting it spiral out of control.

Questions

What does it feel like to be ignored? Have I ever ignored someone on purpose? Why? Do I ever ignore my intuition? Do I ignore God?

Declarations

I **ignore** naysayers who tell me I can't reach my goals. I leave them in the dust as I run past them. I **ignore** people who say something about me that is inconsiderate. I choose to **ignore** peer pressure. I stay relaxed by **ignoring** the petty little things that upset others.

I **ignore** worrying about the future and enjoy this glorious moment right now. There is absolutely nothing I can do about the past, so I **ignore** dwelling on it. I did what I thought was right at the time. I can learn valuable lessons from my mistakes and **ignore** the rest.

I **ignore** the little voice telling me to quit when I know that victory is right around the corner. I **ignore** looking at others when I am the one who needs the work. I **ignore** frivolous chatter and being a busybody. I am self-confident as I put on the cloak of happiness and **ignore** skepticism. I feel great being free, rich, and **successful**.

I **ignore** the urge to over-indulge in food or drink. I crave healthy foods. I am grateful for baseball, basketball, football, hockey, soccer, and other team sports. I **ignore** the thought of slacking off on my workouts because I feel so alive, healthy, and invigorated afterward.

I hang around positive people and **ignore** negative ones. I **ignore** fearful thoughts as they arise and think on what is lovely. I **ignore** any negative self-talk as I declare something good is going to happen to me today. I take positive action to reach my goals. I recognize and never **ignore** the prompting of the Holy Spirit.

I have a willingness to **ignore** the things I can't control. I allow life to unfold. Even when progress is slow and not going my way, I **ignore** getting frustrated. I **ignore** urgent things to focus on the important. I **ignore** doubts. I **ignore** getting off course by looking at my dreams.

366:
Review
December 31

Bible Verses
"Every day I review the ways he works; I try not to miss a trick." Psalm 18:22 (MSG)

"Let us review the situation together, and you can present your case to prove your innocence." Isaiah 43:26 (NLT)

Word of the Day
Review – The process of giving something a second look. To audit and scan for memorization. To rethink something. Reflect over.

Quotes
"Twice and thrice over, as they say, good is it to repeat and review what is good." Plato

"When we review what has been doing in the world, is it not evident that in all transactions, whether of ancient or of modern date, some strange caprice of fortune turns all human wisdom to a jest?" Publius Cornelius Tacitus

Pam's Perspective
Review is the vehicle for a productive life. By reviewing my progress, I see where I need to make course corrections. Life is not a linear line from birth to death but a boat on an ocean of possibilities that needs a captain to guide it to the right lighthouse. Goals don't get achieved by accident; they take review and action.

Questions
How often do I review my dreams and goals? How often do I review my social media filters and connections? How often do I review my friend list? What do I review, think about and then take action on?

Declarations

I **review** the good I have done in the past and then plan to do more of it. I **review** my disappointments and learn from my mistakes. I know there are no shortcuts to mastery, so I **review** my plans daily to achieve my goals in the best possible way. I **review** my victories.

When I get upset, I **review** in my head the best possible response before I speak. I **review** patience and tolerance as I **review** my values. I **review** my behavior and language. I **review** the kind of person I am and the kind of friend I want to be. I like sending out hand-written notes of appreciation. I **review** my friendships as they shape and influence my life in many ways, so I choose wisely.

I **review** my spending habits to ensure I am a good steward of my finances. I find it rewarding to save. I **review** my investments with a trusted advisor. I am an honest channel through which money easily flows. I **review** the charities I support because I love to give.

I write a **review** of the efforts of my previous year, so I can exceed my wildest expectations in the coming year. I **review** my education to determine what classes I can take next. I **review** the literature I read to enhance my learning. I ask others to **review** my work and critique it. I **review** what I believe and why I believe it. I **review** the commitments I have made so I can be found faithful.

God's **reviews** of me have not changed. I am still His favorite. He is always loving, available, and trustworthy. I **review** God's attributes and emulate them. I **review** my life's purpose of making sure I am on the right course. I **review** my health and look for enjoyable ways to improve it. I **review** all the good things God has blessed me with and give thanks. I know that wherever I turn, goodness and mercy will greet and follow me. I am very grateful for good book **reviews**.

Index - Authors Used in Alphabetical Order
#Numbers correspond to the day of the year.

A

Abigail Adams (November 22, 1744 – October 28, 1818)
https://en.wikipedia.org/wiki/Abigail_Adams
https://www.whitehouse.gov/1600/first-ladies/abigailadams
#228-Rebellion - Adams, A. (1776, March 31). Abigail Adams urges husband to "remember the ladies" - Mar 31, 1776 - HISTORY.com. Retrieved from http://www.history.com/this-day-in-history/abigail-adams-urges-husband-to-remember-the-ladies

John Adams (October 30, 1735 – July 4, 1826)
https://en.wikipedia.org/wiki/John_Adams
https://www.whitehouse.gov/1600/presidents/johnadams
#280-Evidence - Adams, J. (1770). Boston Massacre Historical Society. Retrieved from http://www.bostonmassacre.net/trial/acct-adams3.htm
#171-Exercise - Day, E. P. (1884). Mind. In *Day's collacon: an encyclopaedia of prose quotations: Consisting of beautiful thoughts, choice extracts and sayings, of the most eminent writers of all nations, from the earliest ages to the present time, together with a comprehensive biographical index of authors, and an alphabetical list of subjects quoted* (p. 568). NY, NY: International printing and publishing office.
#111-Rise - Adams, J. (1773, December 17). John Adams - Wikiquote. Retrieved October 12, 2017, from https://en.wikiquote.org/wiki/John_Adams
#90-Weakness - Adams, J. (1787). Letter XXVI Dr. Price. In *A defense of the constitutions of government of the United States of America* (p. 129). London.

John Quincy Adams - 6th U.S. President (July 11, 1767 – February 23, 1848)
https://en.wikipedia.org/wiki/John_Quincy_Adams
https://www.whitehouse.gov/1600/presidents/johnquincyadams
#7-Gratitude - Address of John Quincy Adams. (1842). *Niles' National Register, Volumes 62-63* [Baltimore], p. 136.
#73-Perseverance - Adams, J. Q. (n.d.). John Quincy Adams - Wikiquote. Retrieved October 11, 2017, from https://en.wikiquote.org/wiki/John_Quincy_Adams

Joseph Addison (1 May 1672 – 17 June 1719)
https://en.wikipedia.org/wiki/Joseph_Addison
#260-Abstain - Crabb, G. (1816). Abstain. In *English Synonyms Explained, in Alphabetical Order* (p. 17). London: C. Baldwin. Addison
#247-Design - Addison, J., & Steele, R. (1776). No. 490. Monday, September 22. In *The Spectator. Volume the seventh* (p. 78). Edinburgh.
#331-Disapproval - Deference. (1829). In E. Smedley (Ed.), *The London Encyclopedia, or universal dictionary of science, art, literature, and practical mechanics, comprising a popular view of the present state of knowledge. In twenty-two volumes. Vol. VII* (p. 112). London: Printed for Thomas Tegg, 73, Cheapside.
#344-Inexperience - Allibone, S. A. (1876). Prejudice. In *Prose Quotations from Socrates to Macaulay, with indexes: Authors 544, subjects 571, quotations 8810* (p. 584). Philadelphia, PA: J. B. Lippincott & Co.
#70-Obscurity - Addison, J. (n.d.). Joseph Addison - Christian Classics Ethereal Library - Christian Classics Ethereal Library. Retrieved from https://www.ccel.org/ccel/addison
#199-Thoughts - Addison, J. (n.d.). Joseph Addison - Wikiquote. Retrieved October 13, 2017, from https://en.wikiquote.org/wiki/Joseph_Addison

#303-Whole Whole - Addison, J. (n.d.). Joseph Addison - Wikiquote. Retrieved August 25, 2017, from https://it.wikiquote.org/wiki/Joseph_Addison

Aeschylus (525/524 BC – 456/455 BC)
https://en.wikipedia.org/wiki/Aeschylus
#26-Despair - Aeschylus. (n.d.). Aeschylus - Wikiquote. Retrieved January 22, 2016, from https://en.wikiquote.org/wiki/Aeschylus
#32-Lack - Aeschylus. (n.d.). Aeschylus - Wikiquote. Retrieved March 19, 2016, from https://en.wikiquote.org/wiki/Aeschylus

Aesop (620 BC - 564 BC)
https://en.wikipedia.org/wiki/Aesop
#19-Certain - James, Thomas, 1809-1863, Tenniel, John, Sir, Aesop's fables. English. Selections. (1852). Fable 154 - The Hound And The Hare. In *Aesop's fables [electronic resource]: a new version, chiefly from original sources / by Thomas James ; with more than one hundred illustrations designed by John Tenniel* (p. 107). Philadelphia: John Murray.
#66-Comfort - Wood, J. (1893). Oh how. In *Dictionary of quotations from ancient, modern, English and foreign sources* (p. 326). London and New York: Frederick Warne and Co.
#203-Everything - Aesop. (n.d.). Aesop - Juno and the Peacock. Retrieved October 15, 2017, from https://en.wikipedia.org/wiki/Aesop
#29-Kindness - Aesop. (n.d.). Aesop - Wikiquote. Retrieved January 4, 2016, from https://en.wikiquote.org/wiki/Aesop
#297-Prepare - Aesop. (n.d.). Aesop - Wikiquote. Retrieved March 16, 2016, from https://en.wikiquote.org/wiki/Aesop

Agathon (448 BC - 400 BC)
https://en.wikipedia.org/wiki/Agathon
#84-Past - Agathon - Wikiquote. (n.d.). Retrieved January 8, 2016, from https://en.wikiquote.org/wiki/Agathon

Daniel Akst
http://www.akst.com/index.html
http://www.akst.com/Dan_Akst/Home.html
#324-Reflection

Thomas Bailey Aldrich (November 11, 1836 – March 19, 1907)
https://en.wikipedia.org/wiki/Thomas_Bailey_Aldrich
#218-Outside - Aldrich, T. B. (1897). TWO BITES AT A CHERRY. In *The writings of Thomas Bailey Aldrich* (p. 218). Boston: Houghton, Mifflin, and Company.

James Allen (28 November 1864 – 24 January 1912)
https://en.wikipedia.org/wiki/James_Allen_(author)
#287-Attract - Allen, J. (1903). *As A Man Thinketh*.
#62-Dark - Allen, J. (1908). The way out of undesirable conditions. In *From Poverty to Power: Or, the Realization of Prosperity and Peace* (3rd ed., p. 39). Libertyville, IL: The Sheldon University Press.
#20-Dream - Allen, J. (1903). *As A Man Thinketh*.
#309-Ideal - Allen, J. (1903). *As A Man Thinketh*.
#146-Realities - Allen, J. (1903). *As A Man Thinketh*.
#205-Right - Allan, J. (1907). THE SECRET OF HEALTH, SUCCESS, AND POWER. In *From Poverty to Power: Or, the Realization of Prosperity and Peace* (p. 67).
#199-Thoughts - Allen, J. (n.d.). Your Mental Attitude. Retrieved from http://www.jamesallenlibrary.com/authors/james-allen/above-lifes-turmoil/your-mental-attitude

Michael Althsuler
http://www.michaelaltshuler.com/
#351-Failure - Althsuler, M. (n.d.). Michael's Quotes - Michael Altshuler. Retrieved from http://www.michaelaltshuler.com/michaels-quotes.html
#189-Help - Althsuler, M. (n.d.). Michael's Quotes - Michael Altshuler. Retrieved from http://www.michaelaltshuler.com/michaels-quotes.html
#52-Time - Althsuler, M. (n.d.). Michael's Quotes - Michael Altshuler. Retrieved from http://www.michaelaltshuler.com/michaels-quotes.html

Dr. Robert Anthony
http://www.dranthony.com/
https://www.facebook.com/DrRobertAnthony
https://twitter.com/Dr_R_Anthony
#212-Unload, #86-Risk, #168-Blame

Susan B. Anthony (February 15, 1820 – March 13, 1906)
https://en.wikipedia.org/wiki/Susan_B._Anthony
#248-Destiny - Harper, I. H., & Anthony, S. B. (1898). Women's National Loyal League. In *The life and work of Susan B. Anthony: Including public addresses, her own letters and many from her contemporaries during fifty years. A story of the evolution of the status of woman. Volume I* (p. 227). Indianapolis, IL: The Hollenbeck Press.
#365-Ignore - Harper, I. H., & Anthony, S. B. (1898). Rift in common law - divorce question. In *The life and work of Susan B. Anthony: Including public addresses, her own letters and many from her contemporaries during fifty years. A story of the evolution of the status of woman. Volume I* (p. 204). Indianapolis, IL: The Hollenbeck Press.
#315-Protection - Harper, I. H., & Anthony, S. B. (1898). Chapter XXIII - First trip to the Pacific coast. – 1871. In *The life and work of Susan B. Anthony: Including public addresses, her own letters and many from her contemporaries during fifty years. A story of the evolution of the status of woman. Volume I* (p. 392). Indianapolis, IL: The Hollenbeck Press.
#228-Rebellion - Harper, I. H., & Anthony, S. B. (1898). Chapter XXVII. Revolution Debt Paid-Women's Fourth of July. In *The life and work of Susan B. Anthony: Including public addresses, her own letters and many from her contemporaries during fifty years. A story of the evolution of the status of woman. Volume I* (p. 475). Indianapolis, IL: The Hollenbeck Press.

Antisthenes (445-365 BC)
https://en.wikipedia.org/wiki/Antisthenes
#175-Passionate - Antisthenes. (n.d.). Antisthenes - Wikiquote. Retrieved October 11, 2017, from https://en.wikiquote.org/wiki/Antisthenes

Thomas Aquinas (1225 – 7 March 1274)
https://en.wikipedia.org/wiki/Thomas_Aquinas
#306-Aim - User:SVentura (WMF) - Wikipedia. (n.d.). Retrieved October 11, 2017, from https://en.wikipedia.org/wiki/User:SVentura_(WMF)

Archimedes (287-212 BC)
https://en.wikipedia.org/wiki/Archimedes
#209-Give - Archimedes. (n.d.). Archimedes - Wikiquote. Retrieved October 11, 2017, from https://en.wikiquote.org/wiki/Archimedes

Aristotle (384 - 322 BC)
https://en.wikipedia.org/wiki/Aristotle

#65-Pain - Dalbiac, P. H., & Harbottle, T. B. (1897). Latin Quotations. In *Dalbiac and Harbottle's Dictionary of Quotations (classical)* (2ⁿᵈ ed., p. 451). London and New York: Swan Sonnenschein & Co., Limited. The Macmillan Co., Limited.

#335-Prosperity - Diogenes, L., Yonge, C. D., & University of St. Andrews. (1853). Aristotle. In *The lives and opinions of eminent philosophers by Diogenes Laërtius. Literally translated by C. D. Yonge, B.A* (p. 188). London: Henry G. Bohn, York Street, Covent Garden.

#205-Right - Aristotle. (n.d.). Aristotle - Wikiquote. Retrieved October 12, 2017, from https://en.wikiquote.org/wiki/Aristotle

#125-Share - Aristotle. (n.d.). Aristotle - Wikiquote. Retrieved October 12, 2017, from https://en.wikiquote.org/wiki/Aristotle

#301-Single - Aristotle. (n.d.). Aristotle - Wikiquote. Retrieved October 12, 2017, from https://en.wikiquote.org/wiki/Aristotle

Joan of Arc (6 January 1412 – 30 May 1431)
https://en.wikipedia.org/wiki/Joan_of_Arc
#93-Grace - Joan of Arc. (n.d.). Joan of Arc - Wikiquote. Retrieved October 13, 2017, from https://en.wikiquote.org/wiki/Joan_of_Arc

Angelique Arnauld (8 September 1591 – 6 August 1661)
https://en.wikipedia.org/wiki/Marie_Ang%C3%A9lique_Arnauld
#238-Extraordinary - Edwards, T. (1891). Perfection. In *A dictionary of thoughts* (p. 406). New York, NY: Cassell Publishing Company.

St. Francis of Assisi (1181/1182 – 3 October 1226)
https://en.wikipedia.org/wiki/Francis_of_Assisi
#232-Look - St. Francis of Assisi. (1912). The mystical element in Christianity. What is it and what is its value? In *Annual Baptist Autumnal Conference for the Discussion of ..., Volumes 29-30* (p. 186).

#286-Many - *Journal of Proceedings of the. Annual Meeting, Volume 52 Illinois State Teacher's Association* (p. 127). (1906).

#301-Single - Francis of Assisi. (n.d.). Quote Details: Saint Francis of Assisi: All the darkness in... - The Quotations Page. Retrieved March 9, 2016, from http://www.quotationspage.com/quote/40015.html

St. Athanasius (296-298 – 2 May 373)
https://en.wikipedia.org/wiki/Athanasius_of_Alexandria
#284-Surety - Day, E. P. (1884). Surety. In *Day's collacon: an encyclopaedia of prose quotations: Consisting of beautiful thoughts, choice extracts and sayings, of the most eminent writers of all nations, from the earliest ages to the present time, together with a comprehensive biographical index of authors, and an alphabetical list of subjects quoted* (p. 914). New York, NY: S. Low, Marston, Searle, and Rivington.

William Walker Atkinson (December 5, 1862 – November 22, 1932)
https://en.wikipedia.org/wiki/William_Walker_Atkinson
#107-Attitude - Atkinson, W. W. (1900). Chapter VI. How to become immune to injurious thought attraction. In *Thought Vibration: Or, The Law of Attraction in the Thought World* (p. 44). Chicago, IL: The New Thought Publishing Co.

#46-Hate - Atkinson, W. W. (1900). Chapter I. The Law of Attraction in the Thought World. In *Thought Vibration: Or, The Law of Attraction in the Thought World* (p. 7-8). Chicago, IL: The New Thought Publishing Co.

#166-Sit - Atkinson, W. W. (1900). The transmutation of negative thought. In *Thought Vibration: Or, The Law of Attraction in the Thought World* (p. 57). Chicago, IL: The New Thought Publishing Co.

James Hill Aughey (1828-1911)
http://docsouth.unc.edu/fpn/aughey/aughey.html
#150-Calmness - Aughey, J. H. (1886). *Spiritual gems of the ages* (p. 16). Cincinnati, OH: Elm Street Printing Company.
#362-Sad - Aughey, J. H. (1886). *Spiritual gems of the ages* (p. 201). Cincinnati, OH: Elm Street Printing Company.
#243-Selfish - Aughey, J. H. (1886). Prayer. *Spiritual gems of the ages* (p. 260). Cincinnati, OH: Elm Street Printing Company.
#199-Thoughts - Aughey, J. H. (1886). *Spiritual gems of the ages* (p. 30). Cincinnati, OH: Elm Street Printing Company.

St. Augustine (13 November 354 – 28 August 430)
https://en.wikipedia.org/wiki/Augustine_of_Hippo
#110-Beauty - Saint Augustine of Hippo. (n.d.). Augustine of Hippo - Wikiquote. Retrieved October 15, 2017, from https://en.wikiquote.org/wiki/Augustine_of_Hippo
#261-Perfection - Augustine of Hippo. (n.d.). Perfection - Wikiquote. Retrieved October 12, 2017, from https://en.wikiquote.org/wiki/Perfection
#102-Scatter - Augustine of Hippo. (n.d.). Prayer for the Enlightenment of the Holy Spirit - Prayer Ideas. Retrieved from https://prayerideas.org/how_to_pray/historical/prayer-for-the-enlightenment-of-the-holy-spirit/
#363-Wonder - Augustine of Hippo. (397). Augustine of Hippo - Wikiquote. Retrieved October 15, 2017, from https://en.wikiquote.org/wiki/Augustine_of_Hippo#Misattributed

Marcus Aurelius (26 April 121 – 17 March 180 AD)
https://en.wikipedia.org/wiki/Marcus_Aurelius
#159-Change - Aurelius, M. (n.d.). Marcus Aurelius - Wikiquote. Retrieved October 17, 2017, from https://en.wikiquote.org/wiki/Marcus_Aurelius
#88-Happy - Aurelius, M. (n.d.). Marcus Aurelius - Wikiquote. Retrieved October 17, 2017, from https://en.wikiquote.org/wiki/Marcus_Aurelius
#52-Time - Aurelius, M. (n.d.). Marcus Aurelius - Wikiquote. Retrieved October 17, 2017, from https://en.wikiquote.org/wiki/Marcus_Aurelius
#187-Vice - Aurelius, M. (n.d.). Marcus Aurelius - Wikiquote. Retrieved October 17, 2017, from https://en.wikiquote.org/wiki/Marcus_Aurelius

Jane Austen (16 December 1775 – 18 July 1817)
https://en.wikipedia.org/wiki/Jane_Austen
#225-Early - Smith, G. (1890). Chapter VI. In E. S. Robertson (Ed.), *Life of Jane Austen.* (p. 145). London: Walter Scott.

Avicenna (980 – June 1037)
https://en.wikipedia.org/wiki/Avicenna
#3-Brilliant - DAY, E. P. (1884). Lightning. In *Day's Collacon: an encyclopaedia of prose quotations. Consisting of beautiful thoughts, choice extracts, and sayings, of the most eminent writers of all nations, from the earliest ages to the present times* (p. 516). New York and London: International Printing and Publishing Office, Sampson Low, Marston, Searle, and Rivington.

B

Sir Francis Bacon (22 January 1561 – 9 April 1626)
https://en.wikipedia.org/wiki/Francis_Bacon
#66-Comfort - Bacon, F. (1597). Essays, Of Adversity. Retrieved February 4, 2016, from https://en.wikiquote.org/wiki/Adversity

#57-Content - Bacon, F. (1807). Of Discourse. In *Essays: Moral, economical, and political. By Francis Bacon, Baron of Verulam, and Viscount St. Albans and Lord High Chancellor of England* (p. 126). London: Vernor, Hood & Sharpe, Poultry.

#176-Dull - Bacon, F. (1765). Certain Apophthegms of Lord Bacon. In C. Yorke (Ed.), *The Works of Francis Bacon, Baron of Verulam, Viscount St. Alban, and Lord High Chancellor of England. In five volumes. Vol. 1* (p. 563).

#196-Excessive - Bacon, F. (1765). XIII. Of Goodness, and Goodness of Nature. In C. Yorke (Ed.), *The Works of Francis Bacon, Baron of Verulam, Viscount St. Alban, and Lord High Chancellor of England. In five volumes. Vol. 1* (p. 463).

#286-Many - Bacon, F. (1854). Ornamental Rationalia. In *The Works of Lord Bacon: Philosophical works* (p. 332).

#28-Opportunity - Bacon, F. (n.d.). Essays of Francis Bacon - Of Ceremonies and Respects (The Essays or Counsels, Civil and Moral, of Francis Ld. Verulam Viscount St. Albans). Retrieved from http://www.authorama.com/essays-of-Francis-bacon-52.html

#139-Sleep - Christy, R. (1888). Silence. In *Proverbs, maxims, and phrases of all ages* (p. 269). London: Fisher Unwin.

#144-Surprise - Bacon, F. (1765). Essays civil and moral. In C. Yorke (Ed.), *The Works of Francis Bacon, Baron of Verulam, Viscount St. Alban, and Lord High Chancellor of England. In five volumes. Vol. 1* (p. 478).

#188-Virtue - Bacon, F. (n.d.). Essays of Francis Bacon - Of Adversity (The Essays or Counsels, Civil and Moral, of Francis Ld. Verulam Viscount St. Albans). Retrieved from http://www.authorama.com/essays-of-Francis-bacon-6.html

Walter Bagehot (3 February 1826 – 24 March 1877)
https://en.wikipedia.org/wiki/Walter_Bagehot
#276-Continuous - Bagehot, W., & University of St. Andrews. (1858). Hartley Coleridge. In *Estimates of some Englishmen and Scotchmen, a series of articles reprinted by permission principally from the National Review. By Walter Bagehot* (p. 337).

Mikhail Bakunin (30 May 1814 – 1 July 1876)
https://en.wikipedia.org/wiki/Mikhail_Bakunin
#33-Freedom - Bakunin, M. A. (1871). Mikhail Bakunin - Wikiquote. Retrieved January 22, 2016, from https://en.wikiquote.org/wiki/Mikhail_Bakunin

Clara L. Balfour (21 December 1808 – 3 July 1878)
https://en.wikipedia.org/wiki/Clara_Lucas_Balfour
#184-Opponent - BALFOUR, C. L. (1861). Gifts. In *Sunbeams for all Seasons: a selected series of counsels, cautions, and precepts, relating to the hopes, joys, pleasures, and sorrows of life* (p. 92). London: Houlston & Wright.

Hosea Ballou (April 30, 1771 – June 7, 1852)
https://en.wikipedia.org/wiki/Hosea_Ballou
#7-Gratitude - Douglas, C. N. (1915). Gratitude. In *Forty thousand sublime and beautiful thoughts gathered from the roses, clover blossoms, geraniums, violets, morning-glories, and pansies of literature* (2nd ed., p. 885). New York, NY: The Christian Herald Bible House.

#120-Zeal - Northend, C. (1880). Zeal. In *Gems of thought: Being a collection of more than 1000 choice selections or aphorisms* (p. 227). New York: Appleton.

Honore de Balzac (20 May 1799 – 18 August 1850)
https://en.wikipedia.org/wiki/Honor%C3%A9_de_Balzac
#222-Disrespectful - Douglas, C. N. (1915). Gentleness. In *Forty thousand sublime and beautiful thoughts gathered from the roses, clover blossoms, geraniums, violets, morning-glories, and pansies of literature* (p. 825). New York, NY: Christian Herald.

#246-Less - De Balzac, H. (1829). Part I, Meditation VIII: Of the First Symptoms, aphorism LX. Retrieved March 16, 2016, from https://en.wikiquote.org/wiki/Honor%C3%A9_de_Balzac

#210-Take - De Balzac, H. (1829). Part I, Meditation III: Of the Honest Woman. Retrieved August 30, 2017, from https://en.wikiquote.org/wiki/Honor%C3%A9_de_Balzac

James M. Barrie (9 May 1860 – 19 June 1937)
https://en.wikipedia.org/wiki/J._M._Barrie

#69-Sunshine - Barrie, J. M. (1917). As quoted in Christ's Second Coming Fulfilled (1917) by Marion Morris, p. 144. Retrieved April 21, 2016, from https://en.wikiquote.org/wiki/J._M._Barrie

Cyrus Augustus Bartol (April 30, 1813 – December 16, 1900)
http://oasis.lib.harvard.edu/oasis/deliver/~div00411

#117-Rich - Ballou, M. M. (1886). Ideas. In *Edge-tools of speech: Selected and arranged* (p. 224). Boston, MA: Ticknor and Company.

Clara Barton (December 25, 1821 – April 12, 1912)
https://en.wikipedia.org/wiki/Clara_Barton

#213-Discipline - Barton, C. (n.d.). Clara Barton - New World Encyclopedia. Retrieved from http://www.newworldencyclopedia.org/entry/Clara_Barton

Basil of Caesarea (329 or 330 – January 1 or 2, 379)
https://en.wikipedia.org/wiki/Basil_of_Caesarea

#31-Abundance - Edwards, T. (1891). Good Humor. In *A Dictionary of Thoughts: Being a Cyclopedia of Laconic Quotations from the best authors, both ancient and modern* (p. 199). New York, NY: Cassell Publishing Company.

Henry Ward Beecher (June 24, 1813 – March 8, 1887)
https://en.wikipedia.org/wiki/Henry_Ward_Beecher

#163-Become - Edwards, T. (1891). Parents. In *A Dictionary of Thoughts: Being a Cyclopedia of Laconic Quotations from the best authors, both ancient and modern* (p. 396). New York, NY: Cassell Publishing Company.

#223-Compassion - Handford, T. W. (1890). November thirtieth. In *Two thousand and ten choice quotations in poetry and prose: From the master minds of all ages* (5th ed., p. 339). Chicago, IL: Belford-Clarke.

#348-Conclude - Edwards, T. (1891). Praise. In *A Dictionary of Thoughts: Being a Cyclopedia of Laconic Quotations from the best authors, both ancient and modern* (p. 433). New York, NY: Cassell Publishing Company.

#129-Confidence - Klopsch, L. (1896). Difficulties. In *Many Thoughts of Many Minds A Treasury of Quotations from the Literature of Every Land and Every Age* (p. 67). New York, NY: The Christian Herald.

#200-Deeds - Edwards, T. (1891). Deeds. In *A Dictionary of Thoughts: Being a Cyclopedia of Laconic Quotations from the best authors, both ancient and modern* (p. 108). New York, NY: Cassell Publishing Company.

#71-Healing - Foster, E. (1870). 5796. Trouble, Design of. In *New cyclopedia of prose illustrations adapted to Christian teaching, embracing mythology, analogies, legends, parables, emblems, metaphors, similes, allegories, proverbs; classic, historic, and religious anecdotes, etc.; first series* (p. 638). New York, NY: Thomas Y. Crowell & Co.

#358-Hindrance - Beecher, H. W. (1873). The Spread of Christian Manhood in America. In *The Original Plymouth Pulpit: Sermons of Henry Ward Beecher in Plymouth Church, Brooklyn, Volumes 9-10* (10th ed., p. 31). Boston: The Pilgrim Press Chicago.

#291-Standard - Beecher, H. W. (1902). Beecher's advice to his son. In N. C. Schaeffer (Ed.), *Pennsylvania School Journal, Volume 51* (p. 346). Lancaster, PA: Wickersham Printing Co.

#332-Thanksgiving - Beecher, H. W. (1859). *LIFE THOUGHTS, Gathered from the Extemporaneous Discourses* (p. 115). E. D. Proctor (Ed.). Boston, MA: Phillips, Sampson, and Company.

#340-Yourself - Beecher, H. W. (1902). Beecher's advice to his son. In N. C. Schaeffer (Ed.), *Pennsylvania School Journal, Volume 51* (p. 346). Lancaster, PA: Wickersham Printing Co.

Ludwig van Beethoven (17 December 1770 – 26 March 1827)
https://en.wikipedia.org/wiki/Ludwig_van_Beethoven
#170-Overcome - Beethoven, L. V. (1801, November 16). Ludwig van Beethoven - Wikiquote. Retrieved from https://en.wikiquote.org/wiki/Ludwig_van_Beethoven
Beethoven, L. V. (2011). Fate. In S. Ratcliffe (Ed.), *Oxford Treasury of Sayings and Quotations* (4th ed., p. 163). Oxford: Oxford University Press.
#236-Wisdom - Beethoven, L. V. (1810, May 28). Ludwig van Beethoven - Wikiquote. Retrieved from https://en.wikiquote.org/wiki/Ludwig_van_Beethoven

George Bellows (August 12th or 19th 1882 – January 8, 1925)
https://en.wikipedia.org/wiki/George_Bellows
#43-Spontaneous - The Relation of Painting to Architecture. (1920). In *American Architect and Architecture, Volume 118* (p. 850). New York, CO: The American Architect.

Arnold Bennett (27 May 1867 – 27 March 1931)
https://en.wikipedia.org/wiki/Arnold_Bennett
#193-Sacred - The Human Machine. (1908). In T. P. O'Connor (Ed.), *T. P.'s Weekly, Volume 11* (p. 525).

Hector Berlioz (11 December 1803 – 8 March 1869)
https://en.wikipedia.org/wiki/Hector_Berlioz
#26-Despair - Berlioz, H. (1884). Requiem. In *Autobiography of Hector Berlioz, Volume 1: Member of the Institute of France, from 1803 to 1865; Comprising his Travels in Italy, Germany, Russia, and England* (R. S. Holmes, & E. Holmes, Trans.) (p. 285). London: Macmillan and Co.
#52-Time - Berlioz, L. H. (1865). Hector Berlioz - Wikiquote. Retrieved October 15, 2017, from https://en.wikiquote.org/wiki/Hector_Berlioz

Ambrose Bierce (June 24, 1842 – circa 1914)
https://en.wikipedia.org/wiki/Ambrose_Bierce
#152-Optimism - Bierce, A. (1906). O - Ambrose Bierce - The Devil's Dictionary - for Tablet & Screen. Retrieved from http://www.thedevilsdictionary.com/?o=#!
#194-Profane - Bierce, A. (1906). S - Ambrose Bierce - The Devil's Dictionary - for Tablet & Screen. Retrieved from http://www.thedevilsdictionary.com/?s=#!

Josh Billings (April 21, 1818 – October 14, 1885)
https://en.wikipedia.org/wiki/Josh_Billings
#53-Complete - Billings, J. (n.d.). Josh Billings - Wikipedia. Retrieved June 5, 2016, from https://en.wikipedia.org/wiki/Josh_Billings

Gary Ryan Blair
http://www.everythingcounts.com/
http://www.100daychallenge.com/gary-ryan-blair/
#191-Down, **#203-Everything**

Lady Blessington (1 September 1789 – 4 June 1849)
https://en.wikipedia.org/wiki/Marguerite_Gardiner,_Countess_of_Blessington
#110-Beauty - Winged Words. (1888). In M. Russell, S.J. (Ed.), *The Irish Monthly, Volume 16* (p. 445). Dublin: M. H. Gill & Son, O'Connell Street.

Anicius Manlius Severinus Boethius (480-524 AD)
https://en.wikipedia.org/wiki/Boethius
#88-Happy - Boethius, A. M. (n.d.). Anicius Manlius Severinus Boethius - Wikiquote. Retrieved October 17, 2017, from https://en.wikiquote.org/wiki/Anicius_Manlius_Severinus_Boethius
#187-Vice - Boethius, A. M. (n.d.). Anicius Manlius Severinus Boethius - Wikiquote. Retrieved October 17, 2017, from https://en.wikiquote.org/wiki/Anicius_Manlius_Severinus_Boethius

Horatius Bonar (19 December 1808 – 31 July 1889)
https://en.wikipedia.org/wiki/Horatius_Bonar
#51-Moment - E, J. (1883). Work for God. In *The Voice of wisdom: a treasury of moral truths from the best authors* (p. 165). Edinburgh: W.P. Nimmo & Co.

William Booth (10 April 1829 – 20 August 1912)
https://en.wikipedia.org/wiki/William_Booth
#178-Surrender - The ideal Christian – His Consecration. (1912). In T. L. Gardiner (Ed.), *The Sabbath Recorder, Volume 73* (p. 855).

Louis-Francois de Boufflers (January 10, 1644 – August 22, 1711)
https://en.wikipedia.org/wiki/Louis-Fran%C3%A7ois_de_Boufflers
#183-Warrior - Douglas, C. N. (1915). Abundance. In *Forty thousand sublime and beautiful thoughts gathered from the roses, clover blossoms, geraniums, violets, morning-glories, and pansies of literature* (p. 13). New York, NY: The Christian Herald.

C. Bowles
#41-Cause - DAY, E. P. (1884). Freedom. In *Day's Collacon: an encyclopedia of prose quotations. Consisting of beautiful thoughts, choice extracts, and sayings, of the most eminent writers of all nations, from the earliest ages to the present times* (p. 302). New York and London: International Printing and Publishing Office, Sampson Low, Marston, Searle, and Rivington.

Kate Braestrup
http://www.katebraestrup.com/
Taken from Beginner's Grace: Bringing Prayer to Life by Kate Braestrup. Copyright © (August 9, 2011) by Free Press - Simon and Schuster Publishing. Used by permission of Kate Braestrup. All rights reserved.
#325-Expand - Braestrup, K. (2011). Prayers in the Dark and Quiet. In *Taken from Beginner's Grace: Bringing Prayer to Life* (p. 38). New York, NY: Free Press - Simon and Schuster Publishing.
#245-More - Braestrup, K. (2011). Prayers in the Dark and Quiet. In *Taken from Beginner's Grace: Bringing Prayer to Life* (p. 32). New York, NY: Free Press - Simon and Schuster Publishing.
#240-Refrain - Braestrup, K. (2011). The starting point. In *Taken from Beginner's Grace: Bringing Prayer to Life* (p. 20). New York, NY: Free Press - Simon and Schuster Publishing.
#102-Scatter - Braestrup, K. (2011). Faith. In *Taken from Beginner's Grace: Bringing Prayer to Life* (pp. 229-229). New York, NY: Free Press - Simon and Schuster Publishing.

Robert Brault
http://rbrault.blogspot.com/
#45-Love, #123-See, #365-Ignore

Ebenezer Cobham Brewer (2 May 1810 – 6 March 1897)
https://en.wikipedia.org/wiki/E._Cobham_Brewer
#3-Brilliant - Brewer, E. C. (1854). Theme LXI. In *A guide to English composition, or One hundred and twenty subjects analysed* (p. 227). New York and Boston: C.S. Francis and Company.
#182-Neglect - Brewer, E. C. (1854). Theme LXI. In *A guide to English composition, or One hundred and twenty subjects analysed* (p. 227). New York and Boston: C.S. Francis and Company.

Charles Bridges (1794-1869)
https://en.wikipedia.org/wiki/Charles_Bridges_(theologian)
#24-Unworthy - Bridges, C. (1847). Chapter XIII. 21. In *An Exposition of the Book of Proverbs, Volume 1* (p. 147). New York, NY: Robert Carter.

Richard Gaylord Briley
All quotes Taken from Pray and Grow Rich: 7 Overlooked Secrets from the Bible by Richard Gaylord Briley. Copyright © (June 1, 1998) by Pub in the Glen.
#302-Both - Briley, R. G. (1998). Application III. Success for you & yours on Earth as it is in Heaven. In *Pray and Grow Rich: 7 Overlooked Secrets from the Bible* (p. 131). Glen, NH: Pub in the Glen.
#172-Goal - Briley, R. G. (1998). Application II. Success & master mind groups. In *Pray and Grow Rich: 7 Overlooked Secrets from the Bible* (p. 112). Glen, NH: Pub in the Glen.
#286-Many - Briley, R. G. (1998). Application III. Success for you & yours on Earth as it is in Heaven. In *Pray and Grow Rich: 7 Overlooked Secrets from the Bible* (p. 123). Glen, NH: Pub in the Glen.
#271-Plan - Briley, R. G. (1998). Secret Seven: Success follows faith & faithfulness. In *Pray and Grow Rich: 7 Overlooked Secrets from the Bible* (p. 89). Glen, NH: Pub in the Glen.
#277-Rules - Briley, R. G. (1998). Secret One: Success bows to God's purposes. In *Pray and Grow Rich: 7 Overlooked Secrets from the Bible* (pp. 8-9). Glen, NH: Pub in the Glen.
#24-Unworthy - Briley, R. G. (1998). Secret Three: Success Benefits Others First. In *Pray and Grow Rich: 7 Overlooked Secrets from the Bible* (p. 34). Glen, NH: Pub in the Glen.

Augusta C. Bristol
#28-Opportunity - M. Godin, The founder of the familistere. (1880). In H. S. Drayton & N. Sizer (Eds.), *The Phrenological Journal and Science of Health: Incorporated ..., Volumes 70-71* (p. 312). New York, NY: S. R. Wells & Co.

Henry Brooke (1703 – October 10, 1783)
https://en.wikipedia.org/wiki/Henry_Brooke_(writer)
#203-Everything - Winged Words. (1888). In M. Russell, S.J. (Ed.), *The Irish Monthly, Volume 16* (p. 445). Dublin: M. H. Gill & Son, O›Connell Street.

Richard Bliss Brooke
https://shop.blissbusiness.com/
Taken from Mach II: The Art of Vision and Self-Motivation by Richard Bliss Brooke. Copyright © (March 1, 2006) by Bliss Business. Used by permission of Bliss Business, LLC All rights reserved.
#224-Cruel, #357-Clarity

William Hardcastle Browne (November 14, 1840 -1906)
#314-Protection - Browne, W. H. (1901). Labor. In *Proverbs* (p. 196). Toronto, London, Philadelphia and San Francisco: Drexel Biddle.

Tim Brownson
https://www.adaringadventure.com/
#19-Certain, #195-Enough, #56-Hard

William Jennings Bryan (March 19, 1860 – July 26, 1925)
https://en.wikipedia.org/wiki/William_Jennings_Bryan
#41-Cause - Bryan, W. J. (1896, July 9). Speech at the Democratic National Convention, Chicago, Illinois. Retrieved October 23, 2017, from https://en.wikiquote.org/wiki/William_Jennings_Bryan
#248-Destiny - Bryan, W. J. (1899, February 22). "America's Mission." speech delivered by the leader of the Democratic Party at the Washington Day banquet given by the Virginia Democratic Association at Washington, D.C.,

Retrieved October 23, 2017, from https://en.wikiquote.org/wiki/William_Jennings_Bryan
#51-Moment - Bryan, W. J. (1881). Illinois College Valedictory. Retrieved October 23, 2017, from https://en.wikiquote.org/wiki/William_Jennings_Bryan

James Buckham (February 23, 1844 – September 25, 1930)
https://en.wikipedia.org/wiki/James_Buckham_Kennedy
#358-Hindrance - Constructive force in merchandising. (1918). In *The Nebraska Ironmonger, Volume 6* (p. 27). Lincoln: The Nebraska Hardware Mutual Insurance Co.

Georges-Louis Leclerc, Comte de Buffon (7 September 1707 – 16 April 1788)
https://en.wikipedia.org/wiki/Georges-Louis_Leclerc,_Comte_de_Buffon
#338-Fast - Pat. (1896). In L. Klopsch (Ed.), *Many Thoughts of Many Minds: A Treasury of Quotations from the Literature of Every Land and Every Age* (p. 205). New York, NY: The Christian Herald, Louis Klopsch, Proprietor.

Thomas Bulfinch (July 15, 1796 – May 27, 1867)
https://en.wikipedia.org/wiki/Thomas_Bulfinch
#131-Rude - Bulfinch, T. (1900). Metrical Romances. In J. L. Scott (Ed.), *AGE OF CHIVALRY OR KING ARTHUR AND HIS KNIGHTS* (p. 9).

Edward G. Bulwer-Lytton (25 May 1803 – 18 January 1873)
https://en.wikipedia.org/wiki/Edward_Bulwer-Lytton
#150-Calmness - Power. (1886). In M. M. Ballou (Ed.), *Edge-tools of speech* (p. 385). Boston, MA: Ticknor and Company.

Robert Jones Burdette (July 30, 1844 – November 19, 1914)
https://en.wikipedia.org/wiki/Robert_Jones_Burdette
#149-Worry - Yesterday and Tomorrow. (1912). In J. L. Thomas (Ed.), *Ancient Accepted Sottish Rite of Free Masonry, Brotherhood, Volumes 1-6* (p. 15).

E. C. Burke
#266-Bad - A new leaf. (1908). In J. E & H. S (Eds.), *The Melody of the Heart* (2nd ed., p. 118). New York, NY: Frederick A. Stokes Company.

Edmund Burke (12 January 1730 – 9 July 1797)
https://en.wikipedia.org/wiki/Edmund_Burke
#271-Plan - Conklin, G. W. (1906). Futurity. Letter, Jan. 19, 1791. In *Conklin's who wrote that?: Comprising 3216 prose selections* (p. 86). Philadelphia, PA: Geo. W. Ogilvie & David McKay.

Robert Burns (25 January 1759 – 21 July 1796)
https://en.wikipedia.org/wiki/Robert_Burns
#123-See - Burns, R. (1786). Robert Burns Country: To A Louse: On Seeing One On A Lady's Bonnet, At Church. Retrieved from http://www.robertburns.org/works/97.shtml

Horace Bushnell (April 14, 1802 – February 17, 1876)
https://en.wikipedia.org/wiki/Horace_Bushnell
#237-Ordinary - Gilbert, J. H. (1895). Character. In *Dictionary of Burning Words of Brilliant Writers: A Cyclopædia of Quotations from the literature of all ages* (p. 45). New York, NY: Wilbur B. Ketcham.

Joseph Butler (18 May 1692 – 16 June 1752)
https://en.wikipedia.org/wiki/Joseph_Butler
#44-Deliberate - Wood, J. (1893). Men. In *Dictionary of quotations from ancient, modern, English and foreign sources* (p. 273). London and New York: Frederick Warne and Co.

Charles Buxton (18 November 1823 – 10 August 1871)
https://en.wikipedia.org/wiki/Charles_Buxton
#55-Easy - Buxton, C. (1883). Notes of Thought. Retrieved October 24, 2017, from https://en.wikiquote.org/wiki/Charles_Buxton
#120-Zeal - Ballou, M. M. (1886). Zeal. In *Edge-tools of speech: Selected and arranged* (p. 569). Boston, MA: Ticknor and Company.

Thomas Buxton, 1ˢᵗ Baronet (1 April 1786 – 19 February 1845)
https://en.wikipedia.org/wiki/Fowell_Buxton
#73-Perseverance - Buxton, 1ˢᵗ Baronet, T. F. (1886). *Frank Leslie's Sunday Magazine Vol. XIX, Vol. XIX* (January - June), 89. Retrieved from https://en.wikiquote.org/wiki/Perseverance

William Byrd (1539/40-4 July 1623)
https://en.wikipedia.org/wiki/William_Byrd
#32-Lack - Klopsch, L. (1896). Contentment. In *Many Thoughts of Many Minds: A Treasury of Quotations from the Literature of Every Land and Every Age* (p. 53). New York, NY: The Christian Herald.

Lord Byron (22 January 1788 – 19 April 1824)
https://en.wikipedia.org/wiki/Lord_Byron
#150-Calmness - Walsh, W. S. (1921). Innocence. Werner, Act iv. Se. 1. In *The international encyclopedia of prose and poetical quotations from the literature of the world including the following languages: English, Latin, Greek, French, Spanish, Persian, Italian, German, Chinese, Hebrew and others* (p. 389). Philadelphia, PA: The John C. Winston Company.
#82-Defer - Byron, G. G. (1834). CXXX. In *The works of Lord Byron, including the suppressed poems: Complete in one volume* (p. 80). Paris: A. and W. Galignani.
#84-Past - Pas. (1896). In L. Klopsch (Ed.), *Many Thoughts of Many Minds: A Treasury of Quotations from the Literature of Every Land and Every Age* (p. 204). New York, NY: The Christian Herald, Louis Klopsch, Proprietor.
#125-Share - Byron, G. G. (1819). Don Juan - Stanza 172. Retrieved June 24, 2017, from https://en.wikiquote.org/wiki/Don_Juan_(Byron)

C

E. M. C.
#67-Trust - Perry, S. A. (1905). Courage. In *Spiritual flashlights from godly men and women* (p. 53). Chicago, IL: S.B. Shaw.

Abraham Cahan (July 7, 1860 – August 31, 1951)
https://en.wikipedia.org/wiki/Abraham_Cahan
#260-Abstain - Cahan, A. (1917). *The Rise of David Levinsky*.

Dottie D. Caldwell, MA, LPC
http://www.bridgetolife.org/counseling/dotti-caldwell/
#241-Moving, #79-Truth

William Camden (2 May 1551 – 9 November 1623)
https://en.wikipedia.org/wiki/William_Camden
#225-Early - Camden, W. (2017, July 14). The Early Bird Catcheth the Worme | Quote Investigator. Retrieved from https://quoteinvestigator.com/2017/07/14/early-bird/

George Canning (11 April 1771 – 8 August 1827)
https://en.wikipedia.org/wiki/George_Canning
#350-Honor - *Dictionary of quotations from ancient and modern, English and foreign sources* (p. 193). (1899). J. Wood (Ed.). London: Frederick Warne and Co.

Thomas Carlye (4 December 1795 – 5 February 1881)
https://en.wikipedia.org/wiki/Thomas_Carlyle
#59-Accomplish - Wood, J. (1893). Books. In *Dictionary of Quotations from Ancient and Modern English and Foreign Sources* (p. 32). London and New York: Frederick Warne and Co.
#42-Effect - Alcott, L. M. (n.d.). Laconics. In *Sunday School Library Bulletin: Devoted Exclusively to the Sunday School Library, Volumes 3-6* (p. 26).
#78-Work - Wood, J. (1893). Give. In *Dictionary of Quotations from Ancient and Modern English and Foreign Sources* (p. 123). London and New York: Frederick Warne and Co.

Andrew Carnegie (November 25, 1835 – August 11, 1919)
https://en.wikipedia.org/wiki/Andrew_Carnegie
#36-Community - Carnegie, A. (1889). "The Best Fields for Philanthropy," In North American Review, December 1889 vol. 149, issue 397. Retrieved July 15, 2016, from https://en.wikiquote.org/wiki/Andrew_Carnegie

Dale Carnegie (November 24, 1888 – November 1, 1955)
https://en.wikipedia.org/wiki/Dale_Carnegie
#227-Rules - Retrieved February 7, 2016, from Web Site:
https://en.wikiquote.org/wiki/Dale_Carnegie
On his book *How to Win Friends and Influence People* as quoted in *Newsweek* (8 August 1955); also quoted in *Best Quotes of '54, '55, '56* (1957) by James Beasley Simpson, p. 128.

Lewis Carroll (27 January 1832 – 14 January 1898)
https://en.wikipedia.org/wiki/Lewis_Carroll
#201-Believe - Carroll, L. (n.d.). Carroll, Lewis (1832-1898) (Alice's Adventures in Wonderland). Retrieved from http://www.daviddarling.info/encyclopedia/C/Carroll.html

George Washington Carver (1861 or 1864 – January 5, 1943)
https://en.wikipedia.org/wiki/George_Washington_Carver
#223-Compassion - Carver, G. W. (n.d.). George Washington Carver National Monument--Places Reflecting America's Diverse Cultures Explore their Stories in the National Park System: A Discover Our Shared Heritage Travel Itinerary. Retrieved from https://www.nps.gov/nr/testing/cultural_groups/G_Washington_Carver_Historic_Site.html

Willa Cather (December 7, 1873 – April 24, 1947)
https://en.wikipedia.org/wiki/Willa_Cather
#71-Healing - Cather, W. S. (1927). Death Comes for the Archbishop (1927), Book 1, Ch. 4. Retrieved January 27, 2016, from https://en.wikiquote.org/wiki/Willa_Cather

Catherine the Great (2 May 1729 – 17 November 1796)
https://en.wikipedia.org/wiki/Catherine_the_Great
#168-Blame - In Williams, H. S. (1908). The age of Catherine the Great. In *The historians' history of the world* (p. 423). London and New York: Hooper & Jackson.

Dionysius Cato (3rd or 4th Century AD)
https://en.wikipedia.org/wiki/Distichs_of_Cato
#15-Declare - Walsh, W. S. (1892). Spelling, Eccentricities of. In *Handy-Book of Literary Curiosities* (p. 1024). Philadelphia, PA: J. B. Lippincott Company.

Miguel De Cervantes (29 September 1547 – 22 April 1616)
https://en.wikipedia.org/wiki/Miguel_de_Cervantes
#80-Falsehood - Cervantes, S. M. (1908). Chapter X. In *The history of the ingenious gentleman Don Quixote of La Mancha* (P. A. Motteux, Trans.) (p. 123). Edinburgh: John Grant.
#211-Load - Walsh, W. S. (1921). Ass. In *The international encyclopedia of prose and poetical quotations from the literature of the world including the following languages: English, Latin, Greek, French, Spanish, Persian, Italian, German, Chinese, Hebrew and others* (p. 62). Philadelphia, PA: The John C. Winston Company.
#249-Power - De Cervantes, M. (n.d.). Miguel de Cervantes, Don Quixote (1605-1615), Part I, Section XXI. Retrieved March 23, 2017, from https://en.wikiquote.org/wiki/Begging

Oswald Chambers (24 July 1874 – 15 November 1917)
https://en.wikipedia.org/wiki/Oswald_Chambers
All quotes Taken from *My Utmost for His Highest* by Oswald Chambers. © 1935 by Dodd Mead & Co. renewed © 1963 by the Oswald Chambers Publications Assn., Ltd., and is used by permission of Discovery House Publishers, Box 3566, Grand Rapids MI 49501. All rights reserved.
#44-Deliberate, #216-Doubt, #7-Gratitude, #14-Hypocrite, #232-Look, #250-Powerless, #310-Real, #78-Work, #206-Wrong.

Nicolas Chamfort (6 April 1741 – 13 April 1794)
https://en.wikipedia.org/wiki/Nicolas_Chamfort
#25-Laughter - Pascal, Chamfort, and La Bruyere. (1888). In R. Halkett (Ed.), *The Bookmart, Volume 5* (p. 304). Pittsburg: Bookmart Publishing Company.

Chanakya (350-275BC)
https://en.wikipedia.org/wiki/Chanakya
#241-Moving - Chanakya. (n.d.). Chanakya, in The true aspect of Chanakya (Birth: 350 BC. Death:275 BC). Retrieved October 26, 2017, from https://en.wikiquote.org/wiki/Tranquility
#320-Present - Chanakya. (n.d.). Portal:Bihar. Retrieved October 3, 2017, from https://en.wikipedia.org/wiki/Portal:Bihar

Anton Pavlovich Chekhov (29 January 1860 – 15 July 1904)
https://en.wikipedia.org/wiki/Anton_Chekhov
#121-Idleness - Chekhov, A. P. (1896). My life, by Anton Chekhov. Retrieved August 14, 2016, from https://en.wikiquote.org/wiki/Anton_Chekhov

Lydia M. Child (February 11, 1802 – October 20, 1880)
https://en.wikipedia.org/wiki/Lydia_Maria_Child
#35-Individual - Child, L. M. (n.d.). Child, Lydia, M. Letters from New York, 1943. Retrieved from http://www.sailorthomson.com/child.html
#329-Own - Child, L. M. (1843). Letter to Ellis Gray Loring (1843). Retrieved January 25, 2016, from https://en.wikiquote.org/wiki/Lydia_Maria_Child

Rev. C. W. L. Christian
#215-Faith - Perry, S. A. (1905). Faith. In *Spiritual flashlights from godly men and women* (p. 83). Chicago, IL: S.B. Shaw.

Marcus Tullius Cicero (3 January 106 BC – 7 December 43 BC)
https://en.wikipedia.org/wiki/Cicero
#76-Disgrace - Cicero, M. T. (n.d.). Orator Ad M. Brutum (46 BC). Retrieved January 3, 2016, from https://en.wikipedia.org/wiki/Cicero
#319-Former - Douglas, C. N. (1915). History. In *Forty thousand sublime and beautiful thoughts gathered from the roses, clover blossoms, geraniums, violets, morning-glories, and pansies of literature* (p. 955). New York, NY: Christian Herald.
#182-Neglect - Edwards, T. (1891). Action. In *A Dictionary of Thoughts: Being a Cyclopedia of Laconic Quotations from the best authors, both ancient and modern* (p. 3). New York, NY: Cassell Publishing Company.
#17-Tranquil - Cicero, M. T. (n.d.). Book I, section 6. Retrieved from https://en.wikiquote.org/wiki/Cicero

Claudianus (370 – 404 AD)
https://en.wikipedia.org/wiki/Claudian
#188-Virtue - Halyburton, T., & Hog, J. (1798). Principles of the modern deists. De consulatu Malli Theodorii Panegyris. i. In *Natural religion insufficient, and revealed necessary, to man's happiness in his present state: or, A rational enquiry into the principles of the modern deists: Wherein is largely discovered their utter insufficiency to answer the great ends of religion, and the weakness of their pleadings for the sufficiency of nature's light to eternal happiness* (p. 256). Philadelphia: Printed by Hogan & M›Elroy, no. 1, North Third-Street, and sold by A. Cunningham, Washington, (Penn.) A. M›Donald, Northumberland; C. Davis, New-York; and by J. M›Culloch, and the publishers, Philadelphia.

Luc de Clapiers (6 August 1715 – 28 May 1747)
https://en.wikipedia.org/wiki/Luc_de_Clapiers,_marquis_de_Vauvenargues
#323-Clarity - De Clapiers, L. (1746). Maxim 729, Réflexions et maximes ("Reflections and Maxims"). Retrieved August 3, 2017, from https://en.wikiquote.org/wiki/Luc_de_Clapiers,_Marquis_de_Vauvenargues

Isidore van Cleef (Born March 19, 1859)
#208-Decline - Ballou, M. M. (1899). Toleration. In *Edge-tools of speech: Selected and arranged* (p. 504). Boston, MA: Ticknor and Company.

Jeremy Collier (23 September 1650 – 26 April 1726)
https://en.wikipedia.org/wiki/Jeremy_Collier
#142-Disorder - Edwards, T. (1891). Idleness. In *A dictionary of thoughts* (p. 243). New York, NY: Cassell Publishing Company.

Charles Caleb Colton (1780-1832)
https://en.wikipedia.org/wiki/Charles_Caleb_Colton
#177-Fight - Edwards, T. (1891). Religion. In *A Dictionary of Thoughts: Being a Cyclopedia of Laconic Quotations from the best authors, both ancient and modern* (p. 474). New York, NY: Cassell Publishing Company.
#127-Reply - Ballou, M. M. (1886). Argument. In *Edge-tools of speech: Selected and arranged* (p. 21). Boston, MA: Ticknor and Company.
#279-Say - Allibone, S. A. (1875). Argument. In *Prose Quotations from Socrates to Macaulay* (p. 41). Philadelphia: J.B. Lippincott & Company.

William Congreve (24 January 1670 – 19 January 1729)

https://en.wikipedia.org/wiki/William_Congreve

#176-Dull - Congreve, W. (1693). The Old Bachelor, Act II, scene vii. Retrieved October 29, 2016, from https://en.wikiquote.org/wiki/William_Congreve

#130-Uncertainty - Congreve, W. (1695). Love for Love, Act IV, scene xx. Retrieved September 10, 2016, from https://en.wikiquote.org/wiki/William_Congreve

Confucius (September 28, 551 BC – 479 BC)

https://en.wikipedia.org/wiki/Confucius

#122-Action - Confucius. (n.d.). The Analects, Chapter IV. Retrieved March 11, 2017, from https://en.wikiquote.org/wiki/Confucius

#66-Comfort - Confucius. (n.d.). The Analects, Chapter I. Retrieved May 20, 2017, from https://en.wikiquote.org/wiki/Confucius

#148-Defeat - Douglas, C. N. (1915). Will. In *Forty thousand sublime and beautiful thoughts gathered from the roses, clover blossoms, geraniums, violets, morning-glories, and pansies of literature* (p. 1932). New York, NY: The Christian Herald.

#96-Diligence - Ballou, M. M. (1884). Diligence. In *Treasury of thought: Forming an encyclopedia of quotations from ancient and modern authors* (p. 127). Boston, MA: Houghton, Mifflin.

William Cowper (26 November 1731 – 25 April 1800)

https://en.wikipedia.org/wiki/William_Cowper

#40-Dismiss - Cowper, W. (1824). The winter walk at noon. In *The poems of William Cowper, Esq: With notes from his own correspondence and a bibliographical memoir* (p. 289). London: Printed and published by J. Limbird.

#116-Rest - Wood, J. (1893). Above. In *Dictionary of quotations from ancient, modern, English and foreign sources* (p. 2). London and New York: Frederick Warne and Co.

Rev. Francis W. Cox (January 1817 – 29 March 1904)

https://en.wikipedia.org/wiki/F._W._Cox

#310-Real - Perry, S. A. (1905). Prayer. In *Spiritual flashlights from godly men and women* (p. 211). Chicago, IL: S.B. Shaw.

Frank Crane (1861-1928)

https://en.wikiquote.org/wiki/Frank_Crane

#67-Trust - Crane, F. (n.d.). As quoted in Business Education World, Vol. 15 (1935) p. 172. Retrieved June 28, 2017, from https://en.wikiquote.org/wiki/Frank_Crane

David Crockett (August 17, 1786 – March 6, 1836)

https://en.wikipedia.org/wiki/Davy_Crockett

#317-Ahead - Crockett, D. (1834). In quote on cover of book. In *[A Narrative of the Life of David Crockett ... Written by himself.]*. London: John Limbird.

Thomas Crofton (15 January 1798 – 8 August 1854)

https://en.wikipedia.org/wiki/Thomas_Crofton_Croker

#268-Always - Croker's Popular Songs of Ireland. (1839). In J. Fraser (Ed.), *Fraser's Magazine for Town and Country, Volume 19* (p. 682). London: James Fraser.

Theodore L. Cuyler (January 10, 1822 – February 26, 1902)

https://en.wikipedia.org/wiki/Theodore_L._Cuyler

#220-Useless - Gilbert, J. H. (1895). Decision. In *Dictionary of Burning Words of Brilliant Writers: A Cyclopædia of Quotations from the literature of all ages* (p. 186). New York, NY: Wilbur B. Ketcham.

St. Cyprian (200 - September 14, 258 AD)
https://en.wikipedia.org/wiki/Cyprian
#265-Good - Adversities. (1916). In C. J. Callan (Ed.), *Illustrations for sermons and instructions: Definitions, word-pictures, exemplifications, quotations and stories, explanatory of Catholic Doctrine and practice. Gathered from the Sacred Scriptures, from the works of the Fathers and saints and from the writings of recent authors and preachers of note* (p. 287). New York, NY: Joseph F. Wagner (Inc.).

D

Joos de Damhouder (25 November 1507, Bruges – 22 January 1581 Antwerp)
https://en.wikipedia.org/wiki/Joos_de_Damhouder
#174-Answer - DAY, E. P. (1884). Hearing. In *Day's Collacon: an encyclopaedia of prose quotations. Consisting of beautiful thoughts, choice extracts, and sayings, of the most eminent writers of all nations, from the earliest ages to the present times* (p. 363). New York and London: International Printing and Publishing Office, Sampson Low, Marston, Searle, and Rivington.

W. W. Davies, Ph. D., (Halla). Professor of Hebrew, Ohio Wesleyan University
#37-Growth - Gould, H. D., & Hessenmueller, E. L. (1904). The new biblical criticism. In *Best Thoughts of Best Thinkers: Amplified, Classified, Exemplified and Arranged as a key to unlock the literature of all ages* (p. 345). Cleveland, OH: Best Thoughts Publishing Company.

Leonardo Da Vinci (15 April 1452 – 2 May 1519)
https://en.wikipedia.org/wiki/Leonardo_da_Vinci
#41-Cause - Da Vinci, L. (n.d.). XIX Philosophical Maxims. Morals. Polemics and Speculations. Retrieved November 2, 2017, from https://en.wikiquote.org/wiki/Leonardo_da_Vinci
#254-Stagnant - Da Vinci, L. (n.d.). The Notebooks of Leonardo da Vinci (Richter, 1888). Retrieved June 2, 2017, from https://en.wikiquote.org/wiki/Leonardo_da_Vinci

Clarence Day (November 18, 1874 – December 28, 1935)
https://en.wikipedia.org/wiki/Clarence_Day
#101-Group - Day, Jr., C. (1920). V. In *This simian world* (p. 10). New York, NY: Alfred A Knoph.

Edward Parsons Day (1822-1906)
#3-Brilliant - DAY, E. P. (1884). Oratory. In *Day's Collacon: an encyclopaedia of prose quotations. Consisting of beautiful thoughts, choice extracts, and sayings, of the most eminent writers of all nations, from the earliest ages to the present times* (p. 644). New York and London: International Printing and Publishing Office, Sampson Low, Marston, Searle, and Rivington.

Democritus (460 – 370 BC)
https://en.wikipedia.org/wiki/Democritus
#197-Direction - Dalbiac, P. H., & Harbottle, T. B. (1897). Latin Quotations. In *Dalbiac and Harbottle's Dictionary of Quotations (classical)* (2nd ed., p. 487). London and New York: Swan Sonnenschein & Co., Limited. The Macmillan Co., Limited.

Demosthenes (384 – 12 October 322 BC)
https://en.wikipedia.org/wiki/Demosthenes
#184-Opponent - Demosthenes. (n.d.). Dictator - RationalWiki. Retrieved November 8, 2017, from https://rationalwiki.org/wiki/Dictator
#300-Treachery - Edwards, T. (1891). Power. In *A Dictionary of thoughts: Being a cyclopedia of laconic quotations from the best authors, both ancient and modern* (p. 429). New York, NY: Cassell Publishing Company.

#136-Wish - Gould, H. D., & Hessenmueller, E. L. (1904). Laconics. Best thoughts about Belief. In *Best Thoughts of Best Thinkers: Amplified, Classified, Exemplified and Arranged as a key to unlock the literature of all ages* (p. 369). Cleveland: Best Thoughts Publishing Company.

Sir John Denham (1614 or 1615-19 March 1669)
https://en.wikipedia.org/wiki/John_Denham_(poet)
#234-Acceptance - What. (1899). In J. Wood (Ed.), *Dictionary of Quotations from Ancient and Modern, English and Foreign sources* (p. 536). London and New York: Frederick Warne and Co.
#247-Design - Waller, E., Denham, J., & Gilfillan, G. (1857). Of Prudence. In *The poetical works of Edmund Waller and Sir John Denham. With memoir and critical dissertation, by the Rev. George Gilfillan By Edmund Waller, John Denham (sir.)* (p. 285). Edinburgh, London, Dublin: James Nichol, James Nisbet & Co., W. Robertson.

Rene Descartes (31 March 1596 – 11 February 1650)
https://en.wikipedia.org/wiki/Ren%C3%A9_Descartes
#1-Resolution - Descartes, R. (n.d.). Discourse on the Method - Wikiquote. Retrieved February 22, 2016, from https://en.wikiquote.org/wiki/Discourse_on_the_Method
#219-Use - Descartes, R. (n.d.). René Descartes - Wikiquote. Retrieved May 9, 2017, from https://en.wikiquote.org/wiki/Ren%C3%A9_Descartes

Antoinette Deshoulieres (January 1, 1638 – February 17, 1694)
https://en.wikipedia.org/wiki/Antoinette_du_Ligier_de_la_Garde_Deshouli%C3%A8res
#135-Satisfied - 1831. Reflexions viii (1904). In W. F. King (Ed.), *Classical and foreign quotations: A polyglot manual of historical and literary sayings, noted passages in poetry and prose phrases, proverbs, and bons mots* (3rd ed., p. 235). London: J. Whitaker & Sons, Limited.

Madame de Stael (22 April 1766 – 14 July 1817)
https://en.wikipedia.org/wiki/Germaine_de_Sta%C3%ABl
#355-Creative - Madame de Stael, A. L. (1807). Anne Louise Germaine de Staël - Wikiquote. Retrieved October 7, 2017, from https://en.wikiquote.org/wiki/Anne_Louise_Germaine_de_Sta%C3%ABl

Charles Dickens (7 February 1812 – 9 June 1870)
https://en.wikipedia.org/wiki/Charles_Dickens
http://www.charlesdickensinfo.com/
#133-Safe - Error of English. (1921). In J. T. Baker (Ed.), *Correct English How to use it, Volumes 22-23*(p. 223). Evanston, IL: Correct English Publishing Co.
#220-Useless - Dickens, C. J. (n.d.). Charles Dickens - Wikiquote. Retrieved November 9, 2016, from https://en.wikiquote.org/wiki/Charles_Dickens

John Di Lemme
https://giantgoals.com/
#360-Miracle

Dionysius of Halicarnassus (60 BC-7 BC)
https://en.wikipedia.org/wiki/Dionysius_of_Halicarnassus
#114-Silence - Walsh, W. S. (1892). Silence. In *Handy-book of literary curiosities / by William S. Walsh* (p. 1009). Philadelphia, PA: J. B. Lippincott Company.

Byron Dorgan
http://www.byrondorgan.com
https://en.wikipedia.org/wiki/Byron_Dorgan

#253-Turn - October 25, 1999. (1999). In *Congressional Record, V. 145, Pt. 18, October 14, 1999, to October 25, 1999* (p. 26625). Washington: United States Government Printing Office.

Fyodor Dostoevsky (11 November 1821 – 9 February 1881)
https://en.wikipedia.org/wiki/Fyodor_Dostoyevsky
#195-Enough - Dostoevsky, F. (1864). Chapter VI. In *Notes from the Underground*. Epoch.
http://www.pagebypagebooks.com/Fyodor_Dostoevsky/Notes_from_the_Underground/Part_II_Chapter_VI_p6.html
#309-Ideal - Dostoyevsky, F. (1922). Lacerations. In *The Brothers Karamazov: A Novel in Four Parts and an Epilogue* (p. 178). New York, NY: The Macmillan Company.

Frederick Douglass (February 1818 – February 20, 1895)
https://en.wikipedia.org/wiki/Frederick_Douglass
#228-Rebellion - Reconstruction. (1866). In *The Atlantic Monthly. A Magazine of Literature, Since, Art, and Politics, Volume 18* (p. 763). Boston, MA: Ticknor and Fields.

William Scott Downey
#102-Scatter - Downey, W. S. (1851). Chapter V., 9. In *Proverbs of Rev. William Scott Downey, Baptist Missionary* (3rd ed., p. 13). New Orleans, LA: Printed by Davies, Son & Co.

Henry Drummond (17 August 1851 – 11 March 1897)
https://en.wikipedia.org/wiki/Henry_Drummond_(evangelist)
#171-Exercise - The greatest thing in the world. (1900). In D. J. Brewer (Ed.), *The World's Best Orations* (p. 1951).
#147-Triumph - The greatest thing in the world. (1900). In *Orations of British Orators: Including Biographical and Critical ..., Volume 2* (p. 502). New York, NY: The Colonial Press.

Samuel Willoughby Duffield (September 21, 1843 – May 12, 1887)
https://en.wikipedia.org/wiki/Samuel_Willoughby_Duffield
#322-Stretch - Longing and Listening, February 3, 1904. (1904). In *The Religious Telescope, Volume 70*(p. 129). Dayton, OH: Official Publication of the Church of the United Brethren in Christ.

John Bacchus Dykes (10 March 1823 – 22 January 1876)
https://en.wikipedia.org/wiki/John_Bacchus_Dykes
#200-Deeds - Edwards, T. (1891). Deeds. In *A Dictionary of Thoughts: Being a Cyclopedia of Laconic Quotations from the best authors, both ancient and modern* (p. 108). New York, NY: Cassell Publishing Company.

E

Marie Ebner-Eschenbach (September 13, 1830 – March 12, 1916)
https://en.wikipedia.org/wiki/Marie_von_Ebner-Eschenbach
#49-Ability - Ballou, M. M. (1886). Action. In *Edge-tools of speech: Selected and arranged* (p. 4). Boston, MA: Ticknor and Company.

Jonathan Edwards (October 5, 1703 – March 22, 1758)
https://en.wikipedia.org/wiki/Jonathan_Edwards_(theologian)
#295-Afraid - The religious telescope, August 3, 1904. (1904). In *The Religious Telescope, Volume 70* (p. 973). Dayton, OH: Official Publication of the Church of the United Brethren in Christ.

Tryon Edwards (7 August 1809 – 4 January 1894)
https://en.wikipedia.org/wiki/Tryon_Edwards

#119-Character - Edwards, T. (1891). Education. In *A Dictionary of Thoughts: Being a Cyclopedia of Laconic Quotations from the Best Authors of the World, Both Ancient and Modern* (pp. 114-115). New York, NY: Cassell Publishing Company.

#115-Train - Edwards, T. (1891). Education. In *A Dictionary of Thoughts: Being a Cyclopedia of Laconic Quotations from the Best Authors of the World, Both Ancient and Modern* (p. 134). New York, NY: Cassell Publishing Company.

Albert Einstein (14 March 1879 – 18 April 1955)
https://en.wikipedia.org/wiki/Albert_Einstein
http://einstein.biz/
http://press.princeton.edu/einstein/
#172-Goal, **#74-Lazy**

T. Harv Eker
#1 NY Times Bestselling Author of Secrets of the Millionaire Mind
http://www.harveker.com/
#122-Action - Eker, T. H. (2012, April 5). T. Harv Eker. Retrieved from https://www.facebook.com/HarvEker/posts/10150727947763390

#83-Future - Eker, T. H. (2012, July 10). T. Harv Eker. Retrieved from https://www.facebook.com/HarvEker/posts/10151034673088390

#335-Prosperity - Eker, T. H. (2013, December 10). T. Harv Eker. Retrieved from https://www.facebook.com/harveker/posts/10152059337423390

George Eliot - Mary Ann Evans (22 November 1819 – 22 December 1880)
https://en.wikipedia.org/wiki/George_Eliot
#260-Abstain - Eliot, G. (1879). George Eliot - Wikiquote. Retrieved November 12, 2017, from https://en.wikiquote.org/wiki/George_Eliot

#30-Criticism - Hall, A. W. (1887). The Works of George Eliot. Scenes of Clerical Life. In *Great Thoughts from Master Minds, Volume 8* (p. 68). London: A. Bradley.

#200-Deeds - Edwards, T. (1891). Deeds. In *A Dictionary of Thoughts: Being a Cyclopedia of Laconic Quotations from the best authors, both ancient and modern* (p. 108). New York, NY: Cassell Publishing Company.

#68-Distrust - Eliot, G. (1901). Chapter XLIV. In *The Works of George Eliot : Middlemarch* (p. 318). Edinburgh and London: William Blackwood and Sons.

#241-Moving - Eliot, G. (1858). George Eliot - Wikiquote. Retrieved November 12, 2017, from https://en.wikiquote.org/wiki/George_Eliot

#220-Useless - Douglas, C. N. (1915). Speech. In *Forty thousand sublime and beautiful thoughts gathered from the roses, clover blossoms, geraniums, violets, morning-glories, and pansies of literature* (p. 1659). New York, NY: Christian Herald.

Havelock Ellis (2 February 1859 – 8 July 1939)
https://en.wikipedia.org/wiki/Havelock_Ellis
#281-Adequate - Book Reviews. (1922). In M. Sanger (Ed.), *The Birth Control Review, Volumes 6-7* (p. 95). New York, NY: The Birth Control Review.

James Ellis
#328-Victory - A beautiful thought for each day in July. (1902). In F. Noble (Ed.), *The Treasury. A Magazine of Religious and Current Thought for Pastor and People, Volume 19* (p. 249). New York, NY: E. B. Treat & Co.

Emma C. Embury (February 25, 1806 – February 10, 1863)
https://en.wikipedia.org/wiki/Emma_Catherine_Embury

#39-Meditate - In Griswold, R. W. (1853). Emma C. Embury. Autumn Evening. In *The Female Poets of America* (2nd ed., p. 144). Philadelphia, PA: Henry Baird.

Ralph Waldo Emerson (May 25, 1803 – April 27, 1882)
https://en.wikipedia.org/wiki/Ralph_Waldo_Emerson
http://www.rwe.org/
#306-Aim - Flood, T. L. (1892). The Library Table. In *The Chautauquan, Volume 14* (p. 635). Meadville, PA: The T. L. Flood Publishing House.
#110-Beauty - Emerson, R. W. (1860). Beauty. In *The Conduct of Life* (p. 263). Boston, MA: Ticknor and Fields.
#119-Character - Emerson, R. W. (1860). Chapter 6 - Worship. In *The Conduct of Life* (p. 214). Boston, MA: Ticknor and Fields.
#36-Community - Emerson, R. W. (1875). Conduct of life. III. Wealth. In *The Prose Works of Ralph Waldo Emerson, Volume II* (p. 371). Boston, MA: James R. Osgood and Company.
#33-Freedom - Wood, J. (1899). Thought. In *Dictionary of quotations from ancient, modern, English and foreign sources* (p. 485). London: Frederick Warne and Co.
#226-Late - Emerson, R. W. (1860). The Conduct of Life - Culture. Retrieved from https://en.wikipedia.org/wiki/Ralph_Waldo_Emerson
#10-Misunderstand - Emerson, R. W. (1841). Self-Reliance. Retrieved from https://en.wikipedia.org/wiki/Ralph_Waldo_Emerson
#12-Presence - Emerson, R. W. (1839). Ralph Waldo Emerson - Wikiquote. Retrieved October 12, 2017, from https://en.wikiquote.org/wiki/Ralph_Waldo_Emerson
#144-Surprise - Emerson, R. W. (1904). IX Inspiration. In *Letters and Social Aims* (4th ed., p. 289). Boston and New York: Houghton, Mifflin, and Company.
#67-Triumph - Man the reformer (Peroration of the Address before the Mechanics' Apprentices' Library Association, Boston, January 25th, 1841). (1900). In D. J. Brewer (Ed.), *The World's Best Orations* (p. 2009).
#67-Trust - Emerson, R. W. (1904). IX Inspiration. In *Letters and Social Aims* (4th ed., p. 338). Boston and New York: Houghton, Mifflin, and Company.
#359-Usual - Editor's Study. (1887). In H. M. Alden (Ed.), *Harper's New Monthly Magazine, Volume 75* (p. 803). New York, NY: Harper & Brothers, Publishers.

Epictetus (55 – 135 AD)
https://en.wikipedia.org/wiki/Epictetus
#53-Complete - Epictetus. (135). The Enchiridion - as translated by Elizabeth Carter. Retrieved November 13, 2017, from https://en.wikiquote.org/wiki/Epictetus
#285-Few - Edwards, T. (1891). Wealth. In *A Dictionary of Thoughts: Being a Cyclopedia of Laconic Quotations from the Best Authors of the World, Both Ancient and Modern* (p. 618). New York, NY: Cassell Publishing Company.
#111-Rise - Epictetus. (n.d.). Fragment xxii. Retrieved October 15, 2017, from https://en.wikiquote.org/wiki/Epictetus
#210-Take - Epictetus. (n.d.). Golden Sayings of Epictetus as translated by Hastings Crossley (115). Retrieved November 14, 2017, from https://en.wikiquote.org/wiki/Epictetus
#136-Wish - Epictetus. (n.d.). Golden Sayings of Epictetus as translated by Hastings Crossley (26). Retrieved November 14, 2017, from https://en.wikiquote.org/wiki/Epictetus

Epicurus (341 - 270 BC)
https://en.wikipedia.org/wiki/Epicurus
#335-Prosperity - Epicurus. (n.d.). Epicurus - Letter to Menoeceus. Retrieved October 5, 2017, from http://www.epicurus.net/en/menoeceus.html
#337-Slow - Epicurus. (n.d.). Epicurus - Wikiquote. Retrieved October 13, 2017, from https://en.wikiquote.org/wiki/Epicurus

Desiderius Erasmus (28 October 1466 – 12 July 1536)
https://en.wikipedia.org/wiki/Erasmus
#209-Give - D'Aubigne, J. H., Beveridge, H., & White, H. (1845). Erasmus and Luther Contrast. In *History of the Reformation in the Sixteenth Century, Volume 1* (p. 91). Glasgow: William Collins, London: R. Groombridge & Sons.
#170-Overcome - Benham, W. G. (1914). Latin Quotations. In *Cassell's book of quotations proverbs and household words* (p. 506). London, New York, Toronto, and Melbourne: Cassell & Company, LTD.

Euripides (480 – 406 BC)
https://en.wikipedia.org/wiki/Euripides
#346-Lose - Conklin, G. W. (1906). Learning. In *Conklin's who wrote that?: Comprising 3216 prose selections* (p. 133). Philadelphia, PA: Geo. W. Ogilvie & David McKay.
#127-Reply - Euripides. (n.d.). Unidentified Plays, Fragment 977. Retrieved November 14, 2017, from https://en.wikiquote.org/wiki/Euripides

Edward Everett (April 11, 1794 – January 15, 1865)
https://en.wikipedia.org/wiki/Edward_Everett
#186-Liberty - Everett, E. (1852). *The Common School Journal and Educational Reformer* (p. 28). W. B. Fowle (Ed.).
Edward Everett - Wikiquote. (n.d.). Retrieved February 7, 2016, from https://en.wikiquote.org/wiki/Edward_Everett

F

Frederick William Faber (28 June 1814 – 26 September 1863)
https://en.wikipedia.org/wiki/Frederick_William_Faber
#120-Zeal - Gilbert, J. H. (1895). Kindness. In *Dictionary of Burning Words of Brilliant Writers: A Cyclopædia of Quotations from the literature of all ages* (p. 363). New York, NY: Wilbur B. Ketcham.
#328-Victory - Edwards, T. (1891). Temptation. In *A dictionary of thoughts being a cyclopedia of laconic quotations* (p. 567). New York, NY: Cassell Publishing Company.

Owen Feltham (1602 – February 23, 1668)
https://en.wikipedia.org/wiki/Owen_Feltham
#151-Perspective - Gilbert, J. H. (1895). Meditation. In *Dictionary of Burning Words of Brilliant Writers: A Cyclopædia of Quotations from the literature of all ages* (p. 406). New York, NY: Wilbur B. Ketcham.
#118-Poor - Edwards, T. (1891). Good Humor. In *A Dictionary of Thoughts: Being a Cyclopedia of Laconic Quotations from the best authors, both ancient and modern* (p. 199). New York, NY: Cassell Publishing Company.

Johann Gottlieb Fichte (May 19, 1762 – January 27, 1814)
https://en.wikipedia.org/wiki/Johann_Gottlieb_Fichte
#312-Vocation - Fichte, J. G. (1794). in The Vocation of the Scholar (1794), Lecture I : The Absolute Vocation OF Man. Retrieved October 22, 2017, from https://en.wikiquote.org/wiki/Vocation

Henry Fielding (22 April 1707 – 8 October 1754)
https://en.wikipedia.org/wiki/Henry_Fielding
#37-Growth - Ballou, M. M. (1886). Success. In *Edge-tools of speech: Selected and arranged* (p. 478). Boston, MA: Ticknor and Company.

Sarah Fielding (8 November 1710 – 9 April 1768)
https://en.wikipedia.org/wiki/Sarah_Fielding

#29-Kindness - Sarah Fielding (1710-1768), British novelist. The Adventures of David Simple, Volume the Last, bk. 7, Ch. 10 (1754).

Guy Finley
Life of Learning Foundation
http://www.guyfinley.org/
#54-Incomplete, #9-Understand

J. De Finod
#93-Grace - Ballou, M. M. (1886). Simplicity. In *Edge-tools of speech: Selected and arranged* (p. 455). Boston, MA: Ticknor and Company.

Dr. Clarice Fluitt
http://www.claricefluitt.org/
#279-Say, #100-Want, #270-Word

Richard J. Foster
https://renovare.org/people/richard-foster
#314-Sensitive - Foster, R. J. (August 20, 2002). *Prayer: Finding the heart's true home* (p. 85). San Francisco, CA: HarperOne.
#258-Submission - Foster, R. J. (2008, September 17). Richard Foster on Leadership. How do leaders — who must get subordinates to follow their lead — practice the discipline of submission? Retrieved from http://www.christianitytoday.com/ct/2008/september/27.44.html

Anatole France (16 April 1844 – 12 October 1924)
https://en.wikipedia.org/wiki/Anatole_France
#48-Imagine - France, A. (1881). The Crime of Sylvestre Bonnard, Pt. II, Ch. 2. Retrieved November 14, 2017, from https://en.wikiquote.org/wiki/Anatole_France

Francis Frangipane
http://www.frangipane.org/
#288-Repel

Benjamin Franklin (January 17, 1706 – April 17, 1790)
https://en.wikipedia.org/wiki/Benjamin_Franklin
#225-Early - Franklin, B. (1758). Poor Richard: 1758. Retrieved from https://usa.usembassy.de/etexts/funddocs/loa/bf1758.htm
#95-Excuse - Franklin, B. (n.d.). Benjamin Franklin Quotes - iPerceptive. Retrieved from http://iperceptive.com/authors/benjamin_franklin_quotes_2.html
#285-Few - Franklin, B., & Spofford, A. R. (n.d.). *Autobiography: Poor Richard. Letters* (p. 200). New York, NY: D. Appleton and Company.
#99-Need - Franklin, B. (1742). Poor Richard: 1742. Retrieved from https://usa.usembassy.de/etexts/funddocs/loa/bf1742.htm
#228-Rebellion - Franklin, B. (1853). Benjamin Franklin - Wikiquote. Retrieved November 15, 2017, from https://en.wikiquote.org/wiki/Benjamin_Franklin
#313-Strong - Franklin, B. B. (1914). 650. In *Poor Richard's almanack ... for the year 1807* (p. 61). Waterloo, IA: The U. S. C. Publishing Co.
#4-Stupid - Franklin, B. (n.d.). Benjamin Franklin Quotes - iPerceptive. Retrieved from http://iperceptive.com/authors/benjamin_franklin_quotes_2.html
#300-Treachery - Aphorisms. (1893). In J. Attfield (Ed.), *The Bulletin of Pharmacy* (p. 11). Detroit, MI: George S. Davis, Medical Publisher. https://www.poorrichards.net/

Rev. T. P. Frost
#163-Become - Perry, S. A. (1905). Miscellaneous. In *Spiritual flashlights from godly men and women* (p. 367). Chicago, IL: S.B. Shaw.

Thomas Fuller (1608 – 16 August 1661)
https://en.wikipedia.org/wiki/Thomas_Fuller
#224-Cruel - Fuller, T. (n.d.). Thomas Fuller - Wikiquote. Retrieved August 17, 2017, from https://en.wikiquote.org/wiki/Thomas_Fuller
#356-Distinction - Berkeley, E. (1853). *The world's laconics: Or, The best thoughts of the best authors* (p. 178). New York, NY: M.W. Dodd.

G

Amy Gage
Verbal Consent
#252-Fun

Galileo Galilei (15 February 1564 – 8 January 1642)
https://en.wikipedia.org/wiki/Galileo_Galilei
#156-Find - Galilei, G. (n.d.). Galileo Galilei - Wikiquote. Retrieved March16, 2016, from https://en.wikiquote.org/wiki/Galileo_Galilei
#267-Never - Galilei, G. (n.d.). Galileo Galilei - Wikiquote. Retrieved June 18, 2016, from https://en.wikiquote.org/wiki/Galileo_Galilei

Mahatma Gandhi (2 October 1869 – 30 January 1948)
https://en.wikipedia.org/wiki/Mahatma_Gandhi
http://www.mkgandhi.org/
#269-Humanity - Gandhi, M. (n.d.). Mahatma Gandhi - Wikiquote. Retrieved November 16, 2017, from https://en.wikiquote.org/wiki/Mahatma_Gandhi
#327-Mission - Gandhi, M. (n.d.). Mahatma Gandhi - Wikiquote. Retrieved November 16, 2017, from https://en.wikiquote.org/wiki/Mahatma_Gandhi
#185-Restraint - Gandhi, M. (n.d.). Mahatma Gandhi - Wikiquote. Retrieved November 16, 2017, from https://en.wikiquote.org/wiki/Mahatma_Gandhi
#205-Right - Gandhi, M. (n.d.). Mahatma Gandhi - Wikiquote. Retrieved November 16, 2017, from https://en.wikiquote.org/wiki/Mahatma_Gandhi
#191- Up - Gandhi, M. (n.d.). Mahatma Gandhi - Wikiquote. Retrieved November 16, 2017, from https://en.wikiquote.org/wiki/Mahatma_Gandhi

James A Garfield (November 19, 1831 – September 19, 1881)
https://en.wikipedia.org/wiki/James_A._Garfield
https://www.whitehouse.gov/1600/presidents/jamesgarfield
#153-Begin - It is. (1899). In J. Wood (Ed.), *Dictionary of Quotations from Ancient and Modern, English and Foreign sources* (p. 201). London and New York: Frederick Warne and Co.
#15-Declare - Chaplin, J. (1881). James A. Garfield. In *Chips from the White House: Or, Selections from the Speeches, Conversations, Diaries, Letters, and other writings, of all the Presidents of the United States* (p. 399). Boston, MA: D. Lothrop and Company.
#38-Reduction - Ballou, M. M. (1886). Crime. In *Edge-tools of speech: Selected and arranged* (p. 88). Boston, MA: Ticknor and Company.

Bruce Garner
http://www.faithwired.com/
#201-Believe, #83-Future, #233-Today, #67-Trust

William Lloyd Garrison (December 10, 1805 – May 24, 1879)
https://en.wikipedia.org/wiki/William_Lloyd_Garrison
#95-Excuse - Garrison, W. L. (1831, January 1). The Liberator: "To the Public." Retrieved November 16, 2017, from https://en.wikiquote.org/wiki/William_Lloyd_Garrison

Valerie De Gasparin (13 September 1813 – 16 June 1894)
https://fr.wikipedia.org/wiki/Valérie_de_Gasparin
#220-Useless - Nothing. (1899). In J. Wood (Ed.), *Dictionary of Quotations from Ancient and Modern, English and Foreign sources* (p. 316). London and New York: Frederick Warne and Co.

Shakti Gawain
http://shaktigawain.com/
From the book *Living in the Light*. Copyright © 1998 by Shakti Gawain and Laurel King. Reprinted with permission from New World Library, Novato, CA. www.newworldlibrary.com. #308-Authority

John Gay (30 June 1685 – 4 December 1732)
https://en.wikipedia.org/wiki/John_Gay
#168-Blame - Gay, J., & Coxe, W. (1798). Fable 38. The Turkey and the Ant. In *Fables by John Gay: Illustrated with notes and the life of the author. By William Coxe, Rector of Bemerton* (p. 111). Salisbury: Printed and by J. Easton.

Johann Carl Gehler (17 May 1732 – 6 May 1796)
https://en.wikipedia.org/wiki/Johann_Carl_Gehler
#48-Imagine - Douglas, C. N. (1915). Goodness. In *Forty thousand sublime and beautiful thoughts gathered from the roses, clover blossoms, geraniums, violets, morning-glories, and pansies of literature* (2nd ed., p. 864).

Henry George (September 2, 1839 – October 29, 1897)
https://en.wikipedia.org/wiki/Henry_George
#251-Labor - George, H. (1879). Chapter II. Of the effect upon distribution and thence upon production. In *The Complete Works of Henry George* (p. 442). The National Single Tax League Publishers.

Konrad von Gesner (26 March 1516 – 13 December 1565)
https://en.wikipedia.org/wiki/Conrad_Gessner
#326-Preserve - Edwards, T. (1891). Thankfulness. In *A Dictionary of Thoughts: Being a Cyclopedia of Laconic Quotations from the Best Authors of the World, Both Ancient and Modern* (p. 570). New York, NY: Cassell Publishing Company.

Henry Giles (November 1, 1809 – July 10, 1882)
https://en.wikipedia.org/wiki/Henry_Giles
#26-Despair - Wood, J. (1893). Der Wird. In *Dictionary of quotations: From ancient and modern English and foreign sources* (p. 62). London and New York: Frederick Warne and co.
#221-Respect - Giles, H. (1851). Falstaff. In *Lectures and essays, Volume I* (p. 39). Boston, MA: Ticknor, Reed, and Fields.

Seth Godin
http://www.sethgodin.com/sg/
#246-Less - Godin, S. (2009, August 15). Seth's Blog: Willfully ignorant vs. aggressively skeptical. Retrieved from http://sethgodin.typepad.com/seths_blog/2009/08/willfully-ignorant-vs-aggressively-skeptical.html

William Godwin (3 March 1756 – 7 April 1836)
https://en.wikipedia.org/wiki/William_Godwin
#75-Integrity - Godwin, W. (1830). Chapter II. In *Cloudesley, a tale. By the author of Caleb Williams in three volumes, Volume 3* (2nd ed., p. 36). London: Henry Colburn and Richard Bentley.
#359-Usual - Godwin, W. (1793). Book 1: Chapter V, The voluntary actions of men originate in their opinions. In *Enquiry concerning political justice and its influence on modern morals and happiness*. London: G.G.J. and J. Robinson.

Johann Wolfgang von Goethe (28 August 1749 – 22 March 1832)
https://en.wikipedia.org/wiki/Johann_Wolfgang_von_Goethe
#49-Ability - Wood, J. (1899). Our. In *Dictionary of Quotations from Ancient and Modern, English and Foreign Sources* (p. 338). London and New York: Frederick Warne and Co.
#173-Ask - Thoughts of a believer in the logos. XVI. (1846). In F. R. Lees & G. S. Phillips (Eds.), *The Truth Seeker in Literature, Philosophy, and Religion: Volume 2* (p. 86). London: Chapman Brothers.
#208-Decline - Wood, J. (1899). *Dictionary of quotations from ancient, modern, English and foreign sources* (p. 422).
#77-Play - O How. (1899). In J. Wood (Ed.), *Dictionary of Quotations from Ancient and Modern, English and Foreign sources* (p. 321). London and New York: Frederick Warne and Co.

Oliver Goldsmith (10 November 1728 – 4 April 1774)
https://en.wikipedia.org/wiki/Oliver_Goldsmith
#112-Fall - The growth of beauty. (1908). In J. E & H. S (Eds.), *The Melody of the Heart* (2nd ed., p. 147). New York, NY: Frederick A. Stokes Company.
#230-Intent - Wood, J. (1899). Some. In *Dictionary of quotations from Ancient and Modern, English and Foreign sources* (p. 397). London and New York: Frederick Warne and Co.
#179-Positive - Populus. (1899). In J. Wood (Ed.), *Dictionary of Quotations from Ancient and Modern, English and Foreign sources* (p. 353). London and New York: Frederick Warne and Co.

Baltasar Gracian (8 January 1601 – 6 December 1658)
https://en.wikipedia.org/wiki/Baltasar_Graci%C3%A1n
#98-Condemn - Gracian, B. (1904). ccxlv Original and out of the way views. In *The Art of Worldly Wisdom* (J. Jacobs, Trans.) (pp. 148-149). New York, NY: Macmillan and Co., Limited.
#319-Former - Gracian, B. (1904). ccii Words and deeds make the perfect man. In *The Art of Worldly Wisdom* (J. Jacobs, Trans.) (p. 121). New York, NY: Macmillan and Co., Limited.
#75-Integrity - Gracian, B. (1904). clxxxi The Truth, but not the whole Truth. In *The Art of Worldly Wisdom* (J. Jacobs, Trans.) (pp. 108-109). London: Macmillan and Co., Limited.
#324-Reflection - Gracian, B. (1904). cli Think beforehand. In *The Art of Worldly Wisdom* (J. Jacobs, Trans.) (pp. 89-90). London: Macmillan and Co., Limited.
#139-Sleep - Gracian, B. (1904). cli Think beforehand. In *The Art of Worldly Wisdom* (J. Jacobs, Trans.) (p. 90). London: Macmillan and Co., Limited.

Ulysses S. Grant (April 27, 1822 – July 23, 1885)
https://www.whitehouse.gov/1600/presidents/ulyssessgrant
https://en.wikipedia.org/wiki/Ulysses_S._Grant
#76-Disgrace - Grant, U. S. (n.d.). Ulysses S. Grant Quotes. Retrieved from http://www.totalgettysburg.com/ulysses-s-grant-quotes.html
#338-Fast - Grant, U. S. (n.d.). Ulysses S. Grant Quotes. Retrieved from http://www.totalgettysburg.com/ulysses-s-grant-quotes.html
#162-Gloom - Grant, U. S. (n.d.). Ulysses S. Grant Quotes. Retrieved from http://www.totalgettysburg.com/ulysses-s-grant-quotes.html
#230-Intent - Grant, U. S. (n.d.). Ulysses S. Grant Quotes. Retrieved from http://www.totalgettysburg.com/ulysses-s-grant-quotes.html

Thomas Gray (26 December 1716 – 30 June 1771)
https://en.wikipedia.org/wiki/Thomas_Gray
#154-End - Oldschool, O. (1808). Criticism. Ode on spring - Gray. *The Port Folio, Vol. VI* (p. 406). Philadelphia, PA: Printed by Smith and Maxwell.

Stephan Grellet (2 November 1773 – 16 November 1855)
https://en.wikipedia.org/wiki/Stephen_Grellet
#82-Defer - Grellet, S. (n.d.). Stephen Grellet - Wikiquote. Retrieved November 2, 2016, from https://en.wikiquote.org/wiki/Stephen_Grellet

Dorothy Grenside
#89-Strength - Grenside, D., & Trine, R. W. (1916). The building of strength and beauty. In *Little Builders: New thought talks to children* (p. 96). New York, NY: Dodge Publishing Company.

Jean-Baptiste-Louis Gresset (August 29, 1709 – June 16, 1777)
https://en.wikipedia.org/wiki/Jean-Baptiste-Louis_Gresset
#21-Flow - One or two guesses at one or two truths. (Le Méchant) (1839). In J. Fraser (Ed.), *Fraser's Magazine for Town and Country, Volume 19* (p. 535). London: James Fraser.

Francis Greville, 1ˢᵗ Earl of Warwick (10 October 1719 – 8 July 1773)
https://en.wikipedia.org/wiki/Francis_Greville,_1st_Earl_of_Warwick
#8-Ingratitude - Addington, J. F. (1829). Ingratitude. In *Poetical Quotations: Being A Complete Dictionary of The most elegant Moral, Sublime, and Humorous Passages in the British Poets. Volume 2* (p. 249). Philadelphia, PA: James Kay, Jun. & Co.

Terri Guillemets
http://www.quotegarden.com/terri-guillemets.html
#66-Comfort, #27-Purpose, #183-Warrior, #149-Worry

H

Thomas Chandler Haliburton (17 December 1796 – 27 August 1865)
https://en.wikipedia.org/wiki/Thomas_Chandler_Haliburton
#108-Balance - Haliburton, T. C. (1855). A crittur with a thousand virtues and but one vice. In *Nature and Human Nature* (p. 58). New York, NY: Stringer and Townsend.

G. Stanley Hall (February 1, 1846 – April 24, 1924)
https://en.wikipedia.org/wiki/G._Stanley_Hall
#35-Individual - Hall, G. S. (1908, July). From Generation to Generation. *The American Magazine*, p. 250.

John Hall (1829-1898)
https://en.wikipedia.org/wiki/John_Hall_(Presbyterian_pastor)
#221-Respect - Aughey, J. H. (1886). *Spiritual gems of the ages* (p. 229). Cincinnati, OH: Elm Street Printing Company.

Joseph Hall (1 July 1574 – 8 September 1656)
https://en.wikipedia.org/wiki/Joseph_Hall_(bishop)
#8-Ingratitude - Hall, J. (1837). Meditations and vows. Century II. In *The works of Joseph Hall, with some account of his life and sufferings* (8ᵗʰ ed., p. 34). Oxford: D. A. Talboys.

Alexander Hamilton (January 11, 1755, or 1757 – July 12, 1804)
https://en.wikipedia.org/wiki/Alexander_Hamilton
#123-See - Hamilton, A. (n.d.). Alexander Hamilton - Wikiquote. Retrieved September 17, 2017, from https://en.wikiquote.org/wiki/Alexander_Hamilton
#111-Rise - Hamilton, A. (1775). The Farmer Refuted. Retrieved November 17, 2017, from https://en.wikiquote.org/wiki/Alexander_Hamilton
#193-Sacred - Hamilton, A. (1775). The Farmer Refuted. Retrieved November 17, 2017, from https://en.wikiquote.org/wiki/Alexander_Hamilton
#359-Usual - Hamilton, A. (1787-1788). The Federalist Papers. Retrieved November 17, 2017, from https://en.wikiquote.org/wiki/Alexander_Hamilton

Augustus William Hare (17 November 1792 – 22 January 1834)
https://en.wikipedia.org/wiki/Augustus_William_Hare
#306-Aim - Hare, J. C., & Hare, A. W. (1884). *Guesses at truth* (3rd ed., p. 409). London: Macmillan and Co.

Julius Charles Hare (13 September 1795 – 3 January 1855)
https://en.wikipedia.org/wiki/Julius_Hare
#240-Refrain - Hare, J. C., & Hare, A. W. (1861). *Guesses at truth, by two brothers: From the fifth London ed.* (p. 185). Boston, MA: Ticknor and Fields.

Henry Stanley Haskins (1875-1965)
https://en.wikiquote.org/wiki/Henry_S._Haskins
#318-Behind - Haskins, H. S. (1940). Meditations in Wall Street. Retrieved from https://quoteinvestigator.com/2011/01/11/what-lies-within/

Nathaniel Hawthorne (July 4, 1804 – May 19, 1864)
https://en.wikipedia.org/wiki/Nathaniel_Hawthorne
132- Appreciate - Hawthorne, N. (1876). The custom house. Introductory. In *The complete works of Nathaniel Hawthorne* (2nd ed., p. 32). Boston: James R. Osgood and Company.

William Hazlitt (10 April 1778 – 18 September 1830)
https://en.wikipedia.org/wiki/William_Hazlitt
#295-Afraid - Douglas, C. N. (1915). Friends. In *Forty thousand sublime and beautiful thoughts gathered from the roses, clover blossoms, geraniums, violets, morning-glories, and pansies of literature* (p. 780). New York, NY: Christian Herald.
#275-Cease - "On The Spirit of Controversy," *The Atlas* (30 January 1830), reprinted in *The Collected Works of William Hazlitt* (1902-1904)

Gabriel Heatter (September 17, 1890 – March 30, 1972)
https://en.wikipedia.org/wiki/Gabriel_Heatter
#290-Boss - Heatter, G. (n.d.). Gabriel Heatter - Biography - IMDb. Retrieved from http://www.imdb.com/name/nm0372789/bio

Bettina Heiß
Verbal Confirmation
#109-Celebrate

Anna Held (19 March 1872 – 12 August 1918)
https://en.wikipedia.org/wiki/Anna_Held
#303-Whole - Golden, E. (2000). The Belle of New York. In *Anna Held and the birth of Ziegfeld's Broadway* (p. 68). Lexington, KY: University Press of Kentucky.

William Earnest Henley (23 August 1849 – 11 July 1903)
https://en.wikipedia.org/wiki/William_Ernest_Henley
#342-Death - Henley, W. E. (n.d.). William Ernest Henley - Rhymes And Rhythms, XII. Retrieved October 22, 2017, from https://en.wikiquote.org/wiki/William_Ernest_Henley

O. Henry, (William Sydney Porter) (September 11, 1862 – June 5, 1910)
https://en.wikipedia.org/wiki/O._Henry
#305-Aimless - Henry, O. (1906). The Green Door. In *The Four Million* (4th ed., p. 151). New York, NY: A. L. Burt Company.

Patrick Henry (May 29, 1736 – June 6, 1799)
https://en.wikipedia.org/wiki/Patrick_Henry
#186-Liberty - Henry, P. (1775, March 20). Patrick Henry - Wikipedia. Retrieved December 15, 2016, from https://en.wikipedia.org/wiki/Patrick_Henry

Edward Herbert (March 3, 1583 – August 20, 1648)
https://en.wikiquote.org/wiki/Edward_Herbert,_1st_Baron_Herbert_of_Cherbury
#167-Forgive - Herbert, E., & Lee, S. (1906). *The autobiography of Edward, Lord Herbert of Cherbury* (p. 34). London: G. Routledge.

Brigid E. Herman (1876-1923)
https://www.biblio.com/brigid-e-herman/author/864143
#92-Humility - Herman, B. E. (1921). *Creative prayer.* London: James Clark & Co.
#114-Silence - Herman, B. E. (1921). *Creative prayer.* London: James Clark & Co.

Robert Herrick (24 August 1591 – 15 October 1674)
https://en.wikipedia.org/wiki/Robert_Herrick_(poet)
#84-Past - Mis. (1896). In L. Klopsch (Ed.), *Many Thoughts of Many Minds: A Treasury of Quotations from the Literature of Every Land and Every Age* (p. 181). New York, NY: The Christian Herald, Louis Klopsch, Proprietor.

Hesiod (750–650BC)
https://en.wikipedia.org/wiki/Hesiod
#190-Harm - Hesiod. (n.d.). Works and Days (c. 700 BC), lines 265-266. Retrieved September 27, 2017, from https://en.wikiquote.org/wiki/Hesiod

John Heywood (1497-1580)
https://en.wikipedia.org/wiki/John_Heywood
#57-Content - Heywood, J. (1867). Part I, chapter 4. In *The Proverbs and Epigrams of John Heywood 1562* (3rd ed.). Manchester: Charles Simms and Co.

Napoleon Hill (October 26, 1883 – November 8, 1970)
http://www.naphill.org/
https://en.wikipedia.org/wiki/Napoleon_Hill
#257-Dominate - Hill, N. (1937). Chapter 3 - How to develop faith. In *Think and Grow Rich.* Meriden, CT: The Ralston Society.
#172-Goal - Hill, N. (1937). Chapter 3: Faith. In *Think and Grow Rich.* Meriden, CT: The Ralston Society.
#145-Mind - Hill, N. (1937). Chapter 1 - A fifty-cent lesson in persistence. In *Think and Grow Rich.* Meriden, CT: The Ralston Society.
#339-Myself - Hill, N. (1937). Chapter 3 Faith - Self-confidence formula. In *Think and Grow Rich.* Meriden, CT: The Ralston Society.

#353-New - Hill, N. (1937). Chapter 2 - Desire. In *Think and Grow Rich*. Meriden, CT: The Ralston Society.

#6-Possible - Hill, N. (1937). Chapter 14 – The sixth sense. In *Think and Grow Rich*. Meriden, CT: The Ralston Society.

Hippocrates (460-370BC)
https://en.wikipedia.org/wiki/Hippocrates
#66-Comfort - Reframing Medicine: Cure Sometimes, Treat Often, Comfort · Events at The University of Melbourne. (2017, October 18). Retrieved from https://events.unimelb.edu.au/events/9506-reframing-medicine-cure-sometimes-treat-often-comfort-always

Josiah Gilbert Holland (July 24, 1819 – October 12, 1881)
https://en.wikipedia.org/wiki/Josiah_Gilbert_Holland
#76-Disgrace - Ballou, M. M. (1886). Disgrace. In *Edge-tools of speech: Selected and arranged* (p. 110). Boston, MA: Ticknor and Company

Oliver Wendell Holmes, Sr. (August 29, 1809 – October 7, 1894)
https://en.wikipedia.org/wiki/Oliver_Wendell_Holmes_Sr.
#174-Answer - Holmes, O. W., & Morse, J. T. (1896). To Mrs. Harriet Beecher Stowe. September 13, 1860. In *Life and letters of Oliver Wendell Holmes in two vol. - 1* (p. 264). Boston and New York: Houghton, Mifflin, and Company.

#97-Blessing - Foster, E. (1877). Blessings. In *New cyclopaedia of prose illustrations adapted to Christian teaching, embracing allegories, analogies, anecdotes, aphorisms, emblems, fables, legends, metaphors, parables, quotations, similes, biblical types, and figures, etc. ; second series* (p. 60). New York, NY: Funk & Wagnalls Co.

#176-Dull - Poetry. (1899). In J. Wood (Ed.), *Dictionary of Quotations from Ancient and Modern, English and Foreign sources* (p. 351). London and New York: Frederick Warne and Co.

#333-Halt - Holmes, O. W. (1846). Poem. In *Urania. A rhymed lesson* (p. 16). Boston, MA: William D. Ticknor & Company.

#353-Old - Valedictory Address, delivered to the graduating class of the Bellevue Hospital College, March 2, 1871, By Oliver Wendell Holmes, M.D., Parkman Professor of Anatomy and Physiology in the Medical School of Harvard University. (1871). In E. S. Dunster, M.D. (Ed.), *New York Medical Journal, Volume 13* (p. 426). New York, NY: D Appleton and Company.

#113-Speak - Parker, R. G. (1852). Lesson XV. Language and Dress. - O. W. Holmes. In *National Series of Selections for Reading; Adapted to the Standing ..., Volume 4* (p. 53). New York, NY: A. S. Barnes & Co.

#165-Stand - Holmes Sr., O. W. (1858). The Autocrat of the Breakfast Table Chapter IV. Retrieved November 18, 2017, from https://en.wikiquote.org/wiki/Oliver_Wendell_Holmes_Sr

Barten Holyday (1593-1661)
https://en.wikipedia.org/wiki/Barten_Holyday
#363-Wonder - Trench, R. C. (1870). Distiches by Barten Holyday. In *A Household Book of English Poetry. Selected and arranged, with notes* (2nd ed., p. 103). London: Macmillan and Co.

Homer (Born 1102 BC or 850 BC)
https://en.wikipedia.org/wiki/Homer
#125-Share - Roberts, K. L. (1923). Help. Iliad. Bk. XII. L. 493. Bryant's Trans. In *HOYT'S NEW CYCLOPEDIA OF PRACTICAL QUOTATIONS* (p. 364). New York and London: Funk & Wagnalls Company.

Winslow Homer (February 24, 1836 – September 29, 1910)
https://en.wikipedia.org/wiki/Winslow_Homer
#276-Continuous - Downes, W. H. (1911). The artist and the man. In *The Life and Works of Winslow Homer* (p. 20). Boston and New York: Houghton Mifflin Company.

Emma Curtis Hopkins (September 2, 1849-April 8, 1925)
https://en.wikipedia.org/wiki/Emma_Curtis_Hopkins
#265-Good - Hopkins, E. C. (1894). Nature and office of mind work. In *Spiritual law in the natural world* (p. 163). Chicago, IL: Purdy Publishing Company.
#270-Word - Hopkins, E. C. (1894). Nature and office of mind work. In *Spiritual law in the natural world* (p. 67). Chicago, IL: Purdy Publishing Company.

Erastus Whitford Hopkins
#313-Strong - Hopkins, E. W. (1904). Soul Faculties. In *Science of the new thought* (p. 43). Bristol, CT: The New thought Book Concern.

Horace (December 8, 65 BC – November 27, 8BC)
https://en.wikipedia.org/wiki/Horace
#275-Cease - Roberts, K. L. (1923). Future. Carmina. I. 9. 13. In *HOYT'S NEW CYCLOPEDIA OF PRACTICAL QUOTATIONS* (p. 305). New York and London: Funk & Wagnalls Company.
#34-Confinement - Christy, R. (1888). Happiness. In *Proverbs, maxims, and phrases of all ages* (p. 480). New York and London: G. P. Putnam's Sons.
#42-Effect - The Essayist. (1863). In *The British Controversialist and Literary Magazine* (p. 58). London: Houlston and Wright.
#274-Hurry - Unkindness. (1895). In H. P. Smith & H. K. Johnson (Eds.), *A Dictionary of Terms, Phrases, and Quotations* (p. 711). New York, NY: D. Appleton and Company.
#320-Present - Hoyt, J. K., & Ward, A. L. (1886). Enjoyment. In *The Cyclopædia of Practical Quotations. English and Latin, with an appendix containing proverbs from the Latin and modern foreign languages* (8th ed., p. 519). New York and London: Funk & Wagnalls.
#126-Retain - Wooléver, A. (1878). Prejudice. In *Treasury of wisdom, wit and humor, odd comparisons and proverbs* (3rd ed., p. 324). Philadelphia, PA: Claxton.

Elbert Hubbard (June 19, 1856 – May 7, 1915)
https://en.wikipedia.org/wiki/Elbert_Hubbard
#30-Criticism - Ferguson, J. W., Carnegie, A., Helps, A., Fenton, W. T., Bacon, F., & Hubbard, E. (n.d.). Get Out, or Get in Line - Elbert Hubbard. In *The Transaction of Business, Sir Arthur Helps. How to Win Fortune, Andrew Carnegie* (p. 161). Chicago, IL: Forges & Company.
#238-Extraordinary - Hubbard, E. (1911). *A thousand & one epigrams, selected from the writings of Elbert Hubbard* (p. 151). East Aurora, NY: The Roycrofters.
#202-Get - Hubbard, E. (1916). Epigrams. In *The Philosophy of Elbert Hubbard* (p. 173). East Aurora, NY: The Roycrofters.
#180-Negative - Looking for the good by Elbert Hubbard. (1918). In *Hearst's, Volumes 27-28* (p. 481). New York, NY: Hearsтs.
#204-Nothing - Looking for the good by Elbert Hubbard. (1918). In *Hearst's, Volumes 27-28* (p. 481). New York, NY: Hearsтs.
#135-Satisfied - Notes. (1897). In H. P. Taber & E. Hubbard (Eds.), *The Philistine, Volume 5 edited by Harry Persons Taber, Elbert Hubbard* (p. 23). East Aurora, NY: B C. Hubbard.
#303-Whole - Hubbard, E. (1916). Epigrams. In *The Philosophy of Elbert Hubbard* (p. 173). East Aurora, NY: The Roycrofters.

Cheri Huber
http://www.cherihuber.com/
#203-Everything - Huber, C. (1988). *How you do anything is how you do everything – A Workbook*. Chicago, IL: Keep It Simple Books.

Victor Hugo (26 February 1802 – 22 May 1885)
https://en.wikipedia.org/wiki/Victor_Hugo
http://www.visitguernsey.com/victor-hugo
#309-Ideal - Hugo, V. (1907). Supreme contemplation. In *Intellectual autobiography: (postscriptum de ma vie) being the last of the unpublished works and embodying the author's ideas on literature, philosophy and religion* (L. O›Rourke, Trans.) (p. 331). New York and London: Funk and Wagnalls Company.
#354-Old - Hugo, V. (1862). Jean Valjean - IV The Grandson and the Grandfather. In *Les Miserables, Volumes 13-17* (p. 533). New York, NY: Dod, Mead and Company Publishers.
#261-Perfection - Hugo, V. (1907). Genius and Taste. In *Intellectual autobiography: (postscriptum de ma vie) being the last of the unpublished works and embodying the author's ideas on literature, philosophy and religion* (L. O›Rourke, Trans.) (p. 94). New York and London: Funk and Wagnalls Company.
#6-Possible - Hugo, V. (1907). Promontorium Somnii. In *Intellectual autobiography: (postscriptum de ma vie) being the last of the unpublished works and embodying the author's ideas on literature, philosophy and religion* (L. O›Rourke, Trans.) (p. 125). New York and London: Funk and Wagnalls Company.
#336-Poverty - Hugo, V. (1907). Thoughts II. In *Intellectual autobiography: (postscriptum de ma vie) being the last of the unpublished works and embodying the author's ideas on literature, philosophy and religion* (L. O›Rourke, Trans.) (p. 357). New York and London: Funk and Wagnalls Company.
#63-Responsibility - Hugo, V. (1907). Supreme contemplation. In *Intellectual autobiography: (postscriptum de ma vie) being the last of the unpublished works and embodying the author's ideas on literature, philosophy and religion* (L. O›Rourke, Trans.) (p. 340). New York and London: Funk and Wagnalls Company.
#187-Vice - Hugo, V. (1907). Thoughts. In *Victor Hugo's Intellectual Autobiography* (L. O›Rourke, Trans.) (p. 362). New York & London: Funk & Wagnalls Company.

Jonathan Lockwood Huie
www.jlhuie.com
http://www.jonathanlockwoodhuie.com/
www.facebook.com/jonathan.lockwood.huie
#356-Distinction, #305-Aimless, #7-Gratitude

Jan Edward Hulett
Verbal Confirmation
#101-Group

Joan Hunter
http://joanhunter.org/
https://www.facebook.com/4cornersconferencecenter/
All Quotes from:
Taken from Power To Heal by Joan Hunter. Copyright © (June 8, 2009) by Whitaker House. Used by permission of Whitaker House. All rights reserved.
#364-Expectation - Hunter, J. (2009). Chapter 7. What's in your house? Anger. In *Power to Heal. Experiencing the Miraculous* (pp. 83-84). New Kensington, PA: Whitaker House.
#341-Life - Hunter, J. (2009). Chapter 14. Use what you have learned. 6. Give Thanks! In *Power to Heal. Experiencing the Miraculous* (p. 185). New Kensington, PA: Whitaker House.
#91-Pride - Hunter, J. (2009). Chapter 7. What's in your house? In *Power to Heal. Experiencing the Miraculous* (p. 74). New Kensington, PA: Whitaker House.

Thomas Huxley (4 May 1825 – 29 June 1895)
https://en.wikipedia.org/wiki/Thomas_Henry_Huxley
#250-Powerless - Ballou, M. M. (1886). Time. In *Edge-tools of speech: Selected and arranged* (p. 500). Boston, MA: Ticknor and Company.

Hypatia (350-370; died 415 AD)
https://en.wikipedia.org/wiki/Hypatia
#9-Understand - Vol. 1 December 1908 No. 9. (1908). In E. F. Bigelow (Ed.), *The Guide to Nature and to Nature Literature, Volume 1, Issues 1-11* (p. 311). Stamford, CT: The Agassiz Association.

I

St. Ignatius of Loyola (October 23, 1491 – July 31, 1556)
https://en.wikipedia.org/wiki/Ignatius_of_Loyola
#93-Grace - Ignatius, Young, W. J., & Centrum Ignatianum Spiritualitatis. (1959). Rome, March 18, 1542. In *The spiritual diary of St. Ignatius: (February 2, 1544, to February 27, 1545)* (p. 55). Chicago, IL: Loyola University Press.

Robert Ingersoll (August 11, 1833 – July 21, 1899)
https://en.wikipedia.org/wiki/Robert_G._Ingersoll
#132-Appreciate - Ingersoll, R. G., & Farrell, C. P. (1900). Voltaire. In *The works of Robert G. Ingersoll In Twelve Volumes. Volume Three. Lectures* (p. 188). New York, NY: The Ingersoll Publishers, Inc., C. P. Farrell.
#290-Boss - Ingersoll, R. G. (1907). Intellectual development. In *Lectures: Including his letters on The Chinese god. Is suicide a sin? The right to one's life. Etc., etc., etc.* (pp. 631-632). Chicago, IL: Rhodes & McClure Publishing Co.
#148-Defeat - Ingersoll, R. G., & Farrell, C. P. (1900). Abraham Lincoln. In *The works of Robert G. Ingersoll In Twelve Volumes. Volume Three. Lectures* (p. 150). New York, NY: The Ingersoll Publishers, Inc., C. P. Farrell.
#350-Honor - Ingersoll, R. G. (1882). Col. Ingersoll's Decoration Day Oration. In *Tracts* (p. 6). Washington, D. C.: C. P. Farrell, Publisher.
#193-Sacred - Ingersoll, R. G. (1876). Arraignment of the church. In *The Gods, and Other Lectures* (p. 21). New York, NY: D. M. Bennett, Liberal and Scientific Publishing House.
#155-Seek - Ingersoll, R. G. (1907). Voltaire. In *Lectures of Col. R. G. Ingersoll: Including his letters on The Chinese god. Is suicide a sin? The right to one's life. Etc., etc., etc.* (p. 797). Chicago, IL: Rhodes & McClure Publishing Co.
#188-Virtue - Ingersoll, R. G. (1902). A Lay Sermon. In *Works* (p. 232). New York, NY: Dresden Pub. Co., C.P. Farrell.

Washington Irving (April 3, 1783 – November 28, 1859)
https://en.wikipedia.org/wiki/Washington_Irving
#34-Confinement - Irving, W. (1835). The sketch book, A Royal Poet. In *The complete works of Washington Irving in One Volume, with a memoir of the author* (p. 251). Francfort on the Main: Sigismond Schmerber.
#335-Prosperity - Walsh, J. P. (1889). Miscellaneous extracts for analysis. In *A Practical English Grammar: With Lessons in Composition and Letter-writing* (p. 106). Philadelphia, PA: Christopher Sower Company.

Gary Isham
Verbal Confirmation
#289-Employee, #347-Initiate

Silius Italicus (28-103)
https://en.wikipedia.org/wiki/Silius_Italicus
#334-Advance - Hamerton, P. G. (1894). Silius Italicus. In *The Greatest Works of the Greatest Authors, Ancient and Modern* (p. 600).

J

Harriet Ann Jacobs (February 11, 1813 – March 7, 1897)
https://en.wikipedia.org/wiki/Harriet_Ann_Jacobs
#281-Adequate - Jacobs, H. A. (1861). Sketches of neighboring slaveholders. In L. M. Child (Ed.), *Incidents in the life of a slave girl. Jacobs, Mrs. Harriet (Brent): Written by herself. Edited by L. Maria Child* (p. 79). Boston: Pub. for the author.

Henry James (15 April 1843 – 28 February 1916)
https://en.wikipedia.org/wiki/Henry_James
#142-Disorder - Douglas, C. N. (1915). Government. In *Forty thousand sublime and beautiful thoughts gathered from the roses, clover blossoms, geraniums, violets, morning-glories, and pansies of literature* (p. 874). New York, NY: Christian Herald.
#217-Inside - Kellogg, J. A. (1883). *Philosophy of Henry James: A digest* (p. 9). New York, NY: John W. Lovell Company.

John Angel James (6 June 1785 – 1 October 1859)
https://en.wikipedia.org/wiki/John_Angell_James
#162-Gloom - Gilbert, J. H. (1895). Spiritual Progress. In *Dictionary of Burning Words of Brilliant Writers: A Cyclopædia of Quotations from the literature of all ages* (p. 565). New York, NY: Wilbur B. Ketcham.

William James (January 11, 1842 – August 26, 1910)
https://en.wikipedia.org/wiki/William_James
#189-Help - James, W. (1897). The Will to Believe and Other Essays in Popular Philosophy (. Retrieved November 20, 2017, from https://en.wikiquote.org/wiki/William_James
#2-Indecision - James, W. (1890). Principles of Psychology, Ch. 4 (. Retrieved November 20, 2017, from https://en.wikiquote.org/wiki/William_James
#231-Overlook - James, W. (1890). Principles of Psychology, Ch. 22 (. Retrieved November 20, 2017, from https://en.wikiquote.org/wiki/William_James

Criss Jami
http://crissjami.wixsite.com/criss-jami
#259-Indulge, #35-Individual, #134-Vulnerable

Thomas Jefferson (April 13, 1743 – July 4, 1826)
https://en.wikipedia.org/wiki/Thomas_Jefferson
https://www.whitehouse.gov/1600/presidents/thomasjefferson
#181-Care - Jefferson, T. (1809). Thomas Jefferson to Maryland Republicans, 1809. Retrieved from https://en.wikipedia.org/wiki/Good_government
#33-Freedom - Jefferson, T. (1900). 3632. Happiness, Conditions of. Notes on Virginia. (1782). In J. P. Foley (Ed.), *The Jeffersonian cyclopedia: A comprehensive collection of the views of Thomas Jefferson classified and arranged in alphabetical order under nine thousand titles relating to government, politics, law* (p. 398). New York and London: Funk and Wagnalls Company.
#186-Liberty - Jefferson, T. (1776, July 4). The Declaration of Independence: Full text. Retrieved from http://www.ushistory.org/declaration/document/
#133-Safe - Jefferson, T. (1816, January 6). Thomas Jefferson, Letter to Colonel Charles Yancey. Retrieved November 21, 2017, from https://en.wikiquote.org/wiki/Freedom_of_the_press
#113-Speak - Jefferson, T. (1825, February 21). Founders Online: From Thomas Jefferson to Thomas Jefferson Smith. Retrieved from https://founders.archives.gov/documents/Jefferson/98-01-02-4987

#69-Sunshine - Rayner, B. L., & Jefferson, T. (1834). Chapter XIV. In *Life of Thomas Jefferson, with selections from the most valuable portions of his voluminous and unrivaled private correspondence* (p. 423). Boston: Lilly, Wait, Colman, & Holden.

Richard Jefferies (6 November 1848 – 14 August 1887)
https://en.wikipedia.org/wiki/Richard_Jefferies
#152-Optimism - The pageant of summer. By Richard Jefferies. (1883). In *The Eclectic Magazine of Foreign Literature, Science, and art. Volume 38; Volume 101* (p. 147). New York, NY: E. R. Pelton.

Dr. Ron Jenson
http://www.ronjenson.com/
Taken from Achieving Authentic Success by Ron Jenson. Copyright © (2002) by Future Achievement International. Used by permission of Ron Jenson. All rights reserved.
#311-Ought, #312-Vocation

Jerome K. Jerome (2 May 1859 – 14 June 1927)
https://en.wikipedia.org/wiki/Jerome_K._Jerome
#121-Idleness - Jerome, J. K. (1886). Idle Thoughts of an Idle Fellow. Retrieved January 21, 2016, from https://en.wikiquote.org/wiki/Jerome_K._Jerome

St. Jerome (27 March 347 – 30 September 420)
https://en.wikipedia.org/wiki/Jerome
#145-Mind - Saint Jerome. (n.d.). Letter 54. Retrieved November 21, 2017, from https://en.wikiquote.org/wiki/Jerome
#267-Never - Saint Jerome. (n.d.). Letter 52. Retrieved November 21, 2017, from https://en.wikiquote.org/wiki/Jerome

Samuel Johnson (18 September 1709 – 13 December 1784)
https://en.wikipedia.org/wiki/Samuel_Johnson
#334-Advance - Ballou, M. M. (1882). Perfection. In *Pearls of Thought* (p. 196). Boston, MA: Houghton, Mifflin, and Company.
#164-Choice - Johnson, S. (1856). Chapter XXIX. The debate on marriage continued. In *Rasselas* (p. 55).
#294-Demand - Douglas, C. N. (1915). Coward. In *Forty thousand sublime and beautiful thoughts gathered from the roses, clover blossoms, geraniums, violets, morning-glories, and pansies of literature* (p. 390). New York, NY: The Christian Herald.
#167-Forgive - Johnson, S., & Murphy, A. (1840). The Rambler. In *The Works of Samuel Johnson, LL.D* (p. 278).
#75-Integrity - Johnson, S. (1820). Chapter XLI. The astronomer discovers the cause of his uneasiness. In *The history of Rasselas, Prince of Abissinia* (p. 108).
#182-Neglect - Ballou, M. M. (1882). Neglect. In *Pearls of Thought* (p. 184). Boston, MA: Houghton, Mifflin, and Company.
#141-Order - Broswell, J. (1791). *The Life of Samuel Johnson, LL.D.: Comprehending an Account of His Studies and Numerous works in chronological order* (p. 476). London: Henry Baldwin.
#155-Seek - Edwards, T. (1891). Happiness. In *A Dictionary of Thoughts: Being a Cyclopedia of Laconic Quotations from the Best Authors of the World, Both Ancient and Modern* (p. 216). New York, NY: Cassell Publishing Company.
#206-Wrong - Johnson, S. (1750, December 18). The Rambler (1750-1752), No. 79. Retrieved November 8, 2017, from https://simple.wikiquote.org/wiki/Samuel_Johnson

David Starr Jordan (January 19, 1851 – September 19, 1931)
https://en.wikipedia.org/wiki/David_Starr_Jordan

#297-Prepare - The suddenness of war. (1913). In H. Holt (Ed.), *The Independent Weekly, Inc., Volume 75*(p. 681). New York, NY: Hamilton Holt.

Rebecca Barlow Jordan
www.rebeccabarlowjordan.com
#153-Begin, #255-Hope

Joseph Joubert (7 May 1754 – 4 May 1824)
https://en.wikipedia.org/wiki/Joseph_Joubert
#306-Aim - Joubert, J. (1883). The Notebooks of Joseph Joubert. Retrieved February 7, 2016, from https://en.wikiquote.org/wiki/Joseph_Joubert
#197-Direction - Joubert, J. (1883). The Notebooks of Joseph Joubert. Retrieved February 7, 2016, from https://en.wikiquote.org/wiki/Joseph_Joubert
#272-Settle - Joubert, J. (1883). The Notebooks of Joseph Joubert. Retrieved February 7, 2016, from https://en.wikiquote.org/wiki/Joseph_Joubert
#214-Undisciplined - Joubert, J. (1883). The Notebooks of Joseph Joubert. Retrieved February 7, 2016, from https://en.wikiquote.org/wiki/Joseph_Joubert

Benjamin Jowett (15 April 1817 – 1 October 1893)
https://en.wikipedia.org/wiki/Benjamin_Jowett
#292-Great - Plato. (1901). Translator's introduction. Lii. In *The World's Greatest Literature: Masterpieces of the World's ..., Volume 58. The Republic by Plato* (B. Jowett, Trans.) (p. 284). New York and London: The Colonial Press.

Julian of Norwich (8 November 1342 - 1416)
https://en.wikipedia.org/wiki/Julian_of_Norwich
#263-Joy - Julian of Norwich. (1395). Prayer Written by Julian of Norwich. Retrieved from https://www.cenaclesisters.org/houston/Prayers-Meditations/

K

Immanuel Kant (22 April 1724 – 12 February 1804)
https://en.wikipedia.org/wiki/Immanuel_Kant
#224-Cruel - Kant, I. (n.d.). From Lectures on Ethics. Retrieved from http://faculty.smu.edu/jkazez/animal%20rights/IMMANUEL%20KANT.htm
#216-Doubt - Kant, I., & Stirling, J. H. (1881). The Kritik of Pure Reason. In *Text-book to Kant. The critique of pure reason: Aesthetic, categories, schematism. Translation, reproduction, commentary, index* (p. 115). Edinburgh: Oliver and Boyd.

Jean-Baptiste Alphonse Karr (24 November 1808 – 29 September 1890)
https://en.wikipedia.org/wiki/Jean-Baptiste_Alphonse_Karr
#150-Calmness - Ballou, M. M. (1886). Politeness. In *Edge-tools of speech: Selected and arranged* (p. 378). Boston, MA: Ticknor and Company.

John Keats (31 October 1795 – 23 February 1821)
https://en.wikipedia.org/wiki/John_Keats
#329-Own - Locke, J. S. (1884). Letter of John Keats, the Poet, to Fanny Brown. In *The Art of Correspondence: How to construct and write letters according to approved usage* (p. 144). Boston, MA: DeWolfe, Fiske, and Company.

Thomas à Kempis (1380 – 25 July 1471)
https://en.wikipedia.org/wiki/Thomas_%C3%A0_Kempis
#278-Amend - Kempis, T. A. (1913). Chapter XVI - Of Bearing Other Men's Infirmities and Faults. In E. Rhys (Ed.), *The Imitation of Christ* (2nd ed., p. 27). London: J.M. Dent & Sons Ltd.
#108-Balance - Kempis, T. A. (1903). Book I. Chapter XVI. Of bearing with the defects of others. In *The Imitation of Christ: Four Books* (p. 42).
#168-Blame - Kempis, T. A. (1850). Book II. Chapter VI. Joy of a good conscience. In *The Imitation of Christ: Four Books* (p. 67). London: Samuel Bagster and Sons Limited
#177-Fight - Overcoming ourselves. (1916). In C. J. Callan (Ed.), *Illustrations for Sermons and Instructions* (p. 306).
#262-Imperfection - Selections Apr. 16, 1891. (1891). In H. F. Williams (Ed.), *Young Men's Era, Volume 17* (p. 243).
#137-Peace - Kempis, T. A. (1866). Book 3. Chapter XXVIII. Against the Tongues of Slanderers. In *Of the Imitation of Christ, in four books* (p. 182). Oxford: J. N. & J. Parker.
#136-Wish - Kempis, T. A. (n.d.). Thomas à Kempis - Wikiquote. Retrieved October 17, 2017, from https://en.wikiquote.org/wiki/Thomas_%C3%A0_Kempis

Thomas Ken (July 1637 – 19 March 1711)
https://en.wikipedia.org/wiki/Thomas_Ken
#21-Flow - Ken, T. (1674). Doxology - "Praise God, from whom all blessings flow." Retrieved from https://en.wikipedia.org/wiki/Doxology

Søren Kierkegaard (5 May 1813 – 11 November 1855)
https://en.wikipedia.org/wiki/S%C3%B8ren_Kierkegaard
#294-Demand - Kierkegaard, S. (n.d.). Either/Or Part I, Swenson Translation p. 19. Retrieved October 31, 2017, from https://en.wikiquote.org/wiki/Talk:S%C3%B8ren_Kierkegaard

Charles Kingsley (12 June 1819 – 23 January 1875)
https://en.wikipedia.org/wiki/Charles_Kingsley
#191-Down - Sense and Nonsense. (1904). In *The Phrenological Journal and Science of Health (1838): Incorporated with the Phrenological Magazine (1880), Volume 117* (p. 170). New York, NY: Fowler & Wells Co.
#87-Miserable - Handford, T. W. (1890). 504. How to be miserable. Charles Kingsley. In *Two thousand and ten choice quotations in poetry and prose: From the master minds of all ages* (5th ed., p. 117). Chicago, IL: Belford-Clarke.

Kip Kint
http://kipkint.com/
#49-Ability
Taken from You Can If You Will: How to Succeed Through Commitment & Accountability by Kip Kint. Copyright © (June 24, 2015) by CreateSpace Independent Publishing Platform. Used by permission of Kip Kint. All rights reserved.

Jarod Kintz
https://jarodkintz.com/
#25-Laughter

Rudyard Kipling (30 December 1865 – 18 January 1936)
https://en.wikipedia.org/wiki/Rudyard_Kipling
#351-Failure - The progress of the world. (1901). In W. T. Stead (Ed.), *The Review of Reviews, Volume 24* (p. 137). London: Mowbray House.

#10-Misunderstand - Kipling, R. (1900). The light that failed. In *Selected works of Rudyard Kipling* (p. 61). New York, NY: Peter Fenelon Collier & Son.

Brian Klemmer (1950-2011)
http://www.klemmer.com/
Taken from The Compassionate Samurai: Being Extraordinary in an Ordinary World by Brian Klemmer. Copyright © January 1, 2009, by Hay House Publishing. All Rights Reserved.
#302-Both - Klemmer, B. (2009). Chapter 2: Personal Responsibility. This isn't a blame game. In *The compassionate samurai: Being extraordinary in an ordinary world* (p. 47). Carlsbad, CA: Hay House, Inc.
#239-Practice - Klemmer, B. (2009). Chapter 1: Commitment. Everyone is committed whether they know it or not. In *The compassionate samurai: Being extraordinary in an ordinary world* (p. 23). Carlsbad, CA: Hay House, Inc.
#298-Pretending - Klemmer, B. (2009). Chapter 2: Personal Responsibility. Options and Liberty In *The compassionate samurai: Being extraordinary in an ordinary world* (p. 36). Carlsbad, CA: Hay House, Inc.
#243-Selfish - Klemmer, B. (2009). Chapter 1: Commitment. Quit making excuses – just say it and do it. In *The compassionate samurai: Being extraordinary in an ordinary world* (p. 5). Carlsbad, CA: Hay House, Inc.

Kelly Kotarski
Verbal Confirmation
#109-Celebrate

C. Baxter Kruger
https://www.perichoresis.org/
Taken from Across All Worlds: Jesus Inside Our Darkness by C. Baxter Kruger. Copyright © (January 1, 2007) by Regent College Publishing. Used by permission of C. Baxter Kruger. All rights reserved.
#11-Absence - Kruger, C. B. (2007). Chapter 12. Running. In *Across all worlds: Jesus inside our darkness: an essay on reconciliation in honor of Professor James B. Torrance* (p. 61). Jackson, MS: Perichoresis Press.
#343-Experience - Kruger, C. B. (2016, March 18). The Story Behind the Story. Retrieved from https://www.perichoresis.org/the-story-behind-the-story/

L

Jean de La Fontaine (8 July 1621 – 13 April 1695)
https://en.wikipedia.org/wiki/Jean_de_La_Fontaine
#248-Destiny - La Fontaine, J. D. (1678-1679). Book VIII, fable 16 (The Horoscope). Retrieved November 8, 2017, from https://en.wikiquote.org/wiki/Jean_de_La_Fontaine
105-Patience - De La Fontaine, J. (1668). Fables, Book II, fable 11. Retrieved October 31, 2017, from https://en.wikiquote.org/wiki/Jean_de_La_Fontaine

Alphonse de Lamartine (21 October 1790 – 28 February 1869)
https://en.wikipedia.org/wiki/Alphonse_de_Lamartine
#362-Sad - Edwards, T. (1891). Poetry. In *A Dictionary of Thoughts: Being a Cyclopedia of Laconic Quotations from the best authors, both ancient and modern* (p. 417). New York, NY: Cassell Publishing Company.

Charles Lamb (10 February 1775 – 27 December 1834)
https://en.wikipedia.org/wiki/Charles_Lamb
#104-Respond - DAY, E. P. (1884). Childhood. In *Day's Collacon: an encyclopaedia of prose quotations. Consisting of beautiful thoughts, choice extracts, and sayings, of the most eminent writers of all nations, from the earliest ages to the present times* (p. 99). New York and London: International Printing and Publishing Office, Sampson Low, Marston, Searle, and Rivington.

John Lanahan (1815-1903)

https://en.wikiquote.org/wiki/John_Lanahan

#305-Aimless - Gilbert, J. H. (1895). God's Sovereignty. In *Dictionary of Burning Words of Brilliant Writers: A Cyclopædia of Quotations from the literature of all ages* (p. 284). New York, NY: Wilbur B. Ketcham.

Walter Savage Landor (30 January 1775 – 17 September 1864)

https://en.wikipedia.org/wiki/Walter_Savage_Landor

#40-Dismiss - Landor, W. S. (1875). VII. Diogenes and Plato. In J. Forster (Ed.), *Works and Life of Walter Savage Landor: Imaginary conversations: ser. I. Examination of Shakespeare.* (p. 65). London: Chapman and Hall.

Sophie von La Roche (6 December 1730 – 18 February 1807)

https://en.wikipedia.org/wiki/Sophie_von_La_Roche

#72-Hurt - Litterae. (1899). In J. Wood (Ed.), *Dictionary of Quotations from Ancient and Modern, English and Foreign sources* (p. 251). London and New York: Frederick Warne and Co.

William Law (1686 – 9 April 1761)

https://en.wikipedia.org/wiki/William_Law

#287-Attract - Law, W. (1893). The grounds and reasons of Christian regeneration. In *The works of the Reverend William Law, M.A: 1. A demonstration of the gross and fundamental errors of a late book, called 'A plain account of the nature and end of the sacrament of the Lord's supper, etc.' 2. The grounds and reasons of Christian regeneration* (p. 168). Brockenhurst, NH: G. Moreton.

Brother Lawrence (1614 – 12 February 1691)

https://en.wikipedia.org/wiki/Brother_Lawrence

#255-Hope - Mrs. Carson's Settlement Work. (1902). In *Northwestern Christian Advocate, Volume 50* (p. 16). Cincinnati, Chicago, Kansas City: Jennings & Pye.

#128-Prayer - Tarbell, M. (1909). Third Quarter, Lesson IV July 25. The Practice of the Presence of God. In *Tarbell's teachers' guide to the International Sunday-school lessons improved uniform course for* (p. 272). New York, Chicago, Toronto, London, and Edinburgh: Fleming H. Revell Co.

#12-Presence - De la Résurrection, L., & Pearsall Smith. (1904). Letters. In *The Practice of the Presence of God: Being Conversation and Letters of ... By Laurent de la Résurrection* (p. 25). London: James Nisbet & Co., Limited.

#326-Preserve - De la Résurrection, L., & Pearsall Smith. (1904). Letters. In *The Practice of the Presence of God: Being Conversation and Letters of ... By Laurent de la Résurrection* (p. 35-36). London: James Nisbet & Co., Limited.

T. E. Lawrence (16 August 1888 – 19 May 1935)

https://en.wikipedia.org/wiki/T._E._Lawrence

#6-Possible - Lawrence, T. E. (1922). Seven Pillars of Wisdom. Retrieved December 21, 2017, from https://en.wikiquote.org/wiki/T._E._Lawrence

Robert E. Lee (January 19, 1807 – October 12, 1870)

https://en.wikipedia.org/wiki/Robert_E._Lee

#308-Authority - Lee, R. E. (n.d.). As quoted in General Robert E. Lee After Appomattox (1922), by Franklin Lafayette Riley, p. 18. Retrieved from https://en.wikiquote.org/wiki/Robert_E._Lee

#224-Cruel - Lee, R. E. (1862, December 25). Letter to his wife on Christmas Day, two weeks after the Battle of Fredericksburg. Retrieved November 22, 2017, from https://en.wikiquote.org/wiki/Robert_E._Lee

#61-Light - Men and the Bible, June 1909. (1909). In *Association Men, Volume 34*(p. 430). New York, NY: Young Men's Christian Associations of North America.

Mikhail Lermontov (October 15, 1814 – July 27, 1841)
https://en.wikipedia.org/wiki/Mikhail_Lermontov
#138-Turbulence - Lermontov, M. (1841). A Hero of Our Time (1840; rev. 1841). Retrieved November 22, 2017, from https://en.wikiquote.org/wiki/Mikhail_Lermontov

Mrs. Frank Leslie (June 5, 1836 – September 18, 1914)
https://en.wikipedia.org/wiki/Miriam_Leslie
#144-Surprise - Leslie, F. (1892). Is marriage a failure? In *Are We All Deceivers? The Lover's Blue Book By Mrs. Frank Leslie* (p. 86). London and New York: F. Tennyson Neely.

George Henry Lewes (18 April 1817 – 30 November 1878)
https://en.wikipedia.org/wiki/George_Henry_Lewes
#228-Rebellion - Lewes, G. H., & Scott, F. N. (1891). The principle of sincerity. In *The Principles of Success in Literature* (3rd ed., p. 94). Boston: Allyn and Bacon.

Tokugawa Ieyasu (January 31, 1543 – June 1, 1616)
https://en.wikipedia.org/wiki/Tokugawa_Ieyasu
#337-Slow - Tokugawa, L. (n.d.). Tokugawa Ieyasu - Wikipedia. Retrieved October 12, 2017, from https://en.wikipedia.org/wiki/Tokugawa_Ieyasu

Joseph Barber Lightfoot (13 April 1828 – 21 December 1889)
https://en.wikipedia.org/wiki/Joseph_Lightfoot
#307-Messenger - Lightfoot, Bishop of Durham, J. B. (1890). Ordination addresses. In *Ordination addresses and counsels to clergy* (p. 24). London and New York: Macmillan and Co.

L. W. Lightly
York County, PA
#266-Bad - *RURAL AND WORKMAN, A journal for farmers, mechanics, and workmen. Vol. XIV* (p. 7). (1890). H. Nowlin (Ed.). Little Rock, AK: H. Nowlin, Son & Co.

Abraham Lincoln (February 12, 1809 – April 15, 1865)
https://en.wikipedia.org/wiki/Abraham_Lincoln
https://www.whitehouse.gov/1600/presidents/abrahamlincoln
#41-Cause - Lincoln, A. (1894). *Speeches & Letters of Abraham Lincoln, 1832-1865, Volume 64* (15th ed.). M. Roe (Ed.). London and New York: J. M. Dent & Sons Limited, E. P. Dutton & Co. Inc.
#129-Confidence - Schell, S. (1910). Quotations from Lincoln. In *Werner's Readings and Recitations, Issue 45 Lincoln celebrations - Part 1* (p. 167). New York, NY: Edgar S. Werner & Company.
#282-Inadequate - Lincoln, A., & Hobson, J. T. (1912). The quiet past and stormy present. (Extract from the second annual message to Congress, December 1, 1862). In *The Lincoln year book: Containing immortal words of Abraham Lincoln spoken and written on various occasions, preceded by appropriate Scripture texts and followed by choice poetic selections for each day in the year, with special reference to anniversary dates* (p. 358). Dayton, OH: Press of United Brethren Pub. House.
#63-Responsibility - Lincoln, A., & Hobson, J. T. (1912). I must do the best I can (Remarks at Cabinet meeting, September 22, 1862, concerning the Emancipation Proclamation). In *The Lincoln year book: Containing immortal words of Abraham Lincoln spoken and written on various occasions, preceded by appropriate Scripture texts and followed by choice poetic selections for each day in the year, with special reference to anniversary dates* (p. 358). Dayton, OH: Press of United Brethren Pub. House.

Mike Lipkin
http://www.mikelipkin.com/
#99-Need

John Locke (29 August 1632 – 28 October 1704)
https://en.wikipedia.org/wiki/John_Locke
#154-End - Locke, J. (1689). Second Treatise of Government, Ch. VI, sec. 57. Retrieved September 16, 2017, from https://en.wikiquote.org/wiki/John_Locke
#343-Experience - Locke, J. (1689). *An Essay Concerning Human Understanding,* Book II, Ch. 1, sec. 19. Retrieved September 16, 2017, from https://en.wikiquote.org/wiki/John_Locke
#353-New - Locke, J. (1689). *An Essay Concerning Human Understanding,* Dedicatory epistle. Retrieved September 16, 2017, from https://en.wikiquote.org/wiki/John_Locke
#199-Thoughts - Locke, J. (1689). *An Essay Concerning Human Understanding,* Book 1, Ch. 3, sec. 3. Retrieved September 16, 2017, from https://en.wikiquote.org/wiki/John_Locke

Henry Wadsworth Longfellow (February 27, 1807 – March 24, 1882)
https://en.wikipedia.org/wiki/Henry_Wadsworth_Longfellow
http://www.hwlongfellow.org/
#59-Accomplish - E, J. (1883). Patience. In *The Voice of wisdom: a treasury of moral truths from the best authors* (p. 110). Edinburgh: W.P. Nimmo & Co.
#148-Defeat - Douglas, C. N. (1915). Character. In *Forty thousand sublime and beautiful thoughts gathered from the roses, clover blossoms, geraniums, violets, morning-glories, and pansies of literature* (p. 233). New York, NY: Christian Herald.
#333-Halt - Longfellow, H. W. (1887). The Theologian's Tale. In *The poetical works of Henry Wadsworth Longfellow. Household edition with illustrations* (p. 286). Boston and New York: Houghton, Mifflin, and Company.
#226-Late - Longfellow, H. W. (1887). Birds of passage. In *The poetical works of Henry Wadsworth Longfellow. Household edition with illustrations* (p. 358). Boston and New York: Houghton, Mifflin, and Company.
#264-Sorrow - Longfellow, H. W. (1857). Driftwood. Retrieved November 22, 2017, from https://en.wikiquote.org/wiki/Henry_Wadsworth_Longfellow

R. A. Longman
Superintendent Children's Home
#40-Dismiss - The advantages of placing out homeless children, October 26, 1904. (1904). In *The Religious Telescope, Volume 70* (p. 1352). Dayton, OH: Official Publication of the Church of the United Brethren in Christ.

Samuel Lover (24 February 1797 – 6 July 1868)
https://en.wikipedia.org/wiki/Samuel_Lover
#229-Circumstance - Winged Words. (1888). In M. Russell, S.J. (Ed.), *The Irish Monthly, Volume 16* (p. 445). Dublin: M. H. Gill & Son, O›Connell Street.

James Russell Lowell (February 22, 1819 – August 12, 1891)
https://en.wikipedia.org/wiki/James_Russell_Lowell
#161-Cheer - Edwards, T. (1891). Anxiety. In *A Dictionary of Thoughts: Being a Cyclopedia of Laconic Quotations from the best authors, both ancient and modern* (p. 23). New York, NY: Cassell Publishing Company.
#81-Decide - Lowell, J. R. (1844). The Present Crisis. Retrieved October 22, 2017, from https://en.wikiquote.org/wiki/James_Russell_Lowell
#343-Experience - Conduct. (1911). In G. B. Strand (Ed.), *Conduct, health, good fortune* (p. 20). Chicago, IL: A.C. McClurg & Co.
#90-Weakness - Ballou, M. M. (1886). Pride. In *Edge-tools of speech: Selected and arranged* (p. 394). Boston, MA: Ticknor and Company.

Sir John Lubbock (30 April 1834 – 28 May 1913)
https://en.wikipedia.org/wiki/John_Lubbock,_1st_Baron_Avebury
#161-Cheer - Lubbock, J. (1889). Preface. In *The Pleasures of Life, Volume 1* (p. vi). London and New York: Macmillan and Co.
#342-Death - Lubbock, J. (1889). The destiny of man. In *The Pleasures of Life, Volume 1* (p. 277). London and New York: Macmillan and Co.
#231-Overlook - McGuffey, W. H. (1889). The Duty of Happiness by Sir John Lubbock. In *McGuffey's Alternate Sixth Reader, Volume 6* (p. 428). Cincinnati and New York: Van Antwerp, Bragg, and Company.

Lucan (39 – April 30, 65 AD)
https://en.wikipedia.org/wiki/Lucan
#296-Daring - 180. (1904). In W. F. King (Ed.), *Classical and foreign quotations: A polyglot manual of historical and literary sayings, noted passages in poetry and prose phrases, proverbs, and bons mots* (3rd ed., p. 24). London: J. Whitaker & Sons, Limited.

Lucretius (15 October 99 BC – 55 BC)
https://en.wikipedia.org/wiki/Lucretius
#73-Perseverance - Edwards, T. (1891). Perseverance. In *A Dictionary of Thoughts: Being a Cyclopedia of Laconic Quotations from the best authors, both ancient and modern* (p. 407).

Martin Luther (10 November 1483 – 18 February 1546)
https://en.wikipedia.org/wiki/Martin_Luther
#143-Promise - A Happy Easter Time. (1898). In *School Education, Volume 17* (p. 22). Minneapolis, MN: School Education Company.

Rev. Milford H. Lyon
#299-Accountability - April 20, 1905, The prayer meeting, by Rev. Milford H. Lyon. (1905). In *The Advance, Volume 49* (p. 505). Chicago: Advance Publishing Company.

M

John F. MacArthur, Jr.
https://www.gty.org/
Taken from, Worship: The Ultimate Priority by John Macarthur, Jr., Page 176. Copyright © (February 1, 2012) by Moody Publishers.
#349-Dishonor - MacArthur Jr., J. (2012). *Worship: The ultimate priority: John Macarthur, Jr. on worship* (p. 176). Chicago, IL: Moody Publishers.

Thomas Babington Macaulay (25 October 1800 – 28 December 1859)
https://en.wikipedia.org/wiki/Thomas_Babington_Macaulay
#272-Settle - Free Press Extra. (1915). In W. W. Prescott & W. A. Spicer (Eds.), *The Protestant Magazine, Volume 7* (p. 102). Washington D.C.: The Protestant Magazine.

George Macdonald (10 December 1824 – 18 September 1905)
https://en.wikipedia.org/wiki/George_MacDonald
#234-Acceptance - Handford, T. W. (1890). May nineteenth. 640. In *Two thousand and ten choice quotations in poetry and prose: From the master minds of all ages* (5th ed., p. 144). Chicago, IL: Belford-Clarke Co.
#164-Choice - MacDonald, G. (1867). Unspoken Sermons, First Series. Retrieved February 29, 2016, from https://en.wikiquote.org/wiki/George_MacDonald

Ian Maclaren – Rev. John Watson (3 November 1850 – 6 May 1907)
https://en.wikipedia.org/wiki/Ian_Maclaren
#316-Battle - Maclaren, I. (2010, June 29). Be Kind; Everyone You Meet is Fighting a Hard Battle | Quote Investigator (1898). Retrieved from https://quoteinvestigator.com/2010/06/29/be-kind/

James Madison (March 16, 1751 – June 28, 1836)
https://en.wikipedia.org/wiki/James_Madison
https://www.whitehouse.gov/1600/presidents/jamesmadison
#133-Safe - Madison, J. (1884). 14. Property, 1792. In *Letters and other writings of James Madison: Fourth president of the United States. Vol. IV, 1829-1836* (p. 478). New York, NY: J. B. Lippincott & Co.

Maimonides (1135 or 1138 – December 12, 1204)
https://en.wikipedia.org/wiki/Maimonides
#79-Truth - Maimonides. (n.d.). Talmudist - Jewish History - Moreh Nevuchim 2:15. Retrieved from http://www.chabad.org/library/article_cdo/aid/107771/jewish/Talmudist.htm

Pam Malow-Isham
www.Tranquilpower.com
#49-Ability, **#31-Abundance**, **#59-Accomplish**, **#299-Accountability**, **#295-Afraid**, **#306-Aim**, **#305-Aimless**, **#268-Always**, **#132-Appreciate**, **#287-Attract**, **#13-Authentic**, **#308-Authority**, **#140-Awake**, **#318-Behind**, **#150-Calmness**, **#109-Celebrate**, **#18-Chaos**, **#357-Charity**, **#66-Comfort**, **#129-Confidence**, **#34-Confinement**, **#30-Criticism**, **#81-Decide**, **#208-Decline**, **#200-Deeds**, **#16-Deny**, **#331-Disapproval**, **#76-Disgrace**, **#349-Dishonor**, **#142-Disorder**, **#257-Dominate**, **#176-Dull**, **#225-Early**, **#95-Excuse**, **#42-Effect**, **#325-Expand**, **#364-Expectation**, **#343-Experience**, **#351-Failure**, **#47-Focus**, **#7-Gratitude**, **#333-Halt**, **#56-Hard**, **#269-Humanity**, **#72-Hurt**, **#365-Ignore**, **#2-Indecision**, **#35-Individual**, **#347-Initiate**, **#64-Irresponsible**, **#263-Joy**, **#94-Judgment**, **#226-Late**, **#246-Less**, **#61-Light**, **#124-Miss**, **#10-Misunderstand**, **#51-Moment**, **#245-More**, **#99-Need**, **#180-Negative**, **#182-Neglect**, **#353-New**, **#70-Obscurity**, **#157-Obstacle**, **#28-Opportunity**, **#218-Outside**, **#170-Overcome**, **#329-Own**, **#65-Pain**, **#304-Part**, **#73-Perseverance**, **#151-Perspective**, **#6-Possible**, **#336-Poverty**, **#143-Promise**, **#335-Prosperity**, **#27-Purpose**, **#146-Realities**, **#240-Refrain**, **#85-Refuge**, **#288-Repel**, **#104-Respond**, **#221-Respect**, **#205-Right**, **#111-Rise**, **#86-Risk**, **#131-Rude**, **#277-Ruin**, **#362-Sad**, **#133-Safe**, **#135-Satisfied**, **#123-See**, **#155-Seek**, **#243-Selfish**, **#244-Selfless**, **#272-Settle**, **#306-Single**, **#113-Speak**, **#254-Stagnant**, **#4-Stupid**, **#352-Success**, **#332-Thanksgiving**, **#52-Time**, **#115-Train**, **#169-Transcend**, **#130-Uncertainty**, **#191-Up**, **#134-Vulnerable**, **#100-Want**, **#303-Whole**, **#236-Wisdom**, **#136-Wish**, **#363-Wonder**, **#206-Wrong**, **#340-Yourself**

Horace Mann (May 4, 1796 – August 2, 1859)
https://en.wikipedia.org/wiki/Horace_Mann
#330-Borrow - Punctuality. (1896). In L. Klopsch (Ed.), *Many Thoughts of Many Minds: A Treasury of Quotations from the Literature of Every Land and Every Age* (p. 240). New York, NY: The Christian Herald, Louis Klopsch, Proprietor.
#70-Obscurity - Biography. (1896). In L. Klopsch (Ed.), *Many Thoughts of Many Minds: A Treasury of Quotations from the Literature of Every Land and Every Age* (p. 30). New York, NY: The Christian Herald, Louis Klopsch, Proprietor.
#218-Outside - Gems of Thought. (1873). In R. D. Lewin (Ed.), *The New Era: A Monthly Periodical Devoted to Humanity, Judaism, and Literature. Volume 3* (p. 368). New York, NY: The New Era Publishing Company.

Brennan Manning (April 27, 1934 – April 12, 2013)
https://en.wikipedia.org/wiki/Brennan_Manning
https://brennanmanning.com/

Taken from Abba's Child: The Cry of the Heart for Intimate Belonging by Brennan Manning. Copyright © 2002 by NavPress Publishing Group (first published 1994). Used by permission of Tyndale House Publishers, Inc. All rights reserved.

#13-Authentic - Manning, B. (2002). Chapter 2. The Imposter. In *Abba's child: The cry of the heart for intimate belonging* (p. 26). Carol Stream, IL: A NavPress resource Publishing in alliance with Tyndale House Publishers, Inc.

Katherine Mansfield (14 October 1888 – 9 January 1923)
https://en.wikipedia.org/wiki/Katherine_Mansfield
https://www.katherinemansfield.com/
#141-Order - Mansfield, K. (1922, January 29). Published in The Journal of Katherine Mansfield (1927). Retrieved March 23, 2016, from https://en.wikiquote.org/wiki/Katherine_Mansfield

Mary Jane Mapes
http://maryjanemapes.com/
#153-Begin, **#340-Yourself**

Steve Maraboli
http://stevemaraboli.net/
#323-Clarity, **#294-Demand**, **#209-Give**,

Turkish Spy (Giovanni Paolo Marana) (1642 - 1693)
https://en.wikipedia.org/wiki/Letters_Writ_by_a_Turkish_Spy
#34-Confinement - Christy, R. (1888). Freedom. In *Proverbs, maxims, and phrases of all ages* (p. 401). New York and London: G. P. Putnam's Sons.

Orison Swett Marden (1848 - March 10, 1924)
https://en.wikipedia.org/wiki/Orison_Swett_Marden
#317-Ahead - Marden, O. S. (1907). IX. Learn to expect a great deal of life. In *The Optimistic Life* (p. 43).
#355-Creative - Marden, O. S. (1910). I. The Divinity of Desire. In *The miracle of right thought* (pp. 11-12).
#172-Goal - Marden, O. S. (1910). III. Working for one thing and expecting something else. In *The miracle of right thought* (p. 62). New York, NY: T.Y. Crowell & Co.
#217-Inside - Marden, O. S. (1910). XI. The Great Within. In *The miracle of right thought* (p. 229).
#32-Lack - Marden, O. S., & Devitt, G. R. (1901). Tact and Common sense. In *Success Library, Volume 8, Parts 22-24* (p. 4479). New York, NY: The Success Company.
#152-Optimism - Peace, Power and Plenty. (1910). In B. O. Flower (Ed.), *The Arena, Volume 41* (p. 597).
#170-Overcome - Marden, O. S., & Devitt, G. R. (1901). Overcoming Obstacles. In *Success Library, Volume 8, Parts 22-24* (p. 4429). New York, NY: The Success Company.
#175-Passionate - Marden, O. S. (1897). Chapter 1. Enthusiasm. In *Success: A Book of Ideals, Helps, and Examples for All Desiring to Make the Most of Life* (p. 16).
#291-Standard - Make the most of yourself. (1910). In E. E. Stevens (Ed.), *Labor Digest: A National Magazine for the Advocacy of Industrial Peace, Volume 3* (p. 13).

Frederick Marryatt (10 July 1792 – 9 August 1848)
https://en.wikipedia.org/wiki/Frederick_Marryat
#142-Disorder - DAY, E. P. (1884). Nature. In *Day's Collacon: an encyclopaedia of prose quotations. Consisting of beautiful thoughts, choice extracts, and sayings, of the most eminent writers of all nations, from the earliest ages to the present times* (p. 613). New York and London: International Printing and Publishing Office, Sampson Low, Marston, Searle, and Rivington.

Ralph Marston
http://greatday.com
http://greatday.com/nmot/ralph.html
#287-Attract

Martial (38 and 41 CE - between 102 a d 104CE)
https://en.wikiquote.org/wiki/Martial
#286-Many - Smith, H. P. (1895). Fortune. In H. K. Johnson (Ed.), *A Dictionary of Terms, Phrases, and Quotations* (p. 572). New York, NY: D. Appleton Company.

Mary, Queen of Scots (8 December 1542 – 8 February 1587)
https://en.wikipedia.org/wiki/Mary,_Queen_of_Scots
#116-Rest - Service salad, April. (1893). In L. R. Hamersly (Ed.), *The United Service. A monthly review of military and naval affairs. Volume 9* (p. 400). Philadelphia, PA: L. R. Hamersly & Co.

Abraham H. Maslow (April 1, 1908 – June 8, 1970)
https://en.wikipedia.org/wiki/Abraham_Maslow
Taken from Religions, Values, and Peak-Experiences by Abraham H. Maslow Copyright © 1964 by Columbus: Ohio State University Press
Used by permission of Columbus: Ohio State University Press, Inc. All rights reserved.
#237-Ordinary

Berniece Matejcek (November 1, 1922 – May 18, 2017)
http://obits.mlive.com/obituaries/flint/obituary.aspx?pid=185491453
http://www.faithwired.com/about/faith-history/
Verbal confirmation
#207-Much

Latin Maxim
#206-Wrong - Trayner, J. (1894). Nullius. In *Latin Maxims and Phrases: Collected from the Institutional Writers on the law of Scotland and other sources* (4th ed., p. 407). Einburgh: William Green & Sons.

Giuseppe Mazzini (22 June 1805 – 10 March 1872)
https://en.wikipedia.org/wiki/Giuseppe_Mazzini
#327-Mission - Roberts, K. L. (1923). Eagle. In *HOYT'S NEW CYCLOPEDIA OF PRACTICAL QUOTATIONS* (p. 208). New York and London: Funk & Wagnalls Company.

Rev. Charles S. Macfarland, Ph. D.
#329-Own - Three stern truths. (1901). In J. N. Hallock (Ed.), *Christian Work: Illustrated Family Newspaper, Volume 70* (p. 74). New York, NY: The Christian Work.

Anna Agnes McGinley
#256-Hopeless - McGinley, A. A. (1907). New things and old in the householder's treasure. In *The profit of love: Studies in altruism* (p. 15). New York, NY: Longmans, Green, and Co.
#269-Humanity - McGinley, A. A. (1907). The passion for perfection. In *The profit of love: Studies in altruism* (p. 81).

Kate Mcveigh
http://katemcveigh.org/
#68-Distrust

William Melmoth (1665/66 - 1743)

https://en.wikipedia.org/wiki/William_Melmoth

#135-Satisfied - Mason, J., Melmoth, W., & Dodsley, R. (1824). Of Human Life. In *Mason on self-knowledge: Melmoth's Great importance of a religious life considered [and] Dodsley's Economy of Human life* (p. 249). London: Printed by J.F. Dove for the Proprietors of the English classics.

Menander of Athens (342/41 - 290 BC)

https://en.wikipedia.org/wiki/Menander

#96-Diligence - Menander. (2016, November 15). Menander. Retrieved from https://en.wikipedia.org/wiki/Menander

#293-Contribution - Menander. (1921). *Menander, the principal fragments* (F. G. Allinson, Trans.) (p. 445). London: W. Heinemann, G. P. Putnam›s Sons.

#267-Never - Menander. (1921). Labor Omnia Vincit. *Menander, the principal fragments* (F. G. Allinson, Trans.) (p. 445). London: W. Heinemann, G. P. Putnam›s Sons.

Mencius (372 - 289 BC)

https://en.wikipedia.org/wiki/Mencius

#81-Decide - Mencius. (n.d.). Mencius, Works, Book IV, Part II, Chapter VIII. Retrieved October 22, 2017, from https://en.wikiquote.org/wiki/Decisions

#292-Great - Mencius. (n.d.). Mencius, Book 4, pt. 2, v. 12. Retrieved April 22, 2016, from https://en.wikiquote.org/wiki/Mencius

Frederick Brotherton Meyer (8 April 1847 – 28 March 1929)

#242-Staying - A beautiful thought for each day in July. (1902). In F. Noble (Ed.), *The Treasury. A Magazine of Religious and Current Thought for Pastor and People, Volume 19* (p. 249). New York, NY: E. B. Treat & Co.

Joyce Meyer

https://www.joycemeyer.org/

#145-Mind - Meyer, J. (2004). *Audio CD, Where the mind goes, the man follows.* Fenton, MO: Joyce Meyer Ministries.

Paul J. Meyer (May 21, 1928 – October 26, 2009)

http://pauljmeyer.com/

Permission granted by The Meyer Resource Group * Inc.

#48-Imagine

John Stuart Mill (20 May 1806 – 8 May 1873)

https://en.wikipedia.org/wiki/John_Stuart_Mill

#278-Amend - Mill, J. S., & Taylor, H. (1875). Nature. In *Nature, The utility of religion and theism. 4th ed.* (p. 54). London: Longmans, Green, Reader, and Dyer.

#16-Deny - Mill, J. S. (n.d.). John Stuart Mill - Wikiquote. Retrieved October 11, 2017, from https://en.wikiquote.org/wiki/John_Stuart_Mill

#87-Miserable - Mill, J. S. (1862). "The Contest in America," Fraser's Magazine (February 1862). Retrieved October 26, 2017, from https://en.wikiquote.org/wiki/John_Stuart_Mill

Rev. J. R. Miller, D. D. (20 March 1840 – 2 July 1912)

https://en.wikipedia.org/wiki/J._R._Miller

#207-Much - Perry, S. A. (1905). Miscellaneous. In *Spiritual flashlights from godly men and women* (p. 374). Chicago, IL: S.B. Shaw.

#353-New - Perry, S. A. (1905). Character of Christ. In *Spiritual flashlights from godly men and women* (p. 19). Chicago, IL: S.B. Shaw.

Moliere (15 January 1622 – 17 February 1673)
https://en.wikipedia.org/wiki/Moli%C3%A8re
#127-Reply - Ballou, M. M. (1886). Repartee. In *Edge-tools of speech: Selected and arranged* (p. 419). Boston, MA: Ticknor and Company.

Michel de Montaigne (28 February 1533 – 13 September 1592)
https://en.wikipedia.org/wiki/Michel_de_Montaigne
#129-Confidence - De Montaigne, M. (n.d.). Michel de Montaigne - Wikiquote. Retrieved October 13, 2017, from https://en.wikiquote.org/wiki/Michel_de_Montaigne
#204-Nothing - Socrates. (n.d.). *The Essays of Montaigne*, Vol. 2, p. 593. Retrieved December 5, 2016, from https://en.wikiquote.org/wiki/Socrates
#219-Use - De Montaigne, M. (n.d.). Michel de Montaigne - Wikiquote. Retrieved October 13, 2017, from https://en.wikiquote.org/wiki/Michel_de_Montaigne
#236-Wisdom - Wooléver, A. (1876). Cheerfulness. In *Encyclopaedia of quotations: a treasury of wisdom, wit and humor, odd comparisons and proverbs: Authors, 931; subjects, 1393; quotations, 10,299* (6th ed., p. 58). Philadelphia, PA: David McKay, Publisher.

Charles de Montesquieu (18 January 1689 – 10 February 1755)
https://en.wikipedia.org/wiki/Montesquieu
#59-Accomplish - Montesquieu, C. (n.d.). Montesquieu - Wikiquote. Retrieved September 14, 2017, from https://en.wikiquote.org/wiki/Montesquieu
#220-Useless - Montesquieu, C. (n.d.). Montesquieu - Wikiquote. Retrieved July 8, 2017, from https://en.wikiquote.org/wiki/Montesquieu

James Montgomery (November 4, 1771 - April 30, 1854)
https://en.wikiquote.org/wiki/James_Montgomery
#173-Ask - Ballou, M. M. (1886). Perseverance. In *Edge-tools of speech: Selected and arranged* (p. 365). Boston, MA: Ticknor and Company.

Thomas Moore (28 May 1779 – 25 February 1852)
https://en.wikipedia.org/wiki/Thomas_Moore
#140-Awake - Moore, T. (n.d.). O! think not my spirits are always as light, St. 1. Retrieved November 24, 2017, from https://en.wikiquote.org/wiki/Thomas_Moore

Hannah More (2 February 1745 – 7 September 1833)
https://en.wikipedia.org/wiki/Hannah_More
#277-Ruin - Peerage and Baronetage Charts. (1824). *A dictionary of quotations from the British poets, by the author ..., Volume 1* (p. 99). London: G. and W. B. Whittaker. Hannah More›s Belshazzar, p. 2.
#312-Vocation - More, H. (1810). *Cœlebs in Search of a Wife: Comprehending Observations on ..., Volumes 1-2*(3rd ed., p. 113). New York, NY: T. & J. Swords.

Sir Thomas More (7 February 1478 – 6 July 1535)
https://en.wikipedia.org/wiki/Thomas_More
#347-Initiate - Allibone, S. A. (1876). Industry. In *Prose Quotations from Socrates to Macaulay, with indexes: Authors 544, subjects 571, quotations 8810* (p. 352). Philadelphia, PA: J. B. Lippincott & Co.

L. Morris
#15-Declare - Larcom, L. (1887). Among the sheaves. 8 October. In *[Beckonings for every day. A calendar of thought, arranged by L.L.]* (p. 171). Boston and New York: Houghton, Mifflin, and Company.

Joe Morton
https://www.facebook.com/joe.morton.9022
Verbal confirmation
#341-Life

John Muir (April 21, 1838 – December 24, 1914)
https://en.wikipedia.org/wiki/John_Muir
#202-Get - John Muir - Wikiquote. (n.d.). Retrieved October 11, 2017, from https://en.wikiquote.org/wiki/John_Muir
#209-Give - Muir, J. (1912). *The Yosemite* (p. 256). New York, NY: The Century Co.
#245-More - John Muir - Wikiquote. (n.d.). Retrieved October 11, 2017, from https://en.wikiquote.org/wiki/John_Muir
#69-Sunshine - "The Yellowstone National Park." *The Atlantic Monthly*, volume LXXXI, number 486 (April 1898) pages 509-522 (at pages 515-516); modified slightly and reprinted in *Our National Parks* (1901), chapter 2: *The Yellowstone National Park*

Andrew Murray (9 May 1828 – 18 January 1917)
https://en.wikipedia.org/wiki/Andrew_Murray_(minister)
#215-Faith - Perry, S. A. (1905). Faith. In *Spiritual flashlights from godly men and women* (p. 86). Chicago, IL: S.B. Shaw.

Miyamoto Musashi (1584 – June 13, 1645)
https://en.wikipedia.org/wiki/Miyamoto_Musashi
#183-Warrior - Musashi, M. (1645). Miyamoto Musashi - Wikiquote. Retrieved November 24, 2017, from https://en.wikiquote.org/wiki/Miyamoto_Musashi

N

Sir Isaac Newton (25 December 1642 – 20 March 1726/27)
https://en.wikipedia.org/wiki/Isaac_Newton
#283-Confusion - Newton, I. (n.d.). Isaac Newton - Wikiquote. Retrieved October 26, 2017, from https://en.wikiquote.org/wiki/Isaac_Newton
#349-Dishonor - Nichols, J. (1822). Miscellaneous Letters of Sir Isaac Newton to Francis Aston, Esq. (1669). In *Illustrations of the Literary History of the Eighteenth Century ..., Volume 5* (p. 43). London: John Nichols and Son.

Benjamin Elliott Nicholls (1796 – 1846)
#264-Sorrow - Nicholls, B. E. (1842). *The Book of Proverbs, Explained and Illustrated* (p. 63). London: Printed for J. G. F. & J. Rivington.

Florence Nightingale (12 May 1820 – 13 August 1910)
https://en.wikipedia.org/wiki/Florence_Nightingale
http://www.florence-nightingale.co.uk
#95-Excuse - Nightingale, F. (1861). I Attribute My Success to This:—I Never Gave or Took an Excuse | Quote Investigator. Retrieved from https://quoteinvestigator.com/2016/07/30/excuse/

Rev. J. H. Norris
#301-Single - Perry, S. A. (1905). Trust. In *Spiritual flashlights from godly men and women* (p. 327). Chicago, IL: S.B. Shaw.

Novalis (2 May 1772 - 25 March 1801)
#50-Inability - Taylor, J. (1837). 711. The True End of Intellectual Cultivation. In *Materials for thinking: Extracted from the works of ancient and modern authors* (220th ed.). London: J. Starie.

O

Kane O'Hara (1711 or 1712-17 June 1782)
https://en.wikipedia.org/wiki/Kane_O%27Hara
#313-Strong - Pre. (1896). In L. Klopsch (Ed.), *Many Thoughts of Many Minds: A Treasury of Quotations from the Literature of Every Land and Every Age* (p. 229). New York, NY: The Christian Herald, Louis Klopsch, Proprietor.

Stormie Omartian
https://www.stormieomartian.com/
Taken from: THE PRAYER THAT CHANGES EVERYTHING®. Copyright © 2004 by Stormie Omartian. Published by Harvest House Publishers. Eugene, Oregon. Used by Permission
#115-Train - Omartian, S. (2004). Why we need to know God better. In *The prayer that changes everything* (p. 37). Eugene, OR: Harvest House Publishers.

Frances Sargent Osgood (June 18, 1811 – May 12, 1850)
https://en.wikipedia.org/wiki/Frances_Sargent_Osgood
#251-Labor - Labor. By Mrs. Frances S. Osgood. (1846). In J. L. O'Sullivan (Ed.), *The United States Democratic Review, Volume 17* (p. 220). New York, NY: J. L. O'Sullivan & O. C. Gardiner.

Sir William Osler (July 12, 1849 – December 29, 1919)
https://en.wikipedia.org/wiki/William_Osler
#235-Ignorance - Osler, W. (n.d.). William Osler - Wikiquote. Retrieved November 1, 2016, from https://en.wikiquote.org/wiki/William_Osler
#169-Transcend - September 30, 1905, St. Louis Medical Review. (1905). In K. W. Millican & B. A. Camb (Eds.), *St. Louis Medical Review, Volumes 51-52* (p. 275). St. Louis, MO: St. Louis Medical Review Association.

Ouida (Marie Louise de la Ramée) (1 January 1839 – 25 January 1908)
https://en.wikipedia.org/wiki/Ouida
#314-Sensitive - Rame, M. L. (1875). Chapter IX. In *Signa: A Story* (p. 208). London: Chapman and Hall.

Ovid (20 March 43 BC-AD 17/18)
https://en.wikipedia.org/wiki/Ovid
#184-Opponent - Dalbiac, P. H., & Harbottle, T. B. (1897). Latin Quotations. De Arte Amandi, II., 197. In *Dalbiac and Harbottle's Dictionary of Quotations (classical)* (2nd ed., p. 26). London and New York: Swan Sonnenschein & Co., Limited. The Macmillan Co., Limited.

Jafree Ozwald
https://www.enlightenedbeings.com/
#263-Joy, #261-Perfection, #178-Surrender

P

Thomas Paine (February 9, 1737 – January 29, 1809)
https://en.wikipedia.org/wiki/Thomas_Paine

#299-Accountability - Stockham, A. (1900). Selections from Pain's Rights of Man. In *The Fearful Outlook Or the Impending Crisis. God's Dynamite. To Whom it May Concern* (7th ed., p. 43). Scioto County, OH: Waits.

#224-Cruel - Paine, T. (1797, May 12). "A Letter: Being an Answer to a Friend, on the publication of The Age of Reason" (12 May 1797), published in an 1852 edition of The Age of Reason, p. 205. Retrieved from https://en.wikiquote.org/wiki/Thomas_Paine

#80-Falsehood - Paine, T. (1826). Falsehood. In *Aphorisms, Opinions, and Reflections of T. Paine. To which is prefixed, an Essay on his Life. By Juvencus* (p. 45). London.

#186-Liberty - Paine, T. (1795). Dissertation on First Principles of Government (July 1795), published in an 1852 edition of The Age of Reason, p. 205. Retrieved from https://en.wikiquote.org/wiki/Thomas_Paine

#321-Shrink - Duyckinck, E. A., & Duyckinck, G. L. (1856). Thomas Paine. In *The Cyclopedia of American Literature Vol. 1* (p. 204). New York, NY: Charles Scribner.

#147-Triumph - Paine, T. (1835). No. 1. In *The American Crisis* (p. 3).

Rev. W. J. Palm, Alexis, Illinois

#58-Discontent - BALFOUR, C. L. (1861). Making the best of things. In *Sunbeams for all Seasons: a selected series of counsels, cautions, and precepts, relating to the hopes, joys, pleasures, and sorrows of life* (p. 527). London: Houlston & Wright.

J. Parker

#174-Answer - E, J. (1883). Prayer, not dictation. In *The Voice of wisdom: A treasury of moral truths from the best authors* (p. 116). Edinburgh: William P. Nimmo & Co.

Theodore Parker (August 24, 1810 – May 10, 1860)
https://en.wikipedia.org/wiki/Theodore_Parker

#160-Unchanging - Walsh, W. S. (1921). Government. Speech at the N. E. Anti-slavery Convention. Boston, May 20, 1850. In *The international encyclopedia of prose and poetical quotations from the literature of the world including the following languages: English, Latin, Greek, French, Spanish, Persian, Italian, German, Chinese, Hebrew and others* (p. 323). Philadelphia, PA: The John C. Winston Company.

Charles Henry Parkhurst (April 17, 1842 – September 8, 1933)
https://en.wikipedia.org/wiki/Charles_Henry_Parkhurst

#317-Ahead - Douglas, C. N. (1915). Discoveries. In *Forty thousand sublime and beautiful thoughts gathered from the roses, clover blossoms, geraniums, violets, morning-glories, and pansies of literature* (p. 509). New York, NY: Christian Herald.

#211-Load - How much do you love? (1885). In S. Jackson (Ed.), *Presbyterian Home Missionary, Volume 14, Issue 6 edited by Sheldon Jackson* (p. 139). New York, NY: The Board of Home Missions of the Presbyterian Church.

Blaise Pascal (19 June 1623 – 19 August 1662)
https://en.wikipedia.org/wiki/Blaise_Pascal

#80-Falsehood - Pascal, B. (1910). Polemical Fragments, 864. In C. W. Eliot (Ed.), *Thoughts, Letters, and Minor Works* (W. F. Trotter, M. L. Booth, & O. W. Wight, Trans.) (p. 307). New York, NY: P.F. Collier & Son.

#292-Great - Pascal, B. (1910). Proofs of Jesus Christ, 797. In C. W. Eliot (Ed.), *Thoughts, Letters, and Minor Works* (W. F. Trotter, M. L. Booth, & O. W. Wight, Trans.) (p. 281). New York, NY: P.F. Collier & Son.

#207-Much - Northend, C. (1853). Chapter VI. Kindness, gentleness, and forbearance. In *The teacher and the parent: A treatise upon common-school education; containing practical suggestions to teachers and parents* (p. 42). Boston: Jenks, Hickling, & Swan.

#237-Ordinary - Pascal, B. (1910). Section I Thoughts on Mind and on Style, 7. In C. W. Eliot (Ed.), *Thoughts, Letters, and Minor Works* (W. F. Trotter, M. L. Booth, & O. W. Wight, Trans.) (p.10). New York, NY: P.F. Collier & Son.

#240-Refrain - Pascal, B. (1803). *Thoughts on religion and other important subjects* (T. Chevalier, Trans.) (p. 48). London: Printed for Samuel Bagster.

#328-Victory - Pascal, B. (1910). Misery of man without God, 135. In C. W. Eliot (Ed.), *Blaise Pascal* (W. F. Trotter, M. L. Booth, & O. W. Wright, Trans.) (p. 51). New York, NY: P F Collier & Son.

Saint Patrick (385 – March 17, 461)
https://en.wikipedia.org/wiki/Saint_Patrick
#318-Behind - Saint Patrick. (n.d.). The Lorica of Patrick. Retrieved June 18, 2017, from https://en.wikiquote.org/wiki/Saint_Patrick

#358-Hindrance - Patrick. (1868). Appendix containing his confession and epistle to coroticus. In *St. Patrick: Apostle of Ireland in the Third Century* (R. S. Nicholson, Trans.) (p. 117). Dublin, London, Belfast: M›Glashan and Gill, John Russell Smith, Archer & Sons.

Jean Paul (21 March 1763 – 14 November 1825)
https://en.wikipedia.org/wiki/Jean_Paul
#211-Load - Gould, H. D., & Hessenmueller, E. L. (1904). *Best Thoughts of Best Thinkers: Amplified, Classified, Exemplified and Arranged as a key to unlock the literature of all ages* (p. 579). Cleveland, OH: Best Thoughts Publishing Company.

Steve Pavlina
https://www.stevepavlina.com/
#179-Positive - Pavlina, S. (2015, November 18). Creative Observation - Steve Pavlina. Retrieved from https://www.stevepavlina.com/blog/2006/08/creative-observation/
#340-Yourself - Pavlina, S. (2005, November 14). What Will Other People Think of You? - Steve Pavlina. Retrieved from http://www.stevepavlina.com/blog/2005/11/what-will-other-people-think-of-you/

William Penn (14 October 1644 – 30 July 1718)
https://en.wikipedia.org/wiki/William_Penn
#235-Ignorance - Wakefield, P., & Penn, W. (1833). Reflections, 307. In *A brief memoir of the life of William Penn: Compiled for the use of young persons* (p. 114). New-York, NY: Printed and sold by M. Day.
#105-Patience - Penn, W. (1699). Part I, Industry. In *Some fruits of solitude: In reflections and maxims relating to the conduct of human life, the fifth edition, with additions. Licensed, May 24. 1693*. London: Printed for Thomas Northcott, in George-Alley in Lombard-street.
#146-Realities - Douglas, C. N. (1915). Ostentation. In *Forty thousand sublime and beautiful thoughts gathered from the roses, clover blossoms, geraniums, violets, morning-glories, and pansies of literature* (p. 1272). New York, NY: Christian Herald.

Rev. Pennington (1807 – October 22, 1870)
https://en.wikipedia.org/wiki/James_W.C._Pennington
#242-Staying - Perry, S. A. (1905). Perseverance. In *Spiritual flashlights from godly men and women* (p. 194). Chicago, IL: S.B. Shaw.

Frankie Waldo Perez
https://www.facebook.com/MindGym/
#22-Overflow

Mattie Perry
#215-Faith - Perry, S. A. (1905). Faith. In *Spiritual flashlights from godly men and women* (p. 85). Chicago, IL: S.B. Shaw.

<u>Tiffany Peterson</u>
http://thelighthouseprinciples.com/
#122-Action, **#20-Dream**

<u>J. Petit-Senn</u> (1792-1870)
https://en.wikipedia.org/wiki/Jean_Antoine_Petit-Senn
#31-Abundance - Douglas, C. N. (1915). Abundance. In *Forty thousand sublime and beautiful thoughts gathered from the roses, clover blossoms, geraniums, violets, morning-glories, and pansies of literature* (p. 13). New York, NY: The Christian Herald.

<u>Petrarch</u> (July 20, 1304 – July 19, 1374)
https://en.wikipedia.org/wiki/Petrarch
#94-Judgment - Robinson, J. H. (1906). The Italian Cities and the Renaissance. In *Readings in European history. (A collection of extracts from the sources chosen with the purpose of illustrating the progress of culture in Western Europe since the German invasions)* (p. 223). Boston, New York, Chicago, London: Ginn & Company.

<u>Wendell Phillips</u> (November 29, 1811 – February 2, 1884)
https://en.wikipedia.org/wiki/Wendell_Phillips
#37-Growth - Ballou, M. M. (1886). Want. In *Edge-tools of speech: Selected and arranged* (p. 534). Boston, MA: Ticknor and Company.

<u>Arthur Tappan Pierson</u> (March 6, 1837 – June 3, 1911)
https://en.wikipedia.org/wiki/Arthur_Tappan_Pierson
#5-Impossible - The Glory of the God-man, delivered at Northfield, Mass, August 4, 1901. (1902). In F. Noble (Ed.), *The Treasury. A Magazine of Religious and Current Thought for Pastor and People, Volume 19* (p. 521). New York, NY: E. B. Treat & Co.

<u>William Pinkney</u> (March 17, 1764 – February 25, 1822)
https://en.wikipedia.org/wiki/William_Pinkney
#64-Irresponsible - Douglas, C. N. (1915). Oppression. In *Forty thousand sublime and beautiful thoughts gathered from the roses, clover blossoms, geraniums, violets, morning-glories, and pansies of literature* (p. 1267). New York, NY: Christian Herald.

<u>Plato</u> (428/427 or 424/423 - 348/347 BC)
https://en.wikipedia.org/wiki/Plato
#174-Answer - Ballou, M. M. (1886). Conversation. In *Edge-tools of speech: Selected and arranged* (p. 82). Boston, MA: Ticknor and Company.
#196-Excessive - Plato (1901). Book VIII, Four forms of government. In *The Republic of Plato* (B. Jowett, Trans.) (p. 264). New York and London: The Co-operative Publication Society.
#171-Exercise - Selections from great educators throughout the ages. (1933). In E. D. Mitchell (Ed.), *The Journal of health and physical education Vol. IV, No. 1* (p. 50). Ann Arbor, MI: American Physical Education Association.
#350-Honor - Plato. (1901). On wrong or right government, and the pleasures of each. In *The World's Greatest Literature: Masterpieces of the World's ..., Volume 58. The Republic by Plato* (B. Jowett, Trans.) (p. 284). New York and London: The Colonial Press.
#311-Ought - Gould, H. D., & Hessenmueller, E. L. (1904). *Best Thoughts of Best Thinkers: Amplified, Classified, Exemplified and Arranged as a key to unlock the literature of all ages* (p. 79). Cleveland, OH: Best Thoughts Publishing Company.
#271-Plan - Edwards, T. (1891). Self-reliance. In *A Dictionary of Thoughts: Being a Cyclopedia of Laconic Quotations from the best authors, both ancient and modern* (p. 519). New York, NY: Cassell Publishing Company.

#366-Review - Plato. (1907). Gorgias. In *The Dialogues of Plato, Volume 3* (B. Jowett, Trans.) (p. 89).
#284-Surety - Douglas, C. N. (1915). Abstinence. In *Forty thousand sublime and beautiful thoughts gathered from the roses, clover blossoms, geraniums, violets, morning-glories, and pansies of literature* (p. 12). New York, NY: Christian Herald.
#100-Want - Gentle Speech. (1908). In J. E & H. S (Eds.), *The Melody of the Heart* (2nd ed., p. 191). New York, NY: Frederick A. Stokes Company.
#363-Wonder - Dalbiac, P. H., & Harbottle, T. B. (1897). In *Dalbiac and Harbottle's Dictionary of Quotations (classical)* (2nd ed., p. 411). London and New York: Swan Sonnenschein & Co., Limited. The Macmillan Co., Limited.

Plautus (254 - 184 BC)
https://en.wikipedia.org/wiki/Plautus
#316-Battle - Edwards, T. (1891). Courage. In *A Dictionary of Thoughts: Being a Cyclopedia of Laconic Quotations* (p. 93).

Plutarch (46-120 AD)
https://en.wikipedia.org/wiki/Plutarch
#230-Intent - Edwards, T. (1891). Misery. In *A Dictionary of Thoughts: Being a Cyclopedia of Laconic Quotations from the* (p. 352). New York, NY: Cassell Publishing Company.
#70-Obscurity - Klopsch, L. (1896). Contentment. In *Many Thoughts of Many Minds: A Treasury of Quotations from the Literature of Every Land and Every Age* (p. 54). New York, NY: The Christian Herald, Louis Klopsch, Proprietor.

Edgar Allan Poe (January 19, 1809 – October 7, 1849)
https://en.wikipedia.org/wiki/Edgar_Allan_Poe
#42-Effect - Woodberry, G. E. (1885). In New York. In C. D. Warner (Ed.), *American Men of Letters. Edgar Allan Poe* (pp. 211-212). Boston and New York: Houghton, Mifflin, and Company. The Riverside Press, Cambridge.

Alexander Pope (21 May 1688 – 30 May 1744)
https://en.wikipedia.org/wiki/Alexander_Pope
#91-Pride - Wood, J. (1893). Precepts. In *Dictionary of quotations: From ancient and modern English and foreign sources* (p. 356). London and New York: Frederick Warne and co.

Winkie Pratney
https://www.winkiepratney.net/
#197-Direction, #238-Extraordinary

Samuel Irenaeus Prime (1812-1885)
https://en.wikipedia.org/wiki/Samuel_I._Prime
#88-Happy - Gilbert, J. H. (1895). Kindness. In *Dictionary of Burning Words of Brilliant Writers: A Cyclopædia of Quotations from the literature of all ages* (p. 363). New York, NY: Wilbur B. Ketcham.

John Critchley Prince (21 June 1808 – 5 May 1866)
https://en.wikipedia.org/wiki/John_Critchley_Prince
#17-Tranquil - Hours with the Muses - John Critchley Prince. (1842). In *Christian Teacher; A Theological and literary journal. Volume fourth* (p. 196). London: John Green.

Matthew Prior (21 July 1664 – 18 September 1721)
https://en.wikipedia.org/wiki/Matthew_Prior
#268-Always - Allibone, S. A. (1878). Talk. In *Poetical quotations from Chaucer to Tennyson. With copious indexes: authors, 550; subjects, 435; quotations, 13,600* (p. 545). Philadelphia, PA: J. B. Lippincott & Co.

Marcel Proust (10 July 1871 – 18 November 1922)
https://en.wikipedia.org/wiki/Marcel_Proust
#198-Journey - Proust, V. M. (n.d.). Vol II: Within a Budding Grove (1919), Ch. IV: "Seascape, with a Frieze of Girls." Retrieved from https://en.wikiquote.org/wiki/Marcel_Proust

Proverb

#60-Abandon - Bechtel, J. H. (1902). Watchfulness, Care, Caution. In *Proverbs: Maxims and phrases drawn from all lands and times; carefully selected and indexed for convenient reference* (p. 173). Philadelphia, PA: The Penn Publishing Company.

#167-Forgive - Wood, J. (1893). The. In *Dictionary of quotations: From ancient and modern English and foreign sources* (p. 445). London and New York: Frederick Warne and co.

#255-Hope - Manser, M. H. (2002). He that lives in hope dances to an ill tune. In R. Fergusson & D. Pickering (Eds.), *The Facts on File Dictionary of Proverbs* (2nd ed., p. 120). New York, NY: Facts On File, Inc. An imprint of InfoBase publishing.

#198-Journey - Wood, J. (1899). Practically. In *Dictionary of quotations from ancient, modern, English and foreign sources* (p. 355). London and New York: Frederick Warne and Co.

#251-Labor - Browne, W. H. (1901). Labor. In *Proverbs* (p. 196). Toronto, London, Philadelphia and San Francisco: Drexel Biddle.

#166-Sit - Bechtel, J. H. (1902). Health, Life, Livelihood. In *Proverbs: Maxims and phrases drawn from all lands and times; carefully selected and indexed for convenient reference* (p. 86). Philadelphia, PA: The Penn Publishing Company.

#233-Today - Browne, W. H. (1901). Error. In *Proverbs* (p. 132). Toronto, London, Philadelphia and San Francisco: Drexel Biddle.

#79-Truth - Bechtel, J. H. (1902). Truth, Virtue, Vice. In *Proverbs: Maxims and phrases drawn from all lands and times; carefully selected and indexed for convenient reference* (p. 167). Philadelphia, PA: The Penn Publishing Company.

English Proverb

#108-Balance - Benham, W. G. (1914). Latin Quotations. In *Cassell's book of quotations proverbs and household words* (p. 506). London, New York, Toronto, and Melbourne: Cassell & Company, LTD.

#181-Care - Lantz, M. S. (1884). *The acme cyclopedia and dictionary: A practical compendium of useful information, and book of reference for everyone* (p. 185). Philadelphia, PA: Globe Bible Publishing Co.

#72-Hurt - Many. (1899). In J. Wood (Ed.), *Dictionary of Quotations from Ancient and Modern, English and Foreign sources* (p. 270). London and New York: Frederick Warne and Co.

#5-Impossible - Preston, T. (1880). 851. Impossible. In *Dictionary of English Proverbs and Proverbial*. The Library of Alexandria.

#346-Lose - Fresh-water fish and their associations. (1890). In S. Urban (Ed.), *The Gentleman's Magazine, Volume 268* (p. 22). London: Chatto & Windus, Piccadilly.

#124-Miss - Christy, R. (1888). Shot, Shooting. In *Proverbs, maxims, and phrases of all ages* (p. 263). New York and London: G. P. Putnam›s Sons.

#311-Ought - Wooléver, A. (1891). Indolence of. In *Treasury of wisdom, wit and humor, odd comparisons and proverbs:* (5th ed., p. 514). Philadelphia, PA: David McKay, Publisher.

French Proverb

#140-Awake - Macdonnel, D. E. (1826). VE-VE. In *A Dictionary of Quotations in most frequent use, taken chiefly from the Latin and French, but comprising many from the Greek, Spanish, and Italian languages, translated into English* (9th ed., p. 407). London: Printed for Geo. B. Whittaker.

Haitian Proverb

#158-Path - Bigelow, J. (1877). XXXIV. In *The wit and wisdom of the Haytians* (pp. 68-69). New York, NY: Scribner & Armstrong.

Latin Proverb
#114-Silence - Ali-Alt. (1866). In H. T. Riley (Ed.), *Dictionary of Latin quotations, proverbs, maxims, and mottos, classical and medieval, including law terms and phrases. With a selection of Greek quotations* (p. 17). London: Bell & Daldy.

Rev. John Pulsford (1815-1897)
#218-Outside - Hall, A. W. (1887). Gems from the Rev. John Pulsford. In *Great Thoughts from Master Minds, Volume 8* (p. 12). London: A. Bradley.

Pythagoras (570 – 495 BC)
https://en.wikipedia.org/wiki/Pythagoras
#135-Satisfied - Berkeley, E., & Sprague, W. B. (1853). Doing well. In *The world's laconics: Or, The best thoughts of the best authors* (p. 71). New York, NY: M.W. Dodd.

Q

Francis Quarles (8 May 1592 – 8 September 1644)
https://en.wikipedia.org/wiki/Francis_Quarles
#332-Thanksgiving - *The Saturday Magazine, Volume 6, under the direction of the committee of general literature and education, appointed by the society for promoting Christian knowledge* (p. 149). (1835). London: John William Parker.

Nido Qubein
http://www.nidoqubein.com/
#249-Power

Pasquier Quesnel (14 July 1634 – 2 December 1719)
https://en.wikipedia.org/wiki/Pasquier_Quesnel
#120-Zeal - Wood, J. (1893). Youth. In *Dictionary of quotations: From ancient and modern English and foreign sources* (p. 569). London and New York: Frederick Warne and co.

Quintilian (35 – 100 AD)
https://en.wikipedia.org/wiki/Quintilian
#98-Condemn - Hoyt, J. K., & Ward, A. L. (1886). Philosophy. In *The Cyclopædia of Practical Quotations. English and Latin, with an appendix containing proverbs from the Latin and modern foreign languages* (8th ed., p. 553). New York and London: Funk & Wagnalls.
#131-Rude - HOYT, J. K., & Ward, A. L. (1894). Music. In *The Cyclopædia of Practical Quotations. English and Latin, with an appendix containing proverbs from the Latin and modern foreign languages* (12th ed., p. 550). Toronto, New York, London: Funk & Wagnalls Company.

R

Sir Walter Raleigh (1554 – 29 October 1618)
https://en.wikipedia.org/wiki/Walter_Raleigh
#142-Disorder - Raleigh, W. (1829). The cabinet council. In *The Works of Sir Walter Ralegh, Kt. Now first collected: To which are prefixed the lives of the author, by Oldys and Birch in eight volumes. Vol. VIII. Miscellaneous Works* (p. 122). Oxford: At the University Press.

W. Rathbone
#213-Discipline - DAY, E. P. (1884). Self-Reliance. In *Day's Collacon: an encyclopaedia of prose quotations. Consisting of beautiful thoughts, choice extracts, and sayings, of the most eminent writers of all*

nations, from the earliest ages to the present times (p. 843). New York and London: International Printing and Publishing Office, Sampson Low, Marston, Searle, and Rivington.

Publius Flavius Vegetius Renatus (Died 450AD)
https://en.wikipedia.org/wiki/Publius_Flavius_Vegetius_Renatus
#214-Undisciplined - Simes, T. (1780). The Roman Discipline, the Cause of their Greatness. In *A treatise on the military science: which comprehends the grand operations of war, and general rules for conducting an army in the field* (p. 253). London: Printed for John Millan.

Jean Paul Richter (7 June 1847 – 25 August 1937)
https://en.wikipedia.org/wiki/Jean_Paul_Richter
#211-Load - *Friends' Intelligencer, Volume 65* (p. 343). (1908). Philadelphia, PA: Friends Intelligencer Association, Limited.

Sonia Ricotti
http://www.leadoutloud.ca/
#229-Circumstance, **#253-Turn**

Mike Robbins
https://mike-robbins.com/
#13-Authentic

Frederick W. Robertson (3 February 1816 – 15 August 1853)
https://en.wikipedia.org/wiki/Frederick_William_Robertson
#21-Flow - ROBERTSON, F. W., Richards, W. C., & TUPPER, K. B. (1881). Atonement. In *Robertson's living thoughts. A thesaurus. By K.B. Tupper. With an introduction by … W.C. Richards* (p. 14). Chicago, IL: S.C. Griggs and Co.
#269-Humanity - Robertson, F. W., & Brooke, S. A. (1871). Chapter VIII. Brighton, October 1849, to December 1850. In *Life, letters, lectures, and addresses of Fredk. W. Robertson, M.A., incumbent of Trinity Chapel, Brighton, 1847-1853* (p. 167). New York, NY: Harper & Brothers Publishers.
#151-Perspective - Robertson, F. W. (1873). VI. The Illusiveness of Life. In *Sermons preached at Trinity Chapel, Brighton* (p. 489). New York, NY: Harper & Brothers, Publishers.
#185-Restraint - Robertson, F. W. (1873). The Pre-eminence of Charity. In *Sermons preached at Trinity Chapel, Brighton* (p. 784). New York, NY: Harper & Brothers, Publishers.
#89-Strength - ROBERTSON, F. W., Richards, W. C., & TUPPER, K. B. (1881). Love. In *Robertson's living thoughts. A thesaurus. By K.B. Tupper. With an introduction by … W.C. Richards* (p. 115). Chicago, IL: S.C. Griggs and Co.
#313-Strong - Robertson, F. W. (1873). XXI. The skepticism of Pilate. In *Sermons preached at Trinity Chapel, Brighton* (p. 234). New York, NY: Harper & Brothers, Publishers.
#345-Win - ROBERTSON, F. W., Richards, W. C., & TUPPER, K. B. (1881). Love. In *Robertson's living thoughts. A thesaurus. By K.B. Tupper. With an introduction by … W.C. Richards* (p. 122). Chicago, IL: S.C. Griggs and Co.

Bud Robinson (January 27, 1860 – November 2, 1942)
http://snu.edu/bud-robinson
#292-Great - Perry, S. A. (1905). Miscellaneous. In *Spiritual flashlights from godly men and women* (p. 360). Chicago, IL: S.B. Shaw.
#10-Misunderstand - Perry, S. A. (1905). Miscellaneous. In *Spiritual flashlights from godly men and women* (p. 363). Chicago, IL: S.B. Shaw.

François De La Rochefoucauld (15 September 1613 – 17 March 1680)
https://en.wikipedia.org/wiki/Fran%C3%A7ois_de_La_Rochefoucauld_(writer)
#11-Absence - Wooléver, A. (1891). Absence. In *Treasury of wisdom, wit and humor, odd comparisons and proverbs* (5th ed., p. 2). Philadelphia, PA: David McKay.
#331-Disapproval - Woolever, A. (1891). Approbation. In *Treasury of Wisdom, Wit, and Humor, Odd Comparisons and Proverbs* (5th ed., p. 18).
#76-Disgrace - Ballou, M. M. (1886). Disgrace. In *Edge-tools of speech: Selected and arranged* (p. 110). Boston, MA: Ticknor and Company.
#349-Dishonor - May 1880, Wisdom. (1880). In H. S. Drayton & N. Sizer (Eds.), *The Phrenological Journal and Science of Health: Incorporated ..., Volumes 70-71* (p. 280). New York, NY: S. R. Wells & Co.
#325-Expand - Wooléver, A. (1891). Indolence of. In *Treasury of wisdom, wit and humor, odd comparisons and proverbs:* (5th ed., p. 280). Philadelphia, PA: David McKay, Publisher.
#205-Right - Wooléver, A. (1878). Minds of narrow views. In *Treasury of wisdom, wit and humor, odd comparisons and proverbs* (3rd ed., p. 281). Philadelphia, PA: Claxton.

Will Rogers (November 4, 1879 – August 15, 1935)
https://www.cmgww.com/historic/rogers/
https://en.wikipedia.org/wiki/Will_Rogers
#350-Sit

Fernando de Rojas (1465/73 – April 1541)
https://en.wikipedia.org/wiki/Fernando_de_Rojas
#200-Deeds - Edwards, T. (1891). Deeds. In *A Dictionary of Thoughts: Being a Cyclopedia of Laconic Quotations from the best authors, both ancient and modern* (p. 108). New York, NY: Cassell Publishing Company.
#219-Use - Rojas, F. D. (1499). Fernando de Rojas - Wikiquote. Retrieved October 21, 2017, from https://en.wikiquote.org/wiki/Fernando_de_Rojas

Theodore Roosevelt (October 27, 1858 – January 6, 1919)
https://en.wikipedia.org/wiki/Theodore_Roosevelt
https://www.whitehouse.gov/1600/presidents/theodoreroosevelt
#30-Criticism - Roosevelt, T. (1918, May 18). Theodore Roosevelt on Criticizing the President. Retrieved from https://www.snopes.com/theodore-roosevelt-on-criticizing-the-president/

Joseph Roux (19 April 1834 – February 1905)
https://en.wikiquote.org/wiki/Joseph_Roux
#256-Hopeless - Douglas, C. N. (1915). Labor. In *Forty thousand sublime and beautiful thoughts gathered from the roses, clover blossoms, geraniums, violets, morning-glories, and pansies of literature* (2nd ed., p. 1063). New York, NY: Christian Herald.

Nicholas Rowe (20 June 1674 – 6 December 1718)
https://en.wikipedia.org/wiki/Nicholas_Rowe_(writer)
#296-Daring - The nobility of work. (1908). In J. E & H. S (Eds.), *The Melody of the Heart* (2nd ed., p. 15). New York, NY: Frederick A. Stokes Company.

Gretchen Rubin
http://gretchenrubin.com/
#357-Charity - Rubin, G. (2009, March 13). Happiness Myth No. 10: It's Selfish To Try To Be Happier. Retrieved from http://www.slate.com/blogs/happinessproject/2009/03/13/happiness_myth_no_10_the_biggest_myth_it_s_selfish_to_try_to_be_happier.html
#244-Selfless - Rubin, G. (2014, April 10). Celebrating Happiness / The Selflessness of Being Happy. Retrieved from https://thecelebrationofhappiness.wordpress.com/tag/gretchen-rubin/

#273-Procrastination - Rubin, G. (2014, July 8). Secret of Adulthood: Working Is One of the Most Dangerous Forms of Procrastination. Retrieved from https://gretchenrubin.com/2014/07/secret-of-adulthood-working-is-one-of-the-most-dangerous-forms-of-procrastination/
#340-Yourself - Rubin, G. (2012, December 19). 7 Tips for Sticking to Your New Year's Resolutions. Retrieved from https://gretchenrubin.com/2012/12/7-tips-for-sticking-to-your-new-years-resolutions/

Friedrich Ruckert (16 May 1799 – 31 January 1866)
https://en.wikipedia.org/wiki/Friedrich_R%C3%BCckert
#115-Train - Wood, J. (1893). Licht. In *Dictionary of quotations: From ancient and modern English and foreign sources* (p. 246). London and New York: Frederick Warne and co.

Alanus de Rupe (1428 – 8 September 1475)
https://en.wikipedia.org/wiki/Alanus_de_Rupe
#236-Wisdom - Quarles, F., & WILSON, R. (1824). *Emblems, Divine and Moral … A new edition carefully, revised and corrected in two volumes. Vol. I* (p. 57). London: J. Robins & Co.

John Ruskin (8 February 1819 – 20 January 1900)
https://en.wikipedia.org/wiki/John_Ruskin
#201-Believe - The test of a truly great man. (1819). (1883). In *The Royal Readers: Special Canadian Series. Fifth book of reading lessons* (p. 106). Toronto: Thomas Nelson and Sons, and James Campbell and Son.
#208-Decline - Ruskin, J. (1849). Chap. IV. The lamp of beauty. In *The Seven Lamps of Architecture, Volume 1* (p. 120). London: Smith, Elder, and Co.
#262-Imperfection - Patrick, D. (1903). Perfection in Art (From the Stones of Venice.). In *Chambers's Cyclopaedia of English Literature, New Edition. Volume 3* (p. 574). London and Edinburgh: W. & R. Chambers, Limited.

Lord John Russell (18 August 1792 – 28 May 1878)
https://en.wikipedia.org/wiki/John_Russell,_1st_Earl_Russell
#236-Wisdom - Allibone, S. A. (1876). Proverb. In *Prose Quotations from Socrates to Macaulay, with indexes: Authors 544, subjects 571, quotations 8810* (p. 594). Philadelphia, PA: J. B. Lippincott & Co.

Samuel Rutherford (1600 – 29 March 1661)
https://en.wikipedia.org/wiki/Samuel_Rutherford
#160-Unchanging - Ryle, J. C. (1860). Assurance. Rutherford's Letter. 1637. In *Home truths: Being miscellaneous addresses and tracts, volume 1* (6th ed., p. 266). Ipswich: William Hunt.
#123-See - E, J. (1883). Faith, trial of. In *The Voice of wisdom: a treasury of moral truths from the best authors* (p. 52). Edinburgh: W.P. Nimmo & Co.

Jeff Ryal
http://www.goodjustice.com/
#33-Freedom

J.C. Ryle (10 May 1816 – 10 June 1900)
https://en.wikipedia.org/wiki/J._C._Ryle
#286-Many - Ryle, J. C. (1880). John XX. 24-31. In *Expository Thoughts on the Gospels: For Family and Private Use with the text complete, St. John. Volume 3* (p. 406). New York, NY: Robert Carter and Brothers.

S

Saadi (1208 - 1291 or 1292)
https://en.wikipedia.org/wiki/Saadi_Shirazi

#266-Bad - Edwards, T. (1891). Fortune. In *A Dictionary of Thoughts: Being a Cyclopedia of Laconic Quotations from the best authors, both ancient and modern* (p. 183). New York, NY: Cassell Publishing Company.

#55-Easy - Ethics of intellect. - CCCXVI. Nature. (1877). In M. D. Conway (Ed.), *The Sacred Anthology (Oriental): A Book of Ethnical Scriptures* (5th ed., p. 231). New York, NY: Henry Hold and Company.

Bhagavan Sathya Sai Baba (23 November 1926 – 24 April 2011)
https://en.wikipedia.org/wiki/Sathya_Sai_Baba
#317-Ahead - Sai Baba, S. (2014). *Sathya Sai Teachings* (p. 143). Dr. Purushothaman (Ed.). Kollam, Kerala, India: Centre for human perfection.

Jacques-Henri Bernardin de Saint-Pierre (19 January 1737 – 21 January 1814)
https://en.wikipedia.org/wiki/Jacques-Henri_Bernardin_de_Saint-Pierre
#141-Order - Saint-Pierre, B. (1835). Recapitulation. In *St. Pierre's Studies of nature* (H. Hunter, Trans.) (p. 393). Philadelphia, PA: Joseph J Woodward.

Saint Francis de Sales (21 August 1567 – 28 December 1622)
https://en.wikipedia.org/wiki/Francis_de_Sales
#105-Patience - De Sales, F. (n.d.). Quoted by Bishop Jean-Pierre Camus in The Spirit of Saint Francis de Sales, section "Upon Discouragement". Retrieved October 31, 2017, from https://en.wikiquote.org/wiki/Francis_de_Sales

Sallust (86 – 35 BC)
https://en.wikipedia.org/wiki/Sallust
#316-Battle - DAY, E. P. (1884). Oratory. In *Day's Collacon: an encyclopædia of prose quotations. Consisting of beautiful thoughts, choice extracts, and sayings, of the most eminent writers of all nations, from the earliest ages to the present times* (p. 644). New York and London: International Printing and Publishing Office, Sampson Low, Marston, Searle, and Rivington.

Mr. Savanar
#177-Fight - 268. (1772). In *A Cluster of Canaan's Grapes. Being select sentences and extracts from the most Evangelical old Divines* (p. 53). London: Printed for Joseph Gurney.

Friedrich Schiller (10 November 1759 – 9 May 1805)
https://en.wikipedia.org/wiki/Friedrich_Schiller
#59-Accomplish - Wood, J. (1893). He who. In *Dictionary of Quotations from Ancient and Modern English and Foreign Sources* (p. 152). London and New York: Frederick Warne and Co.

#51-Moment - Ballou, M. M. (1886). Present. In *Edge-tools of speech: Selected and arranged* (p. 329). Boston, MA: Ticknor and Company.

#77-Play - W. (1899). In J. Wood (Ed.), *Dictionary of Quotations from Ancient and Modern, English and Foreign sources* (p. 518). London and New York: Frederick Warne and Co.

#4-Stupid - Ballou, M. M. (1886). Stupidity. In *Edge-tools of speech: Selected and arranged* (p. 475). Boston, MA: Ticknor and Company.

Sir Walter Scott (15 August 1771 – 21 September 1832)
https://en.wikipedia.org/wiki/Walter_Scott
#107-Attitude - Scott, W. D. (1911). Chapter VI. Wages. In *Increasing Human Efficiency in Business, a contribution to the psychology of business* (p. 134). New York, NY: The Macmillan Company.

George de Scudery (22 August 1601 – 14 May 1667)
https://en.wikipedia.org/wiki/Georges_de_Scud%C3%A9ry

#86-Risk - 202. (1904). In W. F. King (Ed.), *Classical and foreign quotations: A polyglot manual of historical and literary sayings, noted passages in poetry and prose phrases, proverbs, and bons mots* (3rd ed., p. 26). London: J. Whitaker & Sons, Limited.

#328-Victory - Douglas, C. N. (1915). Victory. In *Forty thousand sublime and beautiful thoughts gathered from the roses, clover blossoms, geraniums, violets, morning-glories, and pansies of literature* (p. 1875). New York, NY: Christian Herald.
http://www.giga-usa.com/quotes/authors/george_scuderi_a001.htm

John Selden (16 December 1584 – 30 November 1654)
https://en.wikipedia.org/wiki/John_Selden
#57-Content - Wood, J. (1899). Humility. In *Dictionary of quotations from ancient, modern, English and foreign sources* (p. 163). London: Frederick Warne and Co.

Seneca - Lucius Annaeus Seneca (4 BC-AD 65)
https://en.wikipedia.org/wiki/Seneca_the_Younger
#213-Discipline - Wood, J. (1899). No Artist. In *Dictionary of quotations from ancient, modern, English and foreign sources* (p. 301). London and New York: Frederick Warne and Co.

#158-Path - Walsh, W. S. (1921). Experience. Seneca. (Epistolae. vi. 5) In *The international encyclopedia of prose and poetical quotations from the literature of the world including the following languages: English, Latin, Greek, French, Spanish, Persian, Italian, German, Chinese, Hebrew and others* (p. 243). Philadelphia, PA: The John C. Winston Company.

#118-Poor - Hamerton, P. G. (1894). Seneca. In *The Greatest Works of the Greatest Authors, Ancient and Modern* (p. 597).

#113-Speak - Hamerton, P. G. (1894). Seneca. In *The Greatest Works of the Greatest Authors, Ancient and Modern* (p. 595).

#147-Triumph - Hamerton, P. G. (1894). Seneca. In *The Greatest Works of the Greatest Authors, Ancient and Modern* (p. 591).

#79-Truth - Hamerton, P. G. (1894). Seneca. In *The Greatest Works of the Greatest Authors, Ancient and Modern* (p. 594).

#130-Uncertainty- Southgate, H. (1862). Time-Loss of. In *Many thoughts of many minds: Being a treasury of reference consisting of selections from the writings of the most celebrated authors, from the earlies to the present time* (3rd ed., p. 624). London: Griffin, Bohn, and Company.

Kim Serafini
https://www.mindpt.com/mindpt
#140-Awake

Marquise De Sevigne (5 February 1626 – 17 April 1696)
https://en.wikipedia.org/wiki/Marie_de_Rabutin-Chantal,_marquise_de_S%C3%A9vign%C3%A9
#298-Pretending - DAY, E. P. (1884). Thought. In *Day's Collacon: an encyclopaedia of prose quotations. Consisting of beautiful thoughts, choice extracts, and sayings, of the most eminent writers of all nations, from the earliest ages to the present times* (p. 941). New York and London: International Printing and Publishing Office, Sampson Low, Marston, Searle, and Rivington.

William Shakespeare (26 April 1564 - 23 April 1616)
https://en.wikipedia.org/wiki/William_Shakespeare
http://shakespeare.mit.edu/index.html
#318-Behind - Shakespeare, W., Johnson, S., Stevens, G., Clark, W. G., Wright, W. A., & Cross, J. (1891). Concordance of familiar gems. In *The complete works of Shakespeare: With life, compendium, and concordance: illustrated with seventy-one photogravures* (p. 275). Philadelphia, PA: Gebbie & Co., Publishers.

#168-Blame - Douglas, C. N. (1915). Guilt. In *Forty thousand sublime and beautiful thoughts gathered from the roses, clover blossoms, geraniums, violets, morning-glories, and pansies of literature* (p. 909).

#16-Deny - Berkeley, E. (1853). *The world's laconics: Or, The best thoughts of the best authors* (p. 416). New York, NY: M.W. Dodd.

#216-Doubt - Shakespeare, W. (1602). Troilus and Cressida - Act II. Retrieved October 4, 2017, from https://en.wikiquote.org/wiki/Troilus_and_Cressida

#325-Expand - Edwards, T. (1891). Virtue. In *A Dictionary of Thoughts: Being a Cyclopedia of Laconic Quotations from the Best Authors of the World, Both Ancient and Modern* (p. 609). New York, NY: Cassell Publishing Company.

#112-Fall - Shakespeare, W. (1603). Measure for Measure - Act II. Retrieved October 4, 2017, from https://en.wikiquote.org/wiki/Measure_for_Measure

#285-Few - Shakespeare, W. (1623). SCENE I. Rousillon. The COUNT's palace. Retrieved from http://shakespeare.mit.edu/allswell/allswell.1.1.html

#226-Late - Shakespeare, W. (1602). SCENE II. A room in the Garter Inn. Retrieved from http://shakespeare.mit.edu/merry_wives/merry_wives.2.2.html

#25-Laughter - Shakespeare, W. (1600). SCENE I. Venice. A Street. Retrieved from http://shakespeare.mit.edu/merchant/merchant.1.1.html

#246-Less - Conduct. (1911). In G. B. Strand (Ed.), *Conduct, health, good fortune* (p. 20). Chicago, IL: A.C. McClurg & Co.

#346-Lose - Shakespeare, W. (1623). SCENE IV. A nunnery. Retrieved from http://shakespeare.mit.edu/measure/measure.1.4.html

#329-Own - Shakespeare, W. (1602). SCENE III. A room in Polonius' house. Retrieved from http://shakespeare.mit.edu/hamlet/hamlet.1.3.html

#103-Question - Shakespeare, W. (1602). SCENE I. A room in the castle. Retrieved from http://shakespeare.mit.edu/hamlet/hamlet.3.1.html

#204-Nothing - Shakespeare, W. (1602). SCENE II. A room in the castle. Retrieved from http://shakespeare.mit.edu/hamlet/hamlet.2.2.html

#120-Zeal - Griffiths, R., & Griffiths, G. E. (1824). Howard on Wolsey and his times. In *The Monthly Review* (p. 294). London: A. & R. Spottiswoode, New-Street-Square.

Henry Wheeler Shaw (1818- October 11, 1885)
https://pfaffs.web.lehigh.edu/node/54286

#279-Say - Wom. (1896). In L. Klopsch (Ed.), *Many Thoughts of Many Minds: A Treasury of Quotations from the Literature of Every Land and Every Age* (p. 296). New York, NY: The Christian Herald, Louis Klopsch, Proprietor.

#4-Stupid - Ballou, M. M. (1886). Stupidity. In *Edge-tools of speech: Selected and arranged* (p. 475). Boston, MA: Ticknor and Company.

Mary Shelley (30 August 1797 – 1 February 1851)
https://en.wikipedia.org/wiki/Mary_Shelley

#18-Chaos - Shelley, M. W. (1818). In the Introduction to Frankenstein. Retrieved October 22, 2017, from https://en.wikiquote.org/wiki/Chaos

Percy Bysshe Shelley (4 August 1792 – 8 July 1822)
https://en.wikipedia.org/wiki/Percy_Bysshe_Shelley

#161-Cheer - Ward, A. L. (1889). Poets. In *A Dictionary of Quotations in Prose: From English and Foreign Authors Including Translations from Ancient Sources* (p. 424). New York, NY: Thomas Y. Crowell Company.

#48-Imagine - American Literature. (1850). In W. H. Bidwell (Ed.), *The Eclectic Magazine of Foreign Literature, Science, and Art, Volume 20* (p. 330). New York, NY: Edward O. Jenkins, Printer.

Marci Shimoff
http://www.marcishimoff.com/
Professional Speaker
#1 *NY Times* Bestselling Author,
Happy for No Reason, Love For No Reason, and Chicken Soup for the Woman's Soul
#27-Purpose

Anna Shipton (1815-1901)
https://en.wikiquote.org/wiki/Anna_Shipton
#53-Complete - Gilbert, J. H. (1895). Kindness. In *Dictionary of Burning Words of Brilliant Writers: A Cyclopædia of Quotations from the literature of all ages* (p. 362). New York, NY: Wilbur B. Ketcham.

Albert B. Simpson (December 15, 1843 – October 29, 1919)
https://en.wikipedia.org/wiki/Albert_Benjamin_Simpson
#173-Ask - Simpson, A. B. (1895). Chapter XXI. The Spirit and the resurrection. In *The Holy Spirit, or Power From On High. An unfolding of the doctrine of the Holy Spirit in the old and new testaments. Part 1. The Old Testament* (p. 335). New York, NY: The Christian Alliance Publishing Co.
#364-Expectation - Simpson, A. B. (1895). Chapter XXI. The Spirit and the resurrection. In *The Holy Spirit, or Power From On High. An unfolding of the doctrine of the Holy Spirit in the old and new testaments. Part 1. The Old Testament* (pp. 334-335). New York, NY: The Christian Alliance Publishing Co.
#361-Rejoice - Simpson, A. B. (1890). The larger life. In *A Larger Christian Life* (pp. 101-102). New York, NY: The Christian Alliance Publishing Co.
#254-Stagnant - Simpson, A. B. (1890). Filled with the spirit. In *A Larger Christian Life* (p. 81). New York, NY: The Christian Alliance Publishing Co.

Samuel Smiles (23 December 1812 – 16 April 1904)
https://en.wikipedia.org/wiki/Samuel_Smiles
#198-Journey - E, S. P., & Punshon, W. M. (1874). Hope. In *The new handbook of illustration; or, Treasury of themes, meditations, anecdotes, analogies, parables, similitudes, types, emblems, symbols, apologues, allegories, and expositions of scripture truth and Christian life* (p. 180). London: Elliot Stock.
#352-Success - Allibone, S. A. (1876). Industry. In *Prose Quotations from Socrates to Macaulay, with indexes: Authors 544, subjects 571, quotations 8810* (p. 352). Philadelphia, PA: J. B. Lippincott & Co.

Adam Smith (16 June 1723 – 17 July 1790)
https://en.wikipedia.org/wiki/Adam_Smith
#304-Part - Smith, A. (1902). Of the wages of labor. In *The wealth of nations, Part 1* (p. 139). New York, NY: P. F. Collier & Son.

Logan Pearsall Smith (18 October 1865 – 2 March 1946)
https://en.wikipedia.org/wiki/Logan_Pearsall_Smith
#312-Vocation - Smith, L. P. (1931). In Afterthoughts (1931), Art and Letters. Retrieved October 22, 2017, from https://en.wikiquote.org/wiki/Vocation

Tobias Smollett (19 March 1721 – 17 September 1771)
https://en.wikipedia.org/wiki/Tobias_Smollett
#113-Speak - Smollett, T., & Anderson, R. (1806). The Regicide: A Tragedy. In *The miscellaneous works of Tobias Smollett, M.D with memoirs of his life and writings* (3rd ed., p. 416). Edinburgh: Mundell, Doig & Stevenson.

Socrates (470 – 399 BC)
https://en.wikipedia.org/wiki/Socrates

#56-Hard - The value of good reading. (1884). In T. Powner & W. Groves (Eds.), *Our Country and Village Schools, Volume 6* (p. 345). Decatur, IL: Powner, Ackerman & Co., Publishers.
#270-Word - Socrates. (n.d.). Socrates - Wikiquote. Retrieved December 5, 2016, from https://en.wikiquote.org/wiki/Socrates

Sophocles (497/6 – 406/5 BC)
https://en.wikipedia.org/wiki/Sophocles
#365-Ignore - Sophocles. (n.d.). Ajax, Line 964. Retrieved December 17, 2016, from https://en.wikiquote.org/wiki/Sophocles

Robert Southey (12 August 1774 – 21 March 1843)
https://en.wikipedia.org/wiki/Robert_Southey
#141-Order - Wood, J. (1893). Optimum. In *Dictionary of quotations from ancient, modern, English and foreign sources* (p. 336). London and New York: Frederick Warne and Co.

Edmund Spenser (1552/1553 – 13 January 1599)
https://en.wikipedia.org/wiki/Edmund_Spenser
#118-Poor - Spencer, E. (1758). Canto IX., XXX. In *The Fairy Queen, Volume 2* (p. 413). London: Printed for J. and R. Tonson in the Strand.

Herbert Spencer (27 April 1820 – 8 December 1903)
https://en.wikipedia.org/wiki/Herbert_Spencer
#243-Selfish - Ballou, M. M. (1886). Law. In *Edge-tools of speech: Selected and arranged* (p. 267). Boston, MA: Ticknor and Company.

Rev. Francis Spirago - Professor of Theology
#203-Everything - Spirago, F. (1899). The Precepts of the Love of God. The Commandments. In R. F. Clarke (Ed.), *The Catechism Explained: An Exhaustive Exposition of the Christian Religion, with special reference to the present state of society and the spirit of the age* (p. 292). New York, Cincinnati, Chicago: Benziger Brothers.

Charles Haddon Spurgeon (June 19, 1834 – January 31, 1892)
https://simple.wikiquote.org/wiki/Charles_Spurgeon
http://www.spurgeon.org/
#207-Much - Spurgeon, C. H. (1885). Though he were dead. In *Return, O Shulamite! And other sermons preached in 1884* (p. 185). New York, NY: Robert Carter & Brothers.
#304-Part - Perry, S. A. (1905). Miscellaneous. In *Spiritual flashlights from godly men and women* (p. 359). Chicago, IL: S.B. Shaw.
#240-Refrain - Spurgeon, C. H. (1858). Chapter III. Jesus Desired. In *The Saint and his Saviour; or, The progress of the soul in the knowledge of Jesus. By the Rev. C. H. Spurgeon* (p. 129). New York, Boston, and Chicago: Sheldon, Blakeman & Co., Gould & Lincoln., S. C. Griggs & Co.

Philip Dormer Stanhope, 4th Earl of Chesterfield (22 September 1694 – 24 March 1773)
https://en.wikipedia.org/wiki/Philip_Stanhope,_4th_Earl_of_Chesterfield
#55-Easy - Stanhope Earl of Chesterfield, P. D. (1799). Letter writing. In *Maxims selected from the writings of Philip Dormer Stanhope, Earl of Chesterfield* (p. 52).
#210-Take - Conklin, G. W. (1906). Prudence. In *Conklin's who wrote that?: Comprising 3216 prose selections* (p. 186). Philadelphia, PA: Geo. W. Ogilvie & David McKay.

Dean Stanley (13 December 1815 – 18 July 1881)
https://en.wikipedia.org/wiki/Arthur_Stanley_(priest)

#253-Turn - Hall, A. W. (1887). Thoughts from Dean Stanley's "Life of Thomas Arnold." In *Great Thoughts from Master Minds, Volume 8* (p. 282). London: A. Bradley.

Sir Richard Steele (12 March 1672 – 1 September 1729)
https://en.wikipedia.org/wiki/Richard_Steele
#211-Load - Addison, J., & Steele, R. (1860). No. 100. Monday, June 25, 1711. In *The Spectator. A new edition with biographical notices of the contributors complete in one volume* (p. 148). Cincinnati, OH: Applegate & Co.

Laurence Sterne (24 November 1713 – 18 March 1768)
https://en.wikipedia.org/wiki/Laurence_Sterne
#106-Impatience - Wood, J. (1893). Imagination. In *Dictionary of quotations from ancient, modern, English and foreign sources* (p. 183). London: Frederick Warne and Co.

Abel Stevens (1815 - 1897)
https://en.wikipedia.org/wiki/Abel_Stevens
#251-Labor - Douglas, C. N. (1915). Abstinence. In *Forty thousand sublime and beautiful thoughts gathered from the roses, clover blossoms, geraniums, violets, morning-glories, and pansies of literature* (p. 12). New York, NY: Christian Herald.

Robert Louis Stevenson (13 November 1850 – 3 December 1894)
http://robert-louis-stevenson.org/
https://en.wikipedia.org/wiki/Robert_Louis_Stevenson
#47-Focus - A new leaf. (1908). In J. E & H. S (Eds.), *The Melody of the Heart* (2nd ed., p. 118). New York, NY: Frederick A. Stokes Company.
#274-Hurry - An apology for idlers. (1877). In G. Smith & W. M. Thackeray (Eds.), *The Cornhill Magazine, Volume 36 edited by George Smith, William Makepeace Thackeray* (p. 85). London: Smith, Elder & Co.
#182-Neglect - An apology for idlers. (1877). In G. Smith & W. M. Thackeray (Eds.), *The Cornhill Magazine, Volume 36 edited by George Smith, William Makepeace Thackeray* (p. 84). London: Smith, Elder & Co.

Gregory Stock
http://www.gregorystock.net/
#228-Reduction

Thomas Stott (1755-1829)
#129-Confidence - Oldschool, O. (1808). Ode to Columbia. *The Port Folio, Vol. VI* (p. 406). Philadelphia, PA: Printed by Smith and Maxwell.

Harriet Beecher Stowe (14 June 1811 – 1 July 1896)
https://en.wikipedia.org/wiki/Harriet_Beecher_Stowe
#202-Get - The Schoolroom. (1898). In H. R. Pattengill (Ed.), *Michigan School Moderator, Volume 19*(p. 18). Lansing, MI: Michigan State Teachers Association.
#74-Lazy - Stowe, H. B. (1864). Household Papers and Stories, Ch. 6. Retrieved December 6, 2017, from https://en.wikiquote.org/wiki/Harriet_Beecher_Stowe

Charles Sumner (January 6, 1811 – March 11, 1874)
https://en.wikiquote.org/wiki/Charles_Sumner
#45-Love - The religious telescope, September 28, 1904. (1904). In *The Religious Telescope, Volume 70* (p. 1245). Dayton, OH: Official Publication of the Church of the United Brethren in Christ.

Lester Sumrall (February 15, 1913 – April 28, 1996)
https://en.wikipedia.org/wiki/Lester_Sumrall
https://lesea.com/about-us/legacy/
Taken from Faith Can Change Your World by Lester Sumrall. Copyright © (1984, second printing 1991) by Lester Sumrall Evangelistic Assn, Inc. Used by permission of LeSEA Publishing. All rights reserved.
#202-Get, #304-Part, #126-Retain

Billy Sunday (November 19, 1862 – November 6, 1935)
https://en.wikipedia.org/wiki/Billy_Sunday
#41-Cause - Ellis, W. T., & Sunday, B. (1917). Speech - seasoned with salt. In *"Billy" Sunday, the man and his message* (p. 72). Philadelphia, PA: The John C. Winston Company.
#280-Evidence - Ellis, W. T., & Sunday, B. (1917). The Christian's Daily Helper. In *"Billy" Sunday, the man and his message* (p. 365). Philadelphia, PA: The John C. Winston Company.
#304-Part - Ellis, W. T., & Sunday, B. (1917). Chapter XXII. The revival on trial. In *"Billy" Sunday, the man and his message* (p. 295). Philadelphia, PA: The John C. Winston Company.
#267-Never - **Question:** Ellis, W. T., & Sunday, B. (1917). Speech - seasoned with salt. In *"Billy" Sunday, the man and his message* (p. 79). Philadelphia, PA: The John C. Winston Company.
#249-Power - Ellis, W. T., & Sunday, B. (1917). Chapter XXII. The revival on trial. In *"Billy" Sunday, the man and his message* (p. 288). Philadelphia, PA: The John C. Winston Company.

Publilius Syrus (85 – 43 BC)
https://en.wikipedia.org/wiki/Publilius_Syrus
#336-Poverty - E, S. P., & Punshon, W. M. (1874). Avarice. In *The new handbook of illustration; or, Treasury of themes, meditations, anecdotes, analogies, parables, similitudes, types, emblems, symbols, apologues, allegories, and expositions of scripture truth and Christian life* (p. 29). London: Elliot Stock.
#245-More - Bartlett, J. (1895). Publius Syrus, Maxim 528. In *Familiar quotations: A collection of passages, phrases, and proverbs traced to their sources in ancient and modern literature* (9th ed., p. 711). Boston, MA: Little, Brown, and company.
#23-Worthy - Wood, J. (1893). Beneficium. In *Dictionary of quotations: From ancient and modern English and foreign sources* (p. 28). London and New York: Frederick Warne and co.

T

M. T.
#211-Load - Perry, S. A. (1905). Miscellaneous. In *Spiritual flashlights from godly men and women* (p. 324). Chicago, IL: S.B. Shaw.

Publius Cornelius Tacitus (56 – 120 AD)
https://en.wikipedia.org/wiki/Tacitus
#130-Uncertainty - Macdonnel, D. E. (1826). VE-VE. In *A Dictionary of Quotations in most frequent use, taken chiefly from the Latin and French, but comprising many from the Greek, Spanish, and Italian languages, translated into English* (9th ed., p. 407). London: Printed for Geo. B. Whittaker.
#366-Review - Hamerton, P. G. (1894). Tacitus. In *The Greatest Works of the Greatest Authors, Ancient and Modern* (p. 603).

Jeremy Taylor (15 August 1613 – 13 August 1667)
https://en.wikipedia.org/wiki/Jeremy_Taylor
#106-Impatience - Taylor, J., & Patterson, J. B. (1834). Of contentedness in all estates and accidents. In *The beauties of Jeremy Taylor, D.D. bishop of Down, Connor, and Dromore. Selected from his works, with an essay on his life and writings* (p. 359). Glasgow: Glasgow: Blackie & Son.

#264-Sorrow - Richardson, C. (1875). Bal. vol ii. Ser. 17. In *A new dictionary of the English language, combining explanation with etymology: And illustrated by quotations from the best authorities* (p. 126). London: G. Bell and Sons.

Tamara Taylor
Verbal Confirmation
#316-Battle

Sir William Temple (25 April 1628 – 27 January 1699)
https://en.wikipedia.org/wiki/Sir_William_Temple,_1st_Baronet
#338-Fast - Pat. (1896). In L. Klopsch (Ed.), *Many Thoughts of Many Minds: A Treasury of Quotations from the Literature of Every Land and Every Age* (p. 205). New York, NY: The Christian Herald, Louis Klopsch, Proprietor.
#117-Rich - Hall, A. W. (1887). Our Life. In *Great Thoughts from Master Minds, Volume 8* (p. 25). London: A. Bradley.

Terence (195/185 – 159 BC)
https://en.wikiquote.org/wiki/Terence
#294-Demand - Walsh, W. S. (1908). Argument - Terence. Phormio. Viii. 2. 6. In *The International Encyclopedia of Prose and Poetical Quotations* (p. 55). Philadelphia, PA: The John C. Winston Company.

Saint Teresa of Avila (28 March 1515 – 4 October 1582)
https://en.wikipedia.org/wiki/Teresa_of_%C3%81vila
#21-Flow - Teresa, & Zimmerman, B. (1912). The first mansions. II The human soul. In *The interior castle: Or The mansions. Translated from the autograph of Saint Teresa by the Benedictines of Stanbrook. Revised with introd. and additional notes by Benedict Zimmerman* (Stanbrook Abbey, Trans.) (2nd ed., p. 14). New York, Cincinnati, Chicago: Benziger Brothers.

William Makepeace Thackeray (18 July 1811 – 24 December 1863)
https://en.wikipedia.org/wiki/William_Makepeace_Thackeray
#252-Fun - If any. (1899). In J. Wood (Ed.), *Dictionary of Quotations from Ancient and Modern, English and Foreign sources* (p. 172). London and New York: Frederick Warne and Co.

Theophrastus (371 – 287 BC)
https://en.wikipedia.org/wiki/Theophrastus
#94-Judgment - DAY, E. P. (1884). Oratory. In *Day's Collacon: an encyclopaedia of prose quotations. Consisting of beautiful thoughts, choice extracts, and sayings, of the most eminent writers of all nations, from the earliest ages to the present times* (p. 644). New York and London: International Printing and Publishing Office, Sampson Low, Marston, Searle, and Rivington.

Henry David Thoreau (12 July 1817 – 6 May 1862)
https://en.wikipedia.org/wiki/Henry_David_Thoreau
https://www.walden.org/
#132-Appreciate - Thoreau, H. D., In Sanborn, F. B., & Emerson, R. W. (1906). John Brown's Deed. In *The writings of Henry David Thoreau, Volume 1. A week on the Concord and Merrimack Rivers* (p. 423). Boston and New York: Houghton Mifflin Company.
#62-Dark - Thoreau, H. D. (1906). Accident in the best things March 11, 1859. In B. Torrey (Ed.), *The Writings of Henry David Thoreau. Journal. Volume XII. March 2, 1859-November 30, 1859* (p. 39). Boston and New York: Houghton, Mifflin, and Company.
#20-Dream - Thoreau, H. D. (1910). Conclusion. In *Walden* (p. 427). New York, NY: Thomas Y. Crowell & Company.

#235-Ignorance - Thoreau, H. D., In Sanborn, F. B., & Emerson, R. W. (1906). Wednesday, The Good how can we trust. In *The writings of Henry David Thoreau, Volume 1. A week on the Concord and Merrimack Rivers* (p. 301). Boston and New York: Houghton Mifflin Company.

#344-Inexperience - Thoreau, H. D., In Sanborn, F. B., & Emerson, R. W. (1906). Wednesday, Lately, alas, I knew a gentle boy. In *The writings of Henry David Thoreau, Volume 1. A week on the Concord and Merrimack Rivers* (p. 278). Boston and New York: Houghton Mifflin Company.

#226-Late - Thoreau, H. D. (1910). Economy. In *Walden* (p. 8). New York, NY: Thomas Y. Crowell & Company.

#51-Moment - Thoreau, H. D. (1906). Times and seasons. In B. Torrey (Ed.), *The Writings of Henry David Thoreau Journal* (p. 159). Boston and New York: Houghton, Mifflin & Co.

#85-Refuge - Thoreau, H. D., In Sanborn, F. B., & Emerson, R. W. (1906). Friday. All things are current found. In *The writings of Henry David Thoreau, Volume 1. A week on the Concord and Merrimack Rivers* (p. 418). Boston and New York: Houghton Mifflin Company.

#166-Sit - Thoreau, H. D. (1851, August 19). Journals (1838-1859). Retrieved August 20, 2016, from https://en.wikiquote.org/wiki/Henry_David_Thoreau

#210-Take - Thoreau, H. D. (1910). Economy. In *Walden* (p. 11). New York, NY: Thomas Y. Crowell & Company.

#303-Whole - Thoreau, H. D. (1840, April 20). Journals (1838-1859). Retrieved August 26, 2016, from https://en.wikiquote.org/wiki/Henry_David_Thoreau

T. Thompson
#239-Practice - Thompson, T. (1884). Wisdom. In *Thoughts on men and things; or, Essays on familiar topics* (p. 141). Manchester: John Heywood.

W. Gardner Thrall
#39-Meditate - Value of Religious Meditation in Every-day Life. (1907). In J. N. Hallock (Ed.), *The Christian Work and the Evangelist, Volume 82* (p. 552). New York, NY: The Christian Work and the Evangelist.

John Tillotson (October 1630 – 22 November 1694)
https://en.wikipedia.org/wiki/John_Tillotson
#75-Integrity - Allibone, S. A. (1876). Consistency. In *Prose Quotations from Socrates to Macaulay, with indexes: Authors 544, subjects 571, quotations 8810* (p. 127). Philadelphia, PA: J. B. Lippincott & Co.

Frank Tipler
http://129.81.170.14/~tipler/
#348-Conclude

Leo Tolstoy (28 August 1828 – 20 November 1910)
https://en.wikipedia.org/wiki/Leo_Tolstoy
#159-Change - Tolstoy, L. (1900). "Three Methods Of Reform" in Pamphlets: Translated from the Russian (1900) as translated by Aylmer Maude, p. 29. Retrieved November 14, 2017, from https://en.wikiquote.org/wiki/Leo_Tolstoy
#341-Life - Tolstoy, L. (n.d.). War and Peace (1865–1867; 1869), Bk. XIV, Ch. 15. Retrieved August 28, 2017, from https://en.wikiquote.org/wiki/Leo_Tolstoy

Charlotte Elizabeth Tonna (1 October 1790 – 12 July 1846)
https://en.wikipedia.org/wiki/Charlotte_Elizabeth_Tonna
#258-Submission - Gilbert, J. H. (1895). Cross bearing. In *Dictionary of Burning Words of Brilliant Writers: A Cyclopædia of Quotations from the literature of all ages* (p. 170). New York, NY: Wilbur B. Ketcham.

Richard Chenevix Trench (9 September 1807 – 28 March 1886)
https://en.wikipedia.org/wiki/Richard_Chenevix_Trench
#38-Reduction - Punshon, W. M. (1874). Fall of man. In *The new handbook of illustration; or, Treasury of themes, meditation, anecdotes, analogies, parables, similitudes, types, emblems, symbols, apologues, allegories, and expositions of scripture truth and Christian life* (p. 138). London: Elliot Stock.

Ralph Waldo Trine (October 26, 1866 – November 8, 1958) In, *In tune with the infinite or fullness of peace, power and plenty by Ralph Waldo Trine* (p. 24). New York, NY: Thomas Y. Crowell & Co.
#165-Stand - Trine, R. W. (1897). Wisdom and interior illumination. In, *In tune with the infinite or fullness of peace, power and plenty by Ralph Waldo Trine* (p. 109). New York, NY: Thomas Y. Crowell & Co.
#90-Weakness - Trine, R. W. (1897). The realization of perfect peace. In, *In tune with the infinite or fullness of peace, power and plenty by Ralph Waldo Trine* (p. 148). New York, NY: Thomas Y. Crowell & Co.

Vironika Tugaleva
http://www.vironika.org/
#23-Worthy

Martin Farquhar Tupper (17 July 1810 – November 1889)
https://en.wikipedia.org/wiki/Martin_Farquhar_Tupper
#307-Messenger - Douglas, C. N. (1915). Baby - Babyhood. In *Forty thousand sublime and beautiful thoughts gathered from the roses, clover blossoms, geraniums, violets, morning-glories, and pansies of literature* (p. 140). New York, NY: The Christian Herald.
#233-Today - Douglas, C. N. (1915). Today. In *Forty thousand sublime and beautiful thoughts gathered from the roses, clover blossoms, geraniums, violets, morning-glories, and pansies of literature* (p. 1802). New York, NY: The Christian Herald.

John Tyndall (2 August 1820 – 4 December 1893)
https://en.wikipedia.org/wiki/John_Tyndall
#61-Light - Tyndall, J. (1870). On the Methods and Tendencies of Physical Investigation, p. 7. Retrieved November 24, 2017, from https://en.wikiquote.org/wiki/John_Tyndall

Lao Tzu (6th-5th C. BCE – Died 531BCE)
https://en.wikipedia.org/wiki/Laozi
#55-Easy - Government. (1886). In M. M. Ballou (Ed.), *Edge-tools of Speech* (p. 190).

U

Author Unknown
#293-Contribution - *The Dayspring - Volume 10* (p. 136). (1881). Boston, MA: Unitarian Sunday-School Society
#255-Hope - Facts, hints, gems, and poetry. (1866). In J. F. Winks (Ed.), *The Christian pioneer; A monthly magazine, Issued in numbers, one halfpenny each. Volumes XX* (p. 50). London: Simpkin, Marshall, and Co.
#263-Joy - Butler, H. E. (1900). New practical methods. In *The Occult and Biological Journal, Volume 1* (p. 466). Applegate, CA: Esoteric Publishing Company.
#61-Light - Just Shine. (1907). In R. A. Bischoff (Ed.), *The Lutheran Pioneer, Volume 29* (p. 56). St. Louis, MO: The Evangelical Lutheran Synodical Conference of North America.
#137-Peace - La Clochette - Wikipedia. (n.d.). Retrieved October 13, 2017, from https://en.wikipedia.org/wiki/La_Clochette

#73-Perseverance - Wooléver, A. (1891). Perseverance and Obstinacy. In *Encyclopaedia of quotations: a treasury of wisdom, wit and humor, odd comparisons and proverbs: Authors, 931; subjects, 1393; quotations, 10,299* (p. 314). Philadelphia, PA: D. McKay.

#297-Prepare - Strengthening deficient faculties. (1907). In General Board of the Church of Jesus Christ of Latter-day Saints (Ed.), *The Children's Friend, Volume 6* (p. 109). Salt Lake City, UT: The Desert News.

#320-Present - Bric-A-Brac. (1882). In G. M. Adam (Ed.), *Rose-Belford's Canadian Monthly and National Review, Volume 8; Volume 21* (p. 440). Toronto: Rose-Belford Publishing Company.

#143-Promise - Gleanings. (1898). In H. R. Pattengill (Ed.), *Michigan School Moderator-topics, Volume 18* (p. 425). Lansing, MI: Timely Topics.

#1-Resolution - EXTRACTS, & KNOX, V. (1800). 273 - Inconstancy. In *Elegant Extracts; or, Useful and entertaining passages in prose. [Edited by Vicesimus Knox.] Book third & fourth* (p. 372). London.

#17-Transcend - Quote of the Day: 130 Years v. 3 Years – Theological Jon. (n.d.). Retrieved from https://theologicaljon.com/2017/05/20/quote-of-the-day-130-years-v-3-years/

#340-Yourself - An alphabet for beginners, on the beginning of each month. (1857). In J. D. Caldwell (Ed.), *The Ohio Journal of Education, Volume 6* (p. 348). Columbus, OH: Follett, Foster, and Company.

Thomas Cogswell Upham (January 30, 1799 – April 2, 1872)
https://en.wikipedia.org/wiki/Thomas_Cogswell_Upham
#283-Confusion - Upham, T. C. (1841). The sense of sight. In *Elements of Mental Philosophy Embracing the Two Departments of the Intellect and the Sensibilities, Volume 1* (p. 119). New York, NY: Harper & Brothers.

George P. Upton (1834-1919)
#69-Sunshine - Douglas, C. N. (1915). Love. In *Forty thousand sublime and beautiful thoughts gathered from the roses, clover blossoms, geraniums, violets, morning-glories, and pansies of literature* (p. 1106). New York, NY: The Christian Herald.

V

Virgil (October 15, 70 – September 21, 19 BC)
https://en.wikipedia.org/wiki/Virgil
#277-Ruin - Hoyt, J. K., & Ward, A. L. (1886). Philosophy. In *The Cyclopædia of Practical Quotations. English and Latin, with an appendix containing proverbs from the Latin and modern foreign languages* (8th ed., p. 553). New York and London: Funk & Wagnalls.

#322-Stretch - Action. (1895). In H. P. Smith & H. K. Johnson (Eds.), *A Dictionary of Terms, Phrases, and Quotations* (p. 522). New York, NY: D. Appleton and Company.

Voltaire (21 November 1694 – 30 May 1778)
https://en.wikipedia.org/wiki/Voltaire
#33-Freedom - Voltaire. (1730). Source Brutus, act II, scene I. Retrieved January 11, 2017, from https://en.wikiquote.org/wiki/Voltaire

#190-Harm - Wheeler, J. M., & Foote, G. W. (1894). His Character and Services. In *Voltaire: a Sketch of His Life and Works: With Selections from His Writings* (p. 64). London: Robert Forder.

#103-Question - Fothergill, J. M. (1883). What to ask. Introduction. In *Aids to diagnosis: Part I-Semeiology* (p. 8). New York, NY: G.P. Putnam's Sons.

#79-Truth - Voltaire. (1738). Deuxième discourse: de la liberté," Sept Discours en Vers sur l'Homme (1738). Retrieved from https://en.wikiquote.org/wiki/Voltaire

Ann Voskamp

http://annvoskamp.com/

Taken from One Thousand Gifts: A Dare to Live Fully Right Where You Are by Ann Voskamp Copyright © 2012 by Zondervan. Use by permission of Zondervan. www.zondervan.com

#124-Miss - Voskamp, A. (2012). First flight. In *One thousand gifts: A dare to live fully right where you are* (p. 57). Zondervan.

#268-Always - Voskamp, A. (2012). A sanctuary of time. In *One thousand gifts: A dare to live fully right where you are* (p. 74). Zondervan.

W

Waldorf

#275-Cease - The Devil's Diary; or, Temptations. (1839). In J. Fraser (Ed.), *Fraser's Magazine for Town and Country, Volume 19* (p. 659). London: James Fraser.

Lew Wallace (April 10, 1827 – February 15, 1905)

https://en.wikipedia.org/wiki/Lew_Wallace

#196-Excessive - Good Fortune. (1911). In G. B. Strand (Ed.), *Conduct, health, good fortune* (p. 56). Chicago, IL: A.C. McClurg & Co.

Booker T. Washington (April 5, 1856 – November 14, 1915)

https://en.wikipedia.org/wiki/Booker_T._Washington

#229-Circumstance - Washington, B. T. (1896, September 30). "Democracy and Education." speech, Institute of Arts and Sciences, Brooklyn NY. Retrieved from https://en.wikiquote.org/wiki/Booker_T._Washington

#170-Overcome - Washington, B. T. (1901). Up from slavery – Chapter II: Boyhood days. Retrieved from https://en.wikiquote.org/wiki/Booker_T._Washington

George Washington (February 22, 1732 – December 14, 1799)

https://en.wikipedia.org/wiki/George_Washington

https://www.whitehouse.gov/1600/presidents/georgewashington

#259-Indulge - Edwards, T. (1908). Morality. In *A Dictionary of Thoughts: Being a Cyclopedia of Laconic Quotations from the best authors, both ancient and Modern* (p. 361). Detroit, MI: F.B. Dickerson Co.

#194-Profane - Edwards, T. (1891). Profanity. In *A Dictionary of Thoughts: Being a Cyclopedia of Laconic Quotations from the best authors, both ancient and modern* (p. 447). New York, NY: Cassell Publishing Company.

#27-Purpose - Texas Bankers' Association. Address of President McAshan. (1903). In *The Bankers Magazine, Volume 66* (p. 861). New York, NY: The Bankers Publishing Co.

#138-Turbulence - Washington, G., & Sparks, J. (1840). To Timothy Pickering, Secretary of War. Mount Vernon, 27 July 1795. In *The writings of George Washington: Being his correspondence, addresses, messages, and other papers, official and private. Volume XI* (p. 40). Boston, MA: Ferdinand Andrews, Publisher.

#188-Virtue - Washington, G. (1788, August 28). George Washington Letter to Alexander Hamilton. Retrieved from https://en.wikiquote.org/wiki/George_Washington

Martha Washington (June 13, 1731 – May 22, 1802)

https://en.wikipedia.org/wiki/Martha_Washington

https://www.whitehouse.gov/1600/first-ladies/marthawashington

#339-Myself - Washington, M. (1789, December 26). Martha Washington - Wikiquote. Retrieved October 20, 2017, from https://en.wikiquote.org/wiki/Martha_Washington

Bishop Watson (1737 - 1816)
https://en.wikipedia.org/wiki/Richard_Watson_(bishop_of_Llandaff)
#103-Question - Wooléver, A. (1878). Discussion. In *Treasury of wisdom, wit and humor, odd comparisons and proverbs* (3rd ed., p. 112). Philadelphia, PA: Claxton.

Doug Wead
http://www.dougwead.com/
#336-Poverty

William Wells
#232-Look - Wells, W. (1854). From Vienna to Venice. In D. W. Clark (Ed.), *The Ladies' Repository* (14th ed., p. 266). Cincinnati: R. P. Thompson.

Charles William Wendte (June 11, 1844 – September 9, 1931)
http://www.harvardsquarelibrary.org/biographies/charles-william-wendte/
#352-Success - Linn, S. P. (1883). Chapter VI. White-Heat. In *Golden Gleams of Thought from the words of leading orators, divines, philosophers, statesmen and poets* (p. 47). Chicago, IL: Jansen, McClurg, & Company.

John Wesley (17 June 1703 – 2 March 1791)
https://en.wikipedia.org/wiki/John_Wesley
#278-Amend - Wesley, J. (1821). *A Plain Account of Christian Perfection* (p. 41). New York, NY: James & John Harper.
#181-Care - Wesley, J. (1821). *A plain account of Christian perfection* (p. 18). New York, NY: James & John Harper.
#128-Prayer - Wesley, J. (1821). *A Plain Account of Christian Perfection* (p. 42). New York, NY: James & John Harper.

Edith Wharton (January 24, 1862 – August 11, 1937)
https://en.wikipedia.org/wiki/Edith_Wharton
#231-Overlook - Wharton, E. (1907, November 19). Edith Wharton - Letter to Robert Grant. Retrieved from https://en.wikiquote.org/wiki/Edith_Wharton

Edwin Percy Whipple (March 8, 1819 – June 16, 1886)
https://en.wikipedia.org/wiki/Edwin_Percy_Whipple
#213-Discipline - Watson, J. M. (1875). Cheerfulness. In *Independent Sixth Reader: Containing a Complete Treatise on elocution, both scientific and practical, illustrated with diagrams ..., Book 6*(p. 271). New York and Chicago: A. S. Barnes & Company.

Henry Benjamin Whipple (February 15, 1822 – September 16, 1901)
https://en.wikiquote.org/wiki/Henry_Benjamin_Whipple
#156-Find - Illustrative quotations and anecdotes. (1886). In J. W. Kirton (Ed.), *The Lay Preacher. A magazine for all Christian workers. Helps for the study, pulpit, platform, and desk* (p. 48). London and New York: F. E. Longley and A. D. F. Randolph & Co.

John H. Whipple (June 13, 1845 – March 23, 1922)
https://dellwoodcemetery.org/2016/09/26/john-h-whipple-past-masonic-grand-master-dead/
#345-Win - Redway, T. H. (1896). Vermont, 1895. In *Proceedings By Freemasons. New Jersey. Grand Lodge* (p. 206). Trenton, NJ: MacCrellish & Quigley, Book, and Job Printers.

Walt Whitman (May 31, 1819 – March 26, 1892)
https://en.wikipedia.org/wiki/Walt_Whitman

#62-Dark - Whitman, W. (n.d.). Walt Whitman - Miracles. Retrieved August 9, 2017, from https://en.wikiquote.org/wiki/Walt_Whitman

John Greenleaf Whittier (December 17, 1807 – September 7, 1892)
https://en.wikipedia.org/wiki/John_Greenleaf_Whittier
#362-Sad - Sermons by a Non-Reverend. Regret. (1864). In J. H. Agnew (Ed.), *The American Monthly. The Knickerbocker, devoted to literature, art, science, and politics. Volume 64* (p. 44). New York, NY: Published at the office of the magazine.

Smith Wigglesworth (8 June 1859 – 12 March 1947)
https://en.wikipedia.org/wiki/Smith_Wigglesworth
#31-Abundance - Wigglesworth, S. (1924). Chapter six. Himself took our infirmities. In *Ever Increasing Faith* (p. 43). Springfield, MO: GOSPEL PUBLISHING HOUSE.

Ella Wheeler Wilcox (November 5, 1850 – October 30, 1919)
https://en.wikipedia.org/wiki/Ella_Wheeler_Wilcox
#159-Change - Wheeler Wilcox, E. (1908). Ignore Misfortune. In *New Thought Common Sense and What Life Means to Me* (p. 47). Chicago, IL: W. B. Conkey Company.
#58-Discontent - Recent chapters in the story of liberty VIII. (1910). In S. Y. Gillan (Ed.), *Western Teacher: Devoted to Schoolroom Methods. Practical ..., Volumes 17-18* (p. 309). Milwaukee: S. Y. Gillan and Company.
#274-Hurry - Wheeler Wilcox, E. (1908). Every-Day Opportunities. In *New Thought Common Sense and What Life Means to Me* (p. 230). Chicago, IL: W. B. Conkey Company.
#165-Stand - Wheeler Wilcox, E. (1908). The Onward March. In *New thought common sense and what life means to me* (p. 157). Chicago, IL: W.B. Conkey Company.
#206-Wrong - Wheeler Wilcox, E. (1908). What is a good woman? In *New thought common sense and what life means to me* (p. 108). Chicago, IL: W.B. Conkey Company.

Oscar Wilde (16 October 1854 – 30 November 1900)
https://en.wikipedia.org/wiki/Oscar_Wilde
#195-Enough - Wilde, O. (1905). An Ideal Husband. In *Epigrams & aphorisms* (p. 30). Boston, MA: John W. Luce and Company.
#85-Refuge - Wilde, O. (1905). A woman of no importance. In *Epigrams & aphorisms* (p. 57). Boston, MA: John W. Luce and Company.
#212-Unload - Douglas, C. N. (1915). Chrysanthemum. In *Forty thousand sublime and beautiful thoughts gathered from the roses, clover blossoms, geraniums, violets, morning-glories, and pansies of literature* (p. 301). New York, NY: The Christian Herald.

Marianne Williamson
https://marianne.com/
#155-Seek - Williamson, M. (2005). *A return to love: [reflections on the principles of a Course in miracles]*. New York, NY: Harper Audio.
#71-Healing - Williamson, M. (2009). Chapter 5. Miracles. 1. Forgiveness. In *A Return to Love: Reflections on the Principles of A Course in Miracles* (p. 70). New York, NY: HarperCollins.

Nathaniel Parker Willis (January 20, 1806 – January 20, 1867)
https://en.wikipedia.org/wiki/Nathaniel_Parker_Willis
#288-Repel - Lovell, J. E. (1860). *Lovell's progressive readers, no. 5: A class book for the use of advanced pupils, in public and private schools: comprising a very large selection of lessons, a treatise on the principles of elocution, and a full explanatory index, etc.* (p. 81). Philadelphia, PA: H. C. Peck & Theo. Bliss.

Robert Eldridge Aris Wilmott (30 January 1809 – 27 May 1863)
https://en.wikipedia.org/wiki/Robert_Aris_Willmott
#250-Powerless - WILLMOTT, R. A. (1860). Criticism enforces unity of purpose. In *Pleasures of Literature* (5ᵗʰ ed., p. 74). London: Bell and Daldy.

Woodrow Wilson (December 28, 1856 – February 3, 1924)
https://en.wikipedia.org/wiki/Woodrow_Wilson
https://www.whitehouse.gov/1600/presidents/woodrowwilson
#330-Borrow - Wilson, W. (1914, March 20). Woodrow Wilson - Speech to the National Press Club. Retrieved from https://en.wikiquote.org/wiki/Woodrow_Wilson

John Winthrop (12 January 1587/88 – 26 March 1649)
https://en.wikipedia.org/wiki/John_Winthrop
#293-Contribution - DAY, E. P. (1884). Character. In *Day's Collacon: an encyclopaedia of prose quotations. Consisting of beautiful thoughts, choice extracts, and sayings, of the most eminent writers of all nations, from the earliest ages to the present times* (p. 94). New York and London: International Printing and Publishing Office, Sampson Low, Marston, Searle, and Rivington.

Carol Woods
Verbal consent
#307-Messenger, #136-Wish

William Wordsworth (7 April 1770 – 23 April 1850)
https://en.wikipedia.org/wiki/William_Wordsworth
#156-Find - Wordsworth, W. (1891). Poems of the fancy. Stray pleasures. In *The "Abilon" Edition. The Poetical Works of Wordsworth. With Memoir, Explanatory Notes &c* (p. 84). London & New York: Frederick Warne and Co.
#29-Kindness - Wordsworth, W. (1891). Poems of the imagination. Lines, July 13, 1798. In *The "Abilon" Edition. The Poetical Works of Wordsworth. With Memoir, Explanatory Notes &c* (p. 115). London & New York: Frederick Warne and Co.

Mathew Wren (3 December 1585 – 24 April 1667)
https://en.wikipedia.org/wiki/Matthew_Wren
#49-Ability - Ballou, M. M. (1886). Ability. In *Edge-tools of speech: Selected and arranged* (p. 1). Boston, MA: Ticknor and Company.

Y

Philip Yancey
https://philipyancey.com/
#246-Less - Philip Yancey, *What's So Amazing About Grace?* (Grand Rapids, MI: Zondervan Publishing House, 1997), p. 70.

Edward Young (3 July 1683 – 5 April 1765)
https://en.wikipedia.org/wiki/Edward_Young
#13-Authentic - Addington, J. F. (1829). Heavens. In *Poetical Quotations, Volume 2* (p. 174).
#273-Procrastination - DAY, E. P. (1884). Procrastination. In *Day's Collacon: an encyclopaedia of prose quotations. Consisting of beautiful thoughts, choice extracts, and sayings, of the most eminent writers of all nations, from the earliest ages to the present times* (p. 731). New York and London: International Printing and Publishing Office, Sampson Low, Marston, Searle, and Rivington.

Z

Dan Zadra
http://zadracreative.com/
#299-Accountability

Zimmerman
#195-Enough - E, S. P., & Punshon, W. M. (1874). Contentment. In *The new handbook of illustration; or, Treasury of themes, meditations, anecdotes, analogies, parables, similitudes, types, emblems, symbols, apologues, allegories, and expositions of scripture truth and Christian life* (p. 99). London: Elliot Stock.

Zoroaster (2nd millennium BCE)
https://en.wikipedia.org/wiki/Zoroaster
#260-Abstain - Doubt. (1881). In A. Woolbever (Ed.), *Treasury of Wisdom, Wit, and Humor, Odd Comparisons and Proverbs:* (4th ed., p. 114). Philadelphia, PA: E. Claxton & Company.

Index 1-366 Days

23	January	23	Worthy	1 Timothy 5:17 (NIV), Hebrews 3:3 (NIV)	Publilius Syrus, V. Tugaleva
24	January	24	Unworthy	Deuteronomy 15:9 (ESV), Matthew 10:13 (HCSB)	R. G. Briley, C. Bridges
25	January	25	Laughter	Jeremiah 31:13 (CEB), 1 Peter 1:8 (MSG)	J. Kintz, N. Chamfort, Shakespeare
26	January	26	Despair	Psalm 40:2 (NLT), 2 Corinthians 4:8 (GNT)	Aeschylus, H. Berlioz, H. Giles
27	January	27	Purpose	Romans 8:28 (WEB), 1 Timothy 1:5 (NKJV)	M. Shimoff, G. Washington, T. Guillemets, P.M.I.
28	January	28	Opportunity	Galatians 6:10 (NKJV), Ephesians 5:16 (NLT)	P.M.I., A. C. Bristol, F. Bacon
29	January	29	Kindness	John 1:17 (GW), Ephesians 1:8 (GW)	Aesop, W. Wordsworth, S. Fielding
30	January	30	Criticism	Proverbs 15:31 (NLT), Proverbs 28:23 (NLT)	G. Eliot, T. Roosevelt, E. Hubbard, P.M.I.
31	January	31	Abundance	Job 36:31 (AMP), Psalm 37:11 (KJV)	S. Wigglesworth, J. Petit-Senn, St. Basil, P.M.I.
32	February	1	Lack	Psalm 23:1 (NIV), Psalm 34:9-10 (NIV)	Orison Swett Marden, Aeschylus, Byrd
33	February	2	Freedom	Psalm 119:45 (ERV), Galatians 5:1 (ERV)	J. Ryal, M. Bakunin, R. W. Emerson, Voltaire
334	February	3	Confinement	Isaiah 42:7-8 (CJB), Micah 2:13 (MSG)	Turkish Spy, W. Irving, P.M.I., Horace
35	February	4	Individual	Job 34:29 (HCSB), Colossians 4:6 (CJB)	G. S. Hall, P.M.I., L. M. Child, C. Jami
36	February	5	Community	Acts 2:41 (CEB), Ephesians 4:29 (CEB)	R. W. Emerson, A. Carnegie
37	February	6	Growth	1 Corinthians 3:6 (NASB), 1 Corinthians 3:7 (RSV)	W. Phillips, Fielding
38	February	7	Reduction	Exodus 5:11 (HCSB)	Trench, G. Stock, J. A. Garfield
39	February	8	Meditate	Psalm 119:15 (WEB), Psalm 145:5 (NIV)	St. Francis de Sales, Emma C. Embury
40	February	9	Dismiss	Psalm 102:17 (MSG), Luke 2:29-30 (NIV)	W. S. Landor, R. A. Longman, W. Cowper
41	February	10	Cause	Psalm 118:7 (VOICE), Isaiah 1:17 (NIV)	L. da Vinci, W. J. Bryan, B. Sunday, C. Bowles, A. Lincoln
42	February	11	Effect	Romans 4:14 (CEB), James 1:4 (NET)	T. Carlyle, P.M.I., E. A. Poe, Horace
43	February	12	Spontaneous	Deuteronomy 15:10 (MSG), Psalm 119:108 (CEB)	George Bellows
44	February	13	Deliberate	Acts 2:23 (NIV), Acts 15:6 (NET)	B. Butler, O. Chambers
45	February	14	Love	1 Corinthians 13:4-7 (NLT)	R. Brault, C. Sumner
46	February	15	Hate	Luke 6:27 (NLT), 1 John 2:9 (NLT)	William W. Atkinson
47	February	16	Focus	Proverbs 22:17 (AMP), 1 Timothy 4:16 (GW)	P.M.I., R. L. Stevenson

48	February	17	Imagine	Genesis 11:6 (AMP), Ephesians 3:20 (CEB)	P. J. Meyer, A. France, J. C. Gehler, P. Bysshe Shelley
49	February	18	Ability	Numbers 22:28 (NLT), Acts 11:29 (NKJV)	Goethe, K. Kint, M. Wren, P.M.I., M. Ebner-Eschenbach
50	February	19	Inability	Romans 4:19-20 (ISV), Philippians 2:30 (NET)	Novalis
51	February	20	Moment	Proverbs 12:19 (ERV), Luke 8:44 (ERV)	H. Bonar, H. D. Thoreau, F. Schiller, J. Bryan, P.M.I.
52	February	21	Time	Ecclesiastes 3:1-8 (NIV)	M. Althsuler, H. Berlioz, P.M.I., Marcus Aurelius
53	February	22	Complete	Ephesians 1:23 (NLT), James 2:22 (NLT)	J. Billings, Anna Shipton, Epictetus
54	February	23	Incomplete	1 Corinthians 13:12 (NLT)	Guy Finley
55	February	24	Easy	Proverbs 1:33 (NLV), Matthew 11:30 (NLT)	Saadi, C. Buxton, Lao Tzu, P. Stanhope
56	February	25	Hard	Ecclesiastes 2:10 (NLT), 2 Thessalonians 3:8 (NLT)	P.M.I., T. Brownson, Socrates
57	February	26	Content	Proverbs 13:25 (NIV), 1 Timothy 6:6 (GW)	J. Selden, J. Heywood, F. Bacon
58	February	27	Discontent	Deuteronomy 15:10 (LEB)	Rev. W. J. Palm, Alexis, Illinois, Ella Wheeler Wilcox
59	February	28	Accomplish	Psalm 57:2 (WEB), Ephesians 1:9 (CEB)	C. de Montesquieu, P.M.I., H. W. Longfellow, T. Carlyle, F. Schiller
60	February	29	Abandon	Deuteronomy 31:8 (NLT), Psalm 27:10 (NLT)	Proverb
61	March	1	Light	Matthew 5:16 (NIV), Ephesians 5:8 (NIV)	Tyndall, Unknown, Gen. Robert E. Lee, P.M.I.
62	March	2	Dark	2 Chronicles 6:1 (NIV), Psalm 139:12 (NIV)	J. Allen, W. Whitman, H. D. Thoreau
63	March	3	Responsibility	Deuteronomy 22:1 (NLT), Ezra 10:4 (NASB)	V. Hugo, A. Lincoln
64	March	4	Irresponsible	Romans 13:2 (MSG), 1 Thessalonians 5:14 (HCSB)	P.M.I., W. Pinkney
65	March	5	Pain	Psalm 32:10 (LEB), Revelation 21:4 (NKJV)	P.M.I., Aristotle
66	March	6	Comfort	Psalm 71:21 (NIV), Psalm 119:50 (AMP)	F. Bacon, Aesop, P.M.I., T. Guillemets, Hippocrates
67	March	7	Trust	Proverbs 16:20 (GW), Nahum 1:7 (NIV)	R. W. Emerson, B. Garner, E. M. C., F. Crane
68	March	8	Distrust	Matthew 6:22-23 (MSG), Romans 4:20 (AMP)	G. Eliot, K. Mcveigh
69	March	9	Sunshine	Job 11:17 (GNT), Isaiah 18:4 (CEB)	J. Muir, G. P. Upton, T. Jefferson, J. M. Barrie
70	March	10	Obscurity	Deuteronomy 5:22 (DARBY), Isaiah 29:18 (DRA)	Joseph Addison, Plutarch, H. Mann, P.M.I.
71	March	11	Healing	Malachi 4:2 (NRSV), Acts 10:38 (NLV)	M. Williamson, H. W. Beecher, W. Cather

72	March	12	Hurt	Jeremiah 7:19 (NLT), Luke 6:28 (NLT)	S. von La Roche, P.M.I., Proverb
73	March	13	Perseverance	Hebrews 12:1 (NIV), James 1:3-4 (NIV)	J. Q. Adams, Lucretius, T. Buxton, P.M.I., Unknown
74	March	14	Lazy	Ecclesiastes 10:18 (ERV), Hebrews 6:12 (NLV)	A. Einstein, H. B. Stowe
75	March	15	Integrity	Job 1:1 (NLT), Proverbs 10:9 (NIV)	S. Johnson, W. Godwin, J. Tillotson, B. Gracian
76	March	16	Disgrace	Psalm 25:3 (NLT), Psalm 37:19 (NLT	La Rochefoucauld, J. G. Holland, U. S. Grant, Cicero, P.M.I.
77	March	17	Play	Exodus 32:6 (KJV), Proverbs 12:9 (GNT)	F. Schiller, Mephisto
78	March	18	Work	2 Chronicles 15:7 (NASB), 1 Thessalonians 1:3 (NIV)	O. Chambers, T. Carlyle
79	March	19	Truth	John 8:32 (NIV), 3 John 1:4 (NIV)	D. D. Caldwell, MA, Proverb, Voltaire, Seneca, Maimonides
80	March	20	Falsehood	Deuteronomy 5:11 (AMP), Proverbs 12:17 (LEB)	M. De Cervantes, B. Pascal, T. Paine
81	March	21	Decide	Job 22:28 (NET), John 7:24 (AMP)	J. R. Lowell, P.M.I., Mencius
82	March	22	Defer	Leviticus 19:15 (NASB), Leviticus 19:32 (NRSV)	Stephan Grellet, Lord Byron
83	March	23	Future	Job 5:21 (TLB), Psalm 16:5 (HCSB)	T. Harv Eker, B. Garner
84	March	24	Past	Ezekiel 33:16 (NLT), Romans 11:33 (ESV)	Agathon, R. Herrick, Lord Byron
85	March	25	Refuge	2 Samuel 22:31 (NASB), Proverbs 14:26 (GW)	H. D. Thoreau, P.M.I., O. Wilde
86	March	26	Risk	John 10:11 (AMP), Romans 16:3-4 (CEB)	P.M.I., R. Anthony, G. de Scudery
87	March	27	Miserable	Psalm 32:3 (VOICE), Proverbs 15:15 (MSG)	C. Kingsley, J. S. Mill
88	March	28	Happy	Psalm 144:15 (RSV), John 13:17 (NLV)	Marcus Aurelius, S. I. Prime, Boethius
89	March	29	Strength	Psalm 18:32 (ESV), Psalm 59:17 (YLT)	D. Grenside, F. W. Robertson
90	March	30	Weakness	2 Corinthians 12:9 (CEB), Hebrews 4:15 (GNT)	J. Adams, J. R. Lowell, R. W. Trine
91	March	31	Pride	Psalm 10:4 (NIV), James 1:9 (NIV)	J. Hunter, Pope
92	April	1	Humility	Proverbs 22:4 (HCSB), Philippians 2:5 (AMP)	B. E. Herman
93	April	2	Grace	Proverbs 22:11 (NKJV), Ephesians 2:8 (NASB)	St. Ignatius of Loyola, Joan of Arc, De Finod
94	April	3	Judgment	Proverbs 3:21 (NIV), John 8:15 (NIV)	Petrarch, P.M.I., Theophrastus
95	April	4	Excuse	Romans 1:20 (NIV), Romans 2:1 (NIV)	B. Franklin, P.M.I., F. Nightingale, W. L. Garrison

96	April	5	Diligence	Romans 12:8-11 (ASV)	Confucius, Menander
97	April	6	Blessing	Genesis 12:2 (NLT), Ezekiel 34:26 (KJV)	O. W. Holmes
98	April	7	Condemn	Job 15:6 (NRSV), Luke 6:37 (NRSV), John 3:17 (NRSV)	B. Gracian, Quintilian
99	April	8	Need	Romans 1:12 (NLV), Philippians 4:19 (NLV)	B. Franklin, M. Lipkin, P.M.I.
100	April	9	Want	Psalm 34:9 (NLV), Matthew 6:10 (NLV)	Plato, Dr. Clarice Fluitt, P.M.I.
101	April	10	Group	Acts 5:14 (NLV), 1 Peter 2:9 (NLV)	Jan Edward Hulett, Clarence Day
102	April	11	Scatter	Deuteronomy 28:7 (NLT), Psalm 68:1 (GNT)	St. Augustine, K. Braestrup, W. S. Downey
103	April	12	Question	Mark 2:8 (NLT, 1 Timothy 3:16 (NLT)	Voltaire, B. Watson, Shakespeare
104	April	13	Respond	Hosea 6:3 (NLT), Matthew 8:26 (NLT)	P.M.I., C. Lamb
105	April	14	Patience	Proverbs 15:18 (ERV), Luke 21:19 (NKJV)	W. Penn, St. F. de Sales, J. de La Fontaine
106	April	15	Impatience	Proverbs 14:29 (CEB), Romans 8:24-25 (PHILLIPS)	L. Sterne, J. Taylor
107	April	16	Attitude	Proverbs 18:14 (ERV), Philippians 2:5 (NLT)	W. W. Atkinson, W. Scott
108	April	17	Balance	Proverbs 16:11 (GW), Job 31:6 (ASV)	T. Kempis, T. C. Haliburton, Proverb
109	April	18	Celebrate	Psalm 135:3 (NLT), Luke 15:32 (NLT)	B. Heiß, P.M.I., K. Kotarski
110	April	19	Beauty	Proverbs 31:30 (NLT), Romans 12:17 (MSG)	Lady Blessington, R. W. Emerson, St. Augustine
111	April	20	Rise	Proverbs 24:16 (AMP), Luke 18:33 (AMP)	A. Hamilton, P.M.I., Epictetus, J. Adams
112	April	21	Fall	Psalm 7:15 (NOG), Psalm 66:9 (NOG)	William Shakespeare, Oliver Goldsmith
113	April	22	Speak	Proverbs 29:20 (NIV), Titus 2:15 (NASB)	P.M.I., O. W. Holmes, Sr., Seneca, T. Smollett, T. Jefferson
114	April	23	Silence	Mark 4:39 (NLT), 1 Peter 2:15 (NIV)	Dionysius, Proverb, B. E. Herman
115	April	24	Train	Proverbs 22:6 (KJV), 1 Timothy 4:7 (NLT)	T. Edwards, P.M.I., F. Ruckert, S. Omartian
116	April	25	Rest	1 Kings 5:4 (NKJV), Job 11:18 (CEV)	Mary, Queen of Scots, Bill Johnson
117	April	26	Rich	Psalm 49:16 (RSV), Proverbs 8:18 (NIV)	C. A. Bartol, W. Temple
118	April	27	Poor	Job 34:19 (AMP), Psalm 34:6 (KJV)	Seneca, E. Spenser
119	April	28	Character	Isaiah 32:8 (NET), Ephesians 5:13 (GW)	R. W. Emerson, T. Edwards

120	April	29	Zeal	Romans 10:2 (ESV), 1 Corinthians 14:12 (NKJV)	F. W. Faber, P. Quesnel, C. Buxton, Shakespeare, Henry VIII, H. Ballou
121	April	30	Idleness	Proverbs 6:6 (KNOX), Ecclesiastes 10:18 (NLT)	A. Pavlovich Chekhov, J. K. Jerome
122	May	1	Action	Ezra 10:4 (NOG), 1 John 3:18 (NIV)	Tiffany Peterson, Confucius, T. Harv Eker
123	May	2	See	Psalm 27:13 (NLV), Matthew 5:8 (NLV)	A. Hamilton, R. Brault, S. Rutherford, R. Burns, P.M.I.
124	May	3	Miss	Proverbs 19:2 (NIV), Hebrews 12:15 (NLV)	Proverb, P.M.I., A. Voskamp
125	May	4	Share	1 Chronicles 16:23 (CEB), Hebrews 13:16 (NKJV)	Aristotle, Homer, Lord Byron
126	May	5	Retain	John 20:23 (NKJV), 2 Timothy 1:13 (NASB)	L. Sumrall, Horace
127	May	6	Reply	Proverbs 15:23 (NIV), Luke 21:15 (NLT)	Moliere, Euripides, C. C. Colton
128	May	7	Prayer	Matthew 21:22 (NASB), James 5:16 (NASB)	Brother Lawrence, J. Wesley
129	May	8	Confidence	Psalm 118:8 (RSV), Hebrews 4:16 (CEB)	M. de Montaigne, H. Beecher, T. Stott, A. Lincoln, P.M.I.
130	May	9	Uncertainty	1 Timothy 6:17 (KJV), James 3:17 (RSV)	Tacitus, W. Congreve, Seneca, P.M.I.
131	May	10	Rude	Proverbs 18:13 (MSG), Proverbs 22:10 (VOICE)	T. Bulfinch, Quintilian, P.M.I.
132	May	11	Appreciate	Proverbs 15:12 (GW), 1 Thessalonians 4:4 (MSG)	N. Hawthorne, R. G. Ingersoll, H. D. Thoreau, P.M.I.
133	May	12	Safe	Proverbs 18:10 (NIV), Proverbs 29:25 (AMP)	T. Jefferson, C. Dickens, J. Madison, E. C. Stanton, P.M.I.
134	May	13	Vulnerable	Proverbs 22:22 (VOICE), Proverbs 31:8 (CEB)	C. Jami, P.M.I.
135	May	14	Satisfied	Deuteronomy 8:10 (CEB), Proverbs 12:14 (AMP)	W. Melmoth, E. Hubbard, P.M.I., A. Deshoulieres, Pythagoras
136	May	15	Wish	Proverbs 23:18 (NCV), Romans 12:14 (NCV)	Epictetus, T. à Kempis, C. Woods, Julius Caesar, P.M.I.
137	May	16	Peace	Psalm 4:8 (NIV), Proverbs 16:7 (NKJV)	T. à Kempis, Anonymous
138	May	17	Turbulence	Psalm 46:3-4 (CJB), 2 Corinthians 7:4 (VOICE)	M. Lermontov, G. Washington
139	May	18	Sleep	Psalm 3:5 (RSV), Psalm 127:2 (AMP)	F. Bacon, B. Gracian
140	May	19	Awake	Psalm 119:148 (NKJV), 1 Thessalonians 5:10 (CEB)	K. Serafini, P.M.I., Proverb
141	May	20	Order	Psalm 50:23 (NKJV), 1 Corinthians 14:40 (NKJV)	F. Bacon, B. de St. Pierre, K. Mansfield, S. Johnson
142	May	21	Disorder	1 Thessalonians 5:14 (WEB), James 3:16 (NRSV)	J. Collie, W. Raleigh, F. Marryatt, H. James, P.M.I.

143	May	22	Promise	Acts 2:39 (HCSB), 1 John 2:25 (HCSB)	Unknown, P.M.I., M. Luther
144	May	23	Surprise	Habakkuk 1:5 (NLV), 1 John 3:13 (NIV)	R. W. Emerson, F. Bacon, Mrs. F. Leslie
145	May	24	Mind	Psalm 16:8 (HCSB), 1 Corinthians 2:16 (HCSB	N. Hill, St. Jerome, J. Meyer
146	May	25	Realities	1 Corinthians 2:13 (NIV), Revelation 22:20 (VOICE	J. Allen, P.M.I., W. Penn
147	May	26	Triumph	Psalm 118:7 (NLT), 2 Corinthians 2:14 (AMP)	H. Drummond, T. Paine, R. W. Emerson, Seneca
148	May	27	Defeat	Psalm 116:8 (GNT), 1 John 5:4 (NLT)	Confucius, H. W. Longfellow, R. G. Ingersoll
149	May	28	Worry	Proverbs 1:33 (GW), Luke 12:29 (GW)	T. Guillemets, R. J. Burdette
150	May	29	Calmness	Proverbs 25:15 (AMP), Isaiah 30:15 (CJB)	J. H. Aughey, P.M.I., Lord Byron, A. Karr, E. G. Bulwer-Lytton
151	May	30	Perspective	Colossians 3:2 (MSG), 1 Peter 2:4 (CEB)	P.M.I., O. Feltham, F. W. Robertson
152	May	31	Optimism	Psalm 28:7 (NIV), Galatians 1:11-12 (MSG)	O. S. Marden
153	June	1	Begin	Proverbs 9:6 (NLT), Lamentations 3:23 (NLT)	M. J. Mapes, J. Garfield
154	June	2	End	Job 8:7 (NLT), Daniel 7:18 (NLT)	J. Locke, T. Gray
155	June	3	Seek	Matthew 6:33 (NKJV), Matthew 7:8 (NASB)	S. Johnson, M. Williamson, R. G. Ingersoll, P.M.I.
156	June	4	Find	Proverbs 3:4 (KJV), Proverbs 8:17 (YLT)	W. Wordsworth, G. Galilei, B. Whipple
157	June	5	Obstacle	Proverbs 4:12 (VOICE), Daniel 2:22 (TLB)	P.M.I.
158	June	6	Path	Psalm 119:105 (ASV), Proverbs 4:26 (AMP)	Seneca, Haitian Proverb
159	June	7	Change	Matthew 18:3 (NIV), Romans 11:29 (GW)	E. W. Wilcox, Leo Tolstoy, Marcus Aurelius
160	June	8	Unchanging	Isaiah 41:4 (AMP), Hebrews 6:18 (VOICE)	T. Parker, S. Rutherford
161	June	9	Cheer	Proverbs 12:25 (NLT), James 5:13 (YLT)	P. Bysshe Shelley, J. Lubbock, J. R. Lowell
162	June	10	Gloom	Job 12:22 (NLT), Isaiah 58:10 (NET)	John Angel James, Ulysses S. Grant
163	June	11	Become	Proverbs 13:20 (NIV), 2 Corinthians 5:21 (NIV	H. W. Beecher, T. P. Frost
164	June	12	Choice	Deuteronomy 30:19 (NLT), Proverbs 2:11 (NLT)	S. Johnson, G. Macdonald
165	June	13	Stand	Ephesians 6:14 (NLT), Revelation 13:10 (MSG)	R. W. Trine, O. W. Holmes, Sr., E. W. Wilcox
166	June	14	Sit	Isaiah 42:7 (NLT), Revelation 3:21 (GNT)	W. W. Atkinson, H. D. Thoreau, W. Rogers, Proverb

190	July	8	Harm	Psalm 37:8 (NKJV), Proverbs 3:30 (DARBY)	Voltaire, Hesiod
191	July	9	Up	Psalm 63:4 (GW), Proverbs 31:9 (NLT)	P.M.I., Gandhi
192	July	10	Down	Psalm 51:6 (GW), Hebrews 10:12 (NCV)	C. Kingsley, G. R. Blair
193	July	11	Sacred	Matthew 7:6 (AMP), 1 Thessalonians 5:26 (AMP)	A. Hamilton, R. G. Ingersoll, A. Bennett
194	July	12	Profane	Leviticus 19:12 (NASB), Malachi 2:10 (NASB)	A. Bierce, G. Washington
195	July	13	Enough	Psalm 14:3 (MSG), Proverbs 25:16 (NIV)	T. Brownson, O. Wilde, F. Dostoevsky, Zimmerman
196	July	14	Excessive	Ecclesiastes 7:16-17 ((NET), Ephesians 5:18 (VOICE)	F. Bacon, Plato, L. Wallace
197	July	15	Direction	Proverbs 22:6 (MSG), James 3:4 (VOICE)	J. Joubert, W. Pratney, Democritus
198	July	16	Journey	Judges 18:6 (NIV), Psalm 121:8 (CEB)	M. Proust, S. Smiles, Proverb
199	July	17	Thoughts	Proverbs 4:23 (ERV), Isaiah 55:8-9 (NIV)	J. H. Aughey, J. Allen, J. Addison, J. Locke
200	July	18	Deeds	Psalm 107:8 (WEB), Psalm 143:5 (CEB)	Dykes, H. W. Beecher, P.M.I., Rojas, G. Eliot
201	July	19	Believe	Mark 11:24 (RSV), John 3:16 (NIV)	J. Ruskin, L. Carroll, B. Garner
202	July	20	Get	Genesis 13:17 (NET), Genesis 34:10 (WEB)	E. Hubbard, L. Sumrall, H. B. Stowe, J. Muir
203	July	21	Everything	Genesis 9:3 (CEB), 1 Corinthians 10:23 (NET), Philippians 2:14 (NET)	Gary Ryan Blair, Aesop, Cheri Huber, Henry Brooke, Voltaire
204	July	22	Nothing	Psalm 119:165 (NET), Ecclesiastes 1:9 (NET)	Shakespeare, M. de Montaigne, E. Hubbard
205	July	23	Right	Romans 21:2 (NLT), Galatians 6:9 (MOUNCE)	J. Allen, Gandhi, Aristotle, La Rochefoucauld, P.M.I.
206	July	24	Wrong	Leviticus 19:18 (ERV), 1 Thessalonians 5:15 (GNT)	O. Chambers, E. W. Wilcox, S. Johnson, P.M.I.
207	July	25	Much	Proverbs 23:20 (NOG), Luke 16:10 (KJV)	B. Matejcek, J. R. Miller, C. Spurgeon, B. Pascal
208	July	26	Decline	Proverbs 4:5 (KJV), Isaiah 38:8 (RSV)	P.M.I., Goethe, I. van Cleef, J. Ruskin
209	July	27	Give	Psalm 16:5 (ERV), Luke 6:38 (NKJV)	D. Erasmu, Archimedes, John Muir
210	July	28	Take	Romans 12:10 (NLT), Ephesians 2:8 (NLT)	Earl of Chesterfield, H. de Balza, Epictetus, H. D. Thoreau
211	July	29	Load	Psalm 68:19 (NKJV), Matthew 11:30 (NLV)	C. H. Parkhurst, M. T., J. P. Richter, Cervantes, R. Steele
212	July	30	Unload	Psalm 43:4 (VOICE), Ezekiel 27:33 (HCSB)	R. Anthony, O. Wilde

213	July	31	Discipline	Psalm 94:12 (NIV), Proverbs 19:20 (GW)	Seneca, E. P. Whipple, C. Barton, W. Rathbone
214	August	1	Undisciplined	Proverbs 29:15 (NLT), 2 Thessalonians 3:7 (NASB)	J. Joubert, Publius Flavius Vegetius Renatus
215	August	2	Faith	Hebrews 11:1-3 (RSV)	C. W. L. Christian, M. Perry, A. Murray
216	August	3	Doubt	Matthew 11:6 (GNT), John 20:27 (NIV), Jude 1:22 (NLV)	O. Chambers, Shakespeare, I. Kant
217	August	4	Inside	Psalm 16:7 (ERV), 2 Corinthians 4:16 (ERV)	H. James, O. S. Marden
218	August	5	Outside	Matthew 23:28 (GW), Ephesians 2:19 (GW)	J. Pulsford, H. Mann, T. B. Aldrich
219	August	6	Use	Ecclesiastes 10:11 (GNT), Mark 4:24 (GNT)	M. de Montaigne, R. Descartes, F. de Rojas
222	August	7	Useless	Psalm 127:1 (CEV), 2 Timothy 2:16 (CEV)	T. L. Cuyler, G. Elliot, C. de Montesquieu, C. Dickens, Mm. De Gasparin
221	August	8	Respect	Leviticus 19:32 (NIV), 1 Peter 2:17 (NIV)	H. Giles, P.M.I., J. Hall
222	August	9	Disrespectful	Exodus 22:28 (GW), Titus 3:2 (CEB)	Balzac
223	August	10	Compassion	Psalm 145:9 (NLT), Micah 7:19 (NLT)	G. W. Carver, H. W. Beecher
224	August	11	Cruel	Proverbs 12:10 (ERV), Proverbs 27:4 (WEB)	R. B. Brooke, T. Paine, I. Kant, R. E. Lee, T. Fuller
225	August	12	Early	Mark 1:35 (EXB), James 5:7 (AMP)	B. Franklin, J. Austen, W. Camden, P.M.I.
226	August	13	Late	Psalm 127:2 (NLT), Habakkuk 2:3 (GW)	R. W. Emerson, Shakespeare, H. W. Longfellow, H. D. Thoreau, P.M.I.
227	August	14	Rules	Psalm 96:10 (MSG), 2 Timothy 2:5 (GW)	D. Carnegie, R. G. Briley
228	August	15	Rebellion	Jeremiah 3:22 (CEB), 1 John 3:4 (CEB)	A. Adams, G. H. Lewes, F. Douglass, B. Franklin, S. B. Anthony
229	August	16	Circumstance	Psalm 125:1 (TLB), Isaiah 60:1 (AMP)	S. Ricotti, S. Lover, B. T. Washington
230	August	17	Intent	Psalm 25:14 (GW), Hebrews 4:12 (DRA)	O. Goldsmith, U. S. Grant, Plutarch
231	August	18	Overlook	Proverbs 19:11 (NIV), Hebrews 6:10 (VOICE)	W. James, E. Wharton, J. Lubbock
232	August	19	Look	Psalm 37:37 (NLT), Ecclesiastes 9:8 (GNT)	W. Wells, O. Chambers, Francis of Assisi
233	August	20	Today	Proverbs 22:19 (NLT), 2 Corinthians 6:2 (NLT)	Proverb, B. Garner, M. F. Tupper
234	August	21	Acceptance	Job 33:26 (VOICE), Romans 5:17 (PHILLIPS)	G. MacDonald, Denham

235	August	22	Ignorance	Proverbs 12:23 (GNT), 1 Peter 2:15 (NKJV)	H. D. Thoreau, W. Penn, W. Osler
236	August	23	Wisdom	Job 12:13 (NLT), James 1:5 (NLT)	M. de Montaigne, J. Russell, Beethoven, P.M.I., A. de Rupe
237	August	24	Ordinary	1 Corinthians 10:3 (TLB), 1 Corinthians 1:28 (GW)	A. H. Maslow, H. Bushnell, B. Pascal
238	August	25	Extraordinary	Job 8:7 (CEB), Acts 19:11 (AMP)	E. Hubbard, W. Pratney, A. Arnauld
239	August	26	Practice	Matthew 7:26 (CEB), Luke 11:28 (CEB)	B. Klemmer, T. Thompson
240	August	27	Refrain	Psalm 37:8 (NRSV), 1 Peter 3:10 (KJV)	K. Braestrup, B. Pascal, J. C. Hare, Spurgeon, P.M.I.
211	August	28	Moving	Job 17:9 (NLT), Psalm 69:35 (TLV)	Chanakya, Dottie D. Caldwell, G. Eliot
242	August	29	Staying	James 5:11 (MSG), Revelation 14:12 (MSG)	F. B. Meyer, J. Pennington
243	August	30	Selfish	Philippians 2:3 (GW), Romans 8:5 (CEB)	J. H. Aughey, B. Klemmer, Herbert Spencer, P.M.I.
244	August	31	Selfless	Romans 5:6-8 (MSG)	G. Rubin, P.M.I.
245	September	1	More	Psalm 4:7 (GW), Psalm 71:14 (GW)	Kate Braestrup, Publilius Syrus, J. Muir, P.M.I.
246	September	2	Less	Proverbs 13:11 (NLV), 1 Timothy 4:12 (NLT)	P.M.I., S. Godin, H. de Balzac, P. Yancey, Shakespeare
247	September	3	Design	Proverbs 25:11 (GNT), Ephesians 1:11 (CEB)	J. Addison, J. Denham
248	September	4	Destiny	Psalm 16:5 (CEB), Psalm 73:24 (NLT)	P. L. Hirsch, J. de La Fontaine, W. J. Bryan
249	September	5	Power	Psalm 20:7 (GNT), Luke 10:19 (NASB)	M. de Cervantes, Billy Sunday, Nido Qubein
250	September	6	Powerless	Proverbs 14:31 (CEB), Isaiah 40:29 (CJB)	O. Chambers, T. Huxley, R. E. A. Wilmott
251	September	7	Labor	Psalm 128:2 (NLT), 1 Corinthians 3:8 (NKJV)	H. George, Proverb, Mrs. F. S. Osgood, A. Stevens
252	September	8	Fun	Ecclesiastes 8:15 (NLT), Ecclesiastes 10:20 (NLT)	Thackeray, Amy Gage
253	September	9	Turn	Psalm 22:27 (DARBY), Psalm 119:36 (NRSV)	D. Stanley, S. Ricotti, B. Dorgan
254	September	10	Stagnant	Proverbs 10:31 (MSG), Jeremiah 2:13 (VOICE)	Leonardo da Vinci, A.B. Simpson, P.M.I.
255	September	11	Hope	Isaiah 40:31 (NIV), Jeremiah 29:11 (NLT)	Brother Lawrence, G. Herbert, R. Barlow Jordan
256	September	12	Hopeless	Mark 12:44 (CEB), Romans 4:18 (CEV)	A. A. McGinley, J. Roux
257	September	13	Dominate	1 Corinthians 6:12 (ESV), Colossians 3:7-8 (GNT)	N. Hill, P.M.I.
258	September	14	Submission	Job 26:24 (AMP), 2 Corinthians 9:13 (LEB)	C. E. Tonna, R. Foster

259	September	15	Indulge	Proverbs 18:21 (AMP), Luke 22:26 (VOICE)	George Washington, Criss Jami
260	September	16	Abstain	1 Corinthians 8:8 (CJB), 1 Peter 2:11 (HCSB)	G. Eliot, Zoroaster, A. Cahan, J. Addison
261	September	17	Perfection	Psalm 119:96 (TLV), 1 John 4:17 (AMP)	J. Ozwald, M. Zaher, Augustine, V. Hugo
262	September	18	Imperfection	Song of Solomon 4:7 (HCSB), 1 Peter 1:19 (GW)	T. à Kempis, J. Ruskin
263	September	19	Joy	Luke 1:47 (GW), Romans 4:7 (NLT)	J. Ozwald, Julian of Norwich, Unknown, P.M.I.
264	September	20	Sorrow	Proverbs 10:22 (RSV), Revelation 21:4 (KJV)	J. Taylor, H. W. Longfellow, B. E. Nicholls
265	September	21	Good	Genesis 1:4 (KJV), Romans 8:28 (TLV)	E. C. Hopkins, St. Cyprian
266	September	22	Bad	Matthew 22:10 (NLT), 1 Corinthians 15:33 (NLV)	E. C. Burke, Saadi, L. W. Lightly
267	September	23	Never	Proverbs 23:2 (ERV), 1 Corinthians 13:7 (ERV)	St. Jerome, G. Galilei, Menander, B. Sunday
268	September	24	Always	Exodus 15:18 (CEB), Psalm 48:14 (CEB)	Ann Voskamp, Prior, Thomas Crofton, P.M.I.
69	September	25	Humanity	Genesis 1:27 (VOICE), Psalm 36:7 (NLT)	Gandhi, F. W. Robertson, A. A. McGinley, P.M.I.
270	September	26	Word	Mark 4:20 (NIV), John 1:1 (CEB)	C. Fluitt, E. C. Hopkins, Socrates
271	September	27	Plan	Psalm 20:4 (NIV), Proverbs 16:3 (GNT)	R. G. Briley, Plato, E. Burke
272	September	28	Settle	Numbers 33:53 (GNT), Proverbs 25:9 (GNT)	T. B. Macaulay, P.M.I., Joseph Joubert
273	September	29	Procrastination	Proverbs 13:4 (NOG), Luke 9:62 (MSG)	Edward Young, G. Rubin
274	September	30	Hurry	Psalm 119:60 (CEB), Proverbs 21:5 (CEB)	E. W. Wilcox, Horace, R. L. Stevenson
275	October	1	Cease	Genesis 8:22 (CEB), Proverbs 22:10 (KJV)	W. Hazlitt, Horace, Waldorf
276	October	2	Continuous	Zechariah 14:6-7 (MSG), 1 Corinthians 1:4 (VOICE)	W. Homer, W. Bagehot
277	October	3	Ruin	Proverbs 10:14 (NOG), Proverbs 11:9 (NOG)	Hannah More, Virgil, P.M.I.
278	October	4	Amend	Proverbs 14:9 (NIV), Jeremiah 7:3 (RSV)	J. Wesley, T. à Kempis, J. S. Mill
279	October	5	Say	Exodus 3:14 (CEB), Psalm70:4 (KJV), Proverbs 18:20 (CEB)	C. Colton, H. W. Shaw, C. Fluitt
280	October	6	Evidence	Psalm 89:1 (GW), 1 Corinthians 12:7 (GW)	John Adams, Billy Sunday
281	October	7	Adequate	2 Corinthians 3:5 (MOUNCE), 1 Thessalonians 3:9 (AMP)	H. Ellis, H. A. Jacobs
282	October	8	Inadequate	1 Corinthians 2:3-5 (MSG)	Abraham Lincoln

283	October	9	Confusion	Psalm 83:16 (ASV), 1 Corinthians 14:33 (ASV)	T. C. Upham, I. Newton
284	October	10	Surety	Proverbs 11:15 (NKJV), Proverbs 17:18 (NRSV)	St. Athanasius, Plato
285	October	11	Few	Psalm 90:12 (TLB), 17:27-28 (TLB)	Epictetus, Shakespeare, Benjamin Franklin
286	October	12	Many	Job 9:10 (ERV), Job 11:19 (TLB)	F. Bacon, Francis of Assisi, R. G. Briley, Martial, J. C. Ryle
287	October	13	Attract	John 6:65 (TLB), John 12:32 (NLV)	P.M.I., W. Law, R. Marston, J. L. Allen
288	October	14	Repel	Proverbs 10:3 (DARBY), Luke 7:23 (AMP)	P.M.I., F. Frangipane, N. P. Willis
289	October	15	Employee	John 13:12-17 (MSG)	Gary Isham
290	October	16	Boss	Ecclesiastes 10:4 (NLT), Romans 8:6 (NLV)	Gabriel Heatter, R. Ingersoll
291	October	17	Standard	Ephesians 4:13 (CEB), 3 John 1:3 (TLB)	H. W. Beecher, O. S. Marden
292	October	18	Great	Psalm 18:35 (TLB), Psalm 86:10 (TLB)	Mencius, B. Pascal, B. Robinson, B. Jowett
293	October	19	Contribution	Exodus 25:2 (NLT), Exodus 36:7 (NLT)	Unknown, Menander, J. Winthrop
294	October	20	Demand	Matthew 5:41 (TLB), John 15:12 (TLB)	S. Kierkegaard, S. Maraboli, S. Johnson, Terence
295	October	21	Afraid	Job 3:25 (CEB), Mark 5:36 (NIV)	P.M.I., J. Edwards, W. Hazlitt
296	October	22	Daring	Philippians 1:14 (VOICE)	Lucan, N. Rowe
297	October	23	Prepare	Proverbs 24:27 (NRSV), 1 Peter 1:13 (NRSV)	D. S. Jordan, Aesop, Unknown
298	October	24	Pretending	Romans 12:9 (CEB), 2 Timothy 3:5 (ERV)	B. Klemmer, Marquise De Sevigne
299	October	25	Accountability	Matthew 23:36 (GW), James 2:10 (ESV)	T. Paine, P.M.I., D. Zadra, M. H. Lyon
300	October	26	Treachery	Psalm 5:6 (HCSB), 1 Peter 3:10 (AMP)	Demosthenes, B. Franklin
301	October	27	Single	Matthew 6:22 (KJV), Luke 12:25 (NIV)	J. H. Norris, Aristotle, P.M.I., St. Francis of Assisi
302	October	28	Both	Psalm 115:13 (KJV), James 3:11 (NLT)	B. Klemmer, R. G. Briley
303	October	29	Whole	Proverbs 11:10 (TLB), Mark 8:36 (TLB)	P.M.I., A. Held, H. D. Thoreau, J. Addison, E. Hubbard
304	October	30	Part	Psalm 139:13 (TLB), Proverbs 3:9 (GW)	L. Sumrall, B. Sunday, A. Smith, C. Spurgeon, P.M.I.
305	October	31	Aimless	Jeremiah 17:5-6 (MSG)	J. Lanahan, P.M.I., O. Henry, J. L. Huie
306	November	1	Aim	Romans 14:19 (AMP), 2 Corinthians 8:21 (AMP)	T. Aquinas, R. W. Emerson, A. W. Hare, J. Joubert, P.M.I.
307	November	2	Messenger	Proverbs 13:17 (HCSB), John 13:16 (NRSV)	J. B. Lightfoot, C. Woods, M. F. Tupper

308	November	3	Authority	Matthew 9:6 (NASB), Mark 16:17-18 (GW)	R. E. Lee, S. Gawain, P.M.I.
309	November	4	Ideal	Romans 3:23 (TLB), Colossians 3:14 (AMP)	F. Dostoyevsky, J. L. Allen, V. Hugo
310	November	5	Real	Proverbs 4:21-22 (TLB), Luke 12:15 (TLB)	O. Chambers, Rev. F. W. Cox
311	November	6	Ought	Ecclesiastes 7:11 (GNT), Luke 12:12 (AMP)	Phaedrus, Proverb, R. Jenson
312	November	7	Vocation	1 Corinthians 7:20 (KNOX), Ephesians 4:1 (DRA)	R. Jenson, H. More, L. P. Smith, J. G. Fichte
313	November	8	Strong	Deuteronomy 31:6 (RSV), Ephesians 6:10 (NKJV)	B. Franklin, E. W. Hopkins, F. W. Robertson, K. O'Hara
314	November	9	Sensitive	Ezekiel 11:19 (AMP), Romans 12:16 (CJB)	R. J. Foster, Ouida
315	November	10	Protection	2 Samuel 22:3 (NLT), Psalm 91:4 (NLT)	S. B. Anthony, W. H. Browne
316	November	11	Battle	Exodus 23:27 (ERV), 1 Samuel 17:48 (AMP)	I. Maclaren, Sallust, T. Taylor, Plautus
317	November	12	Ahead	2 Samuel 7:3 (NLT), Job 22:28 (NLT)	D. Crockett, C. H. Parkhurst, Sai Baba, O. S. Marden
318	November	13	Behind	Psalm 37:8 (CEB), Romans 12:9 (VOICE)	H. S. Haskins, Shakespeare, P.M.I., St. Patrick
319	November	14	Former	Ecclesiastes 7:10 (NRSV), Isaiah 43:18-19 (ESV)	Cicero, B. Gracian
320	November	15	Present	2 Corinthians 10:11 (NRSV), Galatians 1:3-4 (HCSB)	Chanakya, Horace, Unknown
321	November	16	Shrink	Proverbs 3:11 (AMP), Hebrews 10:38-39 (NRSV)	T. Paine
322	November	17	Stretch	Psalm 21:4 (NLT), Isaiah 45:12 (NLT)	S. W. Duffield, Virgil
323	November	18	Clarity	Psalm 19:8 (VOICE), Romans 1:19 (VOICE)	R. B. Brooke, Luc de Clapiers, S. Maraboli
324	November	19	Reflection	Psalm 49:3 (VOICE), Proverbs 8:12 (DARBY)	D. Akst, B. Gracian
325	November	20	Expand	Psalm 34:1 (MSG), Psalm 119:32 (VOICE)	Shakespeare, P.M.I., La Rochefoucauld, K. Braestrup
326	November	21	Preserve	Proverbs 18:21 (GNT), Ephesians 4:3 (GNT)	Brother Lawrence, K. von Gesner
327	November	22	Mission	Joshua 22:3 (NIV), Isaiah 48:15 (NIV)	Gandhi, G. Mazzini
328	November	23	Victory	Exodus 15:2 (NLT), 1 Corinthians 15:57 (NASB)	J. Ellis, G. De Scuderi, B. Pascal, F. W. Faber
329	November	24	Own	Deuteronomy 8:17 (NRSV), Proverbs 16:2 (NRSV)	J. Keats, L. M. Child, Shakespeare, Gandhi
330	November	25	Borrow	Proverbs 22:7 (ERV), 2 Corinthians 8:12 (VOICE)	H. Mann, W. Wilson
331	November	26	Disapproval	Luke 19:6-7 (PHILLIPS), 1 Timothy 4:7 (AMP)	La Rochefoucauld, J. Addison, P.M.I.

332	November	27	Thanksgiving	Psalm 69:30 (NIV), 1 Timothy 4:4 (NIV)	P.M.I., F. Quarles, H. W. Beecher
333	November	28	Halt	1 Kings 18:21 (KJV), Luke 7:14 (NASB)	P.M.I., O. W. Holms, H. W. Longfellow
334	November	29	Advance	Proverbs 9:6 (ERV), Ephesians 1:11 (NLT)	Silius Italicus, S. Johnson
335	November	30	Prosperity	Deuteronomy 28:11 (NLT), Proverbs 21:21 (NIV)	W. Irving, Epicurus, T. H. Eker, Aristotle, P.M.I.
336	December	1	Poverty	Psalm 102:17 (ERV), Proverbs 14:23 (CEB)	P.M.I., V. Hugo, Doug Wead, Publius Syrus
337	December	2	Slow	Proverbs 16:32 (AMP), James 1:19 (AMP)	T. Leyasu, Epicurus
338	December	3	Fast	Proverbs 28:22 (CEB), 1 Thessalonians 5:21 (KJV)	U. S. Grant, W. Temple, G.-L. Leclerc, C. de Buffon
339	December	4	Myself	Genesis 22:15-17 (TLB)	M. Washington, N. Hill
340	December	5	Yourself	Job 5:2 (GNT), Galatians 5:14 (GNT)	M. J. Mapes, Proverb, S. Pavlina, H. W. Beecher, G. Rubin, P.M.I.
341	December	6	Life	Psalm 16:11 (NLT), John 11:25 (NLT)	J. Morton, J. Hunter, L. Tolstoy
342	December	7	Death	Acts 2:24 (NLV), Revelation 21:4 (NIV)	W. E. Henley, J. Lubbock
343	December	8	Experience	Psalm 16:11 (TLB), Proverbs 15:33 (MSG)	C. B. Kruger, J. Locke, P.M.I., Lowell
344	December	9	Inexperience	1 Samuel 17:33 (MSG), Acts 4:13 (CEB)	J. Addison, H. D. Thoreau
345	December	10	Win	1 Corinthians 9:24 (NLT), Revelation 21:7 (GNT)	B. Whipple, F. W. Robertson
346	December	11	Lose	Matthew 16:25 (GW), Hebrews 10:35 (GW)	Shakespeare, Proverb, Euripides
347	December	12	Initiate	Hebrews 12:2 (NLT)	G. Isham, T. More, P.M.I.
348	December	13	Conclude	Ecclesiastes 3:12 (TLB), Romans 3:28 (KJV)	F. Tipler, H. W. Beecher
349	December	14	Dishonor	Exodus 22:28 (NLT), Isaiah 61:7 (NLT)	I. Newton, La Rochefoucauld, J. MacArthur, P.M.I.
350	December	15	Honor	Matthew 19:19 (NIV), 1 Timothy 1:17 (NIV)	Plato, R. G. Ingersoll
351	December	16	Failure	Matthew 6:14 (GW), Ephesians 1:7 (CEB)	R. Kipling, M. Althsuler, G. Canning, P.M.I.
352	December	17	Success	1 Samuel 18:14 (NRSV), Proverbs 15:22 (NLT)	S Smiles, P.M.I, C. W. Wendte
353	December	18	New	Lamentations 3:23 (NIRV), 2 Corinthians 5:17 (NIRV)	J. Locke, Rev. J. R. Miller, D. D., P.M.I., N. Hill
354	December	19	Old	Psalm 37:25 (NRSV), Psalm 92:14 (NRSA)	O. W. Holmes, Sr., Victor Hugo
355	December	20	Creative	Galatians 6:1 (MSG), Galatians 6:5 (MSG)	Mm. de Stael, R. W. Trine, O. S. Marden
356	December	21	Distinction	Romans 10:12 (DRA), 1 Corinthians 12:4-6 (DARBY)	J. L. Huie, T. Fuller

357	December	22	Charity	Ecclesiastes 11:1 (MSG), 1 Corinthians 16:14 (KNOX)	P.M.I., G. Rubin
358	December	23	Hindrance	Matthew 16:23 (ESV), Acts 28:31 (NIV)	J. Buckham, St. Patrick, H. W. Beecher
359	December	24	Usual	Acts 24:4 (CEB), James 5:18 (AMP)	A Hamilton, R. W. Emerson, W. Godwin
360	December	25	Miracle	Acts 19:11 (NIV)	J. Di Lemme
361	December	26	Rejoice	Psalm 118:24 (NLT), Philippians 4:4 (NKJV)	A.B. Simpson
362	December	27	Sad	Psalm 42:11 (NLT), Romans 12:15 (NLV)	J. G. Whittier, P.M.I., Lamartine, J. H. Aughey
363	December	28	Wonder	Mark 7:37 (CEB), Hebrews 2:4 (NLT)	Plato, St. Augustine, P.M.I., B. Holyday
364	December	29	Expectation	Proverbs 23:18 (AMP), 2 Corinthians 8:5 (NIV)	A.B. Simpson, P.M.I., J Hunter
365	December	30	Ignore	Proverbs 12:16 (NRSV), Proverbs 13:18 (NLT)	R. Brault, S. B. Anthony, Sophocles, P.M.I.
366	December	31	Review	Psalm 18:22 (MSG), Isaiah 43:26 (NLT)	Plato, Tacitus

Index Words Used in Alphabetical Order

About the author Pam Malow-Isham

Pam has searched for a straightforward and accessible way to live happily and fulfilled. She has found the answer in Jesus Christ... simply trusting God, believing what He says and then declaring it over your life.

She has changed her inner dialog from self-condemnation and shame to self-confidence and courage. Pam is convinced that you too can wake up to your own greatness and appreciate your value and individual gifts. She believes you can live every day knowing you are loved, adored, and a co-creator of your destiny in partnership with the most powerful Source in the universe. When you realize you are responsible for your own happiness and how you respond to every thought and experience, there really is no reason ever to have a bad day again.

Pam loves to help people feel good and has channeled this gift in many ways. She has been practicing as a Licensed Massage Therapist since 1988. Pam taught ballroom dancing for 17 years and loves to exercise and dance regularly. Pam has been on the National Ski Patrol since 2003 at Mt. Holly Ski & Snowboard Resort in Michigan. After Pam received her Certification as a Life Coach in 2012, she has assisted people in reaching their dreams and goals through tranquil power.

In her free time, Pam is an advanced master gardener and loves working in her flower and vegetable gardens. She also volunteers at her church, Faith Tabernacle, with the food pantry ministry, encouraging girlfriend group, altar team ministry and is a trustee on their board.

Pam married Gary Isham in 2002, and she adores his two dynamic, loving children, Logan and Sagen. Pam and Gary love to play with their dogs, Minnie and Tinkerbell, hike the woods in northern Michigan, kayak the Pine River, share about the benefits of positive declarations and travel around the world.

CPSIA information can be obtained
at www.ICGtesting.com
Printed in the USA
LVHW040845300720
661936LV00001B/2